Underlying the apparent diversity shown by the thousands of mutually incomprehensible languages of the world, there is a remarkable, elegant and principled unity in the way that these languages exploit the phonetic resources of speech. It is these principles that Professor Laver sets out to describe in this major new textbook. Assuming no previous knowledge of the subject, it is designed for readers who wish to pursue the study of phonetics from an initial to an advanced stage, equipping them with the necessary foundations for independent research. The classificatory model proposed unifies the description of linguistic, paralinguistic and certain extralinguistic aspects of speech production. The book moves from a presentation of general concepts to a total of eleven chapters on phonetic classification, and it includes discussion of other issues such as the relationship between phonetics and phonology, the nature of accent, dialect and language, and the description of voice quality and tone of voice. Every descriptive category is illustrated by words in phonetic transcription from over 500 of the world's languages.

Principles of Phonetics will be required reading and an invaluable resource for all serious students and scholars of speech and language.

Andrew Linn

Cambridge 1995

D1434564

CAMBRIDGE TEXTBOOKS IN LINGUISTICS

General Editors: J. BRESNAN, B. COMRIE, W. DRESSLER, R. HUDDLESTON, R. LASS, D. LIGHTFOOT, J. LYONS, P. H. MATTHEWS, R. POSNER, S. ROMAINE, N. V. SMITH, N. VINCENT

PRINCIPLES OF PHONETICS

In this series

PRINCIPLES OF
PHONETICS

JOHN LAVER

PROFESSOR OF PHONETICS
UNIVERSITY OF EDINBURGH

CAMBRIDGE
UNIVERSITY PRESS

Published by the Press Syndicate of the University of Cambridge
The Pitt Building, Trumpington Street, Cambridge CB2 1RP
40 West 20th Street, New York, NY 10011-4211, USA
10 Stamford Road, Oakleigh, Melbourne 3166, Australia

First published 1994

Printed in Great Britain at the University Press, Cambridge

A catalogue record for this book is available from the British Library

Library of Congress cataloguing in publication data

Laver, John.
Principles of phonetics / John Laver.
  p. cm. – (Cambridge textbooks in linguistics)
Includes bibliographical references and index.
ISBN 0-521-45031-4 (hardback) ISBN 0-521-45655-X (paperback)
1. Phonetics. I. Title. II. Series.
P221.L293 1994
414–dc20 93-18183 CIP

ISBN 0 521 45031 4 hardback
ISBN 0 521 45655 X paperback

TAG

For Sandy, Nick, Michael, Claire and Matthew

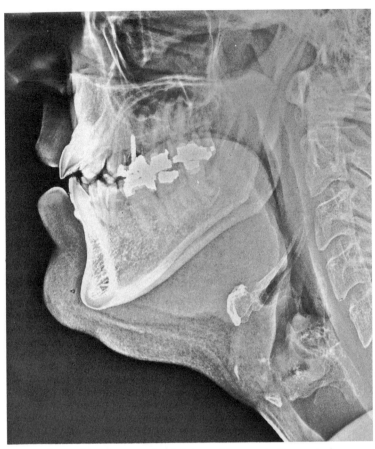

Xeroradiographic photograph of the vocal organs in the neutral
configuration, during the pronunciation of a mid-central vocoid [ə]

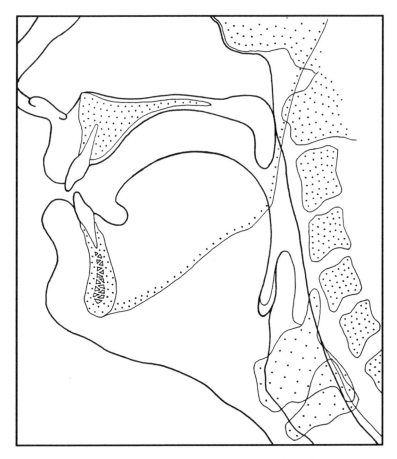

The neutral configuration of the vocal tract, drawn from the
xeroradiographic photograph on the opposite page

CONTENTS

Contents

FIGURES

TABLES

PREFACE

In a preface, one can perhaps be allowed to make some personal remarks. In my own training in the Department of Phonetics of the University of Edinburgh, I had the great privilege of being taught by some of the leading phoneticians of the century. Foremost amongst these were David Abercrombie and Peter Ladefoged. Ian Catford was also in Edinburgh at that time, at the School of Applied Linguistics. The hallmarks of their teaching were a scrupulous attention to objective phonetic detail, the development of excellent practical skills of phonetic performance and perception, and a rigorous concern for the architecture of phonetic theory. The abiding motivation of their work was always the linguistic relevance of speech.

These attitudes were and are strongly held, but they are not novel. They have been a characteristic of professional phoneticians in what one might call the British school since the days of Henry Sweet in the nineteenth century (Henderson 1971). One may not completely agree with the full implications of Sweet's claim when he wrote in his Preface to *A Handbook of Phonetics* (1877), that 'The importance of phonetics as the indispensable foundation of all study of language – whether that study be purely theoretical, or practical as well – is now generally admitted.' There are some aspects of linguistics (defined as the study of language) where the connection with speech as such is very tenuous; phonetics is undoubtedly indispensable, however, to the study of any aspect of spoken language. Daniel Jones emphasized the utility of phonetics for this and other purposes when he wrote that 'Phonetics is a means to an end' (Jones 1937). But I believe that the approach to phonetics implicit in the teaching of Abercrombie, Ladefoged and Catford goes a long way further than this, and I would wish to insist on the merit of phonetics, not only as providing tools for a variety of applications, but also as an end in itself – as a subject worthy of study in its own right and as an equal of other university-level disciplines.

ACKNOWLEDGEMENTS

In writing this book, I have had the benefit of help, advice and critical comment from many friends and colleagues: Marie Alexander, Brian Annan, Ron Asher, Saiqa Asif, Janet Mackenzie Beck, André-Pierre Benguerel, Art Blokland, Gunilla Blom, Adam Brown, Fouzia Bukshaisha, Guy Carden, John Clark, Bruce Connell, Alan Cruttenden, Jonathan Dalby, Gerard Docherty, Hartvig Eckert, John Esling, Ahmed Ferhardi, Arne Foldvik, Helen Fraser, Lindsay Friedman, Osamu Fujimura, John Gilbert, Jonathan Harrington, Jimmy Harris, Tom Harris, Dick Hayward, Katrina Mickey Hayward, Eugénie Henderson, Jo-Ann Higgs, Steve Hiller, Sandy Hutcheson, Mervyn Jack, Carolyn Johnson, Yasuo Kato, John Kelly, Alan Kemp, Handan Kopkalli, Bob Ladd, Peter Ladefoged, Roger Lass, Timo Lauttamus, Nick Laver, Björn Lindblom, Jim Lubker, Sudaporn Luksaneeyanawin, Fergus McInnes, Angus McIntosh, Geoff Nathan, Paroo Nihalani, Francis Nolan, John Ohala, Sallyanne Palethorpe, Jeff Pittam, Peter Roach, Sheila Rowe, Edmund Rooney, Ann Sutherland, Robin Thelwall, Elizabeth Uldall, Jo Verhoeven, Nigel Vincent, Briony Williams, Ken Winch and Colin Yallop.

Jo-Ann Higgs and Gerard Docherty used early versions of the text as a support for their advanced undergraduate course in phonetic theory in the Department of Linguistics at the University of Edinburgh over a number of years, and their comments have been of special value to me. I have also used later drafts of the book in teaching this course myself, and in teaching one on phonetics for postgraduate students of the Department of Applied Linguistics at the University of Edinburgh, and I am very grateful to all the students who discussed their response to the text with me.

Eugénie Henderson and Peter Ladefoged both contributed editorial advice during the preparation of the book, and their guidance has been very welcome. It is a matter of extreme regret to me that Eugénie Henderson's death in July 1989 prevented her seeing the full outcome of her characteristically benevolent advice. Lindsay Friedman helped to bring the book through the middle stages of its preparation, and her critique of early theoretical matters was invaluable. In the final stages, Marie Alexander worked very hard in helping to check the consistency of the text, the figures, the appendices and the language statistics. I very much appreciated her meticulous and knowledgeable help. Doreen Cairns typed early versions of the manuscript, and Jan Wallace helped more recently with references.

Frances MacCurtain of the Middlesex Hospital in London made the xeroradiographic photograph of my production of the neutral configuration of the vocal organs shown as the frontispiece, from which Janet Mackenzie Beck created the drawing reproduced on the page facing it. She also drew the schematized version reproduced as figure 5.12, which has been used as the basis for many of the articulatory diagrams throughout the book. Tom Harris took the fiberoptic telelaryngoscopic pictures reproduced in figure 7.4.

Nigel Vincent offered some particularly constructive criticisms as a reviewer of the manuscript for Cambridge University Press. Some of the suggestions made by several anonymous reviewers have also been incorporated. Penny Carter, Marion Smith and Judith Ayling have been the staunchest (and surely the most patient) of editors. Jenny Potts made a very significant contribution as copy-editor for the Press. Fiona Barr composed the indexes. I offer my warmest thanks to all these colleagues and friends. I am responsible for the unwitting or wilful mistakes that remain.

In a textbook of this sort I also owe a special debt to all those writers whose clarity of phonetic commentary has allowed me to draw examples from their work on the phonetics and phonology of individual languages. I am especially grateful to John Esling of the University of Victoria and Speech Technology Research Ltd of Victoria, Canada, and to Kay Elemetrics Corporation of New Jersey, USA, for their kind permission to cite phonetic examples from the twenty-five languages illustrated in their joint project on the *University of Victoria Phonetic Database* (Esling 1991). The language database was developed at the Phonetics Laboratory of the University of Victoria, and sound recordings are available on floppy disks for use with an IBM PC and Kay Elemetric Corporation's *Computerized Speech Lab*. For more information, contact Dr John Esling at the Phonetics Laboratory, Department of Linguistics, University of Victoria, PO Box 3045, Victoria, BC V8W 3P4, Canada, or Kay Elemetrics Corporation at 12 Maple Avenue, PO Box 2025, Pine Brook, NJ 07058-2025, USA.

I am grateful to Marconi Speech and Information Systems, our industrial partner in the IED/SERC (Alvey) Large Scale Demonstrator Project on Integrated Speech Technology, for consent to the publication of the phonetic distance matrices in chapter 13. I thank the Alvey Directorate and the Information Engineering Directorate of the Department of Trade and Industry, and the Science and Engineering Research Council for their support of this project over the period 1984–91 (IED/SERC Grants GRD/29604, GRD/29611, GRD/29628, GRF/10309, GRF/10316, and GRF/70471). I also thank the Medical Research Council for its support of our work on vocal profiles (MRC Grant G987/1192/N: 1979–82), and our work on microperturbatory aspects of laryngeal function (MRC Grant 8207136N : 1982–5), parts of which are described in this book. Permission to adapt material from copyright publications for a number of figures and tables is gratefully acknowledged, as indicated in the list attached below.

Tolerance and support have been provided by many people in connection with the preparation of this book, not least by my colleagues in the Centre for Speech Technology Research in the University of Edinburgh, especially Mervyn Jack and Ron Asher. The highest price for a book, however, is always paid by an author's family. For their enduring love and support, I dedicate this book to my wife and colleague Sandy Hutcheson and to my children Nick, Michael, Claire and Matthew.

'IBM' and 'PC' are registered trademarks of International Business Machines Corporation. 'Computerized Speech Lab' is a registered trademark of Kay Elemetrics Corporation.

Permission to reproduce copyright material is gratefully acknowledged for the following figures, tables and appendices: Academic Press (fig. 15.8, table 6.3); Edward Arnold (figs. 15.14, 15.19); Professor T. Balasubramanian (figs. 8.3a, 8.3b); Basil Blackwell (figs. 3.3, 3.4, 6.2, 7.6); Professor L. Cagliari (fig. 10.16); Cambridge University Press (figs. 3.1, 4.1, 7.1, 7.2, 7.3, 10.9, 15.5, 15.6, 15.7, 15.11, 15.12, 15.16, 15.20, tables 12.1, 19.1 and the map of language families in appendix II); Chulalongkorn University Press (fig. 15.9, table 15.3); Croom Helm (fig. 3.2); Edinburgh University Press (figs. 10.3, 10.4, 10.6); Lawrence Erlbaum Associates (fig. 12.4); Professor G. Fant and Dr A. Kruckenberg (fig. 15.4); Foris (fig. 11.4); Julius Groos Verlag (figs. 10.18, 10.20); T. Harris (fig 7.4); Heffer (figs. 10.4, 10.5); Dr S. Hiller (fig. 15.18); the *International Journal of American Linguistics* (table 12.2); the *International Phonetic Association* (figs. 10.7, 10.14, 15.15a and b, appendix I); S. Karger (fig. 10.17, table 15.2); Longman (fig. 14.1); Marconi Speech and Information Systems (fig. 13.1); Dr F. McInnes (fig. 13.2); Penguin (fig. 15.13); Prentice-Hall (fig. 6.1, table 6.1); Springer-Verlag (figs. 4.3, 10.19, 15.2, 17.1); University of Chicago Press (fig. 12.2).

Introduction

This book is designed to equip the reader with a foundation for independent research in the phonetic study of speech. It makes no assumptions about prior knowledge of the subject, and is meant to be suitable as a comprehensive reference textbook on phonetics for graduates with no previous direct experience in the subject, who are following conversion courses to prepare themselves for research in phonetics and related subjects. It can also be used as a textbook supporting undergraduate courses on phonetics from elementary to advanced levels.

The book is thus addressed to readers who wish to pursue the subject from an initial to an advanced stage. I have tried to offer a general orientation, and a framework which provides a guide to navigation through some of the central territory of phonetics. Above all, I hope that the book may stimulate readers to reflect on the theoretical foundations of the subject.

Speech is our most human characteristic. It is the most highly skilled muscular activity that human beings ever achieve, requiring the precise and rapid co-ordination of more than eighty different muscles, many of them paired. Even the expertise of the concert pianist pales into relative insignificance beside the intricately co-ordinated muscular vocal skills exercised by a ten-year-old child talking to friends in the school playground. A pianist playing a rapid arpeggio makes about sixteen finger strokes per second, each the product of multiple motor commands to the muscles of the fingers, wrist and arm. Speech is both faster and more complicated (Boomer 1978). The process of speaking at a normal rate is achieved by means of some 1,400 motor commands per second to the muscles of the speech apparatus (Lenneberg 1967). As children, we take a number of years to acquire the skills of producing and perceiving speech, but once we have learned these abilities, only pathology or accident deprives us of their use.

Speech is the prime means of communication for virtually every social group, and the structure of society itself would be substantially different if we had failed to develop communication through speech (Bickerton 1990:

240). Furthermore, our social interaction through speech depends on much more than solely the linguistic nature of the spoken messages exchanged. The voice is the very emblem of the speaker, indelibly woven into the fabric of speech. In this sense, each of our utterances of spoken language carries not only its own message, but through accent, tone of voice and habitual voice quality it is at the same time an audible declaration of our membership of particular social and regional groups, of our individual physical and psychological identity, and of our momentary mood.

A comprehensive understanding of a phenomenon as complex and multi-stranded as speech necessarily has to draw on the resources of a large number of different disciplines. Given the prime communicative function of spoken language, one discipline that lies at the heart of any adequate study of speech is linguistics. But speech, as just indicated, is a carrier of more information than solely the meaningful patterns of individual utterances of spoken language. A vast amount of social and personal information about the speaker is carried as well. In this century, the horizons of communication through speech have expanded greatly, through telecommunications, broadcasting and computing. To reach a full understanding of the nature of communication through speech one would therefore have to appeal to concepts not only from linguistics, but also from sociology, anthropology, philosophy, psychology, anatomy, physiology, neurology, medicine, pathology, acoustics, physics, cybernetics, electronic engineering, computer science and artificial intelligence. The study of speech in this broad view thus covers a remarkably wide domain, embracing aspects of the social sciences, the life sciences, the physical sciences, the engineering sciences and the information sciences.

All the disciplines mentioned above take speech as part of their professional domain, though their principal focus is elsewhere. Phonetics is the discipline that takes speech as its central domain, and which stands at the intersection of all these disciplines. In the definition to be promoted in this book, phonetics is the scientific study of all aspects of speech. Phonetics and linguistics are seen here as sister sciences, together making up 'the linguistic sciences'. This allows one to say that phonetics is the scientific study of speech, and that linguistics is the scientific study of language. Their domains overlap in the area of spoken language, but each has legitimate concerns outside the professional remit of the other.

More traditional definitions of phonetics content themselves with a narrower range of territory, usually limiting the domain of phonetics to the study of those aspects of speech relevant to language, which locates phonetics within the encompassing discipline of linguistics. One candid objective of this book is to persuade the reader that it is possible and reasonable for phonetics to have wider horizons. Embedding spoken language in a wider context of communicative behaviour, and integrating it within a wider descriptive model, brings a double benefit: it not only gives us a better understanding of the communicative texture of speech in general, but also gives us a better insight into the nature of spoken language itself. Unfortunately, space does not permit a full discussion of all the aspects of speech that accompany and complement spoken language, and the first priority of this book will be the exploration of the nature of spoken language. But every reasonable opportunity will be taken to exemplify the non-linguistic functions of each type of phonetic phenomenon in conjunction with the description of its use in spoken language.

Phonetics is sometimes thought by practitioners of other disciplines (and by the occasional phonetician, it has to be said) to be somehow a chiefly 'practical' subject, more properly conceived as an art than a science, preoccupied with the description of data but without a central interest in theoretical matters. It is certainly true that good phoneticians should be masters of the art of pronouncing and perceiving any and every speech sound used communicatively in the languages of the world. The term 'practical' is hence clearly applicable to the skills of performance and perception widely practised by phoneticians. The term 'practical' also applies, however, to the empirical speech data described by phonetics. To imagine that an interest in data can be sustained without the support of theory is to misunderstand the fundamental relationship between data and theory. As a basic aspect of the philosophy of science it is quite illusory to conceive of 'data' except in the context of a theory within whose framework the data are characterized.

Halle and Stevens (1979: 335) quote a comment addressed by Einstein (1933) to theoretical physics, which is as germane to phonetics, on the relationship between data and theory:

> We are concerned with the eternal antithesis between the two
> inseparable components of knowledge, the empirical and the rational
> ... The structure of the system is the work of reason; the empirical
> contents and their mutual relations must find their representation
> in the conclusions of the theory. In the possibility of such a
> representation lie the sole value and justification of the whole
> system, and especially the concepts and fundamental principles
> which underlie it.

In phonetics just as much as in physics, the empirical should be married to the theoretical, each forming a balancing and inseparable reflection in the mirror of the other.

The core of phonetics as a scientific discipline is the architecture and content of its descriptive theory. The focus of this book is the principles on which such a theory can be constructed. As with any comparable subject, phonetics can and should be judged by the adequacy of coverage offered by this theory, and by the degree to which, within the limits of current knowledge, the nature of its descriptive concepts furnishes an efficient explanation of the underlying relations which bind the data into a coherent and (provisionally) truthful whole.

A primary task of phonetics is therefore to provide an objective description of speech. The most widely accepted theory for doing this is the one that underlies the symbols of the phonetic alphabet of the International Phonetic Association, which was founded just over 100 years ago. The theory has been modified in detail since that time, but the basic structure of the accepted descriptive model is not substantially different (Ladefoged 1987b). Just after its centenary in 1986, the Association re-evaluated the stock of standard symbols in its phonetic alphabet and, by implication, reconsidered the shape of the underlying descriptive theory (MacMahon 1986). A convention of the International Phonetic Association in Kiel in August 1989 made a set of recommendations about a standard set of notational symbols to be used in phonetic transcription, which has recently been ratified by the Council of the Association for international use. These recommendations have almost all been adopted here. The descriptive theory which is put forward in this book is fully compatible with the implications of the Kiel decisions, though there are a number of further innovations, each of which is fully explained at the relevant point in the text. The 1989 version of the International Phonetic Association's phonetic alphabet is reproduced as appendix I.

A basic purpose of this book is thus to help people interested in speech to think about the subject in an objective way, with a concern for the architecture and efficiency of the descriptive theory being proposed, and with an appreciation of the full range of the subject. The book is inevitably concerned in part with specifying sets of symbols and diacritics for phonetic transcription, and with their relationship to descriptive phonetic concepts and labels. It is crucial that students of phonetics learn these concepts, labels and symbols of phonetic description as an interlinked set. It deserves emphasis, however, that the descriptive labels and transcriptional symbols are only the visible part of a large section of phonetic theory about the substance of speech. Each label, with its associated symbol, is a reflection of an underlying network of theoretical concepts and assumptions. Learning the appropriate use of the descriptive vocabulary of symbols and labels can only be properly achieved by simultaneously absorbing the underlying structure of phonetic theory. For convenience of reference, the sets of symbols and labels relevant to each chapter are gathered together at the end of that chapter.

The sequence of presentation of the descriptive theory merits some comment. The book is divided into eight parts. Part I consists of three introductory chapters explaining general concepts used in the analysis of spoken language. Chapter 1 presents elementary ideas helpful in understanding the coded nature of spoken language and the different types of information available to the listener, and introduces a number of different levels of analysis. Chapter 2 offers a basic view of the relationship between phonetics and phonology, as the abstract set of sound-patterns that constitute the coded nature of linguistic communication through speech. Chapter 3 explores the distinction between an 'accent', a 'dialect' and a 'language', and touches on a number of linguistic disciplines to which phonetics makes a contribution, such as sociolinguistics, dialect geography and historical linguistics.

The two chapters of Part II then launch the more technical core of the book. Chapter 4 begins by considering the relationship between biological aspects of the speech apparatus and its phonetic use. It then explores different conceptual approaches to the question of how the stream of speech can be segmented for analysis, and proposes some fundamental units of phonetic analysis: features, segments, syllables, settings, utterances and speaking turns. The concept of the segment, as the phonetic manifestation of the linguistic units of consonants and vowels, is probably the one initially most familiar to readers of this book. Chapter 4 concludes with a preliminary identification of the six basic strands of speech production: initiation of an airstream, phonation, articulation, temporal, prosodic and metrical organization.

Chapter 5 is a pivotal chapter in the design of the book. Because chapters 6–17 look in turn at each strand of vocal performance in fairly extensive detail, it was thought helpful to the reader to have an initial summary overview of the whole architecture of the descriptive theory proposed in the book, before launching into the local detail of each of the following chapters. Chapter 5 is therefore designed to give the reader an architectural frame of reference within which to locate the remaining chapters of the book. By its nature it can only give a skeletal outline of a large and detailed area. But its summary form may also allow it to function as a review of the design of the descriptive theory to which the reader can return as desired. The principal innovations in the architecture of the descriptive theory presented in this book are the concepts of 'aspect of articulation', 'intersegmental co-ordination' and featural 'settings'.

Part III consists of two chapters explaining initiation and phonation. Chapter 6 on initiation describes the mechanisms for setting a flow of air in motion for the purposes of speech. Chapter 7 on phonation explains the ways that the larynx can impose a variety of patterns of vibration on the flow of air from the lungs, to provide a source of acoustic energy which the articulatory apparatus can then further modify to produce the segments of speech.

The four chapters of Part IV present an analysis of the segmental performance of the sounds representing consonants and vowels. Stop articulations are described in chapter 8, fricative articulations in chapter 9 and resonant articulations in chapter 10. Chapter 11 explains the articulatory basis of segments made with more than one major articulatory constriction.

Part V explores the relationships between segments next to or near to each other in the stream of speech. Chapter 12 looks at how the articulation of adjacent segments is co-ordinated, especially in the events at the junction of the two sounds. Chapter 13 explores in more detail than is usual in phonetic textbooks the topic of phonetic similarity between segments, invoking the concept of a 'setting' as a feature running through several segments to explain degrees of similarity, and using setting-analysis as a basis for constructing descriptive 'vocal profiles' of the voices of individual speakers.

Part VI presents a temporal, prosodic and metrical analysis of speech. Chapter 14 considers matters of the temporal duration of segments. Chapter 15 moves to the prosodic description of the use of pitch, in tonal and intonational functions of speech melody. It also discusses the control of loudness in speech. Chapter 16 integrates the temporal and prosodic material of the preceding two chapters, and presents a metrical analysis of speech where the focus is on stress and rhythm. Chapter 17 then presents a description of the way that speech can vary in its rate and continuity, as a final part of the temporal organization of speech.

Part VII examines the principles by which different types of transcription can be classified. Chapter 18 includes numerous examples of detailed phonetic transcriptions of utterances from native speakers of each of a number of languages from widely different parts of the world. These transcriptions were made jointly by the author and a colleague in the University of Edinburgh (Sandy Hutcheson), for the purpose of teaching postgraduate courses in the use of phonetic transcription for fieldwork. The transcriptions called potentially on the entire repertoire of general phonetic notation. The chapters leading up to chapter 18 explain the meanings and use of all the

6

transcriptional symbols available in this repertoire, and the relationships between them. If, when chapter 18 is reached, the transcriptions in this chapter are able to be interpreted by the reader with full and confident understanding, then the book will have succeeded in a significant part of its objective of providing a foundation for independent phonetic research. Learning the meaning and use of the phonetic symbols has an obvious practical value, but the most important consequence of acquiring a deep understanding of the notation is the accompanying insight that is gained into the underlying theoretical architecture that binds the concepts represented by the symbols into a coherent framework.

Part VIII rehearses the main principles of phonetic description that have been presented, placing them in a broader context of other approaches to the description of speech. In addition, chapter 19 considers the question of empirical justification for the architectural design of a descriptive phonetic theory, by appeal to statistical facts about the relative frequency of occurrence of the different phenomena described.

Phonetic concepts presented in the book are illustrated from as wide a range of different languages as feasible, drawn from reliable sources in the literature of the subject and from personal experience. The linguistic examples are co-ordinated with the introduction of phonetic concepts and symbols, and illustrations in phonetic transcription are offered from over 500 different languages. There are several reasons for choosing to illustrate the book with copious examples drawn from this wealth of languages. A central part of the motivation in drawing on a wide range of linguistic material is to offer objective evidence to support the generality of the descriptive theory being put forward. A related objective is to give the reader an appreciation of the paradox that, underlying the apparently extraordinary diversity of the patterns of spoken language, there is a remarkable unity in the phonetic resources exploited by the languages of the world. The challenge of writing this book lay above all in the attempt to capture the range and elegance of this combination of diversity and unity.

Every effort has been made to account for all phonetic processes known to be exploited by spoken language. If any reader knows of phonetic phenomena in some language which are either not covered, or inadequately described, I would be most grateful to receive information about the nature of the phonetic process concerned, with phonetic transcriptions and glosses of illustrative words, for possible inclusion in a later edition.

Another motivation for frequently drawing on illustrations from real languages is that the theoretical discussion of phonetic principles can become very abstract without continual renewal of connection with the linguistic material that the theory seeks to illuminate. A final part of the motivation is the belief that readers who experiment with their own ability to pronounce the illustrative material are more likely to reach an integrated understanding of the underpinning theoretical concepts. Readers are encouraged to use the linguistic examples for practical performance, especially (but not only) if the material can be practised with the help of an experienced phonetician.

The language material is normally presented in phonetic (rather than 'phonemic') transcription. Where no source is indicated for language examples, the illustration is offered from my own experience. The symbols used in the transcriptions of examples drawn from the work of other phoneticians and phonologists have been standardized wherever necessary to fit the conventions of this book. Where examples from a particular language have been borrowed from another writer, specific reference is always given, to give due acknowledgement and to allow consultation for further details.

Particular care has been taken to indicate, wherever feasible, the original source of technical concepts. I feel that it is important for students and professionals alike to appreciate the intellectual continuities in the broad landscape of the rich and well-populated literature of phonetics. Any reader fortunate enough to acquire the majority of the publications listed in the References to this book would possess the nucleus of a very good phonetics library. Recommended further reading is indicated at the end of chapters.

Wherever practicable, the language-family and the part of the world in which the language is spoken is given. Names of countries are as up-to-date as political developments at the time of going to press allowed. Each of the languages mentioned in the text is listed in appendix II, together with its language-family and geographical location. The affiliation identified in appendix II is normally the major language-group of which the language is a member; the language-family given in the body of the text usually indicates a lower-level grouping. Appendix II also serves as a Language Index, giving the page numbers of all mentions of the language concerned. The appendix is prefaced by a map of the world on which the locations of the major language-families are indicated (Crystal 1987: 294–5).

Examples are drawn from the language-families of every inhabited continent, but the languages of three particular areas tend to recur. One is Europe, with its relatively familiar (mostly Indo-European) languages. The other two are Africa and the Americas. The languages of Africa have received a good deal of attention from phoneticians and phonologists, and Africa (particularly the languages of the Niger-Congo family) is the area with which I am myself most familiar. The languages of North and South America and the Mesoamerican Indian languages of Central America have received particular attention from the phoneticians and linguists trained in the American tradition, especially from the many linguists associated with the Summer Institute of Linguistics. Both Africa and the Americas are areas rich in phonetic processes unfamiliar to the languages of Europe. For comprehensive information on the language-families of the world, the reader might like to consult the publications listed in the section on Further Reading at the end of chapter 3 and at the beginning of appendix II.

The language examples offered in the first four chapters are deliberately taken mostly from English. This is because it is likely to be the native or second language of the large majority of readers of this book, and therefore the examples will perhaps have a greater immediacy for these readers than they might otherwise have. But it is also directly because the detailed discussion of matters of pronunciation of less familiar languages really requires a prior understanding of the descriptive articulatory concepts offered in the later chapters, in which the examples drawn from languages other than English are concentrated.

The English examples are normally taken from an accent of England called Received Pronunciation (RP). RP is a non-regional accent of England, and is probably most familiar to the readers of this book as the accent used by most announcers and newsreaders on national and international BBC broadcasting channels. If no further identification is given to the term 'English', it can be assumed that reference is being made to English pronounced with an RP accent. RP is discussed more fully in chapter 3.

Words in many languages are contrastively identified by different patterns of pitch, or 'tone'. Diacritic symbols marking such tonal characteristics are often included in the transcriptions of the linguistic examples, when known, for review purposes. They typically consist of acute or grave accent-diacritics, placed above the symbols representing vowels. They can perhaps be left unremarked during the first reading of the text until chapter 15, where tone is discussed in more detail.

Figures are numbered in sequence throughout each chapter, as are tables. Technical terms, on introduction and definition, and as topic identifiers in the recommendations for Further Reading at the ends of chapters, are printed in **bold-face**. The Subject Index prints the page numbers of these boldened items also in bold, for convenience of review.

PART I

General concepts

1

The semiotic framework

The point of departure for this book is that speech is the most subtle and complex tool of communication that man has ever developed. The aim of this chapter is to discuss the nature of spoken communication, and to offer a broad framework within which the analysis of speech in general, and of spoken language in particular can be set. Some basic concepts are defined for use throughout the book.

One of the most important concepts to be introduced is the notion of the acts of spoken language as artefacts, used as elements of a coded system of **signs**. As a **code**, spoken communication can only be successful when used between people skilled in the production and interpretation of the relevant signs. Another very important concept discussed in this chapter is the many-layered nature of speech, with each layer carrying a different type of information. The framework proposed here for the analysis of these concepts comes originally from the discipline of semiotics.

1.1 Semiotics as the general theory of signs

Semiotics is the study of all aspects of sign systems used for communication. The term 'semiotic' was first used in ancient Greek medicine, to refer to the theory of medical symptoms used in the diagnosis and prognosis of disease (Morris 1946: 285). The Stoic philosophers then used the term to refer to the general theory of signs. The semiotic analysis of speech can involve a consideration not only of the communicative signs themselves, but also of the mechanisms by which the signs are produced by the **speaker** and perceived by the **listener**, using the auditory and visual channels of communication. Also of semiotic interest are the ways in which the manufacture and use of particular signs can carry information about the characteristics of their producers.

There is a continual flow of information between participants in any conversation. The first step in setting up a convenient semiotic framework for the discussion of how speech works is to distinguish between three major types of information exchanged. In order, these will be called 'semantic', 'evidential' and 'regulative' information.

1.2 Semantic, evidential and regulative information in speech

The largest part of this book will be about the analysis of the aspects of speech that convey the first type of information mentioned above – **semantic information**. This is what most people think of as the direct 'meaning' of a spoken utterance. It is the propositional content of the communicative acts of conversation, and the more complex the proposition the more likely it is to rely on being communicated by spoken words. Simple semantic information can often be exchanged by other means, however. A message corresponding to the potential utterance 'Come here' can often be communicated perfectly unambiguously by a beckoning gesture, for instance, within the interpretive conventions of the particular culture for interpreting 'meaning'. More indirect aspects of meaning, such as **pragmatic meaning** (where an utterance such as *It's cold in here* is taken to constitute a request to shut the door rather than solely to offer a comment about the local temperature), will not be dealt with directly in this book. References to work on pragmatics can be found in the recommended publications for Further Reading at the end of the chapter.

Evidential information can be said to be conveyed by signs in speech which act as attributive **markers** (Laver and Trudgill 1979: 3). These are used by the listener as the basis on which to attribute personal characteristics to the speaker. The attributes of the speaker fall into three groups:

> **physical markers** – those that indicate physical characteristics such as sex, age, physique and state of health;
>
> **social markers** – those that indicate social characteristics such as regional affiliation, social and educational status, occupation and social role;
>
> **psychological markers** – those that indicate psychological characteristics of personality and affective state or mood.

Markers of physical characteristics lie, for example, in a speaker's **voice quality**. Social markers often include such features as **accent** and choice of vocabulary. Psychological markers of personality and mood are often taken to reside in a speaker's (habitual and momentary) **tone of voice**. In the sense that evidential markers of this sort can be said to be **symptoms** of a speaker's individual characteristics, their semiotic status is close to the diagnostic role of signs in the medical origins of semiotic theory in ancient Greece.

The meaning of the term 'marker' as presented here is derived from the concept that Abercrombie (1967: 6) introduced to the semiotic study of speech under the name 'index'. Abercrombie drew this term, with its related adjective 'indexical', from the semiotic writings of Charles Peirce, the late-nineteenth-century American pragmaticist philosopher (Buchler 1940).

The markers that serve to identify an individual's membership of a given social group are of especial interest to the sector of linguistics usually called **sociolinguistics** or the **sociology of language**. Seminal work in this area was done by Labov (1966, 1972a, 1972b), and by Hymes (1974, 1977) and Trudgill (1974), to which interested readers are directed. Other useful sources on sociolinguistics are given in the list of Further Reading at the end of the chapter.

There is one particular sort of evidential information that it is helpful to label separately, which identifies the speaker's desire to retain or to yield the role of speaker in the time-course of a given conversation. This can be called **regulative information**, and it is used by the participants in a conversation to control the time-sharing of the interaction. In most conversations the participants take turns to occupy the role of speaker, and conventional mechanisms exist for managing smooth transitions at turn-boundaries. These are well understood by adult participants native to the culture. They are normally exercised outside conscious awareness, but the temporal structure of speaking-turns in conversation is a skilled product of co-operative work between the participants. The skill has to be learned by each speaker as part of his or her socialization into the use of spoken language. It is hence a skill whose details are specific to the language community concerned. Yielding the floor to the other speaker is managed in English by a variety of conventional signals. Some of them use the visual channel (head-movements and eye-contacts), and some of them use speech (mostly particular types of intonation and timing).

Having drawn this triple distinction between the semantic, evidential and regulative types of information exchanged in conversational interaction, we can now turn to a more detailed consideration of the different means available to speakers for transmitting this information. The chief distinction to be drawn here is that between vocal and non-vocal behaviour. By definition, vocal behaviour is audible, while non-vocal behaviour is visible.

1.3 Vocal and non-vocal behaviour

It will be clear from the discussion in the section above that the information imparted by the **vocal behaviour** of speech consists of more than the audible elements of spoken language. When we listen to a speaker, we perceive not only semantic information conveyed by the words the speaker is producing, but also regulative information about the conversational structure of the utterance. We also perceive evidential information marking the speaker's identity and his or her affective state. In the definitions used in this book, the analysis of speech covers the study of this whole complex of vocal behaviour – the coded vocal material of spoken language, the vocal shaping of conversational structure, and the vocal marking of speaker-attributes.

Conversation itself consists of more than just vocal behaviour, however. In all normal circumstances of face-to-face conversation, there is a constant two-way traffic of information on the visual channel (particularly of evidential and regulative information), communicated by **non-vocal behaviour**. Gesture, posture, head-movements, body-movements, facial expression, gaze and eye-contact behaviour are continually in play, complementing and supporting speech activity. These non-vocal aspects are themselves elements of a coded system of communication, which users have to learn. A small part of non-vocal communication (notably some aspects of facial expression) is thought to be of universal human significance, but most non-vocal communication consists of behaviour that is particular to the culture of the speaker. This too is therefore a skill whose performance has to be learned, albeit a somewhat less complex skill than that involved in spoken language. The analysis of non-vocal material lies outside the study of speech as such, but it is integral to the study of the communicative context in which speech is almost always performed.

1.4   Verbal and non-verbal behaviour

The second distinction to be drawn between different means of communicating information is that between verbal and non-verbal means. These terms are interpreted in many different ways in books on speech and conversational interaction. In this book, **verbal** elements are defined as any aspects of communicative behaviour that serve to identify individual words as units of spoken language; **non-verbal** elements are then any features of communicative behaviour that serve functions other than that of verbal identification. **Vowels** and **consonants**, for example, serve the verbal function, as does **word-stress**. **Intonation**, as pitch-melody associated with units of spoken language usually longer than individual words, is a non-verbal element, as is the use of stress for purposes of emphasis (**emphatic stress**). Linguistic communication is thus served by both verbal and non-verbal devices. Verbal devices are solely linguistic, but non-verbal communication includes both linguistic and non-linguistic processes (Key 1980). One such non-linguistic process is communication through **tone of voice** (discussed below in section 1.10) as a non-verbal vocal element. Examples of non-verbal non-vocal means of communication include gesture, posture, looking-behaviour and facial expression.

1.5 Signs and symbols

The semiotic framework used in this book, following the precedent set by Abercrombie (1967), is largely derived from some of the key concepts in the writings of Charles Peirce, the pragmaticist philosopher mentioned earlier. Peirce defined semiotics as 'the formal doctrine of signs ... [where] ... a sign is something which stands to somebody for something in some respect or capacity' (Hartshorne and Weiss 1931–5, vol. II: 227–8). A three-way relationship is implied between a person, an entity and the sign used to refer to the entity. The referential link between the entity and the sign can be either non-arbitrary or arbitrary. The link between wind-direction and a weathercock is non-arbitrary, for example, and many signs which are used to communicate evidential information are of this non-arbitrary kind. The habitual pitch of a person's voice, for instance, is often fairly direct evidence of the overall size of the vocal folds in the speaker's larynx.

More tenuously, a non-arbitrary link is often claimed to exist between certain **onomatopoeic signs** used in language, such as the words *clink* and *clank*, and the entities to which they refer. But such onomatopoeic signs are a tiny minority of the signs used for linguistic purposes. Linguistic signs virtually all show a culturally determined, arbitrary link between the sign and the entity (or **referent**) to which reference is made. Linguistic signs of this latter sort are usually called **symbolic signs**. A **symbol** is a sign whose reference is arbitrary, and governed only by social convention. The meaning of a symbolic sign can thus only be appreciated by someone who has learned the appropriate referential convention. There is no element of necessity in the referential link between the linguistic sign *cat* and the feline animal which is its conventional referent in English, for example. The arbitrary convention linking such symbolic signs with their referents is a convention to which all users of a given language tacitly subscribe.

Words are symbolic signs, and the semiotic status of these linguistic elements is relatively clearcut. But the semiotic status of the individual consonants and vowels which make up the verbal means for differentiating one word from another is less obvious. It is helpful to draw a sharp theoretical distinction between an entity such as an individual consonant, and the actual event of pronunciation. We can call the act of pronunciation a **speech-sound**, for convenience. The semiotic position to be adopted here is that it is the speech-sound that 'stands for' the consonant, and that a conso-

17

nant has the status of an abstract element of the linguistic code. This may be clearer if we consider the fact that any given consonant is represented in different contexts of utterance and in different speakers by a large number of differentiable speech-sounds.

First, a given native speaker of English will produce two speech-sounds of different quality for the English consonant *s*, for example, in the words *soon* and *seen*. The former will typically be pronounced with a slightly rounded opening of the lips compared with a more neutral position for the latter. Second, the same speaker will very often (randomly) adopt slightly varying positions for the shape of the lip-opening for repeated pronunciations of the '*s*' consonant in any particular word. Third, different speakers nominally sharing the same accent of English will often nevertheless show idiosyncratic differences of pronunciation, each having slightly different productions of *s* in the same word. Yet native listeners ascribe the same linguistic value to all these differing speech-sounds – namely, that of the English consonant *s*. Speech-sounds can hence be thought of as representing, or 'symbolizing' abstract linguistic units such as consonants and vowels, in a many-to-one relationship.

1.6 Dual-level structure in the linguistic code

Two quite different levels of symbolization combine to give language a unique semiotic nature. The higher level will be called here the **grammatical level**. The grammatical level is made up of units which are capable of having external reference to the semantic world, such as words, phrases, clauses and sentences. The lower level is usually called the **phonological level**. This is made up of units such as consonants and vowels whose sole function is to act as building blocks for the construction of those higher-level grammatical units. This double level of grammatical and phonological structure in the linguistic code is a defining characteristic of language, and has been variously called 'double structure', 'double articulation' or 'dual structure' (Hockett 1958: 574–5, Lyons 1972: 65). To summarize this **dual structure**, speech-sounds (as acts of pronunciation) represent abstract phonological units in the language concerned. Grammatical units (made up of combinations of phonological units) are the devices of the language whose function it is to represent entities in the external semantic world.

This picture of the dual structure of spoken language is simplified, in order to present the duality principle with clarity. However, it will be necessary later in the book to allow the phonological level to consist not only of 'segmental' consonants and vowels, but also of a hierarchy of superordinate, 'suprasegmental' entities. These suprasegmental entities include syllables, rhythmic units and units of intonation and tone. The syllable is a phonological entity which gives structure to sequences of consonants and vowels. Rhythmic units give form to sequences of syllables. Intonational and tonal units serve to relate the segmental, syllabic and rhythmic material to the higher-order grammatical level, and to the pragmatic level of interaction between the speaker and the listener. The grammatical level, made up of lexical, morphological, syntactic and semantic entities, will not be discussed in detail in this book except to the extent that it is relevant to phonological and phonetic distinctions. (Discussion of the different areas contributing to this grammatical level can be found in the publications indicated in Further Reading below.) The function of the present book is rather to explain how speech-sounds can be described, and to explore their relationship with the phonological level of structure. The later chapters offer a comprehensive account of the first objective, and we can turn now to an initial consideration of the relationship between acts of pronunciation and the phonological units they are held to represent.

1.7 Form and substance

Two crucial notions underlying the perception of spoken language are **variability** and **pattern**. It was said earlier that variability (some of it principled and some of it apparently random) is an inherent characteristic of pronunciation, both within and between speakers. For spoken language to work effectively, it is imperative that despite the variability of the speech produced the perceiver should be able to discern the **distinctive patterns** in the speech-sounds that identify the phonological units involved.

This is not to say that the full complement of relevant distinctive patterns is unfailingly represented in the speech-sounds produced in every linguistic utterance. On many occasions of real, spontaneous speech, the speech material produced is somewhat impoverished of relevant patterning, for many different reasons. Through lifelong experience, however, the human perceptual system is very adept at making educated guesses at the intended message from only partial clues. This usually involves the use of phonological and grammatical knowledge as a predictive resource. Listeners can normally reconstitute the full message with ease from a reduced, everyday utterance, as would be the case in the following example in which some of the speech sounds might be omitted by a speaker:

Reduced utterance   She sh---d --v- giv-n -im the package
Full message   She should have given him the package

We can leave aside this normal state of affairs for the moment, however, and focus in the remainder of this chapter on the more ideal situation. This is one where the relevant distinctive pattern is fully available to the listener in the actual pronunciation of the material concerned.

Pattern as such is an abstract concept. To exist in the real world, a given pattern has to have a physical **embodiment** (or **realization**, or **manifestation**). Terms often associated with pattern and embodiment are 'form' and 'substance' respectively (Abercrombie 1967). **Form** is to do with the identity of the pattern as a representative of a linguistic unit, and **substance** is to do with the medium in which linguistic patterns are embodied. In this connection, **phonology** is often said to be the study of the form of spoken language, and **phonetics** to be the study of the substance of spoken language. It would be rather more accurate, in terms of some of the attitudes espoused by this book, to say that phonology and phonetics both concern themselves with the form and substance of spoken language, though they vary in their primary focus. Phonology has a primary interest in the form of spoken language, while phonetics has a primary interest in the substance of spoken language. This book, however, goes further than this. It presents phonetics as a subject that also takes a legitimate interest in facets of the substance of speech other than solely those that embody the formal symbolic patterns of spoken language. Two of these facets have already been mentioned. One (the evidential aspect of speech) concerns the way that evidence about the identity of the speaker is carried in speech. Another (the regulative aspect of speech) concerns the way that participants in a conversation co-operate with each other in the management of taking turns to occupy the role of speaker.

1.8 Code and medium

Formal aspects of speech make up the code of spoken language. A speaker **encodes** a message into its particular linguistic form by creating appropriate patterns through his or her manipulation of the **medium** of speech (Abercrombie 1967: 1). Since the code must be embodied in a physical medium, all instances of coded linguistic messages are necessarily transmitted as artefacts created out of the substance of that medium. The listener **decodes** the message partly by attending to the distinctive patterns available in the artefacts of the substance of the utterance, and partly through predictive knowledge of probable grammatical sequences and likely choices of vocabulary.

The events of speech are artefacts of the spoken medium, just as the events of writing are artefacts of the written medium. Because these events are artefacts, they not only embody patterns, they also carry with them clear evidential information about their manufacture. This information indicates both the type of apparatus used to create the artefacts, and the personal style of the artisan who made them. Evidence of the nature of the vocal apparatus lies in the characteristic voice quality of the speaker, and evidence of personal style lies for example in the details of the speaker's habitual pronunciation. When we perceive a spoken message, therefore, we are able not only to decode the linguistic form of the message, but may also be able to identify the speaker, through his or her voice and accent. The symbolic information communicating the linguistic message and the evidential information marking the identity of the speaker are hence two sides of the same coin.

1.9 Communicative and informative behaviour

The term 'communicative' has been used so far without definition. It may now be helpful to make the meaning of this term more explicit. An important semiotic distinction can be drawn between 'communicative' and 'informative' aspects of signals used in speech. A signal is **communicative** if 'it is intended by the sender to make the receiver aware of something of which he was not previously aware'. A signal is **informative** if, regardless of the intentions of the sender, 'it makes the receiver aware of something of which he was not previously aware' (Lyons 1977: 33). Linguistic activity is thus both communicative and informative, under these definitions.

1.10 Linguistic, paralinguistic and extralinguistic behaviour

It is convenient to draw a second set of distinctions between different means for conveying information in speech, differentiating between linguistic, paralinguistic and extralinguistic behaviour. All three types of behaviour are informative, in the terms introduced immediately above, but only linguistic and paralinguistic behaviour is coded and communicative.

The term **linguistic** is familiar from everyday use as an adjective associated with **language**. The commonest form of linguistic behaviour is communicative behaviour which uses the dual-level code of spoken language made up of the phonological and grammatical units discussed above. Other forms of linguistic behaviour are found in writing systems (and sign language), but it is worth pointing out that literate communication is still a minority activity in the language communities of the world.

Paralinguistic behaviour in speech is communicative behaviour that is non-linguistic and non-verbal, but which is nevertheless coded, and which is designed to achieve two goals of conversational interaction. These are the communication of the speaker's current affective, attitudinal or emotional state (such as anger, sadness, excitement, disappointment, happiness, cordiality etc.), and the regulation of the time-sharing of the conversation. The adjective 'paralinguistic' derives from the term 'paralanguage', which was first suggested by the American linguist Archibald Hill. Paralinguistic behaviour includes communication by tone of voice. As the label 'paralinguistic' suggests, it is in some respects similar to linguistic behaviour, and in some other respects dissimilar. It is similar to linguistic behaviour in that paralinguistic signs form a coded type of communication whose meaning is not necessarily obvious to all human perceivers on some universal basis. It is particular to the culture of the speaker, and its conventional interpretation must be learned. For example, the interactional meaning of the use of a falsetto tone of voice by an adult male speaker is not necessarily the same from one culture to another. One paralinguistic use of falsetto in English by male speakers is as a mocking device, where mimicking another participant's utterance with a falsetto phonation counts as an accusation of either effeminacy or whining complaint. In Tzeltal, a Mayan language of Mexico, however, the use of falsetto in greeting someone is a marker of honorific respect (Brown and Levinson 1978: 272). In Shona, a language of Zimbabwe, falsetto is used to mock someone thought to be boasting (B. Annan, personal communication).

Sequential structure is crucial to the way that language works, with grammatical units being given their distinctive shape by differing linear combinations of phonological units. Paralinguistic communication differs from linguistic behaviour in this respect, in that no meaningfulness is imparted by sequence, and there is therefore no possibility of meaningful structure. The choice from a conventional repertoire of a given paralinguistic tone of voice, for instance, involves no consideration of what the immediately earlier choice was, nor of what the next one might be, in terms of any 'tone of voice' structure. The only way in which sequential relationships carry any significance in paralinguistic communication is in judgements about the relative degree of manifestation of a feature. A judgement by the listener that a speaker has started to speak more slowly, for example, clearly depends on the speaker's earlier rate of articulation. But such a relationship is merely sequential and not structural, in the technical sense of 'structure' to be described in the next chapter.

Paralinguistic behaviour is also different from the linguistic behaviour of spoken language in that non-vocal elements play a very large part. Gesture, posture, body-movement, facial expressions and looking-behaviour all form part of the elaborate, coded, paralinguistic system of communication together with the vocal strand of tone of voice. Facial expression is the strand amongst these paralinguistic resources that is most similar to that of tone of voice.

Extralinguistic behaviour in speech is then the residue of the speech signal after analysis of all coded linguistic and paralinguistic aspects is complete. Non-coded, extralinguistic aspects of speech are often rich in evidential information about the identity of the speaker, particularly with respect to habitual factors such as the speaker's voice quality, and overall range of pitch and loudness (Laver 1980). Extralinguistic behaviour is thus informative, in the terms introduced earlier, but not communicative.

One might think that conclusions about social characteristics are more likely to be drawn from linguistic and paralinguistic sources, since by definition social characteristics are learned, not innate. Similarly, conclusions about psychological states and attributes might be thought to depend on linguistic and paralinguistic information. Equally, conclusions about physical attributes might be assumed to rely mostly on organic, extralinguistic information. The attribution of social, psychological and physical characteristics from speech cannot, however, be correlated directly with linguistic, paralinguistic and extralinguistic information respectively. In drawing conclusions about the personality of a speaker, for example, a listener may impute psychological attributes to the speaker (sometimes mistakenly) from evidence taken from any or all of the three sources of information (Sapir 1927). A listener might conclude, for instance, that a loud, resonant voice is correlated with an authoritative personality. But if that voice were solely the outcome of a large and powerful physique, then the listener would erroneously be drawing psychological conclusions from extralinguistic sources. The cognitive processes of attribution by listeners of social, psychological and physical characteristics to speakers from the rich variety of markers in their speech remains a fertile potential area for research (Laver and Trudgill 1979).

1.11 The domain of phonetics

Many traditional approaches to phonetics take the domain of the subject to be the description of spoken language. As evident from the Introduction, and from the comments offered in this chapter, this book urges a wider semiotic perspective, in the belief that the proper domain of phonetics as a discipline is the study of all aspects of speech. We shall return in chapter 4 to a more detailed consideration of the specific objectives of the discipline of phonetics.

Further reading

Sebeok (1991) is a readable and wide-ranging book about semiotics in general. Hartshorne and Weiss (1931–5) is a substantial edition of the collected writings of the pragmaticist philosopher Charles Sanders Peirce. The most accessible general introduction to Peirce's philosophy is Feibleman (1970). Burks (1949) continues some of Peirce's semiotic themes in his article on iconic, indexical and symbolic signs.

Useful textbooks and edited collections of articles about **sociolinguistics** are Chaika (1989), Fasold (1984, 1989), Fishman (1968), Gumperz (1983), Gumperz and Hymes (1986), Hudson (1980), Hymes (1974), Milroy (1980, 1987), Romaine (1982), Saville-Troika (1989), Trudgill (1978) and Wardhaugh (1986). Ager (1990) is a commentary on contemporary sociolinguistic variation in French in both France and Canada. Barbour and Stevenson (1990) outline sociolinguistic variation in German. Cheshire (1991) considers sociolinguistic matters in English in different countries in the world. For more references to sociolinguistic variation in English around the world, further recommended reading is suggested in chapter 3.

Topics in **general linguistics** are covered in the Cambridge University Press series of Textbooks in Linguistics, and in its other series on linguistics, in such publications as Allwood, Anderson and Dahl (1977) on logic in linguistics; Bauer (1983) on English word formation; Brown and Yule (1983) on discourse analysis; Bynon (1977) on historical linguistics; Comrie (1976) on aspect and (1985) on tense, and Palmer (1986) on mood and modality; Corbett (1991) on grammatical gender; Croft (1990) and Shopen (1985) on the typology of languages, and on typical grammatical features; Elliot (1981) on child language; Huddleston (1984, 1988) on the grammar of English; Hurford and Heasley (1983), Kempson (1977) and Lyons (1977) on semantics, and Cruse (1986) on lexical semantics; Levinson (1983) on pragmatics; Matthews (1974, 1981, 1991) on morphology and syntax respectively and Radford (1981, 1988) on transformational syntax. Newmeyer (1988, vol. I) is a review of most of these foundational areas of linguistic theory. Lyons (1968) is a comprehensive account of linguistic theory for students pursuing a specialized interest in the discipline; Lyons (1991) is a volume of essays on linguistic theory; and Lyons (1981) offers an overall view of linguistics for the educated non-specialist reader. Other recommended publications on **pragmatics** are Austin (1962), Blakemore (1992), Brown and Levinson (1978), Searle (1969) and Sperber and Wilson (1986).

The organization of behaviour in face-to-face **conversational interaction** is discussed in Atkinson and Heritage (1984), Kendon (1981), Laver (1976), Laver and Hutcheson (1972), Nofsinger (1991) Scherer and Ekman (1982) and Siegman and Feldstein (1978). A more detailed discussion of non-vocal behaviour and its relationship to vocal facets of conversation can be found in Buck (1984), Chaika (1989: 75–97), Coulmas (1981), Hinde (1972, 1974), Kendon (1981), Key (1980), Laver and Hutcheson (1972), Poyatos (1983) and Weitz (1974). Sacks, Schegloff and Jefferson (1974) is one of the foundational publications on strategies for conversational turn-taking.

Pioneering publications in **paralinguistics** were Abercrombie (1967, 1968),

Birdwhistell (1961), Crystal (1969), Crystal and Quirk (1964), Henry (1936), Pittenger, Hockett and Danehy (1960), Sapir (1927) and Trager (1958, 1960, 1961). Key (1975) contains a good bibliography of this pioneering stage. Crystal (1975) discusses the paralinguistic phonetic phenomena of **tone of voice** exploited by English. Scherer (1982) gives a useful account of the methodological principles of experiments on the communication of emotion by paralinguistic features of tone of voice, and van Bezooyen (1984) describes an interesting range of experiments on this topic. A classic earlier work on the signalling of emotional states in man and animals is Darwin (1872). Other useful sources that can be consulted on the vocal expression of emotion and affect are Scherer (1984, 1986a, 1986b, 1989), and Scherer, Wallbott and Summerfield (1986).

Major publications on **facial expression** are Ekman (1984), Ekman and Friesen (1978), Ekman, Friesen and Ellsworth (1982) and Izard (1971). Further references on **voice quality** include Catford (1964), Laver (1991) and Nolan (1983), and discussion of the attribution by listeners of physical, social and psychological characteristics of identity can be found in Darby (1981), Laver (1968, 1991) and Scherer and Giles (1979).

2

The relationship between phonetics and phonology

The point has now been reached where it is necessary to develop in more detail the concept of a number of levels of analysis of the material of speech production. This will be used throughout the rest of the book as a basic framework. The major part of the chapter will then focus on the discussion of the phonological level of analysis, and its relationship to phonetic analysis. A number of basic phonological concepts will be introduced, amongst which those of the phoneme and the allophone, together with the idea of phonological structure and system, are the most central.

2.1 The acoustic level

The initial level of analysis of speech production, closest to the physics of the original speech material itself, is the **acoustic level**. Two speech events can be considered to be different at the acoustic level, in either quality or timing, when an instrumental acoustic analyser of any sort can register discernible evidence of the difference. Two repetitions by a single speaker of vocal material that is linguistically and paralinguistically identical are most unlikely to be acoustically exactly the same. Two such utterances from two different speakers are virtually certain, except by the most random operation of chance, to be acoustically different (Perkell and Klatt 1986).

This level of analysis is the subject matter of **acoustic phonetics**, and will not be the principal concern of this book. Many good introductions to acoustic phonetics exist, including Baken (1987), Borden and Harris (1980), Fry (1979) and Ladefoged (1962). Other works on acoustic phonetics are suggested in the Further Reading at the end of the chapter.

2.2 The perceptual level

This level of analysis concerns the registration by the perceiver of sensory data of all relevant types. The sensory system which will figure most often in discussion in this book will be the auditory system and the sense of hearing, as a resource common to both the speaker and the listener.

But the senses of touch, pressure, muscle-tension and joint-position are all also relevant to considerations of how speakers control and monitor the actions of their vocal apparatus in the production of speech.

The auditory system is subject, as are all sensory systems, to psychophysical ranges and limits of sensitivity, and these are discussed at more length in chapter 15. The term **perceptual** will be used in the remainder of this book, if offered without further qualification, to refer specifically to auditory perception.

There are four perceptual domains available to the human auditory system which are exploited in listening to speech. These are the domains of perceptual **quality, duration, pitch** and **loudness**. The only way that sounds can differ audibly from each other is in terms of these four perceptual attributes. Chapters 6–13 offer a description of the ways that a speaker can control the production of sounds which differ in their perceptual quality. Chapters 14 and 17 describe the ways in which the units of speech can differ in terms of their **temporal** characteristics (duration, rate and continuity). Chapter 15 describes the **prosodic** attributes of speech (pitch and loudness). Chapter 16 then explores the way that facets of all four domains – quality, duration, pitch and loudness – are integrated to form the **metrical** structure of speech, in terms of its stress and rhythm.

2.3 The organic level

The next level of analysis to be discussed is the **organic level**. Speakers differ organically from each other in anatomical factors such as the dimensions, mass and geometry of their vocal organs. They will differ in such details as the overall length of the vocal tract; the volume and shape of the pharynx, mouth and nasal cavities; the nature of the dentition, the size and shape of the lips, tongue and lower jaw; the three-dimensional geometry of the structures in the larynx; and the volume and power of the respiratory system. People differ in the organic basis of their vocal apparatus no less than they do in the details of their facial appearance. That this should be so is less surprising than it might seem at first, given the anatomical connection that necessarily exists between the two.

More minor physiological factors may also play a role at the organic level, when the degree of muscular tonus changes for reasons outside the voluntary control of the speaker (such as excitement or fatigue), or when endocrinal or hormonal states have an effect on the detailed quality of the speaker's vocal performance. A speaker may produce utterances which differ to some small degree in these more minor physiological factors, while still being identical in linguistic and paralinguistic respects. Utterances from a single speaker may also differ on a more striking organic basis when his or her state of health varies. A cold in the head, for instance, can often change a person's voice rather dramatically.

Two different speakers will almost always differ on the organic level, even though they may be judged to be producing linguistically and paralinguistically identical utterances. Only in the case of identical twins is it at all likely that the organic anatomical make-up of any two speakers could be more closely similar.

The extremely low probability of two speakers being organically the same, and therefore having the potential to produce very close copies of each other's utterances, has implications for the nature of imitative mimicry. Since mimics and impostors cannot change the organic basis of their vocal apparatus, even though they can to some extent compensate for organic differences by muscular adjustments, they are obliged to select individual features for imitation from the complex of features that characterize their target speaker. Mimicry is therefore necessarily a stereotyping process, not one of exact copying. The process of imitation, and by extension the process of a child's initial acquisition of patterns of speech, therefore depend on activities at the next level of analysis, the 'phonetic' level, which concerns voluntary, learnable movements of the vocal apparatus.

2.4   The phonetic level

If the organic foundation of a speaker's vocal apparatus endows him or her with quasi-permanent voice characteristics, the voluntary use the speaker can learn to make of the apparatus is much more plastic. The term **phonetic** will be used in this book to refer to any learnable aspect of use of the vocal apparatus. One could alternatively construe this as the aspect of speech under 'potential muscular control', but it is probably more helpful to insist on the 'learnability' of phonetic activity. This has the advantage of emphasizing the fact that the individual speaker acquires phonetic behaviour in a social context, guided by norms of phonetic similarity to the speech behaviour of the community in which the child grows up.

It is one of the most basic assumptions of phonetic theory that two organically different speakers should be able to produce phonetically identical utterances. This amounts to claiming that two spoken events can be phonetically identical but nevertheless sound acoustically different. The basis for maintaining this is that the phonetic level of description is abstract, not concrete. An assertion about **phonetic sameness** between two sounds is an assertion of comparability of particular abstract features in the sounds, rather than a claim about complete acoustic identity. To say that two sounds are phonetically equivalent rests on an idealizing assumption that organic differences between speakers can be ignored in evaluating phonetic quality, as if both speakers could be held to be producing their performance on the same notional vocal apparatus. Phonetic sameness, which has to be conceded as a possibility before descriptive phonetic theory can work at all, is thus not a simple concept.

A speech event capable of displaying **phonetic equivalence** between speakers will be called a **phone**. The adjective from 'phone' will be taken in this book to be 'phonetic'. The notion of phonetic equivalence is one extreme of the scale of **phonetic similarity**. This concept of phonetic similarity is explored in detail in chapter 13.

Phonetic description is said to be based on the assumption that the process of description does not require knowledge about the formal, linguistic value that the event being described might have as a coded, communicative element in some particular language. In this sense, phonetic description of a given stretch of speech is held to be independent of the phonological description of the language involved. This forms the basis on which descriptive phonetic theory can be regarded as a general theory capable of application to the sounds of any language in the world.

It is not completely true, however, that the categories of phonetic description have evolved entirely independently of experience of typical correspondences between phonological units and their phonetic manifestations in languages in general. The structure of general phonetic theory is inevitably coloured to a certain extent by general phonological considerations. This point is explored further in chapter 4, in the discussion of the concept of phonetic units as basic descriptive categories.

2.4.1 *Phonetic notation*

One of the chief resources of phonetics is **phonetic notation**, as a set of written symbols used for transcribing the phones of actual pronunciation. In order to distinguish **phonetic transcription** from orthographic and other symbols, a widely followed convention will be adopted in this book of enclosing phonetic symbols in **square brackets**. The orthographic representation *seen* will be transcribed phonetically as [sin], for example. The detailed meaning of all the different phonetic symbols used will be introduced more fully in appropriate chapters. When an understanding of the phonetic meaning of a symbol is necessary for an appreciation of the theoretical point under discussion in this chapter, a brief description will be offered. Chapter 18 provides a general discussion of different types of transcription, and suggests principles for their classification.

2.5 The phonological level

The next level of analysis to be considered is the **phonological level**. Phonology is a very large and active subject with a very substantial literature, some of which is recommended in the section on Further Reading at the end of the chapter.

We have seen that the function of phonology is to relate the phonetic events of speech to **grammatical units** operating at the morphological, lexical, syntactic and semantic levels of language. Phonology is intimately connected with the phonetic study of speech – indeed it is not unreasonable to suggest that neither good phonology nor good phonetics is feasible without an adequate understanding of the other. For more comprehensive accounts of phonological theory as such, the references cited immediately above should be consulted. The central concern of this book is rather to give an account of a descriptive phonetic theory which will be of use in relating phonetic material to the study of phonology. The exposition given in this chapter on the relation between phonetics and phonology is therefore limited to an outline of the basic concepts necessary to understand the phonological roles of speech-sounds discussed in the later chapters on general phonetic description.

At the phonological level of analysis, two utterances are held to be different if the phonetic differences between them serve to identify the two utterances as representing different grammatical units of a given language. When two utterances are phonologically identical except for one distinctive difference, the two grammatical units involved are said to form a **minimal pair** of contrasting forms.

Limiting exemplification in the remainder of this chapter to grammatical units at the word level (**lexical units**), and to phonological units at the level of consonants and vowels, we can say, for instance, that a minimally different pair of words in English is *pan* and *tan*. The relevant phonetic difference that distinguishes them is that the consonant at the beginning of the first word is pronounced with the lips momentarily closing off the escape of the breath from the mouth, while the consonant at the beginning of the second word is pronounced with the tip or blade of the tongue sealing off the escape of the airflow. The two initial consonants, when they serve to distinguish different words in this way, are said to have a **contrastive function**, and to be in **opposition** to each other in the phonological code of which they are elements. The process of substituting one element for another to establish that an opposition exists in the language under examination is sometimes called a **commutation test**, and the elements which display such an opposition are said to have a **commutative relationship** with each other.

In order to be quite explicit about the level of analysis concerned, whenever phonological elements with a contrastive grammatical function are being discussed, their transcription will be enclosed in **slant brackets**. This convention is used very widely by linguists and phoneticians. The minimal lexical pair in English mentioned above, *pan* and *tan*, would be transcribed phonologically as /pan/ and /tan/ respectively. This means that comment on contrastive phonological elements involved, through the use of slant brackets, can be distinguished from the provision of detailed information on their pronunciation, for which square phonetic brackets are used.

Using the type of brackets as a signal of the level of analysis concerned allows not only a very desirable explicitness, but also provides a means for making concise statements about the phonetic manifestations of phonological elements. It is possible, for instance, to say that the word *pan* /pan/ in a given accent of English is pronounced as [pʰan], where the phonetic meaning of [ʰ] is that the onset of voicing for the vowel after [p] is audibly delayed for a fraction of a second. (Voicing, which is the buzzing sound which can be heard when the vocal folds in the larynx are made to vibrate, is fully explained in chapter 7.) A yet more compact version of the statement about the phonetic manifestation of the phonological elements would be the formula:

$$/pan/ \Rightarrow [p^han]$$

where the arrow '$\Rightarrow$' (or its equivalent '$\rightarrow$') stands for the relation 'is pronounced as', or 'is manifested phonetically as', or 'is realized phonetically as'. The formulaic device of the arrow will be used in the rest of this book in this realizational sense.

As with phonetic symbols, the meaning of phonological symbols will be explained in this chapter only if they are crucial to an understanding of the discussion. Otherwise they are merely illustrated here, and explained in detail in later chapters. Before going further, it is necessary to discuss three major facets of phonological organization. Appeal will be made to the notions of 'system', 'structure' and 'context'.

2.5.1 *Phonological system*

We have seen that there is a contrastive opposition in English between the initial consonants of the words *pan* /pan/ and *tan* /tan/. In fact, the list of consonants which are in potential opposition at this initial place in the set of such words in English is larger than merely /p/ and /t/. Other minimal pairs are provided by the availability, for example, of /k/ in *can*, /b/ in *ban*, /d/ in *Dan*, /m/ in *man*, /n/ in *Nan*, /f/ in *fan*, /v/ in *van*, /ð/ in *than* and

/r/ in *ran*. This list of consonants in potential distinctive opposition to each other is called a **phonological system**, and the items in such a list can be said to be in **systemic contrast**. Similar vowel systems exist in word sets such as *heed* /hid/, *hid* /hɪd/, *head* /hɛd/, *had* /had/ etc. The minimally contrasting word-sets which display permutations of possible consonants (or vowels) at one place in structure are said to constitute a **paradigm** of such words, and **paradigmatic opposition** is a synonym for 'contrastive opposition' as introduced above.

A different system operates at each different place in the structure of a given set of minimally contrasting words. So, for instance, a system of choices of vowels serves to contrast *pan* /pan/ with *pin* /pɪn/, *pen* /pɛn/, *pawn* /pɔn/ and *pun* /pʌn/. Similarly, a system of consonants (different from the initial-place system just described) yields contrasts at the final place in the word, between *pan* /pan/, *Pam* /pam/, *pang* /paŋ/, *pal* /pal/, *pap* /pap/, *pat* /pat/, *pack* /pak/, *patch* /patʃ/ and *pad* /pad/. The elements of each of these systems can be thought of as being in potential competition with the other elements of the same system to fill the relevant place in the structure of the word.

2.5.2 *Phonological structure and the phonological syllable*

The examples in the preceding section were all of words of identical **phonological structure**. All were words made up by a sequence of an initial consonant, followed by a vowel, followed by a final consonant. But words can differ from each other not only in the matter of which item is chosen from a relevant system for occupancy of a given place in the structure of the word, but also in terms of the chosen sequence of consonants and vowels that gives the word its structural shape. The three words in English *tuck*, *truck* and *struck* (transcribed phonologically as /tʌk/, /trʌk/ and /strʌk/) are all structurally different. Using **C** to mean 'a consonant' and **V** to mean 'a vowel', structural formulae for these three words are CVC, CCVC and CCCVC respectively.

Formulae of this sort are usually used to comment on the phonological structure of individual **syllables**. The examples in the previous paragraph happen to be **monosyllabic** words. When a syllable ends in a vowel, with no final consonant, it is said to be an **open syllable**. The English word *bee* /bi/ is an open syllable of CV structure. Another way of putting this is to say that the syllable ends in zero consonants. A general symbol for 'zero' is '∅'. The syllable-structure formula for an open syllable would then be CV∅. Conversely, when the syllable is terminated by a consonant, it is said to be a **closed syllable**. The English word *bit* /bɪt/ is a closed syllable of CVC structure. (The **phonological syllable** is a concept discussed at greater length in chapter 4; it is sufficient here simply to note that one of its principal uses is to frame descriptive statements about the mutual distribution of vowels and consonants.)

Languages differ in the different syllabic structures they allow, in terms of how many consonants can begin or end a syllable, whether vowels can begin syllables, and whether both open and closed syllables are possible. It is a **structural** fact about the accents of the English language, for instance, that the maximum number of consonants that can make up the leading edge of a syllable at the beginning of an isolated word is three. The first of these can only be /s/, the second has to be selected from /p, t, k/, and the third from /r, l, w, j/, giving such words as the following:

Three-consonant syllable onsets in English
/spleɪd/ splayed   /streɪd/ strayed   /skreɪp/ scrape
/spjum/ spume   /stjud/ stewed   /skjud/ skewed
/skwɪʃ/ squish   /skwɔk/ squawk   /skwil/ squeal

The syllables in all the words in the above examples show the structure CCCVC. Notice that when the third consonant is /w/, then the first two consonants in English are obliged to be /s/ and /k/. There are some further **combinatorial constraints** between these units in an initial cluster of three consonants: /spr-/ and /str-/ are both permitted in English, but /spw-/ and /stw-/ are not legitimate occurrences within the same syllable.

English is somewhat unusual in allowing syllabic onsets of a maximum of three consonants. Most languages do not allow as many. Another example of a language in which three-consonant onsets are permitted (though rare) is Qatari Arabic, which nevertheless has a somewhat different pattern from English. The first consonant must be /s/, as in English; the second can only be /t/; but the third can be drawn from a wider range, which includes /q, ʃ, ʕ, m/ (Bukshaisha 1985: 33):

Three-consonant word onsets in Qatari Arabic
/stqiːl/ 'resign!'   /stʃiːr/ 'consult'
/'stʕaːraː/ 'borrowing'   /'stmaːra/ 'a form'

Serbo-Croatian is similar to English in allowing three-consonant onsets, but the choice of consonants in this language is less restricted. Sloat, Taylor and Hoard (1978: 64) make the following comments about the Serbo-Croatian rules: 'In Serbo-Croatian, the first consonant of a three-part onset is not limited to *s*, but may be any of the fricatives [s, z, ʃ, ʒ, h] or [ɡ]; the second may be a voiced or voiceless stop, or [m] or [v]; and the third may be a glide ([w] or [j]), a liquid ([r] or [l]), or [v] or [n].' They give the following examples to illustrate their comments (*ibid.*). The transcription is enclosed here in square phonetic brackets because the exact phonological status of their transcription is unspecified.

> *Three-consonant syllable onsets in Serbo-Croatian*
> [smraad] 'filth'   [ʒdrijebac] 'stallion'
> [svjedok] 'witness'   [ʒglob] 'joint'
> [ʃtrik] 'rope'   [htjeti] 'to want'
> [ʃkrina] 'box'   [gdje] 'where'
> [zgneetʃiti] 'to crush'   [zdvojiti] 'to get together'

The classic examples of languages with very long clusters of consonants as permissible syllable-onsets are the languages of the Caucasus. In Georgian, a South Caucasian (or Kartvelian) language, syllable-initial clusters of consonants can range from two to six, as in the following examples (Catford 1977b: 292):

> *Multiple consonant clusters as syllable-onsets in Georgian*
> [prts'kvna] 'to peel'   [ts'vrtna] 'to train'   [brts'q'inva] 'to shine'

The sequence 'ts'' in these Georgian examples functions as a single consonant in that language, so the word meaning 'to peel' has an initial consonant cluster of six consonants, the word for 'to train' has five, and the word for 'to shine' has four. The diacritic sign ['] means that the sound immediately preceding it is an 'ejective' sound; this is described in detail in chapter 6.

A vowel can be regarded as the **nucleus** of a phonological syllable. Every syllable in every language must obligatorily have a nucleus (though we shall see that in some circumstances in some languages the nuclear place in a given syllable may be filled by what some readers may prefer to call a consonant). However, even though every syllable must have a nucleus, it is not obligatory in every language that the syllable must have a consonantal onset. If the onset of a syllable is regarded as the initial place in the structure of the syllable, potentially fillable by one or more consonants, it is also possible for this place to be left empty (i.e. to be filled by zero consonants). Thus in English (RP), the syllable structure of a word such as 'end' /ɛnd/ can be represented as VCC (or ØVCC). Other examples of words with syllable structures showing zero-consonant onsets are:

> *Zero-consonant onsets to words in English*
> /ant/ 'ant'   /ilz/ 'eels'
> /ist/ 'east'   /ɒks/ 'ox'

Some languages, such as Quileute, Coeur d'Alène and Puget Salish, which are all Amerindian languages, do not allow this vowel-onset structure, and word-initial syllables all have a consonantal onset. The majority of the languages of the world, however, do permit zero-consonant onsets to word-initial syllables, as in the following illustrations from Hawaiian and Finnish (Sloat, Taylor and Hoard 1978: 64):

> *Zero-consonant onsets to words in Hawaiian*
> [ahi] 'fire'   [ola] 'life'
>
> *Zero-consonant onsets to words in Finnish*
> [on] 'is'   [iso] 'large'

Hawaiian, and Finnish differ from English, however, in that while their syllables may begin with either a consonant or a vowel, they cannot begin with more than one consonant.

English, as we have seen, allows open syllables and closed syllables. The number of final consonants in closed syllables in English can range from one to four consonants, as in 'sick' /sɪk/ (CVC), 'six' /sɪks/ (CVCC), 'sixth' /sɪksθ/ (CVCCC) and 'sixths' /sɪksθs/ (CVCCCC). In many West African languages, however, such as Etsako (Laver 1969: 49) and Urhobo (Kelly 1969: 157), only open syllables are phonologically permitted, as in the following instances:

> *Open syllables in Etsako*
> [uta] 'to say'   [una] 'to run'
> [usa] 'to shoot'   [ozi] 'crab'
>
> *Open syllables in Urhobo*
> [se] 'read!'   [so] 'sing!'
> [si] 'write!' [hɔ] 'wash!'

In Etsako, the words are made up in these cases of two open syllables of structure V + CV. When words originally made up of closed syllables are borrowed into Etsako from another language, as in the case of a **loanword** borrowed from English with a structure -VC such as *bread* (CCVC), Etsako speakers regularize the syllable-structure pattern to conform to the rules of Etsako phonology. They insert an extra vowel in the appropriate places, thereby creating a CV+CV+CV syllable structure, to give the form /burɛdi/ (Laver 1969: 55). Firth (1948) refers to this process as **naturalization**, and gives the example of the English loanword *screwdriver* being naturalized in Hausa, a language of Northern Nigeria and sub-Saharan Africa, as [sukuru direba], in which all the syllables are made into open syllables. (The symbol 'r' in the above loanword examples in Etsako and Hausa is a general symbol for an 'r-sound', with no specific implication as to the exact phonetic realization). A similar example comes from Turkish, where the English loan-word *sport* is naturalized as [si'por] (Waterson 1956), because of sequential consonantal constraints in Turkish not allowing [s] and [p] to occur next to each other at the beginning of a syllable.

2.5.2.1 *Definition of a minimal pair of words*

Now that the concept of phonological structure has been established, the notion of a **minimal pair** of words can be amplified into a definition:

> *A minimal pair of words consists of two words of identical structure in a given accent of a language, which differ in the systemic choice made at only one place in that structure.*

While /pan/ and /tan/, both of CVC structure, form a minimal pair in English, /pan/ and /tap/ do not, though both are also of CVC structure, because they differ in more than one structural place. The words /span/ and /tan/ do not form a minimal pair either, because their structures (CCVC and CVC) are not identical.

2.5.3 *Phonological context*

When considering the characteristics of individual phonological units such as consonants and vowels, it is important to know in which contexts they can be found. One aspect of **context** is the structural position in which the unit can occur. This can be referred to as the unit's **structural context**. In English, for instance, /h/ can occur in syllable-initial position, as in *hat* /hat/, or in *perhaps* /pəhaps/ (structurally CV + CVCC), but nowhere else. The consonant /ŋ/, usually spelt *ng*, as in *hang* /haŋ/ and *hanging* /haŋɪŋ/ (structurally CVC + VC), can occur in syllable-final position, but nowhere else. Unlike either /h/ or /ŋ/, /p/ can occur in either syllable-initial or syllable-final position, as in *pip* /pɪp/, and so can /t/, as in *tot* /tɒt/, and /k/, as in *cook* /kʊk/.

Another aspect of context is the identity of elements adjacent to the individual phonological unit such as a given consonant or vowel. This can be referred to as the unit's **environment**, or **environmental context**. In terms of preceding environmental context of this sort (**left-context**), in single words in English /ŋ/ can only occur after vowels of relatively short duration. There are many examples of words like *sing* /sɪŋ/ and *long* /lɒŋ/. But there are no words in English which have relatively long vowels preceding /ŋ/, which would have to be spelt *seeng* or *lawng* or *voong*, for instance. Similarly, at the beginning of a word, /l/ can only occur either by itself, as in *long* /lɒŋ/, or after /p, b, k, g, f, s/, as in *played* /pleɪd/, *blade* /bleɪd/, *clay* /kleɪ/, *glade*

/gleɪd/, *flayed* /fleɪd/ or *slay* /sleɪ/. There are a few words used by English speakers which break this rule, such as *shlep* and *zloty*, but these are loan-words from other languages, and are signalled as such by having contextual shapes that are not a native part of the phonology of English.

In terms of succeeding environmental context (or **right-context**), in some accents of English /r/ is not able to be followed by another consonant within the same syllable, whereas in others (the majority) this is permitted. For example, the word *port* is pronounced /pɔt/ in RP and many accents of England, but /port/ in many American accents.

The importance of taking phonological context into account lies not least in the influence it has on the detailed phonetic manifestation of the phono-logical unit concerned. The pronunciation of a given consonant or vowel can be sensitive to either or both structural and environmental context. In English, /p/ has a number of different pronunciations depending on these two factors. As mentioned earlier, in initial position in a word like *pan* /pan/ ⇒ [pʰan], there is a moment of relative silence after the lips open for the release of the consonant, when only the outflowing breath is audible (sig-nalled by the [ʰ] in the phonetic transcription), before the pronunciation of the vowel can be heard. We shall use the phonetic term **aspiration** to refer to this detail of pronunciation, and the [p] can therefore be said to be **aspirated**. In *span* /span/, pronounced typically as [span], there is no such momentary silence, and the onset of audible voicing for the vowel is simultaneous with the opening of the lips. The pronunciation of /p/ is therefore said to be **unaspirated** in English in this position. Aspirated and unaspirated sounds are discussed at greater length in chapter 12.

Different adjacent elements have their effect also. The pronunciation of /p/ in *span* /span/ ⇒ [span] is different from that in *spoon* /spun/ ⇒ [spʷun], with the lips being held momentarily in a more rounded position for /p/ in *spoon* [spʷun] than for /p/ in *span* [span], (with the rounded position of the lips being signalled by the diacritic [ʷ] in the phonetic tran-scription). This is because in the pronunciation of the /p/ of *spoon* the mus-cles that control the position of the lips are being made to anticipate the rounded posture needed for the pronunciation of the following /u/ vowel. We shall use the phonetic term **lip-rounded**, for the moment, to refer to this detail of pronunciation. The precise area and shape of the opening of the lips varies with that of the sound whose anticipatory influence is being exerted on the sound in question, but this fine degree of detail is not usually annotated by using different transcriptional diacritics. Lip-rounding (under the more technical label 'labialization') is discussed at greater length in chapter 11.

2.5.4   *Phonological distribution*

An individual consonant or an individual vowel in the phonology of a given language can occur in different locations. This contextual concept has been expressed above in terms of the possibilities of location in different syllable structures and different environmental contexts. For any given consonant or vowel, the range of possible locations is constrained by the phonology of the language. This range of permitted locations constitutes the **phonological distribution** of that consonant or vowel. It is knowledge of constraints on such distributions that enables a speaker to decide that *zloty* cannot be a native word in English, because the sequence /zl-/ breaks the rules about contextual occurrences in syllable-initial structural position of the /z/ and /l/ consonants. The distributional range of contextual occurrences of a given consonant or vowel in an accent is said to constitute its **phonotactic range**.

The distributions of two consonants (or two vowels) are often compared, for purposes of describing the phonological function of the segments in question. When two consonants or two vowels share the same distribution exactly (that is, when they can be said to have exactly the same phonotactic range), they are said to be in **parallel distribution**, or to be **distributionally equivalent** (Lyons 1968: 70). When they share no locations, they are said to be in **complementary distribution**.

Consonants which are in parallel distribution are in contrastive opposition to each other, since by definition they are competing for occupancy of the same places in structure. Consonants which are in complementary distribution are not in contrastive opposition to each other, since by definition they are never in competition for occupancy of the same places in structure. There are also, however, many instances in languages where the consonants show an **overlapping distribution**, where some contexts are shared and some are not (Lyons 1968: 71). All the statements in this paragraph hold equally true for relationships between vowels.

In English, almost no two consonants (or two vowels) show precisely the same phonotactic range, and the condition of parallel distribution can therefore normally be achieved only on the more restricted consideration of overlapping distribution. Even /p/ and /b/ differ in their phonotactic range in English, though they are otherwise rather similarly distributed, in that /b/ cannot occur in syllable-final position after /m/, though /p/ can, as in *lamp* /lamp/ and *jump* /dʒʌmp/.

2.5.5   *The phoneme as a contrastive and distributed phonological unit made up of phonetically similar allophones*

The discussion above has made appeal to the notion of a given consonant (or vowel) participating in two axes of interaction with other consonants (or vowels). The two axes are the **systemic axis** and the **contextual axis**.

First, taking consonants as representative, each consonant is firstly a member of a number of consonantal systems whose other members compete with that consonant for occupancy of the relevant structural place in sets of English words. The systemic axis can be figuratively thought of as a 'vertical' axis of interaction, in that the system operating at syllable-final position for the sequence /pa__ / in the **paradigm** of existing monosyllabic English words in an American accent (*pap, pat, pack, pad, patch, path, pass, Pam, pan, pang* and *pal*) can be represented graphically in the following way:

p
t
k
d
ʧ
θ
s
m
n
ŋ
l
/pa__ /

This systemic, vertical axis is sometimes called the **paradigmatic axis**.

Second, each consonant participates in a 'horizontal' axis of contextual distribution into different phonotactic possibilities. This horizontal axis is sometimes called the **syntagmatic axis**, because of the underlying idea of 'chaining' that is implicit ('syntagma' is derived from the Greek word for a link in a chain). This notion of a linear 'chained' sequence of units is of course general to the different levels of linguistic analysis, and is of major importance at the phonological level. It was first explicitly introduced into linguistics by the structuralist teachings of the great Swiss linguist Ferdinand de Saussure nearly a century ago (Crystal 1985: 299). The general concept of a syntagma was described by de Saussure in an illustration of word-sequences (though the argument holds equally well for the sequence of phonological units):

> words acquire relations based on the linear nature of language because
> they are chained together ... The elements are arranged in sequence
> on the chain of speaking. Combinations supported by linearity are
> *syntagms*. The syntagm is always composed of two or more

> consecutive units (e.g. French *re-lire* 're-read', *contre tous* 'against everyone', *la vie humaine* 'human life', *Dieu est bon* 'God is good', *s'il fait beau temps, nous sortirons* 'if the weather is nice, we'll go out' etc.). In the syntagm a term acquires its value only because it stands in opposition to everything that precedes or follows it, or to both.
> (de Saussure 1916 (1966): 123)

We have seen that, from the perspective of different contextual possibilities, different consonants are often subject to different syntagmatic constraints. The consonant /j/, for instance, as in *yet* /jɛt/ can only occur syllable-initially in English by itself, or in consonantal contexts after /p, t, k, b, d, g, m, n, f, v, θ, s, z, l/. The consonant /w/, on the other hand, as in *wet* /wɛt/ can only occur by itself, or in consonantal contexts after /t, k, d, g, θ, s/. A partial syntagmatic constraint in English on /w/, therefore, is that it cannot occur syllable-initially in native English words immediately after a consonant from the set /p, b, m, f, v/, whose pronunciation, like that of /w/, involves the participation of the lips. This is true of English, but is not true of many other languages, such as French, where a pronunciation such as *moi* /mwɑ/ ('me') is fully orthodox.

The phrase introduced by de Saussure for the paradigm of choices made at any one place in a syntagmatic chain was an 'associative opposition'. He recognized that the two fundamental concepts of syntagmatic and paradigmatic organization expressed relationships that are not only ones of opposition, but also ones that serve to limit the otherwise apparently arbitrary multiplicity of the type and number of linguistic signs in a language. The structures and systems of a language (or of an accent) are finite in number and characteristic of that language. In a discussion of the 'motivation' of the design of language, de Saussure commented that:

> The notion of relative motivation implies: (1) analysis of a given term, hence a syntagmatic relation; and (2) the summoning of one or more other terms, hence an associative relation ... Up to this point units have appeared as values, i.e. as elements of a (system or structure), and we have given special consideration to their opposition; now we recognize the solidarities that bind them; they are associative and syntagmatic, and they are what limits arbitrariness. *Dix-neuf* is supported associatively by *dix-huit*, *soixante-dix*, etc. and syntagmatically by its elements *dix* and *neuf* ... This dual relation gives it a part of its value ... In fact, the whole system of language is based on the irrational principle of the arbitrariness of the sign, which would lead to the worst sort of complication if applied without restriction. (*ibid.*, pp. 132–3)

2.5.5.1 *Definitions of the phoneme and the allophone*

It is now possible to introduce two very widely used phonological concepts, that of the **phoneme** and the **allophone**. The notion of the phoneme has its roots in the alphabetic tradition of writing (Jones 1957), and there are almost as many definitions of the phoneme as there have been phoneticians and phonologists. It is a very convenient concept, but definitions of the phoneme should be understood as exemplary rather than theoretically strict.

In this book, a definition of the phoneme can be approached by invoking the phonological ideas introduced above of contrastive function, system, structure, context, parallel distribution, complementary distribution and overlapping distribution. The paradigmatic and syntagmatic axes of interaction described immediately above furnish the basis for the definition, which is presented here in two parts. The first part of the definition focuses on the issue of contrastiveness between one phoneme and another, and the second part on the issue of the contextually-distributed nature of the members of a phoneme conceived as a set of sounds.

The first part of the definition of a **phoneme** is as follows:

> *Two speech sounds are said to be manifestations of different phonemes in a given accent of a language when they act as the basis of a contrastive opposition that distinguishes a pair of words of identical phonological structure, differing in the systemic choice made at a single place in that structure.*

In order to satisfy these conditions, the two speech sounds must thus show parallel distribution over the context in question, in that both sounds must have the potential of occupying the single place in structure concerned. Phonemes can be transcribed using symbols enclosed in slant brackets, as in the transcription of the English word *cat* /kat/, and such **phonemic transcription** will be treated as an instance of a **phonological transcription**, as introduced earlier.

This first part of the definition is idealistic in that it makes appeal to the notion of minimal pairs of words of identical structure, whereas in any accent of a given language such minimal pairs may be only sparsely available, through the accidental circumstances of the lexical evolution of the language. English is relatively rich in such minimal pairs, as it happens. Where minimal pairs of words are not available, then the weaker condition of overlapping (rather than fully parallel) distribution over the relevant subpart of the words in question can apply.

The second part of the definition of a **phoneme** is as follows:

> *Speech sounds regularly occurring in a number of different*
> *structures and contexts may be classified as members of a given*
> *phoneme if their occurrences are in complementary distribution,*
> *and if they display sufficient phonetic similarity to make it*
> *plausible to class them together as members of a common set.*

The members of a given phoneme are called **allophones**. Allophones can be transcribed by using phonetic symbols enclosed in square brackets, as in the pronunciation of the English word *peep* as [pʰipˑ]. The [ʰ] element of this transcription means that, after the tiny but audible explosion when the lips separate at the end of the pronunciation of the first [p], there is a perceptible delay of about a twentieth of a second before the buzzing sound technically called **voicing** begins for the following vowel; this is the same process as exemplified by [ʰ] in the transcription of *pan* [pʰ an] discussed earlier. The [ˑ] element of the transcription means that the second [p] sound typically lacks this audible explosion, when it is in final position in an utterance. We shall use the phonetic term **unreleased** to refer to this detail of pronunciation. Unlike the unreleased pronunciation of [pˑ], the pronunciation of [pʰ] is **released**, as well as being **aspirated**. The concept of release of particular types of sounds is discussed at greater length in chapter 12. In this example, the two [p] sounds are in complementary distribution, in that under the rules governing the phonetics of English [pʰ] is appropriate for the pronunciation of the /p/ phoneme as a single consonant at the beginning of a syllable, while [pˑ] is appropriate for a pronunciation of the /p/ phoneme in utterance-final position.

It is important to note that the concept of an allophone is itself an abstract concept, and is not to be equated directly with that of a phone, which is a single differentiable phonetic event. The phonetic manifestation of a given allophone may vary slightly, on a random basis. On each occasion that a phonetic difference is perceptible, a different phone is involved. To take the example given immediately above, the [pʰ] element in the allophonic transcription [pʰipˑ] can on different occasions represent several slightly different phones, where the duration of delay in the onset of voicing is fractionally but audibly different.

A more extended example of allophones in a Southern British English accent which satisfy the conditions of complementary distribution and phonetic similarity mentioned in the definition of the phoneme, and which are therefore candidates for being grouped into a single phoneme, can be found in the following illustration. This shows different phonetic realizations of the phoneme /p/ (coincidentally always spelled 'p' in the orthography of English) in words such as:

peat /piːt/ ⇒ [pʰiːt], where the [pʰ] is aspirated, but where the lips are not rounded, because the lip position for the following vowel is unrounded;

pot /pɒt/ ⇒ [pʰʷɒt], where the [pʰʷ] is aspirated and lip-rounded;

spot /spɒt/ ⇒ [spʷɒt], where the [pʷ] is lip-rounded but unaspirated;

pop /pɒp/ ⇒ [pʰʷɒp˺], where the lips can in some circumstances at the end of an utterance remain closed rather than opening to release the compressed air built up during the final [p], so that the [p˺] is unreleased;

port /pɔːt/ ⇒ [pʰʷɔːt], where the [pʰʷ] is aspirated and lip-rounded (with a degree of rounding of the lips which is slightly more extreme for *port* than for *pot*, because the lip position for the following vowel has a smaller, more rounded opening in the case of *port*).

In the above cases, the pronunciations of /p/ show a strong degree of phonetic similarity to each other, in that they all involve the lips momentarily closing completely, with a simultaneous absence of voicing. They also show a variety of phonetic differences from each other (differences of aspiration versus non-aspiration, release or non-release, and differences in the presence and degree of lip-rounding).

These phonetic differences can all be described in the accent concerned as tied either to particular structural contexts or to statable environmental contexts. For example, in terms of responsiveness to particular structural constraints, the aspirated version of /p/ occurs in these English examples when it is a single consonant onset at the beginning of a word, and the pronunciation of /p/ is (optionally) unreleased when it is in a final position in the utterance. In terms of being subject to the influence of environmental context, the pronunciations of /p/ in the above examples show lip-rounding in anticipation of vowels whose performance requires a lip-rounded position (in *pot*, *spot*, *pop* and *port*). Equally, lip-rounding is absent from the pronunciations of /p/ when the following vowel shows no lip-rounding (in *peat*).

The different pronunciations discussed above can therefore be regarded as satisfying the requirements for allophonic grouping into a single phoneme. These requirements are, in summary, that the different pronunciations are complementary in their distribution, that they show close phonetic similarity, and that their phonetic differences can be attributed either to their structural position, or to interaction with their environmental context.

Daniel Jones gives many examples of allophonic groupings into phonemes in his book on the phoneme (Jones 1950), and in many articles (e.g. Jones 1944a, 1957). The following illustrations are taken from Jones (in W.E. Jones and Laver 1973: 170):

> If one isolates the sounds of **g** in the words **goose** and **geese**, one hears them to be different, and one can feel that they have different tongue articulations: the second has a fronter articulation than the first. But from the point of view of the structure of the language the two sounds count as if they were one and the same. In the terminology I find it convenient to use they are 'members of a single phoneme'. One of the sounds is the variety appropriate in English to a following [uː], while the other is conditioned to the following [iː].

Jones gives another example, from Italian, which shows that the allophones of a given phoneme can show tangible differences in some of the phonetic features involved, so long as a substantial degree of phonetic similarity exists in the remaining features. He also shows that the classification of particular allophones into a given phoneme is specific to the given language only:

> In Italian and some other languages our English **ng**-sound occurs, but only in specific phonetic contexts, namely before [k] and [ɡ]; it is used in these contexts to the exclusion of [n]. Thus the **n**'s in the Italian words **banca** and **lungo** are pronounced [ŋ], and an Italian never uses an ordinary [n] in such a situation. He is not like a Russian who uses [n] before [k] and [ɡ] as well as in other positions. The result is that an Italian whose attention has not been called to the fact is unaware that the sound of **n** before [k] and [ɡ] is in any way different from that of any other **n**. To him these nasal consonants are one and the same, and for all linguistic purposes they count as if they were one and the same – the sounds [n] and [ŋ] are 'members of the same phoneme' in Italian. (They are not so in English or German). (in Jones and Laver 1973: 171)

It has to be acknowledged that the part of the definition of the phoneme which relates to phonetic similarity is clearly more convenient than rigorous, and gives the individual analyst more latitude. But it is an important practical ingredient in the definition, none the less. It is the case, for instance, that the sounds which typically represent consonants are in complementary distribution with those normally representing vowels, in that they seldom compete for the same place in the structure of a syllable. If the only relevant criterion were one of complementary distribution, then it would be theoretically possible to collapse the manifestations of consonants and vowels together into single phonemes (and some phonologists have indeed made such proposals for some languages – Kuipers (1960), for instance, suggests that Kabardian, a language of the Caucasus, can be analysed on this basis as if it had no independent vowel-phoneme at all). Most phoneticians would resist such a solution, however, not least because it contravenes a reasonable application of this second criterion of phonetic similarity. The definition is also convenient rather than rigorous in that the idea of 'phonetic similarity' is itself partly a matter of judgement on the part of the analyst as to what model of descriptive phonetic theory should be invoked, and therefore as to what should count as phonetically similar.

2.5.6 *Formulaic phonological rule notation*

The passage quoted above from Jones (1944a), on the status of [ŋ] in Italian as an allophone of /n/ in the context preceding /k/ or /g/, affords the opportunity to introduce a useful expansion of the formulaic device ' ⇒ ', explained in section 2.5 as meaning 'is realized phonetically as'. It is often convenient to be able to express contextually or structurally determined allophonic variation in a given language or accent as a formulaic rule, as introduced into linguistics by generative phonology. More extensive descriptions of the conventions of such rules are available in Clark and Yallop (1990: 156–69), Kaye (1989: 32–5) and Sommerstein (1977: 114–42). Formulaic rules of this sort give a compact way of summarizing the conditions under which phonological processes such as realization rules operate. Using A, B, C, D as notional symbols, the most general form for a realization rule is:

$$A \Rightarrow B \,/\, C \_\_ D$$

The single slash symbol '/' means 'in the context of'. The symbol '_' is called an **environment bar**, and is a device for helping to identify the structural or contextual location of the item on which the rule is to operate. In conjunction with a symbol placed to the left of the environment bar, left-context can be specified, and right-context is indicated by a symbol placed to the right. The rule as written above is thus interpreted to mean 'A is realized as B when A occurs in a sequence with C as its left-context and D as its right-context'. As well as this joint condition of both left- and right-contexts being prescribed, this formalism allows the specification of a more limited contextual condition, where the elements that trigger the realizational rule are simply the occurrence of C as left-context, with D null (i.e. zero), or the occurrence of D as right-context, with C null.

The entities in the formalism represented here by A, B, C and D may be phonemes, phonetic events, groups of phonological or phonetic features etc., but for our immediate purposes we shall limit them to phonemic and phonetic symbols. A version of the above rule might then read:

$$/X/ \Rightarrow [y] \,/\, /C/ \_\_ /D/$$

meaning 'the phoneme /X/ is realized as the phonetic event [y] when the phoneme /X/ occurs in a sequence with the phonemes /C/ as its left-context and /D/ as its right-context'. The contextual specification can be made more comprehensive by including alternative realizations in different contexts in a composite rule, as follows:

$$/X/ \Rightarrow \left\{ \begin{array}{l} [y] \ / \ /C/\_\_ \ /D, \ E/ \\ [z] \ / \ /F/\_\_ \\ [x] \end{array} \right\}$$

This is to be interpreted as 'the phoneme /X/ is realized as its allophone [y] when the phoneme /X/ occurs in a sequence with the phonemes /C/ as its left-context and /D/ or /E/ as its right context, as its allophone [z] after the phoneme /F/, and as its allophone [x] everywhere else'. The use of the curly braces indicates options of choice subject to the constraints expressed by the placement of the environment bar relative to the symbols adjacent to it. Thus '__ /D, E/' specifies the contextual position as 'preceding /D/ or /E/', and 'F __' as 'following /F/'. Absence of the environment bar indicates that the occurrence of the specified allophone is without contextual constraint except for the conditions listed above it inside the braces.

The specification of [n] and [ŋ] in Italian as contextually determined allophones of the /n/ phoneme in Italian can then be expressed formulaically as:

$$/n/ \Rightarrow \left\{ \begin{array}{l} [\eta] \ / \ \_\_ \ /k, \ g/ \\ [n] \end{array} \right\}$$

The symbols [ŋ], [k] and [g] are all called 'velar' sounds, specifying that part of their pronunciation in each case involves the back of the tongue touching the underside of the soft palate (or 'velum', to give it its technical anatomical name). It is this velar element of the pronunciation of [ŋ] that reflects the allophonic adaptation of /n/ to its contextual environment in this example.

Such an allophonic rule would apply in Spanish, but would not apply in German, nor in most accents of English (including RP). It would, however, apply in some accents of English, as Clark and Yallop (1990: 127) comment:

> [there are] varieties of English in which ... words such as <u>sing</u>, <u>rang</u>, <u>singer</u> are pronounced with [g] following the velar nasal (e.g. <u>sing</u> is [sɪŋg]). These varieties of English (chiefly found in the Midlands and north of England) are like Italian and Spanish in that [ŋ] occurs only immediately before a velar consonant and can therefore be analysed as a conditioned variant of /n/.

This general constraint in such accents of requiring velar allophones of /n/

before velar consonants can be expressed in a slightly more abstract form, as:

$$/n/ \Rightarrow \left\{ \begin{array}{l} [\eta] \ / \ \underline{} \ /C_{velar}/ \\ [n] \end{array} \right\}$$

A similar general constraint, this time on the occurrence of nasality on the realizations of vowel phonemes before nasal consonants in English, can be signalled by using a wider range of generic symbols. Thus

$$/V/ \Rightarrow \left\{ \begin{array}{l} [\tilde{V}] \ / \ \underline{} \ /C_{nas}/ \\ [V] \end{array} \right\}$$

means that any vowel phoneme in English is pronounced with nasality when placed before a nasal consonant, and without nasality elsewhere. An equivalent formula could have replaced the general symbol $/C_{nas}/$ with a corresponding general symbol /N/ meaning 'any nasal consonant' (i.e. in English /m, n, ŋ/).

2.5.7 *Polysystemic and monosystemic approaches to phonology*

The notion of a (phonemic) system was introduced above in a two-part definition. The first part of the definition constrained the segments in a given system to show contrastive opposition in parallel distribution in comparable structures. If this strict definition were maintained, then a given accent could be partly defined by multiple, separate systems, each operating at a different place in structure. Such an approach is sometimes called a **polysystemic** approach. The second part of the definition, where the criterion of phonetic similarity is invoked to group phones showing complementary distribution into class-membership of a given phoneme, is actually in tension with the first part of the definition, and pulls the perspective towards what has been called the **monosystemic** approach. This is where the multiple, separate systems of the polysystemic approach are treated as if they were welded into a single, monolithic system. In this monosystemic approach, phonetic similarity is the unifying principle which justifies allocating a single phonemic symbol to all the members of the complementarily distributed set of allophones. It has to be said immediately that a monosystemic approach often forces anomalies on the description of the data. Having to set up a notion of **defective distribution**, for instance (where one phoneme is in other respects in parallel distribution to another, but fails to occur in a particular contextual or structural place), is the consequence of taking a distorting monosystemic view of patterns of phonology.

In the monosystemic approach, it is possible to speak broadly of 'the consonant system of English' and 'the vowel system of English' (or of Zulu, or of any given language). In the polysystemic approach, one has to speak in a more restricted and specific compass, of a given system operating at a particular place in the structure of a given type of larger linguistic unit such as the syllable, or the word. The monosystemic approach lends itself to a panoramic view of the sound-system of a language at large, and its transcriptional devices tend to be alphabetic in nature. The polysystemic approach perhaps favours a more microscopic attention to phonological and phonetic detail, and its transcriptional formulae are seldom devised with easy legibility in mind – that is not their prime purpose, which is rather to act as a powerful tool for professional phonologists.

A polysystemic approach of this sort has been associated with the work of J.R. Firth and his associates in the School of Oriental and African Studies in the University of London, in the approach usually called 'Prosodic Analysis' (though the term 'prosodic' is used in that approach in a somewhat different sense than in this book, mostly to refer to what we shall be calling 'features'). The single most influential paper in this tradition was probably Firth's own 'Sounds and prosodies' (Firth 1948), reprinted in Firth's collected papers (Firth 1957). There is only a limited opportunity in the present book to refer to the work of this school in any detail, but the serious student of phonetics and phonology is urged to become familiar with these publications, which explore a very wide range of oriental and African languages. Although most of the scholars actively subscribing to the Prosodic Analysis approach have now retired, the contributions achieved under the aegis of this tradition still reflect some of the theoretically most sophisticated ideas in the history of the British school of phonetics and phonology. In particular, their rejection of the validity of a monosystemic approach to phonology, in favour of a polysystemic perspective, is increasingly finding echoes in the work of modern phonologists.

The comments that follow in later chapters will mostly be based on the monosystemic approach, explicitly relying on the concepts of the phoneme and the allophone. It will sometimes be convenient, nevertheless, to consider the systems operating at different structural places separately from each other. To the extent that separate sub-systems are under consideration at any point, we will have moved away from a fully monosystemic approach towards a polysystemic approach.

2.6 Language-system and language-behaviour

It may be helpful to conclude this chapter on the relationship between phonetics and phonology with a brief mention of a basic but somewhat problematic distinction that readers are likely to encounter in their wider reading of textbooks on general linguistic theory. Different linguists use different terms, but the concept is long-established in modern linguistics. It is characterized by Lyons (1981: 10) as a distinction between a **language-system** and **language-behaviour**: 'A language-system is a social phenomenon, or institution, which of itself is purely abstract, in that it has no physical existence, but which is actualized on particular occasions in the language-behaviour of individual members of the language-community.' The distinction was originally introduced by de Saussure (1916 (1959)), in his differentiation of *langue* and *parole*, and was reinforced by Chomsky (1965) in a broadly comparable distinction between 'competence' versus 'performance'. De Saussure, in the fragmentary notes on his work collected by his editors Bally, Sechehaye and Riedlinger (de Saussure 1916 (1966)), gives only discursive descriptions of the concepts of *langue* and *parole*, but the essence of his concept of *langue* refers to the collective language-system shared by a community of speakers, and *parole* to concrete utterances produced in the act of speaking by an individual in actual situations (Crystal 1991: 194, 251). *Langue* is a social fact, while *parole* is an individual act, said de Saussure (1916 (1966): 13).

Chomsky (1965) called the tacit operational knowledge of the language-system possessed by typical speaker/listeners their linguistic **competence**, and called the exploitation of such knowledge by speakers and listeners in actual language-behaviour their linguistic **performance**. The description of linguistic competence, which many theoretical linguists take to be their primary task, concentrates on a highly idealized perspective of language. Chomsky and Halle (1968: 3), for example, describe the distinction between competence and performance in the following terms:

> The performance of the speaker or hearer is a complex matter that involves many factors. One fundamental factor involved in the speaker-hearer's performance is his knowledge of the grammar that determines an intrinsic connection of sound and meaning for each sentence. We refer to this knowledge – for the most part, obviously, unconscious knowledge – as the speaker–hearer's 'competence'. Competence, in this sense, is not to be confused with performance. Performance, that is, what the speaker–hearer actually does, is based not only on his knowledge of the language, but on many other factors as well – factors such as memory restrictions, inattention, distraction, nonlinguistic knowledge and beliefs, and so on. We may, if we like, think of the study of competence as the study of the potential performance of an idealized speaker–hearer who is unaffected by such grammatically irrelevant factors.

Chomsky (1965: 3) offered a more outright indication of the way that this distinction focuses the objectives of linguistic study: 'Linguistic theory is concerned primarily with an ideal speaker–listener, in a completely homogeneous speech community, who knows its language perfectly and is unaffected by such grammatically irrelevant conditions as memory limitations, distractions, shifts of attention and interest, and errors (random or characteristic) in applying his knowledge of the language in actual performance.' An important difference between de Saussure's *langue* and Chomsky's 'competence' is thus that while *langue* as a social concept emphasizes the institutional character of a language-system as a property of the whole language-community, 'competence' as a cognitively oriented concept refers not so much to the speaker-general language-system as such, but to the 'typical speaker's knowledge of the language-system' (Lyons 1981: 10). An intrinsic part of competence, for Chomsky and for the whole generativist tradition of linguistics, is that it reflects the fact that the generative 'capacity to produce and understand syntactically well-formed sentences is a central part – indeed, the central part – of a speaker's linguistic competence' (Lyons 1981: 234). The notion of competence in this respect is especially valuable in that the rule-governed ability which is the basis for producing and understanding a virtually infinite potential number of sentences begins to explain the 'creative' nature of language.

The distinction between competence and performance has been widely adopted by generative linguistics, though scholars such as Hymes (1971a) have argued for an enrichment of the concept of competence to include not only narrowly linguistic but a wider range of knowledge about other sociocultural communicative systems relevant to the use of language in different circumstances and for different purposes, in the notion of **communicative competence**. Others, such as Linell (1979: 17–26), have contested the psychological validity of the distinction.

The general concepts of language-system and language-behaviour are clearly useful for the discipline of phonetics. Phonetics has a part to play in the study of spoken language in both perspectives. It may be relevant, however, to signal some reservations about the full utility of these and related concepts for the discipline of phonetics. First, all three pairs of distinctions (language-system and language-behaviour, *langue* and *parole*, competence and performance) incorporate an assumption that it is sufficient to frame the concepts in terms of the typical speaker/listener, and to seek to characterize the linguistic attributes of the language-community. But phonetics, while being centrally interested in speaker-general phenomena in the same way, is also necessarily interested in the individual speaker/listener. Some very important applications of phonetics, such as speech pathology and speech technology, have an absolute need to be able to relate the speech patterns of the individual, however idiosyncratic, to the generalized patterns that characterize their sociolinguistic community. This has implications for the need to study and define the language-system that can be taken to underlie the utterances of that individual speaker's language-behaviour, even if he or she is unique in using the systematic patterns concerned. From both a social and a theoretical point of view, it is in any case arguable whether the number of speakers of a given language is at all a relevant measure of the degree of interest that linguists should properly take in the properties of that language. In a discussion of how to choose the world's major languages for a descriptive survey, Comrie (1987: ix–x) offers a salutary comment on this point: 'When the world's linguists learned in 1970 that the last speaker of Kamassian, a Uralic language originally spoken in Siberia, had kept her language alive for decades in her prayers – God being the only other speaker of her language – they may well have wondered whether, for this person, *the* world's major language was not Kamassian.' General phonetic theory should have the capacity, so long as deviations from standard anatomy are not in question, of describing the articulatory strategies of production of any type of speech sound used by any speaker for communication through spoken language, not only by those who conform more closely to the norms of their sociolinguistic group.

Second, to address the specifics of the competence/performance dichotomy, if competence reflects the structure and content of a mental grammar and the operational knowledge necessary to generate sentences by means of this grammar, then any overall model of performance would need to incorporate a component representing this competence, as the quotation above from Chomsky and Halle (1968: 3) indicates. One view of the relationship between competence and performance is thus that the former is included within the latter. The highly abstract view of linguistic competence as taken by the generativist tradition has had the result of promoting a focused interest in a narrow definition of grammar, to the considerable benefit of formal aspects of linguistic study. But such a promotion of interest in competence at the expense of the wider concept of performance has had the inevitable disadvantage of holding performance-related issues other than those of competence somewhat at arm's-length. It remains true, nevertheless, as Chomsky (1965: 15) comments, that although 'there has been a fair amount of criticism of work in generative grammar on the grounds that it slights study of performance in favor of study of underlying competence', the study of competence itself 'can provide some insight into performance'.

Third, the true complexity of an adequately comprehensive model of the performance of utterances of spoken language is astonishing, and phonetics and linguistics are still very far from a full understanding of the cognitive and motor processes involved. The spoken performance of even the most simple sentence necessarily exploits the full depth of a speaker's operational knowledge of neurolinguistic and neuromuscular strategies of planning and executing ideational, pragmatic, semantic, lexical, syntactic, morphological, phonological and motor programs for the production of the utterance involved. It also exploits highly complex perceptual and neurolinguistic strategies of self-monitoring for the orthodoxy of what was actually said against what the speaker intended to say, and of planning and executing appropriate corrective material (Fromkin 1980; Laver 1991). The listener's perceptual and neurolinguistic performance in decoding the linguistic meaning of the acoustic material produced by the speaker is no less complex (Caplan 1987; Flores d'Arcais 1988).

The term 'neurolinguistic' is used here to emphasize the eventual need, at some stage in the modelling of how speakers and listeners process the production and perception of spoken language, to address the question of the real strategies and mechanisms used by the human neurological apparatus in achieving these operations. The more familiar term for the study of such processes is **psycholinguistics** (Garman 1990), reflecting what is sometimes a more abstract cognitive approach to the problem.

Psycholinguistic research in cognitive aspects of spoken language has tended to be atomistic, with individual researchers specializing in a given area, such as syntax, morphology, phonology, phonetics etc. Each of these areas can be hypothesized to be an (internally complex) module in the overall cognitive process which begins with the generation of some initial idea and ends in its eventual articulation as an audible utterance. There is now some evidence, however, that cognitive research into speech production and perception is beginning to address the challenge of modelling the possible links between the different modules, fashioning the beginnings of an understanding of the complete cognitive chain from ideation to articulation (Garrett 1988; Laver 1989).

Within the study of spoken language, phonetics as a discipline needs to be able to describe the phonetic substance of any communicative aspect of speech, as well as accounting for the formal aspects of the phonological level of description. It needs to be able to describe what real speakers actually do on real occasions of utterance, as well as to identify the social value of that performance as a manifestation of a sociolinguistic code. Phonetics thus has the responsibility of providing a well-founded description of the substance of speech, in a descriptive theory whose architecture is shaped in part by the need to provide explicit linkage to phonological use, and in another part by the need to provide descriptors for individual speech behaviour.

Further reading

A book particularly recommended for the reader seeking a comprehensive foundation in **acoustic phonetics** for general purposes in speech science is Kent and Read (1992). More specialized treatments include Fant (1960 and 1973), Fry (1976), N.J. Lass (1976), Lehiste (1967), Lieberman and Blumstein (1988), Markel and Gray (1976) and Rabiner and Shafer (1978). Discussions of aspects of **speech technology**, to which acoustic phonetics makes a central contribution, are available in Ainsworth (1988), Allerhand (1987), Bristow (1984), Dixon and Martin (1979), Fallside and Woods (1985), Flanagan and Rabiner (1973), Holmes (1972, 1988), Jack and Laver (1988), Laver (1993), Parsons (1987) and Saito and Nakata (1985).

Good accounts of the **anatomy and physiology of speech** which are reflected in the **organic level** of speech analysis are available in Dickson and Maue-Dickson (1982), Hardcastle (1976) and Kaplan (1960).

A classic early work on the principles of phonology is Trubetzkoy (1939), which is strongly recommended for readers interested in the history of phonology. General introductions to **phonology** are Anderson (1974, 1985), Fischer-Jørgensen (1975), Lass (1984a), and Sommerstein (1977). Some recent developments can be pursued in Aronoff and Oehrle (1984), Basbøll (1988), Beckman (1986), Clements and Keyser (1983), Durand (1990), Giegerich (1985), Goldsmith (1990), Hogg and McCully (1987), van der Hulst and Smith (1982), Kaye (1989), Kiparsky (1982), Ladd (1980), Liberman (1975), Liberman and Prince (1977) and Selkirk (1984). A seminal work on the phonology of English is Chomsky and Halle (1968), though Ladefoged (1971) properly takes issue with the theoretical architecture they propose, as being over-abstract for the task of phonetic description. An up-to-date introduction to the phonology of English is Giegerich (1992). A good account of the issue of psychological reality in phonology is Linell (1979), and views of the relevance of phonology to the cognitive representation of speech can be found in Myers, Laver and Anderson (1981).

The main articles characterizing the **Prosodic Analysis** approach to phonology, apart from Firth's own work, can be found in a number of collections (Bazell *et al.* 1966; Jones and Laver 1973; Mitchell 1975; Palmer 1970; Robins 1970). The collection edited by Palmer (1970) is particularly valuable, and the article on ' "Openness" in Tigre: a problem of prosodic statement', by the editor himself (Palmer 1956), is a classic statement of the technique of prosodic analysis, as is the article on prosodies in Siamese (Thai) by Henderson (1949). Discussions of Firth's ideas, and the relation between the Prosodic Analysis school of thought and other approaches to phonology can be found in Anderson (1985: 169–93), Fischer-Jørgensen (1975: 59–63), Langendoen (1968) and Sampson (1980: 212–35).

Further publications on **psycholinguistics**, the older references being of particular historical interest, include Aitchison (1987), Clark and Clark (1977), Deese (1984), Fodor, Bever and Garrett (1974), Foss and Hakes (1978), Frauenfelder and Tyler (1987), Fromkin (1973, 1980), Jeffress (1951), Lenneberg (1967), Levelt (1989), McClelland and Rumelhart (1986), McNeill (1987), Miller, Galanter and Pribram (1960), Rumelhart and McClelland (1986) and Studdert-Kennedy (1983).

3

Accent, dialect and language

The purpose of this third preliminary chapter is to introduce some further basic concepts, this time to do with the variations of accent, dialect and language between speakers, and of these aspects of language across space and time. The discussion will include issues in dialectology, sociolinguistics, linguistic geography and historical linguistics. It is necessary to say from the outset that this chapter thus touches on disciplines to which phonetics makes a contribution, but which in themselves are not traditionally central to phonetics as such. It is also the case that the contribution of phonetics to these disciplines has so far not been as extensive as it might profitably be, and there is considerable room for further phonetic research in these areas. The treatment of these neighbouring disciplines is inevitably presented in rather general terms, but readers are likely to encounter in their wider reading in linguistics all the speech-related technical concepts introduced here.

An important initial distinction needs to be introduced between 'accent' and 'dialect'. The technical meanings of both these terms differ from their everyday meanings. The technical meaning of the term **accent** is simply **manner of pronunciation**. In this sense, everyone speaks with an accent. Technically, it is not possible to speak aloud without speaking with an accent. The notion of accent is a phonological and phonetic concept, with some implications for the lexical level of analysis as well.

The technical meaning of the term **dialect** covers the types and meanings of words available and the range of grammatical patterns into which they can be combined. **Dialects** are discernibly different to the extent that they involve different morphological, syntactic, lexical and semantic inventories and patterns. A dialect can be expressed in either spoken or written form. In spoken form, a given dialect can often be associated with more than one accent. Many writers draw no specific distinction between the concepts of dialect and accent, but this book will maintain the distinction where feasible.

A **language** is the entity made up of a group of related dialects and their associated accents. From a technical point of view, it is not only impossible to speak a given language without exhibiting some particular accent, it is also impossible to speak (or write) without exemplifying a choice of dialect, in terms of the vocabulary used and the sequences in which the words are combined. This book exemplifies a written dialect that is very largely common to educated use throughout the English-speaking world. To that extent, it could be referred to as **Standard English**. It is standard in the sense that it is a dialect understood and used in a relatively standard way by a very large number of people. The term 'standard' is here being employed in a **descriptive**, not a prescriptive mode. A **prescriptive attitude** would flavour the definition if 'standard' were to be interpreted to mean 'considered to represent correct and socially acceptable usage for educated purposes'. Such views about 'correctness' and 'social acceptability' would be undesirably self-regulating, in that it would be the self-selected people who use the dialect who would be ruling on its acceptability. Prescriptivist attitudes about 'correctness' have no place in a scientific approach to the description of speech that seeks to maintain objectivity.

3.1 The Standard English dialect, and non-regional and regional accents

An implication might be drawn from the comments above that Standard English is invariant over the English-speaking world. There are of course a number of detailed differences of usage between different national groups. British and American versions of Standard English, for example, will in fact be treated later as different dialects, for the sake of illustrating dialectal differences with familiar material. But such differences as exist between the various national forms of Standard English (American, Australian, British, Canadian etc.) are nevertheless small compared with the differences between these and other dialects of English. For the moment, then, it will be useful to maintain the convenient fiction that Standard English is a single dialect.

Since Standard English is by definition a dialect, unlike other dialects only in its unusually wide geographical scope, it follows that Standard English can be spoken with a variety of accents. Accents always mark the geographical origin of the speaker. Some accents mark regional origin very locally, and some mark only the fact that the speaker is an American, or is Australian, Canadian, English, Irish, Scots, Welsh etc. To the extent that a particular accent marks a speaker as having a very specific regional origin, it can be called a **regional** or **local** accent. Highly localized regional accents of this sort are also often called **broad accents**. To the extent that the speaker's local origin can be marked only within national boundaries, the accent can be said to be a **non-regional accent**.

A given speaker may be able to speak with two or more accents, with one accent often being broader than the other(s). Furthermore, a given speaker may well be able to use more than one dialect. A speaker native to Scotland will normally speak either the Standard English dialect with a regional Scottish accent, or a Scottish dialect of English with either the same or a broader Scottish accent, as the social occasion requires. Equally, a speaker native to Kentucky might speak Standard English with a regional Kentucky accent while working as, say, a receptionist for a multinational corporation, but speak a Kentucky dialect with a broader Kentucky accent when visiting relatives in his or her home town.

Received Pronunciation (RP) is an example of a non-regional accent of British English, which has been described in detail by very many authors, amongst whom Jones (1962) and Gimson (1962, 1989) are outstanding. The pronouncing dictionary specifying the details of RP which has been regarded for very many years as the most authoritative source is the one first published by Daniel Jones in 1917. This has been updated in many successive editions. Gimson, as one of Jones' senior colleagues, and the holder of the Chair of Phonetics at University College London immediately after Jones, was responsible for the 13th and 14th editions (Gimson 1967, 1977). This 14th edition was in turn the basis for a further revision by Ramsaran (1988). Another excellent and up-to-date pronouncing dictionary which describes RP (as well as a number of other accents of English) is Wells (1990). Wells maintains a historical continuity with Daniel Jones, being Gimson's successor in the Chair of Phonetics at University College London.

The term 'Received', in its Victorian sense of being 'received in polite society', gives a historical clue to the origins of the RP accent. According to Abercrombie (1965), RP developed as an accent of the English public schools (i.e. private schools, in the paradoxical usage of the English), and 'is maintained, and transmitted from generation to generation, mainly by people educated at [these] public schools' (Abercrombie 1965: 12). Wells (1982, vol. I: 10) summarizes these characteristics of RP by stating that:

> In England ... there are some speakers who do not have a local accent. One can tell from their speech that they are British (and very probably English) but nothing else ... It is characteristic of the upper class and (to an extent) of the upper-middle class. An Old Etonian sounds much the same whether he grew up in Cornwall or Northumberland.

Although the function of this accent as a marker of socioeconomic status is now a good deal weaker than previously, RP is still perhaps better regarded as marking social rather than narrowly regional aspects of identity

(Ramsaran 1990). The accent is non-regional in that the public schools themselves are regionally distributed throughout England (though it is true to say, demographically, that the population of RP speakers is denser in the south of England than anywhere else).

Petyt (1980: 29) suggests a descriptive link between the regional nature of accents and dialects and the socioeconomic status of the speakers concerned, such that the less regional variation is involved, the higher the status of the speaker. Crystal (1988: 63) comments that RP, like other accents, is subject to change with time:

> Early BBC recordings show the remarkable extent to which RP has altered over just a few decades, and they make the point that no accent is immune to change, not even the 'best'. In addition, RP is no longer as widely used as it was even 50 years ago. Only about 3 per cent of British people speak it in a pure form now. Most other educated people have developed an accent which is a mixture of RP and various regional characteristics – 'modified' RP, some call it, or perhaps we should talk about modified RP's, as in each case the kind of modification stems from a person's regional background, and this varies greatly.

Crystal also points out that the Victorian stigmatization of regional accents by educated British society is now fading, and that 'several contemporary politicians make a virtue out of their regional background, and the BBC employs several announcers with regionally modified accents. Nor is it uncommon, these days, to find educated people expressing hostility towards RP, both within and outside Britain, because of its traditional association with conservative values' (Crystal, *ibid.*). There are of course numerous other accents of British English, and a variety of different regional dialects within Britain. References on this topic are given in the recommended Further Reading at the end of the chapter.

Another example of a non-regional accent is the one that is often called **General American**. This name, according to Van Riper (1973: 232), was first promoted by Krapp (1925) and Kenyon (1930). Krapp characterized General American in the following terms: 'One may say that in America three main types of speech have come to be recognized, a New England local type, a Southern local type, and a general or Western speech covering the rest of the country, and all speakers in the South and New England at the moments when their speech is not local in character' (Krapp 1925, vol. I: 35, cited in Van Riper 1973).

Wells (1982, vol. I: 10) characterizes General American in the following terms, though with a reservation about the complete truth about the standard nature of the accent:

> In the United States, it is true not just of a small minority, but of the majority, that their accent reveals little or nothing of their geographical origins. They are the speakers of General American ... This is a convenient name for the range of United States accents that have neither an eastern nor a southern colouring; dialectologically, though, it is of questionable status.

The claim to generality of the term 'General' American is thus somewhat too sweeping (McDavid and McDavid 1956), but the term is now thoroughly established. In the *Random House Dictionary of the English Language* (1966), the phrase 'General American Speech' is defined as 'a pronunciation of American English showing few regional peculiarities: most U.S. radio and television announcers use General American Speech'. Bowen (1975) gives an outline of the pronunciations associated with General American. Kurath and McDavid (1961) offer an account of the accents associated with the dialects spoken along the eastern seaboard of the United States that are described in Kurath (1949). Kenyon and Knott (1944) cover the pronunciation of accents spoken in the Mid-West and Far West of the States in their pronouncing dictionary of American English. A general treatment of accents of English in both American and British English (RP) is given by Kurath (1964).

A large survey of Australian accents was conducted by Mitchell and Delbridge (1965). A commentator on the unusual uniformity of Australian English accents is Bernard (1969).

Canadian English is discussed by Avis (1986). Wells (1982) is an excellent and very detailed three-volume work on the accents of English round the world. Bailey and Görlach (1982) offer an edited collection of chapters on varieties of English dialects and accents in many different parts of the world, including Africa, Asia, the Pacific and the Caribbean as well as Britain, Ireland, Canada and the United States.

This book is centrally concerned with matters relating to pronunciation, rather than directly with higher-order linguistic phenomena at the level of dialects. But it is important to appreciate the distinction between dialect and accent, so in order to elaborate the distinction it may be helpful now to offer a few examples of specific differences between dialects, then of differences between accents, and then of differences within the accent of a single speaker speaking on different occasions. All the differences discussed below in this chapter fall within a definition of linguistic behaviour – differences due to paralinguistic changes of tone of voice signalling attitudinal and emotional information about the speaker are not considered here.

3.2 Differences of dialect between speakers

We can consider some examples of differences of dialect between speakers, at the morphological, syntactic, semantic and lexical levels of analysis of English. An example of a **morphological** difference between dialects can be found from a comparison of American and British English versions of Standard English. Where British English has only one past participle of the verb *to get*, namely *got*, according to Lass (1987: 7) American English has two, as in *I've got* ('I have') versus *I've gotten* ('I've obtained'). Another example cited by Lass (*ibid.*) is the American English *dove* as the past participle of *to dive*, in contrast with the British English *dived*.

Two speakers speaking the same language but different dialects can also differ **syntactically**, in phrases such as *The kettle needs boiled* in common use in Scots English versus *The kettle needs boiling* or *The kettle needs to be boiled* in most other dialects of English. Further examples of syntactic differences come from the Edinburgh dialect of Scottish English, here illustrated by a transcription of a colloquial Edinburgh accent as described by Brown and Millar (1978: 174, 164). Standard English equivalents are given in parentheses:

> *Syntactic forms in the Edinburgh dialect of Scottish English*
> [ɪf 'ad ʌ bin 'ðer] if I̱'d a been there ('If I had been there')
> [ɪf ʌ 'hʌdne ʌ bin ðer] if I ha̱dnae a been there ('If I hadn't
> been there')
> [ɪf ʌ hʌdʌv 'told ʌm] if I had've to̱ld him ('If I had told him')
> [jʌv 'goʔe no 'go] you've go̱t to no go̱ ('You musn't go')

(The [ʔ] symbol represents a glottal stop, and the meanings of the symbols representing vowels are explained in chapter 10. The underlining of an individual syllable indicates that the syllable was made intonationally prominent in the utterance.)

An example of **semantic differences** between dialects can be found in British and American versions of Standard English where the form of the word is the same but the meaning is different. A lexical example is *momentarily*, which means 'for a moment's duration' in British English and 'in a moment, any minute now' in some dialects of American English. An announcement to passengers by an airline pilot to the effect that *This flight to New York will be taking off momentarily* could have quite different impacts on British and American listeners.

Some semantic differences between Scots English and other versions of Standard English are: *to sort* ('to mend'), *to clap* ('to pet' (an animal)), *messages* ('shopping') and *bramble* (referring to the fruit as well as the plant of the blackberry) (Lass 1987: 261). A phrasal example of semantic differences between dialects is the difference between British and American usages of *just in case*, where this means 'lest' in British English, and 'only in the case where' in (some versions of) American English.

Differences of dialect very often show themselves as a matter of **lexical differences**, usually where two or more different word-forms in the two dialects have approximately the same meaning. An example of this is the very widespread current use in the Scots version of Standard English of the form *outwith*, as in *outwith the competence of this committee*, or *outwith the city limits*, where the comparable word in most dialects of England would be *outside*, or *beyond*.

Two other examples of lexical differences, this time between the colloquial Edinburgh dialect of Scottish English and Standard English, can be seen in the use of the Scottish English words *ken* ('know') and *thole* ('bear, tolerate') in the following phrases (Brown and Millar 1978: 167):

> *Lexical forms in the Edinburgh dialect of Scottish English*
> [ʌ dɪ ne kɛn] I dinnae ken ('I don't know')
> [ʌ kane θol ɪʔ] I cannae thole it ('I can't bear/tolerate it')

Other lexical items specific to Scottish English, cited in the *Concise Scots Dictionary* (Robinson 1985), include *depute* ('deputy'), *dreich* ('dreary, bleak'), *fankle* ('tangle'), *gean* ('wild cherry'), *haar* ('sea-mist'), *peelie-wallie* ('under the weather'), *pech* ('pant breathlessly'), *rone* ('(roof)-gutter'), *roup* ('public auction') and *swither* ('hesitate').

Australian English has its own lexical items, such as *outback* ('wilderness'), *tucker* ('food') and *crook* (adjective) ('not as it should be' or 'ill'). A lexical difference between British English and English in North America is the British form *cattle grid* for the North American phrase *Texas gate*. Lass (1987: 285) mentions a number of lexical items specific to Canadian English. These include *bush* (meaning 'wilderness', shared with Australia, but not with the United States), *corduroy road* ('road made with logs', which is also known in the United States) and *frost boil* (meaning 'a frost-induced eruption on the surface of a road'). Lexical items particular to South African English are often borrowed from Afrikaans, or from Bantu languages (Lass 1987: 307–8). Afrikaans-derived instances are: *mealies* ('maize', which is also known as 'mealies' in East African English), *kloof* ('ravine'), *vlei* ('shallow lake'), *witblits* ('home distilled spirit' (literally, 'white lightning')) and *skolly* ('hoodlum'). Examples derived from Bantu languages (mainly Zulu and Xhosa) are: *fundi* ('expert'), *bundu* ('wilderness'), *songololo* ('millipede') and *muti* ('herbal medicine', 'magical potion'). Loans from Khoi languages include *dagga* ('cannabis') and *gogga* ('bug, creepie-crawlie').

3.3 Differences of accent between speakers

Considerations of differences between accents invoke the concepts of system and structure introduced in chapter 2. It will be recalled that these concepts deal with the stock of phonological units used to distinguish different words in the language – in particular, with their number (the concept of 'system') and the permissible ways the phonological units can be arranged into sequences (the concept of 'structure'). We shall deal here with systems and structures involving phonological units only at the level of consonants and vowels – in other words the phoneme. It should be noted, however, that there are other types of (non-segmental) phonological units, to do with prosodic and temporal features such as intonation, stress and rhythm, which would have to be included in an overall scheme.

At the segmental level of consonants and vowels, the overall inventory of consonant phonemes of a given accent makes up its **consonant system**, and the vowel phonemes its **vowel system**. (It should be remembered, nevertheless, that while this monosystemic approach is convenient for summary presentation, it brings with it the concomitant disadvantage that it obliges us to collapse all the contextually specific sub-systems of such units into a global single system, with a corresponding loss of polysystemic detail). RP has 24 consonants in its consonant system, and 20 vowels in its vowel system. General American, which is less homogeneous than RP, has 24 consonants and 15 or 16 vowels, depending on which sub-type of the General American accent is being considered (Kreidler 1989). Most Scots accents have 25 or 26 consonants and 13 or 14 vowels. Figure 3.1 lists these consonant and vowel systems for the three accents, with illustrative words. Differences between accents which involve the number and type of word-differentiating phonemic distinctions available to the accents are called **systemic differences** (Laver and Trudgill 1979: 16).

Examples of systemic differences can be seen in a comparison between RP and typical accents of Scotland. RP speakers differentiate between *Sam* and *psalm* by having two vowel phonemes available in their vowel system, which yield the pronunciations /sam/ and /sɑm/. Most Scots have only one vowel at this place in their vowel system, so that in their accents the two words have the same pronunciation – that is, they are **homophones**. Similarly, RP distinguishes between *tot* and *taught*, and between *pull* and *pool*, whereas most Scots have the same vowel in each pair of words, such that *tot* and *taught* are homophones, as are *pull* and *pool*. On the other hand most Scots have two vowel phonemes in their system to distinguish words such as *tide* and *tied* as /tʌɪd/ and /taed/, whereas most RP speakers have only one, which can be transcribed as /taɪd/. In the case of such RP speakers, there is therefore

Consonant systems

Keyword	Scottish English	RP	General American
pea	p	p	p
tea	t	t	t
lock	k	k	k
loch	x		
bee	b	b	b
dye	d	d	d
guy	g	g	g
me	m	m	m
knee	n	n	n
song	ŋ	ŋ	ŋ
thin	θ	θ	θ
then	ð	ð	ð
fan	f	f	f
van	v	v	v
see	s	s	s
zoom	z	z	z
she	ʃ	ʃ	ʃ
beige	ʒ	ʒ	ʒ
each	tʃ	tʃ	tʃ
edge	dʒ	dʒ	dʒ
hat	h	h	h
lay	l	l	l
ray	r	r	r
yes	j	j	j
witch	w	w	w
which	ʍ		

Vowel systems

Keyword	Scottish English	RP	General American
bead	i	i	i
bid	ɪ	ɪ	ɪ
bed	ɛ	ɛ	ɛ
Sam	a	a	a
psalm	a	ɑ	ɑ
cot	ɔ	ɒ	ɑ
caught	ɔ	ɔ	ɔ
pull	u	ʊ	ʊ
pool	u	u	u
mud	ʌ	ʌ	ʌ
bird	(ɪr)	3	ɚ
word	(ʌr)	3	ɚ
heard	(ɛr)	3	ɚ
bay	e	eɪ	eɪ
side	ʌɪ	aɪ	aɪ
sighed	ae	aɪ	aɪ
boy	ɔe	ɒɪ	ɔɪ
cow	ʌu	ɑʊ	aʊ
go	o	oʊ	oʊ
beer	(ir)	ɪə	(ir)
bare	(er)	ɛə	(ɛr)
poor	(ur)	ʊə	(ur)

Keyword	Scottish English	RP	General American
taxi	e	I	i
axis	I	I	I
taxes	I	ə	ə
china	ʌ	ə	ə

Figure 3.1 Consonant and vowel systems of Received Pronunciation, Scots and General American English (after Giegerich 1992)

no distinction between these words, which are homophones with the same pronunciation /taɪd/. A minority of RP speakers do maintain a distinction between the two words, but it is a distinction based on vowel quantity (length) rather than vowel quality. The same vowel quality [aɪ] is used in both words, but the vowel in *tide* is pronounced with a shorter duration, and the one in *tied* with a longer duration.

Scots accents have at least one additional consonant in their consonant system compared with RP, in that where RP has only the consonant /k/, Scots has /k/ and /x/. For instance, *lock* and *loch* are pronounced identically in RP as /lɒk/, with a final /k/. All Scots accents pronounce *lock* with a final /k/, where the back of the tongue rises up to contact the underneath of the soft palate, completely blocking off the flow of air from the mouth for a moment. But the word *loch* is pronounced by Scots with a final /x/, for which the back of the tongue is brought close to the soft palate, though without completely closing off the outflow of air from the mouth, which creates a soft hissing/hushing sound technically called a 'fricative' (described in more detail in chapter 9).

Many Scots accents also have an additional consonant /ʍ/ in their systems (sometimes phonemically transcribed /hw/), which is used to distinguish the consonant at the beginning of *whine* /ʍaɪn/ from the one at the beginning of *wine* /waɪn/. The majority of RP speakers (not all) make no such difference, using only /w/. The phonetic difference between /ʍ/ and /w/, which are articulatorily identical, is that the former is voiceless and the latter voiced.

A **structural difference** between accents is a matter of the different rules governing the permissible sequences of phonemes in the phonemic make-up of word-shapes (Laver and Trudgill 1979: 18). It was mentioned earlier that a major structural constraint in RP is that /r/ is never pronounced before another consonant, whereas in very many other accents of English around the world, /r/ can be pronounced in this position. The type of accent where /r/ can be pronounced before consonants is called a **rhotic accent**, and the accents which do not allow this are called **non-rhotic accents**. Rhotic accents include all accents of Scotland, and all of the accents of the Mid-West and West of the United States. In addition to RP, many accents of England, the accents of Australia, New Zealand and South Africa, and many accents of the east and south of the United States are non-rhotic. On this, and related topics, see particularly Wells (1982).

The principal phonological differences between accents typically concern systemic and structural differences of the sort exemplified above. There is, however, a further type of difference of phonological relevance which deserves mention, though it is normally of a minor kind. This type of difference concerns the distribution of phonemic resources over the vocabulary of the dialect, in terms of which phonemes are selected in which words. Differences between two accents which are reflected in such variations of distribution are therefore called **selectional differences**. (These are also sometimes called 'distributional' differences, but to avoid confusion this term will not be used in this sense in this book.) A **selectional difference** is only relevant when the two accents in question share the same phonemic sub-system, but exploit the use of these phonemes differently in given words. A selectional difference can exist between two accents which are otherwise systemically and structurally identical, in the detail of the way that these phonological resources are lexically distributed across small sub-sets of the vocabulary (Abercrombie 1977: 22). An example of a selectional difference concerning vowels, taken from RP and some otherwise comparable accent, is the different distribution of the /a/ and /ɑ/ phonemes found in words like *pat*, *past* and *photograph*. The two accents could both distinguish between *pat* /pat/ and *past* /pɑst/ in the same way, but one might use the /a/ vowel of *pat* in *photograph* /'foʊtəgraf/ where the other uses the vowel /ɑ/ of *past* in *photograph* /'foʊtəgrɑf/.

An example of a selectional difference concerning consonants, taken from RP and General American, is the differing lexical distribution of the /h/ phoneme. General American has preserved the older (seventeenth-century) pronunciation /ɝb/ (or /ɝrb/) of the word *herb* without an /h/, whereas RP invariably uses the newer form /hɝb/. Another consonantal example is the RP pronunciation of *suggest* /sə'dʒɛst/ where some American accents have /səg'dʒɛst/.

All the systemic, structural and selectional differences between accents that have been discussed so far have been differences at the phonological level, concerning the number, sequence and lexical distribution of phonemes characterizing a given accent. The final difference between accents to be discussed is at the phonetic level, and is to do with how speakers of the given accents actually pronounce the phonemes of those accents. Since this is a matter of detailed phonetic realizations, such a difference between accents can be called a **realizational difference**. It was said above that many Scots accents have only one vowel phoneme, which we shall transcribe /a/, in the area of the vowel system where RP has two – /a/ and /ɑ/ – in words such as *Sam* and *psalm*. The detailed phonetic realization of the Scots /a/ phoneme varies widely between accents: if the phonetic realizations of RP /a/ and /ɑ/ ([a] and [ɑ] respectively) were to be regarded as the end-points of a phonetic scale of vowel quality, then the qualities found as realizations of the Scots /a/ phoneme cover the whole of this scale. Where speakers of one Scots accent pronounce both *Sam* and *psalm* as [sam], speakers of another may say the pair as [sɑm], those of a third may use a pronunciation of a vowel mid-way between the two, and those of a fourth may choose a quality nearer one of the end-points.

Realizational differences occur not only between accents, but also between speakers of a single accent who may otherwise share systemic, structural and selectional characteristics. A consonantal example of realizational differences within one accent of English can be found in the rather variable pronunciation of /s/ by different speakers of RP. Some speakers make this sound very high-pitched and piercing, even to the point of producing a momentary soft whistle. Others round their lips. Some (a small minority) raise their bottom lip slightly. Yet others curl the tip of the tongue slightly up and back, which has the effect of making the hissing sound less loud, and the apparent pitch of the hissing sound lower.

Some speakers have one or a small number of phonetic realizations that are sufficiently unlike those of the majority of their accent-group that they strike the listener as notably idiosyncratic, and strongly mark the identity of the speaker as an individual within the group. In extreme cases, such idiosyncrasy is perceived as a **speech defect**. But as a more general comment, it will be apparent on reflection that the phonetic realizations of every phoneme of every speaker have the potential of being slightly different from those of many other speakers even of the same general accent. A lifetime of settling to a habitual mode of speaking has given the personal accent of every speaker an individualizing realizational flavour, within the overall systemic, structural and selectional conventions of his or her own accent-group.

The overall range of phonetic variation between speakers within the accent of a single social or geographical group must not be so extreme as to threaten the classification of the speech patterns of the group as a single group-accent. As a set of working criteria, an accent can be regarded as a unified entity if its speakers share a relevant social or geographical attribute, and if the speakers of the accent successfully maintain a uniform set of systemic and structural characteristics, despite a certain amount of limited realizational variation between speakers. In addition, selectional variation must be very strongly limited. This matter is further discussed in section 3.5 below.

3.4 Differences of style and free variation within the accent of a single speaker

The speech of a single speaker on different occasions and with different conversational partners, within the confines of what would qualify as a single group-accent, may nevertheless differ in two further ways. The first of these types of differences is a matter of the style of speech, and the second concerns free variation of the phonemic and phonetic make-up of individual words within a given style. The approach to the **style of speaking** taken in this book will be to say that speech style is that part of linguistic behaviour that signals the speaker's assessment of the relative formality or informality of the relationship between the participants in the interaction, on the occasion of the conversation. It should be distinguished from para-linguistic matters of tone of voice, signalling emotional and attitudinal information about the speaker such as feelings of anger, grief, complaint, commiseration, joy, amusement or exasperation. All these paralinguistic effects can be overlaid on the linguistic foundation of a speaker's formal or informal style of speaking. It should also be distinguished from matters of **genre**, which are concerned with characteristics of language-use (spoken or written) which are particular to a given situation, such as television news reporting, academic lectures etc. Genres of language-use (particularly those showing variation across speech and writing) are discussed by Biber (1988).

Speech style in English relies on at least three different types of manipulation of the speech material of the utterance: re-organization of the phonemic structure of individual words, modifications of speech rate, and associated prosodic changes of pitch and loudness behaviour. In the progression from a formal to an informal style, the phonemic structure of individual words is often re-organized to reduce the complexity and number of syllables. An illustration of this process can be seen in the following set of progressively informal versions of the word *actually*, as pronounced by RP speakers (J. Harrington, personal communication):

maximally formal	/aktjʊəlɪ/
	/aktʃʊəlɪ/
	/aktʃʊlɪ/
	/aktʃəlɪ/
	/aktʃlɪ/
	/akʃlɪ/
maximally informal	/aʃlɪ/

Polysyllabic words in English have on average about two or three such re-organized pronunciations for use in informal speech (Laver 1989: 50), though some have very many more alternatives. Another form of **phonemic re-organization** for stylistic purposes is **assimilation**, which is discussed in more phonetic detail in chapter 12. Briefly, this process results in consonants at the margins of neighbouring words being made more similar to each other, by the phonetic identity of one consonant (usually the final one in the first word) being subordinated to that of another (usually the first consonant in the second word). Instances of this are the changes in the pronunciations of the final phonemes of the words *horse* and *can* from the formal to the informal versions of the (RP) phrase *Horse shoes can bring you luck* (Laver 1989: 50):

> *formal*   /hɔs ʃuz kan brɪŋ ju lʌk/
> *informal*   /hɔʃ ʃuz kəm brɪŋ jʊ lʌk/

In both cases, the final consonant has been made more like the following initial consonant. In the case of *horse*, the informal version of the word-final consonant /ʃ/ is a result of copying the following word-initial consonant /ʃ/. In the case of *can*, the /n/ has been changed into an /m/ under the influence of the following /b/. The consonant /m/ is like a /b/ in that the consonant articulation in both cases is performed chiefly by the lips closing. Further re-organizational changes can also be seen in the vowels of *can* and *you*, where the pronunciation of these unstressed vowels is reduced (in both duration and vowel quality) compared with their more formal versions. The change in vowel quality, whose basis is explained in more detail in chapter 10, involves a reduction in the distance of the body of the tongue's articulatory travel away from a neutral, central position in the mouth.

An illustration of style differences at a sentence level, showing an assimilatory change, vowel reductions and syllabic simplifications, can be seen in a comparison of two (RP) versions of the sentence *Do you actually know any solicitors?*:

> *formal*   /du ju aktjʊəlɪ nəʊ ɛnɪ səlɪsɪtəz/
> *informal*   /ʤʊ aʃlɪ nəʊ ɛnɪ slɪstəz/

The assimilatory change in this example takes place in the first two words, in a process where the vowel of *do* is dropped, the /d/ of *do* and the /j/ of *you* coalesce to form /ʤ/ (like the final consonant in *hedge*), and the /u/ of *you* changes to a reduced /ʊ/. The [ʒ] element is more similar to [d] than is [j], in that the front of the tongue is closer to the roof of the mouth for [ʒ] than [j], and thus more like the tongue position for [d], where the tongue is in complete contact with the ridge behind the upper teeth. Sounds like [ʤ] (called 'affricates') are described in detail in chapter 12.

As speech style becomes more informal, with syllables often becoming structurally and articulatorily less complex, some authors (e.g. Jones 1962: 13) suggest that there is a tendency in English for the speech rate to increase. However, as mentioned in section 17.2 below, Ramsaran (1978) discovered no such correlation in her experimental investigation of speech style. With increasing informality, it does seem to be the case that associated changes in pitch and loudness behaviour also occur, with pitch levels and ranges rising and loudness levels and ranges dropping (as a very broad generalization). Speech style is still a very under-researched area, however, and the ways in which pitch-patterns may change with increasing informality is not yet well documented for any language.

A final point to be made about the variations in the speech of a single speaker which are attributable to the style of speech used in different circumstances is that the phonological rules underlying casual, informal speech are often different from those applicable to formal speech. One example is the set of phonotactic rules which govern permissible sequences of consonants and vowels in syllable structure. The logical extreme of the reduction process mentioned above is deletion of individual segments from the pattern for individual words and phrases pronounced in isolation. This may give rise to syllable structures which are actually more rather than less articulatorily complex. Couper-Kuhlen (1986: 17) cites examples of this tendency from Bell and Hooper (1978: 18), commenting that '[In] casual speech even the phonotactic rules of a language may be violated: e.g. *potato* /pteɪtə/, *tonight* /tnaɪt/, *fatality* /ftælɪtɪ/', so that the syllable-initial consonantal sequences /pt-, tn-, ft-/ can be found in informal speech in English but not in formal speech. More strictly, one might say that the phonotactic rules governing informal speech are different from those of formal speech, rather than that informal speech 'violates' the rules of formal speech style – since informal speech is no less a legitimate expression of spoken language than is formal speech.

The second type of variation to be discussed in this section is **free variation**. This is where a speaker speaking in a single accent is free to choose between two or more forms of a particular word, without stylistic implications. One instance from RP is the free choice by a speaker on different occasions between the pronunciations /ivə'luʃən/ and /ɛvə'luʃən/ for the word 'evolution'. This is an example where the choice lies between two of the vowel phonemes available in the speaker's vowel system. Free variation also occurs on a microscopic scale at the phonetic level within the speech of every individual speaker, where the exact quality of the realization of any given phoneme in a given context displays small phonetic differences (on an apparently random basis) on different occasions of utterance (Gimson 1962: 47).

3.5 Accent as a marker of the speaker's group-membership and individuality

The accent of a given speaker can be viewed in (at least) two perspectives. It can be seen as a **group-marker** of the speaker's membership of a variety of social groupings, and as an **individuating marker** uniquely identifying the speaker against the mass of other members of the wider group. A term used for an accent which characterizes the speech of a whole social group when speaking in a given style is **sociolect**. Within such a sociolect, the uniquely idiosyncratic accent of a given speaker speaking in a given style is called the speaker's **idiolect**. The term **lect** is then a neutral term for an accent without specific implications for its sociolectal or idiolectal status.

Comment on a sociolect considers the speaker as a member of a particular social group. Comment on an idiolect focuses on the speaker as an individual within his or her social group. A speaker-identifying idiolect typically relies for its individuating power on fine details of phonetic realizations. A group-identifying sociolect is usually chiefly signalled by more systemic, structural and selectional considerations.

Accent is a rich source of inference for the listener about the social attributes of the speaker (though it should be remembered that these judgements by the listener are not always reliably accurate). The syllable structures of the accent, together with the consonant and vowel systems, the lexical distributions of the phonemes and their phonetic realizations, are taken to mark the speaker's membership of a particular sociolinguistic community. As we saw earlier in this chapter, this marking can vary in its degree of geographical specificity, depending on whether the sociolinguistic community is non-regional (as in the case of the General American and Received Pronunciation accents), or regional (as in the case of Texan or Cockney accents).

Accent is also taken to mark a range of social attributes other than merely that of geographical origin. Wells (1970: 248), for instance, comments that 'Accent is still significantly linked to social class in England, and often constitutes an important index of class affiliation.' One particular facet of phonetic performance that serves this function in the accents of England is the detailed quality of the pronunciation of vowels. We shall see in chapter 10 that the pronunciation of vowel quality is an articulatory, auditory and acoustic continuum, and this makes it available to act as a marker of fine gradations of social status (Giles, Scherer and Taylor 1979: 361; Laver and Trudgill 1979).

The work of Labov (1966, 1972a, 1972b) has been very influential in the sociolinguistic study of speech, notably in understanding the role of accent as a sociolinguistic marker. In particular, Labov promoted the understanding that speakers' accents are not fixed and unchanging, but show many linguistic variables which can be manipulated (consciously or unconsciously) as an adaptive response to the changing social situation in which the speakers find themselves. The changing social factors include such details as the relative social status of the speaker and listener, the familiarity of their acquaintance with each other, whether both participants are of the same sex and age, whether the conversation is within the hearing of bystanders, and the nature and purpose of the meeting itself. One of the responses by the speaker to these changing circumstances can be the degree of informality of the speech style adopted.

An example of sociolinguistic variability within an accent is discussed in the following comments:

> Work in the field of sociolinguistics has shown that social groups may differ not simply in terms of their phonological systems or what pronunciation they use but in *how often* they use certain pronunciations. In the pioneering work in this field, Labov (1966) demonstrated that in New York City speech the pronunciation of /r/ in words such as *farm* (where the r occurs before another consonant) and *far* (where it occurs word-finally) is a *linguistic variable*. While very few New York City speakers actually pronounce the /r/ in these positions on every occasion, most pronounce it on some occasions ... In New York City the frequency with which /r/ in *far*, *farm*, etc. is pronounced correlates very clearly with the age and social class of the speaker, and with the social context in which he is speaking ... In the New York City study, counts of how many /r/s were actually pronounced, and how many could have been but were not, showed that middle-class speakers, on average, pronounced a higher percentage of /r/s than working-class speakers, that younger speakers had a higher percentage than older speakers, and that formal styles of speech produced more /r/s than informal styles. Interestingly enough, studies of English towns where /r/ is also a variable, such as Reading, show exactly the reverse pattern (see Trudgill 1975) – a good illustration of the arbitrary nature of linguistic markers of social categories. (Laver and Trudgill 1979: 19–20)

Many comparable sociolinguistic studies of individual cities in the English-speaking world have been stimulated by Labov's (1966) work on the sociolinguistic patterns of lower east side New York speech. A number of publications describing sociolinguistic work on communities in North America, Great Britain and Autralia are given in the section on Further Reading below.

3.6 Dialectology and dialect geography

The customary name for the discipline that studies the phonetic and phonological patterns of accents and dialects of languages, and their geographical distribution in space and time, is **dialectology** (Chambers and Trudgill 1980). It should be said that the general use of this term is not consistent with the practice advocated in this book, where 'dialect' is reserved for description at a higher linguistic level than pronunciation. But 'dialectology' is so well established as a label that it would be counter-productive to insist on a division between 'dialectology' and 'accentology' or the like. Furthermore, the established scope of the term 'dialectology' encompasses more than matters of accent alone, in that it also deals with dialectal patterns of lexical, syntactic and morphological usage. Walters (1988) offers a compact and valuable account of the history and the methods of both the traditional and the more modern sociolinguistically and quantitatively inclined versions of dialectology in North America and Europe.

A very substantial body of work in dialectology has been invested in the mapping of the geographical distribution of different dialectal forms. This part of the subject is therefore sometimes called **dialect geography**, or **regional dialectology**. The traditional practice in dialect geography was for fieldworkers to conduct face-to-face interviews with speakers they had selected as authentic representatives of the sociolinguistic community they were investigating, and to transcribe the utterances the informants produced for the dialectal forms for objects or activities listed in a standard questionnaire or wordlist, in a phonetic notation whose conventions varied somewhat from one project to another. Cross-project comparability was hence somewhat impeded. The process of gathering adequate data for large-scale projects was typically very expensive in both time and effort, and organizing and preparing the data for publication correspondingly difficult. It is perhaps not then surprising that few large-scale projects have succeeded in reaching final publication.

Carver (1987), Chaika (1989) and Walters (1988) consider the history of dialect surveys in North America. A survey of the dialects of the United States and Canada began in 1931 that sought to register both phonetic and linguistic data of dialect variation (Atwood 1963). The project was entitled the Linguistic Atlas of the United States and Canada (LAUSC), and it accomplished a very significant amount of dialectological work. But it was eventually abandoned in 1949, as simply not feasible. McDavid (1958) described the very ambitious objectives of that project in the following terms: 'the American Atlas seeks to record data illustrating the social differences, the dimension of time, and the process of language and dialect mixture that has been going on everywhere since the New World was settled' (cited by Chaika 1989: 226). Walters (1988: 121) describes the history of the

LAUSC project and related dialectological projects in North America as follows:

> In the United States and Canada, dialect geography is usually
> associated with the *Linguistic atlas of the United States and Canada
> (LAUSC)*, an as yet unrealized effort to produce a linguistic atlas
> for each of the regions of the two countries. The project was begun
> in the late 1920's in New England, yielding the *Linguistic atlas of New
> England (LANE)* (Kurath *et al.* 1939–43) and the *Handbook of the
> linguistic geography of New England* (Kurath *et al.* 1939). None of the
> other atlas projects has fared so well, with only the *Linguistic Atlas of
> the Upper Midwest (LAUM)* (Allen 1973–6) and a few fascicles of the
> *Linguistic atlas of the Middle and South Atlantic States (LAMSAS)* (R.
> McDavid *et al.* 1980–) reaching publication ... The single exception is
> the *Linguistic atlas of the Gulf States (LAGS)* (Pederson 1969, 1971,
> 1974, 1976; Pederson, McDaniel and Bassett 1984).

A current project (*DARE*, the *Dictionary of American Regional English*) is an on-going attempt to map the lexical forms of the dialects across the whole of the United States, comparing these forms with those recorded in the survey begun in 1931 (Cassidy 1985). Kurath (1972) gives a brief overall picture of the dialect geography of the whole of the United States.

A major project on lexical and phonetic aspects of dialects and accents in Scotland and nearby areas is the Linguistic Survey of Scotland, whose original design was outlined by McIntosh (1952), which resulted in the *Linguistic Atlas of Scotland* (Mather and Speitel 1975). As an illustration of such work, figure 3.2 is a reproduction of their map showing the distribution in different parts of Scotland, Northern Ireland, Orkney and Shetland of the words for 'splinter' in a number of different dialects (*skelf, stab, splice, stob, splinter, spell, spale, skelve, spelk, spilk* and *skelb*) (Mather and Speitel 1975: 33). The Linguistic Survey of Scotland includes an important Gaelic section, whose continuing work is described in Jackson (1958) and Gillies (1988). Wagner (1964–9) constitutes a monumental survey of the dialects of Irish. A comparable major work on the dialects of England is the *Linguistic Atlas of England*, published by Orton (1962), Orton and Barry (1969–71), Orton and Halliday (1962–3), Orton and Tilling (1969–71) and Orton and Wakelin (1967–8), and by Orton, Sanderson and Widdowson (1978). A dialect survey of Wales is reported by Thomas (1973).

One of the tools of the dialectologist is the isogloss. An **isogloss** is a line on a map drawn round all areas displaying the same pronunciation for a given consonant, vowel or word. A strong implication underlies the use of such a definite boundary – namely, that the phonetic and phonological characteristics of lects on one side of the isogloss are categorically different from

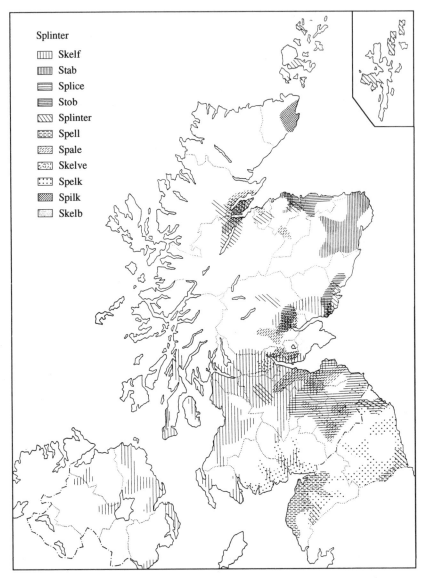

Figure 3.2   The words for 'splinter' in dialects of Scotland, Northern
Ireland, Orkney and Shetland (adapted from Mather and Speitel 1975: 33)

those of lects found on the other side. Figure 3.3 is adapted from Trudgill
(1983: 84), and shows an isogloss on a map of England taken from work by
the Survey of English Dialects, which acts as a boundary dividing the middle of England into two zones. The northern zone contains those lects that

74

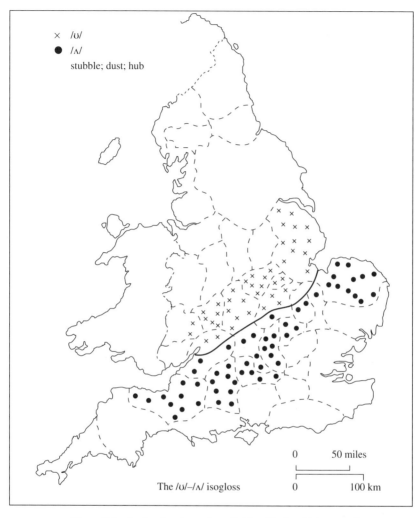

× /ʊ/
● /ʌ/
stubble; dust; hub

0   50 miles

The /ʊ/–/ʌ/ isogloss   0   100 km

Figure 3.3 An isogloss boundary dividing England into a northern zone
using [ʊ] in words such as *dust*, and a southern zone using [ʌ] in these
words (adapted from Trudgill 1983: 84)

use the same vowel in the words *stubble*, *dust* and *hub* as in RP *book*, *push*
and *put* (/ʊ/), rather than the vowel in RP *fuss*, *stud* and *gush* (/ʌ/). The
southern zone contains those lects which share the RP pattern of /ʌ/ in *stubble*, *dust* and *hub*.

The picture offered by such an isogloss map is inadequate in at least two
respects. The first is that the comments quoted in section 3.5 immediately
above from Laver and Trudgill (1979) on sociolinguistic variation are

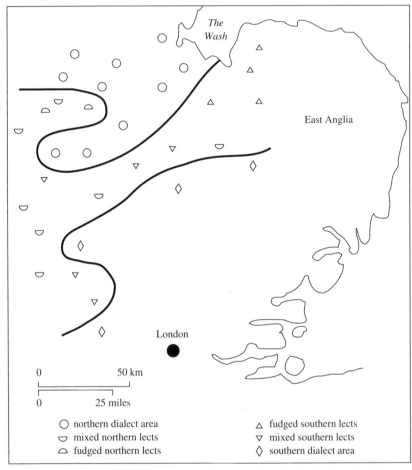

Figure 3.4 Isogloss map showing a corridor of mixed and 'fudged' lects with differing patterns of usage of [ʊ], [ʌ] and [ɤ] in words such as *dust* and *push* (adapted from Trudgill 1983:49–50)

applicable – speakers may vary in how often they choose particular pronunciations within their range of possibilities. The second is that such geographical accent-boundaries are more often gradual than discrete. Figure 3.4 is taken from Trudgill (1983: 49–50), where he comments on previous work by Chambers and Trudgill (1980), to demonstrate that between the northern and southern zones there is actually a corridor of mixed and 'fudged' lects, which forms a transitional zone. He characterizes this 'corridor of variability' as containing the following mixed lects:

(i)   mixed northern lects: /ʌ/ and /ʊ/ alternate, but /ʊ/ predominates;

(ii) fudged northern lects: /ʊ/ alternates with an intermediate vowel [ɤ];

(iii) fudged southern lects: /ʌ/ alternates with an intermediate vowel [ɤ];

(iv) mixed southern lects: /ʌ/ and /ʊ/ alternate, but /ʌ/ predominates. (Trudgill 1983: 49)

The symbol [ɤ] that Trudgill refers to as an 'intermediate vowel' represents a pronunciation whose tongue position is close to that of [ʊ], but with a lip position like that of [ʌ]. The detailed qualities of these sounds are discussed in chapter 10.

3.7   Language differences between speakers

The dialects of a given language can vary in their similarity to each other. Conventionally, the limit that is set to the maximum degree of difference between two dialects is one of **mutual intelligibility**. When two forms of language are mutually unintelligible, they are usually considered to be dialects of two different languages. Any two dialects of English and German, for example, though showing vestigial similarities that reflect their common genetic status as closely related languages in the Indo-European family of languages, are unintelligible to listeners of the other language. But there are many instances where the application of the criterion of mutual intelligibility fails to yield a satisfactory classification of the two language forms concerned. Norwegian and Danish are regarded as different languages, and yet their speakers can hold relatively successful conversations despite the grammatical and phonetic differences that exist. The factor that is decisive in Norwegians and Danes preferring to treat them as different languages rather than different dialects of the same language is less linguistic than political, with differences of language being identified with national differences.

There are other problems with the criterion of mutual intelligibility. One is that intelligibility is a multidimensional scale, when considered within and across the full range of linguistic levels. Setting a limit within such a scale for what counted as a dialect-differentiating versus a language-differentiating degree of intelligibility would be quite arbitrary. Another problem is that matters of intelligibility are themselves subject to the judgemental attitudes of the listeners involved. There are numerous cases where the listeners of language form A find the speakers of language form B quite intelligible, but where the listeners of B claim not to be able to understand the speakers of

A. Once again, factors of social and political attitude dominate the question. It is therefore probably more practical to consider the differentiation of dialects and languages to be primarily a sociopolitical issue. One can perhaps accept the broad proposition that, in general, languages differ linguistically from one another in the same ways that dialects do, even if usually to a more extreme degree.

The concept of intelligibility itself is not a little problematic. A listener who understands French and Italian may be able to make partial sense of utterances heard from speakers of Spanish, because of the general relatedness of the three languages as members of the Romance language-family. But it would not be helpful to suggest that such a listener 'understands Spanish'. The field of cross-linguistic intelligibility offers interesting research possibilities.

3.7.1 *First, second and foreign languages*

Very many speakers, perhaps the majority of speakers in the world, understand at least one language other than their own. A speaker who understands only one language can be described as a **monoglot**, and one who understands two or several a **polyglot**. However, one could be basically a monoglot with only a smattering of knowledge of words and phrases in another language, without qualifying as a polyglot. To clarify the different status of a speaker's experiences of other languages, it is helpful to differentiate between a first language, a second language and a foreign language. A **first language** is a speaker's **native language**, or **mother tongue**, whose learning normally begins in the speaker's earliest experience of language-acquisition as a very small child. A **second language** is any other language that the speaker learns to control, at any time, to a level of near native-like proficiency. Few speakers ever learn to control a second language to the point of being indistinguishable, in every linguistic and phonetic respect, from a native speaker of that language. If they do succeed in attaining this level of expertise, then they can properly be termed **bilingual**. True bilingualism in this strict definition is fairly rare, and most speakers of languages other than their native language show signs of their non-native status in their linguistic and phonetic performance. Any language spoken by a speaker to less than second-language level can be called a **foreign language**, and the state of being able to control more than one language (to any reasonable degree) can be referred to as **multilingualism**. In the literature of applied linguistics, the term bilingualism is often used in this looser sense of multilingualism.

Learning a language other than one's own native language is always a process in which the patterns of the first language interfere with the learning of the foreign language. At any given stage of acquisition of a foreign language, the linguistic competence underlying the utterances performed by the learner will show some amalgam of the patterns of the two languages. Selinker (1972) was amongst the first to develop the concept of an **interlanguage**, to account for the strategies deployed by learners of a foreign language at any given stage in their progressive mastery of that language.

An area where multilingualism is a prime consideration is the teaching of languages. This is a domain where acronyms abound. In the case of English, one encounters acronyms such as **ELT** (English Language Teaching), which is a relatively comprehensive term for teaching English to learners of all types; **TESL** (Teaching English as a Second Language), where the learners addressed are often immigrants to an English-speaking culture; **TEFL** (Teaching English as a Foreign Language), where the learners are normally neither native speakers nor immigrants; and **TESOL** (Teaching English to Speakers of Other Languages), which is a slightly more neutral term encompassing both TESL (mostly) and TEFL, but avoiding some of the potentially prejudicial implications of labels such as 'second language' and 'foreign language'. Accounts of these areas of English-language teaching can be found in Stern (1983).

The very brief sketch above of terms applicable to speakers who understand more than one language does not do justice to the diversity of the topic of multilingualism. In the broad definition as a person's ability to control two or more languages, even to an unequal degree, multilingualism (or 'bilingualism') is currently an intensive research area in applied linguistics (Spolsky 1988).

The deviations in performance of a foreign language by a speaker from native-speaker-like norms of pronunciation are almost all directly attributable to the influence of differences between the phonetic and phonological patterns of the foreign language and the speaker's own native language. The concepts introduced in section 3.3 of structural, systemic and realizational differences between two accents of a language can equally be applied to this situation of speakers trying to pronounce an accent of a language other than their own. When French students beginning to learn English pronounce the phrase *this red cart* as [zis ʁeḏ kaʁt̪], normally pronounced by native speakers of RP as [ðɪs ɹed kɑt], the replacement by the learners of the RP [ð] by [z] in *this* reflects the systemic fact that while the consonant system of RP distinguishes two phonemes /ð/ and /z/, that of French uses only /z/. Similarly, where the RP vowel system distinguishes between /ɪ/ and /i/ (as in *hid* /hɪd/ and *heed* /hid/ respectively), French uses only /i/. The substitution of the RP [ɹ] by [ʁ] has a realizational explanation, in that while the consonant systems of both RP and French include an /r/ phoneme, its realization in RP is (in this syllable-initial position) [ɹ], with the tip of the tongue slightly curled, while that in French is [ʁ], which is made by bringing the back of the tongue near to the end of the soft palate at the back of the mouth. The French learners' use of [d̪] for [d], and [t̪] for [t], also corresponds to realizational differences between the two accents, in that [d̪] and [t̪] in French are made partly by sealing off the flow of air through the mouth by the tip of the tongue against the upper front teeth, while [d] and [t] in English are characteristically made by the seal being made a little further back, on the ridge just above and behind the teeth.

The French insertion of [ʁ] before the consonant /t/ at the end of 'cart', as a pronunciation of an /r/ phoneme thought by the French learners to be implied by the spelling, is a structural matter. Where the RP accent of English is non-rhotic (i.e. excluding the pronunciation of /r/ before consonants, as described in section 3.3), all accents of French are rhotic.

Comparisons in such terms of the phonetic and phonological patterns of the target accent and that of the learner allow the teacher to predict typical errors likely to be made by beginners. They also enable the teacher then to plan appropriate strategies of pronunciation teaching, and to prioritize them in importance and sequence of learning. Two excellent books that have been recently published on learning English pronunciation based on this general approach are Gimson (1989, updated by Ramsaran) and Roach (1991).

3.7.2 *Lingua francas, pidgins and creoles*

Foreign languages are most often used for communication with speakers for whom the language concerned is their native language. A special case is where the language used is the native language of neither the speaker nor the listener, but where it may be the only medium of linguistic communication in common between the two, often for trade purposes. Where this practice is widespread in a given area, the status of the foreign language as an instrument of general communication is recognized by calling it a **lingua franca**.

The orginal 'lingua franca' (literally 'language of the Franks', the Arabic term of the day for all Europeans) came into being in the Eastern Mediterranean at the time of the Crusades about nine centuries ago, and evolved as a composite of Italian, Provençal, French, Spanish and Portuguese (Holm 1989: 607). Lingua francas in use today (or 'lingue franche', to recognize the phrase's Italian origin) notably include English and Mandarin Chinese. Other large-scale lingua francas are Malay in Malaysia and Indonesia, Swahili in East Africa, Hausa in West Africa,

Arabic from West Africa to Afghanistan, Afrikaans in Southern Africa and Spanish in South and Central America. The reader is referred to Holm (1988, 1989) for a very comprehensive account of these and other related language forms around the world.

A lingua franca, despite the originating example above, is often a single homogeneous language. A **pidgin language**, by contrast, though used for much the same purposes of communication between speakers of mutually unintelligible languages (usually in the Third World), is developed out of a mixture of the languages of the communities concerned. Holm (1988: 5) gives one of the clearest definitions of a pidgin language:

> A *pidgin* is a reduced language that results from extended contact between groups of people with no language in common; it evolves when they need some means of verbal communication, perhaps for trade, but no group learns the native language of any other group for social reasons that may include lack of trust or of close contact. Usually those with less power (speakers of *substrate* languages) are more accommodating and use words from the language of those with more power (the *superstrate*), although the meaning, form and use of these words may be influenced by the substrate languages. When dealing with the other groups, the superstrate speakers adopt many of these changes to make themselves more readily understood, and no longer try to speak as they do within their own group. They co-operate with the other groups to create a makeshift language to serve their needs.

Romaine (1988: 3) characterizes the linguistic properties of a pidgin language as follows:

> the vocabulary of a pidgin is usually drawn primarily from the prestige language of the dominant group in a situation of language contact. Its grammar, however, retains many features of the native languages of the subordinate groups. The prestige language which supplies the bulk of the vocabulary is the one which is usually thought of as being pidginized, hence the name Pidgin English.

Mühlhäusler (1986: 4) cites a definition of pidgins by Hall (1966: xii) which emphasizes the reduction in scope of the language and the foreign status of the language for both speakers in a conversation in which 'Two or more people use a language in a variety whose grammar and vocabulary are very much reduced in extent and which is native to neither side'. Romaine (1988: 1) illustrates this reduction in opening her book with an example of an utterance in Tok Pisin (Papua New Guinea Pidgin English) by the Duke of Edinburgh in a speech to the English-Speaking Union Conference in Ottawa in 1958, where he observed that 'I am referred to in that splendid language as "Fella bilong Mrs Queen" (Cohen and Cohen 1971: 67)', (though Romaine (1988: 3) points out that in a more authentic Tok Pisin he should have said 'man' rather than 'fella'). Romaine (1988: 35) gives the following examples of lexical correspondences in Tok Pisin and English:

Lexical structures in Tok Pisin
(New Guinea Pidgin English) and English

Tok Pisin	**English**
gras	grass
mausgras	moustache
gras bilong fes	beard
gras bilong hed	hair
gras bilong pisin	feather
gras antap long ai	eyebrow
gras nogut	weed
han	hand/arm
han bilong diwai	branch of a tree
han bilong pisin	wing of a bird

The characteristic linguistic structure of a pidgin is evident in the following impressionistic example of a text in Solomon Islands Pidgin given by Holm (1989: 534) from a personal communication by E. Lee:

Solomon Islands Pidgin text

Mitufala jes marit   nomoa ia so mitufala no garem
we two   just married only   so we   didn't have
eni pikinini   iet.
any children yet

Mi traehad fo fosim haosben blong mi   fo mitufala go
I   tried   to force husband of   mine for we two   go
long sip   bat taem ia
on   ship but time that

hemi   had tumas fo faendem rum   long sip bikos
it-was hard very to find   room on   ship because
plande pipol wandem
many   people wanted

go-go hom fo Krismas   tu.
to go home for Christmas too

The definitions of a pidgin language quoted above from Holm and Hall specified that a pidgin is native to no speaker. When a pidgin is acquired as the first, native language of a group of speakers (as happened historically to generations of speakers under the social and geographical displacement that accompanied slavery), it is said to constitute a **creole language**. Creole languages typically become more linguistically elaborated than their antecedent pidgins, and become autonomous languages in their own right. The evolution of creole languages, in the process called **creolization**, has claimed a good deal of recent research attention as an arena of creative language acquisition claimed to reveal universal aspects of the language faculty (Hymes 1971b; Romaine 1988). The potential for sociolinguistic research in this topic is also very substantial.

A large number of languages have contributed to the basis of modern creole languages via their parent pidgins, including Arabic, Dutch, English, French, Portuguese, Spanish and Swahili. Hancock (1971: 507–23), reprinted as an Appendix by Romaine (1988: 315–25), lists more than 200 pidgin and creole languages around the world. Well-known examples of creole languages based on English are Krio in Sierra Leone and Jamaican Creole in the Caribbean.

Holm (1989: 475) gives the following illustration of a less-known creole language from the Western Caribbean, Miskito Coast Creole English (the Miskito Coast runs from the northeastern coast of Honduras to the eastern coast of Nicaragua), where Creole English acts as a lingua franca for the various ethnic groups of the population:

Miskito Coast Creole English text

```
wen   i   pik it op           naw i   no     kom  we    a de.
when  he  starts up (drinking) now he  doesn't come where I am
i    tel   mi lay
he tells me lies

wen   i   kom   naw. da    iyvnin  i   sey, 'mama,'  i   sey, 'a
when  he  comes now. in the evening he says mama    he  says I
did     tayad an
ANT    tired and

neva  kom'. a sey, 'yu  dam   lay. siy yu   ay? yu   mi
didn't come I say  you  damn liar see your eye you ANT
dringkin;  das    wai
drinking   that's why

yu  no   mi   wahn   kom  ya.'
you NEG ANT  want to come here
```

83

The discussion above of pidgin and creole languages has concentrated to some extent on the lexical forms involved, but phonetic and phonological considerations also apply. Given the status of a pidgin language as a language foreign to both the speakers in a pidgin conversation, both speakers will pronounce their utterances in ways strongly coloured, if not fully determined, by the phonologies of their own native languages. Romaine (1988: 120–1) gives a very clear description of such differences between speakers of Chinook Jargon, a trade pidgin language of the Pacific Northwest of North America spoken over at least the last 300 years:

> Johnson (1975) describes the phonology of Chinook Jargon as a
> reduction or generalization of the phonological distinctions which
> occur in the speakers' native languages. Speakers generally used
> only those sounds which were present in their native languages. When
> the phonological systems of their native languages permitted, they
> maintained the phonological distinctions of the native American Indian
> languages in words derived from those lexical sources. The distinctions
> made by English in the labial series /b, p, v, f/ were not matched by
> distinctions in the native Indian languages, such as Kwakiutl, which
> has /p, pʰ, p'/. Depending on the language origin of the speaker,
> different allophones may be used, *eg* [p] or [b], [f], [v]. All these
> distinctions were reduced to /p/ in the jargon used by most Indian
> speakers. English and French speakers sometimes maintained these
> distinctions. Thus, for the word 'fish' an English speaker might say
> /fis/, while a Kwakiutl might say /pis/. This means that lexical items
> exist in competing forms, *eg* 'fire' may be /paya/, /faya/ and /baya/.

When such languages become creolized, it seems likely that the phonology of the creole form of the language will acquire an autonomous impetus, and evolve an independent shape, though with traceable affiliations to its parental origins. Holm (1988: 105–37) gives an extensive account of such processes in creole phonologies.

3.8 The genetic relationship between languages

The social basis of every language-form gives it an ever-present momentum for change, given the universal tendency of sociolinguistic communities to adapt their linguistic behaviour towards or away from the accents, dialects or languages of the other groups with which they interact. All accents, dialects and languages are thus in a continuous state of evolutionary change, and describing and explaining the results and causes of such change is the function of **comparative** and **historical linguistics**. When an account of an accent, dialect or language is offered as a snapshot in time, describing its state at a given stage in its historical development, this is usually called a **synchronic** description. When two or more stages in the evolution of a given accent or dialect are compared, this is usually called a **diachronic** description. A comparative interest in accents and dialects can be based on either synchronic or diachronic descriptions. The statements made earlier in section 3.3 about the systemic, structural, selectional and realizational ways that accents can differ from each other are comparative statements made on a synchronic basis. A description of the way that the accents and dialects of English have evolved over the centuries, as offered for instance by Wakelin (1988), involves a diachronic comparison of different stages of each of those accents and dialects. In both the synchronic and diachronic comparisons, we are dealing with the branch of comparative and historical linguistics that is often called **comparative dialectology**. A substantial part of this discipline is set in the older tradition of **comparative philology**. The part that approaches these questions from the perspective of the linguistic sciences is usually called **historical phonology**, as exemplified by Anderson and Jones (1977).

On a small timescale, changes of meaning, vocabulary, syntax and pronunciation are evident even within the lifetime of individual speakers. One of the ways that one can date a commentary by an RP speaker on an old newsreel recorded even in the 1940s, for example, is by the discernibly different realizations of some of the vowels used, in a process called **phonetic drift**. An example is the pronunciation of the /a/ phoneme in words such as *man*, where the quality of the sound used for the vowel is considerably closer to that currently used for the /ɛ/ phoneme in *men* than it would be today in the speech of all except the most conservative speakers. Another example is the change in vocabulary and syntax represented by a spoken phrase of current colloquial English such as *Tabloid sleaze is for real*, which would probably have baffled a reader in the 1940s.

New words, especially in technical domains, are being created in languages such as English every year. New words also enter a dialect or language from other dialects and languages. Conservative speakers of French frequently lament the import of the ever-increasing number of English-based words into French, condemning it as the undesirable growth of a new hybrid 'Franglais'. While new words are created, old words also die. Dictionaries such as the *Oxford English Dictionary* (1989), which reflect historical changes in vocabulary, are full of words which were current in Victorian or slightly earlier times which are now quite obsolete.

The rate of change of a language can be sensed in the development of the accents of North American English from its beginnings in Britain as Elizabethan English. In four centuries, the accents have diverged substantially, even if the versions of Standard English as a dialect spoken in North America are still very largely the same as Standard English spoken in Britain. The forms of English spoken in Britain and North America are still considered to be versions of the same language. But on a longer timescale, had they diverged a thousand years ago they might well by now be candidates for being considered closely related but different languages. A larger difference exists between Yoruba and Igbo, spoken in West Africa, which are thought to have evolved from a common form into different languages several thousand years ago.

The timing of the divergence of language-forms into separate languages is hypothesized in historical linguistics by a comparative method which considers the scale of regular correspondences between the language-forms concerned, drawing on data from **lexicostatistics** and on assumptions about typical rates of language change from **glottochronology**. Gudschinsky (1956) and Hymes (1960) are still good outlines of basic concepts in this area.

The terminology of language classification that results from such enquiries is often couched in terms of a genetic metaphor. Languages such as Yoruba and Igbo are said to have descended from a **parent-language**, and to be genetically related to that ancestral language, to each other and to a number of other languages in a **language-family**. Common membership of a language-family qualifies the languages concerned as **cognate languages**. Within an overall language-family, relationships of varying degree can be established, within **language groups** and **sub-groups**. A language showing no discernible affiliation to other languages, perhaps as a relic of earlier languages displaced by invading populations, is called a **language isolate**. Basque is one such instance. Ainu, a language of Japan, is another.

At the broadest level of comparison, there are thought to be some thirty large, relatively distinct families of languages in the world. The genetic classification of languages is currently an active research field, and statements about the detailed affiliations of many less-researched languages within such large-scale genetic relationships remain hypotheses. **Indo-European** is the name for the language family uniting the **Romance** languages (Latin and its descendants, such as Italian, French, Provençal, Spanish, Catalan and Portuguese), and **Germanic** languages (such as English, German and Danish), with a very wide range of ultimately related languages extending eastwards to the Indian sub-continent, including Greek, Russian, Iranian, Hindi and Sanskrit.

The closer the genetic relationship between two languages, the more abundant the regular correspondences between them at the different linguistic levels of analysis. As an illustration of this phenomenon, table 3.1 presents some of the **sound-correspondences** between Latin, French, Italian and

Spanish (Lyons 1981: 193). If we convert the orthographic forms in Lyons' table to their approximate phonetic equivalents, with allowances for phonetic values known to be valid for earlier periods, then the correspondences shown in table 3.1 can be discerned (Lyons 1981: 195).

Table 3.1 *Sound-correspondences between Latin, French, Italian and Spanish*

	Latin	*French*	*Italian*	*Spanish*
1	[k]	= [ʃ]	= [k]	= [k]
2	[pl, kl]	= [pl, kl]	= [pj, kj]	= [ʎ]
3	[kt]	= [it]	= [tt]	= [tʃ]
4	[f]	= [f]	= [f]	= [h]

(The meaning of the Spanish [ʎ] in these correspondences – a voiced palatal lateral approximant – is explained in chapter 10.) In the case of Latin and its Romance **daughter-languages**, we have good written records that offer direct evidence of the earlier parent-language. But often the details of the parent-language, which may never have developed a writing system, have been lost in unrecorded prehistory. A possible form of a parent-language may nevertheless be reconstructed, through a comparison of such regular sound-correspondences between the surviving descendant languages whose linguistic affiliation to the parent-language is suspected. The resulting hypothesized reconstruction of a parent-language is sometimes called a **proto-language**. Words and other linguistic units of such a **non-attested** reconstruction are conventionally identified as such by prefacing the form by a superscript asterisk, as in Proto-Indo-European */dekm/ 'ten' (Lehmann 1962: 10), and are often referred to as **starred forms**.

The process of phonological reconstruction depends on the assumption that **sound-change** (or **sound-shift**) in a descendant of a parent-language is regular and widespread through the lexical stock of that daughter-language. Gleason (1961: 446) lays out the nature of the argument underlying reconstruction as follows:

> suppose the ancestral language has a phoneme /X/ which by regular change becomes /Y/ in language A, and by a different regular change becomes /Z/ in language B. We might then expect many words with /Y/ in A to correspond with words with /Z/ in language B. Conversely, suppose we observe that many words in language A containing the phoneme /P/ seem similar to words in language B containing /Q/. We may conclude that this is presumptive evidence that there was in the common ancestor a sound (perhaps a phoneme or an allophone) which

by separate changes became /P/ in A and /Q/ in B. We do not know what that sound was, but we may designate it by an arbitrary symbol, say [*R].

Gleason (1961: 447–8) compares sets of corresponding words from four cognate North American Indian Algonquian languages, Fox, Cree, Menomini and Ojibwa as a basis for re-constructing elements of the sound-system of Proto-Central-Algonquian. Gleason's own Americanist phonemic word-transcriptions are preserved in table 3.2 here, since they do not affect the basis of the comparison.

Table 3.2 *Regular sound-correspondences in words in four Algonquian languages*

	Fox	Cree	Menomini	Ojibwa	Meaning
1	pemātesiwa	pimātisiw	pemātesew	pimātisi	'he lives'
2	pōsiwa	pōsiw	pōsew	pōsi	'he embarks'
3	newāpamāwa	niwāpamāw	newāpamaw	newāpamā	'I look at him'
4	wāpanwi	wāpan	wāpan	wāpan	'it dawned'
5	nīyawi	nīyaw	nēyaw	nīyaw	'my body'
6	kenosiwa	kinosiw	kenōsew	kinosi	'he is long'
7	anemwa	atim	anɛm	anim	'dog'
8	nīnemwa	nītim	nēnem	nīnim	'my sister-in-law'
9	ineniwa	iyiniw	enēniw	inini	'man'
10	nēsēwa	yēhyēw	nɛhnew	nēssē	'he breathes'

Assuming that the longer forms in Fox are older, and that the other languages dropped sounds from the corresponding words, it is straightforward to reconstruct a sub-set of Proto-Central-Algonquian sounds [*p], [*m], [*t], [*s], [*w], [*n], [*y] ([j] in IPA terms) and [*k] from the information in rows 1–6 above, which show unusual uniformity of correspondence (Proto-Central-Algonquian [*p] > Fox /p/, Cree /p/, Menomini /p/ and Ojibwa /p/, etc.). The hypothesized words in the proto-language for the first six items would then be [*pemātesiwa, *pōsiwa, *newāpamāwa, *wapānwi, *nīyawi, *kenosiwa] respectively. They happen to be the same as the Fox forms, but Gleason emphasizes that these are merely formulae for the proto-language forms, from which the current forms in the four languages can be predicted. Their status as guesses about the actual pronunciations that characterized the proto-language is only secondary.

The information in rows 7–10 changes the uniformity of the correspondence slightly, in that /n/ in Fox, Menomini and Ojibwa corresponds in Cree to /t/ in rows 7 and 8, and (in some cases) to /y/ in rows 9 and 10. On this basis, Gleason finds it convenient to reconstruct two more Proto-Central-Algonquian forms [*θ] and [*l] (partly because Arapaho, another cognate language, has /θ/ and /l/ as correspondences in these words). The reconstructed words in the proto-language for rows 7–10 above would then read [*aθemwa, *nīθemwa, *elenyiwa, *lēhlēwa]. Gleason (1961: 448) adds that the reconstructed form [*elenyiwa] 'man' in Proto-Central-Algonquian is the precursor (via French) of the modern American English name *Illinois*.

It was suggested earlier that historical sound-change from a phonological pattern in a parent-language was assumed to be regular and widespread through the lexical stock of the descendant language. In reality, such sound-changes are often partial and incomplete, leaving relics of older forms in the descendant language. Lyons (1981: 197) translates a comment by the great historical scholar Jacob Grimm to this effect: 'The sound-shift succeeds in the majority of cases, but never works itself out completely in every individual case; some words remain in the form they had in the older period; the current of innovation has passed them by.' These apparently anomalous cases often turn out to have developed under a different historical timetable, under the influence of different chronological stages of **contact-languages**, or to have been imported from other **source-languages**.

Appendix II lists every language mentioned in the text with an indication not only of where the language is spoken, but also of the major language family to which it is believed to belong. For convenience of reference, appendix II also shows a map of the geographical location of the world's major language families.

Further reading

A good account of attitudes to 'correct' and 'incorrect' language, in a historical perspective of the way that such **prescriptive attitudes** about spoken and written norms in English have changed, is the book by Milroy and Milroy (1985). This also offers a good discussion of the history of the concept of **Standard English**. Trudgill and Hannah (1985) give a good account of national varieties of the Standard English dialect, and of **regional accent** features associated with them. O'Donnell and Todd (1991) are also of interest on this and related topics. A number of accents and dialects of **English in Britain** are described in Hughes and Trudgill (1979), Trudgill (1985, 1990), Trudgill and Chambers (1991), Wakelin (1972, 1977) and Wells (1982). The phonetics and phonology of **Received Pronunciation** are further discussed by Roach (1983a, 1983b, 1991). Lass (1987) considers in some detail the dialects and accents of England and what he refers to as 'the

Celtic countries' – Scotland, Ireland, Northern Ireland and Wales. He also offers a valuable survey of what he calls **extraterritorial English**, with many lexical, phonological and phonetic details. By 'extraterritorial' he means the forms of English spoken in North America (Canada and the United States), Australia, New Zealand and South Africa.

Examples of reliable **dictionaries** which include a specification of pronunciation of **RP** with their lexical information are the *Oxford English Dictionary* (1989), the *Collins English Dictionary* (1986) and the *Longman Dictionary of Contemporary English* (Procter 1978). Dictionaries which include reliable specifications of **General American** pronunciation are *Webster's Ninth New Collegiate Dictionary* (Mish 1983), the *Random House Dictionary of the English Language* (Stein 1983) and the *American Heritage Dictionary* (Morris 1969). An excellent dictionary which includes details of **Australian English** pronunciation is the *Macquarie Dictionary* (Delbridge1981).

Sociolinguistic studies of accents and dialects of English in North America, Great Britain and Australia include de Wolf (1988) and Woods (1979) on Ottawa; Gregg (1984) and de Wolf (1988) on Vancouver; Clarke (1985) on St John's, Newfoundland; Horvath (1985) on Sydney; Macaulay (1977) on Glasgow; Trudgill (1974, 1975) on Norwich and Reading; and Coupland (1988) on Cardiff. Milroy and Milroy (1978) is another city-study, on Belfast, in a volume edited by Trudgill (1978) which offers a collection of articles on sociolinguistic information carried by a variety of other accents and dialects in England, Northern Ireland and Scotland.

An excellent recent collection of articles on principles and practices used in work on the **regional dialectology** of **English in Britain and Ireland** is Kirk, Sanderson and Widdowson (1985). An interesting discussion of work on English dialects is given by Wakelin (1972, 1977).

Amongst other noteworthy publications on dialectology discussing data from **American dialects of English** is Atwood (1962), a dialect atlas of Texas. An account of the word geography of the eastern United States is given in Kurath (1949), which covers the dialects spoken along a thousand miles of the Atlantic coast of the States, from New England to South Carolina, and in adjoining inland areas (see also Kurath and McDavid 1961). Walters (1988: 122) cites Allen (1977) and Pederson (1977) as two well-documented articles summarizing research in the regional dialectology of North America since 1945. McDavid and McDavid (1956) is an earlier survey of investigations of the accent and dialect geography of the whole of the United States. A useful collection of articles on social factors in American dialects is offered by Wolfram and Fasold (1974). Both social and geographical factors in dialect and accent variation are discussed in the volume edited by Allen and Linn (1986). Readings on American dialectology can be found in Allen and Underwood (1971) and Williamson and Burke (1971).

A good introduction to the principles and strategies of **pronunciation teaching** is Kenworthy (1987). **Bilingualism** is discussed in Grosjean (1982), Haugen (1956) and Romaine (1989). Works on **creole languages** and processes of **creolization** are Bickerton (1981) and Mühlhäusler (1986).

Historical phonology is the subject of publications by Jones (1989), Kiparsky (1988), Lass (1976, 1980, 1987), Lass and Anderson (1975) and Swadesh (1951), and is also discussed at length in Bloomfield (1933), one of the classic books on the general study of language. Historical linguistics more broadly is discussed by Bynon (1977) and Lehmann (1962).

Recommended publications on the **language-families** of the world include Asher and Simpson (1993), Bright (1992), Campbell (1991), Comrie (1987), Crystal (1987), Grimes (1988), Maddieson (1984), Meillet and Cohen (1952), Ruhlen (1975, 1987), Sebeok (1963–76) and Voegelin and Voegelin (1977).

PART II

The analytic framework

4

The phonetic analysis of speech

The aim of the first three chapters has been to discuss the nature of spoken communication. A broad framework has been offered for the analysis of speech in general, within which the analysis of those facets of speech that serve to carry spoken language can be set. In this framework, the role of general phonetic theory is to describe and explain the relationship between the medium of speech and the formal code of spoken language. We have seen that this relationship is semiotically rich and complex, and that speech is a vehicle for considerably more information than simply the symbolic communication of spoken language. However, it remains true that the principal traditional focus of general phonetic theory is to provide an objective description of the speech material underlying the contrastive and contextual patterns which constitute spoken language.

The task of this chapter is to give some consideration to the scope and coverage of a general phonetic theory, and to the initial identification of the types of analytic unit that might be recruited for the objective description of the phenomena of speech, especially those of spoken language.

4.1 General phonetic theory and general phonological theory

The purpose of the next thirteen chapters is to develop a descriptive vocabulary for a general phonetic theory that addresses this primary linguistic task, and which can also be extended to the task of describing paralinguistic and extralinguistic events in speech. Success in achieving this will be reflected in the ability to describe and explain the following:

the phonetic basis for the differentiation of words and other linguistic units in every known human language;
the phonetic regularities that serve to distinguish one accent from another accent and make each language sound different from other languages;
the phonetic events that are conventionally used as paralinguistic signals of attitude and emotion in each culture;

the paralinguistic phonetic cues that are conventionally used to claim and yield the floor in the control of speaking-turns in conversational interaction;

the phonetic phenomena that mark each individual speaker's extralinguistic identity.

Within the phrase 'general phonetic theory', the term 'phonetic' is perhaps now understandable. But the term 'general' may deserve some rehearsal. For a phonetic theory to constitute a general theory it has to be as comprehensive as possible. To what degree, in practice, could this be achieved? One could imagine, logically, that at some utopian date in the future, the full range of phonetic phenomena characterizing all languages known at that time might be able to be stated. But two factors conspire to frustrate the absolute comprehensiveness of such a description: first, some previously unknown language might come to light which exploited hitherto undescribed phonetic phenomena; second, spoken language is a social organism, with a life of its own. Like any organism of a more biological sort, it can be thought of as the product of an evolutionary process, subject to growth, change and decay. Consequently, even if it may in principle be possible one day to offer a detailed general phonetic description of all human languages then existing, it will still not be feasible to make completely confident statements about either the origin or the destination of the evolutionary course of the phonetic and phonological characteristics of that language.

There are two approaches to achieving comprehensiveness in phonetic theory. One can either aim to cover all currently known human languages, and allow the descriptive model to expand as new data about the distinctive and contextual properties of languages are discovered, or one can construct an 'anthropophonic' approach to phonetic description. An **anthropophonic approach** entails the construction of a descriptive model capable of accounting for all the sound-making potential of the human vocal apparatus. It is difficult, however, to know how one might set any practical bounds on this latter approach. It is clear that the sound-making capacities of the human vocal apparatus substantially exceed the range exploited by language (assuming that the sample of the languages of the world with which phoneticians are familiar is at least somewhat representative). As Lindblom (1983: 219) suggests, when the range of articulatory gestures is examined 'in relation to the potential capacity of the (physiological) system we note a tendency toward underexploitation'. A crucial question then arises as to the

principles on which linguistic selection from the broader range of anthropophonic possibilities might be evolutionarily based.

One principle might be the selection of those zones of articulatory performance ('quanta') within which the results of minor articulatory variation are
not auditorily perceptible. This is the basis of the 'quantal' theory of speech
(Stevens 1972). A quantal choice from the anthropophonic possibilities confers a valuable degree of stability on the system for spoken communication.
This notion of **quantal properties of speech** is very attractive, but perhaps
needs further development and investigation.

A second principle might be that of adequate perceptual contrast. The use
of a contrast between two sounds of only marginal difference, close to the
limits of psychoacoustic discriminability, is clearly less effective as part of a
communication system than one where the two sounds are comfortably and
easily distinguishable. This principle of adequate perceptual contrast is also
ecologically stronger in that it is likely to yield perceptually robust distinctions which resist masking by environmental noise (including competing
speech from other conversations).

A third principle might be ease and economy of articulatory performance.
As Lindblom (1983: 219) comments, in a consideration of 'pronounceabil-
ity':

> In normal speech the production system is rarely driven to its
> limits. Typically we speak at a 'comfortable' volume or rate and we
> use a degree of articulatory precision that seems 'natural'. On the
> other hand, we are of course occasionally perfectly capable of
> hyperarticulating (and hypoarticulating), that is, of adjusting the
> loudness, tempo, clarity, etc. of our speech to the needs of the
> situation, thereby exploiting more of the full range of phonetic
> possibilities ... this style of behavior can be observed not only
> phonetically in the pronunciation of individual utterances but
> also phonologically in the properties of segment inventories,
> sequences and rules.

Lindblom then goes on to suggest that the underexploitation of the anthropophonic possibilities

> reflects not only speech production constraints but the *concurrent*
> demands of speech perception as well. These conditions interact
> to yield a subset of signals which are sufficiently adapted to their
> communicative purpose but at the same time put reasonable demands
> on the expenditure of physiological energy. In other words,
> underexploitation is, among other things, related to a criterion
> of physiological economy which participates in, as it were, a
> biological 'cost–benefit' conspiracy. (*ibid.*)

The anthropophonic approach is currently gaining ground, not least through the sophistication of Lindblom's own 'ecological' perspective. However, the alternative preferred to date by most phoneticians is to consider general phonetic theory to be a provisional theory limited to known linguistic data. It is provisional, as are all theories with any claim to scientific status, in that it is open to progressive modification in the light of fresh information about the speech material exploited for phonological purposes in languages which are new (or sometimes not so new) to detailed phonetic investigation, or about novel evolutionary developments in languages. The coverage of such a theory is comprehensive, but its limits are set by the range of data for whose description and explanation the theory currently accepts responsibility.

The scope of a general phonological theory is intimately related to that of a general phonetic theory. We have seen that its function is to mediate the connection between phonetic phenomena, as characterized by a general phonetic theory, and linguistic entities at the levels above phonology – morphology, syntax, semantics and pragmatics. The generality of such a theory lies in its ability to describe the phonological relations observed to date in all the known languages of the world. Correspondingly, its coverage extends to all the observed phonological relations in these languages, and its responsibility is as provisional as that of general phonetic theory, needing to be extended or modified only under due cause – namely, the emergence of data incapable of description or explanation in the terms of the established theory.

4.2   The phonetic analysis of speech

The aim of the remainder of this chapter is to set the scene for the main body of the book, which attempts to offer a structured account of the concepts necessary for the comprehensive description of speech production, and of the classificatory labels and transcriptional symbols that are associated with these concepts.

The mastery of phonetic description in this area is a crucial task for every student of phonetics. Such a mastery is not in itself enough, however. Phonetic description is a tool of the subject, and is designed to fulfil a number of functions. The major purposes of phonetic description range from the provision of basic data for the discussion of contrastive and contextual patterns of phonological relevance to spoken language, to furnishing information for speech therapy and communications engineering. All such concerns with speech are less than competent if phonetic description is inadequate.

There are two particular motivations in this book for describing speech production. The first is a desire to understand how speech is produced in the quasi-mechanical phonetic operations of the speaker as an organic and phonetic machine. This constitutes a cybernetic interest in human biomechanics. The second is an interest in wanting to understand how speech functions as a signalling system for exchanging messages with other members of the speech community. This constitutes a semiotic interest in human communication.

At first sight, biomechanics and the semiotics of communication might seem to have only a distant relationship, but in the field of speech they have the most intimate of connections, and we shall see that it is impracticable to keep the two interests rigidly apart. As mentioned earlier, it is extremely difficult to set up descriptive phonetic categories for speech without frequent and necessary recourse at particular points to phonological assumptions about communication. In fact, the attitude is maintained in this book that a general phonetic theory free of general phonological assumptions of any kind is neither desirable nor feasible.

The study of speech production has been set by the comments offered immediately above in a biomechanical and semiotic perspective. Before embarking on a detailed discussion of speech production, it is perhaps worthwhile stepping back for a moment to a fully biological perspective, to pose the question of the status of the anatomical and physiological apparatus for speech as a biological system.

4.3 The biological basis for speech

Textbooks on phonetics typically use the term 'the vocal apparatus' as a basic concept. But in using this phrase, we make a questionable assumption. The phrase 'the vocal apparatus' implies that the organs used for the production of speech are to be thought of as biologically specialized for this purpose. In support of this assumption it could be argued, for instance, that the evolution of the physiological capacity for speech gave mankind a biological advantage that promoted our social and cognitive development to such an extent that it is the very nature of this sociocognitive organization that is the biologically unique characteristic of the species.

Against such a view, however, is the opinion that not one anatomical aspect of the so-called 'vocal' apparatus can be singled out as specialized for the purposes of producing speech as such, apart perhaps from some aspects of the neuroanatomy of the brain. One possible exception to this may be the evolution of one of the paired muscles of the larynx (the posterior cricoarytenoid muscle), whose normal function in animals generally is to help to control the inspiratory intake of breath. In man alone, it is also used to open the laryngeal valve during expiration for speech, as part of the pronunciation of sounds such as the [p] in English 'pet' (Hirose 1976, 1992).

Every action of the apparatus that is involved in speaking could be claimed to exploit the neuromuscular capabilities of an architecture whose primary biological functions are other than articulate speech – breathing, sucking, biting, chewing, swallowing, licking, spitting, sniffing, clearing the throat, coughing, yawning, phonating while laughing, crying, threatening and shouting, and bracing the chest walls while lifting heavy objects. Abercrombie (1967: 20) cites with approval Sapir's comments on this issue, when the latter wrote that 'Physiologically, speech is an overlaid function, or, to be more precise, a group of overlaid functions. It gets what service it can out of organs and functions, nervous and muscular, that have come into being and are maintained for very different ends than its own' (Sapir 1921: 9).

One of the underlying issues in a thoroughgoing approach to the production and perception of speech is therefore the question of whether the brain integrates the performance of a plurality of biologically more primitive functions to serve the singular purposes of speech, or whether it is more valid to propose that speech (and more generally, language), has its own biology.

Alvin Liberman (1984), the distinguished American experimental phonetician, characterizes his earlier work on speech synthesis and the perception of speech as espousing the non-specialized view, for which he suggests the metaphor of a 'horizontal' organization:

> As applied to language, the metaphor is intended to convey that the underlying processes are arranged in layers, none of them specific to language. On that horizontal orientation, language is accounted for by reference to whatever combination of processes it happens to engage. Hence our assumption, in the attempt to find a substitute for speech, that perception of phonological segments is normally accomplished, presumably in the first layer, by processes of a generally auditory sort, by processes no different from those that bring us the rustle of leaves in the wind or the rattle of a snake in the grass ... We were not prepared to give language a biology of its own, but only to treat it as an epiphenomenon, a biologically arbitrary assemblage of processes that were not themselves linguistic. (Liberman 1984: 171)

In his more recent work, Liberman has abandoned this non-specialized view, in favour of an approach to the perception of speech and language as a specialized biological system. Liberman's more recent position that language is a specialized cognitive faculty is probably valid. It may also be that the perceptual system used for the registration and decoding of speech is to some degree specialized for the purposes of linguistic performance. But a corresponding argument at the level of speech production does not yet seem tenable. No phonetic manoeuvre exploited for communicative purposes in speech production seems incapable of explanation as a component of some more primitive biological function. Had the biological apparatus for speech developed independently, perhaps thereby undergoing some process of evolutionary optimization for efficiency of communication, the characteristics of speech itself might well be different.

Until the availability of good evidence offers some resolution of the issue, it is probably safer to assume that speech, as Sapir (1921) maintained, is a function overlaid on more primary biological systems. What then is the objective nature of speech, and how might one go about the process of descriptive phonetic analysis?

4.4 Parametric and linear approaches to segmentation of the stream of speech

The stream of speech within a single utterance is a continuum. There are only a few points in this stream which constitute natural breaks, or which show an articulatorily, auditorily or acoustically steady state being momentarily preserved, and which could therefore serve as the basis for analytic segmentation of the continuum into 'real' phonetic units. On first reading, this statement must seem strange to most readers of this book who have been brought up in an alphabetic culture. Our modes of thought are so strongly conditioned by our literate education that nothing seems more 'natural' than the apparently 'real' phonetic segments of speech, correlated as they manifestly are with the alphabetic symbols of the written language. Yet the view that such segmentation is mostly an imposed analysis, and not the outcome of discovering natural time-boundaries in the speech-continuum, is a view that deserves the strongest insistence.

Given that the complex interaction of the different elements of vocal performance results in a continuously changing acoustic output from the vocal apparatus, with few natural breaks and steady-state stretches, what analytic approaches could be proposed for phonetic segmentation of the stream of speech? There are two chief possibilities, the parametric approach and the linear approach.

4.4.1 *The parametric approach to segmentation*

The first possibility is a **parallel segmentation** of speech, in which each component of vocal performance is treated as a parameter whose value is in a state of constant potential change. This can be called the **parametric**

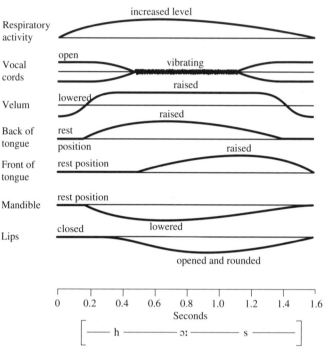

Figure 4.1 Parametric analysis of the articulatory actions of some of the vocal organs in the production of the English (RP) word *horse* /hɔs/ (after Brosnahan and Malmberg 1970: 70)

approach to speech segmentation. An example illustrating this approach is reproduced in Figure 4.1, giving a parametric analysis of the activities of some of the vocal organs for a pronunciation of the English word *horse* /hɔs/, adapted from Brosnahan and Malmberg (1970: 70). In this approach, the individual parameters can be seen rising and falling out of step with each other as their values change in time. Recurring tendencies towards particular combinations of values on the different parameters then represent the patterns of speech. This illustration is a fairly idealized version of the detail of articulatory movements in speech, and figure 4.3 below gives a more realistic picture. Tench (1978) offers a useful discussion of the concept of parameters in phonetic analysis.

A good example of an auditory component which changes parametrically in this way is the pitch of the voice. Another is the loudness of the voice. These are examples of parameters that run virtually throughout an utterance, with their values continually changing, interrupted only by the intermittent stretches where phonation is momentarily switched off. The mutual independence of such parameters can be envisaged through the example of two utterances both of which have a rising pitch-pattern, ending on a high note, but where the loudness parameter has in one case a very high value at the end of the utterance, and in the other case a very low value. Both utterances would have the same pitch-pattern, but one would end in a shout, the other in a murmur.

A parametric approach of this sort is especially helpful in speech technology, when trying to design computer-based machines that can produce or recognize speech. The interest there in the co-variation of phonetic parameters in time lies in the question of how activities on different parameters are co-ordinated to give appropriate temporal patterns of speech. Figure 4.2 is an illustration of a parametric acoustic analysis of the English (RP) utterance *Our lawyer will allow your rule* [ɑ lɔjə wɪl əlaʊ jɔ ɹul], said in an informal style at a moderate rate by the author. The acoustic parameters shown have been measured automatically by computer, by means of the AUDLAB speech-signal processing package developed at the Centre for Speech Technology Research in the University of Edinburgh (Terry *et al.* 1986). The three acoustic parameters identified here are **formants**. They represent the acoustic consequences of the changing shapes of the mouth and pharynx in terms of the varying frequency-values of the resonances of the vocal tract. The three lowest-frequency formants are shown overlaid on a representation of the original acoustic material, called a 'spectrogram'. A **spectrogram** is a three-dimensional display of acoustic energy across a range of frequencies, where the more intense the energy, the darker the display from which the formant-analysis was derived. The 'formants' are represented on this spectrogram by continuous bands of relatively intense energy of changing frequency. The vertical axis shows frequency, and the higher the location of a given formant on the spectrogram, the higher its frequency. Time runs from left to right throughout the spectrogram. There are no voiceless sounds in this utterance, so voicing is present throughout. The approximate alignment of the speech sounds involved is shown by the placement of the phonetic symbols below the parametric display. (The symbols /aa l oo y @ ... / correspond directly to a phonemic transcription, but were designed by the Centre for Speech Technology Research as part of a phonemic alphabet for English (RP) intended to be machine readable. The symbols are made up solely of ASCII characters, and the alphabet is called **MRPA (Machine Readable Phonemic Alphabet).**)

The (partial) parametric statement in this figure could be used as the basis

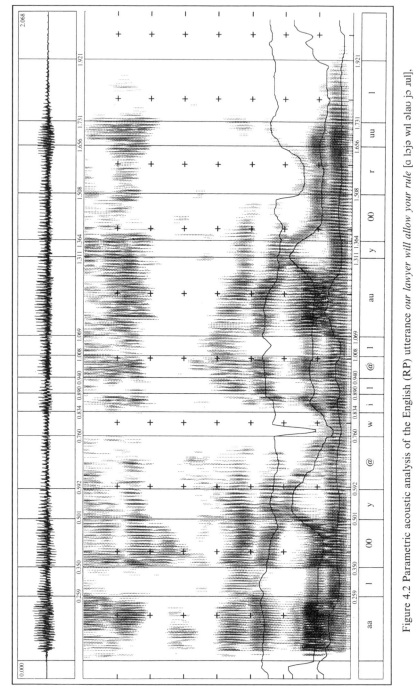

Figure 4.2 Parametric acoustic analysis of the English (RP) utterance *our lawyer will allow your rule* [ɑ lɔjə wɪl əlaʊ jɔ ruːl], automatically analysed by the AUDLAB computer-based signal processing package

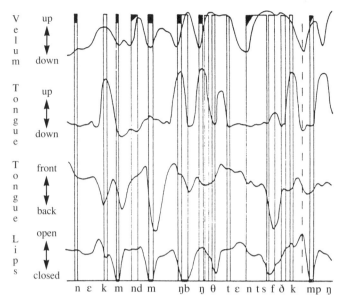

Figure 4.3 Parametric articulatory analysis of the movements of the velum, tongue and lips during the pronunciation of the phrase *next Monday morning bring three tents for the camping (trip)*, recorded by cinefluorography (adapted from Kent 1983: 69)

for specifying the command signals for controlling an acoustic speech synthesizer to produce an intelligible copy of significant aspects of the phrase. Alternatively, it could be used for initial processing of the acoustic input to an automatic speech recognition system, which would then try to recover the identity of the phrase partly on the basis of information associating typical correlations between formant-values and individual speech-sounds.

The changing frequency-values of the formants in figure 4.2, as acoustic parameters, are fairly slow-moving in time, and correspond to our perception of the changing auditory quality of the sounds involved. They are the product of co-ordinated physical movements of articulators in space and time which can individually be rather more rapid. The acoustic consequence of movements of several articulators for the overall shape of the vocal tract depends on the global interaction of these movements, and it is the overall momentary configuration of the whole vocal tract that determines the formant-frequency values that characterize individual sounds. The fast-moving nature of individual articulators, as physiological parameters, can be seen in figure 4.3, showing the respective movements of the velum (the soft palate at

105

the back of the mouth), the tongue and the lips, taken from an analysis of a side-on cinefluorographic view of an American English speaker saying the short phrase *Next Monday morning bring three tents for the camping trip* (Kent 1983: 69). The figure is segmented into a sequence of articulatory events contributing to the identification of some of the individual speech-sounds.

The focus on matters of temporal co-ordination which is promoted by a parametric approach to the description of speech is of interest not only in speech technology, but also in areas like speech pathology, where patients whose speech is defective may often be failing to exercise appropriate timing control over the different parameters. In a related area, it is also relevant to the neurophysiological study of the strategic and tactical control of speech by the brain. The parametric management of the temporal relationships between the activities of different muscle systems constitutes one of the core problems for understanding how the brain controls serial order in particular, and voluntary muscular activity in general (Lashley 1951; Laver 1970, 1991).

4.4.2 *The linear approach to segmentation*

The second major method of segmentation of the stream of speech allows us to stay reasonably close to a quasi-alphabetic approach. This is the **serial approach to speech segmentation**. In the serial segmentation method, the time-continuum of speech is divided without residue into abutting units of varying duration, rather like a train made up of a number of wagons of varying length and type. This serial method of segmentation can alternatively be called the **linear approach to speech segmentation**. Each unit can then be characterized in terms of representative values shown during the production of that unit by the individual phonetic components making up the performance.

It is important to bear constantly in mind here that clues to the identification of an individual segment often lie not only in the properties of the segment itself, but also in properties of adjacent (and sometimes more remote) segments. An English example illustrating this is that the identity of the [u] segment representing the vowel in the English word *soup* [s^{w}up] is signalled not only by the phonetic characteristics of the pronunciation of the vowel itself, but also by the quality of the preceding [s]. The [s^w] in this word is pronounced with a rounded lip-position which anticipates the one needed for the [u] segment to follow, and which affects the audible quality of the [s] sound. In addition, the quality of the [s] sound is also affected by the way in which the body of the tongue itself begins to anticipate the position necessary for the articulation of the oncoming vowel.

The distributed nature of the phonetic properties identifying individual segments also has an importance for speech perception, in that it allows speech communication to retain robustness of intelligibility in noisy environments. This springs from the fact that the identity of a segment is perceptually recoverable not only from the acoustic material internal to the segment itself, but also to a certain degree from the external clues to the segment's interaction with other segments nearby.

The concept that is shared between the linear and the parametric approaches is the notion of speech as the product of the action of a number of independently controllable components co-varying in time. We can refer to the product of each independently controllable component as a **phonetic feature**. The principal difference between the linear and the parametric approaches lies in the relation between a feature and its possible values. In a linear approach, a given feature can have only a limited number of values, or **categories**. For example, the phonetic feature **pitch-height** might be given solely the values 'high', 'mid' and 'low', and analysts would then have only these categories at their disposal for the description of the relative height of the momentary pitch of a speaker's voice.

Linear categories are thus discrete, not continuous. Conversely, in the parametric approach, the potential values that a feature may display are continuous, not discrete. They are limited in discriminative power only by the sensitivity of the measuring system available. The feature pitch-height could therefore have any distinguishable value from maximum to minimum. In a parametric approach, continuous feature-values are easy to draw as graphs and hard to talk about. In a linear approach, discrete featural categories are very convenient for use in spoken or written description, but impose a more selective view on the data to be described.

A parametric approach has the advantage over the rather more artificial linear approach that the former more transparently reflects the dynamic, time-varying nature of multi-stranded vocal performance. It has to be acknowledged, however, that a parametric approach, with its feature-values in constant variation, is conceptually distant from the more linear categories of alphabetic writing systems. Perhaps for this reason, the linear approach is the one taken in most textbooks on phonetics, and it will be the one chiefly used in this book from this point onwards.

Phonetic performance, in terms of the activities of the organs of the vocal tract in modifying the flow of an airstream that is set in motion usually by the respiratory system, has both spatial and temporal domains. The spatial domain concerns the geometric configurations taken up by the vocal tract, and the temporal domain concerns the **time-course**, or chronology, over which the changing configurations are organized. It has become conventional in phonetics to represent the segmental production of speech in terms of spatial configurations taken up by the vocal organs at selected intermittent points in the linear sequence of the time-course. The dynamically changing configurations are effectively reduced to a small, selected number of 'frozen', 'static' frames, represented as a linear sequence of spatial targets that the vocal apparatus achieves serially in an unspecified time-course.

A tempting analogy for the use of 'static' descriptive targets of this sort would be the frames of a cine-film. Taken individually, these frames 'freeze' the action they record into apparently immobile states. Replayed serially at the right speed, their images combine perceptually in time to give the illusion of the original action. The analogy is slightly misleading, however, because cine-films rely for their realism on a standard speed of playback being maintained. In speech, the 'linear sequence of spatial targets' mentioned above does not represent a sampling of the actions of speech at a standard time-interval; the frames of speech are abstractions of target positions achieved by articulatory actions of differing durations. The exact duration will depend on many factors, described in more detail in chapters 14–17. This linear mode of phonetic analysis can thus give a misleading impression if care is not taken to spell out some of the underlying theoretical assumptions, particularly those concerned with matters of timing.

For illustrative purposes, we can consider the way that a linear phonetic representation would conventionally analyse the performance of the English word *fish* [fɪʃ]. This utterance would be represented initially as a sequence of three target states of the vocal organs: one for the configuration corresponding to the [f], one for the [ɪ] and one for the [ʃ]. The three target configurations are shown diagrammatically in figure 4.4. But underlying this very reduced representation of the dynamic vocal performance of [fɪʃ] there remains the theoretical understanding that the vocal organs have to manage complex transitions from and to the silence that borders the utterance, and to move within the utterance through each of the specified configurations in the specified sequence. In addition, there is the understanding that these events have to be performed in a time-course whose complexity research has still not entirely unravelled.

Some aspects of timing spring from organic factors of mechanical and neuromuscular limitations. Other aspects reflect the phonetic manifestation of linguistic and paralinguistic rules. To the extent that factors of timing, and detailed trajectories of transitions from one state to another, arise directly and inevitably from organic properties of the vocal apparatus, they

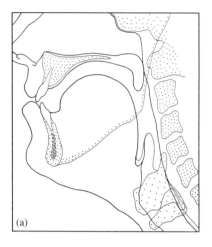

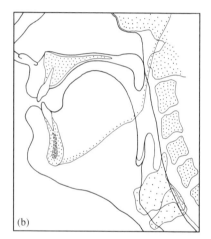

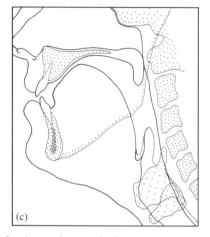

Figure 4.4 Target configurations for the vocal organs in the
articulation of segments in the production of the English word *fish* [fɪʃ]:
(a) [f]; (b) [ɪ]; (c) [ʃ]

form part of its mechanical operational characteristics. As such, they do not
need to be accounted for in the part of phonetic theory that deals with the
control of the apparatus, except as imposing limiting conditions within
which the control system has to operate. To the extent that spatial transitions and factors of timing are susceptible to control, a comprehensive
description of the resources of speech production should ideally be able to

specify them. Some of the prime phonetic differences between languages lie in the segmental control of transitions from one phonetic state to the next and in the detailed control of timing.

It is true, none the less, that in a linear representation of speech many of these phonetic factors of transition and timing are left to be assumed, and are seldom specified explicitly. To that extent, a linear, 'static', frame-by-frame-based representation of phonetic events gives the impression of being less complete than a parametric, 'dynamic' continuous representation.

The linear approach thus appears to be a less complete way of representing speech than the parametric approach. It is nevertheless normally considered to be a more convenient treatment, not least because of its closer relationship to the assumptions of an alphabetic writing system, as mentioned earlier. The requirements of most applications of phonetics are satisfied by a linear approach, provided its limitations and its underlying assumptions are very clearly understood. In particular, if some of the characteristics of temporal and spatial co-ordination of phonetic activity in speech can be made more explicit, as this book will attempt to do, then some of the deficiencies normally associated with the linear approach will be removed.

4.5 Linear units of phonetic organization: feature, segment, syllable, setting, utterance, speaking-turn

We can begin this account with a discussion of phonetic units set up under a linear approach to segmentation, to provide initial descriptive categories. The first question to be addressed in a linear approach is the decision about the nature and size of the units to be used. The six units chosen at the phonetic level of description are the **feature**, the **segment**, the **syllable**, the **setting**, the **utterance** and the **speaking-turn**, each of them covering a different span in the chain of speech.

4.5.1 *The phonetic and the phonological feature*

The set of general phonetic features constitutes the minimum set of descriptors for accounting for the way that segments, and other phonetic units that have been observed in the languages of the world, differ from each other. Two different segments in a minimal pair of linguistic units in some language may differ from each other, in the limiting case, by only one phonetic feature. This feature can then be considered to be playing a distinctive role in the phonological discrimination of the two linguistic units in the language under consideration. The term **distinctive feature** is normally applied in a phonological usage. The universal set of such distinctive features is made up of the comprehensive set of all such features that have so far been found to have a distinctive phonological function in the languages of the world.

Distinctive phonological features fall into classes, and this gives rise to superordinate (and hence yet more abstract) phonological features. An example is the phonological feature 'sonorant', which applies to the phonological units called vowels (e.g. /i/ and /u/), liquids (e.g. /r/ and /l/), glides (e.g. /j/ and /w/) and nasal stops (e.g. /m/, /n/ and /ŋ /) in English.

It has been conventional in much of phonology over the last forty years to represent the phonological attributes of segments in a particular language as a list of values – usually binary values of the distinctive feature-set, that is, present (+) or absent (–). The phoneme /t/ in English, for instance, can be represented as the product of the following distinctive features, each marked with a binary value: –sonorant, +consonantal, –syllabic, +coronal, +anterior, –high ... etc; while /i/can be represented as the product of: +sonorant, –consonantal, +syllabic, –coronal, –anterior, +high etc. The exact nature of these phonological features need not detain us here. The chief early reference for this theory of feature-based representation is Jakobson, Fant and Halle (1952). Chomsky and Halle (1968) is also a standard reference, and a good discussion of the relationships between such features, in terms of what has been called 'feature geometry', is given by McCarthy (1988).

The set of distinctive phonological features needed to account for the phonological discrimination of linguistic units in the languages of the world is smaller than the set of general phonetic features needed to account for the objective differences between the phonetic realizations of such units. This is because the descriptive function of phonetic features is wider than solely to provide a support role for distinctive phonological differentiation. For example, some non-distinctive phonetic features account for the ways in which segments are allophonically adapted to their context, others distinguish the phonetic details of one community's accent from another, and yet others reflect the phonetic differences between individual speakers.

One source of frequent confusion for students is that distinctive phonological features are often given the same name as general phonetic features, leading to uncertainty about the level of description being applied. In the sense that a given phonological feature is chosen (because of its distinctive phonological role) from the group of phonetic features characterizing a particular segment, the motivation for using the same name for the feature at both the phonetic and the phonological level of description (say, 'labial') is understandable. Phonological discussion is often carried out in terms of the interaction of segments at a phonemic level, however, where phonetic detail about the realization of a given phoneme in all its different contexts is irrelevant. In such cases, the phonological labelling of the phoneme in distinctive feature terms may simply have been chosen on the basis of some instance of the phoneme in a 'typical' context. A particular phoneme may be said to be 'voiced', say, even though some of its allophones, through contextual adjustments, may show no phonetic voicing at all. To avoid this source of confusion, when context is insufficient to indicate the level of discussion, the label for a phonological feature can be printed in capitals, as +VOICE, +LABIAL, –NASAL, for instance.

4.5.2   *The phonetic segment*

The concept of the **segment** is that of a linear unit typically anchored in a short stretch of speech by a set of phonetic feature-values which are relatively unchanging. The segment is a construct of phonetic theory which relies here on a related concept of three different phases of articulation of any segment. We shall see in chapter 5 that segments are articulatorily classified partly in terms of the maximum degree of constriction of the vocal tract reached during the production of the segment. The period during which the maximum constriction is achieved defines the **medial phase** of the performance of the segment. Preceding this medial phase, an **onset phase** embodies the approach of the vocal organs to the medial phase, and an **offset phase** shows the movement of the organs towards the medial phase of the next segment (and hence constitutes an **overlapping phase** with the onset phase of that next segment). A given feature may therefore run right through several segments (as a **suprasegmental** feature), or may be limited to the medial phase of a single segment (as a **segmental** feature). More seldom, it may begin or terminate within a particular phase (as a **subsegmental** feature).

An example of a suprasegmental articulatory feature would be the rounded lip position that runs throughout the pronunciation of all the segments in the word *forceful* ⇒ [fʷɔsʷfʷʊlʷ]. An instance of a segmental feature would be the audible friction that characterizes the medial phase of the sound [s] in the word *east* ⇒ [ist]. An illustration of a subsegmental feature would be the nasality that can be heard beginning in the late part of the pronunciation of the vowel in *soon* [sūn], in anticipation of the production of the following nasal consonant.

It would be intellectually satisfying to be able to offer a strict definition of the segment as a descriptive unit established on solely phonetic grounds. Phonetic criteria of course play a major part. Appeal will be made in chapter 5 to criteria of 'strictural' degrees of relative constriction of the vocal tract, as mentioned earlier. Such discontinuities as can be discovered in the time-continuum of speech production and perception will also be invoked in support of the notion of segmental boundaries. But general phonological considerations necessarily weigh heavily in traditional notions of segment-types, as discussed earlier. A **segment** will therefore be considered as a phonetic unit of description, defined as far as possible on strictural and temporal grounds, supported by general phonological considerations. Segments will be classified in terms of the co-occurrence and relative timing of their constituent features. Utterances will be treated as being made up of a linear sequence of segments, which will be phonetic events of normally very short duration, manifesting the phonological units of consonants and vowels. A typical duration for a speech segment, at normal speaking rates, lies approximately between 30 and 300 milliseconds.

4.5.3 *The phonetic and the phonological syllable*
The syllable is a unit often posited at both the phonetic and the phonological levels of analysis. The notion of a phonetic unit the size of a syllable is a very attractive one, and it exercises a perennial attraction for phonetic research. But it is difficult to offer a definition of the phonetic syllable as a natural unit of analysis which has a claim to rigour, and which can show any demonstrable, objective correlates on physically measurable parameters. As Brosnahan and Malmberg (1970: 140–2) comment:

> The syllable ... is by no means a simple concept. Within the one
> language a child can usually count on its fingers the number of
> syllables in a sequence, but no phonetician has succeeded so far in
> giving an exhaustive and adequate description of what the syllable
> is ... No physiological theory of the syllable so far developed
> seems sufficiently well founded instrumentally to be acceptable as
> definitive and exhaustive.

Attempts to provide acoustic or auditory definitions have so far proved equally unsatisfactory.

One of the chief difficulties lies in determining the possible boundaries of such a phonetic unit. In an utterance such as *Eight sheep can each eat cheaply* [eɪtʃipkanitʃittʃiplɪ] (transcribed without word boundaries to reinforce the point), a decision about the syllabic affiliation of the segments corresponding respectively to the spelling sequences *-ght sh-*, *-ch*, and *-t ch-* cannot be taken with only phonetic criteria in mind. Phonological and lexical criteria necessarily play their part.

A different approach to the definition of a phonetic syllable will be taken in this book. No attempt will be made to justify the notion of a phonetic syllable as a natural unit of analysis. The concept of a phonetic syllable will be treated rather as a construct of general phonetic theory useful in explaining a number of co-ordinatory relations between segments. The phonetic definitions of 'aspiration' and 'final release', for example, will be seen in chapter 12 to appeal to the idea of a phonetic syllable as a framing concept.

The concept of the syllable as an entity at the phonological level enjoys no more general a consensus than that of the phonetic syllable. As Bell and Hooper comment, 'The syllable has a long and troubled history in the development of phonology. While the evidence for the syllable as a unit for segment organization exists all around in great abundance the various aspects of the syllable that have been investigated are kaleidoscopic and the pieces have not fallen into place' (Bell and Hooper 1978: 4). Some scholars, such as Chomsky and Halle (1968), dispense with the phonological syllable altogether, relying on the segment and the word as basic units.

This book is not the relevant place for a detailed survey of the abundant theories of the phonological syllable, however. For this the interested reader should rather consult the references listed under Further Reading at the end of this chapter. We shall simply regard the phonological syllable as another convenient construct, following scholars such as Fudge (1969). In Fudge's view, the phonological syllable fulfils two chief functions. The first is to act as the domain of linguistically relevant prosodic properties such as pitch, and the second is to give a basis for organizing and expressing constraints on possible phoneme sequences (Fudge 1969: 254). The attitude to be espoused in this book is therefore also sympathetic to that of O'Connor and Trim, who give a definition of the phonological syllable in a distributional mould from their statistical examination of the incidence of phoneme sequences in English: 'the syllable may be defined as a minimal pattern of phoneme combination with a vowel as nucleus, preceded and followed by a consonant unit or permitted consonant combination' (O'Connor and Trim 1953).

The concept of the **phonological syllable** will hence be adopted as a construct helpful for organizing the explanation of rhythmic and prosodic facts at levels above the segment, and as a convenient domain for expressing the mutual distribution of phonemic segments. The phonological syllable will be defined in this book as a complex unit, made up of nuclear and marginal elements. Nuclear elements, as phonological entities, are what we have been calling **vowels**. Marginal elements are what we have been calling **consonants**. Phonetic segments that manifest nuclear elements of the phonological syllable will be called **syllabic** segments. Those that manifest marginal elements of the phonological syllable will be called **non-syllabic** segments. When the term 'syllable' is used in this book, it will be assumed to refer to the phonological syllable, unless explicit mention is made of its status as a phonetic syllable.

4.5.4 *The phonetic setting*

If one examines an utterance from a single speaker delivered in a characteristic voice quality, it is often evident that the speaker is imposing a muscular bias on the vocal performance, tending to make the vocal organs keep returning during speech towards some habitual state (Honikman 1964). Examples would be the tendency of a particular speaker to keep the jaw in a relatively close position, or to set the lips in a habitually rounded position, or to have a rather whispery type of phonation. It is such biasing tendencies that constitute **settings** (Laver 1980, 1991). A setting is thus a featural property of a stretch of speech which can be as long as a whole utterance; but it can also be shorter, characterizing only part of an utterance, down to a minimum stretch of anything greater than a single segment.

Given that a setting is defined as a persistent tendency towards adopting some particular state, it follows that the presence in the chain of speech of a given setting in an utterance is likely to be continual rather than continuous. The example of a speaker having a rather whispery type of phonation makes this clear. Because voicing will typically be present intermittently, on phonetically voiced segments only, the setting of whispery voicing is unlikely to be continuously present. It will be audible on the pronunciations of about three-quarters of all the sounds in English (all vowels and a narrow majority of consonants).

In a parametric description, a setting could be characterized as the average value of a given parameter. In a linear description, a setting has to be specified in terms of a featural property shared by two or more segments which are either adjacent in the stream of speech or in close proximity. Settings (particularly those which are semi-permanently present) are frequently used as extralinguistic indicators of an individual speaker's identity, and as social indicators of regional group-membership. A smile, performed on part or all of an utterance, would be an example of the use of a medium-term setting for paralinguistic purposes of attitudinal communication. We shall also see that very short-term settings can be used as manifestations of phonological units of various sizes, often as a characteristic of the phonological syllable, or of some group of segments within it. Settings can also form part of the manifestation of higher-level units of language such as the morph, the word and the phrase, in such phenomena as vowel harmony, consonant harmony and co-articulatory feature-spreading.

The substance of both segments and settings is made up of phonetic features. A major difference between a segment and a setting is that of span, with a setting being by definition multisegmental. A feature, on the other hand, is not constrained to any particular span. One of the benefits of setting up the concept of a setting is that it can be used as a theoretical device to explain the basis of phonetic similarity between segments. Any two segments that share a given setting are thereby phonetically more similar to each other than two segments that display no setting in common. The relationship between settings and segments, and the general issues underlying the idea of phonetic similarity, are discussed at length in chapter 13.

4.5.5 *The utterance and the speaking-turn*

The **utterance** is a stretch of speech by a single speaker bounded by silence and containing no internal pauses. The **speaking-turn** consists of one speaker's contribution to a conversation, up to the point in time where the floor is yielded to another participant. Each speaking-turn contains one or more utterances. Both the speaking-turn and the utterance are natural units of analysis. The other four phonetic units – the feature, the segment, the syllable and the setting – are analytically imposed. Speaking-turns from two or more participants may of course overlap, as when a previously silent participant starts talking before the current speaker has finished his or her speaking-turn. This is one way of **seizing the floor**, and competition to **hold the floor** will then continue until one or other speaker **yields the floor** by terminating his or her speaking-turn and falling silent.

4.6 Elements of speech production: initiation, phonation, articulation, temporal, prosodic and metrical organization

The production of audible speech is literally a superficial process. The changing shape of the passage formed by the vocal organs through which air flows is the surface product of underlying muscular actions. We shall exclude from our attention the physiological analysis of these muscular actions themselves, and concentrate solely on the nature of this consequential surface product and its audible effects. Even in this restricted frame of reference, however, speech is very far from being a simple activity, requiring the interaction of at least six elements of production.

The first essential for audible speech is an **airstream mechanism**, which initiates a flow of air for further phonetic modification. The second is **phonatory action** by the larynx, injecting various different types of acoustic energy into the vocal tract. The third element is **articulation**. Articulation consists of producing rapidly changing actions of the organs of the vocal tract to create short-lived phonetic patterns which can stand for consonants, vowels and other types of phonological units. The fourth element is the **temporal organization of speech**, in terms of the duration of individual elements and the overall rate and continuity of speaking. The fifth element is the **prosodic control** of pitch and loudness. The sixth element of speech production is the overall **metrical organization** of utterances, which reflects the rhythmic interaction of syllables and stress.

The action of each of these six elements (airstream initiation, phonation, articulation and temporal, prosodic and metrical organization) can produce a number of relatively independently controllable features, or components, of speech. One of the tasks of students of phonetics is to learn to be able to control all of these componential features in their own phonetic production of speech. A competent phonetician, after adequate analysis of the material concerned, should be able to pronounce any sound used in any language of the world to the perceptual satisfaction of a native listener. By extension, the phonetician should be able to do the same for any word, or for any utterance made up of connected words, in the language concerned. The rationale for setting this goal of personal performance is partly the belief that perceptual discrimination is aided by the ability to produce corresponding articulations oneself, and partly a commitment to the view that the development of adequate perceptual skill is a prime prerequisite for competent personal work in phonological analysis.

The ability to produce an accurate pronunciation of any sound used in any language of the world may seem a daunting ambition to the beginner in phonetics, but it is in fact within the reach of virtually every serious student. Reaching this goal is directly facilitated by the componential nature of descriptive phonetic theory. Speech production can be characterized as the composite product of the actions of the independently varying components, and their actions are given correspondingly explicit identification in composite labels for the different sounds produced. A particular Zulu sound [ɓ], for example, does not need to be vaguely and ambiguously called 'a sort of "b"-sound'. An appropriate composite technical label for [ɓ] would be 'a voiced bilabial implosive'. The structure and meaning of such a composite label is discussed in the following chapters. Basically, each term in the composite label constitutes a choice from a small set of alternatives. Once the productive and perceptual meaning of these small sets have been learned, then the full power of descriptive phonetic theory is at the disposal of the user. The theory is powerful precisely because a componential system of this sort can generate very many different composite labels, within the conventions of combinability imposed by general phonetic theory, by the permutation of the members of the small sets of standard labels associated with the separately controllable components (Laver 1968, 1974). The strength of descriptive phonetic theory is hence that it is constructed on a componential base, and that the components have standard productive and perceptual definitions.

Further reading

Quantal properties of speech production and perception were the subject of a special issue of the *Journal of Phonetics*, for which Ohala was the guest editor (1989), and in which Stevens, the originator of the concept of quantal zones in speech production and perception, makes an important contribution. Carré and Mrayati (1990) consider the relationship between articulatory, acoustic and phonetic levels of analysis from a quantal viewpoint.

On the topic of the **phonological syllable,** Bell and Hooper (1978) offer a collection of articles debating the relationship between such a unit and the segment. Kloster Jensen (1963) debates both phonological and phonetic issues surrounding the definition of the syllable. Kohler (1966a, 1966b) can be consulted for the arguments displaying the most polar opposition to the concept of the phonological syllable. A countering, more supportive view is available in Anderson (1969).

5

The architecture of phonetic classification

The immediately following chapters are devoted in turn to a detailed consideration of each strand of vocal performance, from airstream mechanisms, phonation and articulation to prosodic, temporal and metrical organization. But this method of presentation, desirable though it is in other ways, is difficult to absorb without some initial frame of reference in which to integrate the different pieces of information. This chapter therefore begins with a brief sketch of the way that speech is typically performed, in order to give the reader a preliminary orientation.

The body of the chapter is then taken up with a summary of the principles on which speech can be classified at both the segmental and the suprasegmental levels of analysis. This offers the reader an overview of the architecture of the theoretical model to be developed in this book, before embarking on the full detail of segmental and suprasegmental description in the later chapters. Highlighting the main elements of theoretical structure in this way has the disadvantage that this chapter covers a great deal of ground very cursorily. But it may also have the compensating advantage of providing a summary to which the reader can return for review purposes after reading the later chapters.

5.1   A frame of reference for the production of speech

The basic function of the vocal apparatus in producing speech is to create audibly different patterns of sound. This can only be achieved by using the vocal apparatus to produce noises whose auditory quality, pitch, loudness and duration can be varied at will. We can begin to explore how the vocal apparatus is used to do this, and a first step is to become familiar with the anatomical landmarks of the vocal organs. A preliminary comment is that as part of the substantial organic variation between individuals, both the geometry and the relative proportions of the vocal organs can vary widely between individual speakers.

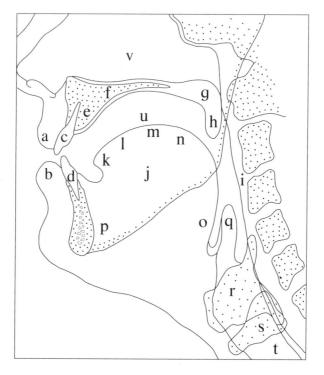

Figure 5.1 Sagittal view of the vocal apparatus, identifying different vocal organs and their parts

a. Upper lip	i. Pharynx wall	q. Epiglottis
b. Lower lip	j. Body of the tongue	r. Thyroid cartilage
c. Upper teeth	k. Tip of the tongue	s. Cricoid cartilage
d. Lower teeth	l. Blade of the tongue	t. Trachea
e. Alveolar ridge	m. Front of the tongue	u. Oral cavity
f. Hard palate	n. Back of the tongue	v. Nasal cavity
g. Soft palate	o. Root of the tongue	
h. Uvula	p. Lower jaw (mandible)	

5.1.1 *Anatomical landmarks in the vocal apparatus*

Figure 5.1 is a view of a **sagittal section** of the vocal apparatus – that is, seen from the side, with the head sectioned from front to back along the mid-line – which shows each of the different vocal organs and identifies some of their sub-parts. The parts that make major contributions to the performance of

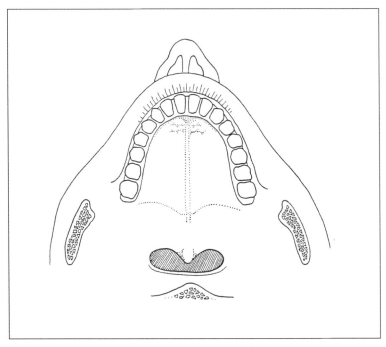

Figure 5.2 Schematic view of the roof of the mouth from below

speech are the **lungs**, the **larynx**, the **vocal tract** (made up of the **pharynx** and the **oral cavity**, the **tongue**, the **lips** and the **jaw**), and the nasal system (made up of the **soft palate** and the **nasal cavity**). Other vocal structures that play a role in speech, albeit passively, are the **teeth**, the **hard palate** and the **epiglottis**.

The sagittal view of the speech organs in figure 5.1 affords an opportunity for a brief discussion of the tongue and its parts. The **body of the tongue** is divided for phonetic discussion into the **root**, the **back** and the **front**. The root of the tongue lies opposite the back wall of the pharynx, in front of the epiglottis. The back of the tongue and the front of the tongue lie under the soft palate and the hard palate respectively. The tongue ends in a rounded **tip**, and the zone just behind the tip is called the **blade of the tongue**. Many students have the initial impression that the tongue is basically a flat structure, somewhat like the deck of an aircraft carrier. In reality, the body of the tongue, which is made up of a nearly globular mass of a densely interlocking set of muscles, is much more like three quarters of a tennis ball, with a very highly extensible and manoeuvrable tip. The tongue is the most versatile and mobile of all the organs of speech, and gains its speech capacity for agile and precise positioning from its primary biological role in moving food around the mouth and pharynx during chewing and swallowing.

Figure 5.2 is a view of the roof of the mouth, looking directly upwards from below. It may be helpful for readers, while reading the following account, to explore the roof of their own mouth (looking in a mirror with the head back, and gently feeling the surfaces mentioned with the tongue tip, thumb or finger). The upper jaw (called the 'maxilla' by anatomists) frames the palate and is the carrier of the upper teeth. The inner surfaces of each of the central upper teeth (the **incisors**) are gently curved, both vertically and from side to side. In most speakers, just behind the junction of these central upper teeth and the gum (or **alveolus**), is a rounded ridge. This is the **alveolar ridge**, and many sounds representing consonants in English and very many other languages are pronounced by placing the tip or blade of the tongue on or near this ridge. Just behind the alveolar ridge, the **hard palate** steepens into a slope that curves up to the highest point of the roof of the mouth. At the beginning of the slope, on the back part of the alveolar ridge, there are usually small corrugations. These are important in allowing the tongue to move food about in the mouth during eating, so that sticky food does not adhere unduly to the palatal surface, but they may also play a role in speech by providing small obstacles to the outflowing air, helping to make the airflow turbulent. This turbulence is responsible for the hissing noise that characterizes sounds such as [s] and [ʃ] in English *see* and *she*.

Most speakers have a thin central line running from the front to the back of most of the length of the hard palate. This is a relic of the growth pattern of the tissue and bones of the palate fusing before birth, and has no function in speech. But at the point where this line fades, towards the top of the palate, the tactile nature of the surface changes to from hard to soft. Gently pressing the beginning of this softer surface, one can still feel the hard bone of the vault of the palate above the fleshy tissue, until it ends abruptly in an edge more or less at a level with the rearmost (**molar**) teeth. The soft tissue further back in the roof of the mouth is the **soft palate**, or **velum**, and is made up of a complex of interwoven muscles. Exploring the feel of this yielding tissue of the body of the velum by touch should be done cautiously and slowly, because of the sensitivity in many speakers of the gag reflex. The soft tissue of the velum thus slightly overlaps the underlying bone of the hard palate, with the transitional zone being the forward attachment of the tissue of the velum. Elementary textbooks tend to imply that the soft palate begins where the hard palate ends, but this would in fact be an unusual anatomical arrangement. The velum ends in the **uvula**, which in most speakers is a single red-tipped extension hanging down as the tip of the soft palate in the centre of the back of the mouth. A very small minority of speakers will have a divided (double) uvula like an inverted 'V', which is the

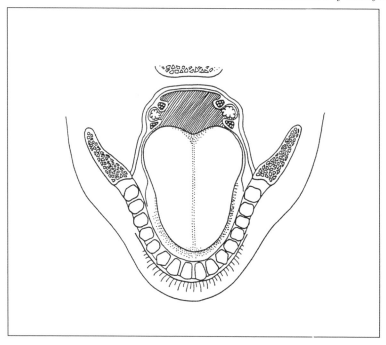

Figure 5.3 Schematic view of the surface of the tongue from above

most minimal version of a cleft palate. The uvular tip of the velum is often not visible unless the body of the tongue is held low in the mouth.

Returning to the sagittal view shown in figure 5.1, and continuing down the pharynx, we finally come to the epiglottis, the esophagus, the larynx, the trachea and the lungs. The chief function of the epiglottis, which is the relatively stiff, leaf-shaped cartilage at the base of the tongue, is to act as a deflector of food and drink in swallowing, thus acting as a protective lid for the larynx. When one swallows, the epiglottis folds down backwards over the larynx and diverts food into the **esophagus**, which normally lies flat, and whose opening is just behind the larynx. The esophagus expands, and muscular action provides a ring-like travelling wave to take the food down to the stomach. In relaxing from the swallow mechanism, the epiglottis then resumes its relatively upright position.

The chief biological action of the larynx is to act as a valve for the respiratory system. The speech functions of the respiratory system are discussed in chapter 6 on airstream mechanisms, and those of the structure and function of the larynx in chapter 7 on phonation, but one general point to make is that the larynx sits on a cartilaginous ring (the cricoid cartilage) at the top of the **trachea**, which leads to the lungs. The trachea is a tube reinforced by a series of horseshoe-shaped, incomplete rings of cartilage. The gap in each cartilaginous tracheal ring faces backwards, and the tissue that seals it forms a common wall with the front part of the esophageal tube, giving the respiratory system and the digestive system a rather intimate connection.

Figure 5.3 is the opposite view from figure 5.2, looking downwards at the top surface of the tongue from directly above. If one opens one's mouth as wide as possible with the lips well spread apart, one can get a somewhat similar view. The lower jaw, or the **mandible**, is the carrier of the lower teeth. Like the upper teeth, these are usually slightly curved, both vertically and from side to side. They very seldom play a direct role in speech, except passively as an obstacle to airflow. The mandible can be thought of as the carrier of the tongue, and makes visible movements during the speech of most speakers as the body of the tongue rises and falls. The tongue is of course capable of articulatory movement independently of the jaw, and a minority of speakers keep their jaw relatively immobile during speech. Perhaps the best way to think of the typical relationship between the tongue and the jaw is to consider the tongue as normally semi-independent of the jaw.

Looking carefully at the surface of the tongue, in most speakers one can see that the very tip is slightly redder than the surface of the blade and the body. In addition, the distribution of touch sensors just below the surface of the tongue is at its most dense around the tip, giving the tip and the blade an acute sensitivity to touch. In the large majority of speakers, one can see a central line running over the body of the tongue towards the back, dividing the body of the tongue into two longitudinal halves. This reflects the fact that the muscles of the tongue are mostly paired, and each side is capable of acting somewhat independently. This capacity to take unilateral action which differs from the contralateral action on the other side of the tongue can contribute to the articulatory performance of sounds such as those at the beginning and end of the English word *lull* [lʌl].

The surface of the tongue is highly adjustable in both the sagittal plane and in the **transverse plane** (the side-to-side dimension). The transverse profile of the body of the tongue can be adjusted to any curvature from a convex to a concave shape. It can also be more finely adjusted, especially in the region of the blade, to form a narrow central groove important for creating a jet of turbulent air in the formation of sounds like [s]. Looking further back to where the body of the tongue curves down into the pharynx at the very back of the mouth, the central line is usually lower than the two sides, giving the surface of the tongue facing the back wall of the pharynx a concave rather than a convex profile in the side-to-side dimension.

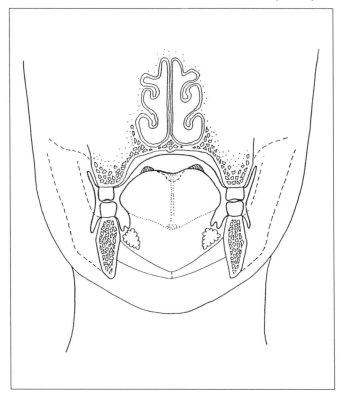

Figure 5.4 Frontal view of the back of the mouth, schematically
sectioned through a plane just forward of the last molar teeth

The representation in figure 5.3 of the horizontal cross-section of the
pharynx, looking down into it from above, shows the cut outlines of two
pairs of muscles at the sides, enclosing the tonsils. The function of these two
pairs of muscles is to pull the soft palate downwards, opening the back
entrance to the nasal cavity when this is required (for breathing, or for
speech purposes). The muscles form the pillars of two pairs of arches at the
back of the mouth. These can be seen in a somewhat more familiar shape in
figure 5.4, which is a **transverse** view of the head, schematically sectioned
through a plane just forward of the last molar teeth. The arches on either
side of the uvula run down into the forward set of pillars at the sides of the
tongue (which eventually insert into the sides of the body of the tongue).
Further back, and normally only clearly visible if one looks at oneself head-
on in a mirror, and yawns with the body of the tongue as low as possible,
is a posterior set of pillars. These run the length of the pharynx, and

125

eventually insert into the top edges of the large cartilage that shields the larynx.

Together, the two sets of pillars are called the **faucal pillars**. When these muscles contract, they not only serve to pull the soft palate downwards, they also tend to narrow the side-to-side diameter of the pharynx. The faucal pillars are mentioned here partly to explain the visible geography of the vocal organs, but also to indicate that they are a prime example of a structure which acts as a physical linkage between the soft palate, the tongue, the pharynx and the larynx. Because of such muscular linkages, almost no articulatory action can take place in speech without some repercussion on the state of the vocal organs somewhere else. Muscular interactions of this sort in speech are described in more detail in Laver (1980).

One other structure in figure 5.4 should be explained. The convoluted areas at the top of the figure are part of the internal structures of the middle part of the nasal cavity. They are covered with mucal tissue like the inside walls of the cheeks, and their elaborately curled shapes maximize their surface area and enhance their ability to warm and clean the incoming air for respiration.

5.1.2 *An illustration of respiratory, articulatory and phonatory action*

In the production of a typical utterance, the respiratory system provides an outward flow of air from the lungs. On its way, the flow of air passes in turn through the larynx, up the pharynx, and out through the mouth and/or the nasal cavity. If the airflow is exclusively through the mouth, the articulation is said to be **oral**. If the air escapes through the nose either instead of through the mouth or as well as through the mouth, the articulation is said to be **nasal**. The flow of air can be directed to escape from the nose instead of the mouth, or vice versa, by means of the movable soft palate acting as a valve at the back of the mouth.

The outflowing air can be made to generate audible acoustic energy by the passage through which it has to flow being made to adopt various different shapes. For example, a hissing noise can be produced by suitably narrowing the vocal tract at any one of a number of different places. The oral sound [s], for instance, as in English *soon* [sun], is produced by narrowing the tract just behind the front teeth, using the tip or blade of the tongue to create an aperture for the escape of the outflowing air that is so small that the flow through it is made into a jet. This jet then hits the downstream obstacle of the inner surfaces of the upper and/or lower central incisor teeth, and the flow becomes turbulent, audibly causing a hissing sound. The sound for [s] is oral because the soft palate closes off the entry at the back of the mouth to the nasal cavity. The articulatory configuration for [s] is shown in a sagittal view in figure 5.5.

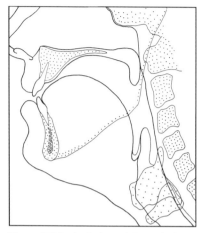

Figure 5.5 Sagittal view of the articulatory
configuration for the production of [s]

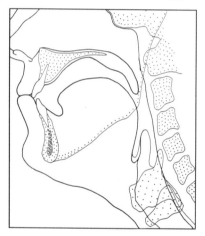

Figure 5.6 Sagittal view of the articulatory
configuration for the production of [m]

In the production of [s], the vocal folds in the larynx (which are two ledges
of muscular tissue with a forwards-pointing, horizontal V-shaped space
between them) are held wide apart, letting the air flow through the larynx relatively silently. This gives a **voiceless** effect. The vocal folds can also be used
to modify the area of this space, which is called the **glottis**. When the two
vocal folds are adjusted to touch each other along their full length, closing the
glottis and momentarily sealing off the escape of air from the lungs, any current of air which through increased respiratory effort succeeds in pushing its
way up through the vocal folds sets them into vibration, and this is heard as a

127

buzzing noise called **voicing**. If this buzzing noise from the larynx is added to the production of [s], the **voiced** sound [z] is made instead, as in English *zoom* [zum]. This difference between voiceless [s] and voiced [z] can be heard very easily if one pronounces these sounds while covering the ears with the hands.

In the production of a sound such as the [m] in *zoom* [zum], the closed lips prevent the air escaping from the mouth, and the soft palate, in an open position, allows the air to flow through the nose instead, giving [m] its characteristic nasal quality. A sagittal view of the articulatory configuration for [m] is shown in figure 5.6. At the same time, the vocal folds are vibrating, giving the typical buzzing sound of voicing, so that [m] can be made to sound quite loud. The **loudness** of the voice can be flexibly manipulated, as can the **duration** of the segment. The **pitch** of the voice can also be altered, so that if [m] is prolonged, melodies can be hummed.

The following summary picture emerges from these illustrative comments about typical respiratory, phonatory and articulatory actions. Air is made to move by the action of the respiratory system, and flows out through the vocal apparatus. The larynx can allow the air to flow through the glottis freely, creating voicelessness, or it can adjust the vocal folds to modify the airflow to produce audible voicing of variable pitch and loudness. The tongue and lips can change the shape of the vocal tract, and further modify the detailed route of the airflow, creating different patterns of auditory and acoustic quality as a result. The soft palate, acting as a valve for controlling the route taken by the escaping airflow, can also participate in this process. The duration of all these activities is also open to control.

The full range of vocal performance of course has many more options of phonetic control than those described above. Air can be made to flow inwards instead of outwards, and the airflow can be created by the activity of other organs than the respiratory system. **Airstream mechanisms** are explored in chapter 6. The vocal folds can be adjusted to give other effects than voicelessness and voicing. The glottal space can be slightly narrowed rather than completely closed, giving rise to a whispery effect, for instance. All of these modes of laryngeal control are discussed in chapter 7 on **phonation**.

The position of the tip, blade, body and root of the tongue, and the shape of the tongue's surface, can also be used in a wider variety of ways than so far mentioned, to give different three-dimensional configurations to the corridor through which the air flows, and the lips can take up different positions, as can the lower jaw. In combination with the action of the velum controlling the entry of air to the nasal cavity, the continually changing shapes given to the vocal tract by the activities of the tongue, lips and lower jaw are the basis for most of the audible differences of the sounds of speech, other than those created by the larynx. These differences are explained in chapters 8–12 on **articulation** and **co-ordination**.

Chapters 13–16 look upwards from the segment towards whole utterances, in a more suprasegmental view of speech. Chapter 13 explores the relationship between settings, features and segments. Chapter 14 discusses the **temporal organization of speech**, in terms of factors of duration, rate and continuity. Chapter 15 considers the **prosodic organization** of pitch and loudness, in the variation of melody and sonority in speech. Chapter 16 examines the interaction of syllables and stress in the **metrical organization of utterances**. Chapter 17 returns to matters of temporal organization, and considers suprasegmental questions of continuity and rate of speech. After the chapters outlining the descriptive theoretical model being offered in this book, chapter 18 looks at principled ways of classifying different types of phonetic and phonological transcription.

We come now to the overall architectural design of the classificatory model for segmental description, whose individual components are the focus of chapters 6–12.

5.2 The traditional design of the classificatory model for segmental description

It is necessary to begin by making it clear that this book will depart to some degree from the traditional way of classifying segments. Some very brief preliminary comments about the traditional method may therefore be appropriate. Abercrombie describes it in his discussion of the analysis of articulatory action in segments representing consonants:

> We can arrive at a description of a consonant segment adequate enough for most practical purposes by answering *seven* questions about it (though we must remember that the answers to these questions will certainly not tell us *everything* about the segment in question). These questions are as follows:
>
> Q1   What is the airstream mechanism?
> Q2   Is the airstream ingressive or egressive?
> Q3   What is the state of the glottis?
> Q4   What is the position of the velum?
> Q5   What is the active articulator?
> Q6   What is the passive articulator?
> Q7   What is the degree and nature of the stricture? (1967: 42)

The answers to these questions result in the choice of labels from a series of limited sets to give a composite label. An example would be: a 'pulmonic egressive voiced labial nasal' for [m], where the labels refer successively to the fact that air from the lungs ('pulmonic') is flowing outwards ('egressive'), through a vibrating larynx ('voiced'), with the oral exit to the outside air closed off by the lips ('labial') and the airflow being routed through the nasal cavity by the soft palate being in an open position ('nasal').

This widely followed method of classifying segments is usually called **classification by place and manner of articulation**. By 'place' is meant the location of the maximum constriction (or 'stricture') of the air-channel. Abercrombie (1967: 47) describes 'manner' as meaning 'primarily the type of stricture which the articulators are making to produce the segment (i.e. the answer to question (7) above), but it may in addition include reference to the position of the velum (question (4)) and to the airstream (questions (1) and (2))'. As labels for the classes of segment to be described under 'manner', Abercrombie (1967: 48–50) lists the terms 'stop', 'nasal', 'fricative', 'trill', 'flap', 'lateral' and 'approximant'. These are not entirely mutually exclusive, in that the system Abercrombie describes allows combinations such as 'fricative-lateral', for instance. Other writers tend to use a closely similar classificatory design, and provide a comparable set of labels.

The classificatory architecture more or less as described by Abercrombie in the comments above has been current for over a century (Ladefoged 1987a: 10), and with minor differences is enshrined in the present structure of the International Phonetic Association's phonetic alphabet, even after the 1989 Kiel Convention's revisions. It is clear that the traditional concept of 'manner' is fairly complex, and makes appeal to a variety of cross-cutting classificatory criteria – see, for example, the criticisms offered by Roach (1987). The same general criticisms could be levelled at the traditional concept of 'place of articulation'. The traditional approach has not been exhaustively described here, because one clearcut objective of this book is to propose a more structured and coherent design for the classification of the phenomena normally covered by the terms 'manner of articulation' and 'place of articulation'. The analysis presented here is nevertheless not far from orthodox, and incorporates the essence of the very large majority of the Kiel revisions. In particular, the Kiel Convention proposals for phonetic symbols are adopted here.

5.3 Classification of segments by initiation, phonation, articulation and co-ordination

The suggested classification of segmental phonetic quality in this book identifies four major descriptive elements: initiation, phonation, articulation and co-ordination. The articulation element is the most heavily sub-divided of the four, and is made up of a triple sub-classification of segments in terms of 'place of articulation', 'degree of stricture' and 'aspect of articulation'. A sum-

Major categories of segmental classification

Initiation	airstream mechanism airflow direction
Phonation	phonation type
Articulation	place of articulation degree of stricture aspect of articulation
Co-ordination	co-ordinatory option

Figure 5.7 Schematic diagram of the four major descriptive elements of speech production: initiation, phonation, articulation and co-ordination

mary schematic diagram of these elements and their sub-divisions is given in figure 5.7. The phenomena traditionally covered by 'manner of articulation' are partly redistributed in this book among the last two of these, 'degree of stricture' and 'aspect of articulation'. The remaining phenomena under the traditional 'manner of articulation' are described here under the rubric of 'co-ordination', rather than under articulation as such. The restructuring proposed is not radical, but reveals a greater degree of order in the phenomena of speech.

Initiation concerns the nature of the mechanism that is responsible for setting the airstream in motion, and the consequent direction of the airflow. The **airstream** can be pulmonic, glottalic or velaric. The **initiator** of the **pulmonic airstream** is the respiratory mechanism. In the case of the **glottalic airstream**, the initiator is the vertically moving larynx, with the glottis closed (in voiceless sounds) or vibrating (in voiced sounds), compressing or rarefying the air-pressure in the vocal tract above it. In the **velaric airstream**, the tongue is the initiator, trapping a body of air within the mouth and compressing or rarefying the pressure of the air so enclosed.

The **direction of the airstream** can be **egressive** (outwards from the body) or **ingressive** (inwards to the body). Most sounds are made on a pulmonic egressive airstream. Sounds made on a glottalic egressive airstream are called **ejective** sounds, and sounds made on a glottalic ingressive airstream **implosive** sounds. Sounds made with a velaric ingressive airstream are called **click** sounds. Sounds can also be made on some combinations of airstream mechanisms, in that pulmonic egressive voicing can be added to either velaric ingressive sounds (to give **voiced clicks**) or to glottalic ingressive sounds (to give **voiced implosives**). The different initiatory possibilities,

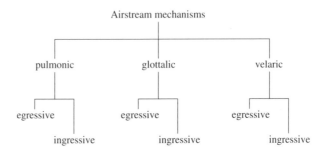

Names for stop segments made on single and combined airstreams

Name	Airstream	Name	Airstream
Plosive	pulmonic egressive	Implosive	pulmonic ingressive
Ejective	glottalic egressive	Voiced implosive	pulmonic egressive + glottalic ingressive
Click	velaric ingressive	Voiced click	pulmonic egressive + velaric ingressive

Ejective fricative segments are also found

Figure 5.8 Summary of the categories of the initiation of speech production, and the associated segment-types

together with the direction of airflow, and the names for the consequent segment-types, are summarized in figure 5.8.

Phonation concerns the generation of acoustic energy (including zero energy) at the larynx, by the action of the vocal folds. The different major **phonation types** are **voicelessness, whisper** and **voicing**. Voicelessness is divided into **nil phonation** and **breath phonation**. Voicing is divided into **normal voicing, creak** and **falsetto**. Combinations such as **whispery voice** and **creaky voice** are possible and are used for phonological purposes in a variety of languages, and for paralinguistic purposes. More elaborate combinations, such as **whispery creaky falsetto**, are physiologically possible, but are not used for linguistic or paralinguistic purposes. The varieties of phonation type, and their possible combinations, are summarized in section 7.7.

Articulation concerns the contribution which organs along the vocal tract from the larynx to the lips make to shaping the airflow in audibly different ways. In addition, **co-ordination** is to do with articulatory and temporal co-ordination between neighbouring segments, and is explicitly linked to articulatory analysis. It is emphasized that articulation and co-ordination are seen as interlocked parts of the theoretical model.

Articulation and co-ordination are the most complex of the four major elements of segmental performance, and it may therefore be helpful to make slightly more extensive comments on the design of the classificatory system for these topics.

There are three sub-classifications of articulation that characterize the performance of any segment. First, the **place of articulation** is identified as the location of the maximum constriction, or **stricture** of the air-channel, that the configuration of the vocal tract imposes on the moving airstream. Second, the type of constriction is identified in terms of the **degree of stricture** involved. Third, comments can be made about a number of additional **aspects of articulation**.

It is convenient first to deal with the nature of the different degrees of stricture, then to discuss the technical vocabulary for describing the place of articulation, and then finally to come to the question of the different aspects of articulation.

5.4   Degree of stricture and phases of articulation

The definition of the relative degree of stricture achieved in any given segment requires the introduction of a general concept of a number of different **phases of articulation** of a segment, as mentioned in section 4.5.2 in the previous chapter. We shall distinguish three different phases, in all types of segments. The first is an **onset phase** where a moving articulator is approaching the position where its maximum degree of vocal-tract constriction is to be reached. The second is a **medial phase** where the target degree of constriction is reached (and sometimes held for a moment in an approximately steady state). The third is an **offset phase** where the vocal organs show a transitional move-

articulatory sequence of a two-segment single-word utterance *saw* [sɔ]

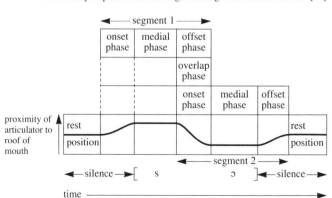

Figure 5.9 Phases of segmental performance

ment away from the medial-phase position. In continuous speech, the onset phase of a particular segment will be the same as the offset phase for the previous segment, in an **overlapping phase**. The identifying degree of stricture for any given segment is the one reached in the medial phase. Figure 5.9 shows these phases of articulation of the performance of a segment.

The description of segment-types that follows will for the moment ignore any contextual effects of neighbouring segments on a segment's marginal phases, and each segment-type will be described as if it were performed in isolation (that is, with silence as the surrounding context). The contextual adjustments between neighbouring segments that are in reality such a characteristic part of the articulation of continuous speech will be dealt with separately, in the discussion of co-articulation below and in chapter 12.

All segments will be described as having one of only three **degrees of stricture**. The maximum possible degree of stricture is the one where there is complete **closure** at some point along the vocal tract. When the medial phase of a segment shows this type of stricture it is called a **stop** segment. Because the outflowing air is momentarily prevented during this medial phase from escaping to the outside atmosphere, a rise in pressure occurs, and this is usually then released during the offset phase of the stop with a small but audible explosion.

The next degree of stricture to be distinguished is the constriction where there is a small aperture, sufficient to allow the airstream to escape continuously, but with a turbulent flow. Turbulence of this sort, because of the 'friction' of the air molecules, is audible as a hissing noise. Articulations whose medial phase is made with audible aerodynamic friction in this way are therefore called **fricative** segments. Because fricative articulations necessarily bring one articulator into very close proximity to another, they are said technically to show **close approximation** of the articulators.

Figure 5.10 The classification of segment-types on the basis of degree of stricture

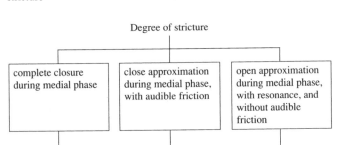

The third degree of stricture is any aperture that is large enough for air-flow through it to be smoothly laminar, without significant turbulence. Segments whose medial phase is made with a relatively open stricture of this sort are therefore said to be made with an **open approximation** of the articulators. In this condition, the configuration of the vocal tract is optimal for being made to resonate, for example by injection of the periodic pulses of acoustic energy created by the voicing process. Segments made with open approximation of the articulators will therefore be called **resonant** segments. Not all resonant segments are voiced, but they are by definition free of audible local friction. Figure 5.10 shows this classification of segment-types on the basis of the degree of stricture involved.

A number of sub-divisions of these categories will be introduced below, but all segments in all languages fall without exception into one of these three structural classes of stop, fricative or resonant.

5.5 Place of articulation

One way of identifying the place of maximum articulatory constriction that is sometimes used in acoustically oriented investigations is to specify its precise distance along the length of the vocal tract from the glottis. For a convenient articulatory labelling system, however, it is preferable to have a manageable list of labels that merely identify the main zones of the vocal tract that are typically involved in segmental articulation. Figure 5.11 shows these zones, in relation to the individual vocal organs. The articulatory zones are labelled from the lips to the glottis as follows: **labial** for articulatory

Figure 5.11 Labels for some of the principal zones of segment-articulation

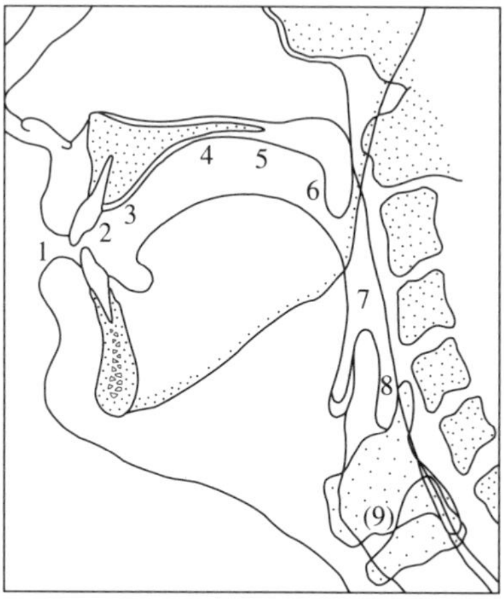

1	Labial
2	Dental
3	Alveolar
4	Palatal
5	Velar
6	Uvular
7	Pharyngeal
8	Epiglottal
9	Glottal

constrictions made at, near or opposite the lips; **dental** at the upper teeth; **alveolar** at the ridge just behind the upper front teeth; **palatal** at the hard palate; **velar** at the velum (soft palate); **uvular** at the uvula (the very tip of the soft palate); **pharyngeal** in the middle of the pharynx; **epiglottal** in the lower part of the pharynx; and **glottal** in the glottis.

More specific positions can also be identified in the margins of these zones, by prefacing the relevant label with **pre-** for a constriction made slightly further forwards towards the lips, and **post-** for one made slightly further back towards the glottal end of the tract. This yields labels such as **post-alveolar**, **pre-palatal** and **pre-velar**, for example. These modifiers signal small adjustments of the exact place of maximum constriction away from the centres of the zones identified by the chief labels. But in one case it is convenient to identify a place of articulation between two of the main zones that are relatively close together. These two zones are dental and alveolar, and **denti-alveolar** is the label given to the place of articulation at the junction of the upper teeth and the alveolar ridge. Another intermediate zone is helpful to break the large span between the alveolar and palatal zones. This intermediate zone is called **palato-alveolar**. The progression of main labels for place of articulation, moving backwards along the vocal tract from labial to glottal, is thus labial, dental, denti-alveolar, alveolar, palato-alveolar, palatal, velar, uvular, pharyngeal and glottal.

One further label that needs to be added to this list is 'alveolo-palat . . This is used in different textbooks in a variety of ways, sometimes referi...g to a place of articulation between alveolar and palato-alveolar, more often to one between palato-alveolar and palatal. The term **alveolo-palatal** will be adopted here to refer to the articulatory zone between palato-alveolar and palatal. For articulations between alveolar and palato-alveolar, we shall use the modifier 'post-' to give **post-alveolar**, and for articulations between alveolo-palatal and palatal, we shall use the modifier 'pre-' to give **pre-palatal**.

All the above locations relate normally to articulations where the constriction is achieved by an articulating organ, usually the tongue, moving upwards towards the roof of the mouth. The moving articulator is called the **active articulator**, and the stationary part of the vocal tract that it moves towards is called the **passive articulator**. Segmental constrictions, considered in isolation, are normally made by the active movement of the articulator that lies anatomically directly below the passive articulator. Velar segments such as the [k] in the English word *cat* [kat], for example, are made by the back of the tongue as the active articulator rising into complete closure with the undersurface of the soft palate as the passive articulator. Alveolar segments such as the [t] of *cat* are made by the tip or blade of the tongue as the

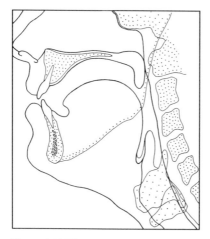

Figure 5.12 The neutral configuration of
the vocal tract, drawn from a
xeroradiographic photograph

active articulator rising into complete closure with the surface of the ridge just behind the upper front teeth.

This configuration of the vocal organs, where the active articulator is able to create constrictions by interaction with the passive articulator that lies anatomically directly opposite, constitutes an important reference configuration. It will be given technical status, and called the **neutral configuration** of the vocal tract. Figure 5.12, which is based on a xeroradiographic photograph of the author, shows this anatomically neutral position. It should be noted that the vocal tract is as nearly as anatomy allows in a posture giving equal cross-section to the tract along its full length, that the tongue is in a regularly curved convex shape, that the velum is in a position of closure with the back wall of the pharynx except for phonemically nasal segments, and that the lower jaw is held slightly open, as are the lips. Segments made by an active articulator interacting with its anatomically neutral passive articulator will be said to produce **place-neutral articulations**.

A smaller number of segment types are made with what is called **displaced articulation**, where the active articulator is displaced from its anatomically neutral position. These will be described in detail in the relevant chapters, but one familiar example is a **labiodental** articulation, where the lower lip is displaced from its neutral position opposite the upper lip to form a constriction with the biting edge of the upper front teeth, in segments such as the [f] in the English word *fish*.

Another (rare) example of displaced articulation is a **linguo-labial** articulation, where the tip or the blade of the tongue is displaced forwards from its neutral position opposite the alveolar ridge to make a constriction with the upper lip. This is found in some languages of the Pacific.

Further examples of displaced articulations concern some articulations of the tip and blade of the tongue. In the neutral disposition, the tip lies opposite the upper front teeth, and the blade lies below the alveolar ridge. Displacement would therefore be involved when the tip of the tongue (technically called the **apex of the tongue**) is used as the active articulator in segments where the passive articulator is not the upper front teeth, or where the blade of the tongue (technically the **lamina** of the tongue) is used in segments for which the passive articulator is not the alveolar ridge. **Apico-dental** segments are thus neutral with respect to displacement, as are **lamino-alveolar** segments. **Apico-alveolar** segments, on the other hand, are displaced articulations, as are **lamino-dental** segments. Equally, when the tip or blade of the tongue is brought forward to protrude between the upper and lower teeth, in an **interdental** place of articulation, this too counts as displaced.

As general labels, **apical** will be the label used for segments made with the tip of the tongue as the active articulator, and **laminar** will be the label for those made with the blade of the tongue as the active articulator. Articulations made by the body of the tongue can be divided into those made by the upper part of the body, or **dorsum**, which will therefore be called **dorsal** articulations, and those made by the root, or **radix**, which will be called **radical** articulations.

A segment can be characterized by simultaneous strictures made at more than one place of articulation. When there are two major constrictions of the vocal tract, a distinction can be drawn in terms of the relative degree of the strictures concerned. Where the two strictures are of equal degree, the segment is said to show a **double articulation**. Where one stricture is of less degree than the other, the stricture of greater degree is called the **primary stricture**, and the one of lesser degree is called the **secondary stricture**. A segment made in this way is said to show **secondary articulation**. The question of how many strictures need to be accounted for by the concepts of degree of stricture and place of articulation is a matter of a 'conformational aspect of articulation', which is discussed in section 5.6 below.

A familiar example of a segment made with a double articulation is the resonant segment [w], in the English word *wet* [wɛt]. Here, one (labial) stricture of open approximation is made by a rounded position of the lips. The other (lingual) stricture of open approximation is made by the back of the tongue being raised close to the soft palate (though not close enough, by definition, to cause audible friction). In cases of double articulation, both strictures are given their own label for place of articulation, giving rise to a two-part label: in the example quoted, the label for the place of articulation of [w] would be **labial velar**. Other examples of similar labels for segments with double articulation exploited by different languages of the world are **labial alveolar** and **labial palatal**.

In the case of a segment with secondary articulation, the places of articulation of both the primary and the secondary stricture are identified in the composite label, but the secondary stricture is given the suffix **-ized** to indicate its non-primary nature. An example of this is the pronunciation of *s* in the English word *soup*. This word was described earlier as being pronounced as [sʷup], which indicates that the [s] is produced with the lips being in a rounded position. The primary (alveolar) stricture is of greater degree, being one of close approximation. The secondary (labial) stricture is one of open approximation. The sound is labelled as 'a **labialized** voiceless alveolar fricative'. Other typical labels for secondary articulations encountered in languages, which are discussed in detail in chapter 11 on segments made with multiple articulations, are **labiodentalized, palatalized, velarized, pharyngealized** and **laryngealized**.

Figure 5.13 The labels for place-neutral, displaced, double and secondary articulations

Place of articulation
(for segments representing consonants)

Neutral	Displaced	Double	Secondary
		– labial alveolar	
– labial	– linguo-labial	– labial palatal	– labialized
	– labiodental	– labial velar	
	– interdental		
– dental	– lamino-dental		
– denti-alveolar			
– alveolar	– apico-alveolar	– labial alveolar	
– palato-alveolar			
– alveolo-palatal			
– palatal		– labial palatal	– palatalized
– velar		– labial velar	– velarized
– uvular			
– pharyngeal			– pharyngealized
– epiglottal			– laryngealized
– glottal			

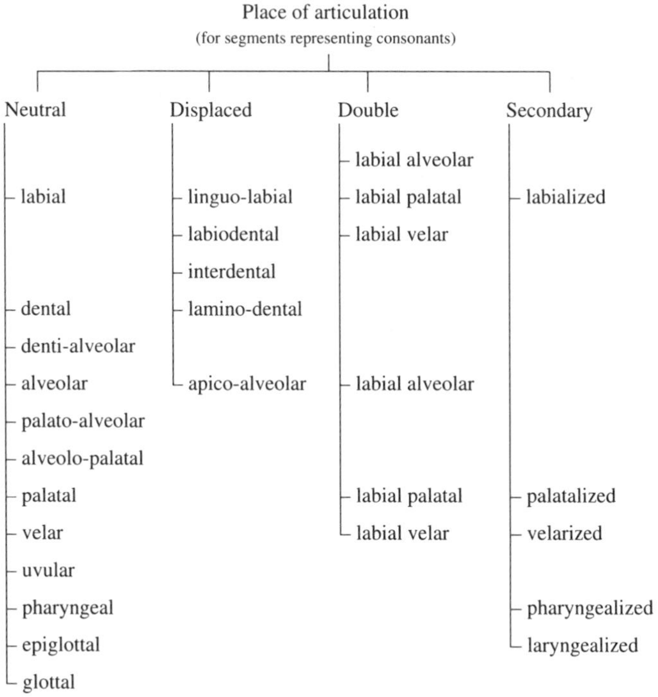

Modifiers: pre-, post-, as in pre-velar, post-velar, pre-palatal, post-alveolar, etc.

Figure 5.13 shows the relationship between all the labels for neutral, displaced and double segments which typically represent consonants, together with a list of labels for secondary articulations.

5.6 Aspect of articulation

It is often helpful or necessary to make explicit reference in a segmental label to factors of articulation over and above those relating merely to the location and degree of stricture. These factors can include matters of general conformation of the total air-channel, details of the topographical shape of the surface of the active articulator, and the nature of articulatory transitions and their timing.

All of these **conformational**, **topographical** and **transitional** factors of segmental performance will be described under the general rubric of **aspect of articulation**, which is a term originally suggested (in a much more restricted sense) by Elizabeth Uldall. Each particular aspect of articulation will be described fully at the point in the text where it first becomes directly relevant, and comment here is restricted to an outline of the basis for classification under the different aspects.

The underlying motivation in setting up the concept of aspect of articulation, apart from making the overall classification of segments more rational, is the fundamental conviction that the concept of degree of stricture is articulatorily, acoustically and auditorily dominant in the way that languages exploit the phonetic possibilities of speech. Stops, fricatives and resonants, as defined above, are regarded in this book as the basic entities in the structure of every spoken language. The phenomena covered under aspect of articulation appear to be different in kind from those discussed under degree of stricture, and therefore deserve to be separately described in the structure of the classificatory phonetic theory. Chapter 19 will return to the question of differences in the statistical take-up by the languages of the world of the various aspects of articulation, compared to the exploitation of the basic categories of stops, fricatives and resonants.

Conformational aspects cover the detailed routing of the air channel. The categories of conformational aspects of articulation include **oral** versus **nasal** patterns of airflow, and **central** versus **lateral** routing of the air-channel. The decision about how many strictures need to be accounted for in single and double articulations, and in occurrences of secondary articulations, is also handled as a matter of a conformational aspect of articulation.

Logically, segments are not limited to a maximum of two degrees of stricture of equal rank, nor to one secondary articulation being applicable. It is physiologically possible to produce a triple articulation, with stop closures at three places of articulation. An example would be a triple oral stop combining velar, alveolar and labial closures. A quadruple articulation could actually be produced by adding a simultaneous glottal stop to the triple velar, alveolar and labial example. Multiple fricative articulations combining several strictures of close approximation can similarly be produced. In practice, however, languages do not seem to exploit the option of multiplicity of strictures beyond double articulations. Multiplicity of secondary articulations on a given segment is perhaps less constrained in language use, but combinations of more than two simultaneous secondary articulations (for example simultaneous labialization and velarization) have seldom been noted in the linguistic phonetic literature.

Topographical aspects concern categories of the shape of the tongue surface which are distinct from its convex curvature in the neutral configuration. There are two major divisions of topographical aspects of articulation, relating to two of the planes of the vocal tract. The first is a group of deviations from the longitudinally regular neutral curve of the tongue's profile in the sagittal front-to-back plane; the second is a group of deviations from the side-to-side cross-sectional curvature of the front and blade of the tongue in its convex neutral configuration.

Longitudinal topographical aspects are made up of four individual categories. First, **retroflexion** of the tongue tip, curling it so that it points either upwards or slightly backwards, presenting either the tip or the undersurface of the tip as the active articulator to some part of the palate as the passive articulator. Retroflexion, as well as involving adjustment away from the longitudinal convexity of the neutral tongue configuration, also involves displacement of the active articulator relative to the neutral passive articulator. The second of the longitudinal categories is bunching of the anterior part of the tongue, which is produced by withdrawing the tongue tip into the body of the front of the tongue. The articulatory consequence of this **withdrawn tongue tip** is to enlarge the volume of the front oral cavity. This is also normally a consequence of retroflexion, and bunching and retroflexion have a very similar acoustic and auditory effect when applied to resonant segments, as discussed in chapter 10. The third longitudinal aspect is **extension** of the tongue tip, in the production of displaced segments such as interdental and linguo-labial articulations. Extension of the tip may also be a concomitant of extreme retroflexion.

The fourth longitudinal category is **advancement of the tongue root** (sometimes abbreviated to 'ATR' in the phonological literature). This has the effect of enlarging the middle and lower pharynx, and gives the longitudinal profile of the root of the tongue a tighter curve than it has in its neutral configuration. In this regard it is articulatorily somewhat similar to bunching of the anterior part of the tongue, which comparably produces a tighter-than-neutral curve to the tip/blade part of the tongue. Advancement of the tongue root is a modification which some languages apply to the production of sub-sets of resonants representing vowels. This is a basis in a number of languages for the phonological process called **vowel harmony**, where all the vowels in a given word are chosen from one of two mutually exclusive (or partially exclusive) sub-sets of the overall inventory – in this case one set using a neutral position of the tongue root and the other an advanced tongue-root position which expands the front-to-back diameter of the pharynx.

Transverse topographical aspects of articulation consist of two categories of adjustment of the surface of the tongue away from the neutral convex shape of its side-to-side cross-section. The first is **grooving** of the surface of the blade of the tongue, in which a more or less deep and narrow furrow is formed, through which a jet of air flows in the production of fricative segments such as the alveolar [s], as described in section 5.1 above. The function of the groove in the blade of the tongue in the production of [s] is both to produce the accelerating effect necessary to create the jet, and to steer it onto the inner surfaces of the upper (and/or lower) teeth, where the flow is made turbulent (and hence noisy) by its impact on this obstacle. It is possible to make fricatives at the alveolar place of articulation which do not have such a grooved aspect, but a grooved [s] (and its voiced counterpart [z]) is overwhelmingly the more common of these two alveolar possibilities.

The second transverse aspect of articulation is **cupping** of the tongue surface, which gives a concave hollowed shape to the tongue body by allowing the midline of the tongue body to drop lower than the sides. Cupping often involves the whole body of the tongue, and does not involve the formation of a narrow local groove as such (though cupping may be combined with local grooving of the tongue blade for an alveolar fricative [s]. Retroflexion may also involve cupping.

Transitional aspects of articulation concern the articulatory manoeuvres of the vocal organs when a steady state is not maintained during the medial phase of segments. Transitional processes include **flapping**, where the active articulator hits the passive articulator in passing; **tapping**, where the active articulator is thrown very rapidly against the passive articulator in a ballistic action; and **trilling**, where the active articulator is momentarily positioned in such a way that aerodynamic forces can set it into regular vibration against the passive articulator. Many of these transitional aspects of articulation can give rise to sub-divisions of the major segmental categories of stop, fricative

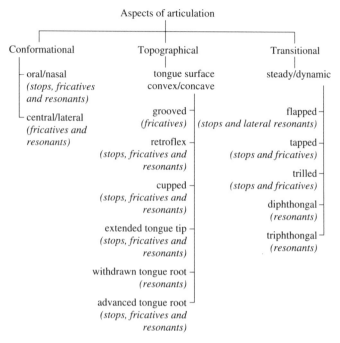

Figure 5.14 The applicability of different aspects of articulation to types of segments

and resonant. Stops and fricatives can be trilled, tapped and flapped. Lateral resonants can be flapped or tapped.

A central resonant representing a vowel can also be subject to transitional aspects of articulation, in that (as a single segment representing a single vowel within a single phonological syllable) it can show either a relatively unchanging quality through the medial phase of its production (producing a **monophthong**), or it can display changing qualities through the medial phase. A unidirectional change gives a **diphthong**, and a double change within the same medial phase gives a **triphthong**.

Figure 5.14 summarizes the structural relationships between all the different aspects of articulation and the segment-types to which they potentially apply.

5.7 Major aspects of articulation

There are three widely occurring aspects of articulation among the groups just described, which merit a fuller treatment. For clarity, they will be illustrated as far as possible from English. Two of these are conformational aspects, which can potentially modify virtually all the basic cate-

143

gories of stop, fricative and resonant. The first concerns a distinction between a **central** versus a **lateral** course for the airflow channel. The second concerns a distinction between an **oral** versus a **nasal** routing of the airflow channel. The third aspect of articulation to be given more extended discussion here is the transitional aspect, concerning the processes of **trilling, tapping, flapping, diphthongization** and **triphthongization**.

5.7.1 *Central versus lateral aspects of articulation*

The routing of the airflow channel in those segments where air can escape orally during the medial phase of the segment is **central** for the great majority of sounds in each of the languages of the world. In other words, in a head-on view of the speaker, air flows out of the vocal tract along the longitudinal mid-line of the tract. This is true of all the sounds in the English words *see* [si], *shoe* [ʃu], *ease* [iz] and *thief* [θif], for instance. But it is also possible to use the active articulator to form a partial blockage in the vocal tract in such a way that the air is forced to escape round one or both sides of the obstacle, with a **lateral** routing of the airflow. In English, the [l] segment at the beginning of the word *law* [lɔ] shows a lateral aspect of articulation of this sort, while [ɔ] is characterized by a central aspect.

This distinction between central and lateral airflow logically applies to all degrees of stricture except that of complete closure, where there is no escape of oral airflow anyway. Fricative and resonant categories can both be affected, giving **central fricatives**, **lateral fricatives**, **central resonants** and **lateral resonants.** In English, [s] in the word *seat* [sit] is a central fricative, [j] in *young* [jʌŋ] is a central resonant, and [l] in *leaf* [lif] is a lateral resonant.

When the conformational aspect of routing of airflow is not explicitly specified in a segment label of this sort, then it is to be assumed that the fricative or the resonant displays a central aspect of articulation.

5.7.2 *Oral versus nasal aspects of articulation*

Virtually all segment-types can be made in an oral or a nasal aspect. When a segment is **oral**, air flows only through the mouth, and not through the nose. When it is **nasal**, air flows through the nose. Whether air flows through the mouth as well as the nose in nasal segments will depend on whether or not there is a simultaneous closure in the oral cavity. The factor that controls whether air flows through the nasal cavity is the position of the soft palate (the **velum**) relative to the back wall of the pharynx. In oral segments, the velum is held in a raised position, making a closure against the

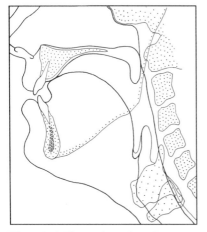

Figure 5.15 The configuration of the vocal organs during the production of [d], a pulmonic egressive voiced oral stop with alveolar and velic closure

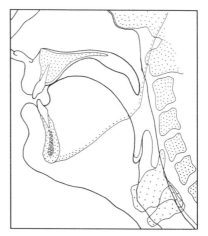

Figure 5.16 The configuration of the vocal organs during the production of [n], a pulmonic egressive voiced nasal stop with alveolar closure and velic opening

back wall of the pharynx. This is called a **velic closure**. In nasal segments, the velum is held in a position of **velic opening**. Figures 5.15 and 5.16 show the vocal organs during the performance of [d], a pulmonic egressive voiced oral stop with alveolar and velic closure, together with one for [n], its nasal counterpart with alveolar closure and velic opening.

5.7.3 *Transitional aspects of articulation: tapping, flapping, trilling, monophthongs, diphthongs and triphthongs*

Tapping and flapping are aspectual processes that concern the speed or nature of the articulatory transitions involved. In **tapping**, the active articulator moves at a higher speed, and for a shorter duration, in all three phases (onset, medial and offset phases) than in the corresponding non-tapped articulation. This tapping process can be applied to at least some of the members of all segment-categories except central resonants. The languages of the world thus include not only **tapped stops**, but also **tapped fricatives**. **Tapped lateral resonants** can also occur phonetically, but seem not to be used as the basis for phonemic oppositions in the languages of the world.

Flapping is an aspectual process that is also normally characterized by a higher speed of articulation, but in addition involves the active articulator striking the passive articulator in a passing trajectory. Flapping is found as an aspect of articulation applied to stops and lateral resonants. When a stop is flapped, the active articulator makes a brief, sliding contact of complete closure with the passive articulator. When a lateral resonant is flapped, the contact between active and passive articulators, though brief and sliding, is only partial, making a central contact, and air can flow continuously through the open lateral approximation. Logically, fricatives (central or lateral) could be flapped, but flapped fricatives do not seem to be used contrastively in languages.

Trilling is a rather different aspectual mechanism. Here the active articulator is positioned either in contact with or close to the passive articulator, in such a way that an egressive flow of air sets the active articulator into regular vibration. Both trilled stops and trilled fricatives can be found in linguistic use.

A transitional aspect of articulation also applies to central resonants representing vowels. These can show a stable medial phase of relatively unchanging quality, in which case they are classified as **monophthongs**, as in the (RP) pronunciation of the vowel in the English word *met* [mɛt]. When the medial phase shows an audible change of quality, with the change consistently progressing towards a single target, as it were, then the sound is classified as a **diphthong**. An example can be found in the (RP) pronunciation of the vowel in the English word *might* [maɪt], where the starting-point for the diphthong is [a], and the target end-point is [ɪ].

Monophthongs and diphthongs are both common types of articulations in the languages of the world, though diphthongs are considerably rarer than monophthongs. The third type of transitional aspect applicable to central resonants representing vowels is much rarer yet. This is the case of **triphthongs**, where an audible change of quality in the medial phase moves first towards one target and then undergoes a change of target in mid-course. An example of a triphthong in English is the (RP) pronunciation of the vowel in the English word *flower* when pronounced as a monosyllable [flaʊə] (often with a starting-point closer to [ɑ], giving [flɑʊə]). Another example comes from the (RP) pronunciation of the vowel in the English word *dire* when pronounced as a monosyllable [daɪə] (sometimes with a starting-point closer to [ɑ], giving [dɑɪə]). It should be noted that the description of a triphthong here is a phonetic definition, not a prescription of how RP speakers necessarily pronounce the illustrative words. In the idiolects of some individual speakers of the RP accent, these triphthongs can be reduced to diphthongs, as in [flaə] and [daə], or even long monophthongs, as in [flɑː] and [dɑː]. In such idiolects, words such as *tire* and *tower* become indistinguishable **homophones**, both pronounced as [taə] or [tɑː].

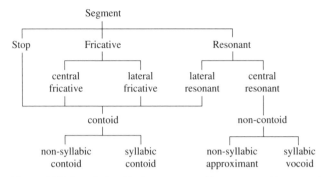

Figure 5.17 The relationship between contoids, non-contoids, approximants and vocoids

5.8   Contoid, approximant and vocoid segments

The distinction between central and lateral aspects of articulation will be applicable in the chapters below on fricatives and resonants, but they were mentioned in section 5.7.1 in order to set up helpful superordinate distinctions between several general classes of segment which will be useful in later discussion – namely, distinctions between **contoids** and **non-contoids**, and within **non-contoids**, between **approximants** and **vocoids**.

The relationship between contoids, non-contoids, approximants and vocoids is represented in Figure 5.17. The term 'contoid' is taken from Pike (1943) and, although its phonetic meaning is slightly different, it is used for a similar purpose – that is, to help to distinguish the phonetic versus the phonological status of segments. A **contoid** will be defined here as any segment other than a central resonant, and includes, therefore, all stops, fricatives and lateral resonants. All central resonants will be called **non-contoids**.

Contoids are most frequently found in the marginal positions in the syllable, in which case they will be classified as **non-syllabic contoids**. When they are in the syllable-nuclear position, they will be called **syllabic contoids**. The initial and final segments of the English (RP) pronunciations of the words *cat* [kat], *dog* [dɒg], *seize* [siz] and *loop* [lup] are all non-syllabic contoids in this definition. Examples of syllabic contoids in English (RP) are the nasal stop [n̩] in *garden*, when this word is pronounced with no segment intervening between the [d] and the [n̩], as in [ɡɑdn̩] (the diacritic symbol [n̩] being used to make the syllabic nature of [n] explicit). A similar example is the syllabic lateral resonant [l̩] in the word *cattle*, pronounced as [katl̩]. A less obvious example is the syllabic fricative [s̩] in the phrase *operatic society* pronounced as [ɒpəɹatɪk s̩saɪtɪ], when the segment normally representing the *o* in the spelling of the first syllable of *society* has been lost in the elision process associated with informal style.

The **non-contoid** class of segments (i.e. all central resonants), can also occur in marginal or nuclear positions in the syllable. When they are marginal (i.e. **non-syllabic**), they will be called **approximants**. Examples of approximants are the initial segments [j], [w] and [ɹ] of the (RP) pronunciations of the English words *yes* [jɛs], *went* [wɛnt] and *red* [ɹɛd]. When non-contoids are nuclear in the syllable (i.e. **syllabic**), they will be called **vocoids**. The category of vocoid is exemplified by the segments making up the pronunciations of the English (RP) words *awe* [ɔ], *E* (name of the letter) [i], *I* (personal pronoun) [aɪ] and *ah* (exclamation) [ɑ]. Further examples are the non-final segments [i], [aʊ] and [ɪə] in the English (RP) pronunciations of *ease* [iz], *owl* [aʊl] and *ears* [ɪəz]. The terms 'approximant' and 'vocoid' are borrowed from Ladefoged (1964) and Pike (1943) respectively, though both are defined here in senses slightly different from their original meanings.

By keeping these phonetic classes of segments distinct in both their articulatory classification and their phonological positioning, it is possible to use 'consonant' and 'vowel' as unambiguously phonological terms. Given that consonants are marginal and vowels nuclear in the syllable, consonants are phonetically manifested by (non-syllabic) contoids and by approximants. Vowels are phonetically manifested most frequently by vocoids, and, less frequently, by (syllabic) contoids. Figure 5.18 exemplifies these relationships with instances of relevant segments from English (RP).

The pronunciations of [θ] and [l] in the English (RP) words *thief* [θif] and *leaf* [lif] are both non-syllabic contoids representing the consonants / θ/ and /l/ respectively. The (RP) pronunciations of [j], [w] and [ɹ] in the English words *yen* [jɛn], *when* [wɛn] and *wren* [ɹɛn] are all non-syllabic approximants

Figure 5.18 Examples from English of syllabic and non-syllabic contoids and vocoids

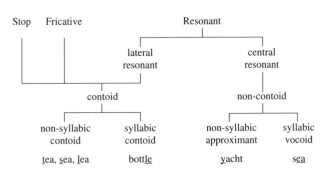

representing the consonants /j/, /w/ and /r/ respectively. Both [ɑ] and [n̩] in the RP pronunciation of *garden* /gɑdn/ cited above as [gɑdn̩], where the [n̩] is acting as the nucleus of the second syllable, are syllabic – [ɑ] is a vocoid and [n] is in this case a syllabic contoid. Both represent vowels, therefore, from a strict phonological point of view.

5.9 Articulatory co-ordination

The classification of segments so far has concentrated on the internal articulatory properties of the segments themselves. There are some articulatory and timing processes, however, that are better described as properties of a co-ordinatory relationship between adjacent segments, rather than as an internal matter specific to a single segment. These include the **devoicing** process, **stop release** modes, **aspiration** and **affrication**.

5.9.1 *Co-ordination between adjacent segments*

All these co-ordinatory processes concern articulatory and timing events during the **overlapping phase** of adjacent segments, where the offset of the first segment completely overlaps with the onset phase of the second. Utterance-marginal silence is here treated as if it were a segment, for the purposes of the classification. In **partial devoicing**, an otherwise voiced segment loses voicing (becoming whispered or voiceless) in one of its marginal phases under the influence of a neighbouring voiceless segment or utterance-marginal silence. The partial devoicing can be **initial devoicing** or **final devoicing**. Devoicing is symbolized by a subscript [̥]. If fine detail is needed, the diacritic can be displaced to the left of the segmental symbol, as in [̥z], to represent initial devoicing. If it is displaced to the right, as in [z ̥], this indicates final devoicing.

In matters of the release of oral stops, the co-ordinatory options are for the compressed air built up during the medial phase either to be **released** during the offset phase, or to be **non-released**. Release is symbolized by adding a superscript [ʰ] between the stop and the following segment, when this is required to be made explicit, as in /at/ ⇒ [atʰ], and non-release is symbolized by means of the superscript [̚] in the same position, as in /at/ ⇒ [at ̚]. When the compressed air is not released, because the overlapping phase with a following stop prevents the escape of air (as in some pronunciations of the [k] in the English word *act* /akt/ ⇒ [ak ̚tʰ]), the stop involved is said to be auditorily **incomplete**, in that it lacks an audible offset phase. In this example, [k ̚] is non-released and incomplete, but [tʰ] is released and complete.

Additionally, stop releases can be **oral** or **nasal**, **central** or **lateral**. This means that the compressed air built up during the medial phase of an oral stop is released during the overlapping offset phase, called **plosion** in this case, either through the mouth in **oral plosion**, or through the nasal cavity in **nasal plosion**. Oral plosion is assumed to be the neutral case, and nasal plosion is symbolized by inserting a superscript [ⁿ] between the stop and the next segment, as in English [gɑdⁿn̩]. In the case of central versus lateral plosion, the compressed air built up during the medial phase of an oral stop segment can be released during the offset phase either centrally (the neutral case), or laterally. In **lateral plosion**, the air escapes through a lateral channel, guided by the appropriate conformational aspect of tongue articulation. It is symbolized by means of a superscript [ˡ] added between the stop and the following segment, as in English *bottle* [bɒtˡl̩].

Both voiceless stops and voiceless fricatives can have an **aspirated** relationship in the overlapping phase with their following voiced neighbour. This involves an audible delay in the onset of voicing for the second segment after the release of the first segment, and is symbolized by insertion of a superscript [ʰ] between the two segments, as we saw in chapter 2 in English words such as *peat* /pit/ ⇒ [pʰit]. Voiced stops and fricatives can also have **voiced aspirated** relationships with their following neighbours, in which case the delay is in the onset of normal voicing, and the preceding phonation shows breathy or whispery voice, symbolized by [ɦ], as in Sindhi [dɦəro] 'a kind of measurement'.

Some languages show **pre-aspiration**, in which a delay in the offset of normal voicing occurs in the overlapping phase between a syllable-nuclear vocoid and a succeeding voiceless stop. It is symbolized by either a superscript [ʰ] being placed between the two relevant segments, as in Gaelic [kʰaʰt] 'cat' (which shows both aspiration and pre-aspiration), or by a corresponding [ɦ] when the phonation shows whispery voice, as sometimes happens in particular accents of Gaelic.

Oral stops can have an **affricated** co-ordinatory relationship in the overlapping phase with their following neighbours, in that the offset phase of the stop can be released slowly enough to allow a moment of audible friction, made **homorganically** (i.e. at the same place of articulation as the preceding stop). This is symbolized by means of a superscript small fricative symbol inserted between the stop and its neighbour, as in [tˢa] 'grass' in Sherpa (alternatively by using a linker diacritic ('‿') placed over the stop and the fricative symbols, as in [t͡sa], or by joining the symbols together, as in [tsa]).

It is also possible for **pre-affrication** to occur as a particular type of co-ordinatory relationship in the overlapping phase between a syllable-nuclear vocoid and a following syllable-marginal voiceless stop. This is where the onset phase of the stop is produced slowly enough to allow a moment of audible friction, made at the same place of articulation as the stop. Once again, this is symbolized by inserting a superscript symbol for the relevant fricative between the two segments, as in [aˣk]. Pre-affrication of this sort is sometimes found in languages as a correlate of pre-aspiration in cognate languages.

5.9.2 Co-ordination between multiple segments

Co-ordinatory relationships can also exist between two or more segments, in adaptive phenomena such as co-articulation. In **co-articulation**, there is a discernible degree of accommodation between the articulatory features of a given string of adjacent segments. This reflects the fact that in the neuromuscular planning and execution of speech, there is a tendency for the performance of a segment to anticipate the articulatory characteristics of one or more nearby segments yet to be pronounced. The span of this influence can be as few as two segments, or as many as all the segments in a short utterance. This is an example of an **anticipatory co-articulatory** influence being exercised. To a weaker extent, **perseverative co-articulatory** effects show themselves as well, where the prolonged influence of a given segment is exercised on segments which follow it in the stream of speech.

An example of anticipatory co-articulation can be seen in the English (RP) word *zoom* [zʷum], where the lip position for [z] anticipates to some degree that for [u]. An example of perseverative co-articulation lies in [ik̟] in the English word *eke*, where the articulation of [k̟] is further forward, under the influence of the front articulation of the [i] preceding, than would be the case in the RP pronunciation of *arc* as [ɑk̠], where the articulation of [k̠] is further back, under the influence of the back articulation of the preceding [ɑ].

5.10 The duration of segments

The duration of a segment can vary for a number of reasons, explored in detail in chapters 14–17. The first reason for variations of duration is phonological contrast. Many languages exploit relative duration as a contrastive cue. To identify the level of analysis used, **duration** can be reserved for phonetic description and **length** for contrastive phonemic use. The colon can be used at the phonemic level to indicate contrastively greater length, as in Finnish /kisa/ 'a game' versus /kisːa/ 'a cat' . Both consonants and vowels can exploit contrastive length. In some languages several degrees of contrastive length are used, with a double colon being used to mark the longest degree. Scottish Gaelic shows a triple length contrast on the representation of some vowels, as in /tuɫ/ 'to go', /uːɫ/ 'apple' and /suːːɫ/ 'eye' (Ternes 1973).

The duration of a segment can also be subject to allophonic adjustments which are part of the pattern appropriate to its given context. In most accents of English, the duration of the segment representing the vowel in *bead* /biːd/ is longer than that representing the vowel in *beat* /biːt/, even though the same vowel phoneme is involved in the two cases. Greater relative duration of this sort can be indicated transcriptionally by use of a colon to mark the longer allophone, giving *bead* /biːd/ ⇒ [biːd], versus *beat* /biːt/ ⇒ [bit].

The duration of a segment is also affected by whether it occurs in a stressed or unstressed syllable. In English syllables of otherwise identical phonemic make-up, the segment representing the vowel in the stressed syllable will be of greater duration than the allophone of the same vowel in the unstressed syllable. When the stressed syllable happens also to have been made the perceptually most prominent syllable of the whole utterance, by intonational means discussed in chapter 15, then the duration of the stressed vowel allophone will be even greater.

Finally, the duration of all segments will be affected by any variation in the overall rate of speaking, though not necessarily in a linear proportion.

5.11   The suprasegmental analysis of speech

The suprasegmental level of the description of speech considers all factors which can potentially be prolonged beyond the domain of the segment. An analysis of **settings** explores the suprasegmental distribution and relation of features which run through sequences of two or more segments, up to whole utterances. The analysis of settings is summarized in section 5.11.1 below. Other suprasegmental factors are normally regarded as properties of units larger than the segment, such as the syllable and the utterance. Examples of these are the suprasegmental patterns of pitch, loudness, rate, continuity and rhythm. **Pitch** and **loudness** are the perceptual correlates of the frequency of vibration of the vocal folds and the acoustic intensity of the voice respectively. **Rhythm** is the complex perceptual pattern produced by the interaction in time of the relative prominence of stressed and unstressed syllables. **Rate** is the overall tempo of speaking. **Continuity** is a matter of the incidence of pauses in the stream of speech. The prosodic analysis of pitch is outlined in section 5.11.2 below, and the metrical interaction of loudness, stress, rhythm, rate and continuity is summarized in section 5.11.3.

5.11.1   *Settings*

A setting, as defined in section 4.5.4 in the previous chapter, is constituted by any tendency for the vocal apparatus to maintain a given configuration or featural state over two or more segments in close proximity in the stream of speech. Any segments sharing a given setting are to that extent **phonetically similar** to each other.

Settings can be used for a wide variety of semiotic purposes. Linguistically, a setting can be the vehicle for a co-ordinatory adjustment towards greater phonetic similarity in **co-articulation** between adjacent segments within a word, and in **assimilation** between adjacent segments across a word boundary. Paralinguistically, a setting can be used as the basis for a particular **tone of voice**. A smile held while talking was one paralinguistic example of a setting given in section 4.5.4 above. Using a whispery voice for signalling confidentiality over a whole utterance would be another. Extralinguistically, phonetic settings characterize the habitual **voice quality** of individual speakers. The idea of a setting is hence sufficiently productive that a slightly extended summary here may be helpful.

The notion of a setting is applicable at every level of phonetic description from **articulation, phonation** and **overall muscular tension** factors to **prosodic** activities in speech. Each of these groups of settings can be related to an appropriate **neutral reference setting**, as a baseline from which to measure the deviation of the individual setting concerned. The amount of deviation can be labelled in terms of a **scalar degree** of deviation on a scale of 1 to 3, where 1 is a slight deviation, 2 is moderate and 3 is as extreme a deviation as is found in typical sociolinguistic accent-characterizing functions. In the idiosyncratic or pathological speech characterizing individual speakers, settings can take on more extreme degrees.

Individual segments are influenced by each type of setting in a gradient of **susceptibility** ranging from maximally susceptible to non-susceptible. This susceptibility depends chiefly on the physiological relationship between the muscle-systems concerned in the production of the segment and the setting. Vocoid production is heavily susceptible, for example, to the effects of a setting which constrains the body of the tongue to try to stay relatively close to the hard palate in a **palatalized voice**. In this case, the vocoid space would be compressed towards the roof of the mouth, and vocoids which in another speaker might be very open, such as the [a] in *bat* [bat], might become so raised as to be phonetically almost [ɛ], for instance. Listeners unfamiliar with such a speaker might then think, on hearing the speaker's pronunciation of *bat* as [bɛt], that the word *bet* was intended. Only greater familiarity would allow listeners to retune their perceptual registrations of the speaker's utterances to make allowance for the distorting effects of the setting on the vocoid segments.

Different settings co-occur in the speech of a given individual. Only physi-

Category	Setting	Scalar degrees			
		neutral	1	2	3
Longitudinal	Laryngeal				
	raised larynx				
	lowered larynx				
	Labial				
	labiodentalization				
	labial protrusion				
Cross-sectional	Labial				
	lip-rounded				
	lip-spread				
	Mandibular				
	close jaw				
	open jaw				
	Lingual tip blade				
	advanced tip blade				
	retracted tip blade				
	Lingual body				
	advanced body				
	retracted body				
	raised body				
	lowered body				
	Lingual root				
	advanced root				
	retracted root				
Velopharyngeal	Velic coupling				
	nasal				
	denasal				

Category	Setting	Scalar degrees	
		neutral	non neutral
Articulatory range	Labial		
	narrow range		
	wide range		
	Mandibular		
	narrow range		
	wide range		
	Lingual		
	narrow range		
	wide range		

Category	Setting	Scalar degrees			
		neutral	1	2	3
Supralaryngeal tension	tense				
	lax				
Laryngeal tension	tense				
	slightly harsh				
	moderately harsh				
	lax				
	slightly breathy				
	moderately breathy				

Category	Setting	Scalar degrees	
		neutral	non neutral
Phonatory	modal voice		
	falsetto		
			1 2 3
	creak(y)		
	whisper(y)		

Category	Setting		Scalar degrees			
			neutral	1	2	3
Prosodic	Pitch					
	mean	high				
		low				
	range	wide				
		narrow				
	variability	high				
		low				
	Loudness					
	mean	high				
		low				
	range	wide				
		narrow				
	variability	high				
		low				

Figure 5.19 Protocol for annotating the scalar degrees of settings of articulation, phonation, overall muscular tension and prosodic performance shown by an individual speaker's vocal profile

ological **compatibility** constrains the combinability of such settings, in principle, although in the very large majority of cases only a few settings in the speech of a single speaker will show any substantial deviation from the neutral reference settings.

Key susceptible segments for analysing the effect of a setting deviating from neutral to each particular scalar degree are given in chapter 13, where settings are discussed in detail. The different types of settings are too numerous to be discussed further here, but the complete range of settings is named in Figure 5.19. This is a **protocol** allowing written annotation of the settings analysed in the speech of any given individual of normal anatomy, divided into settings of articulation, phonation, overall muscular tension and prosodic behaviour. The record for each setting allows judgements of 'neutral', 'scalar degree 1', 'scalar degree 2' or 'scalar degree 3' to be registered. By appropriately filling in the complete protocol for the individual speaker, the analyst gains a record of the speaker's **Vocal Profile**.

5.11.2 *The prosodic analysis of speech*

The pitch of a speaker's voice varies within the physiologically imposed limits of an **organic pitch range** which derives from his or her personal laryngeal anatomy. The habitual range of pitch exploited by a speaker in ordinary conversation can be called the speaker's **linguistic pitch range**. If this range is adjusted for purposes of paralinguistic communication, it can be called the speaker's **paralinguistic pitch range**.

Within a speaker's linguistic range, the momentary **pitch values** of the voice during a given utterance will vary between a local maximum and minimum. This can be called the speaker's **pitch-span**. Individual pitch values tend to become progressively lower through the course of an utterance, in a process called **declination**. The exact placement of the pitch of a syllable within a given pitch span is termed its **pitch-height**, and the shape of the pitch value within the duration of the syllable can be referred to as its **pitch-contour**. Pitch-height can be **high**, **mid** or **low**, or have an intermediate value such as **high-mid** or **mid-low**. The pitch-contour can either be **level**, or can **fall** or **rise**, or display more complex shapes such as **fall–rise**, **rise–fall**, **fall–rise–fall** or **rise–fall–rise**.

Different linguistic functions of pitch can be distinguished. If standard patterns of pitch contribute to the identification of words over a variable number of syllables, this is referred to as **word-based tone**. If the domain over which pitch is distinctive is the syllable, this will be called a use of **syllable-based tone**. Many languages of Africa, Southeast Asia and the Americas exploit this syllable-based use of pitch. Both lexical tone and syllable tone can be regarded as fulfilling a **tonal function**.

Patterns of significant pitch movement over domains longer than the word, that is, word-groups, phrases or whole utterances, fulfil an **intonational function**. All languages show intonational uses of pitch, whether they display tonal functions or not. An example of an intonational function of pitch can be seen in English, where a strongly rising pitch-contour at the end of an utterance such as *Seal-culling is humane* carries a different message from the same phrase said with a strongly falling pitch-contour at the end of the utterance.

Matters of the mean value, overall ranges and the typical degree of fluctuation which characterize the pitch behaviour of a speaker can be described alternatively as types of setting. Such **pitch-settings** are considered at the end of chapter 15.

Analogously to pitch, loudness varies within the speaker's **organic loudness range**, **linguistic loudness range**, **paralinguistic loudness range** and **loudness-span**. Loudness values also show a somewhat similar **declination** effect. Such loudness effects have received very little research to date. The inherent loudness of individual segment-types has been called their **sonority**. A hierarchy of such sonority has been proposed as a basis for explaining a number of phonological issues such as syllable-structure constraints on the syllabic location of particular segment-types, discussed in chapter 15.

5.11.3 *The metrical analysis of speech*

The prosodic and metrical properties of speech are described in this book on the basis of their musical attributes. Thus the prosodic analysis of speech, summarized in the preceding section, considers matters to do with the melodic performance of speech. Metrical factors are taken to include stress and rhythm. The domain of stress is the syllable, and in those languages which exploit stress linguistically we can refer to **syllable-stress**. Broad divisions are normally made between a maximum of three degrees of **lexical word-stress** – **primary stress**, **secondary stress** and **unstressed**. In some languages lexical stress falls on a fixed syllable in the structure of the word, and in others it is more variable. Lexical word-stress, as part of the make-up of individual words, should be distinguished from **emphatic stress**, which is a property of utterances, with optional location on the syllables of the utterance.

Stress is one way of making a syllable perceptually more **prominent**. Another way is **syllable weight**, where the prominence of the syllable derives from its segmental and structural make-up. **Heavy syllables** are those, for example, with either a long vowel, or a short vowel followed by a long consonant or at least two consonants. **Light syllables** are those which do not fulfil these conditions.

The interaction of syllabic timing with stress and syllable weight gives speech a perceived **rhythm**, and different types of interaction lead to different perceptions of rhythm. A tenacious but controversial view of rhythm in speech suggests that all speech tends to be performed in an **isochronous** way, that is, with given units of speech recurring on a regular basis. When a language shows a tendency for every syllable to be heard as lasting very approximately for the same amount of time (at a given rate of speaking), it is said to exploit a **syllable-based rhythm**. An example of such a language is said to be Spanish. When a language shows a rhythmic patterning perceived as based on the intervals between stressed syllables tending to sound approximately equal, it is said to use a **stress-based rhythm**. English is often said to use a stress-based rhythm, and a typical consequence for unstressed syllables following a stressed syllable within the rhythmic unit in English is for these unstressed syllables to be compressed in time, more or less in proportion to the number of syllables in the rhythmic unit (the 'foot'). This compression can be facilitated by processes of **syllable re-organization**, and/or by mechanisms of **vowel reduction** (making the pronunciation of a vowel shorter, less loud, lower in pitch and more central in quality). In some languages the perception of rhythm is said to be constrained by considerations of syllable weight, rather than stress. Such languages are said to show a **mora-based rhythm**, and an often-cited example is Japanese.

The timing constraints on which these categories depend are in fact extremely difficult to establish empirically by instrumental measures of actual speech production. Hypotheses about isochronous rhythmic phenomena in speech are then sustainable only by appeal to a number of factors (such as syllabic structure, and utterance-marginal effects which act as a brake on the rate of speech at the beginnings and ends of the utterances) which can be held to exercise a perturbing influence on the supposed rhythm of a given utterance. The concept of speech rhythm as isochronous then entails positing an underlying regularity which can be recaptured only on a perceptual basis, and normally only by native listeners, through their deep knowledge of the phonological forms of the lexicon of the language. A more profitable view is that perceived rhythm is a property of speech arising from the interaction of segmental sonority, syllable structure, syllable weight and lexical stress, in the timing relationships and fluctuations of prominence perceived as existing between successive syllables. The view that the rhythm of speech is dominated by perceptual, cognitive and phonological factors, and that in addition listeners have a universal tendency to impose a certain degree of rhythmicity on their perception of speech material, will be explored in chapter 16.

5.11.4 *The temporal organization of speech*

The speaking-turns of real speech vary in their continuity, with the speaker signalling hesitation by pausing, or by pronouncing various hesitation noises. Equally, real speech varies in its speed of utterance. The continuity and the rate of speech are non-linguistic factors, available for signalling both paralinguistic information about the speaker's attitudinal or emotional state, and/or extralinguistic information about attributes of speaker-identity and personality.

5.11.4.1 *Continuity of speech*

Pauses in speech can be divided into filled pauses and silent pauses. **Filled pauses** are pauses during which some non-linguistic material such as *er, um, mm* is pronounced. **Silent pauses** contain no such fillers. **Continuous speech** can then be described as a speaking-turn without pauses of any sort (and without the prolongation of linguistic material that is another sign of hesitation). **Non-continuous speech** is any speaking-turn which includes one or more of these signals of hesitation. Chapter 17 also discusses the further matter of **fluent** versus **interrupted speech** (which is not quite synonymous with continuous and non-continuous speech respectively).

5.11.4.2 *Rate of speech*

Two different concepts are necessary to come to grips with the rate (or tempo) of speech. One is **articulation rate**, which is the rate at which a given utterance is produced. The speech material measured by articulation rate therefore excludes silent pauses by virtue of the definition of an utterance, which begins and ends with silence. But it includes all audible speech material within the utterance – the syllables (however prolonged they might be for reasons of hesitation) that make up the linguistic message of the utterance, together with any filled pauses. **Speaking rate**, on the other hand, relates to the rate of speech of the whole speaking-turn. It therefore includes all speech material (linguistic or non-linguistic), together with any silent pauses, that are contained within the overall speaking-turn.

Articulation rate can be measured in units such as syllables per second, and speaking rate in words per minute. For English, a medium articulation rate is about 5.3 syllables per second, and a medium speaking rate a little over 200 words per minute. It is probably necessary to distinguish only between three tempos of speech, **slow**, **medium** and **fast**, and two changes of tempo, **accelerating** and **decelerating**. Articulation rate and speaking rate are not necessarily dependent on each other, because of the role played by pauses in their definitions. Nor are fast rates necessarily correlated with informality of speech style.

Further reading

Orthodox treatments of the **classification by place and manner of articulation** of segmental description, along the lines of the traditional International Phonetic Association model, can be found in most phonetic textbooks, such as Abercrombie (1967), Gimson (1989) and Ladefoged (1975).

PART III

Initiation and phonation

6

Airstream mechanisms

All speech is made by setting a flow of air in motion, and then modifying its progress by superimposing on it some phonatory and articulatory configuration of the vocal organs. The purpose of this chapter is to describe the different ways in which such a flow of air can be made to move, either outwards from the body to the outside atmosphere, or inwards.

There are several different mechanisms for setting a sufficient volume of air in motion to allow audible speech to be produced by phonatory and articulatory modification of the airflow. By far the most common mechanism exploited by the languages of the world is the use of the respiratory system, to provide an outward-flowing stream of air which the larynx and supralaryngeal organs then modulate by phonatory and articulatory action. There are, however, two other mechanisms which are used in a number of different languages to provide the airflow for a usually rather limited number of sounds; one involves the larynx being used as a kind of piston, moving vertically in the cylinder of the pharynx; the other involves the tongue trapping a volume of air between the velum and some point further forward in the mouth.

Two important concepts in classifying the generation of airflow are firstly the identity of the organ that is operative in making the air move, and secondly, the direction of flow of the airstream that is thereby set into motion. The organ that sets the airstream into motion can be called the **initiator** of the airstream, and the different airstream mechanisms can be identified by the initiator concerned. The airstream mechanism which uses the respiratory system as the initiator will be called the **pulmonic airstream mechanism**; the one that uses the larynx as a piston moving in the pharynx will be referred to as the **glottalic airstream mechanism,** and the one that uses the tongue to trap air in the mouth will be referred to as the **velaric airstream mechanism**. The direction that the airflow takes can be labelled with respect to whether it moves outwards from the body, in which case it will be referred to as an **egressive airflow**, or inwards into the body, which will be called an **ingressive**

airflow. Combining the labels for the airstream mechanism and the direction of airflow gives the possibility of discriminating between pulmonic egressive, glottalic egressive and velaric ingressive airstreams, for example. In these cases, the airstream mechanisms are single; but it is also not uncommon for languages to use, for some of their articulations, a simultaneous combination of different airstream mechanisms.

6.1 The pulmonic airstream mechanism

The respiratory system is the initiator of the pulmonic airstream mechanism, providing a flow of air which can be modified by phonatory and articulatory action. The activities of the respiratory system during speech are very different from those during quiet breathing. In quiet breathing, most people breathe in and out about twelve times a minute, with the act of breathing out (expiration) taking only slightly longer than that of breathing in (inspiration). In speaking, the expiratory phase is very much longer than the inspiratory phase. In addition, where quiet breathing chiefly exploits muscular action for inspiration, and largely mechanical and elastic recoil forces as the principal means of expiration, the pulmonic egressive mechanism in speaking depends on positive muscular action as well as on these recoil factors.

Few textbooks on speech give more than the most cursory account of the working of the respiratory system. The impression often given is that the function of the respiratory system in producing an outflowing stream of air of sufficient volume for the needs of speech is relatively simple, and that the significant complexity in speech production lies more in the articulatory domain. An outstanding exception to this tradition is the chapter by Hixon (1973: 73–125). As he comments, 'actually, there is great complexity in the events of respiration during speech, complexity that equals and in many respects surpasses that of events in other parts of the speaking machinery' (*ibid.*: 99). This foundational textbook is not the place to explore the full intricacy of this complexity, but the comment offered by Hixon is a salutary reminder that the customary focus of phonetic textbooks on largely articulatory matters is a highly partial view of the complex physiology that the brain routinely controls to produce the patterns of speech.

The account offered here will be limited to a simplified presentation of the main mechanical, muscular and aerodynamic principles of controlling the pulmonic egressive airstream predominantly used in speech. (Readers for whom this may seem too detailed could move now to section 6.1.1.)

The principal task of the respiratory system in its role as a contributor to the performance of a given utterance is to provide an outflowing stream of pulmonic air at the required pressure and flow-rate, against the dynamically changing moment-to-moment resistance superimposed on the flow by phonatory and articulatory actions. There are three concepts related to air-pressure that will be useful here. One is **atmospheric pressure**, the general external pressure caused by the weight of air in the atmosphere above the speaker. Another is **intra-oral pressure**, the air-pressure inside the mouth which rises and falls under the joint influence of the pulmonic (or other) airstream and the presence of articulatory constrictions preventing the easy outflow (or inflow) of air to (or from) the external atmosphere. The third concept is air-pressure in the lungs, which can be called **pulmonic pressure**. Pulmonic pressure can be equated to **sub-glottal pressure**, a phrase more normally found in phonetics textbooks to mean the air-pressure in the pulmonic airstream just below the vocal folds. Sub-glottal pressure variation in speech has been extensively investigated, and it is possible to say on this basis that perceived loudness is broadly proportional to sub-glottal pressure (Isshiki 1964; Ladefoged 1967), though in a non-linear way.

Clark and Yallop (1990: 26) suggest that sub-glottal pressure is 'relative to the overall level of vocal effort'. This notion of 'vocal effort' is well established in the phonetic literature, but it is highly underspecified. We shall see below, for example, that a given sub-glottal pressure could well be generated on different occasions by different degrees of counter-balancing inspiratory and expiratory muscular effort, depending on the current state of inflation of the lungs.

In order to approach a description of the mechanisms exploited by the respiratory system in producing various flow-rates and sub-glottal pressures, it will be helpful to begin with a small number of technical distinctions between the capacity of the lungs and different volumes within this capacity. (In the discussion below, the term 'lung' will be taken to mean 'lungs and airways'.) Figure 6.1, after Hixon (1973: 95) (who adapted it in turn from Pappenheimer *et al.* 1950), shows four different lung volumes and four different lung capacities. A concept applied to normal breathing is that the regular **respiratory cycle** of inspiration and expiration can be regarded as 'tidal'. The **tidal volume** is then the volume of air breathed in and out during this cycle. This volume is responsive to the current oxygen requirements of the body. When the person is at rest, normal patterns of breathing are realized as **quiet tidal breathing**. The minimum value of this quiet tidal breathing can be called the **resting expiratory level**.

There is a limit to how much air a person can take in by inspiration beyond the peak of the tidal volume, set by anatomical and physiological constraints. This volume is called the **inspiratory reserve volume**. Similarly,

163

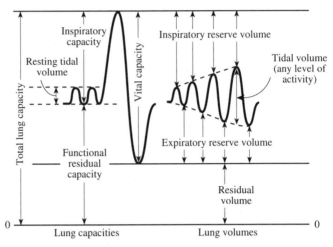

Figure 6.1 Classification of lung volumes and capacities in the respiratory system (adapted from Hixon 1973: 95, after Pappenheimer *et al.* 1950)

there are anatomical and physiological constraints on how much air an individual can breathe out in expiration beyond the minimum values of the tidal volume. This is called the **expiratory reserve volume**. Exhausting the expiratory reserve volume – using up all the available air in breathing out from the minimum of the tidal volume – is nevertheless not the same as exhausting the total capacity of the lungs. A **residual volume** always remains.

The **inspiratory capacity** of the lungs is the maximum amount of air that can be breathed in from the minimum value of the tidal volume. The inspiratory capacity is thus made up of adding the inspiratory reserve volume to the tidal volume. The **vital capacity** of the lungs is the maximum amount of air that can be exhaled after a maximum inspiration. The vital capacity is therefore made up of the combination of the tidal volume, the inspiratory reserve volume and the expiratory reserve volume. The **functional residual capacity** is the amount of air in the lungs at the minimum of the tidal volume – it hence includes the expiratory reserve volume and the residual volume. Finally, the **total lung capacity** is the volume of air in the lungs after a maximum inspiration. Table 6.1 shows all of the above lung volumes and capacities in litres, for a typical healthy young adult male speaker, standing upright, in atmospheric pressure at sea level (Hixon 1973: 96). It is important to specify that the speaker is standing, since lung volumes and capacities change when a speaker changes posture, because of the effect of gravity on the configuration of the respiratory system. It is also relevant to indicate that atmospheric pressure is a factor, since it is the relative balance between atmospheric pressure and the air-pressure in the respiratory system that determines whether pulmonic air flows egressively or ingressively.

Table 6.1 *Lung volumes and capacities*
for a young, healthy, adult male speaker,
standing upright

Lung volume or capacity	Magnitude in litres
Tidal volume	0.5
Inspiratory reserve volume	2.5
Expiratory reserve volume	2.0
Residual volume	2.0
Inspiratory capacity	3.0
Vital capacity	5.0
Functional residual capacity	4.0
Total lung capacity	7.0

Source: After Hixon (1973: 96)

A key concept in understanding how the respiratory system works is that of **relaxation pressure**. This is the pressure in the lungs and airways which is produced by non-muscular forces. Whether the pulmonic air will flow egressively or ingressively whenever the respiratory muscles are relaxed will depend on whether the lungs are currently expanded or contracted relative to their volume at the resting expiratory level. If the lungs are more inflated than the resting expiratory level, then non-muscular relaxation forces generated by elastic and mechanical recoil factors in the lungs, chest, diaphragm and abdomen will have the effect of compressing the lungs back to the resting level, and expiration will result. If the lungs are relatively deflated compared to their volume at the resting expiratory level, then the same non-muscular relaxation forces will have the effect of allowing the lungs to reflate back to the resting level, and inspiration will occur. In either case, unless positive muscular effort is recruited to over-ride the relaxation pressure effect, the return to a resting level is involuntary and automatic.

The action of relaxation pressure can be thought of as exercising a spring-like effect on lung-volume. The result of the spring is to cause expiration at high lung-volumes and inspiration at low lung-volumes, relative to the resting expiratory volume. Relaxation pressure is in direct proportion to lung-volume in the middle of the volume range, while in the extremes of the range pressure changes more abruptly. It follows that 'the amount of muscular pressure required at a given instant during speech depends upon the

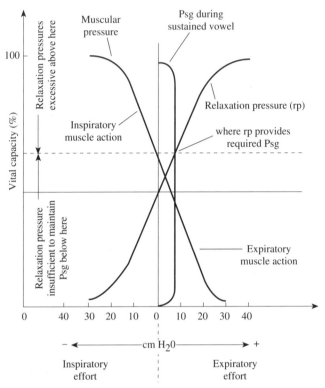

Figure 6.2 The relationship between counter-balancing expiratory and inspiratory forces and relaxation pressure in the respiratory system's contribution to the production of a sustained vocoid (adapted from Clark and Yallop 1990: 28, after Hixon 1973: 102 and Agostoni and Mead 1964)

[pulmonic] pressure needed and the relaxation pressure available at the prevailing lung volume' (Hixon 1973: 97). The type of muscular control needed for pulmonic egressive airflow during speech is hence a collaboration between expiratory and inspiratory efforts, being used in a balanced 'pushing' versus 'checking' mode. After taking a relatively deep breath, for example, a speaker is likely to need to use a partly 'checking' action of the inspiratory muscle system in the early part of a long utterance, to control the expiratory contribution of the relaxation pressure in a fine-tuned way for the purposes of speech, before switching over to a predominantly 'pushing' action of the expiratory muscle system to counter-act the now-inspiratory effect of relaxation pressure once that pressure becomes less than the atmospheric pressure.

Figure 6.2 gives a graphical example of this counter-balancing process, in describing the way in which inspiratory effort switches over to expiratory effort at the point where relaxation pressure becomes inadequate to support the steady outflow of air required for the production of a sustained voiced vowel. The figure is adapted from Clark and Yallop (1990: 28), in which they incorporate information from Hixon (1973: 102) and Agostoni and Mead (1964), showing the change-over point from inspiratory checking to expiratory pushing relative to the contribution from relaxation pressure, against the steadily dropping percentage of vital capacity after a maximum inspiration. In this figure, the timecourse of the production of the vowel can be read as running from top to bottom, as the remaining percentage of vital capacity decreases. The abbreviation 'Psg' in the figure stands for 'sub-glottal pressure'.

It is therefore much too simplistic to suggest that the positive muscular action needed to control egressive pulmonic airflow is exercised by the expiratory muscle system alone. As Hixon (1973: 106) comments:

> the respiratory pump accomplishes the task which speech imposes upon it by adding, at each instant, a muscular pressure that is precisely equal to the difference between the (pulmonic) pressure desired and the relaxation pressure available. The important implication of this statement is that *each (pulmonic) pressure produced in speech demands a different muscular pressure at each lung volume.*
> (emphasis as in original)

The complexity of the brain's task in controlling the muscular support for an aerodynamic situation that dynamically changes throughout an utterance is evident.

6.1.1 *Respiratory support for syllables, stress and loudness*

A distinction can be drawn between the use of the respiratory system to provide a continual flow of air as the basis for whole utterances of normal pulmonic egressive speech, and the more momentary requirements of individual syllables. Many writers on phonetics from the time of Stetson (1928, 2nd edn 1951) have made appeal to what Hixon (1973: 119) calls 'pulsatile' variations in the pulmonic flow for speech, with each muscularly initiated pulse corresponding to a phonetic syllable. Ladefoged (1967) and his co-workers, however, have shown very clearly that in normal speech there is no clear one-to-one correlation between syllables at a phonological level and pulsed, muscular acts of the respiratory system at a phonetic level.

It may be that in conditions of unusual emphasis, such as in a sergeant-major's shouted commands on the parade ground, a more clearcut relationship exists. For everyday speech, nevertheless, it seems unnecessary to posit a respiratory pulse as an obligatory part of the phonetic manifestation of each phonological syllable. Broad tendencies for the respiratory system to increase expiratory effort when phonologically stressed syllables are being uttered can characterize the phonology of many languages, but this is the only type of pulsatile respiratory variation to which explicit appeal will be made here. Chapter 16 discusses in more detail the respiratory support for the production of stressed syllables. The use of the respiratory system for controlling loudness as a part of paralinguistic behaviour will also be discussed below, in chapter 15.

6.1.2   *The pulmonic ingressive airstream*

Speech is possible on a pulmonic ingressive airstream – speaking on an indrawn breath – but this has not so far been found to operate systematically for distinctive phonological purposes in any language of the world. There is, however, one speaker of one language who has been reported as using a pulmonic ingressive airstream on an allophonic basis, and that is a speaker of the Punguu accent of the Tfuea dialect of Tsou, an Austronesian language spoken on the slopes of Mount Ali in Southern Taiwan (Fuller 1990: 9). Tsou has three dialects, spoken by some 3,500 speakers distributed in eight villages, but Fuller notes that the use of this airstream 'may be a sub-dialectal feature unique to the village of Punguu'.

Punguu Tsou is said to use the pulmonic ingressive airstream on two structurally conditioned allophonic segments. Using the diacritic [ɥ] to represent an ingressive pulmonic airstream, placed after the relevant segmental symbol, these are [fɥ] and [hɥ]. These labiodental (fricative) and glottal (approximant) segments occur word-initially before stops (usually glottal stops, but including affricated stops), and pulmonic egressive segments occur everywhere else. Expressed in phonological rule notation, this constraint could be summarized as:

$$/f/ \Rightarrow \left\{ \begin{array}{l} [fɥ] \: / \: \#\_\_\_ \: \text{Stop} \\ [f] \end{array} \right.$$

where the symbol '#' means a preceding word boundary. The only other voiceless fricative phoneme in Punguu Tsou is /s/, and this has only pulmonic egressive allophones, as in [smoftoŋə] 'to hit' and [sɓe'oxə] 'to fall'. Examples of the ingressive and egressive segments given by Fuller (1990: 10–11) are:

Pulmonic ingressive and egressive labiodental segments in one
Punguu Tsou idiolect

['fˀuhu] 'back'   [mafuˈiŋu] 'woods'
['fˀtsuju] 'egg'   ['fo] 'meat/fish'
['fˀhŋu] 'head'   [fuiˈfuu] 'sand'
['fˀisi] 'hair'   [fioˀu] 'tree bark'
['fˀkoi] 'snake'   ['fˀue] 'sweet potato'

Pulmonic ingressive and egressive glottal segments in one
Punguu Tsou idiolect

['hˌuju] 'blood'   [tsuˈhumu] 'water'
[hˌˀisi] 'ashes'   [paˈhisi] 'wing'
['hˌˀtsuju] 'mountain, hill'   [hɔˈfɔia] 'yellow'

As noted above, these articulations were identified in the speech of a single speaker. Subsequent investigation has shown, however, that these patterns are at least partly inconsistent with those of fourteen other speakers of Punguu Tsou who were interviewed, all of whom pronounce a labiodental ejective [f'] where this speaker uses a pulmonic ingressive fricative (P. Ladefoged, personal communication).

6.1.2.1   *Paralinguistic use of the pulmonic ingressive airstream*

Pulmonic ingressive speech is used paralinguistically in a number of Western cultures. In Norwegian, for example, there is a not uncommon pulmonic ingressive pronunciation of *ja* [jˌɑː] ('yes') and *nei* [nˌæɪ] ('no'), where the whole syllable is pronounced on an indrawn breath. It may be voiceless throughout, or may be made with breathy or whispery voice for the first part. (Breathy and whispery voice are described in detail in the next chapter). The word *ja* pronounced in this way expresses sympathy, agreement or commiseration, and *nei* expresses surprise (A. Foldvik, personal communication). In Danish, a pulmonic ingressive [jˌaˌ] for 'yes' is commonly used in the same way as in Norwegian. In addition, a pulmonic ingressive pronunciation of [nˌaɪ] for 'no' can be used in Danish to express sympathy. This pronunciation can also apparently be used as a 'weak rejection by children of an accusation by parents, implying that the accusation is correct' (J. Verhoeven, personal communication), as in:

Parent : 'You did take the money, didn't you'
Child   : [nˌaɪ] 'No'

A somewhat similar usage occurs in English, where *yes* [jɛs] can be pronounced with the [jˌɛˌ] sequence performed on a pulmonic ingressive airstream (often with breathy voice), followed by [s] being uttered on a normal pulmonic egressive airflow. The paralinguistic meaning of pronouncing *yes* in this way seems to be to communicate an attitude of reluctant and slightly exasperated compliance with the exigent wishes or assertions of an insistent interlocutor. Ohala (1983: 192) describes 'pulmonic ingressive vocalization' as 'a stylistic variant of pulmonic egressive speech', giving the example of 'Swedish [ja] (on ingressive voice) "yes" (emphatic), French [wi] (ingressive voice) "yes" (used primarily by females)'. A more extended example comes from Finnish, where speakers who run out of breath towards the end of a long utterance sometimes complete it on a pulmonic ingressive airstream, often substituting whisper for voicing (A. Foldvik, personal communication).

Speech performed on a pulmonic ingressive airstream typically uses a slightly different phonatory quality from speech produced on a pulmonic egressive airstream, with ingressive phonation showing a less efficient mode of vibration than the more habitual and practised egressive mode. Perhaps because of this difference, pulmonic ingressive speech is sometimes used for the purpose of ritual disguise. Catford (1977a: 68) cites Dieth (1950) as discussing the Swiss-German custom of 'Fensterle', in which a village boy speaks to his sweetheart through her window, conventionally disguising his voice from her parents by using a pulmonic ingressive airstream. A similar function of ritual voice disguise during courtship is reported by Conklin (1959) as occurring in the Hanunóo culture of the Philippines, where a suitor is said to hide his visible identity from a girl's parents by covering his head with a blanket, and to conceal his audible identity by speaking on an ingressive pulmonic airstream.

A somewhat similar usage in Greek is described by Catford in a later book (1988: 31), where he comments that pulmonic ingressive speech can be used to disguise the voice, and that he has 'heard Greek spoken with pulmonic suction initiation for precisely this purpose by disguised mummers on a feast-day in a village in Cyprus'. In his earlier book, he also mentions a segmental case of the pulmonic ingressive airstream being used in Damin, an Australian (North Queensland) ritual language of the Lardil of Mornington Island, but thinks that this use (to create a 'pulmonic suction' [l]) may have been a deliberate invention (Catford 1977a: 65).

6.1.3 *Segmental use of the pulmonic egressive system*

A pulmonic egressive airstream is overwhelmingly the most common airstream used in speech, and the majority of sounds in every language are performed on this basis. Unless explicit mention is made to the contrary, it will be taken from this point onwards that the airstream involved in the production of any sound under discussion is provided by the pulmonic egressive mechanism.

Some sample symbols for sounds made with a pulmonic egressive airstream, which may be helpful in interpreting the comments below on non-pulmonic sounds, are as follows. The symbols [p, t, k, q] all represent voiceless oral stops made on the pulmonic egressive airstream mechanism, with the vocal tract being momentarily closed to allow air-pressure to build up before being released with a tiny but audible burst of noise. The closures are made for the stop sounds mentioned above by the action of the lips closing against each other (voiceless labial stop [p]), or the tongue against the alveolar ridge just behind the upper teeth (voiceless alveolar stop [t]), against the underside of the velum (voiceless velar stop [k]), or against the uvula at the very end of the velum (voiceless uvular stop [q]). The pulmonic egressive voiced oral stop counterparts respectively to these sounds are labial [b], alveolar [d], velar [ɡ] and uvular [ɢ]. Other pulmonic egressive symbols (voiceless alveolar fricative [s], voiced alveolar fricative [z] and voiced labial nasal stop [m]) were mentioned in the previous chapter.

6.2 The glottalic airstream mechanism

The initiator in the **glottalic airstream mechanism** is the whole larynx, which is either pulled upwards by the laryngeal elevator muscle groups, in the production of sounds made on a glottalic egressive mechanism, or downwards by the laryngeal depressor muscle groups, for sounds made with a glottalic ingressive mechanism (Abercrombie 1967: 28; Catford 1977a: 68). When the glottalic mechanism is the sole airstream mechanism involved, the glottis is closed, with the vocal folds together, blocking off the volume of air in the lungs from air in the rest of the vocal apparatus. During this time, speakers are in effect 'holding their breath'. Because the larynx moves vertically in the pharynx in this mechanism, it has also been called the 'pharyngeal' airstream mechanism (Pike 1943:90). The term 'glottalic' is preferred here because it more memorably reflects the involvement of the closed or nearly closed glottis.

Sounds made on a glottalic egressive airstream are called **ejectives**. These are usually made with the vocal tract momentarily either completely blocked, or nearly blocked, by the tongue or the lips at some location along its length. The velum blocks off escape of air through the nasal tract, so that the effect of the abrupt rise of the larynx, with the glottis closed and the upper larynx possibly constricted, is to compress the air in the vocal tract. If the vocal tract is completely closed (in a stop articulation), when the closure is released the compressed air bursts out in a vigorous explosion. If the vocal tract is only nearly closed, leaving a very narrow gap (in a fricative articulation), the compressed air hisses out briefly but audibly through the constricted passage.

It is also physically possible to make a variety of other types of sound on a glottalic egressive mechanism, such as tongue trills of a short duration, but the only ejective sounds that have been found in languages so far have been those described above – **ejective stops** and **ejective fricatives**, together with **ejective affricates**, a type of articulation where a stop is released with a short fricative offset phase.

Ejectives are found in many languages in Africa, and in North, Central and South America. They are found occasionally in Asia, for example in the Indian sub-continent in one dialect of Gujarati, in Bishnupriya and some East Bengali dialects (Masica 1991: 104). They are also characteristic of the Caucasian languages, such as Georgian and Circassian (Adyghe) (Catford 1977b: 70). The transcriptional convention for identifying ejective sounds is to put an apostrophe after the segmental symbol, as in [k'] for an ejective velar stop with a closure made by the back of the tongue against the velum, or [t'] for an ejective alveolar stop with a closure made by the tip or blade of the tongue against the alveolar ridge, or [s'] for an ejective alveolar fricative where the air is forced through a very narrow constriction between the blade of the tongue and the alveolar ridge. Examples of ejective sounds used in Zulu are:

> *Ejectives in Zulu*
> [ɪt'wɛːt'wɛ] 'nervousness'   [umt'ːaːt'a] 'a bay'
> [ɪsɪk'ɛːbɛ] 'boat'   [k'aːk'ɑ] 'surround'

Examples of a contrast between pulmonic egressive voiceless stops and glottalic egressive ejective stops in K'ekchi, a Quichean language of Guatemala (Pinkerton 1986: 130) are:

> *Ejectives in K'ekchi*
> [t'oqok] 'to throw'   [toqok] 'to break'
> [faːt'ok] 'you threw it'   [faːtok] ' you broke it'

Sounds made with a glottalic ingressive airstream mechanism are called **implosives**. The larynx, with the glottis closed, is pulled downwards, and any air trapped between the larynx and any closure higher up the vocal tract is rarefied in pressure. When the vocal-tract closure is released, the outside air flows in at atmospheric pressure to fill the relative vacuum. Only oral stops seem to be made on this mechanism for linguistic use. Ashby (1990) describes a range of other implosive articulations which are articulatorily feasible, but which do not seem to be used in spoken languages.

The transcriptional convention for identifying a (voiceless) implosive is to add a right-curling diacritic to the top corner of the segmental symbol, as in the voiceless velar implosive symbol [ƙ]. We shall see that this is the same diacritic device as is used in voiced implosives, and the generalization of the right-curling diacritic being added to the top corner of the segmental symbol to mean 'implosive', rather than as previously merely 'voiced implosive', was one of the innovations recommended by the 1989 Kiel IPA Convention on phonetic symbols.

Voiceless implosives of this sort are rare in languages. Tojolabal, a language spoken in Mexico, and Cakchiquel, another Quichean language of Guatemala in Central America, are said to use them (E. Pike 1963: 104, 107). Campbell (1973), cited by Pinkerton (1986: 126), notes that in fact all the Quichean languages, spoken in the area round Guatemala city, make phonologically contrastive use of [ɗ], a voiceless uvular implosive made by rarefying the pressure between the larynx and a closure made between the very back of the tongue and the uvula (the rearmost part of the velum). Illustrations from Tojolabal and Cakchiquel are shown in the following examples:

Voiceless ejectives and voiceless implosives in Tojolabal
[ɓoɓ] 'to be able'   [pʰopʰ] 'straw mat'
[sk'a'ɓi] 'her sleeve'   [ɓa'k'ɛtʰ] 'meat'

Voiceless ejectives and voiceless implosives in Cakchiquel
['k'olonɬ] 'a gatherer'   ['kʰolonɬ] 'a deceiver'
['ɗolonɬ] 'Saviour'   ['qχolonɘɬ] 'a stripper of bark'

(In the above examples, the symbol [ɬ] means a voiceless type of [l] produced with friction, and [χ] refers to a voiceless fricative made at the same uvular place as [q]. Both [ɬ] and [χ], as examples of fricative segments, are explained in detail in chapter 9.)

Implosives which are made on a complex airstream mechanism, combining a glottalic ingressive mechanism with egressive pulmonic voicing to give a **voiced implosive**, are much more frequently found than implosives made only on a glottalic ingressive airstream. The production of these voiced implosives is discussed below in section 6.4 on combined airstream mechanisms. The production of **voicing** is discussed separately, in chapter 7.

6.3 The velaric airstream mechanism

This mechanism is sometimes called the 'oral' airstream mechanism, because all the actions involved happen in the mouth. It might reasonably be called the 'lingual' airstream mechanism, since the prime initiator is the tongue, but it is commonly called the **velaric airstream mechanism**. This is because a major ingredient in the production of the airstream is a complete closure made by the back of the tongue against the velum. A second closure is also made, further forward in the mouth, either by the tip, blade or front of the tongue, or by the lips. The back of the tongue, maintaining its contact with the soft palate, is then drawn backwards and downwards along the slope of the roof of the mouth. Alternatively or simultaneously, the front of the tongue is drawn downwards. This action expands the volume of air trapped between the two closures, rarefying the intra-oral air-pressure. When the more forward of the two closures is released, the outside air at atmospheric pressure flows in to fill the partial vacuum.

Sounds made on this ingressive velaric mechanism are called **clicks**, and only stops and affricates have been found in phonological use in languages. The use of the term 'click' already indicates that the velaric airstream mechanism is being used to perform a stop articulation, so it is not normally necessary to specify 'velaric ingressive' or 'stop' in the label for such a segment. There are no reports so far of any linguistic use of sounds made with a velaric egressive airstream mechanism, though it is physiologically possible to make sounds in this way.

Examples of languages that use clicks as part of their consonantal stock are the Khoisan languages of Southern Africa, such as: Bushman; Nama (previously called Hottentot, e.g. by Beach 1938, which is now regarded as a pejorative name); !Xóõ which is spoken in Botswana and Namibia (Ladefoged and Traill 1993); and !Xũ, spoken in Angola and Botswana (Snyman 1969; Traill 1973). Clicks are also found in the Southern Bantu languages Xhosa and Zulu (Doke 1926, Ladefoged 1971: 28). Two East African languages which use clicks are Sandawe and Hadzapi (Hatsa), in Tanzania (Catford 1977a: 72).

The original IPA-approved phonetic symbols for click segments at different places of articulation used to have the form [⊙, ɹ, ʗ, ʖ]. These symbol shapes (except for the shared [⊙]) are at typographical odds with the symbols [⊙, ǀ, ǃ, ǁ, ǂ] originally devised for transcribing clicks by Lepsius (1855), and traditionally used by Africanists. Köhler *et al.* (1988) made a proposal to the 1989 Kiel Convention of the IPA that the Lepsius symbols should be substituted, because of the widespread use of these symbols in the extensive literature on the predominantly African languages using click segments. This proposal was accepted by the IPA, and is now incorporated in the IPA phonetic alphabet reproduced in appendix I. Köhler *et al.* (1988:140–1) lists a summary of the Lepsius-based symbols actually used by a number of Africanist and phonetician authors for their accounts of the Khoisan languages. For mnemonic convenience, to help in interpreting pre-1989 non-

Africanist writings on clicks, a comparison of the old and the new IPA symbols is given in table 6.2.

Table 6.2 *A comparison of the old (pre-1989) IPA symbols for click segments and the current symbols recommended by the 1989 Kiel Convention of the IPA*

Place of articulation	Old IPA symbol	Current IPA symbol
labial	[ʘ]	[ʘ]
dental	[ʇ]	[ǀ]
alveolar	([ʇ])	[ǃ]
post-alveolar	[C]	[ǃ]
alveolar lateral	[ʖ]	[ǁ]
palato-alveolar or palatal	([C])	[ǂ]

Source: Adapted from Köhler *et al.* (1988: 140)

Clicks are also used in a paralinguistic function. Because of the wide familiarity of these paralinguistic clicks to many readers, these will be described before transcriptions of linguistic examples are introduced, to facilitate understanding of the articulatory actions involved. In English, and in many Western cultures, a click made with the front closure on the inner surfaces of the front upper teeth, with the influx of air flowing in over the central part of the tongue blade, signifies impatience or exasperation. Orthographically it is often written *tut tut*, or *tsk tsk*, and the recommended IPA phonetic symbol given in table 6.2 is [ǀ]. The phonetic label for this sound is a **voiceless dental click**, and the sequence of initiatory actions used to produce the click are shown in figure 6.3a–c. Because of the necessity in clicks of two closures being formed simultaneously in the mouth, one of them always being a velar closure, clicks are by definition **double articulations**. The category of double articulations is dealt with in detail in chapter 11, but to give recognition to the essential velar closure in clicks, the symbol for voiceless clicks used in this book will follow the precedent set by Ladefoged and Traill (1984, 1993) of including [k] in the formation of a more explicitly complete symbol, as in [k͡ǀ], rather than the more implicit IPA convention of the single [ǀ] etc.

The composite shapes of other click symbols to be used in this book are [k͡ʘ] (labial), [k͡ǃ] (alveolar or post-alveolar), [k͡ǁ] (alveolar lateral), and [k͡ǂ] (palato-alveolar or palatal). The most universally familiar of these clicks is the **voiceless labial click** [k͡ʘ], which represents the action of kissing, with the front closure made and released by the lips. In the **voiceless alveolar** or **post-alveolar click** [k͡ǃ], the influx of air occurs centrally over the

175

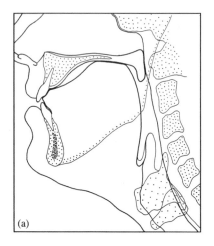

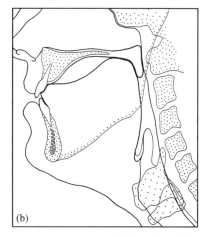
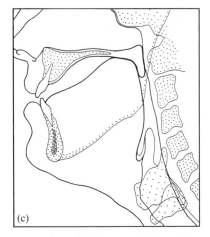

Figure 6.3 The action of the vocal organs in producing a velaric ingressive voiceless dental click [k͡ǀ]: (a) first stage, velic and anterior closure; (b) second stage, expansion of the enclosed oral space; (c) third stage, release of the anterior closure

tip or blade of the tongue as it is released from full contact with the alveolar ridge or the post-alveolar region. In the voiceless post-alveolar click [k͡!], the tongue tip/blade is sometimes allowed to be sucked upwards and inwards by the negative intra-oral pressure created by the velaric mechanism, while still maintaining complete post-alveolar closure. When the tongue tip/blade is removed from complete contact, the tongue is in a slightly curled retroflex position, and in uncurling, the underside of the tip of the tongue often (but not necessarily) strikes the floor of the mouth with a resonating percussive effect. It is this resonant percussion, following an instant after the release of the front oral closure, that gives the voiceless post-alveolar retroflex click the onomatopoeic basis that children exploit in their imitations of the clacking and clopping of horses' hooves. The full phonetic label for a click performed in this way would be a **voiceless post-alveolar retroflex click**. The shape of the earlier IPA symbol [ʗ] gave mnemonic recognition to this retroflex possibility, in that the symbol for the alveolar/post-alveolar click shared with other retroflex symbols such as [ʈ] a descender curling to the right.

In the **voiceless alveolar lateral click** [k͡ǁ], the influx of air flows in over the side of the tongue, with the tip or blade of the tongue being held in central contact with the alveolar ridge. In English, this click is used to persuade horses to start or to accelerate (to 'gee-up'), and is used by extension as a paralinguistic signal of similar encouragement to human listeners. The influx of air for the **voiceless palato-alveolar** or **palatal click** [k͡ǂ] is central, as an extensive domed contact formed between the blade and front of the tongue against the palato-alveolar or palatal region is released.

Linguistic examples of some clicks can be found in the following instances from Nama and !Xóõ (Ladefoged and Traill 1993):

Voiceless dental, alveolar, palatal and alveolar lateral clicks in Nama
[k͡ǀoa] 'put into' [k͡ǂais] 'calling'
[k͡ǃoas] 'hollow' [k͡ǁaos] 'writing'

Voiceless labial, dental, alveolar, palatal and alveolar lateral clicks in !Xóõ
[k͡ʘoõ] 'dream' [k͡ǀà] 'move off'
[k͡ǃaa] 'wait for' [k͡ǁaã] 'poison'
[k͡ǂaã] 'bone'

Because the defining initiatory actions for clicks take place in the mouth, the possibility arises of simultaneously using a second airstream with the click. Logically, either a pulmonic or a glottalic airstream could be brought into play, but the only option found to be exploited so far in spoken language is the addition of a pulmonic egressive airstream. In fact, when a velaric ingressive click is embedded in continuous speech made with a pulmonic egressive airstream, it is likely (unless a simultaneous glottal stop intervenes) that pulmonic egressive air will fill the pharynx behind the velar closure, and become compressed in exactly the way that a pulmonic egressive voiceless velar stop [k] is formed. In this sense, all such voiceless clicks not only have a [k] component as part of their status as double articulations, but can also be said to be performed on a double airstream mechanism.

The availability of the pulmonic egressive airstream during the performance of clicks brings with it a further option of adding voicing to the pulmonic air flowing through the glottis. Because the back of the tongue is by definition in a position of velar closure, the result is the simultaneous production of a [ɡ] with the click. This is the basis for the category of **voiced clicks**, and the phonetic symbol for a voiced click is made by joining the appropriate click symbol to a [ɡ] symbol with a linker [͡], to make the composite symbol [ɡ͡ǀ], which represents a **voiced dental click**. Other examples of symbols for voiced clicks are [ɡ͡ʘ] (labial), [ɡ͡ǃ] (alveolar or post-alveolar), [ɡ͡ǂ] (palato-alveolar or palatal) and [ɡ͡ǁ] (alveolar lateral), which are all used in contrast to their voiceless counterparts in !Xóõ (Ladefoged and Traill 1993):

> *Voiced labial, dental, alveolar, palatal and alveolar*
> *lateral clicks in !Xóõ*
> [ɡ͡ʘóu] 'wild cat' [ɡ͡ǁàa] 'rub with hand'
> [ɡ͡ǃ a̤e] 'hunt' [ɡ͡ǁáã] 'thigh'
> [ɡ͡ǂaã] 'conceal'

The [̤] diacritic under the symbols in the !Xóõ word for 'hunt' above signify a whispery voice phonation type, described in the next chapter.

This pattern of combining a velaric ingressive airstream with a pulmonic egressive airstream in a double mechanism has yet another possible expression. Given that the movements necessary to make a click are performed solely within the mouth, the soft palate is free to take up either an open or a closed position, without affecting the articulatory actions of the click itself. If the soft palate is in a lowered position during the performance of the click, and if there is a simultaneous pulmonic egressive airstream, then the result will be a **voiceless nasal click**. The symbol for a voiceless nasal click is made by linking a voiceless velar nasal stop symbol [ŋ̊] to the relevant click symbol with a linker, as in [ŋ̊͡ǁ].

Furthermore, if voicing is added to the pulmonic egressive airflow, then the result will be a **voiced nasal click**. The phonetic symbol for a voiced nasal click is made by linking a voiced velar nasal stop symbol [ŋ] to the relevant click symbol with a linker, as in [ŋ͡ǁ]. Ladefoged and Traill (1993) give the following examples of voiced nasal clicks in !Xóõ:

Voiced labial, dental, alveolar, palatal and alveolar lateral nasal clicks in !Xóõ

[ŋʘâje] 'tree'   [ŋǀàa] 'to suit'
[ŋǀan] 'lie horizontal'   [ŋǁàhā] 'amount'
[ŋǂaū] 'right side'

The articulatory closures for click segments can also be released in a variety of ways, some of them involving variations in the control of their timing relationships with phonatory actions. Some of these modifications are described in chapter 12 on co-ordination.

6.4 Combined glottalic and pulmonic airstream mechanisms

Another example of sounds made with combined airstream mechanisms involves the simultaneous use of a pulmonic egressive and a glottalic ingressive airstream to produce a category of sounds called **voiced implosives**, mentioned briefly in section 6.2. In this type of sound, the larynx is drawn downwards, giving a glottalic ingressive airstream, but with the vocal folds held only lightly closed. At the same time, a pulmonic egressive airflow rises through the vocal folds, setting them into voiced vibration. The influences of the two initiators, the larynx and the respiratory system, are thus exercised in momentarily opposite directions. The egressive effect of the pulmonic mechanism is enough to cause audible voiced vibration of the vocal folds, but not enough to overcome completely the rarefaction of the enclosed volume of air in the vocal tract caused by the descending larynx. The overall effect is for air momentarily to flow ingressively into the vocal tract from the outside atmosphere, when the articulatory closure is released.

A question arises about how the airflow through the vocal folds is actually made to move. Catford (1977a: 75) suggests, on the basis of cineradiographic films, that the pulmonic initiator is not in fact active, but merely static, in a fixated position which only provides an unchanging respiratory pressure. The egressive airflow necessary for voiced vibration of the vocal folds would then be the direct product of the movement downwards of the larynx against this fixed pressure. This is an interesting suggestion, and may characterize the careful performance of voiced implosives in short demonstration utterances. In the dynamic activity of continuous speech, though, it seems more likely that voiced implosives embedded in a context of continuous egressive pulmonic airflow would be performed with a more positive expiratory effort.

179

Catford (*ibid.*) also points out that fully voiced stops ostensibly made solely on an egressive pulmonic mechanism are in fact typically made with a certain amount of progressive lowering of the larynx, in order to preserve transglottal airflow for voicing. The difference between pulmonic egressive voiced stops and voiced implosives lies in the relative speed and distance of the larynx lowering movement, with voiced implosives using a faster, larger movement.

Voiced implosives are found in many languages, including Sindhi, Maidu and Uduk (Ladefoged 1971: 26–7). Greenberg (1970) offers a survey of these and other sounds made on the glottalic airstream mechanism in a wide range of languages. The transcriptional convention for identifying a voiced implosive, invented by Doke (1926: 60), is to take the symbol for the corresponding egressive pulmonic voiced stop, say [b], [d], or [g], and add a right-hand curl to the top corner of the symbol, giving [ɓ], [ɗ] or [ɠ]. (As noted earlier, this use of the right-hand curl diacritic attached to the top corner of the segmental symbol was generalized by the IPA in 1989 to all implosive symbols, whether voiced or voiceless). Examples of voiced implosives can be seen in Zulu, and in the West African languages Hausa, and Margi:

> *Voiced implosives in Zulu*
> [ɓɪːza] 'call'   [bɪːza] 'have concern'
> [ɓuːza] 'ask'   [buːza] 'buzz'
>
> *Voiced implosives in Hausa*
> [ɓaɓe] 'estrangement'   [babe] 'grasshopper'
> [ɗaka] 'inside of house' [daka] 'pounding'
>
> *Voiced implosives in Margi*
> [ɓaɓal] 'hard'   [babal] 'open place'
> [ɗiɗi] 'flatus'   [didi] 'dirt'

One final comment on combinations of airstream mechanisms needs to be made. During continuous speech, the articulatory movements of the tongue are sometimes both swift and of large extent. Under these circumstances, the tongue can act as a piston in the cylinder of the mouth, and either push air out, momentarily adding to the overall egressive flow initiated by the respiratory system, or suck air in, counteracting the egressive pulmonic flow. If the ingressive tendency of the **lingual airstream** (properly so labelled) that is thus initiated by the tongue is vigorous enough, it can briefly overcome the pulmonic egressive outflow, and cause an overall ingressive flow for a moment. Airflow records of syllables such as [kwa] occasionally show an ingressive effect of this sort. Such a contextual effect is the incidental result of particular combinations of suitable segmental articulations, however, and is not used contrastively.

6.5 Phonological use of non-pulmonic airstreams

It was said at the beginning of this chapter that the pulmonic egressive airstream mechanism was by far the most common airstream exploited for phonological purposes. The typology of consonant systems in the different languages of the world is dominated by sounds made on a pulmonic airstream. It also seems to be the case that within any given language that makes phonological use of segments made on a non-pulmonic airstream, such segments are out-numbered in the huge majority of cases by comparable segment-types made on the pulmonic airstream mechanism. Pinkerton (1986: 125) lists the relevant part of the consonant system for Hausa illustrating this:

*Asymmetric pulmonic and non-pulmonic consonant system
(partial) of Hausa*

-	t	k	k^w	k^j
b	d	g	g^w	g^j
-	-	k'	$k^{w'}$	$k^{j'}$
ɓ	ɗ	-	-	-

Pinkerton (1986) also offers a counter-example to this typological tendency towards asymmetry of pulmonic and non-pulmonic stops, from her own investigations. She gives a table of the inventory of stop consonants in phonological contrast in the Quichean (Mayan) languages – Cakchiquel, Chamelco K'ekchi, Quiché, Tzutujil, Carcha K'ekchi, San Cristobal Pocomchí, Coban K'ekchi and Tactic Pocomchí – using the term 'glottalized' for what have here been called 'glottalic' sounds. This is reproduced in table 6.3 (where there is a typologically unusual symmetry between the pulmonic and the glottalic stops).

Pinkerton cites an observation by Campbell (1973) to the effect that implosives in the Mayan languages 'do not seem to have originated from any of the kinds of sources identified in the development of implosives in other languages (e.g. voiced stops, in the case of Sindhi). Campbell provides examples which suggest that many of the implosives in Mayan languages come from original ejectives. Also, in one case, an ejective, a labial one, has come from an implosive' (Pinkerton 1986: 138). Given that the Quichean (Mayan) languages she is discussing are languages closely historically related to each other, Pinkerton goes on to make suggestions about the way that implosives and ejectives may be related to each other in the evolutionary development of language change, illustrating her comments from the data in table 6.3:

Table 6.3 *Stops made on pulmonic and glottalic airstreams in the Quichean (Mayan) languages of Guatemala*

Language	Pulmonic egressive				Glottalic			
Cakchiquel								
voiceless	p	t	k	q	-	t'	k'	ɗ
voiced	-	-	-	-	ɓ	-	-	-
Chamelco K'ekchi								
voiceless	p	t	k	q	-	t'	k'	ɗ
voiced	-	-	-	-	ɓ	-	-	-
Quiché								
voiceless	p	t	k	q	-	t'	k'	ɗ
voiced	(b)	-	-	-	(ɓ)	-	-	-
Tzutujil								
voiceless	p	t	k	q	-	-	k'	ɗ
voiced	-	-	-	-	ɓ	ɗ	-	-
Carcha K'ekchi								
voiceless	p	t	k	q	-	t'	k'	q'
voiced	b	-	-	-	-	-	-	-
San Cristobal Pocomchi								
voiceless	p	t	k	q	β	t'	k'	q'
voiced	-	-	-	-	-	-	-	-
Coban K'ekchi								
voiceless	p	t	k	q	-	t'	k'	q'/ɗ
voiced	-	-	-	-	ɓ	-	-	-
Tactic Pocomchi								
voiceless	p	t	k	q	β	f	k'	ɗ
voiced	-	-	-	-	-	-	-	-

Source: Adapted from Pinkerton (1986: 137)

It is interesting, then, that the dialect data for Pocomchi and K'ekchi also suggest a close relation between ejectives and implosives. In Pocomchi, the alveolar and uvular glottalized stops are ejective in the San Cristobal dialect but implosive in Tactic. In K'ekchi, the uvular glottalized stop is an ejective in Carcha but an implosive in Chamelco. Finally, in Coban K'ekchi, the uvular glottalized stop is an ejective in word-initial position and an implosive in word-medial position. If it is accepted that in order to explain how sound A can develop into sound B, it would be helpful to identify a situation in which both appear as natural, presumably phonetically caused variants, then it is interesting to speculate that the development of implosives from ejectives in these languages may come about due to ... variation in the timing of articulatory gestures (laryngeal, pharyngeal etc.) ... or ... phonetic differences created by position within the word. (Pinkerton 1986: 138)

6.6 Symbols for segments made on various airstream mechanisms

Phonetic symbols for the different types of sounds made on the various airstream mechanisms can be found in appendix I, which reproduces the phonetic alphabet of the International Phonetic Association.

Further reading

Good presentations of the function of the **respiratory system** can be found in Baken (1987), Clark and Yallop (1990), Hixon (1987), Ladefoged (1967) and Warren (1976). Ohala (1990) is a good overall account of respiratory activity in speech. The detailed technical description offered by Hixon (1973) is particularly recommended for further reading.

Further comment on the production of glottalic segments (**implosives** and **ejectives**) can be found in Greenberg (1970). Further discussions of **clicks** are available in Beach (1938), Cruttenden (1992), Doke (1926), Greenberg (1955), Ladefoged and Traill (1984, 1993), Snyman (1969) and Traill (1973, 1985).

7

Phonation

The purpose of this chapter is to describe the different ways that the larynx can produce sound, in the process called phonation. More precisely, **phonation** is the use of the laryngeal system, with the help of an airstream provided by the respiratory system, to generate an audible source of acoustic energy which can then be modified by the articulatory actions of the rest of the vocal apparatus.

The primary biological function of the larynx is to control the airway to and from the lungs, in support of the breathing process. It also has a protective function, to prevent food and liquid from invading the delicate pulmonary tissues of the lungs. In order to achieve these respiratory and protective functions, the larynx has evolved into a compact and intricate muscular organism, built around a framework of three chief cartilages. As a by-product of these biological functions of the larynx, humans have developed a versatile secondary capacity to exploit the laryngeal apparatus for making and controlling sound through phonation.

Figures 7.1, 7.2 and 7.3 show three views of the larynx. Figure 7.1 is a highly schematized diagram of the cartilaginous frame within which the muscular control of phonation is achieved, showing the relationship between

Figure 7.1 The cartilaginous framework of the larynx
(from Laver 1980: 100).
1. Thyroid cartilage.   2. Cricoid cartilage.   3. Arytenoid cartilages.

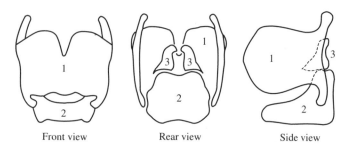

Front view   Rear view   Side view

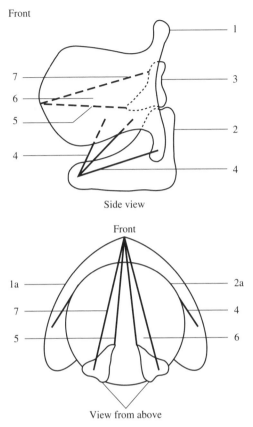

Figure 7.2 Schematic representation of the muscles of the larynx connecting the thyroid cartilage to the cricoid cartilage (from Laver 1980: 102).

1 Thyroid cartilage	4 Cricothyroid muscle
1a External edge of thyroid	5 Glottal border of vocal fold
2 Cricoid cartilage	6 Laryngeal ventricle
2a External edge of cricoid	7 Inner border of ventricular fold
3 Arytenoid cartilages	

the **thyroid**, **cricoid** and **arytenoid cartilages**. Figure 7.2 is similarly schematic, and represents the cartilaginous framework together with some of the associated muscles. This view shows parts of the **vocal folds**, which are the immediately relevant parts of the larynx for this chapter. They are attached at the front of the larynx to the thyroid cartilage and at the back to the arytenoid cartilages. The arytenoid cartilages can be made both to rotate in a swivelling movement, and to slide apart along the thyroid cartilage on which they sit. Both actions open a three-dimensional triangular space between the inner edges of the vocal folds that is called the **glottis**. When the

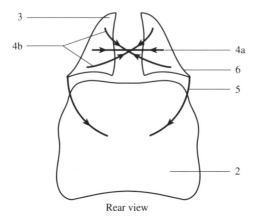

Rear view

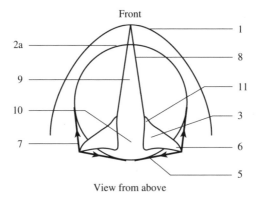

View from above

Figure 7.3 Schematic view of the larynx from behind and from above, showing some of the muscles which control phonation, with labels for parts of the glottis. (from Laver 1980: 105)

1 Thyroid cartilage
2 Cricoid muscle
2a External edge of cricoid
3 Arytenoid cartilage
4 Interarytenoid muscles
4a Transverse arytenoid muscle
4b Oblique arytenoid muscle

5 Posterior cricoarytenoid muscle
6 Muscular process of arytenoid
7 Lateral cricoarytenoid muscle
8 Vocal ligament at edge of vocal fold
9 Ligamental glottis
10 Cartilaginous glottis
11 Vocal process of arytenoid

vocal folds have been drawn apart in this way, they are said to have been **abducted**. When they have been drawn together, obliterating the triangular space of the glottis, they are said to have been **adducted**. Figure 7.3 combines a view of the larynx from behind, showing some of the muscles responsible for moving the arytenoid cartilages on the back edge of the thyroid cartilage, with a schematic view of the glottis from above. Various parts of the glotts are labelled that will be mentioned in the explanation of different ways the vocal folds can be made to vibrate. For more ample detail of how the muscle systems work to adjust the vocal folds for speech, Laver (1980: 93–140) offers a schematized account of the main principles of laryngeal physiology for phoneticians and speech scientists.

The discussion of phonation in this chapter will be largely limited to a consideration of the different types of phonation that have been shown to be used phonologically in languages, together with the use of phonatory settings that serve the purposes of paralinguistic communication. Occasional comment will also be made about the use of phonatory settings for marking extralinguistic speaker identity.

The larynx is capable of producing a wide variety of different modes of phonation. Figure 7.4a–d shows four views of the glottis in action, taken with a Nagashima SFT-1 fiberoptic telelaryngoscope (Harris, personal communication). A detailed discussion of modes of phonation is available in Catford (1964, 1977a: 93–116), who is a major pioneer in the description of phonation types, as well as in Laver (1980). The first distinction to be drawn here is logically the most basic one – that between nil phonation, where the input of acoustic energy into the vocal tract is zero, and phonation where the acoustic energy is more than zero.

7.1 Voicelessness: nil phonation

The larynx can be set in two different modes to achieve **nil phonation**. The vocal folds can be widely abducted (Figure 7.4d), or they can be fully adducted (Figure 7.4b), blocking off any flow of air from the lungs. In the first condition, with the glottis wide open, the acoustic input to the vocal tract will be zero provided that the rate of **transglottal airflow** is below the level that would generate local turbulence at the glottis. A smooth, laminar flow is silent. A turbulent flow creates an audible hiss. Whether the flow is laminar or turbulent depends mainly on two factors: first the rate of airflow, and second the area of the gap, in this case the glottis, through which it is flowing. A man with a large glottis will therefore require a higher absolute rate of airflow to reach the threshold of turbulence than will a woman or a child with a smaller glottis.

In the second condition, where the glottis is held closed, the acoustic input to the vocal tract will be zero only for as long as the glottis is kept closed. In connected speech, if pulmonic egressive effort is being continuously exerted, there will be a surge of transglottal airflow on the release of a short-term glottal closure, usually with a positive, low-level input of acoustic energy

187

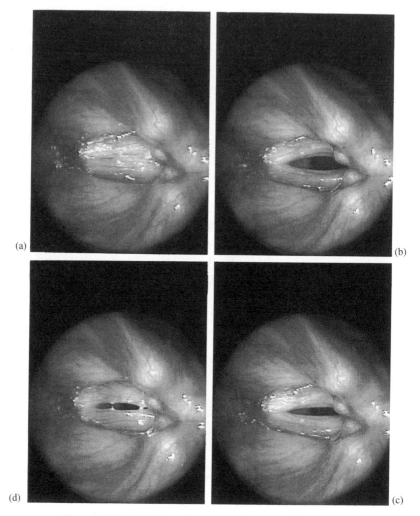

Figure 7.4 The glottis in action: (a) glottal closure; (b) open for voicelessness; (c) open for whisper; (d) vibrating for voicing (T. Harris, personal communication)

into the vocal tract in consequence. The maintenance of a glottal closure is called a **glottal stop**, for which the phonetic symbol is [?].

Nil phonation thus covers only two activities of the larynx: a silent, smooth laminar airflow through a wide open glottis, or zero airflow with the glottis held closed in a glottal stop. All other states of the glottis used in speech generate measurable acoustic energy. Three of these, on a scale of increasing acoustic energy, **breath phonation**, **whisper phonation** and **voiced**

phonation, will be discussed first. Then two types of phonation related to voiced phonation, **creak** and **falsetto**, will be described. Finally, compound phonations showing combinations of the above types will be mentioned.

7.2   Voicelessness: breath phonation

Breath phonation is Catford's term (1977a: 95) for the condition of slightly turbulent flow through the widely abducted glottis described immediately above. He suggests that the threshold of airflow through a typical adult male glottis for creating turbulence is of the order of 200–300 cubic centimetres per second (cc/s). Below this threshold the flow is laminar and silent, giving nil phonation, and above the threshold it is turbulent and audible, though still not loud, giving breath phonation. Impressionistically, the characteristic auditory quality of breath phonation is of a very gentle, rustling sound. The pronunciation of [h] at the beginning of the English word *hat* is an example of breath phonation, and has a volume-velocity flow of about 1000 cc/s (Catford, *ibid.*).

Both nil phonation and breath phonation will be covered by the term **voicelessness**. Voiceless sounds include the (RP) pronunciations of the initial and final English consonants in words like *myth* /mɪθ/ [mɪθ], *buff* /bʌf/ [bʌf] and *hiss* /hɪs/ [hɪs]. Vowels can also be pronounced with voicelessness, but when voiceless almost always show breath phonation rather than nil phonation. It is controversial whether voiceless pronunciations of vowels are used in a contrastive linguistic function, or are only phonetic events whose voicelessness is predictable in terms of their phonological context (Ladefoged 1971: 11). But voiceless pronunciations of vowels occur, on at least the phonetic level of description, in many languages. In some languages, and in individual speakers, a whisper phonation (described in the next section) can be used as a variant of such voicelessness.

Some of these instances of voiceless/whispered pronunciations of vowels are illustrated in chapter 10 on resonants. They are a characteristic of the Amerindian languages of the Plains and the Rockies such as Comanche (Canonge 1957) and Cheyenne (E. Pike 1963). Another example is Nitinaht (called Ditidaht by the speakers themselves), which is a Nootka language of the Pacific Northwest coast of British Columbia. Voiceless/whispered vowels also occur in the contextually predictable 'devoicing' process in many languages discussed in chapter 12, including French, English, Qatari Arabic, Greek, Portuguese, Japanese and Turkana.

Many voiceless sounds have their own transcriptional symbol, such as [p], [t], [s] and [f]. In those cases where there is no independent symbol, voicelessness in a sound can be shown by adding the diacritical marking of a subscript small open circle directly beneath the symbol for the equivalent voiced sound:

Subscript voiceless diacritic for symbols without descenders

[m̥] [n̥]

If the equivalent voiced symbol has a descender, as in [ŋ], which in combination with the voiceless diacritic would make for illegibility, then the diacritic can be centred superscript above the symbol, as in [ŋ̊].

7.3 Whisper phonation

The airflow through the glottis in **whisper** is turbulent, giving a characteristic 'hissing' quality, usually more intense than that in breath phonation. The area of the glottis is smaller, and this is achieved by the vocal folds being positioned much closer together. At a minimum, the only opening of the glottis is at the cartilaginous end, between the two arytenoid cartilages that serve to position the vocal folds, with the rest of the glottis closed. This gives a small triangular opening at the back of the larynx, making up about one third of the full length of the glottis, through which pulmonic air flows in a high-velocity jet into the pharynx, with considerable turbulence (Catford 1964: 31; Laver 1980: 121). Whisper can also be produced with a slightly more open glottis (as in figure 7.4c), so long as the wide-open position for breath phonation is not reached.

Breath and whisper phonation are presented here as different descriptive categories, and this is clearly convenient. But it should not be overlooked that in fact they are really only the product of different degrees of constriction on a scale of decreasing width of glottal opening, as can be seen in figure 7.5, with turbulent airflow. Catford (1977a: 96–7) suggests that the voiceless adjustments of the glottis are typically set to between 60 and 95 per cent of the maximum possible glottal area. The adjustment for whisper is probably normally less than 25 per cent of the area, with characteristic flow rates through the very constricted glottis for whisper being only about 25–30 cc/s.

It was mentioned in the previous section that whisper can be used as a phonation type in the pronunciation of some vowel sounds in some languages of North America. It was also mentioned as a phonetic characteristic of sounds in a number of languages in some pre-pausal and pre-voiceless or post-voiceless contexts, in the devoicing process which will be described in detail in chapter 12. Apart from these rather restricted linguistic uses, whisper is widely used paralinguistically. The use of whisper in a paralinguistic function to signal secrecy and confidentiality, is found in very many cultures (Laver 1980: 122). It is perhaps important to point out that the technical use of the term 'whisper' in the context of paralinguistic communication is dif-

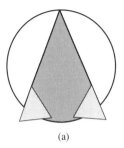 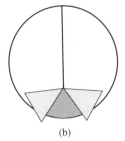

(a)   (b)

Figure 7.5 Schematic views of the glottis showing the configurations for (a) breath and (b) whisper phonation

ferent from the everyday use of that term. In common usage, it is reasonable to use a phrase like *'Come and sit beside me', she whispered secretively.* But technically it would not be the case that every sound in such an utterance would have a whisper phonation. The sounds that are normally voiceless, such as the [s] and [t] of *sit*, remain voiceless, and it is only the sounds that would normally be voiced, such as the pronunciations of the vowels, that become whispered. There are no independent transcriptional symbols for sounds made with whisper phonation. When it is necessary to show whisper, a diacritic subscript of a solid dot, centred underneath the relevant segmental symbol can be used, as in the paralinguistically whispered vowel in *sit* giving [sı̣t]. A more extended example of an utterance that everyday usage would say was 'whispered', which technically shows whisper phonation only on the sounds that would normally be voiced, with [ʃ], [f], [p] and [t] remaining voiceless, is the RP English phrase:

Subscript dot diacritic for marking whisper phonation

Orthographic Where should the flowers be planted?
Transcription [wɛ̣ə ʃʊd ð̣ə flaʊ̣əz bị plɑntəd]

7.4   Voiced phonation

The phonation state called **voicing** is acoustically different from the breath and whisper phonation states in that while breath and whisper inject a continuous acoustic input into the vocal tract, vibration of the vocal folds in voicing creates a **pulsed input**, with the frequency of the pulsing being the interactive product of muscular and aerodynamic factors. The complex interplay of these factors in producing the successive cycles of pulsed energy for voicing created by vocal-fold vibration is briefly summarized here.

The widely accepted model of vocal fold vibration in voicing is called the **aerodynamic–myoelastic model** of phonation. The 'aerodynamic' component refers to the relationship between the air-pressure and airflow factors. The 'myoelastic' component concerns the contribution of mechanical factors in the muscles that position the vocal folds and their associated cartilages. This myoelastic component of the overall model was established by Johannes Müller in 1837, and the aerodynamic elements were first explained by van den Berg and his colleagues in the 1950s and 1960s (van den Berg 1958, 1962).

The aerodynamic–myoelastic model specifies the course of events in one cycle of pulsed energy as beginning with the glottis closed, or nearly closed, by the adductor muscles of the larynx (Laver 1980: 95–9). When closed, a small vertical section of the inner edges of the vocal folds is in contact. In an average male larynx, the depth of this contact section is between 2–5 mm (Fant 1960: 266). Respiratory pressure from the pulmonic egressive airstream mechanism builds up, and subglottal pressure rises in consequence. As soon as the subglottal pressure becomes sufficiently high to overcome the muscular forces which are holding the vocal folds in their closed position, the vocal folds are blown slightly apart (as in figure 7.4d), with the lower parts of the edges of the vocal folds separating before the upper parts, in a vertical **phase difference**, as diagrammed in figure 7.6. The compressed air below the glottis now bursts through the narrow gap into the pharynx, in a jet of air which reaches speeds of between 2,000 and 5,000 cm/s (Catford 1977a: 98). The high velocity of this air-jet is partly the direct product of the subglottal over-pressure, and partly the result of the fact that the narrow constriction bordered by the edges of the separated vocal folds acts as a **venturi tube**, which has the effect of accelerating the flow of air through the constriction. A related aerodynamic factor, called the **Bernoulli effect**, results in a very local drop in air-pressure in the zone of the glottal constriction, so that the action of the high-speed jet itself tends to suck the soft tissue walls of the vocal-fold edges inwards towards renewed contact with each other.

There are thus two factors which are now conspiring towards re-establishing glottal closure: the Bernoulli effect in the transglottal air-jet itself sucking the vocal fold margins back towards renewed closure, and the elastic tension in the laryngeal muscles working to close the glottis against the diminishing subglottal air-pressure, which is leaking away very fast into the pharynx at average flow rates of between 100 and 350 cc/s (Catford 1977a: 99). The point is very rapidly reached where the combined force of these two aerodynamic and myoelastic factors is sufficient to overcome the force of the respiratory pressure, and the vocal folds snap shut. The instant of glottal

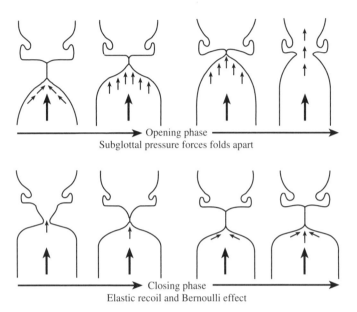

Figure 7.6 Schematic representation of vertical phase differences in the cross-sectional configuration of the vocal folds in one cycle of voiced vibration (after Clark and Yallop 1990: 38, adapted from Schneiderman 1984: 76)

closure sends an acoustic shock-wave travelling up through the air column in the vocal tract. It is this point in the phonational cycle at which the acoustic output of the larynx is at its most intense, and which provides the maximum excitation of the **resonances** of the vocal tract. The detailed values of these resonant frequencies are determined by the overall shape and dimensions of the vocal tract, and form the acoustic counterpart to the audible articulatory quality of the sound being produced. With the vocal folds now successfully closed, the subglottal pressure, driven by the respiratory system, begins to rise once again towards the point where it can overcome the muscular tensions holding the vocal folds closed.

This cycle of events is repeated very fast, and in the voiced phonation of an ordinary adult male larynx recurs on average about 120 times a second. In a typical adult female larynx it repeats itself approximately 220 times per second. (Further discussion of these and related values can be found in chapter 15.) The notation that will be used for indicating the frequency of recurrence of cyclic behaviour of this sort will be **Hz** (after the name of the nineteenth-century German physicist Heinrich Hertz), in preference to the older **cps** (cycles per second). The two notations are equivalent. The

193

frequency of recurrence of these laryngeal pulses can vary in each speaker over a wide range. An average adult male speaker's habitual frequency range typically spans very approximately 50–250 Hz, and an average adult female's 120–480 Hz. The auditory correlate of the frequency of vibration of the vocal folds is the **pitch** of the voice. During normal speech, the pitch of the voice is in continual variation, and in English constitutes the basis of **intonation**, or pitch-melody. This too will be discussed in detail in chapter 15 on the analysis of prosody, as will matters of the loudness of speech.

The interactive relationship between the larynx (as a source of energy-input) and the resonatory system of the vocal tract (as an acoustic filtering process modifying that energy) lies at the heart of the acoustic **source/filter theory** of speech production (Fant 1960). Further reading on this topic is recommended in the list at the end of the chapter.

The distinction between sounds made with voicing and those made with voicelessness is one which is exploited for phonological contrast in all languages. Languages vary in the ratio of voicing to voicelessness that occurs in connected speech: this is a product partly of the types of sounds making up the phonological systems of the language concerned, and partly of the relative incidence of the individual sounds in the words making up the vocabulary of the language. In continuous speech in English, voicing normally makes up a greater proportion of utterances than voicelessness, and Catford (1977a: 107) points out that this is largely true of most West European languages. It is perhaps this predominance of voicing that has led some writers, such as Chomsky and Halle (1968), to regard the voiced state as the 'neutral' or 'unmarked' phonatory state, to which all other states should be compared. This predominance is not necessarily true of all languages, however. Catford (1977a: 107) calculates from samples of text that the voiced:voiceless ratio of phonemes in French is 78:22; in English 72:28; in Russian 61:39; in Abkhaz (a language of the Caucasus) 56:44; and in the Chinese spoken in Canton it is 41:59.

Since voiced sounds are relatively so frequent in European languages, and given that the majority of phoneticians in the history of the subject have been native speakers of European languages, it is perhaps no accident that virtually all the voiced sounds have specific phonetic symbols devoted to them, without the need for a diacritic marking.

7.5 Creak phonation

Creak phonation is also called 'vocal fry' or 'glottal fry' in the American phonetic literature. Like the voiced phonation described above, which we can refer to as **modal voicing**, it provides a pulsed input of energy to the vocal tract, but the pulses occur at a very low frequency, and are usually somewhat irregularly spaced in time. One characteristic pattern that can often be seen in detailed instrumental records is a pulse-grouping into alternations of long and short intervals between pulses. The auditory effect of creak has been compared to hearing a stick being run along railings (Catford 1964: 122). One practical way to produce creak is to pronounce the lowest pitch possible in one's range of voiced phonation, and then try to produce an even lower note. One has the impression of almost being able to hear the individual pulses, in a frequency range that is often as low as 25–50 Hz.

The detailed glottal adjustment for creak is still problematic, with the possibility that different speakers use somewhat different mechanisms (Henton and Bladon 1988: 7–9; Laver 1980: 122–6). Catford (1964: 32) suggests that the low-frequency pulses rise through a small opening near the front end of the glottis, and the very clear photographs taken of the glottis in action by Ohala and Vanderslice, reproduced in Ladefoged (1971: 6), support this view. Hollien *et al.* (1966: 247) say that in the production of creak the vocal folds are loosely pressed together, with a thick vertical contact, giving a highly 'damped' movement of the vibratory opening, and that a very low subglottal pressure, with a very low airflow, is used. Catford (1977a: 101) mentions a flow-rate of 12–20 cc/s.

Creak also seems to be able to occur in simultaneous combination with voicing, to give the compound phonation of **creaky voice.** Compound phonations are discussed in more detail below, but it is appropriate to mention creaky voice here for two reasons. First, it is not certain that the two components one seems to be able to identify perceptually as creak and voicing correspond in fact to separate physiological mechanisms. It may be that creaky voice reflects a particular sub-category of pulse-grouping in creak phonation, and that the impression of two separable auditory components is a perceptual artefact. Second, the distinction between creak and creaky voice does not seem to be exploited for purposes either of linguistic or of paralinguistic contrast. The two labels can be used interchangeably for most purposes.

Ladefoged (1971: 15) mentions that creak/creaky voice (as part of a process he refers to as 'laryngealization') is used for phonological contrast in the Chadic languages of West Africa, such as Hausa, Bura and Margi, to distinguish certain types of consonants, and in the Nilotic languages such as Ateso (Teso) and Lango, to distinguish types of vowels, from sounds with normally voiced phonation.

Creak/creaky voice is also often part of a similar segmentally focused laryngealization process known in Danish as 'stød', discussed in chapter 11.

Because of the relationship between creak and very low pitched voicing, it is also often the case that where linguistic rules prescribe very low pitch, creak or creaky voice is used. In tonal functions of pitch (discussed in chapter 15 on prosody), where words can be contrastively identified by the use of different tonal pitch-patterns on the component syllables, a low falling tone is sometimes terminated phonetically by creak or creaky voice. Such syllables sometimes also end in a final glottal stop.

In intonational functions of pitch (also discussed in chapter 15), where pitch-pattern contrasts are relevant over units longer than a single word, a low falling intonation is also often terminated by creak or creaky voice. In English, termination of this sort is sometimes used for a regulative function, as mentioned in chapter 1, with the speaker using a creaky termination as a signal of yielding the floor to the other speaker, at the end of the speaker-turn. For speakers who adopt this convention, a low falling intonation before a silent pause, but without a creaky termination, and particularly with simultaneous avoidance of eye-contact, signifies that the speaker has not yet reached the end of his or her turn, and is resisting the possibility of take-over of the speaker-role by the other participant.

A creaky phonation is used paralinguistically as a setting in a number of cultures. In English (RP), it can be used to signal bored resignation, when used throughout an utterance (Laver 1980: 126). In Tzeltal, the Mayan language mentioned earlier, creaky voice is used 'to signal commiseration and complaint, and to invite commiseration' (Brown and Levinson 1978: 272). In the Totontepec dialect of Mixe (an Otomanguean language of Central America), Crawford (1963), cited in Suárez (1983: 48), describes creaky voice – which like Ladefoged he refers to as 'laryngealization' – as being used to communicate apology or supplication.

A habitual phonatory setting of creak or creaky voice is also used extralinguistically, as a marker of personal identity. It is not uncommon in American male speakers, for example, and is not infrequently heard in older American female speakers. It is also found in a minority of British speakers as a personal characteristic. In a study of eighty male speakers of RP and an accent referred to as 'Modified Northern' (English), Henton and Bladon (1988: 23) report that ten of these speakers were 'persistent creakers'. In Copenhagen Danish, habitual creaky voice used as a pervasive phonation type throughout voiced segments is said to function as a social marker of upper-class speech (J. Verhoeven, personal communication).

A creaky phonation can be transcribed with a diacritic tilde placed underneath the corresponding voiced symbol, as in:

Subscript tilde diacritic for marking creak/creaky voice phonation

Orthographic Where should the flowers be planted?
Transcription [wɛə ʃʊd ðə fl aʊəz bḭ pl ɑntəd]

An alternative to this, when creak or creaky voice is being used paralinguistically or extralinguistically as a phonatory setting over whole utterances, is to preface the whole transcription with the symbol 'C', or with the general prefacing symbol 'V' with the creak diacritic attached, as in:

Prefacing setting symbols for marking creak/creaky voice phonation

Orthographic Where should the flowers be planted?
Transcription C [wɛə ʃʊd ðə flaʊəz bi plɑntəd]
              or
              V̰ [wɛə ʃʊd ðə flaʊəz bi plɑntəd]

The implication of such a transcription is that all (and only) the segments in the utterance which are susceptible to the effect of the phonatory setting – that is, only the voiced segments, and thus none of [ʃ, f, p, t] – will be pronounced with a creaky phonation.

7.6 Falsetto phonation

Falsetto is another method of providing a pulsed source of phonatory energy. In this case, however, the top of the fundamental frequency range is markedly higher than in ordinary modal voiced phonation. The bottom end of the falsetto range overlaps with the top end of the voiced phonation range: Hollien and Michel (1968: 602) report that the average pitch-range for male falsetto is 275–634 Hz, as against their estimate of 94–287 Hz for ordinary voiced phonation.

In producing falsetto, the vocal folds are stretched longitudinally from front to back, so that they become relatively thin in cross-section, with the glottal margins of the folds being particularly thin-edged. The glottis is often left very slightly open, and this has several results. Firstly, falsetto phonation is often accompanied by a slight whisperiness, as the pulmonic airflow is able to escape continuously through the glottal gap. Secondly, the subglottal pressure is characteristically lower than in ordinary voiced phonation (Kunze 1964), partly because of the continuous transglottal leakage.

Falsetto is not used systematically for contrastive phonological purposes. But it is heard not uncommonly as a phonatory setting in a certain style of male pop singing. Falsetto can also be used paralinguistically. Grimes

(1959), cited in Suárez (1983: 48) notes that 'falsetto in voiced sounds is used in Huichol to express excitement'. (Huichol is a Uto-Aztecan Mesoamerican language of Mexico.) It was also noted in chapter 1 that speakers of Tzeltal can use a sustained falsetto setting as an honorific device. Brown and Levinson (1978: 272) comment that in Tzeltal, such a use of falsetto 'is enjoined in greeting formulae, and may spread over an entire formal interaction'. Finally, it was mentioned in chapter 1 that speakers of Shona in Zimbabwe use falsetto as a setting in utterances mocking someone thought to be boasting (B. Annan, personal communication).

Since falsetto is typically used for whole utterances rather than for individual segments, the domain of transcription for falsetto can be the utterance itself. This can be indicated by prefacing the transcription of the utterance by the symbol 'F', to indicate that all susceptible voiced segments in the transcription are performed with a falsetto phonation, as in:

Prefacing setting symbol for marking falsetto phonation

Orthographic Where should the flowers be planted?
Transcription F[wɛə ʃʊd ðə flaʊəz bi plɑntəd]

7.7 Compound phonation types

Modal voice and falsetto are mutually incompatible, from a physiological point of view. Because they compete for different use of the same laryngeal apparatus, they cannot occur simultaneously. Whisper and creak are not only able to occur alone, but can also modify modal voice and falsetto, and each other. This leads to the possibility of various sorts of **compound phonation types**. Combinations of two phonation types give **whispery voice, whispery falsetto** and **whispery creak**. Triple combinations give **whispery creaky voice** and **whispery creaky falsetto**. The combinability of phonation types is summarized in figure 7.7. All of these may be used extralinguistically, as a personal phonatory setting characteristic, (though falsetto is very rare in any compound combination, at least in male speakers, just as it is rare by itself as a simple phonation type).

The only compound phonation types that are used for linguistic purposes are creaky voice, which has already been discussed, and whispery voice. In whispery voice, the vocal folds are brought close enough to each other to cause vibration, with the Bernoulli effect helping to give the voicing component, but not close enough to seal the glottis between laryngeal pulses. The gap that is left, through which turbulent air flows in a continuous audible stream, can be either between the two arytenoid cartilages at the back of the glottis, or it can be larger, involving part of the glottis further forward as well.

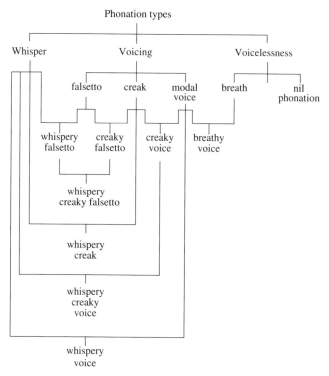

Figure 7.7 Constraints on the combinability of different modes of phonation

The presence of whispery voice can be transcribed by adopting Ladefoged's (1971: 13) convention of putting a double-dot diaeresis diacritic under the symbol:

Subscript diaeresis diacritic for marking whispery voice phonation

Orthographic Where should the flowers be planted?
Transcription [wɛ̤ə ʃʊ̤d ð̤ə fl̤aṳə̤z b̤i̤ pl̤an̤tə̤d]

Alternatively, whispery voiced phonation running through all the susceptible segments of an utterance can be transcribed by means of the general prefacing symbol V, accompanied by the modifying subscript diaeresis, as in:

Prefacing setting symbol for marking whispery voice phonation

Orthographic Where should the flowers be planted?
Transcription V̤ [wɛə ʃʊd ðə flauəz bi plantəd]

	modal voice	i̬
simple phonation types	creak/creaky voice	ḭ
	whisper	i̤
	voicelessness	i̥
compound phonation types	whispery voice	i̤
	whispery creak/creaky voice	i̤̰

Figure 7.8 Diacritic symbols for indicating different phonation types

Ladefoged's term for whispery voice is **murmur**, and he cites murmur as being the basis for segmental contrasts in (Indo-European) languages such as Hindi, Sindhi, Marathi, Bengali, Assamese, Gujarati, and Bihari (Bhojpuri). He also says that murmured consonants figure contrastively in (Niger-Congo) languages such as Shona and Tsonga, and (Benue-Congo) languages such as Ndebele and Zulu (Ladefoged 1971: 12–14). Examples are given in later chapters.

Whispery voice is used in very many cultures (including all European languages) for paralinguistic purposes to signal confidentiality. In the Totontepec dialect of Mixe, however, the Otomanguean language of Central America mentioned in section 7.5, Crawford (1963) states that a whispery or breathy quality marks excitement or emphasis (cited in Suárez 1983: 48).

7.8 Symbols for phonation types

Figure 7.8 gathers together all the diacritics for indicating phonation types that have been discussed in this chapter. Examples will be given in each of the following chapters on stops, fricatives and resonants of the contrastive use of different modes of phonation on individual segments.

Further reading

The **aerodynamic–myoelastic model** of phonation is discussed further in van den Berg (1968), van den Berg, Zantema and Doornenbal (1959), Broad (1973) and von Leden (1961). Details of individual modes of phonation can be found in Hollien (1972), Hollien and Michel (1968) and Moore and von Leden (1958) for **creak** phonation; Hollien (1972) and Hollien and Colton (1969) for **falsetto** phonation; and Catford (1964) and Laver (1980) for compound phonations such as **whispery voice**. Hirano (1981) gives an excellent account of phoniatric investigations of the larynx from a clinical viewpoint, as one of the world's leading laryngologists.

Further description of the **source/filter theory** of the acoustics of speech production is available in Flanagan (1965), Fry (1979), Kent and Read (1992) and Lieberman and Blumstein (1988). More detail about the acoustics of speech in general can be explored by consulting the references recommended in the list of Further Reading in chapter 2.

PART IV

Linear segmental analysis

8

Stop articulations

A **stop segment** is defined as a segment whose medial phase is characterized by a stricture of complete **oral closure** made by the active articulator against the passive articulator. This prevents the escape of air from the mouth, and if a simultaneous **velic closure** is maintained so that the air cannot escape through the nasal cavity either, then under conditions of positive egressive pressure, the **intra-oral pressure** (i.e. the pressure of the air within the vocal tract) will rise. These conditions constitute the minimum requirements for the specification of a pulmonic egressive **oral stop** segment.

When the oral closure is released in the offset phase of an oral stop of this sort, the compressed air escapes to the atmosphere with a small but audible explosion, sometimes referred to in the acoustic phonetic literature as the **stop burst**. In the case of a pulmonic ingressive airstream, the intra-oral pressure of the volume of air which is sealed from the outside atmosphere by the oral and velic closures drops. When the seal is released, the higher-pressure air of the outside atmosphere implodes in to fill the relative vacuum in the vocal tract.

Stops, like other segment-types, have three phases. These all relate to the oral closure that characterizes the medial phase. The onset phase, as the articulatory transition towards complete closure, can be called the **closing phase**. The medial phase of a stop segment (from the moment full closure begins to the moment it ends) can be referred to as the **closed phase**. The offset phase in stop production begins at the instant that complete closure ends, and will be referred to as the **release phase**. In stops made on an egressive airstream, the releasing offset phase is sometimes called **release** or **plosion.** Oral stops made on a pulmonic egressive airstream are therefore often called **plosives.**

Partly because of this triple sequence of their closing, closed and release phases, stops in connected speech can have complex co-ordinatory relationships with their contextual neighbours, especially in the closing and release phases of the stops. These relationships reflect more general principles common to many types of segments concerning both articulatory and temporal co-ordination, and are separately discussed in chapter 12.

Figure 8.6 at the end of this chapter lists the symbols for pulmonic egressive stop articulations. The symbols for non-pulmonic stop segments can be found in the IPA alphabet reprinted as appendix I.

8.1 Place-neutral stop articulations

There are eight chief places of articulation in which stop articulations are performed which are place-neutral, without displacement of the active articulator from its neutral relationship to the passive articulator. These neutral places of articulation, and the symbols for the corresponding voiceless and voiced oral stop segments, are as follows:

Place of articulation	Voiceless oral stops	Voiced oral stops
labial	[p]	[b]
dental	[t̪]	[d̪]
alveolar	[t]	[d]
palatal	[c]	[ɟ]
velar	[k]	[g]
uvular	[q]	[ɢ]
epiglottal	–	[ʡ]
glottal	[ʔ]	–

Since a glottal stop (mentioned in the earlier section on nil phonation) by definition requires complete closure of the vocal folds, it is physiologically impossible to make a voiced glottal stop. On the other hand, although there is no IPA symbol for a voiceless epiglottal stop, this is an articulatorily possible sound. This reflects the more general position that the sound-types associated with the specific IPA symbols listed above do not exhaust the possible range of place-neutral articulations. They happen to be the set of place-neutral stop segments typically found to be exploited by the languages of the world for manifesting phonemic distinctions. But it would be physiologically possible to make place-neutral stop articulations at virtually any point along the continuum of the vocal tract from the lips to the larynx. The general question of the communicative and articulatory principles on which the languages of the world might base this restricted set of choices in this regard remains an open research question.

Figures 8.1a–8.1f respectively show sagittal cross-sections of the vocal organs during the medial phases of the production of a voiceless labial stop [p], a voiceless dental stop [t̪], a voiceless alveolar stop [t], a voiceless palatal stop [c], a voiceless velar stop [k] and a voiceless uvular stop [q].

Examples of place-neutral oral stops made at different places of articulation can be found in probably every one of the world's languages. Contrasts amongst oral stops with labial, alveolar and velar places of articulation are very common, as in the following English examples:

Labial, alveolar and velar plosives in English

[pɪl] pill   [tɪl] till   [kɪl] kill

[bɪl] bill   [dɪl] dill   [gɪl] gill (of a fish)

Labial, dental, alveolar and velar stops are in four-way contrast in Isoko, a Kwa language of midwestern Nigeria (Mafeni 1969: 115–16):

Labial, dental, alveolar and velar stops in Isoko

[épé] 'kind of tree'   [ébé] 'leaves'

[ót̪ú] 'louse'   [ód̪ú] 'farm'

[útí] 'sugar cane'   [údí] 'drink'

[ùkó] 'cup'   [úgó] 'tie-beam (of a house)'

Another four-way contrast, this time between labial, alveolar, palatal and velar places of articulation, can be seen in Urhobo, another language of mid-western Nigeria (Kelly 1969:154–5):

Labial, alveolar, palatal and velar stops in Urhobo

[úpe] 'scar'   [obɔ] 'hand'

[ete] 'ward'   [údu] 'chest'

[océ] 'water-pot'   [oɟa] 'soap'

[ako] 'tooth'   [ɔgɔ́] 'bottle'

Labial, alveolar, palatal and velar stops can also be found in Lhasa Tibetan, in the following illustrations – which are shown without indication of pitch features (Sprigg 1961):

Labial, alveolar, palatal and velar stops in Lhasa Tibetan

[phɑːlə] 'between'   [phʌːtʊ] 'as far as'

[phøgè] 'Tibetan'   [dɹuːgeː] 'Bhutanese'

[ceʥə] 'speech'   [ceːɟuː] 'interpreter'

[maŋbʊ] 'many'   [ʥʌŋgʊ] 'green (adj.)'

A slightly less common instance of a three-way contrast between plosives at the palatal, velar and uvular locations is found in Quechua, a Southern Amerindian language, according to Ladefoged (1972: 9):

Palatal, velar and uvular plosives in Quechua

[caka] 'bridge'   [kara] 'expensive'   [qara] 'skin'

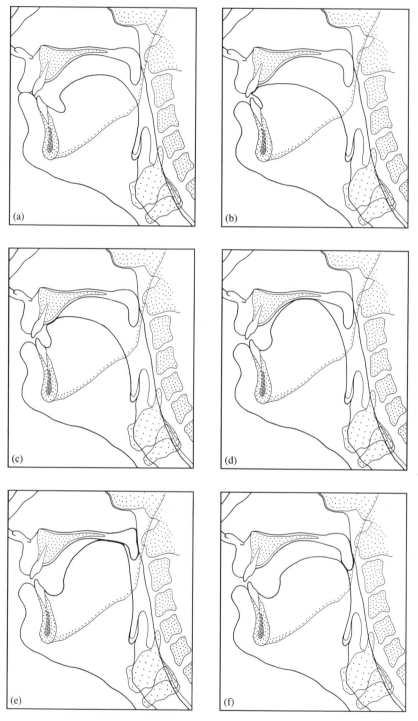

Figure 8.1 Sagittal cross-sections of the vocal organs during the production of the medial phases of a number of oral stop segments: (a) a voiceless labial oral stop [p]; (b) a voiceless dental oral stop [t̪]; (c) a voiceless alveolar oral stop [t]; (d) a voiceless palatal oral stop [c]; (e) a voiceless velar oral stop [k]; and (f) a voiceless uvular oral stop [q]

Another three-way contrast, between labial, dental and velar stops, is shown by Tigre, one of the North Ethiopic Semitic languages spoken in Eritrea (Palmer 1956):

> *Labial, dental and velar stops in Tigre*
> [gəraːɖə] 'scimitar'   [ɗəkʼaːla] 'bastard'
> [kɐbɐroː] 'drum'   [baːɖeːlaː] 'spade'

Labial, dental, palatal and velar stops occur in modern Greek. In the data here, palatal and velar stops are in contrast before [a], but are in complementary distribution elsewhere, in that palatal stops (which may in fact be fronted velar stops) occur only before [i] and [e], and velar stops [k] and [g] occur in other environments (Mackridge 1985: 18–30):

> *Labial, dental, palatal and velar stops in Greek*
> ['paɳɖa] 'always'   [baˈbas] 'daddy'
> ['ṭama] 'vow'   [ḍaˈḍa] 'wet-nurse'
> ['calos] 'and another'   ['kalos] 'corn (callus)'
> ['cerasa] 'I treated (to a drink)' [ṭoɲˈɟeɾasa] 'I treated him (to a drink)'
> [karˈpos] 'fruit; wrist'   [ṣtoŋgarˈpo] 'on the wrist'

Voiceless velar and uvular stops are found in contrast in the Suleimaniya accent of Kurdish of North Eastern Iraq (A. Ferhardi, personal communication):

> *Velar and uvular stops in Kurdish (Suleimaniya accent)*
> [kʰ ir] '(laconically) quiet'   [qʰ ir] 'parched thirstiness'

Examples of voiceless and voiced palatal and velar stops can be seen in Modern Standard Turkish, where they can be treated as allophones of the same phoneme as they are in complementary distribution. Palatal stops occur before front vocoids, and velar stops before back vocoids (H. Kopkalli, personal communication):

> *Palatal and velar stops in Turkish*
> [cɪr] 'dirt'   [ɟɪr] 'come/go in'
> [cœɹ] 'blind'   [ɟœɹ] 'see'
> [cel] 'bald'   [ɟel] 'come'
> [kɑɹ] 'snow'   [ɡɑɹ] 'depot'

8.2 Oral versus nasal aspects of stop articulations

In the default case, where no further specification is made, a stop segment is assumed to be oral, as described above, with one closure made by the active articulator. In stops made with a nasal aspect of articula-

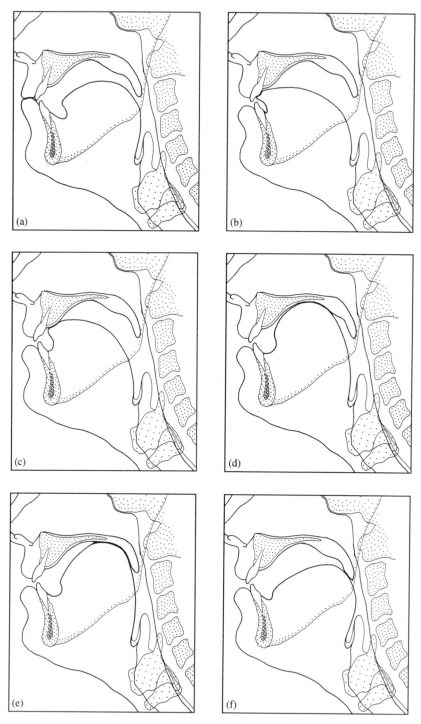

Figure 8.2 Sagittal cross-sections of the vocal organs during the production of the medial phases of a number of nasal stop segments: (a) a voiced labial nasal stop [m]; (b) a voiced dental nasal stop [n̪]; (c) a voiced alveolar nasal stop [n]; (d) a voiced palatal nasal stop [ɲ]; (e) a voiced velar nasal stop [ŋ]; and (f) a voiced uvular nasal stop [ɴ]

tion, the oral closure is not matched by a velic closure. The velum is held in an open position for the medial phase of the stop. The intra-oral air-pressure therefore has no opportunity to rise, and the pulmonic egressive airflow escapes continuously to the outside atmosphere through the nasal cavity. The volume of air in the cul-de-sac formed by the oral cavity behind the oral stricture acts merely as a side-chamber to the main flow.

The size of the side-chamber necessarily varies with the place of articulation of the oral stricture. This side-chamber configuration can be seen in each of figures 8.2a–8.2f, which respectively show sagittal cross-sections of the vocal organs during the medial phases of the production of a voiced labial nasal stop [m], a voiced dental nasal stop [n̪], a voiced alveolar nasal stop [n], a voiced palatal nasal stop [ɲ], a voiced velar nasal stop [ŋ] and a voiced uvular nasal stop [ɴ]. It is the presence of a side-chamber, acting as a side-branch resonator, that gives nasality its characteristic damped acoustic and auditory quality.

Amongst the conformational aspects of articulation, stops are subject only to this oral/nasal dichotomy. They are logically excluded from any choice between central versus lateral routing of the oral airflow since complete oral closure during the medial phase is a prerequisite for being classified as a stop segment.

The very large majority of nasal stops in the languages of the world are made with a voiced phonation type. But voiceless nasal stops can also be found, in languages such as Burmese (Ladefoged 1971: 11) and Oaxaca Chontal of Mexico (Pike 1963: 48):

Voiceless versus voiced nasal stops in Burmese

| [m̥à] 'order' | [n̥à] 'nostril' | [ŋ̊â] 'rent' |
| [mà] 'healthy' | [nà] 'pain' | [ŋâ] 'fish' |

Voiceless and voiced nasal stops in Oaxaca Chontal

| [pam̥pa] 'he sat' | [pan̥ta] 'he will go and stay' |
| [lifum̥pa] 'the fat person' | [panta] 'bag' |

Almost all languages have one or more nasal stops in their phonemic consonantal inventory. Maddieson (1984: 61) mentions that in his survey of 317 of the languages of the world, he found only ten of which this was not true. Of these ten, four not only had no nasal stops, but were said to have no nasal segments of any kind. These were Rotokas (a Bougainville Indo-Pacific language), Quileute and Puget Sound (Pacific Northwest Amerindian languages), and Mura (a Chibchan Southern Amerindian language). The phonological inventory of the other six included either pre-nasal stops (discussed further below in this chapter), or nasal vocoids (described in chapter 10). However, at least one of these languages said to use no nasal segments of any kind (Rotokas) is claimed by other investigators to show voiced nasal stops being used in free variation with voiced oral stops and voiced approximants (Firchow and Firchow 1969, cited by Herbert 1986: 21).

There is one stop where the oral/nasal dichotomy is inapplicable, and that is the glottal stop [ʔ]. Since the outflowing pulmonic airstream meets the glottal closure before coming to the velum, there is logically no possibility of the air escaping, while under subglottal compression, through the nasal cavity. In Terena, an Arawakan language of the Brazilian Matto Grosso, parts of words can be characterized by a setting of nasality as an indicator of the grammatical category of first person: the one segmental exception to this is any glottal stop that participates in the stretch of speech, as in the following example (Bendor-Samuel 1960):

> *Glottal stop interrupting nasality in Terena*
> [emoʔu] 'his word'   [ẽmõʔũ] 'my word'

Nasal stops, as indicated earlier, occur in virtually all the languages of the world. In Brazilian Portuguese (São Paulo accent), three nasal consonants occur whose pronunciations show labial, denti-alveolar and palatal places of articulation (Cagliari 1977: 9–20):

> *Labial, denti-alveolar and palatal nasal stops in Brazilian Portuguese*
> ['somʊ] 'I sum'   ['soṋʊ] 'sleep'   ['soɲʊ] 'dream'

The voiced palatal nasal stop [ɲ] also occurs in other Romance languages, such as French, where it is in contrast with voiced nasal stops at the labial ([m]) and dental ([n̪]) places of articulation (Tranel 1987):

> *Labial, dental and palatal nasal stops in French*
>
> | | | |
> |---|---|---|
> | [mo] 'word' | [n̪o] 'our' | [aɲo] 'lamb' |
> | [pɔm] 'apple' | [pan̪] 'breakdown' | [paɲ] 'loin-cloth' |
> | [vjɛn̪] 'comes' | [fin̪] 'thin' | [ʒwaɲ] 'joins' |
> | (3rd pers. pl.) | | (3rd pers. sg.) |
> | [sœbeɲe] | [lin̪] 'line' | [ɔɲõ] 'onion' |
> | 'to go swimming' | | |
> | [ɲol] 'booze' | [ɲãɲã] 'namby-pamby' | [ɲoɲot̪] 'trash' |

Javanese, like English, uses contrasts between labial, alveolar and velar nasal stops (Clark and Yallop 1990: 138):

Labial, alveolar and velar nasal stops in Javanese
[ana?] 'child'   [maŋanake] 'cause to eat'   [təmɒ?ake] 'cause to
                                                                                  meet'

Sundanese, from West Java, displays an opposition in oral and nasal stops between dental [t̪], alveolar [d] and [n], palatal [ɲ] and velar [ŋ], [k] and [g] (Robins 1953):

Dental, alveolar, palatal and velar oral and nasal stops in
Sundanese

[ɲinum] 'to drink'	[ŋahantʃa] 'to work'
[ŋawidaŋ] 'to dry skins'	[ŋaliwat] 'to pass'
[ɲokot̪] 'to take'	[ŋaboroŋ] 'to buy (an entire stock)'
[ŋadahar] 'to eat'	[ŋadʒawab] 'to answer'
[ŋagan̪t̪i] 'to change'	[ŋusap] 'to stroke'

Tigre, the Ethiopic language mentioned above, contrasts oral and nasal stops at the dental place of articulation (Palmer 1956):

Oral and nasal dental stops in Tigre
[dɐbeːlaː] 'he-goat' [nɐbit̪] 'wine' [t̪ɐkoːbat̪aː] 'her mat'

In Dyirbal, an Australian language of North Queensland, oral and nasal stops are found at the bilabial, alveolar, palatal and velar places of articulation (Dixon 1972: 42):

Oral and nasal bilabial, alveolar, palatal and velar stops in
Dyirbal

[jamani] 'rainbow'	[jamaniga] 'at the rainbow'
[midin] 'possum'	[midinda] 'on the possum'
[jaɹa] 'man'	[jaɹaŋga] 'on a man'
[biɲɟiriɲ] 'small lizard'	[biɲɟiriɲɟa] 'on a small lizard'

In the above examples, Dixon makes it clear that the sounds here represented as palatal are in fact lamino-alveolopalatal stops ; in addition, the velar stop [g] 'normally involves double articulation, the front of the tongue also touching the alveolar ridge' (1972: 37). In the terms of this book, one would have to say that the blade (rather than the front) of the tongue made the anterior contact, and that such a stop was technically a double 'alveolar velar' stop [d͡g]. Stops made with such double articulation are described in detail in chapter 11.

Walmatjari, another Australian language, shows velar oral and nasal stops in syllable initial position (Hudson 1978, cited in Clark and Yallop 1990: 105):

Oral and nasal velar stops in Walmatjari
[ŋapa] 'water'   [kurapa] 'hand'   [ŋarpu] 'father'

One language with the unusually large number of seven different nasal stops is Yanyuwa, another Australian language. Ladefoged (1983a: 180) gives the following illustrations:

Nasal stops in Yanyuwa
[umuwaḍala]   [wuṉunu] 'cooked'   [wunala] 'kangaroo'
  'in the canoe'
[waṇura]   [n̪an̪alu] 'tea'   [luwaɲu] 'strips of fat'
  'white crane'
[waŋulu] 'big boy'

(The symbol [ɳ] immediately above stands for a nasal palato-alveolar stop made with a displaced retroflex aspect of articulation, which is discussed in section 8.4 below.)

8.3   Displaced stop articulations

A number of languages use stop articulations for contrastive phonological purposes where the active articulator is displaced from its neutral position to form the stricture of complete closure. One fairly extreme such articulation has recently been discovered in linguistic use, in V'enen Taut ('Big Nambas'), one of several Austronesian languages spoken in Vanuatu (Fox 1979), of which three at least display the sounds in question. This is a set of 'linguo-labial' sounds in which a stricture is created between the upper lip as the passive articulator and the tip or blade of the tongue as the active articulator. Maddieson (1987a: 26) describes the articulation, on the basis of his personal work with these languages, as 'highly distinctive, with the tongue tip frequently protruding forward of the upper lip'. These linguo-labial sounds are said to have developed from Proto-Oceanic labial sounds in the languages concerned.

Linguo-labial stops (and fricatives) are used in V'enen Taut in a fully contrastive function, competing with sounds of the same degree of stricture at both the labial and alveolar places of articulation. To represent the voiceless linguo-labial oral stop and the voiced linguo-labial nasal stop, the 1989 IPA Kiel Convention proposed the symbols [t̼] and [m̼] respectively. This is a difficult set of sounds to symbolize satisfactorily: the IPA proposal makes a valiant attempt to construct a symbol-shape with intuitive interpretability, combining an element signalling closure achieved by the tip/blade of the tongue with a diacritic implying labiality. The corresponding symbol for a voiced nasal linguo-labial stop, by extension, would be [m̼]. These symbols will be adopted here. Maddieson (1987a: 27) gives the following examples of contrasts involving oral and nasal linguo-labial stop articulations:

> *Oral and nasal linguo-labial stops versus labial and alveolar stops in V'enen Taut*
>
> [tateɪ] 'breadfruit' [pətək] 'my head' [tateɪ] 'father'
> [nəm̼ək] 'my tongue' [nəmək] 'my spirit' [nanɪ] 'goat'

Maddieson (*ibid.*) further states that 'linguo-labial sounds with a more marginal linguistic function are also reported in Chaga (Maddieson 1987b), and in Pirāha (Everett 1982), where a sublaminal linguo-labial occurs with a socio-linguistically restricted function'.

Another example of a displaced stop articulation is the voiced labiodental nasal stop [ɱ], for which the lower lip as the active articulator makes a closure against the upper front teeth as the passive articulator. This is used contrastively in Teke (Paulian 1975), a language of Zaïre. Another example occurs optionally (non-contrastively) before the labiodental consonants /f/ and /v/ in some environments in English, in words such as *envy* and *invade*, when pronounced as [ɛɱvɪ] and [ɱveɪd], instead of the more formal [ɛnvɪ] and [ɪnveɪd]. The symbol [π] can be proposed for a voiced labiodental oral stop, as in some pronunciations of /d/ in English before [f] and [v], in phrases such as [həπfɜst] *head first* and [ɹəʊπvan] *road van*. When a symbol is needed for a voiceless labiodental oral stop, [ƛ] can be used, as in some labiodental realizations of /t/ in English before labiodental fricatives [f] and [v], in utterances such as [hɜ̞π̥fʊl] *hurtful* and [ðaπ̥van] *that van*.

The use of apical articulations at the alveolar place of articulation for stops (and for other categories) can be regarded as examples of slightly displaced articulations. Since the blade of the tongue in the fully neutral position lies directly beneath the alveolar ridge, laminal alveolar articulations can be thought of as neutral with regard to displacement, as mentioned in chapter 5. Speakers of English seem roughly equally divided between those who perform alveolar stops with an apical articulation, and those who use laminal articulations. As far as English is concerned, the choice made by any individual speaker between apical and laminal articulations in the production of alveolar stops has semiotic value only as a marker of personal identity.

8.4 Topographical aspects of stop articulations

Stops are logically excluded from exploiting one of the topographical choices of aspect – namely that of grooving of the tongue blade. But another member of this aspect group, that of retroflexion, is found relatively often in stop articulations. A retroflex stop segment is one where the tip of the tongue is curled upwards and backwards, such that either the tip or the undersurface of the tip makes an airtight seal at the post-alveolar or palato-alveolar place of articulation. By definition, retroflexion also involves a degree of displacement of articulation.

The phonetic symbols for retroflex stops all have descenders of the symbol curling to the right, as in the voiceless retroflex palato-alveolar oral stop [ʈ], the voiced retroflex palato-alveolar oral stop [ɖ] and voiced retroflex palato-alveolar nasal stop [ɳ]. Figure 8.3a shows the configuration of the vocal organs in the formation of [ʈ], and figure 8.3b for [ɳ], based on x-ray data on Tamil from Balasubramanian (1972). Asher (1982: 212), Balasubramanian and Asher (1984: 51) and Soundararaj (1986: 32–4) give some illustrative words:

Dental and retroflex palato-alveolar plosives in Tamil

[paːt̪ˑi] 'flower-bed'	[paːʈˑi] 'grandmother'
[t̪oːʈːō] 'garden'	[ʋaɳɖɪ] 'cart'
[ʋaːn̪d̪i] 'vomit'	[maɳɖe] 'skull'
[pit̪ːəlaːʈō] 'deceit'	[t̪oːʈːaː] 'gun cartridge'

In the transcription here, [ʋ] is a voiced labiodental approximant (see chapter 10), and [ˑ] and [ː] are used as diacritics to indicate slightly versus substantially greater duration respectively (see chapter 14).

A three-way opposition occurs in Malayalam of Southern India, where stops in dental, alveolar and retroflex post-alveolar places of articulation are in phonemic contrast (Ladefoged 1972: 9):

Dental, alveolar and retroflex post-alveolar plosives in
Malayalam

| [kut̪ːi] 'stabbed' | [kutːi] 'peg' | [kuʈːi] 'child' |

Retroflexion is a perceptually striking aspect of articulation, and is strongly characteristic of a number of language groups in the Indian subcontinent and its vicinity, and in many languages in Australia. Masica describes the retroflex aspect of pronunciation as a pan-Asian areal feature which Indo-Aryan languages:

> share with Dravidian, Munda, and also certain nearby Tibeto-Burman and Eastern Iranian languages (and Burushaski). Just as clear is the concentration of this feature (in terms of both systemic development and lexical ... frequency) in the west and south of the subcontinent ... and adjacent Eastern Iranian languages such as Pashto ... and in Dravidian and its fadeout toward the northeast. The latter makes it difficult to connect the sporadic manifestation of the feature in Southeast Asia (Vietnamese) and Indonesia (Javanese), as well as

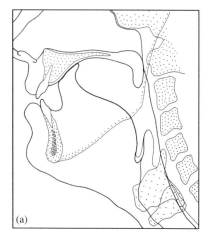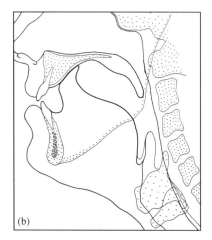

Figure 8.3 Sagittal cross-sections of the vocal organs during the production of the medial phase of (a) a voiceless retroflex palato-alveolar oral stop [ʈ] and (b) a voiced retroflex palato-alveolar nasal stop [ɳ] (both based on X-ray information on Tamil in Balasubramanian 1972)

> its strong development in Australian languages, with the Indian phenomenon. (Masica 1991: 131)

In the above quotation, Burushaski is a remote mountain language which, though sharing some phonetic (and grammatical) features with neighbouring languages, is a language isolate without known genetic affinities. Masica (1991: 41) describes it as being spoken by 'about 30,000 persons in Gilgit-Hunza in the extreme north of Pakistan, in the valleys of two upper tributaries of the Indus'.

Examples of stops made with a retroflex aspect of articulation in Australian languages are given by Breen (1981: 273–97), in a chapter on the Pama-Nyungan language Margany of South Queensland. They contrast with dental, alveolar, palatal and velar oral and nasal stops:

> *Oral and nasal retroflex post-alveolar stops in Margany*
> [baɖi] 'maybe'   [badi] 'to cry'   [waḏin] 'right'
> [baɳa] 'goanna'   [ḏana] 'they (pl.)'
> [guɳma] 'wood duck'   [gunma] 'to break'
> [wakaɳ] 'crow'   [wakan] 'father's sister'

Further illustrations of oral and nasal stops made with a retroflex aspect of articulation are given by Esling (1991), in his discussion of Nyangumarta, another Pama-Nyungan language of about 700 speakers from northern Western Australia:

> *Oral and nasal retroflex palato-alveolar stops in Nyangumarta*
> ['ɳʊɳɖi] 'shoulder'   ['ɳ̃ãɳɳaɳ] 'chin'
> [pʊ'ɖenβʊɖõɳ] 'chest'   ['pɪɳɖɪl] 'back'

Examples from another continent of languages involving retroflexion in stops are found in Herero, a language of Southwest Africa, in contrast to dental stops, and in Ewe, a language of Ghana, in contrast to alveolar stops (Westermann and Ward 1933: 55):

> *Dental versus retroflex palato-alveolar plosives in Herero*
> [t̪a] 'to die'   [ʈa] 'to fit'

> *Alveolar versus retroflex palato-alveolar plosives in Ewe*
> [de] 'to reach'   [ɖe] 'to take away'
> [du] 'town'   [ɖu] 'powder'

8.5 Transitional aspects of stop articulation: tapped, flapped and trilled stops

This is a sub-group of the stop category whose aspects of articulation, as mentioned above, require different aerodynamic or articulatory relationships between the active and the passive articulators than in the stops described so far, though still necessarily requiring a phase of articulatory closure. This is the class of stop segments that in very many different languages have traditionally been regarded as forming part of the phonetic repertoire for manifesting 'r' sounds, in a 'rhotic' phonological role. Trilled and flapped stops are almost always regarded as playing this particular rhotic phonological role.

Tapped stops are also often given a rhotic phonological role, but there are a number of languages where their identity is seen as phonologically closer to that of alveolar plosives. This is the case in American English, for example, where the allophone of /t/ between vowels is realized phonetically in many accents as [ɾ], as in *city* /sɪti/ ⇒ [sɪɾi]. In addition, as mentioned earlier, tapping and flapping can be applied as aspectual processes to more segment-types than merely stops. It is therefore probably sensible to treat the phenomena of trilled, tapped and flapped stops individually, rather than try to force them all into membership of an overall 'rhotic' class of events.

8.5.1 *Trilled stop articulations*

We can consider first the stop usually referred to as a **trill** (which is also sometimes referred to as a 'rolled r'). Because it is regarded here as a stop made with a trilled aspect of articulation, it should strictly be referred to as a **trilled stop**. (For convenience, and in sympathy with the traditional usage, the term 'trill' can be used alone to refer to a trilled stop. For fricative strictures, it will be necessary to add the stricture type and use the full label of a 'trilled fricative' or its alternative 'fricative trill').

Trills can be made in a number of different places of articulation, although alveolar and uvular trills are by far the most common of the trills in the languages of the world. The active articulator in an alveolar trill is usually the blade and sometimes the tip of the tongue, vibrating against the alveolar ridge. In the uvular trill it is the uvula, vibrating in a broad channel formed in the centre of the back of the tongue. The symbol for a voiced alveolar trill is [r], and for the voiced uvular trill is [ʀ].

Trills are made by a mechanism similar to the aerodynamic–myoelastic action of phonation. Taking the alveolar trill as the detailed example, the tongue blade or tip is brought into complete closure with the alveolar ridge (or very nearly so), often in a slightly cupped aspect. Contact pressure is relatively light, and oral pressure builds rapidly to the point of forcing its way through the closure. A high-speed jet of air escapes through the gap, and a combination of elastic muscle forces and the sucking action of the Bernoulli effect in the air-jet bring the tongue surface very quickly back into renewed contact. The cycle is then repeated for as long as the stricture and the air supply are maintained. In those languages that exploit an alveolar trill as part of their phonological repertoire, apical trills are more common than laminal trills, according to Ladefoged, Cochran and Disner (1977: 49).

In connected speech, seldom more than two or three successive cycles are used, at a typical repetition frequency of between 26 and 32 Hz (Ladefoged, Cochran and Disner 1977: 52). These authors analysed the frequency of repetition of the individual cycles in labial trills used in Kele and Titan (Austronesian languages of Papua New Guinea), alveolar trills in Hausa (of Nigeria), Spanish and Italian, and uvular trills in a prestige accent of Italian and in the accent associated with the Scanian dialect of Swedish. There was no statistically significant difference in the rate of vibration of the trills at different places of articulation.

Tigre is an example of a language that uses a voiced alveolar trilled stop (Palmer 1956). The symbol [ʕ] in the transcription of the word for 'sky' refers to a voiced pharyngeal fricative, which is described in chapter 9:

> *Alveolar trill in Tigre*
> [fɐrəd̪] 'revolver'   [ʕastɐr] 'sky'
> [kərɐʃ] 'stomach'   [kərəmbaː] 'cabbage'

219

Another example of a language using a voiced alveolar trilled stop is Sundanese (Robins 1953):

Alveolar trill in Sundanese

[ŋadahar] 'to eat'   [ŋarawaṭ] 'to look after'
[ɲirim] 'to send'   [ŋaboroŋ] 'to buy (an entire stock)'

A voiced labial trill has been reported in contrastive use in Ngwe, a language of Cameroon (Dunstan 1964), in Amuzgo and Isthmus Zapotec (Pike 1963), which are Mesoamerican Amerindian languages, and in Kele and Titan (Ladefoged, Cochran and Disner 1977: 50). The official symbol in the International Phonetic Association alphabet for a voiced bilabial trill is [ʙ], as originally suggested by Ladefoged and his co-workers. (The symbol [ʙ] should not be confused with the typographically similar symbol [β], which is the symbol for a voiced labial fricative, to be more fully described in the next chapter.) An example of a word with a voiced (pre-nasal) labial trill in Kele is [ᵐʙen] 'fruit'. (Pre-nasality of this sort is explained in a later section of this chapter.)

Ladefoged, Cochran and Disner (1977: 49) point out that 'very few languages have any trills at all, and even fewer contrast trills of two different kinds'. They cite the example of Malayalam, which uses two different kinds of trill, both made with the tongue tip as the active articulator. One is slightly advanced from the alveolar place of articulation, and is symbolized [r], and the stricture for the other is post-alveolar (Ladefoged and his colleagues characterize it as 'almost retroflex'). It will be symbolized here as [ɽ]. Sample words are:

Pre-alveolar and retroflex post-alveolar trills in Malayalam

[puɾʌ] 'root'   [kʌɾʌ] 'border'   [maɾʌm] 'tree'
[puɽʌ] 'outer'   [kʌɽʌ] 'stain'   [niɽʌm] 'colour'

Alveolar and uvular trills were said by Coustenoble, a colleague of Daniel Jones, to be in contrast in the Arles accent of Modern Provençal (Coustenoble 1945), in word pairs such as ['sero] 'evening' versus ['seʀo] 'a saw', and [a'ri] 'to cure' versus [a'ʀi] 'oak'. It is not clear that the contrast between alveolar and uvular trills is still maintained in the Provençal spoken today. It is, however, maintained in Modern Northern Tepehuán, a Uto-Aztecan Mesoamerican Indian language (Suárez 1983: 32).

In Dutch, individual speakers vary with respect to alveolar and uvular trills, in that some use one and some the other. The two trills are not, however, in free variation within the speech of single speakers, and the use of one trill versus the other is not restricted either to a given geographical area or to a given social group (J. Verhoeven, personal communication). Examples are:

> *Alveolar and uvular trilled stops as speaker-specific options in Dutch*
> [paːrt] 'horse' varies with   [pɑːʀt] 'horse'
> [ɣrot] 'big'   varies with   [ɣʀot] 'big'

As a member of the overall category of stop contoids, a trill can be either oral or nasal in aspect. The large majority of alveolar trills used in the languages of the world are oral, but Igbo (of Eastern Nigeria) is one example of a language where both nasal and oral trills participate in a minimal pair of words (Williamson 1969a: 87):

> *Nasal and oral alveolar trills in Igbo*
> [ĩr̃ĩ] 'to climb'   [ɪrɪ] 'to creep'

A phonemic transcription might choose to locate the contrastive nasality on the vowel phonemes, reducing the status of the nasality on the trills to contextually specified allophonic value. Nevertheless, nasality on trills in Igbo is part of the complex which signals the distinctive identity of these words.

Another language which uses a nasal (alveolar) trilled stop is Zande, a Ubangi language of Zaïre and the Central African Republic spoken by over a million people (Bright 1992, vol. IV: 204). Herbert (1986: 254), citing Tucker and Hackett (1959), suggests that the [r̃] in Zande [ⁿzõr̃õ] 'bell', for example, is the customary phonetic realization of /ⁿr/, and suggests that 'the group /ⁿv, ⁿz, ⁿr/ functions as a class, as opposed to the pre-nasalized stops /ᵐb, ⁿd, ᵑg,ᵑ͡ᵐg͡b/', noting that /ⁿv/ and /ⁿz/ are similarly often realized phonetically as [ṽ] and [z̃]. Symbols written with a prefaced superscript nasal stop element such as [ᵐb] represent 'pre-nasal' segments (stops and fricatives). Pre-nasal stops are discussed in detail in section 8.6 below on complex oral/nasal stop articulations. The symbol [ᵑ͡ᵐg͡b] stands for a stop made with a simultaneous double stricture of complete closure (velar and labial), prefaced by a homorganic nasal stop element. Segments made with double articulations are described in detail in chapter 11. Nasal and pre-nasal fricatives such as [ṽ] and [z̃] are discussed in chapter 9.

8.5.2 *Flapped stop articulations*

Flapped stops are made by a process which involves the active articulator hitting the passive articulator in passing. The most commonly cited example of this is the flapped stop made in languages such as Hausa, where the tip of the tongue starts from a curled retroflex position, with the tip behind the alveolar ridge. It is made to uncurl forwards rapidly, and in uncurling hits the alveolar ridge, momentarily making an airtight seal against the ridge while sliding forward. For the very short duration of the airtight seal, egressive airflow rises in pressure within the oral cavity. On release of the alveolar closure, as the uncurling tongue allows the tip to continue on its way towards the floor of the mouth (sometimes audibly hitting the floor behind the lower front teeth), the compressed air escapes in a slight, audible plosion. The transcriptional symbol for a retroflex alveolar flapped stop is [ɽ]. A diagram of the actions for [ɽ] is given in figure 8.4a–c. The right-curling descender of the symbol is the indicator that retroflexion is part of the articulation of this segment.

The place of articulation of all other retroflex segments is post-alveolar or palato-alveolar rather than alveolar, and the only relevant property that the flapped stop shares with the other members of the retroflex class of segments is that the onset phase for the flapped stop begins in approximately the same curled position as the rest of the class. As with all other members of the retroflex class of segments, the retroflex flapped stop thus gives a strong 'r-colouring' to the perceptual effect of any preceding vocoid segment, because of the curled shape of the tongue tip/blade in the overlap phase between them.

In this book, 'retroflex' will be reserved for a conformational aspect of tongue shape, and will not be used as a direct identification of place of articulation. The appropriate label for the flapped stop described above would therefore be a **voiced retroflex alveolar flapped stop**. The shorter label 'retroflex flap' can be used for brevity, provided one remembers that the place of maximum stricture is alveolar not palato-alveolar, and that the degree of stricture is that of a (momentary) stop.

Masica (1991: 97) describes the widespread occurrence of the voiced retroflex alveolar flapped stop [ɽ] in the Indo-Aryan languages. He mentions that it is in contrast with a voiced retroflex palato-alveolar stop [ɖ] in Panjabi, as in [saɽi] 'burnt' versus [saɖi] 'our (fem. sg.)', as it is in Sindhi and Modern Standard Hindi. He adds that 'it may be or is reputed as phonemic also in Shina and some other Dardic languages, Dogri, Rajasthani ... various Western Hindi dialects, and in several West Pahari dialects ... It remains subphonemic in Marathi, Gujarati, Eastern Hindi, Bhojpuri, Maithili, Kumauni, Kashmiri ... and probably also Nepali' (Masica *ibid.*).

Amongst Australian languages, Yallop (1982: 61–2) states that a few languages, including Maung and Warlpiri, make contrasts between three rhotic segments, of which one is the voiced retroflex alveolar flapped stop [ɽ]. The

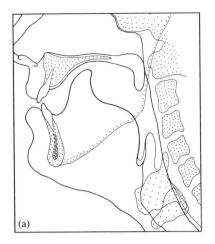

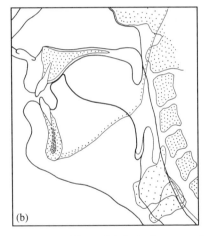
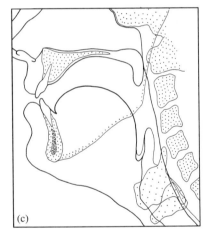

Figure 8.4 Sagittal cross-sections of the vocal organs, showing sequential stages in the production of a voiced retroflex alveolar flapped oral stop [ɽ]: (a) first stage – retroflex onset; (b) second stage – sliding alveolar closure; and (c) third stage – releasing offset

other two are a voiced alveolar tapped stop [ɾ], and a voiced post-alveolar approximant [ɹ]. Amongst the languages of Mexico and Central America, Suárez (1983: 32) cites Huichol, the Uto-Aztecan Mesoamerican Indian language mentioned earlier, as using a voiced retroflex alveolar flapped stop [ɽ] as the phonetic manifestation of the only rhotic segment in the language. Another Mesoamerican Indian language in this area which contrasts a voiced retroflex alveolar flapped stop [ɽ] with a voiced alveolar trilled stop [r] is Tarascan (Suárez 1983: 37).

Trills and flapped stops are in phonemic contrast in a number of African languages. One example comes from Gbaya, a language of the Sudan (Westermann and Ward 1933: 76):

> *Trilled and flapped stops in Gbaya*
> [eɽe] 'hen'   [ere] 'beans'

The flapped stop just mentioned uses the tongue as the active articulator. A second type of flapped stop has been described by Tucker, as used in Gbaya, and by Doke, in Shona (a language of Zimbabwe), both cited in Westermann and Ward (1933: 77). This involves the lower lip as the active articulator against the upper front teeth. Ladefoged (1964: 18) describes a possibly similar flapped labial stop in Margi, a language of Northern Nigeria, used in an 'ideophonic' word [bəvᵇu] (whose sound is supposed to illustrate the concept concerned) to refer to the sudden appearance and flight of a bird, where 'the articulation consists of drawing the lower lip back inside the upper teeth, and then allowing it to flap against the teeth as it returns to its normal position'. There is no conventional symbol for a labial flapped stop. The symbol [vᵇ] is Ladefoged's tentative suggestion (1964: 18).

8.5.3 *Tapped stop articulations*

Tapping as an aspect of articulation is often said to be closely related to trilling. A frequent decription of a **tapped stop** is that it is the limiting case of a trill, with only one contact of complete closure instead of repeated closures. This is rather dubious. In the case of a trill, the tongue is positioned in a near-static posture, and the aerodynamic Bernoulli effect is instrumental in bringing the tongue into repeated contact with the passive articulator in the onset of each individual closure. In the case of a tapped stop, the tongue moves very fast through the onset phase, the closure is extremely brief and the tongue then retreats from closure in a very fast offset phase.

The difference between [d], an ordinary voiced alveolar plosive, and [ɾ], a voiced alveolar tapped stop, may therefore be chiefly speed, as Ladefoged (1975: 147) suggests. If tapped stops and 'one-tap-trills' both occur as phonetic events, it would ideally be necessary, in accounting for phonetic differences between languages, to set up both possibilities as articulatorily and aerodynamically different categories. It is likely that they do occur as different phenomena in the speech of different individuals, but they have never been shown to participate in a contrastive difference within a given accent of any language discovered to date. For convenience it is probably sufficient to include them both under the general category of 'tapped stop', until observed data obliges expansion to separate categories.

Tapped stops are very common in different accents of English. A tapped alveolar stop is widespread in many accents of Scots English, as the manifestation of the /r/ phoneme in various segmental contexts. Tapped stops are also extremely common in North American English, not as manifestations of /r/, but as the pronunciation of /t/ between vowels, as in *latter* [laɾɚ]. These tapped stops can be either voiced or voiceless, depending on regional accent. When the pronunciation of /t/ between vowels is a voiced alveolar tapped stop in North American accents, it can lead to a **neutralization** of phonological contrast with /d/, when this also has the same phonetic manifestation in this position. Pairs of words which are not homophones in other accents, such as *latter* [laɾɚ] and *ladder* [laɾɚ], and *waiting* [weɪɾɪŋ] and *wading* [weɪɾɪŋ], then become auditorily indistinguishable (Wells 1982: 249).

Yoruba, spoken in Nigeria and Benin, is a West African example of a language which uses a voiced alveolar tapped stop, as in [ɾí] 'to see' (Bamgbose 1969: 164). Another Nigerian example is I̩jo̩. The following examples showing the use of [ɾ] as the realization of the single rhotic consonant in the language come from the Kalabari accent of I̩jo̩ described by Williamson (1969b: 103):

> *Tapped stops in Kalabari I̩jo̩*
> [kíɾi] 'ground' [fɪɾí] 'work/message'
> [ɓéɾé] 'case/trouble' [ɓáɾɑ] 'hand/arm'
> [ɓuɾʊ] 'to be rotten' [ɓuɾu] 'yam'

Tapped stops and trills are found in phonemic contrast in the Suleimaniya accent of Kurdish (A. Ferhardi, personal communication), and in European Spanish. In European Portuguese, the tapped stop is alveolar and the trilled stop is uvular (Parkinson 1988: 138):

> *Tapped and trilled stops in Kurdish (Suleimaniya accent)*
> [bɾin] 'wound (injury)' [brin] 'cutting'
>
> *Tapped and trilled stops in European Spanish*
> ['peɾo] 'but (conj.)' ['pero] 'dog'
>
> *Tapped and trilled stops in European Portuguese*
> ['kaɾu] 'dear' ['kaʀu] 'car'

Amongst Mesoamerican Indian languages, Suárez (1983: 36) mentions Coastal Chontal, a Tequistlatec-Jicaque language, as contrasting a voiced alveolar tapped stop [ɾ] with a voiced alveolar trilled stop [r]. In Hausa, the language of Northern Nigeria and other parts of West Africa, tapped stops are found in phonemic contrast with flapped stops, but with the tapped stops being optionally interchangeable with trills in free variation, in examples such as [baɾaː] 'servant' versus [baɾaː] or [baraː] 'begging' (Ladefoged 1964: 30).

An interestingly complex contrast between a flapped stop or trill versus a tapped stop or an approximant is found in Urhobo, the language of Southeastern Nigeria cited earlier. Urhobo uses a distinction between a voiced retroflex alveolar flapped stop 'with a lateral on-glide' (Kelly 1969: 156) which will be symbolized here as [ᴸɽ], and a consonant which is manifested in careful speech by a voiceless alveolar trill [r̥], and in casual speech by a voiced alveolar tapped stop [ɾ], or a voiced post-alveolar approximant [ɹ]. In careful speech in Urhobo, therefore, there is a distinction between [oᴸɽe] 'tsetse fly' and [oɾe] 'plantain' (Kelly 1969: 154).

Esling (1991) describes the accent of Scottish Gaelic spoken on the Hebridean island of Lewis by some 15,000 speakers, where (as a partial allophonic statement) the phoneme /r/ is realized phonetically in a number of different positions as a voiced dental trilled stop [r̪] after voiced oral stops; a voiceless dental trilled stop [r̪̥] or a voiceless tapped stop [ɾ̪̥] after voiceless oral stops; and a voiced dental tapped stop [ɾ̪] intervocalically. The symbol [æ] in the word for 'bread' stands for a slightly closer and nasal version of an [a] vocoid, and is described in more detail in chapter 10:

Tapped and trilled allophones of /r/ in Scottish Gaelic (Lewis)

[ɪn̪ˈdr̪̃ãːsti] 'now'   [t̪ʰr̪̃iː] 'three'
[t̪ʰɾ̪̃iʰkʰj] 'often'   [ˈaɾ̪æ̃n̪] 'bread'

There is no articulatory reason why flapped and tapped stops should not be produced with a nasal aspect of articulation. Nasality in Urhobo is a feature which may extend over the whole of a word, running through phonologically selected consonants. The voiced flapped stop is one of these, and it can therefore occur as a flapped nasal stop, as in [ẽɽ̃ãɥ̃ẽ] 'meat/animal'. The voiceless trill/voiced tapped stop/voiced approximant acts as a phonological block to the spread of nasality, and thus does not occur in a nasal version in Urhobo, as evidenced in the form of words such as [oɾ̥w̃ẽ] 'hunter' (Kelly 1969: 155). The symbols [ɥ] and [w] stand for approximants, and these are explained in chapter 10 below.

Nasality on tapped stops can also be seen in some accents of English, and in Yoruba. Wells (1982: 252) cites Trager (1942: 146) as maintaining that in his own Northern accent of American English, a voiced alveolar tapped nasal stop was in contrast with a voiced alveolar tapped oral stop, in the word-pair *winter* , pronounced [wɪ̃ɾ̃ə], and *winner*, pronounced as [wɪnɚ]. In Yoruba, /r/ before nasal vocoids is manifested phonetically as a voiced alveolar tapped nasal stop, as in [ò̙ɾ̃ũ̀] 'sun' (Bamgbose 1969: 165).

8.6   Complex oral/nasal stop articulations

In section 4.5.2, the concept of the **segment** was described as a 'linear unit consisting of a short stretch of speech of relatively unchanging feature-values'. The implication was allowed to stand that the features whose combination makes up the substance of speech all change their values in synchrony with each other, at the phase-boundaries of the segment. This synchronization of features for the whole of the medial phase of a phonetic segment was a convenient concept for initial presentation, and can be allowed to remain in force for many types of segmental behaviour. In a number of different circumstances, however, there is a greater degree of asynchrony shown by phonetic features than this would suggest. Some of these will be explored in chapter 12 on co-ordination, in the discussion of three areas of the desynchronization of articulatory and phonatory features in phenomena such as aspiration; sub-segmental events being inserted in the overlapping phase between two segments in processes such as affrication; and feature-timing strategies of co-articulation. But we have reached the point in the present chapter where the convenient fiction of feature-synchrony must be modified in order to account for a number of different types of **complex oral/nasal stops**.

The oral stops and nasal stops that have been described so far can be considered to be **simplex stops**. Part of the definition of a **simplex oral stop** is that oral closure and velic closure should co-exist throughout the medial phase of the segment. Similarly, by definition, in a **simplex nasal stop**, oral closure and velic opening must co-exist throughout the medial phase. These timing relationships, where the feature-values are held constant throughout the medial phase, and are allowed the option of synchronized change only at the boundaries of the medial phase, are shown diagrammatically in Figures 8.5a and 8.5b respectively. When the feature of velic state is allowed to change its value within the medial phase of the segment concerned, asynchronously from the continuing oral closure, four candidates for **complex oral/nasal stops** emerge. Diagrams for the relative timings for these are also shown in Figures 8.5c–8.5f. These can be called a **pre-nasal oral stop** (Figure 8.5c), a **post-nasal oral stop** (Figure 8.5d), a **pre-occluded nasal stop** (Figure 8.5e), and a **post-occluded nasal stop** (Figure 8.5f).

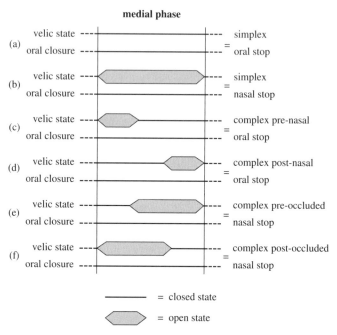

Figure 8.5 The timing relationships of oral closure and velic state during the production of (a) a simplex oral stop; (b) a simplex nasal stop; (c) a complex pre-nasal oral stop; (d) a complex post-nasal oral stop; (e) a complex pre-occluded nasal stop; and (f) a complex post-occluded nasal stop

Whether one classifies a particular sequence of a nasal and an oral element within a complex stop as a pre-nasal oral stop or a post-occluded nasal stop will clearly depend on the relative durational balance of the oral and nasal components within the medial phase of the complex stop. Thus the [m + b] pattern within a complex stop would be classified as a pre-nasal oral stop [ᵐb] if the duration of the oral element predominates, and as a post-occluded nasal stop [mᵇ] if the duration of the nasal element is dominant. A similar criterion of durational balance applies in the comparison between a post-nasal oral stop [bᵐ] and a pre-occluded nasal stop [ᵇm]. Different languages, and speakers of a given language on different occasions, probably vary phonetically to some degree between the members of the relevant pair of possibilities. If the exact phasing of the two elements is less important than the fact of complexity in the production of the stops concerned, then an ambiguous transcription can be tolerated in which both elements are given full status, joined by a linker diacritic. The composite symbol [m͡b] would then stand equally for a pre-nasal oral stop and a post-occluded nasal stop. The composite symbol [b̃m] would stand equally for a post-nasal oral stop or a pre-occluded nasal stop.

One reason for setting up the notion of stops with complex oral/nasal medial phases (in preference to the theoretical alternative of distinguishing between sequences of simplex nasal and oral stop segments of varying durational relationships) is that, in pre-nasal and post-nasal stops the duration of the nasal element is unusually short. Equally, the duration of the oral element in pre-occluded and post-occluded nasal stops is unusually short. Armstrong (1940: 30–1), using oral and nasal airflow measurements, was able to show that in Southern Kikuyu (a language of East Africa) the nasal elements initial in pre-nasal stops are very short, in utterance-initial position at least. Armstrong comments that 'the plosive sounds' [b, d, g] and the voiced pre-palatal affricate [d̠ʑ] 'exist only in conjunction with nasal ... sounds; they are inseparable from the nasal sounds'. (Affricated sounds are described below in chapter 12.) Armstrong continues 'It is phonetically sound to consider [mb, nd, ŋg] and [nd̠ʑ] as single consonant sounds with a nasal "kick-off"' (1940: 31). Words showing these complex segments in Kikuyu are:

> *Pre-nasal stops in Kikuyu*
> [ᵐbura] 'rain'   [ⁿdoːru] 'herds'
> [ᵑgɔrɔ] 'heart'   [ⁿd̠ʑɔrɔ] 'branding irons'

In order further to justify inclusion of these segment-types in a general phonetic theory as complex single segments, as opposed to independent sequences of oral stop followed by nasal stop (or vice versa), it would be persuasive if languages could be found where words are contrastively identified by means of these complex stops versus comparable sequences of their simple nasal and oral stop counterparts. This seems feasible. An illustration is given by Jones (1950: 79–81), in his discussion of the 'compound' nature of pre-nasal stops (though he does not use the term 'pre-nasal') in Sinhalese (a language of Sri Lanka). A triplet of Sinhalese words shows a pre-nasal alveolar stop in contrast to a corresponding sequence of a full nasal stop followed by a full oral stop which is homorganic, versus a word with only the corresponding simplex oral stop. The triplet is:

> *Pre-nasal alveolar stop in Sinhalese*
> [kaⁿdə] 'trunk'
> [kanːdə] 'hill'
> [kadə] 'shoulder pole carrying weights at each end'

(Esling 1991 describes the pre-nasal stops in the cases of the first two words in their current pronunciation as dental for both elements.) Jones states that in the pre-nasal stop the nasal element is so short that the word [ka^{n}də] 'trunk' has the 'same rhythmic pattern as [kadə]. It is not at all like the English word "candour"' (Jones 1950: 78–9). Similar comments are reported for Fijian, discussed further below in this chapter.

Another instance of a complex stop versus a sequence of nasal stop followed by an oral stop can be found in Nyanja, a Bantu language of Malawi, which distinguishes between [^{m}bale] 'plate' and [ṃbale] 'brother' in this way. Using '+' to indicate syllable division, the pronunciation of the first word is disyllabic, as [^{m}ba+le], and the second word is trisyllabic, as [ṃ+ba+le] (Herbert 1986: 161).

Although pre-nasal stops are reported in a number of languages, fully comparable word-pairs are not often included in the summary accounts of phonological systems given in the literature, and constraints on possible syllable structures also often prevent full comparability. Arnott (1969b: 143–51) offers an outline of the consonantal system of Tiv, a language of Northeastern Nigeria, however, where pre-nasal oral stops and pre-nasal oral affricates are in contrast with their simplex stop correspondents:

Pre-nasal stops and pre-nasal affricates in Tiv

[^{m}bara] 'those people'	[bar] 'salt'
[sa^{m}be] 'slap'	[ṃbee] 'I have finished'
[^{n}duhwar] 'hoe'	[daɡi] 'barbed spear'
[^{n}ʤiɣe] 'rubbed between the hands'	[ʤiɣirii] 'straight'
[^{ŋ}guhwar] 'leg/foot'	[ga^{m}be] 'bed'
[^{ŋm}ĝbɔgɔm] 'approached'	[ĝba^{n}de] 'plate'

In many accents of Tiv, [r] is in free variation with [l] (Arnott 1969b: 143). The initial stops in the final pair of words, [^{ŋm}ĝbɔgɔm] 'approached' and [ĝba^{n}de] 'plate' are **double stops** (which are discussed in chapter 11). In [sa^{m}be] 'slap', the syllable-affiliation of the segments is said to be [sa] +[^{m}be], and not [sam] + [be]. The structure of these syllables is thus CV + CV and not CVC + CV. In [ṃbee] 'I have finished', the [ṃ] is both syllabic and carries its own tonal value (syllabic tone is discussed in chapter 15).

Fula, spoken throughout the sub-Saharan belt of West Africa, also has pre-nasal oral stops and pre-nasal affricates in its consonantal system. Arnott (1969a: 57–71) lists [^{m}b, ^{n}d, ^{n}ʣ, ^{ŋ}g]. An example of a language using pre-nasal stops from a very different part of the world is Kalam, spoken by some 13,000 people in Papua New Guinea, on the northern slopes of the central highlands at the junction of the Madang and Western Highlands Provinces.

Foley (1986: 51), in his survey of the Papuan languages of New Guinea, cites the following words from a study by Pawley (1966):

Pre-nasal stops in Kalam

[^{m}benep] 'a man only' [^{m}bim] 'down valley'

[ja^{n}t] 'I' [ki^{n}dɨl] 'sinew'

[wo^{ŋ}k] 'garden' [koriba^{ŋ}gɨp] 'he spoke at the house'

While the nasal element of a pre-nasal stop is necessarily homorganic with that of the oral stop element, it does not follow that the phonatory state is always identical in the two elements, as evident from the words for 'I' and 'garden' in the Kalam example above. However, the nasal element of pre-nasal stops seems most frequently to be voiced. Voiceless exceptions are found in Amahuaca, a Panoan language of the Amazon headwaters spoken by less than 2,000 speakers (Bright 1992, vol. III: 153). Herbert (1986: 202) characterizes the realizations of /p, t, k, θ/ in Amahuaca as 'voiceless stops which are voiced when morpheme-initial after a morpheme ending in a nasalized vowel. When morpheme-initial after a nasalized vowel, /p, t, k, θ/ appear as [mp, nt, ŋk, n̥θ]', as in the following examples:

Voiceless nasal elements of pre-nasal stops in Amahuaca

/wĩpís/ ⇒ [wĩ^{m}pís] 'guayaba' /kɨ̃tí/ ⇒ [kɨ̃^{n}tí] 'cooking pot'

Pre-nasal oral stops at various places of articulation are not extreme rarities in the languages of the world (Herbert 1977, 1986). For the pre-nasal bilabial stop [^{m}b], for example, Maddieson (1981, 1984: 206) cites from his sample of 317 languages: Luvale, Gbeya, Yulu, Sara, Berta, Ngizim, Sedang, Alawa, Hakka, Washkuk, Selepet, Kewa, Wantoat, Nambakaengo, Páez, Apinayé and Sirionó.

Post-occluded nasal stops are reported by Bauernschmidt (1965) in Amuzgo, the Amerindian language mentioned earlier, which she describes as being spoken by some 15,000 speakers in Southeast Guerrero and Southeast Oaxaca in Mexico. For our purposes we can consider two representative contrasts out of a much larger potential set that she offers. The first is between a (tonally equivalent) sequence of a voiced alveolar nasal stop followed by a voiceless alveolar oral stop in [nta] 'liquor' and a post-occluded alveolar nasal stop in [n^{t}a] 'our children', where the post-occluding oral element can be voiceless. The second contrast is between an analogous pair of words: a sequence of two independent consonantal alveolo-palatal segments initial in [ɲcoʔ] 'bread (pl.)' versus a post-occluded alveolo-palatal nasal stop in [ɲ^{c}oʔ] 'itchy'.

Bauernschmidt established durational and voicing facts acoustically by spectrographic measurement. Taking the first pair cited above as representative, she comments that in the sequence of two independent consonants, by contrast with the post-occluded nasal stop, 'the nasal is short, the stop is of greater duration and fortis articulation. There is no carry-over of voicing from the first to the second segment' (Bauernschmidt 1965: 480). She then says that, in the post-occluded nasal stop, by comparison, 'the nasal is longer, the stop shorter and lenis. There is often but not always a carry-over of the voicing from the nasal to the stop.' (The terms 'fortis' and 'lenis' here can be regarded as meaning muscularly tense and lax articulation respectively. The terms are discussed in more detail in section 12.1.)

The mirror-image of pre-nasal stops, namely **post-nasal stops**, are also found occasionally. One example comes from Kaingang, a South American language, where the allophonic realizations of voiced plosive phonemes in final position are [b^m, d^n, g $^\eta$] (Herbert 1986: 206). Another example comes from Içũa Tupí (Abrahamson 1968), a lowland South American language, where 'the voiced stops are [b^m, d^n, g$^\eta$] finally after an oral vowel whereas they are [m, n, ŋ] in this position after a nasal vowel' (Herbert *ibid.*).

Anderson (1976: 332) collapses together the categories of post-nasal oral and pre-occluded nasal stops, and says that they are found 'in a number of South American languages, in some Indonesian languages, in some of the languages of New Caledonia, and in some of the phonologically aberrant languages of Australia, and perhaps elsewhere'. Anderson discusses in some detail (*ibid*: 336–7) data on complex oral/nasal stops in Apinayé, a South American language described originally by Callow (1962). Apinayé is said to have an opposition between a series of voiceless oral stops and a corresponding voiced series. These voiced stops 'can be nasal, pre-nasal, post-nasal or oral depending on the adjacent vowels' (*ibid.* p. 336). Anderson lists two sets of data, one for a VCV sequence where either one or both of the vowels can be oral or nasal, and a corresponding data set for a VCCV sequence where there are two independent consonants. The two sets are:

Contextual conditioning of complex oral/nasal stops in Apinayé

VCV	*VCCV*
[VbV]	[VbdV]
[V̌m̂bV]	[V̌mdV]
[Vbm̂V̌]	[VbnV̌]
[V̌mV̌]	[V̌mnV̌]

The symbols [V, Ṽ, b, d, m, n, m̃b, b̃m] stand respectively for oral vowels ([V]), nasal vowels ([Ṽ]), fully oral stops ([b,d]), fully nasal stops ([m, n]), pre-nasal stops ([m̃b]), and post-nasal stops ([b̃m]). In the case of the second set (VCCV), the oral or nasal status of the adjacent vowel allophonically conditions the oral or nasal status of the consonant next to it. In the case of the first set (VCV), the single consonant has to be regarded as potentially complex. If the two neighbouring vowels are identical in oral or nasal status, then the consonant takes on that status, and is a simple stop, oral or nasal. If the vowels differ in oral/nasal status, then the stop becomes complex, and the oral/nasal status of the individual component of the complex stop is allophonically determined by that of the adjacent vowel. A similar patterning is found in Maxakalí, a language of Brazil (Gudschinsky, Popovitch and Popovitch 1970).

Anderson mentions a further possible degree of oral/nasal complexity, as found in Kaingang, reported by Wiesemann (1972). This involves triple complexity in the medial phase of the stop. Anderson calls the type a 'medio-nasalized stop', and says that such segments 'which occur as conditioned variants of pre-nasalized stops between oral vowels, begin oral, are briefly nasal, and then end oral. They can be transcribed [bmb, dnd] etc.' (Anderson 1976: 335). This triple complexity is the consequence of an adjustment of a pre-nasal stop to a preceding oral context, and is therefore a matter of a particular co-ordinatory allophonic relationship between two segments. However, the internal segmental intricacy of complex oral/nasal stops challenges the theoretical construct of the complex but single phonetic segment to a degree where further discussion is necessary.

It will be recalled that an essential part of the phonetic classification of a given segment is the medial phase where the maximum degree of articulatory stricture is reached and maintained. The notion of this medial phase remains reasonably straightforward in the case of complex oral/nasal stops, even of the triple oral/nasal/oral complexity of the Kaingang data from Wiesemann (1972) and Anderson (1976), provided that the segment-defining medial phase is held to be that of the stricture of oral closure involved. The nasality which then arises from velic opening during any part of this oral closure is a phonetic feature which is physiologically quite independent of the actions needed to maintain the oral closure. The subsegmental timing of the beginning and ending of nasality within the medial phase of the segment defined by the persisting oral closure is correspondingly unconstrained except by factors of maximum speed of velic adjustment and perceptual factors of minimum duration of nasality for audibility.

A similar example is offered by the more familiar case of anticipatory nasality during the medial phase of a vocoid before a nasal stop. This is a phenomenon found in very many languages including English, and is discussed in detail in chapter 10. It is perhaps sufficient to say here that languages vary in the exact subsegmental timing of the onset of nasality within the medial phase of such a vocoid, once again reflecting the physiological freedom of the velic process relative to oral actions.

A theoretical position is thus maintained in this book that the construct of the single phonetic segment, allied to the concept of a defining medial phase, remains a sufficient basis for explaining the articulatory make-up of segments such as complex oral/nasal stops as well as vocoids displaying anticipatory nasality, provided that the relative freedom of the mutual timing of oral and nasal events in such segments is understood. The phonetic complexity of such stops is matched by the intricacy of the phonological considerations that need to be brought to bear on such cases. For discussion of this phonological topic, the reader is referred to Anderson (1974: 267–74) and Herbert (1977, 1986: 201–11).

Complex oral/nasal stops have been plausibly shown to be the product of historical development, in at least some languages, from an original nasal stop. In the Southern Paman languages of Australia's Cape York region, the word for 'man' is hypothesized to have been *[bama] in an earlier form (where it will be recalled that the use of the **asterisk** is a technical means of signalling the hypothesized rather than the **attested** nature of this earlier form). In one Paman language (Olgolo) this has become [aᵇma], with a pre-occluded nasal stop. In another Paman language, Lama-Lama (Lamu-Lamu), it has become [ᵐba], with a pre-nasal oral stop (Dixon 1980: 200).

Pre-nasality participates in an unusual segment-type in Fijian, where in addition to pre-nasal labial, pre-nasal alveolar and pre-nasal velar stops, a pre-nasal post-alveolar stop is found in which the release of the post-alveolar stop is sometimes trilled, as a **pre-nasal post-trilled stop**. Maddieson (1989: 60) gives the following examples:

Pre-nasal stops and pre-nasal post-trilled stops in Fijian

Initial position	Medial position
[ᵐbaka] 'banyan tree'	[kaᵐba] 'climb'
[ⁿdala] 'dal'	[kaⁿda] 'run'
[ⁿdʳata] 'sit'	[taⁿdʳa] 'dream'
[ᵑgara] 'hole'	[raᵑga] 'show off'

From spectrographic measurements on these pre-nasal stops, Maddieson is able to confirm that:

> the role of pre-nasalized stops in the timing pattern of Fijian is generally similar to that of other single segments. They neither have longer duration themselves nor do they shorten a preceding vowel, as might be expected if they had a timing pattern like that of geminate consonants or consonant clusters ... Fijian temporal patterns appear to be strictly based on the CV syllable, place and manner differences in following consonants having no effect on preceding vowel duration. (Maddieson 1989: 64–5)

(Geminate consonants, and contextual influences on allophonic segment duration, are discussed in chapter 14.)

Fully independent pre-nasal trills have also been reported in linguistic use. In Kele, the Austronesian language of Papua New Guinea mentioned earlier, a triple contrast exists between an alveolar trill, a pre-nasal alveolar trill and a pre-nasal labial trill (Ladefoged 1983a: 179; Ladefoged, Cochran and Disner 1977: 50):

Alveolar trilled stop versus pre-nasal alveolar and pre-nasal labial trilled stop in Kele

[riuriu] 'an insect'	[^{n}rikei] 'leg'	[^{m}ʙin] 'vagina'
[rarai] 'a fish'	[^{n}rilɛŋ] 'song'	[^{m}ʙen] 'fruit'
[^{m}ʙulim] 'face'	[^{m}ʙuwen] 'testicle'	

Another Austronesian language of this region, Titan, also uses pre-nasal trills. According to Ladefoged and his colleagues (*ibid.*), in Kele and Titan 'these sounds occur in numerous words in which the neighbouring languages have pre-nasalized /b, d/. In many Austronesian languages the voiced stops are always pre-nasalized. They are the only sequences of consonantal articulations that can occur in these languages, and are usually analyzed as unit phonemes.' The examples from Titan cited by Ladefoged and his colleagues (*ibid.*) are:

Pre-nasal labial trilled stop versus alveolar trilled stop in Titan

[^{m}ʙutukei] 'wooden plate'	[^{n}drakeʔin] 'girls'
[^{m}ʙulei] 'rat'	[^{n} druli] 'sandpiper'

8.7 Stop segments and phonation types

It is physiologically possible to produce stop articulations with a wide variety of phonation types. The phonatory states predominantly exploited by languages for stops are voicelessness or normal voicing. Other phonation types sometimes encountered include whisper, whispery voice, and creak or creaky voice.

Examples of stops made with a creaky voice (or creak) phonation type, in phonemic contrast with stops made with normal voicing and with voicelessness, can be found in Margi, a language of Northern Nigeria (Hoffmann 1963):

> *Stops with creaky voice versus stops with modal voicing and*
> *voicelessness in Margi*
>
> [pádʊ́] 'rain'   [bábál] 'open place'   [b̰ábál] 'hard'
>
> [tátá] 'that one'   [dàlmà] 'big axe'   [dàdàhʊ] 'bitter'

Ladefoged (1971: 14) cites examples suggested by George Fortune of nasal stops produced with a 'murmured' phonation type which in the terms of this book would be called whispery or breathy voice, versus nasal stops made with normal voicing, in Ndebele, a Benue-Congo language:

> *Whispery/breathy voiced nasal stop versus nasal stop made with*
> *modal voicing in Ndebele*
>
> [úm̤âm̤a] 'my mother'   [úmúntu] 'person'

Another example of a Bantu language exploiting murmur versus modal voicing for phonological contrast is Tsonga, spoken in Mozambique and South Africa. Traill and Jackson (1988: 386) offer the following illustrations:

> *Whispery/breathy voiced nasal stops versus nasal stops made with*
> *modal voicing in Tsonga*
>
> [m̤áwúri] 'August'   [mákálà] 'slap'
>
> [m̤àlà] 'type of antelope'   [màsásáǹì] 'righteous person'
>
> [màká] 'matter'   [màsàná] 'sun's rays'
>
> [n̤árù] 'three'   [nàlá] 'enemy'
>
> [ŋ̤wátí] 'type of bird'   [ɲáɲàní] 'type of bird'

The distinction between murmured segments and segments made with normal (modal voice) phonation may in different languages be placed on different parts of the continuum between these polar extremes (Jackson, Ladefoged and Antoñanzas-Barroso 1985; Ladefoged 1983b; Traill and Jackson 1988). This may also be true of different individual speakers within a single language. But in all these cases it also seems to be true that whispery/breathy voice on syllable-initial contoid segments spreads into the following syllable-nuclear vocoid. The phenomenon of murmur will therefore be treated in this book as a matter of co-ordination between a contoid and a following vocoid, under the rubric of 'voiced aspiration', rather than as an attribute solely of a single segment. Both voiceless aspiration and voiced aspiration will be dealt with in chapter 12 on co-ordination.

8.8 Stop articulations and non-pulmonic airstreams

It is often convenient to use special labels for stops made on particular types of airstream mechanism. These have been mentioned in the relevant sections above on airstream mechanisms. They include **ejective stops**, made on the egressive glottalic airstream; **implosive stops**, made on the ingressive glottalic airstream; **voiced implosive stops**, made on the compound mechanism involving both the ingressive glottalic and egressive pulmonic airstreams; and **clicks**, made on the ingressive velaric airstream. Within the overall category of stops, only plosives and clicks have nasal counterparts. Only a limited number of languages use non-pulmonic stops for phonological contrast, however.

Stop segments can be made on both glottalic and velaric airstream mechanisms. Ejective stop segments made on the egressive glottalic airstream can be found in many languages, and a number of examples were given in chapter 6. Further illustrations can be found in Xhosa (Kelly, personal communication), Hausa (Hoffmann and Schachter 1969: 75) and Tigre (Palmer 1956):

Ejective velar stops in Xhosa
[uk'uχula] 'to tow'   [uk'waɬula] 'to divide'

Ejective velar stops in Hausa
[k'jàːmáː] 'aversion'   [k'waɪ] 'egg(s)'

Ejective versus plosive dental stops in Tigre
[ʃənat'aː] 'her haversack'   [salsalataː] 'her bracelet'
[ʃariːt'] 'line'   [nabiːt̪] 'wine'

Another set of contrasts involving ejective versus plosive stops is offered by Esling (1991), in his discussion of Skagit, a northern dialect of Puget Salish (also known by its native name of Lushootseed), which is a Coastal member of the Salish language family, spoken in Skagit County of Western Washington State by a small number of hundreds of speakers. Esling (*ibid.*) also describes a similar set from a related language, Spokane-Kalispel-Flathead, which is an inland member of the Salish language family, spoken in Northeastern Washington, Northern Idaho and Northwestern Montana. The illustrations given below come from Skagit and from the Chewelah accent of Kalispel:

Ejective versus plosive stops in Skagit

[t'ˈqʰad] 'to stick on' [tʰˈqʰad] 'to close it'
[ˈkʷˈilʔ] 'look at it' [kʷʰil] 'pick'
[ˈqʷˈiˑbid] 'to unload it' [ˈqʷibid] 'to fix it'
[qˣəp'] 'bird landing' [qˣəp] 'foolish'

Ejective versus plosive stops in Kalispel (Chewelah)

[p'ɔχʷp'ɔˈχʷotʰ] 'old' [pisˈtɛʔpm̩] 'when'
[qʷˈiˈqʷˈaɪ] 'buffalo' [ˈqʷatsqʰən] 'hat'

The symbol [ʔ͡p] in the Kalispel word for 'when' above is a double stop (see chapter 11), with equal strictures of complete closure made at the glottal and labial places of articulation.

The mechanism for combining the ingressive glottalic and egressive pulmonic airstreams to produce voiced implosive stops was described in section 6.4. In addition to the examples given there, voiced implosives are found in such languages as Fula (Arnott 1969a) and in the Kalabari accent of Ịjọ (Williamson 1969b):

Voiced implosives in Fula

[kiːkiːɗe] 'evening' [ɗiɗi] 'leather loincloths'
[ʃoːɗe] 'herons' [ʃuːɗi] 'huts/rooms'

Voiced implosives in Kalabari Ịjọ

[ɓɛ́rɛ́] 'case/trouble' [ɓárɑ] 'hand/arm'
[ɓʊrʊ] 'to be rotten' [ɓuru] 'yam'

Another example of a language using voiced implosives is Zibiao Guéré, a Kru language spoken in Bangolo Tahouaké in the Ivory Coast. Paradis and Prunet (1989: 339–40) give the following illustrations (tone-marking has been omitted):

Voiced implosive stops in Zibiao Guéré

[kɪɓo] 'rat' [kɪɓe] 'monkey'
[ɓai] 'robe' [būi] 'ashes'
[biɗe] 'swim' [ɗaʊ] 'smoke'

The formation of click segments was described in chapter 6 on airstream production. The comment was made there that it is physiologically possible to make a variety of sound-types using a velaric ingressive airstream mechanism, but that only stops (and affricated stops, as explained in chapter 12) had been found in linguistic use. As an illustration of stop segments made on the velaric ingressive airstream mechanism, we can consider a language which makes considerable use of different click sounds – Xhosa, a Bantu language of the Transkei, spoken by some 4 million speakers. Xhosa exploits voiceless, voiced oral and voiced nasal clicks at the alveolar and palatal locations. In Xhosa, the three voiceless clicks [ǃ, ǁ, ǂ] are each also in contrast with their voiceless aspirated correlates [ǃʰ, ǁʰ, ǂʰ]. We shall confine our attention in this chapter to the non-aspirated contrasts, as exemplified by Esling (1991). (Aspiration is described in detail in chapter 12.) It should be noted that Esling's versions are detailed observations of what he heard on a specific occasion of pronunciation, and some fine discriminations are included that would probably be collapsed in a more phonologically oriented approach. Tonal indications have been omitted, and the transcription modified to fit the conventions of this book:

Voiceless and voiced alveolar, alveolar lateral and palatal oral and nasal clicks in Xhosa

Alveolar click	*Aveolar lateral click*
[kǃɑːkǃɑ̥ˑ] 'to be clear'	[kǁɑːkʼʊ̥] 'to have difficulty; obstruct'
[ukuʔgǃɑːbɑ̥ˑ] 'to apply	[iʔgǁɑːgǁɑː] 'poor man
an ointment'	(uncouth)'
[ŋǃãːŋǃɑ̥ˑ] 'to suck'	[ŋǁəpʰaːjaː] 'anger, displeasure'
Palatal click	
[iʔkǂɑːkǂɑː] 'polecat'	
[uʔgǂiːχʊ̥ˑ] 'doctor'	
[ukuŋǂãːbɑ̥ˑ] 'to be scarce'	

It will be recalled that the diacritic [ː] stands for relatively long duration, and [ˑ] for 'half-long' duration. The subscript diacritic [ḁ] signals (in these cases, utterance-final) devoicing, which is discussed at length in chapter 12 on coordination.

8.9 Syllabic stop segments

Ejectives, implosives and clicks (and of course plosives) are almost entirely found in syllable-marginal positions. One exception to this is found in some of the Amerindian languages of the Pacific coast of Canada and the United States, where a complete syllable may be represented by a single stop. An instance comes from Bella Coola, a Pacific Northwest Indian language, in which even citation forms of some particular words in isolation show no vocoids (Hoard 1978: 67). Syllable boundaries are indicated by '+':

> *Syllabic stops (including ejectives and affrication) in Bella Coola*
> [t̩ɬ' + p̩ʰ + tχ] 'cut it'   [k̩' + x̩ + χ] 'open your eyes'

Two examples from Nez Perce, an Amerindian language of the Sahaptian family (Hoard 1978: 66), spoken in northern Idaho (Bright 1992, vol. III: 178) are:

> *Syllabic voiceless oral stops (plosive and ejective) in Nez Perce*
> [tʰà + qʰɑ + k'ál +k̩ʰ + t̩ʰ] 'to close a door'
> [qʰo + qʰo + qʰeɪˀ + k̩ʰ + t̩ʰ] 'galloped'

One objection to the status of the plosive stops as truly syllabic in the Bella Coola and Nez Perce examples cited above could be that the release of each plosive is followed by a voiceless vocoid, and that such a vocoid might act as the syllabic nucleus. Newman (1947), cited by Hoard (1978: 72), believed that the releases of the stops in Bella Coola were manifested in this way by voiceless vocoids, held to be representing vowels. Hoard's objection to Newman's position is that the quality of such releases, although characteristic of stop releases at the relevant places of articulation, carries no audible information such as would typify the auditory quality of any particular voiceless vocoid following the stop.

Given that Hoard's position is accurate, the use of the [ʰ] diacritic to indicate the release of a stop may be a little misleading here, since [ʰ] is often taken as a kind of cover symbol for stop releases when followed by a voiced vocoid. The auditory quality of the [ʰ] will under those circumstances be coloured by the quality of the vocoid about to follow. It is in that sense that [ʰ] is usually taken to act as a cover symbol for a whole variety of voiceless onsets (of discernibly different vocoid-colouring) to voiced vocoids. A preferable way to transcribe the Bella Coola and comparable examples might therefore be to use some appropriate superscript symbol which merely implied 'release' for the stop, rather than the [ʰ] diacritic. One possibility might be the use of the reversed diacritic ['']. Bella Coola [tʰ + ɬ] ('strong') would then preferably be transcribed as [t' + ɬ], for example.

Examples of a nasal stop segment occurring as the nucleus of a syllable are much more common in languages than syllabic oral stop segments. Syllabic nasal stops are very common in informal speech in English as instances of 'nasal plosion' (a phenomenon discussed in detail in chapter 12 on co-ordination). Briefly, nasal plosion occurs when the oral air pressure built up during the articulation of an oral stop is released through the nasal cavity rather than through the mouth, without an intervening vocoid being pronounced. In such circumstances, the resulting nasal stop (which is necessarily homorganic for place of articulation with the preceding oral stop) functions in a syllabic role. Illustrations are:

> *Syllabic voiced nasal stops in English*
> [itn̩] eaten   [idn̩] Eden
> [beɪkŋ̍] bacon   [kabm̩bɔɪ] cabin-boy

In the case of the transcription for *bacon*, the syllabic diacritic is placed above the [ŋ] symbol because of legibility conflicts with the descender on that symbol.

An interesting occurrence of syllabic nasal stops can be found in Quiotepec Chinantec, an Otomanguean Mesoamerican Indian language of Mexico (Suárez 1983, citing Robbins 1975), where labial nasals, together with glottal stops, can make up entire words. The numbers attached to the following examples are one method of indicating the pitch of tonal contrasts, where five degrees of tone-level (1 representing the highest and 5 the lowest) within the speaker's pitch range are distinguished as end-points (in the case of falling or rising pitches) or as level tones. A more detailed analysis of the contrastive use of pitch in languages is available in chapter 15.

> *Syllabic nasal stops in Quiotepec Chinantec*
> [m̩ʔ¹] 'ant'   [m̩ː²³] 'sandal'
> [m̩ʔ³] 'tomato'   [ʔm̩ː³ m̩ʔ⁴] 'you pinch (pl.)'

In the above examples, the pronunciation of [m] can thus be relatively short or long, may be checked by a glottal stop, may have a voiceless onset, show contrasting tones, and in all four cases is syllabic. The words are pronounced with labial closure throughout, with no intervening vocoids.

8.9.1 *Ejective syllabic trilled stops*

The possibility in Pacific Northwest languages of making stops segments syllabic is combined in Wenatchee-Columbia (Hoard 1978: 63–4), which is a Salishan language spoken in and around the Columbia basin in Washington State, with a rare instance of adding a transitional aspect of trilling to an ejective version of such a stop:

> *Pulmonic egressive trilled stops and syllabic ejective trilled stops in Wenatchee-Columbia*
> [ki+jɛr+kʷ'+'kanʔ] 'cup'   [jɛr'+r̩'] 'tangled up'
> [ʔa+ra+'sikʷ] 'turtle'   [stəˈr'eq+xənʔ] 'mud-hen'

	Place-neutral articulations						Displaced articuations				
	oral stop	nasal stop	oral tap	nasal tap	oral trill	nasal trill	oral stop	nasal stop	oral flap	nasal flap	
labial	p	m̥			ʙ̥	ʙ̥̃					vl
	b	m			ʙ	ʙ̃					vd
linguo-labial							p̺	m̺̥			vl
							b̺	m̺			vd
labio-dental							π̥	ɱ̥			vl
							π	ɱ	ⱱ		vd
dental	t̪	n̥̪									vl
	d̪	n̪									vd
alveolar	t	n̥	ɾ̥	ɾ̥̃	r̥	r̥̃			ɽ̥	ɽ̥̃	vl
	d	n	ɾ	ɾ̃	r	r̃			ɽ	ɽ̃	vd
palato alveolar							ʈ	ɳ̥			vl
							ɖ	ɳ			vd
palatal	c	ɲ̥									vl
	ɟ	ɲ									vd
velar	k	ŋ̥									vl
	g	ŋ									vd
uvular	q	ɴ̥	ʀ̥	ʀ̥̃	ʀ̥	ʀ̥̃					vl
	ɢ	ɴ	ʀ	ʀ̃	ʀ	ʀ̃					vd
epiglottal	ʡ̥										vl
	ʡ										vd
glottal	ʔ										

Single stop segments	diacritics: voiceless, m̥, ɾ̥, m̥ŋ̊ nasal, r̃	dental, t̪, n̪ linguolabial, p̺	retroflex ʈ, ɳ, ɽ

Figure 8.6 Summary of the phonetic symbols for place-neutral and displaced pulmonic egressive simplex stop segments

8.10 Symbols for stop articulations

Figure 8.6 summarizes symbols for pulmonic egressive voiceless and voiced simplex stop segments, for both place-neutral and displaced articulations. The symbols for non-pulmonic simplex stops can be seen in the International Phonetic Association's alphabet reproduced in appendix I.

Further reading

Harrington (1988) contains an extensive bibliography on experimental acoustic investigations of stops in English generally. Zue (1976) can be consulted for details of acoustic characteristics of stop segments in **American English**. Docherty (1992) is recommended for theoretical and quantitative details of stop segments in **British English**, especially on matters of timing of voicing in relation to articulatory events. Keating (1984) discusses both phonetic and phonological considerations of representation of voicing in stop segments.

Herbert (1986) contains a detailed discussion of **complex oral/nasal stop** segments in a variety of languages. For discussion of stops made on nonpulmonic airstreams (**implosives** and **clicks**), see the references listed in the Further Reading section in the preceding chapter. Maddieson (1984) sets out the use of stops of all types in the 317 languages of the UCLA Phonological Segment Inventory Database (UPSID).

9

Fricative articulations

A necessary condition for a segment to be classified as a **fricative** is that the degree of stricture reached and held during the medial phase of the segment must be that of **close approximation**. That is, for any given rate of airflow, the cross-sectional area of the constricted aperture has to be small enough to cause audible friction. This friction (or turbulence of the molecules in the airflow) can either be local, at the exit to the constriction, or it can be caused by the constriction having the effect of directing a jet of air onto a nearby obstacle such as the teeth.

The interaction between airflow and acoustic factors in fricative production is very delicate. For any given small aperture, there is a critical rate of airflow through the gap below which the airflow is laminar and relatively silent, and above which the airflow is turbulent and noisy, producing a 'hissing' or 'hushing' sound. The criteria for classifying a segment as a fricative thus include acoustic/auditory and aerodynamic considerations, as well as articulatory factors. Catford (1977a: 121) suggests that the typical cross-sectional areas of the maximum constriction in a fricative segment range from about 3 sq. mm at a minimum to about 20 sq. mm at a maximum. For normal airflow rates in speech, a gap larger than 20 sq. mm restores laminar, silent flow. In the majority of fricatives, constrictions are estimated to have cross-sectional areas between 6 and 12 sq. mm, with typical airflow rates very roughly of 330 cc/s for a voiceless fricative and 240 cc/s for a voiced fricative (Catford 1977a: 123–4). In addition, the adjustment of the spatial relationship between the active and passive articulators has to be very precisely controlled. Ladefoged and Maddieson (1986) make the following comments:

> in a fricative a variation of one millimeter in the position of the target
> for the crucial part of the vocal tract makes a great deal of difference.
> There has to be a very precisely shaped channel for the turbulent
> airstream to be produced. [In] a stop closure the strength of the closure
> does not have to be constant throughout the gesture. But in many

fricatives .. an exactly defined shape of the vocal tract has to be held for a noticeable period of time. These demands result in a fricative such as *s* having a greater constancy of shape in varying phonetic contexts, in comparison with the corresponding stops *t, d* and nasal *n* (Bladon and Nolan 1977, Subtelny, Oya and Subtelny 1972, Lindblad 1980). (Ladefoged and Maddieson 1986: 57)

9.1 Place-neutral fricative articulations

There are ten places of articulation in which fricative articulations can be performed which are place-neutral, without displacement of the active articulator from its neutral relationship to the passive articulator. These ten neutral places of articulation, and the symbols for the corresponding voiceless and voiced fricative segments, are as follows:

Place of articulation	Voiceless fricatives	Voiced fricatives
labial	[ɸ]	[β]
dental	[θ]	[ð]
alveolar	[s]	[z]
palato-alveolar	[ʃ]	[ʒ]
alveolo-palatal	[ɕ]	[ʑ]
palatal	[ç]	[j]
velar	[x]	[ɣ]
uvular	[χ]	[ʁ]
pharyngeal	[ħ]	[ʕ]
epiglottal	[ʜ]	[ʢ]

Figures 9.1a–9.1j respectively show sagittal cross-sectional diagrams of the vocal organs during the medial phases of the ten voiceless place-neutral fricatives listed above.

The sounds represented by the symbols [h] and [ɦ], which might also be thought to be place-neutral articulations, are often called 'glottal fricatives', because friction can sometimes be heard at the glottal location. But the position to be taken in this book is that this is a category mistake, and that these are better thought of as approximants with whispery phonation. They are therefore discussed in section 10.11.1 and section 10.11.2 in the next chapter.

If no further comment is made in such a classificatory label for a fricative, then the following assumptions apply. These are that the airstream mechanism is **pulmonic**, and the direction of airflow **egressive**; that the conformational aspects of routing of the airflow are **oral** and **central**; that

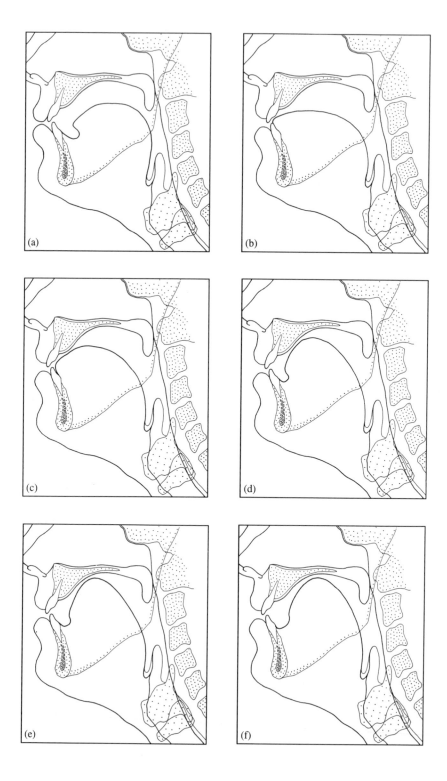

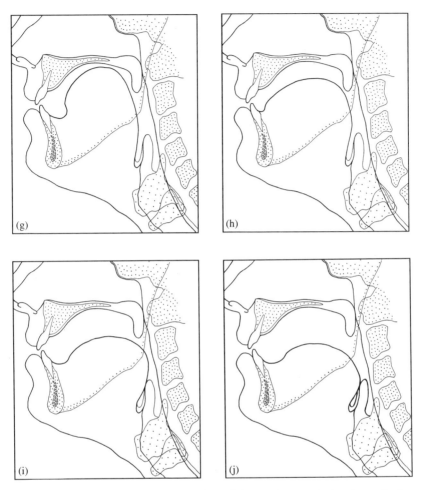

Figure 9.1 Sagittal cross-sections of the vocal organs during the production
of the medial phases of a number of fricative segments: (a) a voiceless
labial fricative [ɸ]; (b) a voiceless dental fricative [θ]; (c) a voiceless alveolar
fricative [s]; (d) a voiceless palato-alveolar fricative [ʃ]; (e) a voiceless
alveolo-palatal fricative [ɕ]; (f) a voiceless palatal fricative [ç]; (g) a voiceless
velar fricative [x]; (h) a voiceless uvular fricative [χ]; (i) a voiceless
pharyngeal fricative [ħ]; and (j) a voiceless epiglottal fricative [H]

the topographical aspect of the shape of the surface of the tongue is neutrally **convex**; that the transitional aspect of the production of the segment is
that the medial phase is momentarily held in a **steady state**; and that only a
single major articulatory stricture is applicable. (Fricatives made with double
strictures are discussed in chapter 11 on multiple articulations.)

Fricative constrictions can potentially be produced at any point along the vocal tract from the lips to the larynx, though the local length of the 'corridor' of close approximation will depend chiefly on the characteristics of the active articulator. Perhaps because so many audibly different fricatives can be produced, there are more transcriptional symbols for fricatives than for any other structural category of contoids.

Fricative segments are used in the very large majority of the world's languages as the basis for contrastive oppositions, though one often-cited exception to this is Hawaiian, which has no fricatives in its eight-consonant system (Hockett 1955: 98, 108). There is however one major language group in which it is rare to find fricatives at all. This is the group of languages found in Australia; of the nineteen Australian languages in Maddieson's (1984) survey of the languages of the world, fifteen have no fricatives.

One uncommon fricative segment, that needs to be mentioned in passing, is a bidental fricative where the upper and lower teeth act as the articulators. Because the upper and lower teeth lie opposite each other in the neutral disposition of the vocal organs, such a segment would not be classified as an example of a displaced articulation. Ladefoged and Maddieson (1986) cite Passy's and Catford's descriptions of this apparently rare articulation in the following terms:

> Passy (1899) describes a fricative in the Shapsug dialect of Adyghe, a Circassian language, which has 'the lips fully open, the teeth clenched and the tongue flat, the air passing between the teeth; the sound is intermediate between ʃ and f.' (Passy 1899: 110, L&M translation.) This sound was noticed independently by Catford who comments that 'the Adyghe (Circassian) bidental fricative is, in fact, a variant of x, occurring for the x in such words as xə "six" and daxə "pretty" in the Black Sea sub-dialect of Shapsug' (Catford, personal communication). (Ladefoged and Maddieson 1986: 64)

There are a number of sub-divisions possible within the overall class of fricative segments. The first concerns displaced articulations. The second includes different aspects of articulation, involving detailed variations of topographical shape of the tongue surface, oral versus nasal airflow routing and central versus lateral airflow routing.

9.2 Displaced fricative articulations

There are at least seven types of fricatives with **displaced articulation**, some of which shown diagrammatically in sagittal cross-section in figure 9.2a–9.2d. The first set are linguo-labial fricatives, which are found as

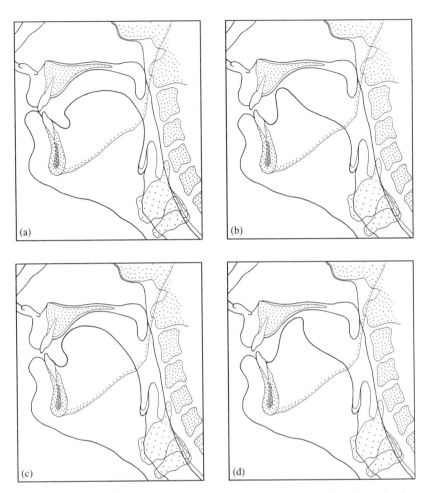

Figure 9.2 Sagittal cross-sections of the vocal organs during the production of the medial phase of a number of oral fricative segments with displaced articulation: (a) a voiceless labiodental fricative [f]; (b) a voiceless apical post-alveolar fricative [ɹ]; (c) a voiceless laminal flat post-alveolar fricative [ʃ.] and (d) a voiceless retroflex palato-alveolar fricative [ʂ]

counterparts to the linguo-labial stops in the Austronesian languages spoken in Vanuatu mentioned in the previous chapter. Just as in the production of the stops, the tongue tip or blade is protruded to articulate with the upper lip, in this case to create a stricture of close approximation with audible friction. Maddieson (1987b: 27) states that in V'enen Taut, a voiced oral linguo-labial fricative [z̼] is in contrast with the corresponding bilabial fricative [β]. The symbol [z̼] for the voiced oral linguo-labial fricative has been constructed here according to the 1989 Kiel IPA Convention recommendations. The examples from V'enen Taut given by Maddieson (*ibid.*) are:

Linguo-labial fricative in V'enen Taut
[naz̼at] 'stone'   [naβal] 'songfest'

The second set of displaced fricatives is made by the lower lip acting as the active articulator against the lower edge of the front upper teeth, with the air flowing out through the small gaps between the curved corners of the biting surfaces of the teeth. These actions produce the **labiodental fricatives** [f] and [v], as in English *fan* [fan] and *van* [van]. Languages differ in the exact location of the contact by the edge of the teeth on the inner or upper surface of the lower lip. In English the contact is mostly on the inner surface.

Examples of labiodental fricatives can be seen in English, Ewe (Ladefoged 1972: 9), Tigre (Palmer 1956) and Portuguese (Johns 1972):

Labiodental and dental fricatives in English
[fat] fat   [vat] vat
[θaɪ] thigh   [ðaɪ] thy

Labiodental and labial fricatives in Ewe
[èvɛ̀] 'two'   [èβɛ̀] 'Ewe'

Labiodental and alveolar fricatives in Tigre
[fɐres] 'horse'   [faləfsʼ] 'wood'
[fɐtəl] 'thread'   [kanfaraː] 'her lip'
[sanduːkʼaː] 'her box'   [kiːs] 'pocket'

Labiodental fricatives in Portuguese
['fɑkɑ] 'knife'   ['vɑkɑ] 'cow'

The third set of displaced fricatives are the **interdental fricatives** made by protruding the tongue tip between the upper and lower teeth, allowing the airflow between the tongue surface and the upper teeth to become turbulent. In the neutral configuration, the tip of the tongue lies behind the lower front teeth, and only has to be raised to achieve the articulation of the (neutral) dental fricatives [θ] and [ð], as in most Southern English speakers' pronunciations of *bathos* ['beɪθɒs] and *bathers* ['beɪðəz]. For interdental fricatives, which are more common as phonetic realizations of /θ/ and /ð/ in speakers of Californian English (Ladefoged 1983a: 187), the tip has to be displaced slightly forwards from its neutral position, as well as upwards, in order to achieve interdental frication. Symbols for the interdental fricatives can be created by adding the centred subscript diacritic [ˌ] to [θ] and [ð], giving [θ̞] and [ð̞], following the suggestion of Ladefoged and Maddieson (1986: 62).

The fourth set of displaced fricatives also concerns dental fricatives (and denti-alveolar fricatives), but where the surface of the tongue is locally grooved rather than flat. They are discussed below under the topographical aspect of grooved fricatives.

The fifth set of displaced fricative articulations consists of segments made with the tongue tip slightly retracted from its anatomically neutral position, creating a constriction in the post-alveolar zone, normally with a slightly cupped aspect to the configuration of the body of the tongue. The symbols for these (apical) cupped **voiceless** and **voiced post-alveolar fricatives** are [ɹ̝̊] and [ɹ̝]. The subscript diacritic [ˌ] is used here, as recommended by the 1989 Kiel IPA Convention, to indicate a closer, fricative adjustment on symbols which would otherwise be taken to represent approximant segments made with strictures of open approximation. The superscript diacritic [°] in the composite symbol [ɹ̝̊] (representing voicelessness) is placed above the symbol rather than below it because of legibility problems that would otherwise be caused by the pre-emptive presence of the raising diacritic. The segments [ɹ̝̊] and [ɹ̝] are heard in many accents of English as manifestations of /r/ in words such as *try* [tɹ̝̊aɪ] and *dry* [dɹ̝aɪ], where the onset of the segments representing /r/ typically show a moment of audible friction before becoming vocoid articulations. Segment-marginal phenomena at the junction of segments of this sort are discussed in chapter 12.

The sixth set of displaced fricatives is closely related to the preceding set of post-alveolar fricatives [ɹ̝̊] and [ɹ̝], in that it consists of fricative strictures made at a place of articulation slightly retracted from alveolar, but without either grooving or substantial cupping. Furthermore, the active articulator is the blade of the tongue rather than the tip, and these are therefore **laminal** articulations. The articulations in question are the (laminal) **voiceless** and **voiced flat post-alveolar fricatives**, which can be symbolized [ʃ̻] and [ʒ̻]. The [ʃ̻] articulation is thus like [ɹ̝̊] in place of articulation, and like [s] in the involvement of the blade of the tongue as active articulator. But it is unlike [ɹ̝̊] in that the articulation is laminal not apical, and unlike [s] in that the surface of the blade of the tongue is flat, not grooved. It is also unlike [ʃ], in that the place of articulation is slightly further forward. This is one justification for retaining 'palato-alveolar' as a term in the place of articulation series, rather than collapsing this category with 'post-alveolar', as the 1989 Kiel IPA Convention urged. But [ʃ̻] is more like [ʃ] with respect to the overall posture of the blade and front of the tongue than it is to [s].

An example of a (voiceless) flat post-alveolar fricative of this sort is found in Standard Chinese as spoken in Beijing (Ladefoged and Wu 1984; Ladefoged and Maddieson 1986: 69), in contrast with (voiceless grooved) alveolar and (voiceless) alveolo-palatal fricatives. All the words in this example are spoken on a high level tone:

Flat post-alveolar fricative in Standard Chinese (Beijing)

[fa] 'to issue'   [sa] 'three' [ʃ̢a] 'sand'
[ça] 'blind'   [xa] 'sound of laughter'

The seventh set of displaced fricative segments is made up of the **voiceless** and **voiced retroflex fricatives** [ʂ] and [ʐ]. These are made, as the the label suggests, by the tongue tip being curled upwards and presented to the roof of the mouth in a stricture of close approximation.

The place of articulation for retroflex fricatives ranges from post-alveolar to palato-alveolar. This is because a retroflex aspect covers three possibilities of adjustment of the tip and blade of the tongue. The tip may be only slightly curled, or pointing vertically, or may be curled right over so that the underside is forming the maximum constriction with the passive articulator. The first two positions give **apical retroflex** articulations, and the third a **sublaminal retroflex** articulation. The degree of curling of the tongue and the degree of retraction of the place of articulation tend to be correlated. Apical retroflex fricatives are usually made at the post-alveolar place of articulation, and sublaminal retroflex fricatives at the palato-alveolar place of articulation.

If no further specification of place of articulation is given on a particular occasion than 'retroflex fricative', it can be assumed either that the place of articulation involved is palato-alveolar, or that it is not necessary for the purposes of the discussion to distinguish between the palato-alveolar and post-alveolar possibilities. On the symbol charts presented in this book, it will be assumed that the retroflex fricatives [ʂ] and [ʐ] are performed at the palato-alveolar place of articulation.

A retroflex fricative stricture at any place of articulation constitutes a 'whistle' stricture for many speakers, and a momentary whistle during the production of these segments is not uncommon, though this will only happen at particular flow rates. The fact that a momentary whistle may be heard in the production of these retroflex fricatives should not lead to their being confused with the so-called 'whistled' fricatives of, for example, the Zimbabwean language Shona. In this language, the whistled fricatives are in fact double labial alveolar fricatives made with a rounded lip position. (The whistled fricatives of Shona are described in detail in chapter 11 on multiple articulations.)

9.3   Examples of fricative segments in languages

Examples of fricative segments at a variety of places of articulation can be seen in the material below from the following languages: Kikuyu of East Africa, Urhobo of Southern Nigeria and Polish (all from J. Kelly, personal communication); Mossi (Mooré) of West Africa, Somali of North-East Africa, Chuana (Tswana) of South Africa, Pedi of Northern Transvaal, Ewe of Ghana (all from Westermann and Ward 1933: 78–85); Tigre (Palmer 1956); Kurdish of Iraq (Arbili accent, A. Ferhardi, personal communication); Isoko of Nigeria (Mafeni 1969); German (Hall 1989); Greek (Mackridge 1985); and European Portuguese (Johns 1972). It may be helpful to emphasize again that these transcriptions are all at the phonetic level – some of the examples (e.g. from German) would be subject to more reduced (and hence more abstract) phonemic analyses. The meanings of all the vowel symbols are explained in chapter 10.

Fricative segments in Kikuyu

[ðovu] 'soup'   [ɣeðima] 'a well'   [ɣekavʊ] 'basket'

Fricative segments in Urhobo

[uɸo] 'throat'   [ɛβe] 'goat'
[efi] 'climbing rope'   [uvi] 'a paddle'
[osa] 'debt'   [uzo] 'bushbuck'
[oʃɔ] 'fear'   [oʒa] 'suffering'
[exa] 'dance'   [aɣa] 'broom'

Fricative segments in Polish

[brɛf] 'eyebrow'   [vrɔna] 'crow'
[pjɛs] 'dog'   [mɛx] 'moss'
[vjɛɕ] 'village'   [vjɛʃ] 'you know (sg.)'
[kaɕa] 'Kate'   [kaʃa] 'buckwheat'
[srɔka] 'magpie'   [ɕrɔda] 'Wednesday'
[ʃrɔn] 'hoarfrost'   [xrɔbri] 'bold (masc.)'
[zrɔbitɕ] 'to do'   [ʒrɛbak] 'foal'   [ʒrɛtu] 'to consume'

[dʑvik] 'a lift'   [dʑvi] 'door'
[zɔwɔ] 'herb'   [ʒɔɲɛʃ] 'soldier'
[tɛɕtu] 'father-in-law'   [dɛʃʧ] 'rain'

Fricative segments in Mossi

[ɕagabo] 'bread, cake'   [moɕe] 'the Mossi people'
[zero] 'soup, sauce'   [zugu] 'head'

Fricative segments in Somali

[saʕ] 'cow' [sɔʕɔtɔ] 'traveller'
[seːhɔ] 'go to sleep' [libæh] 'lion'

Fricative segments in Chuana

[ʃome] 'ten' [diʒɔ] 'food'
[seʃoba] 'bundle' [ʒa] 'to eat'

Fricative segments in Pedi

[ɸoɸa] 'to fly' [ɸeta] 'to pass'
[βɔna] 'to see' [βula] 'to open'

Fricative segments in Ewe

[ɸu] 'bone' [fu] 'feather'
[ɸo] 'beat' [fo] 'to tear off'
[βu] 'boat' [vu] 'to tear'
[βɔ] 'python' [vɔ] 'to be finished'

Fricative segments in Tigre

[harmaːz] 'elephant' [mafaːtəh] 'keys'
[faraʕ] 'clan' [fɐrɐs] 'horse'
[gəndəheː] 'kind of tree' [məhəngaːg] 'scratch'
[ʃənatˤaː] 'her haversack' [haːjuːtʲ] 'lions'
[maŋkaːhuː] 'his spoon' [ʔɐsəgdɐtʲ] 'necks'

Fricative segments in Kurdish (Arbili accent)

[sin] 'letter "s" (Arabic loan)' [zin] 'saddle (for horse)'
[ʃin] 'blue' [ʒin] 'life'
[sɑwɑ] 'young (children)' [zɑwɑ] 'bridegroom'
[dəzi] 'thread' [dəʒi] 'lives (3rd p.sg.)'
[dəkuʃi] 'squeezes' [dəkuʒi] 'kills (3rd p.sg.)'
[bəs] 'enough' [bəz] 'fat (n.)'   [bəʃ] 'share (n.)'

Fricative segments in Isoko

[iβɛ] 'sacrifice' [uɣo] 'money'
[óvu] 'hen' [ofu] 'anger'
[ési] 'horse' [ezi] 'period of time'

Fricative segments in German

[ziːç] 'sickly' [buːx] 'book'
[pɛç] 'bad luck' [kɔx] 'cook'
[høːçlɪç] 'highly' [hoːx] 'high'
[lɛçəln] 'to smile' [mɑxən] 'to make, to do'

[çemiː] 'chemistry'   [knɔxən] 'bone'
[tɑoçən] 'little rope'   [tɑoxən] 'to dive'
[pˤaoçən] 'little peacock'   [pˤɑoxən] 'to hiss'
[koːjə] 'bunk'   [boːjə] 'buoy'

Fricative segments in Greek

['fθino̥] 'I decline'   ['ftino̥] 'I spit'   ['kapsimo]
                                                        'burning'

[efxaɾi'sto̥] 'thank you'   ['kafsimo] 'combustible (n.sg.)'
[mi'sθos] 'salary'   ['sçeðio] 'plan, pattern'
['voɱva] 'bomb'   ['revma] 'current'
[siŋɣɾa'feas] 'author'   ['taɣma] 'battalion'
[ex'θros] 'enemy'   [ekðro'mi] 'excursion'
[sti̥'ço] 'ghost'   [sti̥'çio] 'element, feature'
[komuni̥'sti̥s] 'communist' [komuni̥'zmos] 'communion'
['xoni̥] 'he thrusts'   ['çoni̥] 'snow'

Fricative segments in Portuguese

[ʃa] 'tea'   ['aʃa] 'thinks'   [vɔʃ] 'you (pl.)'
[ʒɑ] 'already'   ['aʒɑ] 'let there be' [vɔʒ] 'voice'

9.4   Conformational aspects of fricative articulations

Fricatives can be made with either oral or nasal aspects of air-flow, and with central or lateral aspects of routing of the flow. Oral and central fricatives have already been considered. The following sub-sections will explore nasal fricatives first, and then lateral fricatives.

9.4.1   *Nasal fricative articulations*

All fricatives have the possibility of being made with a nasal aspect of articulation, giving **nasal fricatives**. This is seldom exploited in spoken language for contrastive purposes. It is more common to find nasality on fricatives in contextual sequences where the fricative is surrounded by or adjacent to other nasal segments. It would not be unusual to hear nasality on the [z] in the English word *damson*, for instance, pronounced as [dãmž̩n]. In Igbo, the language of Eastern Nigeria commented on earlier, nasality is a property of whole syllables, and when [f, v, s, z, ʃ, ʒ] occur in such syllables, they are pronounced as nasal fricatives. The following examples are taken from Williamson (1969a: 87):

Nasal fricatives in Igbo

[ĩf̃ã] 'to shriek'	[ɪfa] 'to wedge in'
[ɪṽõ] 'to hatch'	[ɪvu] 'to be big'
[ɪš̃ã] 'to wash (face/pot)'	[ɪsa] 'to spread out'
[iž̃ũ] 'to steal'	[izu] 'week (of four days)'
[ĩʃ̃ĩĩ] 'six'	[aʃɪ] 'bead'
[eʒ̃ĩ] 'pig'	[oʒi] 'message/errand'

A further example of the use of nasal fricatives comes from Waffa, a language of the East New Guinea Highlands (Stringer and Hotz 1973, cited by Ladefoged and Maddieson 1986: 52). It may be that the nasal fricatives are contextually conditioned by nasality on the following vocoids, but Stringer and Hotz offer no comment on contrastive vowel nasalization in Waffa:

Nasal fricatives in Waffa

[β̃atá] 'ground'	[jaáβ̃ə] 'reed skirt'
[β̃aíni] 'close by'	[óoβ̃ə] '(type of yam)'
[mátee] 'now'	[kamə] 'round taro'

9.4.2 *Pre-nasal fricative articulations*

As in the case of stops, fricatives can occur with pre-nasal onsets. Bendor-Samuel describes Terena, the Arawakan language of the Matto Grosso in Brazil mentioned earlier, as having pre-nasal fricatives [^{n}z] and [^{n}ʒ]. He presents the durational factors of the pre-nasal fricatives in the following terms: 'when sequences such as [i'wuʔiʃo] "he rides" and [i'wuʔi^{n}ʒo] "I ride" are compared, the rhythm and length of the last two syllables are similar' (Bendor-Samuel 1960). Herbert (1986: 202) cites an example from Amahuaca, the language spoken in the area of the headwaters of the Amazon mentioned in the previous chapter, where the nasal element of the pre-nasal fricative is voiceless, agreeing in phonation type with the oral fricative element, in /wõθ̃ĩ/ ⇒ [wõn̥ʔ̞θĩ] 'an animal'. Herbert transcribes the nasal element without indication of dentality, but a dental place of articulation is virtually certain, given the homorganic relations between the elements of adjacent pre-nasal stops and fricatives that are observed in all other known languages.

Zande, the Ubangi language spoken in Zaïre and the Central African Republic mentioned in the previous chapter in connection with an alveolar nasal trilled stop [r̃] as a phonetic realization of /r/, also has pre-nasal fricative phonemes /^{n}v/ and /^{n}z/. In intervocalic position, these are often manifested phonetically as fully nasal fricatives [ṽ] and [z̃], as alternatives to their pronunciation as phonetically pre-nasal fricatives [^{n}v] and [^{n}z] (Herbert 1986: 254, citing Tucker and Hackett 1959).

9.4.3 *Central versus lateral airflow in fricative articulations*

The point has now come where a particularly important aspect of articulation, briefly mentioned earlier, has to be discussed in more detail. This is the distinction between **central** and **lateral** aspects of articulation. The aperture through which the airstream flows in fricative production is located for most segments in the centre of the vocal tract, looking at it from a head-on perspective. This is true of all the fricatives we have considered so far, and these are therefore examples of **central fricatives**. An alternative possibility is to block the central passage and allow the air to escape laterally instead, though still through a stricture of close approximation, with audible friction. This constitutes a **lateral fricative** segment. This is feasible at many points in the vocal tract, but the most frequent examples are found at the alveolar and dental places of articulation.

The symbol for the voiceless alveolar lateral fricative is [ɬ], and for its voiced counterpart is [ɮ]. In these fricatives, the tip or blade of the tongue contacts the central part of the alveolar ridge, and air flows round one or both sides of the partial closure, becoming turbulent as it passes through the constriction(s). The two sounds [ɬ] and [ɮ] are both used contrastively in Zulu (Doke 1926: 99–100), in Xhosa (J. Kelly, personal communication), and in the West African Chadic languages Margi (Hoffmann 1963: 23–5) and Warja (Jungraithmayr 1967: 57):

Alveolar lateral fricatives in Zulu
[ɬuːpha] 'trouble'   [ukuːɮa] 'to eat'
[ɬaβɛlɛːla] 'sing'   [iːɮɛːlɔ] 'pasture-ground'

Alveolar lateral fricatives in Xhosa
[uphaɬa] 'roof'   [iziɬaŋgu] 'shoes'
[umzala] 'cousin'   [umɮalo] 'game'

Alveolar lateral fricatives in Margi
[ɬa] 'cow'   [ɮa] 'fall'   [la] 'to dig'

Alveolar lateral fricatives in Warja
[ɬuni] 'they'   [ɮaɮa] 'eight'

In the above examples, [l] stands for a **voiced alveolar lateral resonant**, and such resonants are discussed in detail in chapter 10.

In North America, in Maddieson's (1984) survey, examples of Amerindian languages using the voiceless dental or alveolar lateral fricative are Navajo, Haida, Tlingit, Tolowa, Hupa, Nootka, Tiwa, Zuni, Wiyot, Yuchi, Alabama, Nez Perce, Kwakw'ala, Quileute, Puget Sound and Diegueño. Eunice Pike (1963: 37–8) gives the following examples from Navajo of the Southwest United States and from Morelos Aztec of Mexico:

Voiceless alveolar lateral fricatives in Navajo

[taʧiltíɬ] 'they eat it'	[toːleːɬi] 'that which will be'
[piɬsekʰe] 'I sat with him'	[tsitɬeɬi] 'match'
[niːniɬ] 'they are placed in a row'	[naːnaɬaʒi] 'the other side'

Voiceless alveolar lateral fricatives in Morelos Aztec

['tspotɬ] 'zapote fruit'	['ʃeɬtɪkʰ] 'coins'
[si'tɬalɪ] 'star'	[si'tɬaɬtɛ] 'stars'

A European language which uses a voiceless alveolar lateral fricative in contrast with a voiced alveolar lateral approximant is Welsh. Examples from North Welsh (Albrow 1966: 2) are:

Voiceless alveolar lateral fricative in North Welsh

[iɬɔŋ] 'her ship'	[ilɔŋ] 'his ship'

9.5 Topographical aspects of the shape of the tongue in fricative articulations

The next aspect of articulation to be discussed concerns the dimensions of the strictural aperture through which the turbulent air flows in fricative production. The size and shape of this aperture are controlled by the surface configuration of the active articulator, which is in most cases the tongue. The neutral condition is one where the tongue is maintained in a convex configuration. For some fricatives whose stricture is made within the front part of the oral cavity, the surface of the tongue is modified to produce a longitudinal, central groove.

In articulating the voiceless and voiced alveolar fricatives [s] and [z], the surface of the blade of the tongue opposite the alveolar ridge is adjusted by the lingual muscles to be deeply grooved, in a narrow, longitudinal furrow. In the voiceless and voiced dental fricatives [θ] and [ð], the surface of the tongue tip or blade is relatively flat in its slightly convex neutral shape, giving a slit aperture whose longer dimension is side to side. Such adjustments then form the basis for a descriptive distinction between **grooved** and **flat fricatives**, as mentioned in section 9.1 above. English exploits a difference between alveolar and palato-alveolar fricatives of this sort:

Grooved alveolar fricatives versus palato-alveolar fricatives in English

[sɪp] sip	[zɪp] zip	[ʃɪp] ship
[lis] lease	[liz] lees	[liʃ] leash
[mɛsə] messer	[mɛʃə] mesher	[mɛʒə] measure
[beɪs] base	[beɪz] baize	[beɪʒ] beige

An important difference between the grooved alveolar and palato-alveolar fricative configurations is that, while the place of articulation is alveolar for [s] and palato-alveolar for [ʃ], the longitudinal 'corridor' of maximum constriction for the audibly 'high-pitched' [s] is much shorter than for the audibly 'low-pitched' [ʃ].

It is possible to make a grooved fricative at the dental place of articulation. A grooved dental fricative of this sort can be transcribed by adding a dental diacritic to the symbol, giving [s̪]. The comparable voiced symbol is [z̪]. A small number of languages exploit contrasts between grooved fricatives at the dental and alveolar places of articulation. Ladefoged and Maddieson (1986: 64) cite two such languages, both from the Amerindian group of languages. One is Karok (Karuk) (Bright 1978), a Hokan aboriginal language of California, and the other is Luiseño, a Uto-Aztecan language:

> *Grooved dental versus grooved alveolar fricative in Karok*
> [s̪úːf] 'creek'   [súːf] 'backbone'

> *Grooved dental versus grooved alveolar fricative in Luiseño*
> [s̪úkat] 'deer'   [sukmal] 'fawn'

When the displacement is of a lesser degree, so that the fricative stricture lies at the junction of the dental and alveolar zones, at the **denti-alveolar** place of articulation, then the [̪] diacritic can be added to [s] and [z] to give [s̪] and [z̪]. Instances of voiceless and voiced grooved denti-alveolar fricatives can be found in English. A voiceless example is in the pronunciation of the word *aesthetic* ⇒ [ɪs̪'θɛtɪk], where the articulation of /s/ is sometimes fronted to the denti-alveolar zone, with the blade of the tongue as active articulator retaining its grooving. The tongue tip is raised towards the upper teeth, taking the fricative stricture slightly further forward in an apical dental articulation for [θ]. A similar voiced example can be heard in informal pronunciations of /z/ in phrases such as *these things* ⇒ [ðiz̪θɪŋz] as a type of assimilatory adjustment. (Assimilation is discussed further in chapter 12 on co-ordination.)

Denti-alveolar fricatives are also used in the Lisbon accent of European Portuguese (Johns 1972):

> *Denti-alveolar fricatives in Portuguese*
> ['s̪elu] 'stamp'   ['z̪elu] 'zeal'
> ['as̪u] 'steel'   ['az̪u] 'pretext'

The frontmost part of the depression for grooving of the tongue surface in dental and alveolar articulations begins in the blade of the tongue just behind the tip. Producing a grooved dental or denti-alveolar fricative there-fore requires the tongue, as the active articulator, to be brought slightly for-ward from the neutral position in which it is the tip rather than the blade that lies opposite the central upper teeth or the teeth–gum junction. Grooved dental or denti-alveolar fricatives also are hence examples of dis-placed fricatives, to add to those mentioned in the earlier section on dis-placed fricative articulations.

It is also possible for alveolar fricatives to be flat rather than grooved. We have seen earlier that flat post-alveolar fricatives occur in the Standard Chinese of Beijing. Flat alveolar fricatives also occur in Icelandic. Ladefoged and Maddieson (1986: 63) quote data from Petursson (1971) showing that the voiceless flat alveolar fricative in Icelandic is made with the blade of the tongue as the active articulator, while the voiced flat alveolar fricative is made by the tip of the tongue. In such a case, the laminal alveolar articula-tion would be place-neutral, while the apical alveolar articulation would count as displaced. The voiceless flat (laminal) alveolar fricative can be sym-bolized as [θ], and the voiced flat (apical) alveolar fricative as [ð̺]. (If atten-tion needs to be drawn to the fact that the voiceless fricative here is laminal and the voiced fricative is apical, then the subscript [˻] laminal diacritic can be added to the voiceless symbol, and the subscript [.] apical diacritic can be added to the voiced symbol.)

> *Flat alveolar fricatives in Icelandic*
> [θakið̺] 'roof'   [vað̺an] 'whence'

Flat alveolar fricatives can also be heard in many accents of Irish English, as phonetic realizations of /t/ in intervocalic and final position, in words such as *patting* [pʰaθm̩] and *cat* [kʰaθ].

9.6   Auditory characteristics of fricatives

Fricative segments can vary, from an auditory perspective, in their apparent 'pitch' and in their intensity. Some, such as [s], sound rela-tively high-pitched and intense, and some, such as [θ], sound low-pitched and less intense. Those that sound high-pitched and intense are character-ized acoustically by displaying greater amounts of energy at higher frequen-cies than those which sound lower-pitched and less intense. Such a scale of **sibilance**, or **stridency**, is a continuum, and the rich contrastive and contex-tual variety of fricative segments of the languages of the world gives the scale a dense population.

Sibilance as an auditory scale could potentially allow the sounds of one lan-guage to be differentiated from those of another, and could be used to help to differentiate the contrastively and contextually different sounds within a single language from each other. But an adequate general phonetic theory should explain as well as describe, and unless the articulatory and aerodynamic bases for such auditory differences are well understood, the use of a solely auditory scale eludes the full obligation of theory to offer due explanation.

One explanatory basis that has been posited for the differences in sibilance shown by fricative segments is that, from an aerodynamic and articulatory perspective, there are actually two ways of creating turbulence in an airstream, as mentioned at the beginning of this chapter. The first involves an adjustment of airflow rate and cross-sectional area of constriction so that the flow through the constriction causes turbulence immediately downstream of the location of the maximum constriction. The voiceless and voiced labial fricatives [ɸ] and [β] would be examples of this. The second method, however, uses the narrow articulatory constriction to form a shaping channel which guides the jet of air onto a downstream obstruction, such as the teeth, where the impact of the air-jet on the obstacle produces edge-effect turbulence at that point. The English fricatives [s] and [ʃ] and their voiced counterparts [z] and [ʒ] are examples of such a process. Fricatives whose turbulence is due to edge effects from airflow hitting an obstruction of this sort are characteristically more sibilant, or strident, in the above terms, than those where the turbulence is due only to the interaction of the airflow and the constriction.

Many phonologists and phoneticians from Jakobson (1949) to Shadle (1985) and Ladefoged and Maddieson (1986) have suggested that a scale of sibilance forms the basis for a phonological feature which has been called STRIDENT/NON-STRIDENT, or SIBILANT/NON-SIBILANT, or OBSTACLE/NON-OBSTACLE. Ladefoged and Maddieson (1986), for instance, following work by Shadle (1985), suggest a distinction between sibilant fricatives and non-sibilant fricatives in which 'sibilant or obstacle fricatives are those such as *s*, *z*, in which the constriction at the alveolar ridge produces a jet of air that hits the obstacle formed by the teeth. In non-obstacle fricatives, such as *θ*, *ð*, the turbulence is produced at the constriction itself' (Ladefoged and Maddieson 1986: 58). Shadle's own terms for these are 'obstacle fricatives' versus 'non-obstacle fricatives'.

Unfortunately, consensus as to where on the scale the division is to be drawn between the two different classes is notably absent. Chomsky and Halle (1968) include English [f, v] with [s, z, ʃ, ʒ] as strident fricatives. Ladefoged and Maddieson (1986: 92) say (properly) that they can see neither phonetic nor phonological justification for this. One problem here is that groupings on a solely acoustic basis will not necessarily give the same results as those based on articulatory and aerodynamic criteria of edge turbulence effects being created by a downstream obstruction.

Since the phonetic difference between the two mechanisms for creating fricative turbulence relies on the detail of the exact routing of airflow, it could potentially be straightforwardly incorporated in the framework for general phonetic theory offered in this book, under the rubric of aspect of articulation.

The book by Ladefoged and Maddieson (1986) is recommended to interested readers. The specific SIBILANT/NON-SIBILANT distinction will not be incorporated here, however. The reason for not yet adopting the suggestion is the absence of a more fully worked-through model of the aerodynamics and acoustics of fricative production. Without such a model, the phonetic basis of the SIBILANT/NON-SIBILANT distinction relies to some unspecified extent on an auditory evaluation. As a phonological feature, +/– STRIDENT (or +/– SIBILANT) remains available, subject to the definitions offered by the analysts concerned.

One important rider to the definition of fricative segments that was offered at the beginning of this chapter emerges from this discussion, however. It was said earlier that, for a segment to be classed as fricative, 'for any given rate of airflow, the cross-sectional area of the constricted aperture has to be small enough to cause audible local friction'. In the light of the comments in this section, the interpretation of what is meant in the definition by 'local' has to be understood to mean turbulence effects which can be caused in two different ways. One is turbulence caused directly by the constriction, occurring immediately downstream of the constricted channel. The second is where the turbulence occurs slightly further downstream, when the impact of the air-jet channelled by the constriction hitting an intervening obstacle causes turbulent edge-effects.

We can nevertheless take note of the general fact that fricatives vary in the frequency-distribution of their energy and in their intensity, and thus vary in their relative perceptual prominence. It is worth briefly considering the case of the fricatives which show low perceptual prominence. Miller and Nicely (1955), in a famous experiment on perceptual confusions among consonants, showed that when noise is used to mask the stimuli, the realizations of /f/ and /v/ versus /θ/ and /ð/ are amongst the most confusable sounds in the English consonant system. Harris (1958) showed that the relatively weak voiceless fricatives used in English to represent /f, v/ and /θ, ð/ rely for their perceptual identification more on transitional information in neighbouring vowel manifestations than on information audible during the medial phase of the fricatives themselves. Heinz and Stevens (1961) confirmed the results reported by Harris for the voiceless fricatives. The English consonants /s, z, ʃ, ʒ/ remain independent and perceptually robust in comparison, which gives some support to the general notion of a sibilant/non-sibilant distinction. However, as Goldstein (1977) cited in Maddieson (1984: 51) has pointed out, the perceptibility of a sound is a product not only of acoustic factors but also of response bias in the subjects. This response bias is directly influenced by the frequency of occurrence of the sounds in question, and /s/ is by far the most frequent of the English sounds concerned, with /ʃ/, /f/ and /θ/ being substantially less frequent, in that order.

9.7   Transitional aspects: flapped, tapped and trilled fricatives

The flapped, tapped and trilled aspects of articulation were described in the preceding chapter on stops. One articulatory difference between a **flapped stop** and a **flapped fricative** would be that instead of the active articulator making a momentary complete closure as it passed through the phase of maximum constriction as it does in a flapped stop, in the case of a flapped fricative it would only come close enough to the passive articulator to cause a momentary stricture of close approximation. A flapped fricative would consequently show a brief period of audible friction and no moment of complete closure. While flapped fricatives are articulatorily feasible, however, they do not seem to be used linguistically. Tapped and trilled fricatives on the other hand, analogous to the flapped fricative just described, can both be found in a number of languages.

A **tapped fricative** is made by a swift movement of the active articulator towards the passive articulator, but where the maximum degree of stricture reached is that of close approximation rather than one of complete closure. Etsako, the Nigerian language mentioned earlier, uses a **tense voiceless tapped alveolar fricative,** which can be symbolized phonetically as T[ɾ̥] in contrast with a **lax voiced alveolar tapped stop** L[ɾ] (Laver 1969: 49). The subscript diacritic element [ˌ] in the composite symbol for the tense voiceless tapped alveolar fricative T[ɾ̥] is meant to indicate that the articulation is more open than the tapped stop symbol alone would imply. The voiceless diacritic (normally subscript) has been placed above the symbol for reasons of legibility:

> *Tense voiceless alveolar tapped fricative versus lax alveolar*
> *tapped stop in Etsako*
> T[aɾ̥u] 'hat'   L[aɾu] 'louse'

In those General American accents that manifest /t/ between vowels as a voiceless alveolar tapped stop rather than as a voiced tapped stop, in words like *city* [sɪɾɪ], the tapped stop is often in free variation with a comparable tapped fricative, giving [sɪɾ̝ɪ] as an alternative.

The case of a **trilled fricative** is more problematic. In the formation of an alveolar trilled stop, in the brief intervals between the repeated closures of the trilling the escaping air normally flows out in a relatively silent, laminar stream. If the respiratory pressure is high, or if the maximum aperture in the intervals between the repeated closures is small enough, this airflow can become turbulent, and cause pulses of audible friction. In traditional terms this is usually called a **fricative trill**, and it is used in Czech, for example. The 'ř' spelling in the name of the Czech composer Dvořak represents this voiced alveolar trilled stop with intermittent friction, and the (pre-Kiel) phonetic symbol for it is [ɼ]. Ladefoged (1971: 49) suggests that 'what characterizes the Czech variant of the trill manner of articulation is that it is a laminal (and not an apical) trill, and that the stricture is held for longer (but probably with a shorter onset and offglide)'. It is physically possible, and may indeed happen occasionally in Czech, that instead of allowing the tongue to make repeated closures in such a trill, it is limited to a vibratory pattern within the zone of close approximation, so that audible friction is continuous rather than intermittent. This would be a true trilled fricative, in strict technical terms. It is probably over-delicate, however, to insist on a descriptive distinction between trilled stops with intermittent friction on the one hand and trilled fricatives with continuous friction on the other, and the traditional term 'fricative trill' can conveniently be used to cover either possibility.

Another example of a fricative trill is [ʁ], the voiced uvular fricative trill used in French in some contexts, as in *rater* [ʁɑt̪e] 'to fail', together with [χ], its voiceless counterpart, as in some pronunciations of *quatre* [kɑt̪χ] 'four'. (The symbols [ʁ] and [χ] are ambiguous between a uvular fricative and a uvular fricative trill. The symbol for a voiced uvular trilled stop without friction is [ʀ].) The active articulator here is not only the tongue, but also the uvula, vibrating in a broad channel formed along the centre of the back and root of the tongue. In addition, unlike the tongue tip/blade in alveolar trills, the uvula sometimes tends to vibrate rather irregularly.

9.8 Syllabic fricatives

Fricatives typically act as consonants, at syllable-margins. But some languages allow fricatives (voiced and voiceless) to fill the nuclear position in syllables in certain circumstances. English is one such language, in that the processes of syllable re-organization in unstressed syllables in informal speech often result in both the deletion of vocoids representing nuclear elements, and the prolongation of a fricative element, which in effect takes over the role of syllable nucleus. An example in British English (RP) is the following:

Syllabic fricatives in informal style in British English (RP)

Orthographic form	No solicitor will ever support that view
Formal utterance	[nəʊ səˈlɪsɪtə wɪl ˈɛvə səˈpɔt ðat vju]
Informal utterance	[nəʊ s̩ˈlɪstəɹ l̩ ˈɛvə s̩ˈpɔt ðat vju]

There are a number of differences between the formal and the informal versions of the above sentence. Some are irrelevant to the present discussion, such as the insertion of a so-called **linking-r** at the end of 'solicitor' once the following /w/ which normally blocks its occurrence has been removed. What is central to the point being made here is that it is reasonable to suggest that the first segments in the pronunciations of both *solicitor* and *support* have taken over a syllable-nuclear role in the informal version. In the case of *support*, the duration of the [s:] segment will tend to be relatively longer, except at the extreme of informal style, than in the corresponding pronunciation of *sport*. In this perspective, the informal pronunciation of the word *support* continues to represent two syllables, with the first syllable being manifested solely by [s̩:].

A small number of languages accept fricatives as syllable-nuclear entities even at the most formal levels of style. One example is Bella Coola, the Pacific Northwest Indian language mentioned in the previous chapter (Hoard 1978: 67). Examples (with '+' once again being used to indicate syllable boundaries) are:

Syllabic fricatives in Bella Coola

[t̩ʰ+ɬ] 'strong'	[ɬ+qʰ] 'wet'
[k̩ʷ+s̩] 'rough'	[p̩ɬ+t̩ʰ] 'thick'
[q̩ʷ+t̩ʰ] 'crooked'	[s+ps] 'north east wind'
[s̩+t̩ʰ+t̩ʰ] 'birthmark'	[ɬ+mi+ɬ] 'it's us'

A longer Bella Coola sequence cited by Hoard (1978: 68) is [nu+jam+ɬ+ɬ+ɬ+ɬ] 'we used to sing', where [nujamɬ] + [ɬ] + [ɬ] + [ɬ] = 'sing', + *past* + *past* + 'we'.

There are many similar instances from other languages of the Pacific Northwest, including Wenatchee-Columbia, Quileute and Puget Salish (or Lushootsheed), and from Nez Perce of the Sahaptian language family (Hoard 1978: 59–68).

9.9   Fricative articulations and phonation types

Voiceless fricatives seem to be more numerous in the consonant systems of the languages of the world than voiced fricatives. In Maddieson's survey of 317 languages, the ratio of voiced to voiceless fricatives is 43:57 (Maddieson 1984: 45).

Fricatives are less versatile than stops in the range of phonation types that are exploited linguistically. While voicelessness and normal voicing are common, whispery voice, creak and creaky voice do not seem to have been established as the basis for contrastive oppositions between pairs of fricatives. At an allophonic level, whisper is sometimes used in the co-ordinatory process of 'devoicing' that is discussed in chapter 12.

9.10   Fricative articulations and non-pulmonic airstreams

Fricative articulations can be made on any airstream that can initiate sufficient airflow through a narrow articulatory constriction to make the resultant escape of air turbulent. The glottalic airstream mechanism is easily capable of doing this, though necessarily for a very short duration, limited to the amount of time during which the larynx is moving in its initiating movement. Only egressive use seems to be made of this possibility in languages, and ejective fricatives are not uncommon. One example comes from Amharic, a language of Ethiopia, where Westermann and Ward (1933: 97) cite the use of a voiceless alveolar ejective fricative in the word [as'e]. meaning 'His Majesty'. Further examples are found in Xhosa (J. Kelly, personal communication), Hausa (Westermann and Ward *ibid.*) and Kabardian (Catford 1984: 33), for instance:

> *Ejective fricative segments in Xhosa*
> [uχ'ot'i] 'bravery'   [uk'uχ'wɛmpa] 'to scratch'

> *Ejective fricative segments in Hausa*
> [s'ara] 'contemporary'   [sara] 'cut down'

> *Ejective fricative segments in Kabardian*
> [bzu'wuf'] 'good bird'   [fə'zef'] 'good woman'

9.11   Symbols for fricative articulations

Figure 9.3 summarizes symbols for pulmonic egressive voiceless and voiced fricative segments, for both place-neutral and displaced articulations.

Further reading

Maddieson (1984) sets out the use of fricatives of all types in the 317 languages of the UPSID database. Shadle (1990) presents an account of the relationship between articulatory and acoustic events in fricative production, and Jassem (1965) describes acoustic cues to place of articulation in

	Place-neutral articulations						Displaced articuations				
	oral fric.	nasal fric.	oral fric. tap	nasal fric. tap	oral fric. trill	nasal fric. trill	oral fric.	nasal fric.	oral fric. flap	nasal fric. flap	
labial	ɸ	ɸ̃			B̥	B̥̃					vl
	β	β̃			B	B̃					vd
linguo-labial							ɸ̪	ɸ̪̃			vl
							β̪	β̪̃			vd
labio-dental							f	f̃			vl
							v	ṽ			vd
dental	θ	θ̃					s̪	s̪̃			vl
	ð	ð̃					z̪	z̪̃			vd
alveolar	s	s̃	ɾ̥	ɾ̥̃	r̥	r̥̃	θ̠ ɹ̥	θ̠̃ ɹ̥̃	ɾ̥	ɾ̥̃	vl
	z	z̃	ɾ	ɾ̃	r	r̃	ð̠ ɹ	ð̠̃ ɹ̃	ɾ	ɾ̃	vd
palato-alveolar	ʃ	ʃ̃					ʂ	ʂ̃			vl
	ʒ	ʒ̃					ʐ	ʐ̃			vd
alveolo-palatal	ɕ	ɕ̃									vl
	ʑ	ʑ̃									vd
palatal	ç	ç̃									vl
	ʝ	ʝ̃									vd
velar	x	x̃									vl
	ɣ	ɣ̃									vd
uvular	χ	χ̃									vl
	ʁ	ʁ̃			ʀ	ʀ̃					vd
pharyn-geal	ħ	ħ̃									vl
	ʕ	ʕ̃									vd
epiglottal	ʜ	ʜ̃									vl
	ʢ	ʢ̃									vd

Single fricative segments	diacritics:	voiceless, r̥ nasal, r̃	fricative, r̝, ɹ̝ retroflex, ʂ, ʐ	flat, θ̱ dental, s̪

Figure 9.3 Summary of the phonetic symbols for place-neutral and displaced pulmonic egressive fricative segments

fricatives. Docherty (1992) is recommended for theoretical and quantitative details of fricative segments in **British English**, especially on matters of timing of voicing in relation to articulatory events.

Phonetic and phonological publications dealing with the notion of fricative **sibilance** as a feature include those by Chomsky and Halle (1968), Jakobson, Fant and Halle (1952), Jakobson and Halle (1956, 1957, 1968), Jakobson and Lotz (1949), Ladefoged (1971, 1975) and Nartey (1982).

10

Resonant articulations

All **resonants** have a stricture of open approximation. A necessary condition for the performance of resonants is that the airstream passes through the vocal tract in a smoothly laminar flow, with no audible local friction. Resonants were said in chapter 5 to be classifiable into **central resonants** and **lateral resonants.** This chapter will begin by describing the production of central resonants. The description of lateral resonants is presented later, in section 10.13.

Resonants which are central are classified as **non-contoid** segments. When non-contoids are marginal in the syllable, the label attached to them in the descriptive model offered in this book is that of **non-syllabic approximants** (or **approximants**, for brevity). When non-contoids are nuclear in the syllable – that is, when they are syllabic, they are classified as **syllabic vocoids** (or **vocoids**, for brevity). Figure 10.1 shows these relationships, replicating part of figure 5.18 for convenience. Approximants by definition always function phonologically as consonants. Vocoids by definition always function phonologically as vowels. In these senses, the pronunciation [j] corresponding to the letter 'y' in the English word *yes* [jɛs] is an **approximant**, and that to the 'e' is a **vocoid**. Similarly, the pronunciation corresponding to the letter 'w' in the English word *wit* [wɪt] is an approximant, and that to the 'i' is a vocoid.

Figure 10.1 The relationship between contoids, non-contoids, approximants and vocoids

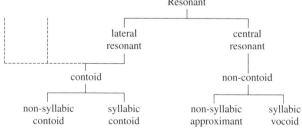

The term 'approximant', which was invented by Ladefoged (1964), is in the usage of this book broadly comparable to the traditional phonetic terms 'semi-vowel' and 'frictionless continuant' (though the category of 'frictionless continuants' is sometimes taken to include the concept of lateral resonants).

The term 'vocoid' corresponds straightforwardly in this book to the traditional phonetic term 'vowel'. But it would be unhelpful to adopt the traditional usage of 'vowel' here as a phonetic term, since the use of the term 'vowel' for units at both the phonological and the phonetic levels reflects an uncomfortable degree of theoretical ambivalence, and can lead to more than a little confusion in the minds of students. Within the definitions proposed above, vocoids will be discussed first and then approximants. Finally, lateral resonants will be considered.

10.1 Syllabic vocoids

The very large majority of vocoid articulations in the languages of the world are voiced. As was stated in chapter 4, when the articulators are in a stricture of open approximation, the vocal tract is in an optimal configuration for it to be made to resonate by the pulsed acoustic energy injected into it by the vibrating larynx.

There are two active articulators in vocoid articulations, the tongue and the lips. Since the stricture to which they jointly contribute must by definition be limited to one of open approximation, neither has structural priority over the other. All such vocoid segments are therefore examples of **double articulation,** a category of place of articulation in which there are two concurrent strictures of equal degree. Double articulation is discussed separately in detail in the following chapter on multiple articulations, but it is mentioned at this point to explain a decision to present the description of vocoids in two sets. The first set of vocoid segments to be presented will be those varying in lingual articulation but with their labial articulation showing non-rounded positions of the lips. The second set of vocoid segments to be presented will be those with the same lingual articulations as the first set but with their labial articulation characterized by lip-rounding.

Almost all vocoids representing vowels show the body of the tongue to have a regularly curved convex surface, with the tip of the tongue held lower than the body. It is possible to modify these articulations by curling the tongue tip up in a retroflex aspect. As was mentioned earlier, this is called 'rhotacization', (or 'r-colouring') (e.g. in Wells 1982: 139). Vocoids pronounced with this retroflex aspect are found in many British and North American accents of English, in words like *bird* and *myrrh*, whose articula-

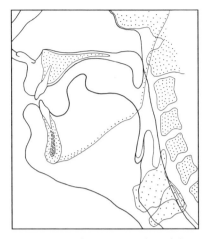

Figure 10.2 Sagittal cross-section of the
vocal organs during the production
of the medial phase of a vocoid
articulated with a retroflex aspect

tory configuration is shown in figure 10.2. The means of transcribing rhotacization on vocoids is to add a right-hook diacritic to the symbol for the
vocoid, as in [ɚ].

Vocoids pronounced with the tongue curved in a convex shape, in both
front-to-back and side-to-side dimensions, are nevertheless overwhelmingly
the most common type. Problems arise when one tries to devise a method
for the unambiguous description of the configuration of the vocal tract
based in some way on the disposition of this regularly curved convex surface
of the body of the tongue. There is a considerable weight of tradition, going
back to Alexander Melville Bell's book on *Visible Speech* published in 1867,
behind the description of the disposition of the tongue in terms of the location in the mouth, vertically and horizontally, of the highest point of its
curved surface. As Ladefoged points out (1980: 488), there is unfortunately
then no way so far proposed of distinguishing between two different configurations of the vocal tract that happen to share a common position for the
highest point of the tongue body. This is a serious drawback, because the
factor determining the resonatory characteristics of the acoustic output, and
hence of the auditory quality of the sound produced, is not the position of
the highest point of the tongue as such, but the overall configuration of the
vocal tract. In other words, two vocoids can share the same position of the
highest point of the tongue and nevertheless still sound different in quality.
A further drawback is that, considering the muscular anatomy of the vocal
tract, the customary vertical and horizontal dimensions of the space within

which the location of the highest point of the tongue falls do not correspond in any direct, simple way to the modes of action of the musculature associated with the tongue.

The traditional 'highest-point' method of description should therefore best be regarded only as a convenient way of discussing the pronunciation of vocoid sounds, well understood and widely used, but with only moderate descriptive power and without strong explanatory insight into the underlying physiology. Because its use is so widespread, a version of the traditional method will be described here; but Ladefoged (1980) and Wood (1977, 1979) have proposed descriptions of tongue action which though less well known are more explanatory and less ambiguous, which are recommended to the reader who wishes to follow the matter further.

10.2 Charts of the vocoid space

The location of the highest point of the regularly curved surface of the body of the tongue falls, in the production of vocoids, into an area which lies below the palatal and the velar zones of articulation. This can be called the **vocoid space.** The actual shape of this space, in the sagittal plane, is that of the tilted ovoid shown in figure 10.3 (adapted from Abercrombie 1967: 157). The limits of the vocoid space are conditioned by the fact that if the highest point of the tongue were raised further, the degree of stricture

Figure 10.3 The tilted oval shape of the vocoid space, within which the highest point of the body of the tongue is placed in the production of vocoids (after Abercrombie 1967: 157)

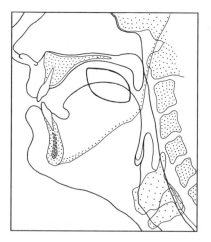

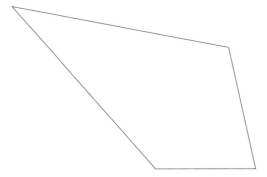

Figure 10.4 Stylized chart of the vocoid space (adapted from Jones 1962:37 and Abercrombie 1967: 157)

would become fricative, as it would if the tongue were retracted into the pharynx so that the highest point of tongue body lay beyond the rearmost boundary of the space. If the highest point of the body of the tongue were advanced beyond the front edge of the vocoid space, front oral friction would be similarly caused. For a given jaw position, anatomical constraints prevent the tongue being lowered beyond the lower limit of the vocoid space. The ovoid shape of this space can be stylized for convenience, and vocoid articulations could be represented by locating the highest point of the tongue as a point in the two dimensions of a slightly stylized **vocoid chart** (adapted from Jones 1962: 37 and Abercrombie 1967: 158), shown in figure 10.4.

In the early part of this century, Daniel Jones made charting the vocoid space into an effective practical instrument for phoneticians, by means of his 'Cardinal Vowel' system. Abercrombie (1967: 176–7) comments that Jones 'used the Cardinal Vowels for identifying the vowels of English in the first edition of [his] *English Pronouncing Dictionary* (1917) [and] they were made use of in the 2nd ed. (1922) of Daniel Jones's *Outline of English Phonetics*, but not in the 1st (mostly in print by 1914, though not published till 1918)'.

The Cardinal Vowel system developed by Jones was a method for locating vocoids on the chart by reference to the relationship between their auditory and articulatory characteristics and those of certain selected vocoids of agreed quality. In particular, Jones made two selected vocoids at the extremes of the vocoid space in his own pronunciation the hinges (hence, 'cardinal', from the Latin *cardo, cardinis*, 'a hinge') of the descriptive system. He described the first of these in the following terms: 'Cardinal vowel No. 1 (**i**) is the sound in which the raising of the tongue is as far forward as possible and as high as possible consistently with its being a vowel ... the lips being spread.' The second was described as follows: 'Cardinal vowel No. 5 (ɑ) is a sound in which the back of the tongue is lowered as far as possible and retracted as far as possible consistently with the sound being a vowel ... and in which the lips are not rounded' (Jones 1962: 31).

Jones then specified a set of six other vocoids – Cardinal Vowels 2 [e], 3 [ɛ] and 4 [a] as a front series on the periphery of the vocoid space dividing the vertical (and auditory) distance between Cardinal Vowels 1 and 5 into equal intervals. Cardinal Vowels 6 [ɔ], 7 [o] and 8 [u] were chosen to continue this series of equal auditory intervals upwards again, along the back periphery of the space, with progressive degrees of lip-rounding, ending in a 'close lip rounding' position for No. 8.

These cardinal vowels were presented as the 'primary' cardinal vowels, and Jones specified a further set of 'secondary' cardinal vowels with reversed lip positions, together with additional secondary cardinal vowels in the central area of the space. Taken together, the primary and secondary Cardinal Vowels thus provided a set of points in auditory and articulatory vocoid space whose location can be conventionally agreed. These then constitute a basis for a chart with a co-ordinate system for locating the auditory and articulatory characteristics of any vocoid segment encountered from any speaker of normal anatomy. According to Windsor-Lewis (1976: 29), the practical chart he devised for the presentation of these Cardinal Vowels, now known as the 'Cardinal Vowel diagram', first appeared as such in Ward (1929). It is shown as figure 10.5, with the highest points of the tongue representing Cardinal Vowel positions falling on the intersections of lines delimiting zones of the chart. The zoning has been adopted by the IPA, as have most of the phonetic symbols for the primary and secondary Cardinal Vowels. The labels given for the different zones are as now recommended by the IPA.

Figure 10.5 The Cardinal Vowel diagram devised by Daniel Jones, with its associated phonetic symbols

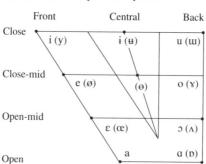

The Cardinal Vowel diagram is yet more stylized than the previous chart shown in figure 10.4. It is worth noting (for purposes of reproduction of the chart) that its trapezoid shape is formed from that of 'a rectangle three units deep and four wide (with) the base, the right-hand upright side and the top ... in the proportions 2:3:4' (Windsor-Lewis 1976: 29–30).

Most professional phoneticians trained in the British tradition are still taught this auditory and articulatory scheme of vocoid description. It will not be dwelt upon here at greater length, partly because, as Jones said, 'The values of the cardinal vowels cannot be learnt from written descriptions; they should be learnt by oral instruction from a teacher who knows them' (Jones 1962: 34). As Abercrombie (1985) comments:

> The system of Cardinal Vowels constitutes a technique, not a theory. It
> is a technique of description, a technique for providing much more
> precise specifications of vowels than the traditional kind of taxonomic
> approach is able to do. It is a technique that is not used in America,
> and not much used by continental phoneticians; it belongs more or less
> exclusively to the British tradition, though, as we know, it was adopted
> by the I.P.A. The *idea* of cardinal vowels was put forward by Ellis, the
> *word* 'cardinal' by Bell, and Henry Sweet, too, spoke of 'cardinal vowel
> positions'. But only Daniel Jones produced a fully worked out system.
> Sweet said that Phonetics is both a science and an art. It should be
> remembered that the Cardinal Vowel technique belongs to the art, and
> not to the science, side of the subject. (Abercrombie 1985: 17–18)

Ellis, Bell and Sweet were all Victorian predecessors of Jones. We can close this brief mention of the Jones Cardinal Vowel technique by noting that the scheme raises some very interesting questions about the theoretical basis of the notion of phonetic equivalence of acts of vocal performance by speakers endowed with very different vocal apparatus, and about concepts of phonetic similarity and phonetic distance.

There are yet other ways of constructing a map which stylizes the tilted oval space of possible locations of the highest point of the tongue shown in figure 10.3, over and above the general method advocated by Daniel Jones and the specific way adopted by the IPA. An additional possibility is offered by Catford (1977a: 184–6), in which he presents the possible space in terms of a segment of a circle of a little more than 90 degrees, pivoted on [a]. The locations of the individual vocoids are represented on a set of polar co-ordinates. This polar chart is reproduced for interest in figure 10.6. One of the advantages of Catford's system, which he agrees has accompanying deficiencies, is that the means of describing vocoids can be unified with the means for describing contoids, with a common method of specifying

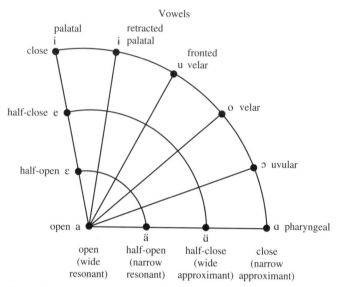

Figure 10.6 Polar chart of the vocoid space (adapted from Catford 1977a: 185)

the location and degree of maximum stricture. The labels given are Catford's.

The symbols currently accepted by the IPA as representing vocoid qualities correspond closely to those used by Jones, and these are shown, in the positions on the vocoid chart to which they relate, in figure 10.7. It should be noted that this chart, authorized by the IPA after the 1989 Kiel Convention, is slightly different (especially in the way that the central area is designed) from the Jones Cardinal Vowel diagram. The Cardinal Vowel diagram will be the one adopted in this book, but we shall adopt the IPA labels for the zoning of the chart. Taking the horizontal dimension first, corresponding to **place of articulation**, there are three divisions, called **front, central** and **back**. The highest point of the tongue in **front vocoids** lies on the front of the tongue, underneath the palatal zone. The highest point in **back vocoids** is on the surface of the back of the tongue, below the velar zone. **Central vocoids** are intermediate between front and back.

The vertical dimension is divided into four areas, in effect sub-dividing the degree of stricture of **open approximation**. Vocoids made in the area closest to the roof of the mouth are called **close vocoids**; those occurring in the lowest part of the chart are called **open vocoids**; the space between the close and open zones is equally divided vertically into two further zones, the upper being called **close-mid** and the lower **open-mid**. The terms 'close-mid' and 'open-mid' were agreed at the 1989 Kiel IPA Convention as replacing

Vowels

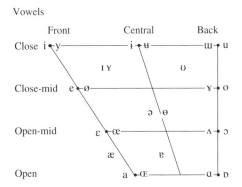

Figure 10.7 Vocoid chart approved by the International Phonetic Association in 1989, with its associated symbols

the former labels 'half-close' and 'half-open' respectively. ('Half-close' and 'half-open' were widely used before 1989 by British-trained phoneticians, though a widespread American practice preferred 'mid'.)

10.3   Phonetic symbols for vocoids

The vocoid space is an articulatory, auditory and acoustic continuum: vocoids can be located in any part of it, and many hundreds of audibly different qualities can be produced by adopting slightly different tongue (and lip) positions. There would be no practical way of inventing independent phonetic symbols for every discriminable vocoid, so a smaller set of symbols has evolved in which each symbol can either be taken to stand for any vocoid occurring in a small, general area of the chart, or can identify more precise locations by the addition of modifying diacritics.

Figure 10.8 shows the phonetic symbols which represent the areas round the intersections of the zone-boundaries on the vocoid chart, all with a non-rounded configuration of the lip-space. Both the area of lip-opening and the vertical position of the jaw are physiologically independent of the position of the tongue body, strictly speaking, but there is a broad tendency for width of the lip space to be correlated with tongue height, with close vocoids having a slightly wider lip-opening than open vocoids. Similarly, the jaw, being the carrier of the tongue, tends not surprisingly to be held in a slightly closer position for close vocoids than for open vocoids.

The modifying diacritics mentioned above signal small adjustments of a vocoid's position from the reference area of the intersection of the zone-boundaries. For a position adjusted towards the front of the mouth, the general diacritic for articulatory 'advancement', [̪], can be used, as a sub-

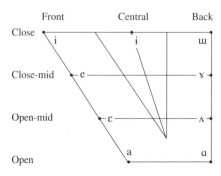

Figure 10.8 Vocoid chart of non-rounded vocoids, with associated symbols

script to a given vocoid symbol. For a retracted position, subscript [ ] can be used. A closer position is indicated by subscript [ ], and a more open position by subscript [ ].

10.4 Labial elements of vocoid segments

In traditional descriptions of vocoid articulations, the configuration of the lips is described with three main labels: **spread, neutral** and **rounded.** In the terms introduced in this section, the non-rounded vocoids shown in figure 10.8 are divided into those with spread and those with neutral lip positions. The vocoids with close tongue positions (front [i], central [ɨ] and back [ɯ]) and close-mid tongue positions (front [e] and back [ɤ]) have a spread lip position; those with open-mid tongue positions (front [ɛ] and back [ʌ]) and open tongue positions (front [a] and back [ɑ]) all have neutral lip positions. There is no currently IPA-approved symbol for a close-mid central vocoid with spread or neutral lips.

Rounded configurations are sometimes further divided into **close rounding** and **open rounding.** For the purposes of describing the phonetic basis of phonological distinctions between vocoid articulations, these labels are probably sufficient. But for describing the articulatory differences between different languages, or between different accents of the same language, or for describing different (extralinguistic) speaker-characterizing settings of the lips or (paralinguistic) attitude-marking settings, we need a more specific vocabulary. This can be achieved by describing the modification of the **interlabial space** in the side-to-side and vertical dimensions (Laver 1980: 35–43). Figure 10.9 shows the neutral configuration of this interlabial space as a dashed outline in a schematized, head-on view. Superimposed on this are the eight general labial configurations that arise from the effect of changing one

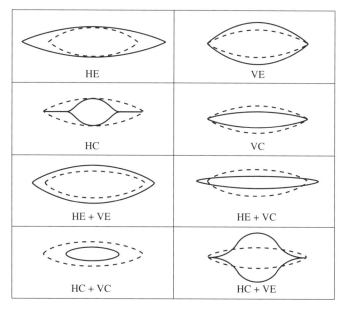

Figure 10.9 Frontal view of the lip position associated with the neutral configuration of the vocal organs (dashed outline). Eight deviations from the neutral configuration arise from expansion or contraction of either or both the horizontal and vertical dimensions of the neutral outline e.g. 'HE' indicates horizontal expansion (after Laver 1980: 37)

or both of the vertical and horizontal axes of the space, either by expansion or by contraction.

Any position with horizontal expansion of the interlabial space corresponds to the traditional descriptive label of a 'spread' lip position. Any position with horizontal contraction of the interlabial space corresponds to a 'rounded' label: 'open rounding' involves contraction of the horizontal dimension and simultaneous expansion of the vertical dimension; 'close rounding' needs either horizontal contraction alone, or horizontal contraction with simultaneous vertical contraction.

In addition to modifications of the area and shape of the interlabial space, the lips can also be protruded forwards from the neutral position. Open rounding tends to protrude the lips to a more marked degree than does close rounding. Figure 10.10 shows the phonetic symbols for vocoids which correspond to the vocoids made with the same tongue positions as those in figure 10.8, but with rounded lip positions. The rounded vocoids made with close tongue positions (front [y], central [ʉ], and back [u]) or close-mid tongue positions (front [ø] and back [o]) have close lip-rounding; those with open-

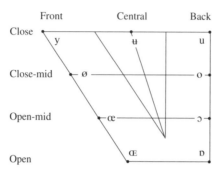

Figure 10.10 Vocoid chart of lip-rounded vocoids, with associated symbols

mid tongue positions (front [œ], and back [ɔ]) and open tongue positions (front [Œ] and back [ɒ]) have open lip-rounding. No current IPA-approved symbols exist for central open-mid or central open vocoids with lip-rounding.

10.5 Intermediate vocoids

Figure 10.11 shows a number of vocoids found fairly frequently in languages, whose positions are distant from the intersections of the zone-boundaries of the vocoid chart. The lip positions for [ɪ], [æ] and [ɐ] are neutral, and for [ɣ] and [ʊ] are slightly more open than for close rounding.

There are two central vocoids whose height is also central (i.e. between close-mid and open-mid). The symbol for this central vocoid made with neutral lips is [ə]. This is the vocoid produced when the vocal tract is in its neutral configuration, and is hence often referred to in other terminologies as 'the neutral vowel'. Another common name for this vocoid is 'schwa' [ʃwa] or 'shva' [ʃva], a term taken from traditional Hebrew grammar (Pullum and Ladusaw 1986: 45). The symbol for a comparable central vocoid made with rounded lips is [ɵ]. Both [ə] and [ɵ] can be used as cover symbols for vocoids in the general central area of the vocoid chart with an appropriate lip position.

An additional symbol for a central vocoid comparable in quality to [ə] is [ɜ]. As a general phonetic symbol, no qualitative difference from [ə] is implied by [ɜ]. Both symbols are often used in phonologically oriented transcriptions of English (RP), as a mnemonic reminder of the stress-status of the syllable concerned, with [ə] being reserved for the realization of the vowel in unstressed syllables and [ɜ] for its manifestation in stressed syllables (where the pronunciation of the vocoid is usually of greater relative duration). Examples of this practice are the transcriptions of the words *bird*

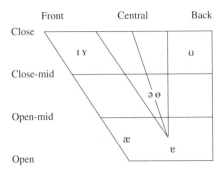

Figure 10.11 Vocoid chart of non-peripheral, intermediate vocoids, with associated symbols

['bɜd], *curler* ['kɜlə] and *murmur* ['mɜmə]. It would be no less phonetically acceptable to transcribe these words as ['bəːd], ['kəːlə] and ['məːmə].

10.6   Exemplification of vocoid symbols

Languages showing the different vocoid articulations mentioned in all the sections above are illustrated below. The examples of Bafang (Fe'Fe) words (a language of Cameroon) are from Westermann and Bryan (1952: 130), the Danish and Ngwe (another language of Cameroon) from Ladefoged (1972), the Dutch from J. Verhoeven (personal communication), the Lhasa Tibetan from Ohala (1981: 184) citing Michailovsky (1975), and the Sindhi from Nihalani (1973). The Kurdish examples are from A. Ferhardi (personal communication) and the Sundanese from Robins (1953).

Vocoids in Bafang
[zák] 'thigh'   [zɔ́k] 'knee'

Vocoids in Danish
[viːɞ̰ə] 'know'   [veːɞ̰ə] 'wheat'
[vɛːɞ̰ə] 'wet'   [vaːɞ̰ə] 'wade'

Vocoids in Dutch
[bit] 'beetroot'   [bet] 'bit (p. participle)'   [bɛt] 'bed'
[byr] 'neighbour'   [bøk] 'beech'   [buk] 'book'
[bot] 'boat'   [bɔn] 'bone'   [bɑt] 'bath'

Vocoids in Ngwe
[mbɨ] 'cowries'   [mbɨ] 'dog'   [mbɣ] 'ivory'

Vocoids in Lhasa Tibetan
[lyː] 'body'   [nuː] 'west'
[pʰøː] 'Tibet'   [qʰøː] 'price'

Vocoids in Sindhi
[pɪ̢ə] 'a curse'   [pʊ̢ə] 'sonny'

Vocoids in Kurdish (Suleimaniya and Arbili accents)
[mir] 'grim-faced'   [mər] 'sheep (sg.)'

Vocoids in Kurdish (Arbili accent)
[bez] 'squeamishness'   [bəz] 'fat (n.)'
[bɑz] 'hawk'   [buz] 'ice (cubes)'
[sɔɾ] 'red'   [suɾ] 'salty'
[siɾ] 'garlic'   [səɾ] 'head'

Vocoids in Kurdish (Suleimaniya accent)
[mil] 'hand of a clock'   [mɨl] 'neck'   [mæl] 'bird'

Vocoids in Sundanese
[ŋokot] 'to take'   [nʏŋgʏl] 'to beat'
[ɲirim] 'to send'   [ŋusul] 'to pursue'

The [ð̞] symbols in the Danish examples (which in Ladefoged's more general transcription are shown as [ð]), represent voiced alveolar approximants, a sound-type discussed later in this chapter. The [ˌ] subscript diacritic placed below the [ð̞] symbol (normally a fricative) is again used to mean 'more open', as in the case of the lamino-lingual vocoid in a Swedish regional dialect accent introduced above.

It perhaps deserves repeating at this point that, in allocating distinct labels, symbols and descriptions to vocoid articulations, one risks giving the impression of 'freezing' into a static representation something that in real, connected speech is a dynamic, continuously changing configuration. Figure 10.12 is revealing in this connection. It is a sequence of tracings from the frames of a cine-film of lip articulation through the time course of two single syllables, one with a lip-rounded vocoid and one with a vocoid without rounding, in Tamil (Balasubramanian 1972: 152). However, the use of discrete labels and symbols is simply intended as a way of selecting and grouping in attention representative facets of articulatory performance.

10.7 Transitional aspects of vocoid production: monophthong, diphthong and triphthong

The involvement of a category of place of articulation involving two strictures of equal degree, in a double articulation of lingual and labial elements has already been noted. Many languages show a transitional aspect of articulation of vocoids which controls the complexity of the articulatory

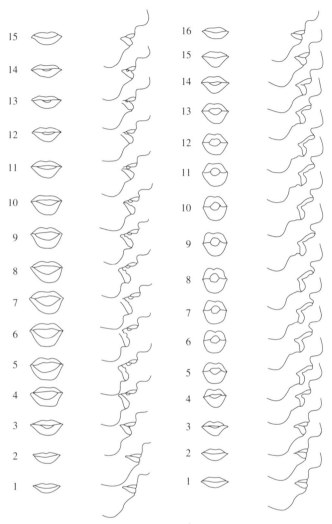

Figure 10.12 Tracings from a cine-film of lip position through the production of two syllables in Tamil, one with and one without lip-rounding (after Balasubramanian 1972:152)

target for individual segments. Like other segment-types, vocoids can be regarded as normally having three component phases: an onset phase during which the body of the tongue is approaching the representative target location in the vocoid space, a medial phase where the target location is reached or most nearly reached, and an offset phase where the vocal organs begin to take up the appropriate articulatory configuration for the performance of the next segment. Labial activity in vocoids shows a similar pattern, and is normally synchronized with lingual activity.

The notion of articulatory transitions forms the basis for making a distinction of aspect of articulation between three auditorily different types of syllabic vocoid, as mentioned in chapter 5. These are **monophthongs, diphthongs** and **triphthongs**. In all three cases, the performance of the vocoid is within the articulatory span of a single syllable.

A **monophthong** is a vocoid where the medial phase shows a relatively stable articulatory position of the tongue and the lips. Auditorily, monophthongs produce an impression of relatively unvarying quality. The open-mid, front unrounded vocoid [ɛ] in *met* [mɛt] is an example of a monophthong in nearly all accents of English. Figure 10.13 shows representations of the articulatory positions of all the twelve monophthongs of RP plotted on a vocoid chart. Another example of a monophthong is the close, front spread vocoid [i] in [ki] *qui* ('who') in French.

Notwithstanding the comments offered immediately above, it should be remembered that this analysis of segmental performance into phases, even though convenient, is at its most arbitrary for vocoids, compared with other segment-types. In the articulation even of monophthongal vocoids, the vocal organs are seldom in a truly static position, and the discussion above concerns relative stability of the vocal tract more than any real tendency to momentary immobility.

A **diphthong** is a vocoid in which the medial phase explicitly consists of an articulatory trajectory across the vocoid space, giving an auditory impression of a changing quality. If the trajectory moves upwards in the vocoid space, the resulting diphthongs are called **closing diphthongs.** Examples are the vocoids in English *flight* [flaɪt] and *flout* [flaʊt], where the body of the tongue starts in the open zone and moves up towards either the close-mid or the close zone. **Centring diphthongs** have articulatory trajectories which start nearer the periphery of the vocoid space, and move towards the central zone. Examples are the diphthongs in Received Pronunciation in British English, where post-vocalic orthographic 'r' has no rhotic pronunciation except before a vocoid, of *pair* [pɛə], *pier* [pɪə] and *poor* [pʊə].

It is customary to transcribe diphthongs by using the symbols that correspond to the start-point and end-point of the trajectory. In the perception of ordinary English speech, the end-point that is inferred as the intended target from the evidence of the trajectory seems to be perceptually more important than the particular end-point actually reached along the articulatory journey towards the goal. Languages differ, however, in the degree to which speak-

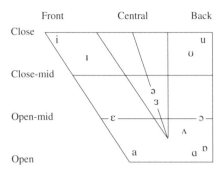

Figure 10.13 Vocoid chart of twelve monophthongs
of English (Received Pronunciation)

ers 'dwell' on either the start-point or the end-point, as compared with the time spent on the trajectory between these points.

The majority of languages of the world do not use diphthongs in their phonological inventory. When two given languages do use diphthongs phonologically, the realizations in the two languages of diphthongal phonemes transcribed with the same phonemic symbol can differ in a number of phonetic respects. The end-points chosen for the diphthongs can differ in the fine detail of their phonetic quality, and the relative speed with which the diphthongal trajectory is performed need not be the same in the two languages. Taking data from Gay (1968) on American English diphthongs, Lindau, Norlin and Svantesson (1990) made an acoustic analysis of the pronunciations representing the diphthongal phonemes /ai/ and /au/ in American English (5 speakers), Arabic (6 speakers from Cairo), Chinese (4 speakers from Beijing) and Hausa (10 speakers from Kano). They selected the /ai/ and /au/ diphthongs because they are by far the most frequent types of diphthong found in the languages of the world. Using a sample of 300 genetically balanced languages taken from Maddieson's (1984) survey of sound-patterns, they found that diphthongs of these two types occur in about one third of the languages sampled. The /ai/ type of diphthong is found in about 75 per cent of the languages showing one or both of these diphthongs, while the /au/ type of diphthong was found in 65 per cent (Lindau, Norlin and Svantesson 1990: 10).

Lindau and her colleagues were able to show that the amount of (acoustic) distance from the start-point of the trajectory to the end of the movement differed between these languages. The amount of time taken to perform these trajectories also varied between the languages, measured as a percentage of the duration of the whole diphthong. Figure 10.14 (adapted from Lindau, Norlin and Svantesson 1990: 13) compares the transition duration percentages against the acoustic distance (measured in the units of a perceptually related 'mel' scale) for the realizations of /ai/ and /au/ in Arabic, Chinese, English and Hausa. It can be seen from this figure that in Arabic and Hausa the transitional trajectory takes up only about 20 per cent of the overall duration of the diphthongs, while in Chinese it occupies about 50 per cent and in English about 70 per cent. It is also noteworthy that the Arabic and Hausa realizations of /au/ are comparable in the time taken to move from the start-point of the trajectory to the end of the diphthongal movement, as a percentage of the overall duration of the diphthongal segment; but the realization of the Arabic /au/ shows a travel over a much greater acoustic (and hence articulatory) distance. Chinese and English realizations of /au/ share about the same acoustic distance measure, but both show a percentage transition measure greater than either Hausa or Arabic, with English having substantially the greatest value.

Some illustrations of languages showing diphthongal pronunciations are given below. The examples from Dutch are from J. Verhoeven (personal communication), Hausa from Schachter (1969: 73–7), omitting tone, and North Welsh from Albrow (1966: 2–3):

Diphthongal vocoids in a number of languages

Diphthongs in Dutch
[ləi] 'lazy'   [lɛi] 'slate'   [lɑu] 'lukewarm'
Diphthongs in Hausa
[ʃɐɪdaː] 'evidence'   [ɓɐunaː] 'bush cow, buffalo'
[k'wɐɪ] 'egg(s)'   [kjɐʊtɜ] 'gift'
Diphthongs in North Welsh
[jaiθ] 'language'   [braud] 'brother'   [nain] 'grandmother'

In the Hausa examples given above and in the next sentence, the transcription has been adapted to the conventions of this book. Schachter (1969: 78) comments on the high degree of variability shown by such diphthongs on different occasions of utterance: '/ai/ varies from [ɐɪ] to [əɪ] to [eɪ] to [eː] in quality ... /au/ varies from [ɐʊ] to [əʊ] to [ɔʊ] to [oː] in quality'.

Diphthongs are characterized by a relatively simple trajectory from one point towards an intended target. **Triphthongs**, by contrast, have a more complex trajectory, involving a change of direction in mid-course. They are transcribed by using a triple phonetic symbol, identifying the start-point, the mid-course target and the intended final target. Examples are Received

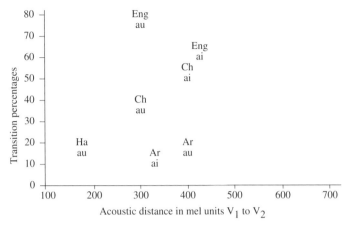

Figure 10.14 Graph of the percentage transition duration against acoustic distance in the realizations of /ai/ and /au/ diphthongs in Arabic, Chinese, Hausa and English (after Lindau, Norlin and Svantesson 1990: 13)

Pronunciation triphthongs in *flour* [flaʊə] and *fire* [faɪə]. (Since the start-point for these triphthongs in RP is a vocoid intermediate between [a] and [ɑ], either could be used in a transcription not making use of modifying diacritics, giving the options of [aʊə] or [ɑʊə], and [aɪə] or [ɑɪə].) It is perhaps not altogether surprising that such articulatory complexity is often simplified in connected speech, and the reduced forms [flaːə] and [faːə], and even [flaː] and [faː] are not uncommon as pronunciations of these words in certain idiolects of RP. Figures 10.15a and 10.15b show examples of the articulatory trajectories of the different types of diphthongs and triphthongs in RP.

As an illustration of another language with monophthongs, diphthongs and triphthongs (many of which can also be contrastively nasal), it may be of interest to consider the following representative phonetic realizations of the Brazilian Portuguese oral vowel system, as spoken in São Paulo (Cagliari 1977: 5–7):

Oral vocoids (monophthongs, diphthongs and triphthongs) in
stressed and unstressed syllables in Brazilian Portuguese

Monophthongs in stressed syllables
['xima] 'rhyme'   ['xema] 'row'
['xɜma] 'boughs'   ['xoma] 'Rome'
['xuma] 'head for'   ['bɛla] 'beautiful'
['bɔla] 'ball'

287

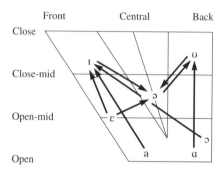

Figure 10.15a Vocoid chart of articulatory trajectories performed for diphthongs in English (Received Pronunciation)

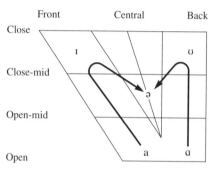

Figure 10.15b Vocoid chart of articulatory trajectories performed for triphthongs in English (Received Pronunciation)

Monophthongs in unstressed syllables

[ilu'zãõ] 'illusion'	[alu'zãõ] 'allusion'
[e'ʈaɾɪa] 'of age'	[o'ʈaɾɪa] 'credulous'
[u'ɾina] 'urine'	[a'ɾena] 'arena'
[kafe'zi̠ɲʊ] 'coffee'	[sɔ'mẽn̪ti] 'only'

Diphthongs ending in [ɪ]

['xeɪs] 'kings'	['xɛɪs] 'cents'
['paɪ] 'father'	['ɖɔɪ] 'it hurts'
['boɪ] 'bull'	['fuɪ] 'I went'

Diphthongs ending in [ʊ]

['viʊ] 's/he saw'	['seʊ] 'yours'
['sɛʊ] 'sky'	['saʊ] 'salt'
['sɔʊ] 'sun'	['soʊ] 'I am'
['suʊ] 'south'	

Diphthongs beginning in [ʊ]
['likʊiɖʊ] 'liquid'   [e'kʊevʊ] 'of the same age'
[e'kʊestri] 'equestrian'   [kʊaliɖaɖɪ] 'quality'

Triphthongs in unstressed syllables
[kʊaɪs'kɛɾ] 'any (sg.)'   [kʊaʊ'kɛɾ] 'any (pl.)'

Triphthongs in stressed syllables beginning in [ʊ] and ending in [ɪ]
[averi'gʊeɪ] 'I examined'   ['kʊaɪs] 'which (pl.)'

Triphthongs in stressed syllables beginning and ending in [ʊ]
['kʊaʊ] 'which (sg.)'   [ɖeli̊ŋ'kʊiʊ] 'offended (3 sg.)'
[averi'gʊoʊ] 's/he examined'

Figure 10.16 shows the articulatory positions of the Brazilian Portuguese
oral triphthongs, plotted on the vocoid chart.

10.8   Tongue-root position in vocoid articulations

A phonetic feature that was first described by Pike (1947: 21–2)
is a modification of (chiefly) vocoid performance that consists of advancing
the root of the tongue. Pike suggested that this modification made vocoids
sound (impressionistically) 'fuller' and 'deeper'. In 1963, as described in his
article published in 1967, the Africanist phonologist Stewart developed this
possibility as a hypothesis for explaining the division in some languages
such as Twi of vowel phonemes into two sets occurring in mutually
exclusive types of words, in the process called 'vowel harmony' (described
in more detail in chapter 12). The pronunciation of one such set, Stewart
suggested, might involve adjustments of the root of the tongue, and this
could be tested by x-ray investigation. In 1962, before Stewart had thought
of the tongue-root hypothesis, he had had a conversation with Ladefoged,
urging him to investigate the physiological basis of distinctions between
vocoids, which were at that time ascribed to differences of lax and tense
muscle tension (Stewart 1967: 198). Ladefoged then independently reached
the conclusion, from x-ray investigations of vowel harmony in the
West African language Igbo, that a tongue-root advancing feature was
indeed instrumental, at least in Igbo, for creating audible and distinctive differences of vocoid-quality (Ladefoged 1964). Tracings from two of
Ladefoged's cineradiographic diagrams for vocoid pairs in Igbo are shown
in figure 10.17.

Adjustment of the root of the tongue in this way constitutes a topographical aspect of articulation. It has come to be called **advanced tongue root**
(often abbreviated to **ATR** , mostly by phonologists using it to characterize

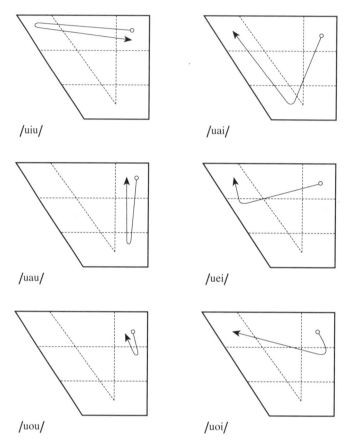

/uiu/   /uai/

/uau/   /uei/

/uou/   /uoi/

Figure 10.16 Vocoid chart of oral triphthongs in Brazilian Portuguese (after Cagliari 1977)

vowel-harmony effects). But the articulatory mechanism is probably better described as a longitudinal bunching of the whole tongue (Ladefoged 1975: 203). Ladefoged uses the terms 'wide' and 'narrow' for advanced versus non-advanced tongue-root positions, reflecting the differences in the front-to-back dimension of the pharynx. Lindau (1979) refers to this feature of pharyngeal diameter as 'expanded'.

Ladefoged comments that:

> In English, there are no pairs of vowels that are distinguished simply by one being wide and the other being narrow. But this aspect of vowel quality does operate to some extent in conjunction with variations in vowel height. The high vowels [i] and [u], as in 'heed' and 'who'd', are wider than the mid high vowels [ɪ] and [ʊ], as in 'hid' and 'hood'. (Ladefoged 1975: 203)

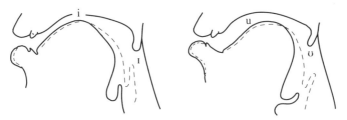

Figure 10.17 Sagittal sections for two vocoid pairs in Igbo, based on cineradiographic analysis by Ladefoged (1964) (from Stewart 1967: 198)

It is the members of pairings of vowels such as these that are often called 'tense' and 'lax' by phonologists working on English and similar languages.

Another term that is sometimes applied to segments with advanced tongue-root positions involved in languages exploiting vowel harmony such as Twi is 'covered', a term adopted from the terminology of singing by writers such as Chomsky and Halle (1968: 314–15). Painter (1973) investigated the articulatory basis of vowel harmony in Twi using cineradiography, and concluded that 'covered' does not usefully add to the descriptive phonological vocabulary, and that while 'tense/lax' might be useful as an abstract feature at the phonological level, vocoids characterized as 'tense' were more accurately described as being pronounced with a widened pharynx.

The IPA-approved diacritic for segments made with an advanced tongue root is a centred subscript [ˌ]. Retraction of the tongue root is discussed below in section 10.11.

10.9 Nasal vocoid articulations

A further aspect of vocoid articulation found in almost every language of the world is nasality. Nasal vocoids occur both in allophonic contextual adjustments to a neighbouring nasal contoid segment (virtually universally), and (less often but still frequently) in phonological contrast to oral vocoids. Examples of vocoids showing contrastive nasality can be found in many languages, including Hindi (M. Ohala 1975: 317), Sioux and Yuchi (J. Harris, personal communication), Yoruba (Bamgbose 1969: 165–6), Polish (Rubach 1977: 17) and Brazilian Portuguese (Cagliari 1977: 31–3). Sioux and Yuchi are both Amerindian languages. Sioux is spoken in the western plains of the United States and Yuchi in the Oklahoma area. Yoruba is a Kwa language spoken widely throughout many parts of West Africa, from Nigeria to Sierra Leone. The following illustrations are

Linear segmental analysis

phonetic in status, and in many cases a variety of phonemic solutions could be devised:

Nasal and oral vocoids in Hindi

[hɛ̃] 'are'	[hɛ] 'is'
[sãs] 'breath'	[sas] 'mother-in-law'
[bãs] 'bamboo'	[bas] 'bad smell'

Nasal and oral vocoids in Sioux

[wḭ] 'woman (abbrev. form)' [wi] 'sun'

Nasal and oral vocoids in Yuchi

[dotũ] 'I will suck' [dotu] 'I suck'

Nasal and oral vocoids in Yoruba

[kṵ̀] 'to be full' [kú] 'to die'

Nasal diphthongs in Polish

[ʒɛ̃ũsa] 'eye-lash'	[klɛ̃ũska] 'defeat'
[kɔ̃ũsat] 'bite'	[vɔ̃ũsci] 'narrow'
[prɛ̃ũʒitɕ] 'tighten'	[dɔ̃ũʒitɕ] 'aspire'
[vɛ̃ũx] 'a sense of smell'	[vzɔ̃ũfʃɨ] 'having taken'

Nasal vocoids (monophthongs, diphthongs and triphthongs) in Brazilian Portuguese

Monophthongs

['siɲ] 'yes'	[ĩsta'laɾ] 'to install'
['seɲ] 'without'	['tɾẽmɪ] 'trembles (3 sg.)'
['sãɲ] 'healthy'	['ɔ̃mẽŋ] 'man'
['sõɲ] 'sound'	[kõm'pɾiɗa] 'long'
['xũŋ] 'rum'	

Diphthongs

['sĩĩɲ] 'yes' (variant pronunciation)	['sẽĩŋ] 'without' (variant pronunciation)
['mãĩɲ] 'mother'	['põĩɲ] 'put'
['pũĩɲʊ] 'fist'	['fĩõmɪ] 'film'
[xẽõma'ʈizmʊ] 'rheumatism'	['sẽõma] 'a name'
['kãõma] 'calm'	['sõũ] 'sound' (variant pronunciation)
['pãõ] 'bread'	['pã̃õ] 'bread' (variant pronunciation)

292

['õ̃ʊ̃mʊ] 'elm'   [kũ̃ũmina'sẽ̃ʊ̃] 'culmination'
[kũ̃iŋkʊe'naʊ] 'quinquennial'   [fɾe'kũ̃ẽ̃ṇṭɪ] 'frequent'
[sa'gũ̃õ̃ŋs] 'lobbies'   ['kũ̃ã̃ṇḍʊ] 'when'

Triphthongs
[sa'gũ̃ã̃õ̃] 'lobby'   [fɾe'kũ̃ẽ̃ĩ̃ṇṭɪ] 'frequent'
                                        (variant pronunciation)
[sa'gũ̃õ̃ĩ̃s] 'lobbies' (variant
pronunciation)

Hombert (1986) offers a commentary on the proportion of languages of the world that exploit nasality on vocoids for contrastive purposes, and their geographical distribution:

> Recent surveys of vowel systems based upon the different language samples indicate that slightly less than one-fourth of the world's languages (24% in Crothers (1978a), 22.4% in Maddieson (1984), 21% in Ruhlen (1978)) have nasalized vowels. Geographically, most of these languages are located on the American continent (North, Central and South), in Northern India and in the western part of Sub-Saharan Africa. Among languages with nasalized vowels, none have more nasalized than oral vowels. In addition, contrary to what was commonly believed, those with an equal number of nasalized and oral vowels are not a rarity since they constitute half of the sample (Crothers 1978a). (Hombert 1986: 359–60)

Co-ordinatory nasal accommodation in contextual adjustments is seen most frequently in an anticipatory mode: where a nasal contoid follows a vocoid articulation, the velum typically opens early, before the beginning of the contoid segment itself, the latter part of the vocoid being made nasal. Different languages vary in the timing of the anticipatory velic opening. English, which has no phonemically contrastive nasal vocoids, shows relatively early opening of the velum in contextual allophonic accommodations of vocoids to nasal contoids. French, which has contrastive nasal vocoids, in words such as *un bon vin blanc* [œ̃ bõ ṽẽ blɑ̃] ('a good white wine'), typically shows later velic opening when a vocoid is succeeded by a nasal contoid, in an utterance like *il a neuf ans* [il ã nøv ɑ̃] ('He is nine years old'). (Placing the superscript tilde diacritic centrally above the vocoid symbol is intended to indicate that the vocoid is fully nasal throughout its duration; displacing it rightwards with respect to the centre of the vocoid symbol signals that the onset of nasality is late.)

Clumeck (1975: 133–4) discusses such timing differences between English and French, citing a study by Ali *et al.* (1971), in which they took English words where vocoids were followed by nasal stops, cut the nasal stops out of the recording and played the remaining vocoids to native listeners. The vocoids were still perceived as nasal in quality, presumably because of the continuing presence of their early anticipatory nasality. When Clumeck repeated this experiment with comparable French words (Clumeck 1971), listeners were unable to judge reliably whether the vocoids had been followed by a nasal stop or not. Clumeck (1975: 141) suggests that the relatively later nasalization of vocoids before nasal stops in French reflects an apparent attempt by speakers of the language to preserve the contrastive power of nasality. Since English does not use nasality for contrastive purposes on vocoids, speakers of English are thus more free to allow early anticipatory nasality for contextual functions.

Kawasaki (1986: 83) suggests that 'In general, a syllable-final nasal nasalizes a vowel more than a syllable-initial nasal. Some languages with anticipatory nasalization are Azerbaijani, Cayapa, Chipewyan, Delaware, English, Hupa, Kashmiri, Malay, Nahuat, Nez Perce, Panamanian Spanish, Tagalog, Tewa, Tolowa, Tunica and Wolof. Languages with perseveratory nasalization are Greenlandic, Kunjen, Kurux, Land Dayak, Loma, Mazatec, Nama, Paez, Sundanese, Ticuna and Yuchi'. Kawasaki (*ibid.*) cites the following examples from this list:

Anticipatory and perseveratory contextual nasality in a number of languages

Tagalog	[mãŋãnãk] 'to give birth'
Tunica	[ʔimapãnʔ] 'I, too'
Cayapa	[ʔɑpãĩŋʔ] 'hurry!'
Kurux	[mẽẽd] 'body'
American English	[kʰǽnt] 'can't'

The allophonic nature of contextual nasality provides one hypothesis for an evolutionary basis for the development of contrastive nasality through sound-change: 'Diachronically, the most general process from which nasalized vowels evolve is through *regressive* assimilation (whereby) an oral vowel becomes phonetically nasalized when it precedes a nasal consonant; after the loss of the nasal consonant, nasalization on the vowel becomes distinctive' (Hombert 1986: 360).

Some languages are said to show two degrees of nasality on vocoid articulations. Typically, the lesser degree is the product of co-ordinatory anticipation or preservation of nasality from a neighbouring nasal segment such as a nasal stop, and the greater degree is reserved for contrastive function. This is claimed to be the case in Scottish Gaelic, as spoken in Applecross on the west coast of Scotland, where the vocoid in [mūr] 'sea' is nasalized under the perseverative influence of the preceding nasal stop, while the vocoid in [mũxk] 'pig', which is contrastively nasal, shows stronger nasality (Ternes 1973: 125). But the dominance in phonetic degree of contrastive nasality over contextual nasality is claimed not to be universal. In commenting on this topic, Ruhlen (1978: 209) suggests that although this pattern of dominance is certainly true for French, for example, it is not the case in some other languages. He cites Jackson (1967: 42) as indicating that in the Léonais dialect of Breton, contextual nasality may be as strong as contrastive nasality, and quotes Ferguson and Chowdhury (1960: 37) as reporting that in Bengali contextual nasality is of even greater phonetic degree than contrastive nasality.

An instance of a language unusually showing two contrastive degrees of nasality is claimed to be Palantla Chinantec, an Otomanguean Mesoamerican Indian Language of Central America, where a triplet of words contrasts an oral vocoid with one which is 'slightly nasal', versus another which is 'strongly nasal' (Suárez 1983: 47, citing Merrifield 1963). The three words are distinguished by the absence or presence of nasality, and its degree. They are identical in their use of other features such as pitch, all having the same tone pattern, a slight rise starting at mid-low and rising to the mid-point of the speaker's pitch range (see chapter 15 for a discussion of the contrastive use of pitch in languages):

> *Two degrees of contrastive nasality in Palantla Chinantec*
> [ʔe] 'leach'   [ʔẽ] 'count'   [ʔẽ̃] 'chase'

A question arises as to how speakers of languages such as Breton, Bengali and Chinantec achieve variations in the audible degree of nasality, in articulatory terms. One way would be through a greater durational proportion of a given vocoid being made nasal in the case of stronger nasality. But there is evidence from combined acoustic and cineradiographic research that slight and heavy nasality is correlated with velic adjustments producing different cross-sectional areas of the velopharyngeal opening into the nasal cavity. Björk (1961) showed that slight nasality was correlated with cross-sectional areas of about 60 mm^2, compared with areas of some 250 mm^2 for heavy nasality.

10.10 Voiceless and whispered vocoids

A minority of vocoid articulations found in the languages of the world are without voicing: vowels represented by voiceless and whispered vocoids are found in phonemic contrast to vowels manifested by voiced vocoids in some Amerindian languages, as mentioned in chapter 7. Casagrande (1954), Canonge (1957), Osborn and Smalley (1949), Riggs (1949) and Smalley (1953) give extensive accounts of voiceless/whispered realizations of vowels in Comanche, for example. The following illustrations are taken from Canonge (1957: 64):

> *Voiceless/whispered versus voiced vocoid in Comanche*
> ['namaka?muki̥kʷai?u̥?] 'he dressed himself and went on'
> ['namaka?mukikʷai?u̥?] 'he went to dress himself'

Maddieson (1984) cites only two languages in his survey of 317 languages as having voiceless vocoids. These are Ik, an Eastern Sudanic language with five voiceless vocoids [i̥, e̥, ḁ, o̥, u̥] in contrast with eight voiced vocoids [i, ɪ, e, ɛ, a, ɔ, o, u] (Heine 1975), and Dafla (Nisi), a Sino-Tibetan Mirish language with two voiceless vocoids [i̥, u̥] in contrast with seven voiced vocoids including [i, u] (Ray 1967). A language from a very different language family which also exploits voiceless vocoids is the Australian language Nyangumarda (Nyangumarta) (Hoard and O'Grady 1976).

Eunice Pike (1963: 41–2) gives examples of voiceless vocoids from Comanche, and from Tlingit (Alaska), Enga (New Guinea), Machiguenga (Peru) (where the voiceless vocoids seem to be in free variation with their voiced counterparts) and from Highland Totonac (Mexico). She makes no comment on whether the phonation type involved is true voicelessness or whisper, and she makes no typographical distinction here between [a] and [ɑ]:

> *Voiceless vocoids in Comanche (length omitted)*
> ['naki̥] 'ear'   [ma'matsɤβaki̥ka] 'when he stuck it'
> ['pakḁ] 'arrow'   [ma'muɸi̥si̥ka] 'when he blew his nose'
>
> *Voiceless vocoids in Tlingit*
> ['naku̥] 'medicine'   [na'daku̥] 'table'
>
> *Voiceless vocoids in Enga*
> [pɛn'doko̥] 'Adam's apple'   ['kɛŋke̥] 'hand'   ['kɪŋki̥] 'name'
>
> *Voiceless vocoids in Machiguenga*
> [pi̥'tomi] 'your son'   ['ako̥tsi̥] 'hand'   [tsi̥βeta] 'flat basket'
>
> *Voiceless vocoids in Highland Totonac*
> ['skutḁ] 'sour'   ['skutḁ] 'to untie'

It seems probable that many of the Amerindian languages actually use whisper rather than voicelessness as the phonation type in non-voiced vocoids. J. Harris (personal communication) represents Cheyenne, an Algonquian language of the western plains of the United States, as using whisper in the following examples:

> *Whispered vocoids in Cheyenne*
> [m̥ɑfiɑəmen̥ɔtse] 'corn/maize'   [m̥ɑhtseʔkɔ̥] 'foot'

Harris also suggests that whisper is used as a phonation type in Malagasy, an Austronesian language spoken in the island of Madagascar:

> *Whispered vocoids in Malagasy*
> [botị] 'a button, an orphan'   [masɔ̥] 'eye'   [etɔ̥] 'here'

Vowels in some pre-pausal contexts in English and French are represented by partially or wholly voiceless or whispered vocoid allophones, in the 'devoicing' process to be discussed in chapter 12. A number of other languages where the allophonic devoicing process has major scope are exemplified in that chapter, including Qatari Arabic, Greek, Portuguese, Russian and Turkana.

10.11   Non-syllabic approximant articulations

Approximants as a group include some segments which are comparable to the syllabic vocoids discussed above in terms of location of the tongue body in the vocoid space and configuration of the lips, but which differ both in their syllabic function and in their timing characteristics. Operating typically at the initial margin of the syllable, these **non-syllabic approximants** are of short relative duration, and act as very brief transitional onsets to the vocoid at the nucleus of the syllable.

An example is the initial segment in the English word *yell* /jɛl/ ⇒ [jɛl]. From an articulatory point of view, the description of the starting-point in the vocoid space for this segment, transcribed as [j], is identical with that of a vocoid in the general articulatory region of [i] and [ɪ]. Perceptually, the essence of [j] as an approximant is that the body of the tongue and the lips start in an [i]-like position and move very quickly to the configuration for the following syllable-nuclear vocoid. Just as there is an articulatory relationship between [j] and [i] (the close front unrounded vocoid), so there are corresponding articulatory parallels between [w] and [u] (the close back rounded vocoid), between [ɰ] and [ɯ] (the close back unrounded vocoid), and between [ɥ] and [y] (the close front rounded vocoid).

The descriptive label for [j] is a **voiced palatal approximant**. Omitting any mention of the lip position permits us to assume that the lips are in a non-rounded position. Similarly, the neutral lip position for [ɰ] allows it to be labelled as a **voiced velar approximant**. In [ɥ] and [w], however, which both have a rounded lip position, the labels have to indicate the labial involvement more explicitly. The label for [ɥ] is therefore a **voiced labial palatal approximant**, and for [w] is a **voiced labial velar approximant**.

French exploits three of these syllable-marginal approximants – the voiced palatal approximant [j], the voiced labial palatal approximant [ɥ] and the voiced labial velar approximant [w], as in the following examples (Tranel 1987: 108–9):

> *Approximants in French*
> [mjɛt̪] 'crumb' [mɥɛt̪] 'mute' [mwɛt̪] 'seagull'
> [bjɛ̃] 'well' [ɥit̪] 'eight' [bwat̪] 'box'
> [pjɛs] 'coin' [lɥi] 'him' [mwa] 'me'
> [pje] 'foot' [nɥi] 'night' [wi] 'yes'

The same set of syllable-marginal approximants is used in the Ngembi accent of Tikar, a language of Cameroon, in the following illustration (Westermann and Bryan 1952: 125–6):

> *Approximants in Tikar*
> [bùkɥê] 'mats' [bùkwɔ̃béji] [bùkwé] 'skins (n. pl.)'
> 'hoes (of) women'

English uses [w] as well as [j], in words such as *west* [wɛst] and *yet* [jɛt], and as elements in clusters of consonants, reserved for the position next to the syllabic vocoid, in words such as *quick* [kwɪk], *cute* [kjut], *squiggle* [skwɪɡl̩] and *skew* [skju]. In detail, when [j] precedes [i] in English, in such words as *yield*, the articulatory starting point for [j] is normally slightly closer and fronter in the vocoid space than for [i]. The same is true when [j] precedes [ɪə], in *year* [jɪə]. A similar relationship holds between [w] and [u] in a word like *woo*, and between [w] and [ʊ], in pronunciations of the word *wood* [wʊd] in the Received Pronunciation accent of British English and in General American. Here the starting point for [w] is both closer and further back in the vocoid space, and the degree of lip-rounding is slightly greater, than for [u] and [ʊ] respectively. Comparable relationships exist between the syllable-marginal approximants and their following syllable-nuclear vocoids in the following instances from the Chengtu accent of Chinese (Chengtu Szechuanese) spoken in Sechuan in Southwest China (Fengtong 1989: 61):

> *Approximants and close vocoids in Chengtu Chinese*
> [ji̋] 'one' [wǔ] 'five' [ɥy̏] 'rain'

The approximants in these positions in English and Chinese can thus act as auditorily distinctive syllable-onsets to the following vocoids.

In addition to the approximants which share articulatory characteristics with syllabic vocoids, it is possible to produce an approximant segment at any place of articulation where a fricative stricture can be made, simply by relaxing the degree of stricture from that of close approximation to one of open approximation. The approximant of this sort that is found most frequently, and which can be found in either syllable-initial or syllable-final position next to the syllable-nuclear vocoid, is the **voiced post-alveolar approximant** [ɹ], used in many British accents as a manifestation of /r/ (e.g. in *red* [ɹɛd]).

There are a number of symbols for other (slightly more rare) approximants, beyond those already mentioned. One is [ʍ], the voiceless equivalent of [w], which is used in many Scots accents of English, in some idiolects of RP and in some other accents of English, to represent the 'wh' spelling in words like *why*, *where* and *when*. The others are: the **voiced labiodental approximant** [ʋ], which occurs in many languages of the Indian subcontinent, such as Tamil (Asher 1985: 217):

> *Voiced labiodental approximant in Tamil*
> [ʋaʐi] 'path'   [kaɽavʋl] 'god'
> [ʋjaːβaːrɔ̃] 'business'   [ʋjaːʐəkˑɛʐəmɛ] 'Thursday'
> [ʋavːaːl] 'bat (animal)' [ovːoɲːʊ] 'one by one'

The half-colon diacritic after the [k] in 'Thursday' above means that this stop is made slightly long in relative duration (but not as long as is indicated by the use of the full-colon diacritic [ː]).

Another symbol for a sound-type that is fairly rare in the languages of the world is the **voiced retroflex palato-alveolar approximant** [ɻ], which is used as a pronunciation of /r/ in a number of American accents of English and of rhotic accents of Southwestern England. The articulation of this sound has the tip of the tongue more curled than is the case in the post-alveolar approximant [ɹ], and presents the tip of the tongue or even the underside of the tip/blade to the palato-alveolar part of the hard palate. In the latter case, the tip may show an extended aspect of articulation. The syllable-nuclear vocoid corresponding to the syllable-marginal retroflex palato-alveolar approximant [ɻ] is [ɚ], the rhotacized vocoid introduced earlier in this chapter.

Having distinguished between the voiced retroflex palato-alveolar approximant [ɻ] and the rhotacized vocoid [ɚ], this is perhaps the appropriate place to introduce a different type of non-retroflex vocoid in a rhotic consonantal function. In Western American accents (and perhaps some other American accents) of English, the consonantal phoneme /r/ in pre-vocalic position can be pronounced either as a voiced retroflex palato-alveolar approximant [ɻ], or as an approximant in the close front or central area of the vocoid space with the tongue tip not retroflex but drawn back from the front oral cavity into the body of the tongue. Such a vocoid, when used in a rhotic consonantal function, is often called a **bunched-r**, because of the bunching caused by the retraction of the tongue tip into the tongue body, or a **molar-r** (Uldall 1958). A justification for the term 'molar' is given by Uldall in the following terms, describing her own articulation:

> [the sound] is articulated by contracting the tongue in a fore-and-aft direction and bunching it up toward the upper back molars. The tip draws back and retreats into the body of the tongue, which presents an almost vertical surface toward the front of the mouth. Some sideways pressure is exerted by the sides of the tongue against the upper molars. (Uldall 1958)

The auditory impression of the two types of sounds, when used as approximant onsets to a syllable-nuclear vocoid, is remarkably similar. This may in part be due to the acoustic effect on higher resonances of the relatively large volume of the front oral cavity, of approximately the same size, in both cases. Delattre (1965: 91) describes the distribution of the two types of sound in these accents:

> The Western American /r/ can be articulated in two different ways, known as *retroflexed* or *bunched*. They are identified by ear as similar sounds, and both cause a lowering of the third formant on spectrograms. For the retroflexed /r/, the palatal constriction is produced by raising back the tip of the tongue towards the hard palate, leaving the tip down or absorbed in the ball-shape of the mass of the tongue. Some American speakers use the retroflexed /r/ in all positions, others use the bunched /r/ in all positions. Still others use both types of /r/, and these speakers use the retroflexed /r/ in strong (pre-vocalic) position, and the bunched /r/ in weak (post-vocalic or inter-vocalic) position.

Lass and Higgs (1984), Lindau (1980) and Zawadski and Kuehn (1980) have confirmed that the bunched vocoid pronunciation of /r/ in fact predominates in pre-vocalic position in these accents. Figure 10.18 shows tracings of frames from a cineradiographic film made by Delattre (1965: 92) of comparable sequences for a Western American speaker pronouncing *rouge* /ruʒ/, with a voiced retroflex palato-alveolar approximant [ɻ] allophone, versus *Arab* /ˈarəb/ with a bunched vocoid allophone. Figure 10.19 is adapted from

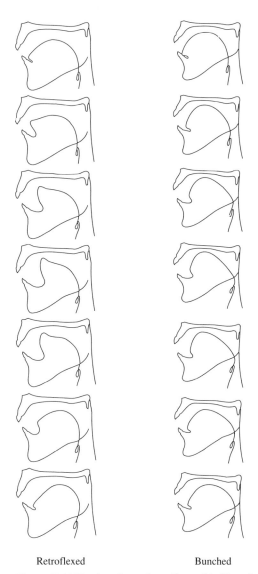

Retroflexed   Bunched

Figure 10.18 Tracings from cineradiographic film of a Western American speaker of English pronouncing *rouge* /ruʒ/ with a voiced retroflex palato-alveolar approximant allophone [ɻ], versus *Arab* /ˈarəb/ with a 'bunched-r' allophone [ɰ] (a voiced labial pre-velar approximant with tongue-tip retraction) (from Delattre 1965: 92)

another x-ray study by Kent (1983: 66–7), showing the two types of segment produced by a single speaker. The lower part of figure 10.19 shows that the bunched vocoid may be produced either in the front part of the vocoid space or further back, in the central part. The solid dot on the surface of the tongue is a radio-opaque pellet, placed there for spatial reference purposes.

Bunching of the tongue in this way, withdrawing the tongue tip into the body of the tongue, is handled in the phonetic framework presented here in terms of a topographical aspect of articulation of the longitudinal profile of the tongue, comparable to adjustments of the tongue root at the other end of the vocal tract in its deviation from the assumption of minimum distortion of the parallel configuration of the neutral vocal tract. No conventional symbol has been allocated by the IPA to a bunched vocoid produced in this way. One possibility would be to use the IPA-approved symbol for tongue root retraction (a centred subscript [ɹ]), but placing it in a centred superscript position, over an existing approximant symbol of suitable lingual and labial attributes. Another possibility would be to suggest a specific new symbol, such as [ɰ]. Lass and Higgs (1984: 96), in a re-examination of Delattre's data, state that all his subjects showed labialization in this pre-vocalic position. They also state that the place of maximum oral stricture, for the largest group of subjects, was at the junction of the hard and soft palates. They describe the place of articulation as 'advanced velar'. The appropriate label for the bunched-r approximant [ɰ] might then be a **voiced labial pre-velar approximant with tongue-tip retraction**.

Lass and Higgs (1984: 107) also describe the vocal-tract configuration for the speakers in Delattre's study as showing a secondary articulation of pharyngeal constriction (as described in more detail in the next chapter). But some British speakers with otherwise similar articulations in the same study displayed no pharyngealization. One can therefore regard pharyngeal constriction as optional for the production of sounds in this general category, rather than a necessary attribute.

Apart from the symbols specified above, all other central approximants can be transcribed by adding a subscript diacritic [˕] to the corresponding fricative symbol, meaning 'more open stricture'. All such symbols, together with the approximant symbols given above, are shown in the IPA phonetic alphabet in appendix I.

Two languages which use many approximants are Spanish and Danish. In Spanish, when compared with other Romance languages, approximants often take the place of voiced fricatives and voiced stops in intervocalic position. An example is the pronunciation of the Spanish word *abogado*

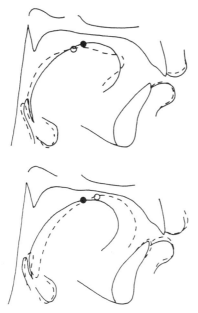

Figure 10.19 Tracings from a cineradiographic film of a single speaker performing a voiced retroflex palato-alveolar approximant [ɻ] compared with a voiced labial pre-velar approximant with tongue-tip retraction [ɥ] (from Kent 1983: 66–7). The solid dot on the surface of the tongue is a radio-opaque pellet placed as a reference

('lawyer') as [aβoɣaðo]. A further example of a voiced alveolar approximant can be found in Danish (J. Verhoeven, personal communication):

Voiced alveolar approximant in Danish
[gæðə] 'street'   [kæðə] 'chain'

The use of the diacritics on the [ð̞] symbol in this Danish example are intended to show that the sound is alveolar not dental, and that it is approximant not fricative.

One approximant for which there is no agreed symbol, and for which a corresponding fricative has not been observed in linguistic use, is the **voiceless bidental approximant** reported by Catford (1977a: 148) as occurring in a variety of Shapsugh, the Western dialect of Adyghe in the Northwestern Caucasus mentioned in the previous chapter.

Central approximants and their corresponding fricatives are not often found in lexical contrast. One example, however, is Margi, the Chadic West African language mentioned earlier. In Margi, a contrast is exploited between a voiced palatal stop, a voiced palatal fricative and its voiced palatal approximant counterpart (Ladefoged and Maddieson 1986: 79), in such triplets of words as:

> *Palatal stop, fricative and approximant contrast in Margi*
> [ɟaʔdi] 'hump of a cow'
> [ʝaʝaʔdʊ] 'picked up'
> [ja] 'give birth'

When it is necessary to distinguish between the voiced palatal fricative and the voiced palatal approximant, and if the [ʝ] symbol for the fricative is not available in the printing technology, then the distinction can be made by using the 'raised' [ˌ] diacritic subscript to the [j] symbol to mean 'fricative'.

A contrast between a voiced palatal fricative and a voiced palatal approximant is also found in Isoko, a Kwa language of mid-western Nigeria (Mafeni 1969: 116):

> *Palatal fricative and approximant contrast in Isoko*
> [ʝá] 'to strive'   [já] 'to swim'

In another more complex opposition, Isoko also contrasts a voiceless post-alveolar fricative [ɹ̝̊] with a voiced post-alveolar approximant [ɹ] and a voiced alveolar tapped stop [ɾ] (in free variation with a voiced alveolar trilled stop [r] (Mafeni *ibid.*):

> *Post-alveolar fricative, approximant and alveolar tapped/trilled stop contrast in Isoko*
> [óɹ̝̊é] 'advice'   [òɹá] 'flight'   [òɾá] / [òrá] 'yours'

Another example of a contrast between an approximant and the corresponding fricative is found in Scottish Gaelic, as spoken in the Isle of Lewis (Shuken, personal communication)

> *Approximant and fricative contrast in Scottish Gaelic (Lewis)*
> [joũsiç] 'learn!'   [joũsiç] 'learned (preterite)'

10.11.1   *Whispered or breathed approximant [h]*

Two special cases of non-syllabic approximants are [h] and [ɦ]. Both of these are performed with the vocal tract in a stricture of open approximation. Both are somewhat unusual in their phonation type. In the case of [h], the phonation type is either whisper, or breath phonation. In the labelling system of this book, [h] can be called a **whispered approximant**, or a **breathed approximant**. No label for place of articulation is given, because [h] is in fact a cover symbol for a whispered or breathed onset to a syllable-nuclear vocoid of any quality, and the quality of the resonance that any laryngeal friction excites in the vocal tract will be that appropriate to the following vocoid, for which the vocal tract will already be in position. In English, the resonant quality of [h] in a word such as *he* [hi] is that of a whispered or breathed version of [i], and in *hoop* [hup], the quality anticipates that of [u].

In a number of other textbooks, [h] is sometimes called a 'voiceless glottal fricative', because the major degree of stricture is thought to be at the glottis. Strictly, one might take the position that this involves a category mistake, in that the fact of glottal friction contradicts identification of the phonatory state of the segment as 'voiceless'. More broadly, it is important to remember that to apply the label 'voiceless' to [h] would be accurate only to the extent that 'voiceless' was being used to mean 'lacking voicing', and was therefore being used as a cover term to include voicelessness (narrowly defined) and whisper.

10.11.2 *Whispery voiced or breathy voiced approximant [ɦ]*

The case of [ɦ] is exactly analogous, in that the phonation type is that of whispery voice ('murmur' in the terminology of some other writers), and it is a cover symbol for a whispery voiced onset to a normally voiced vocoid whose quality determines the resonances heard in the preceding [ɦ]. It can be called a **whispery voiced** or **breathy voiced approximant**, without identification of the place of articulation. The sound [ɦ] sometimes occurs in English, as an allophone of /h/ in intervocalic position, instead of [h], in some pronunciations of such words as *perhaps* [pə'ɦaps], *ahead* [ə'ɦɛd] and *behind* [bɪ'ɦaɪnd].

10.12 Nasal approximants

All approximants may be made with a nasal aspect of articulation. In Terena, the Arawakan Brazilian language of the Matto Grosso mentioned earlier, a voiced palatal nasal approximant [j̃] participates in a contrast with its oral counterpart [j], as does a voiced labial velar nasal approximant [w̃] with its oral counterpart [w] (Bendor-Samuel 1960). It should be noted that the status of the following transcription is phonetic. The phonemic allocation of the nasality to the consonants involved, or to the neighbouring vowels, is a matter of analytic choice:

> *Nasal versus oral approximant contrasts in Terena*
> ['ãj̃õ] 'my brother'   ['ɑjo] 'his brother'
> ['õw̃õŋgu] 'my house'   ['owoku] 'his house'

An example of a nasal/oral contrast involving the whispered/breathed approximant [h] can be found in Igbo, in Nigeria. A similar choice faces the analyst for the phonemic allocation of the nasality. Williamson offers the following comment on the situation in Igbo:

> After a nasalised consonant, a vowel is nasalised. Nasalisation thus runs through the entire syllable. There is therefore a choice as to whether one marks the consonant occurring at the beginning of the syllable as nasalised, with the understanding that this nasalisation is present in the following vowel; or whether one marks the following vowel nasalised, with the understanding that nasalisation is present in the preceding consonant. (Williamson 1969a: 88)

No such problem exists at the phonetic level of notation, where the task is to indicate unambiguously the exact location of the nasality, without regard to its phonemic versus allophonic function in a phonological perspective:

Nasal and oral whispered/breathed approximants in Igbo
[ɪ̃h̃ũ] 'to see'   [ohu] 'twenty'

At a phonetic level of analysis, nasal approximants also occur in English, when embedded in a stretch of speech where no obligatorily oral consonants intervene, as in the following RP utterance:

Nasal approximants in English (RP)
[aɪ həʊp sʌ̃mw̃ʌ̃n j̃ʌ̃ŋ w̃ʌ̃n hʌ̃ndɹədz əv paʊ̃ndz]
I hope someone young won hundreds of pounds

10.13 Lateral resonants

All the classificatory relationships concerning resonants were summarized in figure 10.1. That figure showed that, when lateral, a resonant qualifies as a contoid. The theoretical decision to distinguish between a lateral resonant and a central resonant in terms of making the former a contoid and the latter either an approximant or a vocoid is motivated partly by a criterion connected with stricture-type. While lateral resonants and central resonants both show a degree of stricture which is classified as open approximation, lateral resonants obstruct the airflow to a greater (sub-)degree by interposing a central contact round which air is obliged to flow. In central resonants, the air escapes more directly. In this respect, lateral resonants are articulatorily somewhat more like other contoids than are either approximants or vocoids. Similarly, from this articulatory point of view, the central resonants have more in common with each other than they do with the lateral resonants.

Several different solutions to this general area of the classification of resonant segments could be devised. If lateral resonant segments were to be grouped with non-contoidal segments, as a number of authors suggest, then non-contoids could be distinguished from contoids on a straightforward criterion of major degree of stricture. But one would then either have to abandon the rather convenient position that enables one to use distinct terms ('approximant' versus 'vocoid') for non-contoidal articulations in different syllabic positions, or accept the position that lateral resonants, like central resonants, should be called 'vocoids' when syllabic and 'approximants' when non-syllabic. (It should be acknowledged, in passing, that the position taken in this book is different from that of the consensus of phoneticians reflected in the 1989 Kiel Convention of the International Phonetic Association, which preferred the term 'lateral approximant' over the label advocated here of 'lateral resonant'.)

Lateral resonants constitute an unusual group, from both a phonetic and a phonological point of view. In order to qualify as a resonant segment, the articulation involved has to show a stricture of sufficient aperture that the airflow through it remains laminar and non-turbulent. The lateral escape can vary in location from an anterior position beside the canine teeth to a posterior position opposite the molar teeth.

The lateral resonant segment most commonly found in the languages of the world is the **voiced alveolar lateral resonant** [l], used in most accents of English to represent /l/ (e.g. in lull [lʌl]). A slightly less common lateral segment is the **voiced dental lateral resonant**. Examples from a number of European languages include:

Voiced alveolar and dental lateral resonants in some European languages

English	[leɪk] 'lake'	*French*	[l̪eʒe] 'light (adj.)'
Italian	[l̪upo] 'wolf'	*German*	[libə] 'love'
Portuguese	[l̪iʃu] 'rubbish'	*Spanish*	[l̪etʃe] 'milk'

In some accents of English, including RP and some accents of American English, the pronunciation of pre-consonantal and utterance-final allophones of the /l/ phoneme shows an adjustment of the body of the tongue in a 'velarized' secondary articulation in which the back of the tongue is raised towards the soft palate. This allophonic adjustment in such accents serves to mark the place in syllable structure occupied by the lateral segment. The velarized type of secondary articulation is described in more detail in the next chapter, but it can be seen in the English illustrations in figure 10.20, which is adapted

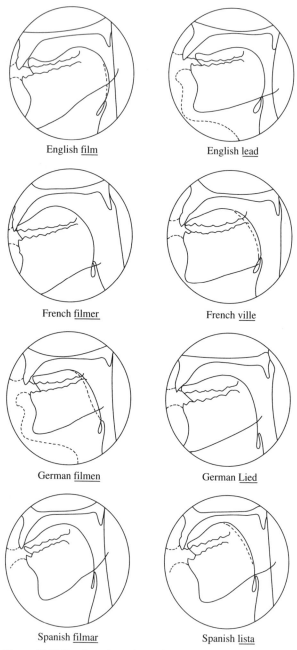

Figure 10.20 Tracings from cineradiographic films showing inter-speaker and inter-language differences in the articulatory configurations for lateral resonants in English, French, Spanish and German (from Delattre 1965: 103, 109)

from Delattre's comparison of the phonetic features of English, French, German and Spanish (Delattre 1965: 103, 109). In figure 10.20, the diagrams are taken from x-ray analysis of speech of native speakers taken at 24 frames per second. The right-hand column shows the tongue configuration for the word-initial [l] in English *lead*, word-final [l] in French *ville*, (in the case of this speaker's pronunciation of this word) denti-alveolar [l] in German *Lied* and Spanish *lista*. The left-hand column shows the pronunciations of /l/ for the same languages in English *film* (in which the velarized secondary articulation can be seen), French *filmer*, German *filmen* (in this case more alveolar than in the same speaker's pronunciation of *Lied*) and Spanish *filmar*. It is evident that different speakers, and different languages (to the extent that these speakers can be taken to be representative), show subtle differences of articulation even within the same overall phonetic category, such as 'dental lateral resonant'.

Some languages have no lateral resonant segment in their inventory. Many languages have one lateral resonant segment, which often shares a phonological distribution with a rhotic segment. It is somewhat unusual for a language to have phonological contrasts between lateral resonant segments at different places of articulation (Ladefoged, Cochran and Disner 1977: 46). The lateral resonants that have been found in linguistic use include segments made at the following places of articulation: dental [l̪]; alveolar [l]; post-alveolar [l̠]; retroflex palato-alveolar [ɭ]; palatal [ʎ]; and velar [ʟ].

Portuguese exploits a phonemic distinction between lateral resonant segments at two places of articulation, alveolar and palatal. Examples from the São Paulo accent of Brazilian Portuguese (Cagliari 1977) are:

> *Alveolar and palatal lateral resonants in Brazilian Portuguese*
> ['mala] 'suitcase'   ['maʎa] 'sweater'

Tamil also exploits a phonemic distinction between lateral resonant segments at two different places of articulation, in this case alveolar and retroflex palato-alveolar (Soundararaj 1986: 32–3):

> *Alveolar and retroflex palatoalveolar lateral resonants in Tamil*
> [baːlaː] '(a proper name)'   [meːɭaː] 'festival'
> [poləʋi] 'fried, spiced rice'   [paɭəsi] 'old, stale'

Melpa, a language of the Eastern Highlands of Papua New Guinea, is a comparative rarity among languages in having a triple contrast of place of articulation between lateral resonants, with dental, alveolar and velar laterals. Ladefoged, Cochran and Disner (1977: 47) give the following illustrations:

Lateral resonants in Melpa
[kiaḻtɪm] 'fingernail'   [lola] 'to speak improperly' [paʟa] 'fence'

Watjarri (Douglas 1981: 207), spoken in the Murchison River area of Western Australia, is another language with a three-way contrast between lateral resonants. In this case, the contrast is between lateral resonants which are (all voiced) dental, alveolar and post-alveolar (slightly retroflex). Instances are:

Lateral resonants in Watjarri
[kuḻu] 'sweet potato'   [kulu] 'flea'
[puli] 'cockatoo'   [puḷi] 'carpet snake'
[kaḻa] 'armpit'   [kaḷa] 'fire'

An interesting example also mentioned by Ladefoged, Cochran and Disner (1977) is Kanite, a Papua New Guinea language related to Melpa, which has only one lateral, but it is the **velar lateral resonant**, for which the 1989 Kiel IPA Convention assigned the symbol [ʟ]. The language exploiting the greatest number of lateral resonant segments is probably Kaititj, an Arandic language of central Australia spoken near Alice Springs, which uses contrasts between interdental, alveolar, retroflex palato-alveolar and palatal lateral resonants. Sample words are (Ladefoged, Cochran and Disner 1977: 49):

Lateral resonants in Kaititj
[aḻuŋ] 'burrow'   [aluŋk] 'to chase'
[aḷat] 'sacred board'   [aʎilk] 'smooth'

The palatal lateral is not confined to contextual positions before palatal (front) vowels, as it is also found in such words as [ʎukuŋk] 'to light' and [ŋkuraʎ] 'rib' (Ladefoged, Cochran and Disner *ibid.*).

There is at least one language which has more than four lateral segments in its phonemic inventory (depending on the phonemic analysis), but in this case only three of them are lateral resonants. The others are voiceless lateral fricatives (together with a laterally affricated ejective stop – see chapter 12 on co-ordination for a discussion of affricated stops). The language in question is Coastal Chontal, a Tequistlatecan Otomanguean Mesoamerican Indian language of Central America (Suárez 1983: 36, citing Waterhouse 1962 and Waterhouse and Morrison 1950). The contrasting lateral segments concerned are [l, lʲ, lʔ, ɬ, ɬ, t͡ɬ'], which are, respectively, a voiced lateral resonant, a voiced palatalized lateral resonant, a glottally checked lateral resonant, a voiceless lateral fricative, a voiceless palatalized lateral fricative, (and a glottally checked laterally affricated ejective stop). In the case of the first five of these, if palatalization and glottal checking were abstracted as separate phonological processes, then the phonemic inventory of lateral segments would drop to two, /l/ and /ʎ/. However, in Suárez's account of this language, while glottal checking is a quite widespread process through the consonant system, palatalization is confined to lateral segments.

Lateral resonants can also be performed without voicing. In French, utterance-final **dental lateral resonants** following a voiceless oral stop have a contextually devoiced phonation type, as in [supl̥] 'supple'. Word-internal lateral resonants in English are also devoiced, in many pronunciations of /l/ after a stressed syllable-initial voiceless oral stop, as in [pl̥iz] 'please'. (An alternative treatment of this as an example of aspiration is given in chapter 12, where the phenomenon of devoicing is also discussed).

Voiceless lateral resonants are occasionally found in contrastive use. One example comes from Burmese (Ladefoged 1971: 11), though Catford (1977a: 132) suggests that this case is in fact fricative not resonant:

> *Voiceless lateral resonants in Burmese*
> [l̥a] 'beautiful'   [la] 'moon'

10.13.1 *Flapped lateral resonant articulations*

Neither trilled nor tapped resonants seem possible, for aerodynamic reasons, given the need to maintain a stricture of open approximation, avoiding audible friction. There are, however, a number of recorded examples of a flapped resonant in linguistic use, with a lateral aspect of articulation. Ladefoged (1971) makes the following comments:

> The central-lateral dichotomy may be applied to flaps, but not to taps and trills. There are a number of languages in which sounds having the characteristic gesture involved in making a flap may have in addition a distinctly lateral quality; when the articulation is formed there is contact only in the center of the mouth, so that momentarily there is a position similar to that of an **l**. This kind of sound often occurs in languages which do not make a contrast between **l** and any form of **r** (e.g. Haya); but it also occurs as a third item contrasting with both **l** and some form of **r** in a number of languages. (Ladefoged 1971: 51–2)

Ladefoged (*ibid.*) then goes on to give some examples from Chaga (Chagga):

> *Alveolar trilled stop and alveolar flapped lateral resonant versus alveolar lateral resonant in Chaga*
> [riha] 'to mash'   [ɺiho] 'exciting'   [liʧa] 'something good'
> [rina] 'a hole'   [ɺika] 'hide something'

Vocoid symbols

	unrounded			rounded		
	front	central	back	front	central	back
close	i	ɨ	ɯ	y	ʉ	u
close-mid	e	ɤ		ø		o
open-mid	ɛ	ʌ		œ		ɔ
open	a	ɑ		Œ		ɒ

Approximant symbols

	unrounded				rounded
	central		lateral		central
	convex	retroflex	convex	retroflex	convex
labio-dental	ʋ				
alveolar			l, ɬ		
post-aveolar		ɹ			
palato-aveolar		ɭ		ɭ	
palatal	j		ʎ		ɥ	labial-palatal
velar	ɰ		ʟ		ʍ w	labial-velar

whispered/breathed approximant [h]
whispery voiced/breathy voiced approximant [ɦ]
('bunched'/'molar' 'r') voiced labial pre-velar approximant
with tongue-tip retraction [ɥ]

	vl	vd

Figure 10.21 Summary of the phonetic symbols for vocoid and
approximant segments of all types

Masica (1991: 97), in his account of Indo-Aryan languages of the Indian
sub-continent, describes a voiced alveolar flapped lateral resonant [ɭ]
contrasting with an 'ordinary' voiced alveolar lateral resonant [l] as 'a
prominent feature of Oriya, Marathi-Konkani, Gujarati, most varieties of
Rajasthani and Bili, Punjabi ... most dialects of West Pahari, and Kumauni'.
He comments that it is absent from most other Indo-Aryan languages.

10.14   Symbols for resonant articulations

The phonetic symbols for resonant segments of all types are summarized in figure 10.21. They can also be found in the IPA alphabet, reproduced in appendix I.

Further reading

The use and value of Daniel Jones' **Cardinal Vowel** scheme are discussed at length by Abercrombie (1967, 1985), Catford (1977a) and Ladefoged (1967).

Laver (1980: 68–92) offers a detailed review of the anatomy, physiology and acoustics of **nasality** on resonants and other segment-types, and of nasality as a personal extralinguistic feature of voice-quality.

Further reading on the typology of **vowel systems** in the languages of the world is given at the end of chapter 19, in the recommendations for phonetic 'universals' involving vowels.

11

Multiple articulations

The notion of **double articulation** has already been mentioned, in connection with vocoids made with simultaneous lingual and labial strictures of open approximation. This conformational aspect of articulation, where a segment is made with strictures of equal degree at two different locations, is applicable not only to vocoids, but also to stops and fricatives. Double articulation is transcribed by putting a superscript linker above the symbols for the two contributory articulations, giving [k͡p], for instance. (The tradition of placing the symbol for the velar element first, against the sequence of the general labelling convention adopted in this book, comes from long-established use in Africanist linguistics.)

11.1 Double stop articulations

Double stops occur in a number of languages, especially those of West Africa. Examples are Idoma (Ladefoged 1971: 59) and Isoko (Mafeni 1969: 116–117), which contrast voiceless and voiced double labial velar stops with the corresponding single labial and velar stops. Another example is Yoruba (Bamgbose 1969: 164–5), where double labial velar stops are in contrast to single velar and (voiced) labial stops:

Labial velar stops in Idoma

[ak͡pa] 'bridge'	[apa] 'lizard'	[aka] 'wheel'
[ag͡ba] 'jaw'	[aba] 'palm nut'	[aga] 'axe'

Labial velar stops in Isoko

[ɒk͡pɒ] 'namesake'	[ɒg͡bɒ] 'plantation/orchard'
[uko] 'cup'	[ugo] 'tie-beam (of a house)'
[epe] 'kind of tree'	[ebe] 'leaves'

Labial velar stops in Yoruba

[k͡pe] 'to call'	[g͡be] 'to carry'
[ke] 'to cry'	[ge] 'to cut'
[bo] 'to peel'	

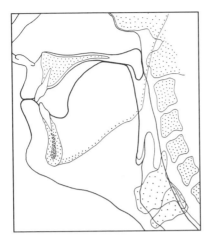

Figure 11.1 Sagittal cross-section of the vocal organs during the production of the medial phase of a voiceless labial velar stop [k͡p]

Figure 11.1 shows a sagittal view of the articulatory configuration of the vocal organs for the medial phase of the labial velar stop [k͡p].

In most West African languages, a nasal stop preceding an oral stop is made homorganic in place of articulation with the oral stop. When this oral stop is a double stop, the preceding nasal is also double. Efik thus has words like [ŋm͡kp͡ep̚] 'I am teaching' (Cook 1969: 39). Efik is also unusual in West Africa in having the possibility of syllable-final consonants, and the situation arises where two single oral stops can follow each other. In such circumstances, the first stop is audibly released, and sequences like [ndɛpʰkɛ] 'I am not buying' occur in Efik (Cook 1969: 38), in distinction to the earlier example.

One type of double stop occurs in English. In many British accents, when a word ending in a single oral stop is in utterance-final position, the oral stop is very often accompanied by a simultaneous glottal stop. In addition, such oral-plus-glottal double stops are not often audibly released (non-release, marked as [p̚], is considered in more detail in chapter 12). The place of articulation of the final segment in each of the three English words *map* [maʔp̚], *mat* [maʔt̚] and *mac* [maʔk̚], is then able to be identified, in this utterance-final position, only by the audible evidence of the articulatory offset transition at the end of the syllable-nuclear vocoid. A different type of double stop occurs in some individual accents of English in the United States. At the end of chapter 3, the example was cited of an American pronunciation of *suggest* as /səɡˈdʒɛst/. As well as the sequential form [səɡˈdʒɛst], the phonetic realization of this can involve a simultaneous double closure, giving an alveolar velar stop [g͡d], resulting in [sə'g͡d͡ʒɛst] (P. Roach, personal communication). A continental European example of double nasal stops comes from modern-day Provençal, the language still spoken by small numbers of speakers in the Provençal area of Southern France. Jones (1950: 43) cites Coustenoble's description (1945) of a labial velar nasal stop in [eɲ͡mple'gaːdo] 'employee', and of an alveolar velar nasal stop in ['kaɲ͡nte] 'I sing'.

The majority of double stops in the languages of the world are probably labial velar combinations. A less frequent example is a possible labial alveolar double stop, said to be found in Bura, another West African language (Ladefoged 1971: 61, basing his comments on information from Carl Hoffman), where a voiceless labial alveolar stop is in contrast with a voiceless labial stop:

> *Labial alveolar stops in Bura*
> [p͡ta] 'hare'   [paka] 'search'
> [p͡tsa] 'roast'   [psa] 'lay eggs'
> [p͡t͡ʃi] 'sun'   [pʃaari] 'spread a net'
> [b͡da] 'chew'   [baɬa] 'dance'

However, Maddieson (1983, basing his comments on an acoustic analysis of data supplied by Schuh and fieldwork tapes supplied by Ladefoged) partly counters this suggestion, stating that the performance of the words in Bura cited above often shows a sequence of a labial stop followed by an alveolar stop rather than a double labial alveolar stop. Maddieson does nevertheless concede that sometimes there is a brief period of simultaneous double closure during an overlap between a preceding labial stop and a following alveolar stop (1983: 290).

Labial alveolar double stops are also found in the Northwest Caucasian languages Abkhaz and Ubykh, where there is a triple contrast between [p͡t], [b͡d] and an ejective double labial alveolar stop [p͡t']. The labial element in these instances corresponds in other Northwest Caucasian languages to a secondary articulation (see section 11.4.1 below) of labialization of alveolar stops (Catford 1977b: 290).

11.2   Double fricative articulations

Double fricatives also occur. The accents associated with some dialects of Swedish are said to use a voiceless alveolar velar double fricative [s͡x], according to Abercrombie (1967: 65). Catford (1977a) reserves his position on the possibility of a double fricative articulation in the accent associated with the Skåne dialect of Swedish, and leans towards analysing it as a secondary articulation. He suggests that 'apico-postalveolarised articulation possibly occurs in the south Swedish (Skåne) variant of [ʃ], which appears to be apico-postalveolarised velar fricative [xʲ] – unless the articulation is actually co-ordinate' (Catford 1977a: 191).

Double labial velar fricatives, made with lip-rounding, occur in Urhobo of Southeastern Nigeria in contrast with double labial velar stops. Kelly (1969: 155) gives the following examples:

Labial velar fricatives in Urhobo

[ox͡ɸʷo] 'person'   [oɣ͡βʷo] 'soup'
[ak͡pʊ] 'world/earth'   [oɡ͡ba] 'fence'

Kelly (1969: 156) describes these double fricatives as 'double articulations, like the plosives /kp/ and /gb/', but uses the symbols [x] and [ɣw].

The so-called 'whistling fricatives' of the African language Shona, spoken in Zimbabwe, are further examples of double fricatives, with one stricture being made at the alveolar place of articulation with a laminal aspect of tongue articulation, and the other at the labial location, with lip-rounding. They have been described by Bladon, Clark and Mickey (1987), Carter and Kahari (1979), Doke (1931a, 1931b), Fortune (1955), Ladefoged (1971) and Pongweni (1977, 1984). Bladon and his colleagues also mention that they have observed whistling fricatives in another language, Jibbali.

Ladefoged (1971: 60) gives examples of Shona contrasts between both voiced and voiceless double fricatives with corresponding single fricatives, one at the alveolar place of articulation with an apical tongue aspect, and the other at the alveolo-palatal place with a laminar aspect (Ladefoged's term for what is here called alveolo palatal is 'prepalatal'). Ladefoged (*ibid.*) says that 'In going from *s* to *ɸ͡s* to *c* there is increasing retardation and flattening of the tongue.' These comments are similar to Doke's, cited by Bladon, Clark and Mickey (1987: 40), where he states that:

> In the formation of these peculiar sounds the tongue is not troughed
> as much as for [s] and [ɸ͡s]; but it is considerably flatter and there is
> a much wider space between the forward tongue-contacts. The main
> difference in sound, however, between [s] and [ɸ͡s] is due to the raising
> of the lower lip and general rounding of the lips in such a way as to
> lessen materially the opening. (Doke 1931a: 47–8)

Carter and Kahari (1979, part II: 3), also cited by Bladon, Clark and Mickey (1987), suggest that the non-labial part of the double fricatives is characterized by some degree of retroflexion.

Ladefoged's examples (suggested to him by George Fortune) are:

> *Double labial alveolar fricatives versus alveolar and alveolo-*
> *palatal fricatives in Shona*
>
> [ɸsoɸsé] 'sugar ant'   [masoro] 'big heads'   [muɕoma] 'be hoarse'
> [βzose] 'all'   [mazoro] 'turns'   [ʐoʐoma] 'tuft of hair'
> [itɸsá] 'new thing'   [tsama] 'handful'   [ɕɕana] 'fat child'
> [idβzá] 'new thing'   [dzamá] 'disappear'   [dʐana] 'turn'

Bladon, Clark and Mickey (1987: 39) use the symbols [sʷ] and [zʷ] for the voiceless and voiced labial alveolar fricatives respectively. This is satisfactory from a language-internal point of view, where the prime need might be for a visible distinction to be simply drawn between the double fricatives and other fricatives in phonological opposition to them. But it is less satisfactory from a general phonetic perspective, in that it fails to acknowledge the double nature of the fricative stricture (whistling is a special case of friction), and is confusable with alveolar fricatives that show only a secondary articulation of labialization.

When the two places of articulation in a fricative segment with a double stricture are next to each other, the result is a longer corridor of constriction, forming a continuous extended stricture. Catford (1977a: 194–5) gives an example of what he calls a 'contiguous' articulation of this sort from the Bzyb dialect of Abkhaz, where a voiceless double uvular–pharyngeal fricative is in contrast with both a single uvular fricative and a single pharyngeal fricative:

> *Voiceless double uvular–pharyngeal fricative versus voiceless*
> *single uvular and pharyngeal fricatives in Abkhaz (Bzyb dialect)*
> [aˈχħə] 'head'   [aˈχə] 'lead (n.)'   [aˈħawə] 'air'

11.3   Resonant articulations with multiple strictures

It was said in chapter 10 on resonants that the performance of every vocoid qualifies by definition as a double articulation, since two strictures of equal rank co-exist (both of open approximation), in the lingual and labial zones. The purpose of this section is to draw attention to the possibility of a third stricture being applied to the performance of certain types of vocoids.

The implication was allowed to stand in chapter 10 that the single active articulator within the mouth for the performance of vocoids was the body of the tongue, in dorsal articulations. For the vast majority of vocoid sounds in the languages of the world this is certainly true (Lindblom 1983: 239). The tip/blade of the tongue is relatively passive during the production of these vocoids, participating only to the extent that it shows traces of the performance of some preceding segment, or begins to anticipate the performance of some following segment. The only exception mentioned was a retroflex vocoid produced with the tip/blade of the tongue curled to present the tip or undertip to the roof of the mouth in a stricture of open approximation.

It is clear from the example of the retroflex vocoid that the tip/blade is sufficiently independent of the action of the body of the tongue that it can make its own contribution to the quality of the sound produced. Indeed, when a voiced alveolar fricative [z] is produced the tip/blade system is the principal active articulator, producing a stricture of close approximation, with the contribution of the body of the tongue being reduced to an enabling role. It is physiologically possible in the production of a vocoid for the tip/blade to be raised to the point where it contributes an audible colouring to the perceived quality of sound produced, but where the degree of stricture remains one of open approximation, at the alveolar place of articulation. In such a situation, one would have to say that a vocoid segment was being produced with a double oral articulation, one (dorsal) made by the body of the tongue and the other (apical or laminal) by the tip/blade. It would be a double **apical dorsal vocoid** (or, correspondingly, a **laminal dorsal vocoid**), where most vocoids are solely dorsal in their production. They are sometimes referred to in the phonetic literature as 'apical vowels', 'coronal vowels' or 'blade vowels'. In the following discussion of an apical dorsal vocoid, the term 'laminal' could be interchanged with the term 'apical'.

An apical dorsal vocoid is relatively rare in the languages of the world, but it occurs in at least two widely different geographical areas: in Szechuanese and (possibly) other dialects of Chinese; and in Swedish. In all four cases, the phonological status of the sound-type is allophonic, not phonemic. In Szechuanese, Scott (1947) states that in the pronunciation of '*si, dzi, tsi* and *zi*', the fricative part of these articulations 'is followed by a voiced sound made with the tip and blade of the tongue in approximately the position for **z**, little or no friction being produced. The sound has some resemblance to a retracted **i**'.

Norman (1988: 194) describes Mandarin Chinese, and especially the accents associated with the Northern and Central groups of Chinese dialects as using 'apical vowels'. His description, however, is not of apical dorsal vocoids as such but of weak syllabic alveolar fricatives. In this description of Mandarin, Norman (1988: 142) writes that /i/ is represented as a weak syllabic [z] after [ts] and [ts^h], but refers to it as an apical vowel. It is not quite clear whether Norman is using the term 'vowel' phonetically or phonologically. Ramsey (1987: 45) describes this Mandarin (Standard Chinese) sound only as 'a syllabic *z* – like the buzzing noise American children make when they imitate the

319

sound of a bee'. To the extent that local friction is audible on any individual occasion, then the phonetic status of the sound would no longer qualify as a vocoid, but straightforwardly as a syllabic fricative segment.

The positioning of the tongue tip/blade in producing an apical dorsal vocoid is quite critical, in that if the tip/blade is raised too little, it will have no audible contribution. If it is raised too much, local friction will be created. It would not be surprising if there were a good deal of free variation between the vocoid and the fricative type of segment in such circumstances, in the speech of an individual speaker. One would also expect that the fricative version would sound palatalized. Palatalization, as a secondary articulation, is explained in the next section.

At least one accent of Swedish is said to use apical dorsal vocoids, to represent a long, stressed /iː/ vowel. This accent is the one found in the eastern and northeastern part of the Östergötland dialect area, on the coast of Sweden, southeast of Stockholm. Pamp (1978, in Swedish) describes the sound involved as a 'strange, muffled buzzing sound' (translated by G. Blom, personal communication). It may be that what Pamp calls a 'buzzing sound' is a transitional element towards the end of the production of the apical dorsal vocoid when a short period of local alveolar friction may be produced.

An apico-dorsal resonant related to the segment described immediately above is also used in syllable-marginal position as an approximant, by speakers of Burushaski, the language isolate spoken by the Burusho tribe in Northwest Kashmir (Crystal 1987: 327), and in part of neighbouring Pakistan and Northwest India. Catford (1977a: 192) describes speakers of the Nagir dialect of Burushaski as using an 'apico-postalveolarized, dorso-palatal approximant', which he symbolizes as [y.], in words such as [ay.a] 'my-father' and [bʌˈy.ʌm] 'mare'.

A possible symbol for this apical dorsal alveolar palatal resonant is [ɒ̰iː]. The subscript diacritic symbol [̰] associated with [ɒ̰] means 'more open', when attached to a symbol normally taken to represent a fricative segment. Another phonetic symbol for the apical dorsal alveolar palatal vocoid sound that has been used, which is probably preferable in its legibility, is [iᶻ] (Lindblom 1986: 40). Catford's symbol [y.], adopted from Lorimer (1935), is also legible, but runs the risk of confusion with the use of [.] as an indicator of phonological syllable division suggested in the 1989 IPA alphabet.

11.4   Secondary articulations

Double stops and double fricatives are comparatively rare in linguistic use. Much more frequently found in the languages of the world are examples of segments made with two simultaneous strictures, but where one is of a lower degree than the other. In these cases, the stricture with the greater degree of constriction is said to be the **primary stricture**, and the one of less degree the **secondary stricture**; the segment concerned is said to be made with **secondary articulation**.

11.4.1   *Labialization*

One very obvious example of segments made with a secondary articulation superimposed on the more primary stricture is that of a stop or a fricative made with the lips in a rounded position of open approximation. Sounds made in this way can be described as labialized sounds. **Labialization** is transcribed with a subscript or superscript 'w', as in English [ʃʷu] 'shoe'.

The segments representing consonants in the English utterance *Who'd choose prune juice?* are all labialized, as

$$[h^wud^w \; \mathfrak{tf}^wuz^w \; p^w\textrm{ɹ}^wun^w \; \mathfrak{dz}^wus^w]$$

An alternative transcription for increased legibility would be one which abstracted the secondary articulation as a setting applying to all susceptible segments in the utterance, giving

$$V^w[\textrm{hud ʧuz pɹun ʤus}]$$

The notion of segmental susceptibility to the effect of individual settings is more fully explained in chapter 13 below.

Labialization is found as a secondary articulation in virtually every language of the world. Labial action of this sort seems less focused in the stream of speech than some other articulatory features, and spreads easily from its major segmental origin to neighbouring segments, particularly in an anticipatory direction (Benguerel and Cowan 1974). In connected speech, when a segment occurs whose phonological identity requires a rounded lip position, it is usually the case that the preceding segments in the same syllable (and sometimes earlier ones) become labialized, provided that a different lip position is not phonologically mandatory for those segments. The relative independence of labialization from the articulatory activities which it colours is easily explained. The control of the lips as an articulatory system is physiologically independent of the control of the tongue and jaw as articulatory systems. Co-ordination in time of the labial system with the lingual and mandibular systems therefore tends to be loose, unless phonological requirements for more precise action are imperative.

Labialization of contoids can play a contrastive phonological role in a number of languages. These include Twi, a language of Ghana (E.K.

Brown, personal comunication), and Luganda, a language of East Africa (Ladefoged 1971: 65):

> *Contrastive labialization in Twi*
> [èc̣c̣ʷi] 'it thrusts'   [èc̣c̃i] 'it fears, shuns'   [èc̣c̃i] 'it wrings'
> [àkʷá] 'a round   [àká] '(somebody)
> about way'   has bitten'

> *Contrastive labialization in Luganda*
> [m̀bʷa] 'dog'   [m̀baala] 'termite'

Labialization also plays a contrastive role on non-labial stops and fricatives in the languages of the Northwest Caucasus, occurring not only on alveolar, alveolo-palatal and velar segments, but also on uvular ones, in such languages as Abkhaz, Abaza and Ubykh (Catford 1977b: 290). It is the contrastive use of secondary articulations that make the consonant systems of the languages of the Northwest Caucasus famously complex. In one analysis, Ubykh, for example, has eighty contrastive elements in its phonemic consonantal system (Comrie 1981:202). To a less extent, this complexity is also characteristic of the languages of the Northeast Caucasus. Tabassaran, a Lezgian language of the Dagestan highlands of the Northeast Caucasus, uses labialization contrastively on uvular ejective stops (Comrie 1981: 201):

> *Labialization on uvular ejective stops in Tabassaran*
> [naqʷ'] 'grave'   [naq'] 'yesterday'

A rather unusual incidence of labialization in a contrastive role is found in the accent of the Bzhedug dialect of Adyghe in the Northwest Caucasus, where it is applied to a glottal stop (Comrie 1981: 203). In a very different language group, Thompson, which is a Salishan language spoken in the southern part of British Columbia, uses labialization contrastively on ejective velar stops (J. Harris, personal communication):

> *Labialization on ejective velar stops in Thompson*
> [ɛːkʷ'tʰ] 'to scrape off (anything)'
> [ɛːk'tʰ] 'to scrape hair off a hide'

11.4.2   *Labiodentalization*

Labiodentalization is a secondary articulation where the lower lip is brought into open approximation with the upper front teeth simultaneously with some other more primary stricture. It is rare in a contrastive role. It is found in Abkhaz in the Northwest Caucasus, on alveolar affricate segments (affricates are explained in chapter 12 below). It is also found in some neighbouring Lezgian languages, including Tabassaran, where [s] and the affricate [ts] are contrastively labiodentalized, according to Catford (1977b: 290).

Labiodentalization, which can be marked with a superscript [ᵛ], is quite common as an extralinguistic idiosyncrasy of particular individuals. In English, it is sometimes heard as a segmental feature modifying [s] and [z], and is not uncommon as a modification of [ɹ].

Two other secondary articulations are also not uncommon in languages, either with a contrastive or a contextual phonological function. These are **palatalization** and **velarization**.

11.4.3 *Palatalization*

Palatalization involves the body of the tongue being used to constrict the vocal tract in a stricture of open approximation at the palatal location, as an accompaniment to a stricture of greater degree. Auditorily, the effect of palatalization is often impressionistically described as giving a segment a 'clear' quality. The body of the tongue is in a position analogous to that of a close front vocoid. In the performance of palatalized segments in many languages, the secondary stricture tends to be relaxed from the palatal location relatively slowly, and this then gives the offset phase of the palatalized segment a characteristically [j]-like offset (or, to put it another way, gives the following segment a [j]-like onset).

Palatalization is transcribed by attaching a small superscript [ʲ] to the relevant segmental symbol, as in [zʲ]. Figure 11.2 shows a sagittal view of the articulatory configuration for the medial phase of a palatalized (voiced)

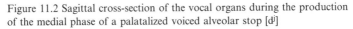

Figure 11.2 Sagittal cross-section of the vocal organs during the production of the medial phase of a palatalized voiced alveolar stop [dʲ]

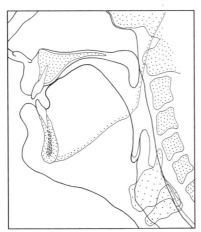

alveolar stop [dʲ]. Catford (1977a) discusses the case of Russian (the symbols quoted here are adapted to the conventions of this book):

> Russian, and several other Slavic languages, opposes a whole series of palatalized consonants to non-palatalized ones. Thus, in addition to [p, b, m, f, v, t, d, n, l, r, s, z] Russian has [pʲ, bʲ, mʲ, fʲ, vʲ, tʲ, dʲ, nʲ, lʲ, rʲ, sʲ, zʲ]. In the bilabial and labiodental series, where the secondary articulation is formed by a quite separate organ from the primary articulation, consonants such as [pʲ, bʲ] simply consist of simultaneous (not successive) articulation of [p, b] and [j]. In the palatalized consonants of the dentalveolar zone some modification of the primary articulation occurs. Thus, while Russian [t] and [d] as in [tot] 'that' and [da] 'yes' are normally apicodental, the [tʲ] and [dʲ] of [tʲọtʲə] 'aunt' and [dʲædʲə] 'uncle' are normally lamino-alveolar or even lamino-postalveolar; moreover, they are often somewhat affricated, sounding rather like palatalized lamino-(post)alveolar [tsʲ, dzʲ]. (Catford 1977a: 192)

Catford (1977a: 183) gives some examples of palatalized and non-palatalized stops in Russian:

Palatalized and non-palatalized stops in Russian
[pʲilˠ] 'drank'   [pilˠ] 'glow'
[tʲʉlʲ] 'tulle'   [tut] 'here'

Among the languages of the Northwest Caucasus, Abkhaz, Abazin and Ubykh all have palatalized uvular stops and fricatives, in contrast with corresponding uvular segments with no secondary articulation. In the palatalized uvular segments, the part of the body of the tongue forward of the primary uvular stricture 'is raised up towards the hard palate, forming a longitudinally extended articulation' Catford (1977b: 290). In the Abdzakh dialect of Adyghe, the Northwest Caucasian language mentioned above, palatalization plays a contrastive role on a glottal stop (Catford 1977b: 289).

Many accents of English use a secondary articulation on [l] involving simultaneous palatal stricture of open approximation, before vocoids and [j], giving 'clear' [l] sounds in words like *leaf* [lʲif], *laugh* [lʲɑf] and *value* [valʲu]. Since [l] is itself a segment made with a stricture of open approximation, this could qualify as an example of double articulation, rather than as secondary articulation. To retain consistency of usage with the majority of textbooks, we can accept that the lateral resonant stricture is of higher (sub-)degree in one respect than the secondary palatalizing stricture, in that lateral aspects of articulation by definition entail a partial blockage in the necessary central contact between active and passive articulators. It was this fact of partial (central) blockage, it will be recalled, that qualified lateral segments as contoids rather than vocoids. A clear [lʲ] can thus perhaps reasonably continue to be called a palatalized [l], maintaining the implication of a primary and secondary articulation, rather than of a double articulation.

Another instance of palatalization comes from the very different group of languages in Australia. Crowley (1978), cited in Hammond (1989: 21), gives an example from Waalubal, a dialect of the Pama-Nyungan language Banjalang:

> *Palatalization in Waalubal Banjalang*
> [bandaŋ] 'other'   [baɲdʲanibe] 'only covered'

It is possible that in the Waalubal word above meaning 'only covered' that what is here transcribed with [d] is in fact rather a voiced palatal stop [ɟ]. This possibility is reinforced by noting that the voiced nasal stop preceding [d] has a palatal place of articulation, and although it is articulatorily possible to make a palatal-to-alveolar-to-palatal segmental sequence in the way transcribed, it is more likely that palatality runs right through the sequence. If what is transcribed is in fact [ɟ], then this would no longer be an example of secondary palatalization, but merely of the palatal off-glide normally associated with the release of a palatal stop into a following vocoid.

11.4.4 *Velarization*

Velarization, where the body of the tongue constricts the vocal tract in a stricture of open approximation at the velar location simultaneously with another stricture of greater degree at some other location, is transcribed by placing a small superscript [ˠ] after the relevant symbol for the primary articulation, as in [lˠ]. (The usage of indicating velarization by writing a tilde through the body of the segmental symbol, as in [ɫ], is also approved under the agreements of the 1989 IPA Kiel Convention, though this sometimes results in relatively illegible composite symbols.)

Velarization is used in Russian. The non-palatalized series of Russian consonants mentioned in the section immediately above 'tend to be velarized, some more than others' (Catford 1977a: 192). Figure 11.3 gives a sagittal view of the articulatory configuration for the medial phase of a velarized (voiced) alveolar stop [dˠ].

The auditory effect of velarization is often said impressionistically to give a 'dark' quality to the segment concerned. When the velarizing component is relaxed relatively slowly, the offset of the primary stricture (or the onset of the following segment) has an [ɯ]-like quality. In many English accents, an [l] which is often described as 'dark' is used in post-vocoid syllable-final position, in words like 'feel' [filˠ] (in some accents, for example of New York

325

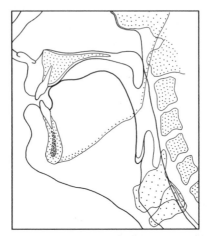

Figure 11.3 Sagittal cross-section of the vocal organs during the production
of the medial phase of a velarized voiced alveolar stop [dˠ]

English, darkness is a characteristic of [l] in all contextual positions). The
same comments apply to the 'secondary' nature of velarization on lateral
resonants as to palatalization.

According to J. Harris (personal communication), contrastive velarization
is used in the accent of the Tarawa dialect of Ikiribati (Gilbertese), an
Austronesian language spoken in the Gilbert Islands, and in Marshallese,
another Austronesian language spoken in the Marshall Islands:

> *Velarization in Ikiribati*
> [mˠiː] 'to dream'   [m̃iː] 'result'
>
> *Velarization in Marshallese*
> [lˠe] 'Mr, Sir'   [le] 'Ms, Madam'

A paralinguistic use of velarization is also reported by Harris (personal
communication), as a marker of a threatening tone of voice in the Bangkok
accent of Thai, in an otherwise identical sequence using the same lexical
tones:

> *Paralinguistic use of velarization in Thai (Bangkok)*.
> [tiːna] '(I'm going to) hit (you)' (neutral statement)
> [tˠiːnˠa] '(I'm going to) hit (you)' (very threatening statement)

11.4.5   *Pharyngealization*

Pharyngealization, where the root of the tongue is drawn back
towards the back wall of the pharynx (or alternatively where the constrictor

muscles of the pharynx reduce its diameter), gives a similar auditory effect as a secondary articulation to that of velarization. Like velarization, pharyngealization is often described impressionistically as imparting a 'dark' quality to segments, and can be transcribed by using a superscript [ˁ] diacritic, as in [nˁ].

Pharyngealization occurs as an important vehicle for phonological contrasts in the different dialects of Arabic, as the manifestation of 'emphasis' (Al-Ani 1970). Emphasis is a common feature of the many different Arabic languages, and of some other Semitic languages. Arab grammarians have commented on the phenomenon since the eighth century, and traditionally ascribe emphasis (*mutbaqa* in Arabic) to consonants rather than vowels, giving rise to the phrase 'emphatic consonants' (Kuriyagawa *et al.* 1988: 117), although pharyngealization of a given consonant inevitably has an influence on the detailed articulation of neighbouring (especially preceding) vocoids.

Emphasis in this sense is a phonological concept, not to be confused with the everyday notion of emphasis meaning 'making more prominent'. Examples of pairs of words from the Arabic of Qatar whose identification depends on the presence versus absence of pharyngealization are (Bukshaisha 1985):

Pharyngealization in Qatari Arabic

Non-emphatic *Emphatic*
[ṯ̣ðir] 'she sprinkles' [ṯˁðˁir] 'she harms'
[χal] 'to leave' [χalˁ] 'vinegar'

The effect of this sort of pharyngealization often spreads considerably back beyond the syllable-final segment, into the syllable-nuclear vocoid, distorting the onset to the vocoid (Norlin 1985). When both initial and final consonants are emphatic, the effect of pharyngealization spreads throughout the syllable, retracting front vowels to a more central position. Further examples of emphasis, manifested as secondary pharyngealization, are found in Tamazight, a Berber language of North Africa (Saib 1978: 940), and in Jordanian Arabic (Kuriyagawa *et al.* 1988):

Pharyngealization in Tamazight Berber

Non-emphatic *Emphatic*
[iβða] 'he divided' [iβˁðˁa] 'he started'
[izi] 'gall-bladder' [izˁi] 'a fly'

Pharyngealization in Jordanian Arabic

Non-emphatic	Emphatic
[siːb] 'let go (imp.)'	[sˤiːb] 'hit a target (imp.)'
[siːh] 'travel (imp.)'	[sˤiːh] 'cry (imp.)'
[tuːb] 'repent'	[tˤuːb] 'bricks (noun)'

Retraction of the body and root of the tongue into the pharynx in pharyngealized segments tends both to retract the position of vocoids, and to lower them. It also tends to cause retraction of the place of articulation of associated contoids. This was made clear by a radiographic study of retraction (*tafkhim*) associated with emphasis in Egyptian (Alexandrian) Arabic by Al-Ani and El-Dalee (1984). Figure 11.4 is a reproduction of their tracings of sagittal sections of the midline of the tongue in comparisons of plain versus emphatic versions of the pronunciation of /t/, in three contexts – before /u/, /i/ and /a/. In all three cases, the emphatic articulation shows not only relative retraction and lowering of the body of the tongue, but also retraction of the tongue tip/blade contact for the alveolar closure.

Pharyngealization is used contrastively in some of the languages of the Caucasus. Catford (1977b: 290) reports that 'pharyngalization occurs with labials and uvulars in Ubykh, and with uvular fricatives only in the Bzyb dialect of Abkhaz. In both these languages we have the usual phenomenon of the co-occurrence of the features labialized and pharyngalized on uvulars'.

Catford (1977a: 182,193) also mentions that pharyngealized 'vowels occur in several Caucasian languages of Dagestan, notably in the Tsez languages Tsez and Khwarshi, and in several of the Lezgian languages'. He gives the example of Tsakhur, in which 'pharyngealized [i, e' a, o, i] all occur, in contrast with non-pharyngealized vowels of the same types'. Catford (1977a: 193) adds that 'pharyngealized sounds involve some degree of contraction of the pharynx either by the root of the tongue, or by lateral compression of the faucal pillars and some raising of the larynx, or a combination of these'. The (rear of the two sets of) faucal pillars are a pair of muscles which link the soft palate to the larynx, whose function is to lower the velum or raise the larynx, depending on which structure is braced against their pull. They run vertically down the side walls of the pharynx, and in contraction narrow the side-to-side dimension of the pharynx.

The auditory effect of pharyngealization gives an impression of slight 'strangulation'. Catford (1977a: 182) describes it as adding a slightly 'squeezed' quality to the Tsez and Lezgian speech-sounds mentioned above, and says that it 'tends to impart a somewhat "fronted" [advanced] quality to back vowels, both in terms of auditory impression and (acoustically)'. An

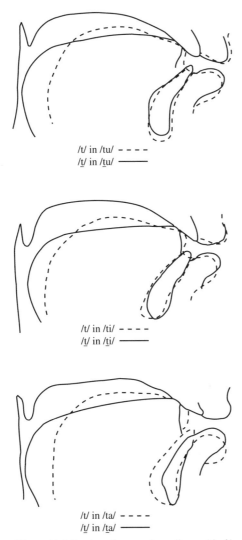

/t/ in /tu/ – – – –
/t̪/ in /t̪u/ ———

/t/ in /ti/ – – – –
/t̪/ in /t̪i/ ———

/t/ in /ta/ – – – –
/t̪/ in /t̪a/ ———

Figure 11.4 Tracings from a cineradiographic film of plain versus 'emphatic' (pharyngealized) allophones of /t/ before /u/, /i/ and /a/ in Egyptian (Alexandrian) Arabic (from Al-Ani and El-Dalee 1984: 388)

apparent contradiction thus exists between the auditory effects of pharyngealization in Arabic (where it supports the articulatory evidence that the tongue body and blade are retracted), and its effects in Caucasian languages (where the auditory effect gives an impression of fronting of the tongue body). There are several possible explanations. One is that pharyngealization in Arabic is chiefly a matter of an articulatory adjustment of the body of the tongue towards the back wall of the pharynx, but that pharyngealization in Caucasian languages is achieved principally by an adjustment of the root of the tongue. If this movement of the root of the tongue is associated with a raising of the larynx, then the consequence for the tongue body could well be a rotational adjustment upwards and forwards, resulting effectively in the articulatory (and hence auditory and acoustic) fronting of vocoids. Another possibility is that retraction of the tongue root combined with vocal-tract shortening by raising the larynx results in an acoustic adjustment which is analogous to (and hence heard as) the acoustic correlate of fronting of the tongue body. This second hypothesis would be an instance of **acoustic equivalence**.

11.4.6   *Laryngealization*

The final type of secondary articulation to be discussed is **laryngealization**. This is a process where the primary supralaryngeal articulation is accompanied by a secondary stricture at the glottal level. This consists of an articulatory tendency to create a glottal constriction, which normally fails nevertheless to reach the maximum stricture of a full glottal stop.

The mode of phonation associated with laryngealization tends to be one of creaky voice or creak. It is therefore a moot point whether laryngealization should be regarded chiefly as a modification of phonation type, as Abercrombie (1977: 101) and Ladefoged (1971: 61) suggest, or whether, because a gesture towards glottal constriction is involved, it should be regarded as having an articulatory component as well. The latter position is adopted in this book. In either characterization, laryngealization is not completely tied to a particular segmental location, and can spread fairly freely into the other parts of the host syllable. Laryngealization which falls short of a complete glottal stop will be symbolized here by using the subscript tilde for creaky phonation. If the laryngealizing gesture results in a complete glottal stop, then the full linear symbol for a glottal stop [?] will be used.

In Danish, laryngealization is given the name 'stød'. Fischer-Jørgensen (1985: 58) offers the following description:

> The Danish stød is a prosodic phenomenon connected with certain syllables. It generally shows up as a decrease in intensity and (often) pitch, in distinct speech ending in irregular vibrations (creaky voice), in very emphatic speech probably sometimes in a glottal closure. A distinction is often made between 'stød in the vowel' and 'stød in the consonant'. But the stød is not, primarily, connected with the specific segments. The irregularities (or dip of the F_0 or intensity curves) are generally found about 10–15 cs after the start of the vowel: therefore,

if the vowel is long they will coincide with the end of the vowel, and if
the vowel is short with the beginning of the following sonorant
consonant. The stød therefore requires for its manifestation a certain
stretch of voicing.

(The term 'sonorant' in the above quotation refers to resonant contoid and
approximant segments. 'F0' stands for the fundamental frequency, or pitch,
of the voice, which is discussed in chapter 15 below.)

Fischer-Jørgensen (1985: 59) and Anderson, Ewen and Staun (1985: 215)
give the following pairs of words testifying to the phonemic status of stød in
Danish:

Laryngealization ('stød') in Danish

[vɛn] 'friend'	[vɛ̰n] 'turn !' (imp.)
[vɛl] 'well'	[vɛ̰l] 'spring!' (imp.)
[du] 'you'	[dṵ] 'tablecloth'
[bœn] 'beans'	[bœ̰n] 'peasants'
[man] 'one' (impers.)	[ma̰n] 'man'
[dɑɪ] 'you' (obl.)	[dɑɪ̰] 'dough'
[sbel] 'play' (noun)	[sbḛl] 'play ' (imp.)

The transcriptions in Anderson, Ewen and Staun (1985) actually use [ʔ]
instead of the symbol [̰], characterizing the use of a glottal stop symbol as a
'broad' usage. Their choice is less desirable than the one made in this book,
because they are choosing to represent a scalar phenomenon by its extreme
value. In addition, Lehiste (1970: 89) cites Ringaard (1960, 1962) in support
of her view that stød should not be analysed as a glottal stop in Danish, in
that there are some dialects where stød is actually in contrast with a glottal
stop. Fischer-Jørgensen (1985: 197) is emphatic that stød in normal Danish
speech is not a glottal stop. She does suggest though, that 'one might
describe an exaggerated stød as a glottal stop, a strong stød as a creak, and
a milder stød as creaky voice' (1985: 181).

The phonology of stød in Danish is complex (Basbøll 1972, 1985), as is its
history (Fischer-Jørgensen 1987), which is probably related to that of word
accents in the Scandinavian languages (Gårding 1977, Liberman 1976,
Ringaard 1978), described in chapter 15. According to Anderson, Ewen and
Staun (1985), who cite the work of Pedersen (1973), the phonetics of stød in
Danish are fairly well agreed to consist of a glottal constriction which seldom reaches complete closure, with creak or creaky voice as the accompanying phonation type. It is clear from the quotation above from Fischer-
Jørgensen (1985), however, that this is only part of the physiological process
associated with the production of stød.

Laryngealization also occurs in English, particularly in Received Pronunciation as pronounced by many speakers, and in a number of other British accents, in a process which has been variously called 'glottal reinforcement', 'pre-glottalization' and 'glottalization' (Andrésen 1968; Christopherson 1952; Higginbottom 1964; O'Connor 1952; Roach 1973). Roach (1973: 10) describes 'glottalization' as follows: 'The essential characteristic of this glottalization is that the oral closure for /p/, /t/ or /k/ is preceded by a glottal closure, but there is much variation from one accent to another in terms both of the distribution of the glottal closure and of its articulatory characteristics (especially the duration of the closure)'. Roach transcribes glottalization by means of a [ʔ] symbol inserted before the relevant voiceless oral stop symbol, and gives the following rule as one amongst several for his own accent: 'the plosives /p/, /t/ and /k/ are glottalized in my accent when they follow a vowel (whether stressed or unstressed) and precede one of certain consonants. This set of consonants comprises plosives, fricatives (including /h/, affricates and nasals), but excludes /l/, /r/, /w/ and /j/' (Roach 1973: 12). He gives the following examples:

> *Laryngealization in British English (RP)*
> ['ɑʔtɪk] 'arctic' ['pɒʔpkɔn] 'popcorn'
> [dɪʔk'teɪʃn̩] 'dictation' [ɪlɛʔktrɪfɪ'keɪʃn̩] 'electrification'
> ['stalə'ʔktaɪt] 'stalactite'

Because glottalization does not occur when the consonant after the /p, t, k/ is one of /l, r, w, j/, words such as *mattress, chocolate, accurate* and *equal* show no inserted glottal element. Another rule Roach gives is that voiceless fricatives before the oral stop suppress glottalization, hence *bests* [bɛsts] and *whisks* [wɪsks]. But a preceding nasal stop or lateral resonant does not suppress the glottalization, hence *belts* [bɛlʔts] and *winks* [wɪŋʔks].

If laryngealization, to revert to the term preferred in this book, were to consist in these cases solely of an inserted glottal stop, then a multiple articulation would exist only as a laryngealizing influence on the preceding segment before the inserted stop. If the form of the laryngealization were a complete glottal closure, and it were to be prolonged into the closure phase of the following oral stop, then this would be an example of a double stop articulation. In some speakers of Received Pronunciation, complete glottal closure does not appear to be reached, at least not before the oral closure for the following stop is achieved. In such cases, the laryngealizing tendency will be audible as a secondary articulation on the segments preceding the oral stop, and will be comparable to the descriptions given above for stød in Danish.

Roach followed his earlier study on laryngealization in British English with an instrumental investigation, examining the actions of the larynx by means of a direct-viewing fiberoptic laryngoscope and cineradiography (Roach 1979). He was able to establish that the process of laryngealization in his own RP accent was achieved by closure not only of the vocal folds but also of the ventricular vocal folds and aryepiglottic folds (structures in the upper part of the larynx above the true vocal folds). He also observed that 'the larynx is raised during the laryngeal closure, causing a rise in intraoral air pressure before release of the closure' (Roach 1979: 2). Laryngealization is thus an appropriate name for the action concerned, since it involves the whole larynx rather than only the vocal folds. Roach also comments that 'complex laryngeal closure similar to this has been observed in Danish (Ringaard, 1960, 1962) and in Swedish (Lindqvist-Gauffin, 1969, 1972; Gauffin, 1977) and in American English (Fujimura and Sawashima, 1971) by means of a fiberscope' (Roach *ibid.*).

Laryngealization has a contrastive status in Bwe Karen, a central dialect of Karen, which is a tonal language of the Tibeto-Burman family spoken in Burma (Henderson 1982: 10–11). Tonal phenomena are more fully discussed in chapter 15, but in this case the contrasts between the words involved also exploit a choice between three patterns of relative pitch on the individual syllables – high level, mid level and low level. Laryngealization in this language is independent of the tonal elements, however.

Laryngealization in Bwe Karen

High level tone	Mid level tone	Low level tone
[ˀwi] 'prophet'	[ˀwi] 'tasty'	–
[wa] 'finished'	[wɛ] 'rain'	[wɛ] 'smelt'

11.5   The phonological patterns of secondary articulations

In languages such as Russian, English and Arabic where secondary articulations like palatalization, velarization or pharyngealization play a contrastive or contextual phonological role, it is more usual for segments with a secondary articulation to be differentiated from segments which have only a single stricture ('plain' segments), rather than from segments with a different secondary articulation. In Arabic, pharyngealized (or velarized) consonants are in contrast with plain segments. In Russian, depending on the accent involved, palatalized consonants are in contrast with plain consonants, or plain consonants in contrast with velarized consonants. An example from the Moscow accent (J. Harris, personal communication) is:

> *Plain versus velarized stops in Russian (Moscow)*
> [dal] 'distance'   [dalˠ] 'gave'

Ward (1964: 389) gives a different transcription (for an unspecified accent of Russian), where he indicates a contrast between palatalized and plain consonants:

> *Plain versus palatalized stops in Russian*
> ['nosʲtitʲ] 'carries'   [nʌ'sʲitʲ] 'to carry'
> ['vɨnəs] 'carrying out'   ['vɨnəsʲitʲ] 'to give birth to'

In Malayalam, a language of South India, however, there is a triple distinction between three different 'r'-sounds, two with secondary articulation. These are 'a short alveolar trill with slight secondary velarization', 'a dentialveolar or dental trill with secondary palatalization' and a retroflex palatoalveolar resonant (Butlin 1936):

> *Secondary articulations in Malayalam*
> [karˠa] 'sap'   [kar̺ʲa] 'coast'   [kaɻa] 'punt-pole'

In Gaelic, as spoken in Applecross on the west coast of Scotland, secondary palatalization is in contrast with secondary velarization, on both nasal stops and lateral resonants (Ternes 1973, reviewed by Wells 1975):

> *Secondary articulations in Scottish Gaelic (Applecross)*
> [taɣuːnə] 'two men'   [taɣuːnˠə] 'two guns'
> [salʲək] 'to salt'   [salˠəx] 'dirty'

In the case of /r/ in Applecross Gaelic, a plain version [r] is in contrast with a velarized [rˠ] (Ternes 1973), as in:

> *Plain versus velarized [r] in Scottish Gaelic (Applecross)*
> [rəiˑn] 'shared'   [rəiˑnˠ] 'to share'

The diacritic [ˑ] in the examples immediately above indicates a slightly longer duration for the vocoid concerned. Matters of relative duration are dealt with in chapter 14.

11.6   The ambiguous use of '-ization' labels

The place of articulation of the secondary stricture is labelled by an appropriate adjective ending in '-**ized**': hence 'labialized', 'palatalized', 'velarized', etc. It is important to be aware that terms such as 'palatalized' are frequently encountered in the literature of general and historical linguistics in a quite different sense. Lass makes a useful distinction, commenting on 'palatalization and the like'. He writes:

These are used in two basic ways: **statically**, as names for secondary articulations (a palatalized consonant has superimposed [i]-colour), and **dynamically**, as names for processes (to palatalize is to impose such colour). But this isn't as troublesome as the ambiguous use of the process sense: 'to palatalize' can not only be to impose [i]-colouring, but to turn a non-palatal into a palatal. Thus not only [t] > [tʲ], but [tʲ] > [c] or [k] > [c] are palatalizations, as traditionally are [k] > [ʧ], [s] > [ʃ], etc. The same holds for the other '-ization' terms. (Lass 1984a: 169)

The use of terms such as 'palatalization' will be reserved in this book to refer only to secondary articulation, whether this is in a static or dynamic sense.

11.7   Symbols for double articulations and secondary articulations

Symbols for double and secondary articulations are presented in the IPA alphabet reproduced in appendix I.

Further reading

Primary, secondary and double articulations are discussed at some length in Brosnahan and Malmberg (1970) and Pike (1943) – both in a slightly different terminology – and in Catford (1977a).

PART V

Articulatory co-ordination and phonetic settings

12

Intersegmental co-ordination

Segments have been described so far as instances of segment-types, and discussion has been focused on the defining characteristics of the segments concerned, as if each were occurring as an individual event isolated in time and independent of neighbouring articulatory context. This was helpful for initial exposition, and at that stage it was unnecessary to say very much about the detailed nature of the onset and offset transitions of segments. We now need to move beyond this initial approach, however, because in real speech segments cannot occur in isolation. As serial elements of a multisegmental utterance of continuous speech, all segments have contextual neighbours. These are either adjacent segments on both sides, or a segment on one side and utterance-marginal silence on the other. Even as single segments, a segment has contextual neighbours of utterance-marginal silence on both sides. In all cases, the articulatory events that make up the segment concerned have to be co-ordinated with those of the neighbouring context.

The detailed mode of this integrating co-ordination is open to phonetic and phonological control, and the articulation of segments can therefore show a variety of co-ordinatory relationships with the contexts in which they are embedded. These relationships involve some of the most interesting and intricate phenomena in the control of speech production, and give rise to issues that have often been found problematic. A range of different types of co-ordination is described in the sections below. The first type to be discussed is the temporal integration of articulatory and phonatory events at the margins of segments in the onset and offset phases, in the **devoicing** process.

12.1   The devoicing process

The timing of voicing relative to that of articulatory events, as a reflection of the interplay between contextual factors and options of phonetic control, is one of the prime examples of intersegmental co-ordination. A wide-ranging review of issues associated with the control of timing of voicing relative to articulatory actions can be found in Docherty (1992).

In the discussion of articulation in the preceding chapters, segments have been characterized as voiced, voiceless or whispered. But because the control of the phonatory system is physiologically independent of that of the articulatory system, segments can vary in the detailed timing of onset or offset of a given phonatory state in such a way that voicing would have to be described as starting late, or as ending early, in relation to the supralaryngeal articulatory events of a segment.

When the voicing for a given segment starts late, or ends early, in the above terms, it is said to be **partially devoiced**. When the voicing starts late, the segment is said to be **initially devoiced**. When the voicing ends early, the segment is said to be **finally devoiced**. Different languages (and different accents within a given language) can partly be characterized by their different choices of such co-ordination of articulatory and phonatory timing.

Instances of different onset and offset timing of voicing within segments

Figure 12.1 Schematic diagram of different categories of devoicing (see also opposite page)

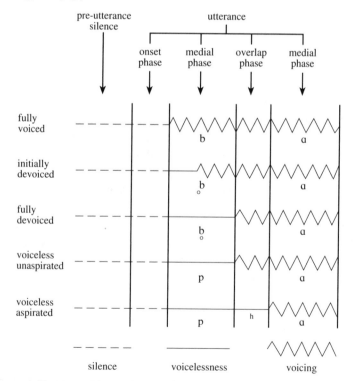

can be seen in the relationship between voicing and alveolar friction in the realizations of /z/ in different contexts in English (RP). In utterance-initial *zoo* (/zu/), voicing for the alveolar fricative [z] typically begins (in most accents) slightly later than the alveolar friction, showing initial devoicing. This late onset can be thought of as an accent-specific accommodation of phonatory behaviour to the preceding silence. The initial devoicing in late voicing-onset can be transcribed by using the subscript 'voiceless' diacritic, placing it to the left of the symbol, giving [ˌzu].

Early offset of voicing can be heard in the realization of /z/ in utterance-final *ooze* (/uz/), where voicing characteristically fades out earlier (in most accents) than the alveolar friction, as a similar accent-specific accommodation to silence. Final devoicing in early voicing-offset of this sort is transcribed by displacing the subscript voiceless diacritic to the right, giving [uzˌ]. Utterance-medial /z/, by comparison, in words like *oozing* /uzɪŋ/, tends in most accents of English to be pronounced with voicing throughout the

Figure 12.1 (for legend, see opposite page)

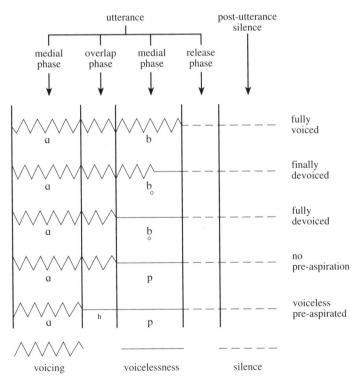

341

fricative duration, as [uzm̥]. The different categories of devoicing are shown diagrammatically in the two parts of figure 12.1.

A distinction can thus be drawn between **full voicing** for a segment, where voicing lasts for the whole duration of the segment, and **partial voicing**, where it lasts for only part of the segment's duration. A small problem of analysis needs to be clarified at this point. When considering the onset and offset of segments internal to an utterance, one segment's offset transition overlaps with the onset of the next segment. This could result in confusion in particular cases about whether devoicing of an individual segment was full or partial, unless some convention about phasing is agreed. It may be helpful, therefore, to emphasize again that the boundaries of the medial phase of approximants and other vocoids are less distinctly identifiable than those in stops and fricatives. In a stop segment, the medial phase lasts from the first to the last instant of complete closure. In a fricative segment, the medial phase lasts from the first to the last instant of close approximation and audible friction.

In both cases, there are clearcut articulatory and auditory criteria for locating the boundaries of the medial phase, and hence for the onset and offset phases. In the case of approximants and other vocoids, however, when these occur in connected speech, it is not as practicable to isolate the precise boundaries of a medial phase. The vocal organs will tend to pass through the articulatory target identified by the representative phonetic label, but the essence of nearly all syllable-marginal approximants, and of all syllable-nuclear vocoids except monophthongs, is that the active articulators are in continuous movement from onset to offset. Even in the case of monophthongs, auditory or instrumental identification of the boundaries of any medial phase can seldom be exact. This difficulty notwithstanding, it remains convenient to persist with the convenient notion of a medial phase in approximants and other vocoids, in order to relate the notion of a representative target position to articulatory action, even if the exact boundaries of the phase cannot be precisely identified on given occasions.

In the light of this discussion, it becomes possible to say that for a stop or a fricative to have full voicing, this voicing must be in evidence throughout the medial phase of the segment. Any devoicing of stops or fricatives therefore has to involve an absence of voicing during some part of the medial phase of such segments. In approximants and other vocoids, full voicing must involve continuous voicing throughout onset, medial and offset phases – throughout the whole segment, in other words. This convention will be particularly helpful when we come to consider the phenomenon of aspiration, or voice-onset delay, in section 12.2.

Partial voicing in the devoicing process is the product of adjustment to a neighbouring voiceless context, (either silence or an adjacent voiceless segment). A classificatory problem potentially arises from the case where, on a particular occasion of utterance, the devoicing process becomes so extensive as to result in a segment entirely without voicing throughout its medial phase. (For convenience of discussion, this might be described as **fully devoiced**; it will be identified by adding a centred subscript voiceless diacritic to the corresponding voiced symbol, as in [z̥].) Should [z̥] and voiceless [s] be regarded as fully identical? Or should [z̥] be classified as a separate type of segment from [s]? This classificatory dilemma typically gives rise to such frequent misunderstanding in the minds of students that a brief discussion may be helpful.

From a phonatory point of view, a fully devoiced segment such as [z̥], and the voiceless segment symbolized as [s], are identical. The phonatory equivalence between fully devoiced and voiceless segments is underlined by the practice of transcribing sounds which are voiceless, but for which no separate voiceless symbols exist, by adding the voiceless diacritic to the corresponding voiced symbol. This creates full ambiguity between the representations of the relevant pair of devoiced and voiceless segments. It will be recalled that voiceless nasal stops, for instance, have no independent symbols. A voiceless labial nasal stop, to take one example, is therefore transcribed by using the symbol [m̥]. A fully devoiced labial stop would also be symbolized as [m̥]. However, when separate symbols are available for the devoiced and the voiceless segments, such as [z̥] and [s], the use of the devoiced symbol [z̥] in such a case, in preference to [s], might have a number of motivations.

First, there is an obvious phonological basis for identifying some particular segment as being devoiced – that is, as having 'lost' the voicing that in some sense 'belongs' to the phonetic manifestation of that phonological unit in other contexts and other circumstances. Using the convention of capitalizing phonological feature labels introduced in section 4.5.1, one could say that in these cases the phonetic realization of a phonological unit characterized as +VOICE had been fully devoiced.

Second, a question is prompted about whether devoiced and voiceless segments are phonetically identical in all respects. One possible ground for maintaining that they are not identical would be that when a segment is fully voiced, various phonetic features (over and above the phonatory difference) have different values than when the corresponding voiceless segment is produced. These differentiating factors may include, potentially, the degrees of muscular effort being exerted throughout the vocal system, particularly in

343

the muscle systems of the supralaryngeal vocal tract. Such differences of overall muscular effort have been posited as the basis for a distinction that is sometimes drawn between **fortis** sounds with high overall muscle tension (normally voiceless) and **lenis** sounds with low overall muscle tension (normally voiced). The argument would then run on to say that if the only change from a lenis voiced segment in producing its devoiced counterpart were a change of phonatory state from vibrating vocal folds to an open glottis, then the lenis devoiced segment would still be differentiated from its fortis voiceless counterpart by factors of overall muscular tension.

The fortis/lenis distinction remains to be confirmed empirically, however, and until it is, a more cautious position would be to accept the equivalence of fully devoiced and voiceless sounds, as a limit to the descriptive power of phonetic theory. Both categories should then be treated as instances of voiceless sounds.

A further point remains to be explained in the relationship between devoiced and voiceless sounds, however. The phonatory state in devoiced segments is not necessarily that of a fully open glottis. In theory, there is a potential continuum of glottal opening from the vibrating position for voicing, where the vocal folds are held lightly together, to the fully open position for voicelessness. Intermediate between these two extremes is the position for whisper, where the glottis is open, but where the vocal folds are still close enough to create turbulence in the transglottal airstream, with audible friction. It is not unusual for the devoicing process to substitute an intermediate, whispered phonation for a voiced one, rather than substituting full voicelessness. In these circumstances, there is of course no phonetic ambiguity between the whispered product of devoicing and the voiceless counterpart. A fully devoiced version of the /z/ in English *zeal* /zil/ where the [z] happened to be pronounced with whisper, giving [ʑil], would remain perceptually distinguishable from *seal* /sil/ [sil].

For maximum clarity, it is therefore probably desirable to limit the implications of devoicing to the phonatory level alone. In the case of segments representing phonological units characterized as +VOICE that are nevertheless pronounced without any phonetic voicing, the only change of phonetic performance that should be implied is a change of phonation type from voicing to either true voicelessness, or whisper.

In summary, in those languages whose phonology exploits a devoicing process, the phonetic products of this process can show partial devoicing or full devoicing. Partial devoicing displays whisper or voicelessness instead of normal voicing either at the beginning of the medial phase (initial devoicing) or at the end of the medial phase (final devoicing). Full devoicing results in a segment whose entire medial phase is characterized by whisper or voice-lessness. A fully devoiced symbol such as [z̥] should be regarded (within the limitations of the descriptive theory advocated in this book) as being synonymous with [s]. It should also be recognized that a preference for the use of a symbol such as [z̥] over [s] on some particular occasion reflects a motivation that is ultimately phonological in nature. It is phonological in that the analyst is thereby drawing attention to the role of such a segment as an allophone of a +VOICE phoneme the majority of whose other allophones are normally phonetically voiced.

12.1.1 *Devoicing as an allophonic process*

Languages differ both in the degree to which devoicing is allowed to affect the proportion of voicing in a segment, and in the detailed glottal adjustment used. French, for instance, shows much less tendency to initial devoicing than English, and utterance-initial + VOICE consonants are often pronounced with full phonetic voicing. In utterance-medial positions, particularly when between two vowels, French + VOICE consonants are almost always pronounced with full phonetic voicing. In final devoicing, French also restricts the glottal adjustment more often to whisper than does English. The French pronunciation of the word *oui* ('yes') in utterance-final position as [wi̥], where the [w] is fully voiced, and the [i] is fully devoiced, but with a whisper phonation as [i̥] rather than a voiceless phonation as [i̥], is common. With the higher airflow-rate that is a consequence of substituting a more open glottis (either in the constricted whisper position or fully open) for the intermittently closed position of the glottis for voicing, one also often hears the pronunciation of the vowel in *oui* in utterance-final position being realized as a fricative, as a whispered or voiceless palatal fricative.

Devoicing is a very common allophonic process in many languages, in the circumstance where a + VOICE consonant finds itself next to a voiceless segment. This process is often constrained to apply under the influence only of preceding context, or only of succeeding context. An optional allophonic rule in the Moscow accent of Russian, for example, has the effect of devoicing the realizations of all word-final occurrences of /l/, /lʲ/, /r/ and /rʲ/ when these phonemes are found after a preceding voiceless (or devoiced) segment. Barry (1989) investigated the phenomena of devoicing by means of acoustic and laryngographic techniques, and clearly showed that these segments can be subject to both partial and sometimes full devoicing in these contexts. Sample words drawn from her data are:

Devoicing after voiceless or devoiced segments in Russian
(Moscow accent)
[mi̯sʲlʲ] 'thought'   [ʒeʐʲlʲ] 'baton'
[vɔplʲ] 'cry'   [vnutʲrʲ] 'inside'

In Qatari Arabic, on the other hand, the following illustrations show the effect of this process on the phonetic realizations of consonantal phonemes where adjacency rather than precedence or succession is a sufficient condition, across syllable boundaries as well as within the syllable (Bukshaisha 1985: 14–25):

Devoiced allophones of consonantal phonemes in Qatari Arabic

/sabt/ ⇒ [sab̥t] 'Saturday'	/ˈbχalʸa/ ⇒ [ˈb̥χalʸa] 'misers'
/dfaːf/ ⇒ [d̥faːf] 'cloaks'	/ˈgtirij/ ⇒ [ˈg̥tərei] 'Qatari (masc.)'
/ʔamˈθaːl/ ⇒ [ʔam̥ˈθaːl] 'examples'	/tlaːl/ ⇒ [tl̥aːl] 'hills'
/traːb/ ⇒ [tr̥aːb] 'earth'	/tðir/ ⇒ [tð̥ir] 'she scatters'
/ħzaːm/ ⇒ [ħz̥aːm] 'belt'	/zkaːm/ ⇒ [z̥kaːm] 'influenza'

In modern Standard Greek, Dauer (1980a, 1980b) has shown instrumentally that, as part of a phonologically conditioned reduction process that also includes the alternatives of extreme shortening or elision, unstressed high vowels /i/ and /u/ in the Athens and Thessalonika accents are often fully devoiced, being realized phonetically as whispered vocoids. She gives the following examples (Dauer 1980b: 18):

Devoicing of unstressed vocoid segments in modern Standard Greek
/ˈisixos/ ⇒ [ˈisi̥xos] 'quiet'   /kiˈtaksane/ ⇒ [ci̥ˈtaksanɛ] 'they watched'

Position in the phrase, and intonational context, are also allophonically relevant in these accents of modern Greek. Dauer states that 'a pause or potential pause indicated by a slowing down at the end of a syntactic group in a sentence will block high vowel reduction', but that 'at the end of a sentence said with a rising intonation pattern, vowel reduction does not usually take place' (Dauer 1980b: 25). She gives examples of two phrases – both presumably said with falling intonation patterns as declarative sentences, so that the unstressed /i/ at the end of the first sentence is phonetically devoiced (whispered). In the first sentence, the vowel in /tus/ is also phonetically devoiced by being whispered, but in the second, the vowel is phonetically voiced, because 'the possessive pronoun /tus/ appears at the end of the subject ... where the speaker has the option of pausing, [and] it is instead stretched out' (Dauer, *ibid.*):

> *Devoicing and blocking of devoicing by phrasal position in*
> *modern Standard Greek*
> /'afisan tis ta'ftoti'tes tus sto 'spiti/
> ['afi̥san tis ta'ftoti'tes tu̥s stɔ 'spiti̥]
> 'they left their identity cards at home'
>
> /i ta'ftoti'tes tus(,) 'vjenun stin astino'mia/
> [i taˌftoti'tes tuˑs 'vjɛnun stin astinɔ'mia]
> 'their identity cards are issued by the police'

In the Lisbon accent of Portuguese, an allophonic rule has the effect of devoicing pre-pausal realizations of consonants, and of /i/ and /u/ in pre-pausal syllables. The devoicing may extend throughout such unstressed syllables, and even into the realizations of certain final consonants of preceding syllables, as in the following examples (Johns 1972: 42–64):

> *Devoicing of pre-pausal segments in Portuguese (Lisbon accent)*
> ['maɫ̩ʲ] 'bad'   [fə 'ʑeɾ̥] 'to do'
> ['meeɣm̥u̥] 'the same'   ['fiʎu̥] 'son'
> [pi̥'ɾigu̥] 'danger'   ['n̥oɾt̥i̥] 'brain'
> ['bwat̥i̥] 'rumour'   ['əm̥u̥] 'I love'
> ['puɾu̥] 'pure'   ['mɔɾt̥i̥] 'death'

One of the best-known examples of a language which shows allophonic devoicing of vowel phonemes is Japanese. Shibatani (1990: 161) discusses the allophonic devoicing of the high vowel phonemes /i/ and /u/ in the Tokyo accent, and states that devoicing occurs when these phonemes are found in a voiceless context in an unaccented (non-prominent) syllable, provided that they are not contiguous to a voiced sound, and that they are not initial in the word. He also suggests that devoicing is also responsive to the tempo of the utterance, in that devoicing in Japanese is less frequent in slow, deliberate speech. Shibatani (1990: 161) gives the following examples of allophonic devoicing applied to /i/ and /u/ in the Tokyo accent of Japanese (where /u/ is realized as [ɯ]):

> *Allophonic devoicing in Japanese*
> [kɯ̥tsɯ] 'shoes'   [haʃi̥] 'chopsticks'   [sɯ̥sɯ̥ki] 'eulalia'

Allophonic devoicing of vowels may well be a source of historical change in a language. Shibatani (1990: 161) comments that 'Vowel devoicing is less noticeable in the Kyōto dialect, but occurs in a number of Kyūshū and

Okinawan dialects, e.g. Kumamoto, Kagoshima, and Bisara. For example, in some of these dialects the process of devoicing has advanced to the extent where the vowels have completely dropped out, e.g. /katu/ ⇒ [kat] "to win".'

12.2 Aspiration

Devoicing has just been described as it applies allophonically to utterance-marginal segments adjacent to silence, and in particular phonological and phonetic contexts. There is a particular type of late onset of voicing which occurs only syllable-internally, and which can play a distinctive phonological role. This is a phenomenon found in many languages of the world, called aspiration, which was briefly mentioned in chapter 2. **Aspiration** is a feature which can manifest a co-ordinatory relationship between a voiceless segment and a following voiced segment at the leading edge of a syllable. In aspiration, the onset of voicing for the second of the two segments is delayed for an audible period of 30–40 msecs or more beyond the end of the medial phase of the preceding segment, giving an onset to the second segment that has a phonatory state that is sometimes whisper but more usually voicelessness. Aspiration is hence sometimes called **voice-onset delay** though 'aspiration' is by definition a term with a more restricted application than the more general 'voice-onset delay'.

In the framework introduced here, aspiration is strictly a property of the relationship between two segments in sequence in the leading edge of a syllable – a voiceless segment followed by a voiced one. But it is customary to say that it is the first of the two segments that is 'aspirated'. The phonetic diacritic for transcribing aspiration, as indicated in chapter 2, is a small superscript 'h' placed to the right of the aspirated segment, as in the English word *pan* [pʰan]. A more extreme degree of aspiration can be transcribed phonetically by writing the [h] symbol on the line, rather than as a superscript diacritic, giving [phan]. Alternatively, the two usages can be regarded as synonymous, with criteria of legibility and printability governing the choice between them.

The auditory quality of the aspiration in any particular instance of an aspirated relationship between a voiceless segment and a following voiced segment is strongly coloured by the articulatory quality of the second segment. This reflects the fact that the relevant articulators are typically already in position for this second segment, or are approaching their target. If the generality of the aspiration process were put on one side, it would therefore be as satisfactorily accurate, from the point of view of phonetic observation, to transcribe the aspirated sequence by means of a superscript devoiced vocoid symbol identical with the linear vocoid symbol immediately following, as in English *peat* [pʲit], *pet* [pᵋɛt], *pat* [pᵃat] and so forth.

As a third alternative approach to the transcriptional problem, the aspirated relationship could be represented by the use of a subscript symbol indicating initial devoicing of the linear vocoid segment, as in *peat* [p̥it], *pet* [p̥ət], *pat* [p̥at], etc. This, too, would be as phonetically accurate as other means of representing aspiration. The use of the [ʰ] or [h] symbols for indicating aspiration is the conventional way, however, of capturing the generalization relevant to phonology.

Hirsh (1959), Pisoni (1977) and Stevens and Klatt (1974) have shown very clearly that two auditory stimuli with relative onset times of 20 msec or less are perceived as simultaneous events. Lisker and Abramson (1964, 1967, 1970) have used instrumental techniques to reveal three general categories of timings of voice onset, as found in stop segments. Taking the moment of release of the articulatory closure as a reference zero point, the continuum of possible relative timings is divided into: long voicing lead onsets, where the beginning of voicing precedes the release of closure by a substantial and perceptible amount (typically more than about 25 msec); a timing relationship where the onset of voicing falls within +/– 20 msec of the stop release, and which therefore counts psychophysically as a simultaneous onset; and long voicing lag (more than about 25 msec), where the relative delay in the onset of voicing is substantial and perceptible. The three perceptual categories are thus: **early onset of voicing**, **simultaneous onset of voicing** and **late onset of voicing**. Only the last of these, late onset with a perceptible voicing lag, qualifies as aspiration.

A phonemic contrast between unaspirated and aspirated voiceless stops is found not infrequently. One instance comes from the Chengtu accent of Chinese (Chengtu Szechuanese) (Fengtong 1989: 63–4). The members of each pair of words in this illustration carry the same tonal pattern, making the role of aspiration fully distinctive:

> *Unaspirated and aspirated voiceless stops in Chengtu Chinese*
> [tou] 'a unit of dry measure   [tʰou] 'to tremble'
> for grain (a decalitre)'
> [kai] 'to cover'   [kʰai] 'to irrigate; general,
>   approximate'

A second example of the distinctive use of aspiration comes from Thai, which distinguishes a tonally equivalent triplet of words by means of a voiced alveolar stop, a voiceless unaspirated alveolar stop and a voiceless aspirated alveolar stop (Ladefoged 1971: 12):

Voiced, voiceless unaspirated and voiceless aspirated alveolar stops in Thai

[dam] 'black'   [tam] 'to pound'   [tʰam] 'to do'

The relationship of aspiration involves a hierarchical ordering of the two segment-types concerned, in that the second segment is always of a more open degree of stricture than the first. There are three general cases. The first, and the most frequent case in the languages of the world, seems to be the one where the first segment is a voiceless stop and the second a voiced syllable-nuclear vocoid. Also common is the second type, where aspiration is a property of a sequence where a voiceless stop is followed by a voiced syllable-marginal resonant such as [j], [w], [ɥ], [ɹ] or [l] and comparable segments. Less common, though still possible, is the third type of sequence, where the first segment is a voiceless fricative, followed by a voiced vocoid. Examples of all three types are given below.

The first general case, where the first segment is a voiceless stop and the second a voiced syllable-nuclear vocoid, is exemplified from the African languages Swahili (East Africa) and Sutu (Tanzania, Mozambique and Malawi) (Westermann and Ward 1933: 50–1):

Voiceless unaspirated and aspirated stops in Swahili
[tembo] 'palm wine'   [tʰembo] 'elephant'
[kata] 'ladle'   [kʰata] 'head pad'

Voiced stops and voiceless unaspirated and aspirated stops in Sutu

[diba] 'encircle'   [tiba] 'to stamp'   [tʰiba] 'to stop up'
[dila] 'to smear with   [tila] 'avoid'   [tʰili] 'udder'
cow-dung'
[dula] 'sit'   [tula] 'crack (a nut)'   [tʰula] 'to butt'

The first segment in this general case of aspiration can also be an ejective stop or a click. The Ndau language of Zimbabwe contrasts (unaspirated) ejective stops with their aspirated pulmonic egressive counterparts (Westermann and Ward 1933: 52):

Unaspirated ejective stops and voiceless aspirated plosives in Ndau
[k'amba] 'be a magician'   [kʰamba] 'leopard'
[p'anda] 'perhaps'   [pʰanda] 'to scratch'

Sutu contrasts an unaspirated palato-alveolar click with an aspirated version of the same segment (Westermann and Ward 1933: 100):

Unaspirated and aspirated palato-alveolar clicks in Sutu

[ǂilaǂila] 'to stamp up   [ǂala] 'to begin'   [ǂɛta] 'to finish'
and down'

[leǂʰeku] 'old man'   [ǂʰala] 'to scatter'   [ǂʰuǂʰa] 'to trot'

English offers another instance of this first general case of aspiration, involving plosive segments. In RP (and the majority, but not all, of the other accents of English), aspiration is an allophonic feature, in that it is contextually predictable. The allophones of voiceless plosives which occur in syllable-initial position in stressed syllables and which are followed by a syllable-nuclear voiced segment are all aspirated. The words *pall*, *tall*, and *call* all have aspirated plosives, as [pʰɔl], [tʰɔl] and [kʰɔl], and voicing for the realizations of the following vowels is audibly delayed. The plosives in *spy*, *sty* and *sky* are unaspirated, however, for the phonological reason that they are not initial in their syllables, and voicing for the vowels is perceived as beginning immediately at the release of the stops concerned, giving [spaɪ], [staɪ] and [skaɪ] respectively.

The second general case of aspiration, where a voiceless stop is followed by a voiced syllable-marginal resonant, is also exemplified from English (RP). We can consider the case of voiceless plosives initial in stressed syllables in English (RP), followed by a voiced syllable-marginal resonant, as in /p/, /t/ or /k/ followed by /r/, /l/, /j/ or /w/, in *pry* /praɪ/, *try* /traɪ/, *cry* /kraɪ/, *play* /pleɪ/, *clay* /kleɪ/, *pure* /pjʊə/, *tune* /tjun/ and *cure* /kjʊə/, *twin* /twɪn/ and *queen* /kwɪn/. In all these cases, the voicing for the second segment begins late. They are frequently described as examples of partial devoicing of the second consonant, and transcribed using the initial devoicing diacritic. Sample transcriptions in this usage would therefore be *cry* [k̥ɹaɪ], *clay* [k̥leɪ], *cure* [k̥jʊə], and *queen* [k̥wɪn], for example. It is as phonetically accurate, and more revealing of a general phonologically-relevant co-ordinatory process of aspiration at work, to transcribe words such as these as *cry* [kʰɹaɪ], *clay* [kʰleɪ], *cure* [kʰjʊə], and *queen* [kʰwɪn] respectively.

The third general case of aspiration, where the first segment is a voiceless fricative followed by a voiced vocoid, can be found in a (relatively small) number of languages. Burmese is one instance. Burmese contrasts voiced, voiceless unaspirated and voiceless aspirated fricatives (Ladefoged 1971: 12):

Voiced, voiceless unaspirated and voiceless aspirated alveolar
fricatives in Burmese

[zãn] 'levitation'   [sãn] 'example'   [sʰãn] 'rice'

[zauŋ] 'edge'   [sauŋ] 'harp'   [sʰauŋ] 'winter'

Affricated stops can also participate in aspirated contrasts. These are discussed in section 12.4.5 below.

Aspiration is sometimes conceived as a limited phenomenon without connection to other phonetic processes. It is more profitable, in terms of a general phonetic theory, to see it as part of the overall topic of co-ordination, and as one application of the general strategy of voice-onset timing. Aspiration therefore has wider potential scope than traditional presentations suggest. In the definition offered in this book, we have seen that delay in the onset of the voice is identified as a phonetic relation between two segments, not the exclusive property of one. This encourages a more general phonological statement to be made about the scope of aspiration in languages such as English, to cover the relation between voiceless stops initial in stressed syllables and any following syllable-marginal resonants as well as the following syllable-nuclear vocoids.

Secondly, it is evident that aspiration is sometimes part of a yet more widely relevant language-characterizing process. For instance, Klatt (1975), Lisker and Abramson (1964) and Zlatin (1974) all show that the aspirated voiceless stops of English are organized in a hierarchy of voice-onset delay not only between themselves on the basis of place of articulation (which had been shown by Peterson and Lehiste (1960) and by Fischer-Jørgensen (1964)), but also relative to the fully or partially devoiced utterance-initial voiced stops that are characteristic of many accents of English in corresponding contexts. Within the 'voiced' and 'voiceless' sub-series, labials show the shortest voice-onset delays, then alveolars, with velars showing the longest.

It is also the case that individual languages differ in the relative timings of voice onset within the general categories. Ladefoged (1971: 20) compares French, English and Thai for their characteristic placement on the continuum of possible voice onset timings. This is shown in figure 12.2.

Figure 12.2 Comparison of timing of typical voice onset in French, English and Thai with respect to medial phase of oral stop (after Ladefoged 1971: 20)

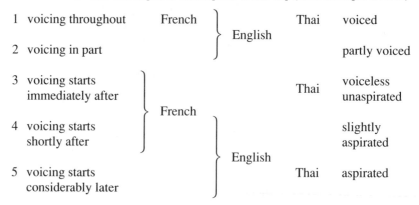

1 voicing throughout   French   Thai   voiced

                           English

2 voicing in part   partly voiced

3 voicing starts   Thai   voiceless
  immediately after   unaspirated

                        French

4 voicing starts   slightly
  shortly after   aspirated

                        English

5 voicing starts   Thai   aspirated
  considerably later

Voice-onset time after voiceless stops varies with the type of vocoid following them (Fischer-Jørgensen 1964). Ohala (1975) discusses evidence from English, Japanese and Russian showing that there is a longer voice onset delay before close vocoids than before open ones. The explanation offered for this is that the high tongue-body position for close vocoids offers greater resistance to the outflow of air from the vocal tract, thus delaying to a greater extent the onset of a transglottal airflow of sufficient volume for voiced vibration of the vocal folds (Kozhevnikov and Chistovich 1965; Ohala 1976).

The relative degree of aspiration can also serve to differentiate two accents of the same language. Fengtong (1989: 63) comments that initial voiceless stops in the Chengtu (Szechuanese) accent of Chinese are 'produced with a stronger puff of air' than in the case of comparable stops in the Beijing accent.

Some languages exploit aspiration to achieve triple distinctions, between unaspirated, moderately aspirated and strongly aspirated segments. Korean is one example (Abberton 1972: 71):

> *Unaspirated versus moderately and strongly aspirated stops in*
> *Korean*
> [pul] 'horn'   [pʰul] 'fire'   [phul] 'grass'

It seems likely in such cases, however, that more phonetic factors are involved in manifesting the phonological distinction than solely the relative duration of voice-onset delay. Abberton shows, using an electrolaryngographic technique which measures the fine detail of each cycle of voicing, that the detailed mode of vibration of the vocal folds is different in the onset of voicing in the three types of words. Kim (1970) proposed that an independent 'tensity' feature is used in Korean, where the unaspirated and the strongly aspirated stops are also 'tense', and the moderately aspirated stop is 'lax'. Abberton (1972:68) cites Lisker and Abramson (1964:442) as concluding, however, that 'voicing, aspiration, and force of articulation seem to be best considered as predictable consequences of a single underlying variable, namely "the differences in the relative timing of events at the glottis and the place of oral occlusion" '.

12.2.1   *Voiced aspiration*

One not infrequently meets the term 'voiced aspiration' in the phonetic literature. Its connection to the notion of aspiration as outlined above needs some explanation. It concerns a phenomenon found in a number of Indo-European languages such as Gujarati, Sindhi, Marathi and

Bengali, and some Central and Southern African languages such as Shona, Zulu and Ndebele, where syllables beginning with a voiced stop (and in some cases a fricative or a lateral resonant) may be pronounced with a whispery or breathy voice phonation, as a phonologically contrastive alternative to ordinary (modal) voicing. This is the same phenomenon that was described in chapter 8, where nasal stops with ordinary voicing in Ndebele and Tsonga were shown in contrast with their murmured (voiced aspirated) equivalents.

Voiced aspiration is usually transcribed phonetically by writing a whispery voiced approximant symbol [ɦ] after the syllable-initial contoid, as in Gujarati [bɦaɾ] (or [bʱaɾ]) 'outside' versus [baɾ] 'twelve'. An alternative method would be to give explicit recognition to the fact that different modes of phonation are involved, with the syllable beginning with whispery or breathy voice and changing in mid syllable to ordinary voicing. Gujarati [bɦaɾ] could thus be phonetically transcribed [b̤aɾ]. The whispery component of the whispery voice tends usually to fade before the end of the vocoid, leaving ordinary voicing, and this can be transcribed explicitly by displacing the whispery voice diacritic to the left of the second symbol, giving [b̤.aɾ]. If it is thought that breathy voice is involved, with its higher airflow, then the diacritic can be correspondingly changed to a subscript diaeresis, to give [b̤aɾ], for instance.

Some languages make contrastive use of both aspiration and voiced aspiration. An example involving oral stops comes from Sindhi (Nihalani 1975: 91):

Contrastive aspiration on voiceless and voiced oral stops in Sindhi

[pəla] 'a kind of fish'	[bəla] 'a snake'	[bɦəla] 'good'
[ʈəɾo] 'bottom'	[ʈʰəɾo] 'a buttock'	
[ɖəɾo] 'a heap'	[ɖɦəɾo] 'a kind of measurement'	
[təɾʊ] 'get away'	[tʰəɾʊ] 'be cool'	
[ɖəɾʊ] 'fear'	[ɖɦəɾʊ] 'slackness'	
[əco] 'come in'	[əcʰo] 'white'	[əɟɦo] 'shelter'
[kɪla] 'fort'	[ɡɪla] 'to speak ill of others	[ɡɦɪla] 'wet'

Sindhi also shows examples of voiced aspiration in syllables with tapped stops, nasal stops and lateral resonants (P. Nihalani, personal communication):

*Voiced aspirated tapped stops, nasal stops and lateral resonants
in Sindhi*

[kaɾo] 'black'	[kaɾɦo] 'a potion'
[mẽ] 'in'	[mɦiẽ] 'a buffalo'
[ali] 'wet'	[sənɦii] 'thin'
[kʌlə] 'a lesson (learned the hard way)'	[kʌlɦə] 'yesterday'
[ʈʰali] 'a dish (plate)'	[ʈʰʊlɦii] 'thick'

One apparent rarity that needs to be mentioned under the general heading of aspiration concerns voiceless stops released with breathy or whispery voice, as a special category of voiced aspiration. Maddieson (1984) cites Chao (1970) and Horne (1961) as describing the occurrence of these sounds in Changchow Chinese (Wu) and Javanese respectively. Maddieson (1984: 206) suggests the diacritic symbol [pɦ] (or [tɦ], [kɦ] etc.) for a voiceless stop released with breathy voice.

12.2.2 *The unification of voiceless and voiced aspiration*

A question that needs to be addressed is whether or not voiceless aspiration and voiced aspiration can profitably be regarded as instances of the same underlying phenomenon. Catford (1977a) proposes that a unifying phonetic definition could be one where aspiration involves a delay in the onset of *normal* voicing. Both voiceless and voiced aspiration meet this condition, in that the phonation type during the aspirated period is not normal voicing (i.e. it is not modal phonation), but voicelessness, whisper or whispery or breathy voice. In addition, Ladefoged *et al.* (1976) have given instrumental data for Igbo, a language of Eastern Nigeria, which show that the aerodynamic events of both sets of aspirated sound-types are similar.

12.2.3 *Aspiration versus final release*

The second point of clarification concerns the notion of 'final release', where [h] can be used as a phonetic diacritic to indicate the audible release of a voiceless stop which is final in the utterance. Release of a stop in this way is dealt with in section 12.4.1, but it is mentioned here because this too is sometimes (misleadingly) referred to as 'aspiration'. The conventional transcription consists, perhaps confusingly, of a superscript small [ʰ] placed after the stop symbol, as in English [itʰ] (*eat* /it/). The description of final release of this sort as 'aspiration' may arise from the shared use of the diacritic [ʰ], but it is important to note that final release is a quite different phenomenon from aspiration as defined in this book. It concerns a co-ordinatory relationship between a stop and utterance-final silence, and not one between two utterance-internal segments. Aspiration in this book will be reserved for the latter phenomenon only.

12.3   Pre-aspiration

Voiceless aspiration has been characterized above as a co-ordinatory relationship between a voiceless segment followed by a voiced one, and examples have been given of this feature occurring in syllable-initial sequences. An analogous feature is occasionally found as a mirror-image process in syllable-final sequences where a syllable-nuclear voiced segment precedes a syllable-marginal voiceless segment. This involves early offset of normal voicing in the syllable-nuclear voiced segment, anticipating the voicelessness of the syllable-final voiceless segment. It is called **pre-aspiration**.

Pre-aspiration can be transcribed in three ways to indicate this early offset of voicing. The first method is to place a subscript [̥] displaced to the right of the syllable-nuclear voiced segment; the second is to put a superscript [ʰ] (or a linear full [h]) in the same place; and the third is to substitute for this a small superscript devoiced vocoid symbol corresponding to the quality of the syllable-nuclear vocoid. Applied to the word for 'grasp! (imp.)' in the Gaelic of the Hebridean island of Lewis (Borgstrøm 1940: 20, cited by Ewen 1982: 58), this would give the following equivalent transcriptions – [ɡlḁk], [ɡlaʰk], [ɡlahk] or [ɡlaᵃk].

Pre-aspiration seems rare among the world's languages. Ní Chasaide and O Dochartaigh (1984: 141) suggest that 'Preaspiration of a postvocalic voiceless stop is found as a phonetic feature in a number of languages which have been called circumpolar languages. These include the Nordic group with Icelandic, Faroese, some West Norwegian dialects, and also Finnish, Lappish and most dialects of Scottish Gaelic.'

A number of authors discuss pre-aspiration phenomena in Icelandic (Arnason 1980; Ewen 1982; Haugen 1958; Malone 1923; Pétursson 1972; Thráinsson 1978). There is a discussion of pre-aspiration in a survey of West Scandinavian and Lappish languages by Kylstra (1972), and Engstrand presents an acoustic investigation of Lappish (Lule Sami) which includes measures of the duration of the 'voice-offset time', which is defined as 'the time lapse between the offset of voicing related to a prestop sonorant sound (e.g. vowel or liquid) and the beginning of the silent interval related to stop closure' (Engstrand 1987: 105).

Ní Chasaide and O Dochartaigh (1984) examine instrumentally analysed data from Icelandic, from the Scottish Gaelic-speaking Outer Hebridean islands of Lewis, Harris and North Uist, and from Irish. Pre-aspiration in

Lewis Gaelic is discussed by Oftedal (1956), and the Gaelic of the Hebrides and North West Scotland by Borgstrøm (1940, 1941), and by Ternes (1973). Ní Chasaide and O Dochartaigh give the following auditorily based comments on the realizations of pre-aspiration in the different languages they examined:

> In Icelandic, with our informant we always hear a voiceless glottal fricative. In the Scottish Gaelic dialects there seemed to be two major groupings of realisations. In Lewis, preaspiration ranges from a period of what we can only describe as silence – that is, with no audible friction – to a weak glottal fricative. In the other Hebridean dialects we hear a stronger glottal fricative, very similar to that heard in the Icelandic realisations, and for the Gaelic velar and palato-velar stops the preaspiration appears as a homorganic fricative. In Irish, the preaspiration has never been noted as such or described by phoneticians. It is barely audible to us and sounds like a very weak glottal fricative or period of silence, somewhat similar to the Lewis varieties. (Ní Chasaide and O Dochartaigh 1984: 142)

(By 'palato-velar' the authors cited here mean a pre-velar place of articulation.) The mention of pre-aspiration (in the Hebridean Gaelic of Uist and Harris) taking the fricative form of what later in their article (1984: 152) they call 'pre-affrication' is interesting. A similar comment is made by Engstrand (1987) for some contexts of Lappish (Lule Sami). Engstrand states that:

> Preaspiration is ... a feature of several northern European languages and dialects. e.g. Icelandic, Faroese and Scottish Gaelic (Pétursson, 1972; Shuken, 1979; Ní Chasaide, 1985), where its detailed phonetic realization may vary with context. In Lule Sami, too, the noise sound in question is frequently fricative rather than aspirative, particularly in palatal and velar contexts. (Engstrand 1987: 105)

Examples of both the 'fricative' and the 'aspirative' types of pre-aspiration given by Engstrand (*ibid.*) are:

Pre-aspiration in Lappish
['paːɬkaːu] '(paid) salary'   ['paːlahkaːn] '(give as) salary'

It is noteworthy that, in the case of the Lappish example above glossed as '(paid) salary', the friction is homorganic not with the following stop, but with the preceding lateral approximant. The general concept of preaffrication will be briefly discussed further in the section below on affrication.

Ewen (1982) cites work by Thráinsson (1978), supported by Arnason

(1980), illustrating word-pairs from Icelandic which show contrasts between aspirated, pre-aspirated and unaspirated stops:

> *Aspirated, pre-aspirated and unaspirated stops in Icelandic*
> [kʰahpɪ] 'hero'   [θahka] 'thank'
> [haːtʰʏr] 'hate'   [hahtʏr] 'hat'   [hatːʏr] 'hair'

In the definition of pre-aspiration, as in that of 'aspiration', it is necessary to use the term 'normal' voicing. This is because Shuken (1980: 455) has shown by instrumental examination of airflow and acoustic details of pre-aspiration that the transition from the voiced state of the preceding segment to the voiceless state of the next segment often passes through an intermediate period of whispery voicing. This is the case in Scottish Gaelic, as spoken in the Isle of Lewis (Shuken *ibid.*), and in Irish (Ní Chasaide and O Dochartaigh 1984: 144). Sample words from Lewis Gaelic are (Shuken 1984: 127):

> *Whispery voiced pre-aspiration in the Hebridean Gaelic of Lewis*
> [pʰɔfik] 'bag'   [paːfitəfih] 'boat'

In addition to the cases of the circumpolar languages, Holmer (1949) states that pre-aspiration is a feature exploited in Guajiro (a Southern Amerindian Arawakan language). Catford (1977a: 114) also mentions that pre-aspiration occurs in the North Caucasian languages Chechen and Ingush.

Pre-aspiration can also be said to occur as a phonetic phenomenon in the Andalucian accent of Spanish, and in some South American accents of Spanish (P. Roach, personal communication). Roach describes a phonological rule of the form

$$/s/ \Rightarrow [h] \ / \ V\!-\!C$$

which is to be interpreted as 'the phoneme /s/ is manifested phonetically as [h] when /s/ occurs in the context of a preceding vowel and a following consonant'. In these circumstances the [h] is of very brief duration. Roach gives the following examples:

> *Phonetic pre-aspiration in Andalucian Spanish*
> *este* /este/ $\Rightarrow$ [eʰt̪e] 'this'
> *es que* /eske/ $\Rightarrow$ [eʰke] 'that is'
> *los dos* /lɔsdɔs/ $\Rightarrow$ [lɔʰd̪o] 'the two'

12.4 Co-ordination of the marginal phases of stop segments

We have already seen that stop segments can participate in a variety of co-ordinatory relationships with the segments that follow them, in terms of the relative timing of articulatory and phonatory activities. Stops also participate in a yet wider range of co-ordinatory relationships with adjacent segments, in several different types of articulatory co-ordination, all involving one or both of the marginal phases of the stop.

12.4.1 *Release and non-release of stop segments*

There are two contextual circumstances in which stops may optionally be **incomplete**, in lacking one of their marginal phases. The first is where the stop is followed by another stop. An example from English would be *stacked* /stakt/, where speakers have two options. The first option is to release the velar closure for [k] before making the alveolar closure for [t], giving [stakʰt], where the [k] represents a complete stop (and where superscript [ʰ] is used to show release of a stop). The second option is to make the alveolar closure for the final [t] before releasing the velar closure for [k], so that the release of the [k] would be auditorily incomplete. It is incomplete in the sense that the compressed air behind the velar closure is prevented from causing an audible explosion by the alveolar closure in front being already established. Oral stops lacking an audible explosion at the release phase can be called **unreleased** stops. These are sometimes called 'unexploded' stops, but it should be noted that this is an asymmetric relationship. All unexploded stops are by definition unreleased, but not all unreleased stops are unexploded. As in the case of the English *stacked* /stakt/ just described, where the release of the velar closure for [k] occurs after the onset of the further forward alveolar closure for [t] has been established, the [k] can be regarded as having been exploded (inaudibly) but not released. The phonetic diacritic for an unreleased stop (strictly defined) is a superscript right-angle placed after the stop symbol, as in [stak˺t].

Examples of unexploded oral stops are found in Bamun, a language of the Bamileke group spoken by some 75,000 speakers in Cameroon. Westermann and Bryan (1952: 131) give the following instances:

> *Unexploded oral stops in Bamun*
> [lwɔ́p˺] 'fish-hook'   [ǹdáp˺ǹdáp˺] 'houses'
> [fúɪfwèt˺] 'winds'   [ŋk'wút˺] 'legs'

In English, the first of two oral stops can optionally be incomplete, even when a word-boundary intervenes. One frequently hears a phrase like *good times* pronounced as [ɡʊd˺tʰaɪmz]. In this example, both stops involved are incomplete, in that the [d˺] lacks an audible explosion, both auditorily and articulatorily, and that the [tʰ] lacks an onset phase, since the tongue tip/blade is already in a position of alveolar closure. The two stops here are

homorganic – that is, they are made at the same place of articulation. In all cases of sequences of two homorganic stops, the second stop is by definition incomplete, in lacking its onset phase. Some of the most widespread examples of this are found in homorganic sequences of a nasal followed by an oral stop. Instances of an oral stop lacking its onset phase in such circumstances would be the [d] in English *band* [band], the [t] in Spanish *fuente* [fuen̪t̪e] ('fountain'), the [b] in Italian *Umberto* [umbɛr̪t̪o], the [d] and the double stop [k͡p] in the West African language Efik in [ndap̚] 'dream' and [ŋ͡mk͡pɛp̚], 'I am teaching' (Cook 1969: 37–9), or the [g] and the [b] in Fula [ŋgaːri] 'bull' and [mbin] 'sound of drum beat' (Arnott 1969a: 60). In cases such as the English phrase *slipped disc*, when pronounced as [slɪp̚t̚dɪskʰ], multiple incompleteness can be analysed.

The second circumstance in which a stop may be incomplete is where, as an alternative to final release, an utterance-final stop is unexploded. This is transcribed in the same way as word-internal unreleased stops, giving *bat* as [bat̚]. In English, utterance-final unreleased voiceless stops are often accompanied by a simultaneous glottal stop, as an unreleased double stop articulation, giving pronunciations like [bat͡ʔ̚]. If no diacritic is attached to a stop, it can be assumed that the stop is either released or that the fact of release/non-release is irrelevant to the point being made. The final release of voiced stops can be explicitly indicated by a small superscript [ᵊ] after the stop symbol.

French tends to differ from English with respect to release versus non-release of oral stops. Table 12.1 compares these, emphasizing the tendency for French to release stops in the positions where English characteristically does not release them.

Table 12.1 *Unreleased stops in English versus released stops in French*

English	French
[kap̚] 'cap'	[kapʰ] 'cape'
[sak̚] 'sack'	[sakʰ] 'bag'
[bag̚] 'bag'	[bagᵊ] 'ring'
[ak̚tə] 'actor'	[akʰtœʁ] 'actor'

Source: Based on Tranel (1987: 133)

12.4.2 *Lateral and central release of oral stop segments*

When an oral stop is followed immediately by a segment made with a lateral aspect of articulation, and which is homorganic in place of articulation, there are two co-ordinatory options for the releasing offset phase of the stop. The air which is compressed during the medial closure phase of the stop segment can be released before the central contact for the homorganic lateral segment is made – in which case, the route taken by the escaping airflow is central. This can be transcribed with a superscript vowel symbol, or a full vowel symbol can be written on the line, as either [bɒtᵊlˠ] or [bɒtəlˠ] for English *bottle*. **Central release** of this sort is sometimes also called **central plosion**. The alternative to this mode of release is to leave the central part of the contact between the active and passive articulators in contact, and release one or both sides of the closure laterally. This can be transcribed by using a superscript [ˡ] after the stop symbol, as in [bɒtˡl̩ˠ] – in English in these conditions the [l] would be pronounced as a syllabic lateral. **Lateral release** of this sort is also called **lateral plosion**.

The articulation of the active articulator is quite different in central versus lateral release. In central release of the sequence [təl], the tip/blade of the tongue makes contact with the alveolar ridge on two separate occasions, with the air escaping centrally between the two moments of contact. In lateral release of [tˡl], the tip/blade makes central contact only once, and the air escapes immediately on the release of the [t] through a lateral channel.

Lateral release is frequent in many accents of English in homorganic sequences of stop plus lateral, even across word boundaries. One thus hears not only *little*, *riddle* and *Atlantic* as [lɪtˡl̩ˠ, ɹɪdˡl̩ˠ, ətˡlantɪk], but also examples such as *cut lip* ⇒ [kʰʌtˡlɪp]. If no diacritic is attached, then lateral release can be assumed if there is no vocoid symbol intervening between the stop and the lateral segment.

Another example of lateral release comes from Qatari Arabic. Bukshaisha (1985: 16) says that /d/ is 'usually realized as a voiced apico-laminal denti-alveolar plosive'. When it is followed by a lateral consonant, it is 'laterally exploded', as in /dlaːl/⇒ [dˡaːl] 'coffee pots'.

12.4.3   *Oral and nasal release of oral stop segments*

When there are two homorganic stops in sequence, the first of which is oral and the second nasal, as in English *hidden* /hɪdn̩/, the air which is compressed during the closure phase of the oral stop can be released in two different options of co-ordinatory control. The first type of release is through the mouth, and **oral release** of this sort is also called **oral plosion**. A short voiced vocoid often intervenes between the two stops in oral release, so that *hidden* can be transcribed as [hɪdᵊn]. After voiceless stops before a word boundary, oral release can be transcribed with the stop release diacritic, as in *cut now* pronounced as [kʰʌtʰnaʊ]. In sequences like this, the active articulator makes two separate contacts with the passive one.

The second type of release is through the nasal cavity, and can be referred to as **nasal release**. It can also be called **nasal plosion**. In nasal release the oral closure for the first stop is maintained through the closure phase of the second, contact being made only once, and it is the lowering of the velum that permits the escape of the compressed air. The nasal stop involved in nasal release is always incomplete, since by definition it is homorganic with the preceding oral stop and therefore lacks an onset phase. Nasal release is explicitly transcribed with a superscript [ⁿ] after the oral stop, giving [hɪdⁿn]. In English in these circumstances the [n] is pronounced as a syllabic nasal. The fact of nasal release can alternatively be left transcriptionally implicit, to be implied by the absence of any orally released segment intervening between the oral stop and the nasal stop.

Nasal release is very frequent in many accents of English, in homorganic sequences of oral plus nasal stops in word-internal and across-word-boundary contexts, though not within a syllable. So one often hears, in informal connected speech at least, not only *happen* as [hapⁿm̩], *ribbon* as [ɹɪbⁿm̩], *kitten* as [kɪtⁿn̩], *bidden* as [bɪdⁿn̩], *bacon* as [beɪkⁿŋ̩] and *bargain* as [bɑgⁿŋ̩], but also *oddness* as [ɒdⁿnəs] and *what name* as [wɒtⁿneɪm].

Nasal release is found in many languages. An example from Qatari Arabic is ['hudⁿni] 'peace'. Another, from German, is *bieten* [bitⁿn̩] 'to offer'. Nasal release is almost always a matter of contextual interaction between an oral stop and a following nasal stop. But nasal release can occasionally be found in a contrastive function. Catford (1977a: 214–15) reports that 'several south Australian languages ... Aranda, Arapana and Wailpi, have a series of nasally released stops contrasting with orally released stops (O'Grady, Voegelin and Voegelin 1966, Wurm 1972)'. Catford (*ibid.*) also cites data from Coustenoble (1929) showing contrastive use of nasal versus oral release from Wolof, the Niger-Congo language spoken in Senegal:

> *Contrastive nasal versus oral release of oral stops in Wolof*
> [lap̚ᵐ] 'to drown' [lapʰ] 'be thin'
> [gɔk̚ᵍ] 'horse's bridle rope' [gɔkʰ] 'white chalk'

12.4.4 *Release requirements of taps, flaps and trills*

The comments offered above have concerned oral and nasal stops in various circumstances. But one aspectual group of stop segments exists to which some of the co-ordinatory options discussed above are not open. This is the group made up of taps, flaps and trills. The aerodynamic requirements of the aspect of articulation for each of these categories are such that an oral airflow is essential during both the onset and the offset phases of the segment in question.

Taps, flaps and trills have the option of having either velic closure or velic opening during their articulation, but even in the latter, nasal case, oral air-flow has to be present throughout all three phases in order to achieve the aerodynamic conditions necessary for the formation of these sounds. Taps, flaps and trills are therefore never incomplete, and are always released orally, whether nasal airflow is present or not.

12.4.5   *Affrication of stop segments*

When a stop is followed by a resonant, the release of the air compressed during the medial phase of the stop normally occurs very rapidly, and it makes its explosive exit to the outside atmosphere so quickly that the moment of release is characterized by a burst of acoustic energy that is only very short-lived. The release of the stop in its offset phase is simultaneous with the onset phase of the resonant that follows, making up the shared overlap phase between the adjacent segments. There is, however, another phonetic option of co-ordinatory control which can be exercised in this overlap phase betwen the two segments. It consists of prolonging the release of compressed air during the overlap phase, by allowing the active articulator to pass slightly more slowly through the zone of close approxi-mation before reaching the stricture of open approximation for the medial phase of the resonant. The brief period of audible friction that results has a perceptible duration, and is necessarily homorganic with the place of articu-lation for the stop. This phonetic process of making the overlap phase between a stop and the following articulation audibly and momentarily fricative is called **affrication**.

In the perspective of the phonetic theory proposed in this book, affrica-tion is a co-ordinatory property of a relationship either between two seg-ments, or between a segment and utterance-final silence. The first element in both cases must be an oral stop. If another full segment follows, then it must be a resonant. This follows from the requirement that the friction in the overlap phase between the two segments (which counts as both the release phase for the stop and the onset phase for the resonant) should be only momentarily audible, dying out as the stricture of the second segment quickly reaches open approximation at the beginning of its medial phase. The same supposition applies in the case of an affricated stop segment fol-lowed by utterance-final silence. The momentary audibility of the friction in utterance-final affrication is terminated by the articulators rapidly relaxing to a position of open approximation.

363

More traditional analysis has conceptualized the process of affrication as a unisegmental property of stop articulation, perhaps because of the fact that the affrication necessarily involves friction during the offset phase of the stop being made at the same place of articulation as the stop. In this more traditional approach, the stop and its affricated release together are conventionally said to form an **affricate**. One can also refer to such stops as **affricated stops**. For expository convenience, we can follow the same practice, while acknowledging the stricter underlying bisegmental relationship of co-ordination.

Affrication is transcribed in any of three ways. One way is to write a small superscript homorganic fricative symbol after the stop symbol, as in [tˢ, tʃ, dʒ, cç, ɟʝ, kˣ, gˠ]. The alternative modes of transcription involve writing both components on the line and either joining them with a linker diacritic, as in [t͡s], or joining the two symbols physically together, as in [ts].

Affricates can be articulated at any place of articulation where oral stops can be formed, and on any airstream mechanism. Two affricates which will be familiar to most readers are the voiceless and voiced palato-alveolar affricates of English [tʃ] and [dʒ]. In the American tradition of phonetics these are also sometimes transcribed as [č] and [ǰ] (Pullum and Ladusaw 1986), though this is not a practice given formal approval by the IPA. These affricates are found in English (RP) as pronunciations for the spellings 'ch-' in *cheer* [tʃɪə], 'j-' in *joy* [dʒɔɪ], 'g-' in *geode* [dʒioʊd], '-ch' in *each* [itʃ], '-tch' in *pitch* [pɪtʃ], '-ge' in *urge* [ɜdʒ] and '-dge' in *hedge* [hɛdʒ] respectively.

Palato-alveolar affricates occur in many languages other than English. Maddieson (1983) lists 141 out of his survey of 317 languages as using the voiceless palato-alveolar affricate [tʃ], with eighty using its voiced counterpart [dʒ]. The illustrations below are from modern Standard Turkish (H. Kopkalli, personal communication) and Sundanese of West Java (Robins 1953):

Palato-alveolar affricates in modern Standard Turkish
[hatʃɯ] 'cross (accusative)' [hadʒɯ] 'pilgrimage (accusative)'

Palato-alveolar affricates in Sundanese
[ŋahantʃa] 'to work' [ŋadʒawab] 'to answer'

Palato-alveolar affricates also occur in Nupe, spoken in the northern states of Nigeria, where a voiceless alveolar affricate is found in limited contrast with a voiceless palato-alveolar affricate. Smith (1969: 135) describes their mutual distribution as follows: '/ts/ normally only occurs before back vowels, /tʃ/ only before front vowels, but both occur and contrast before /a/'. Smith cites the contrasting examples /tsa/ 'to choose' and /tʃa/ 'to begin'.

An example of a contrast between a pair of affricates at the alveolo-palatal place of articulation comes from the Suleimaniya accent of Kurdish (A. Ferhardi, personal communication):

Alveolo-palatal affricates in Kurdish (Suleimaniya accent)
[t͡ɕᶣɛ] 'where'   [ɟ͡zᶣɛ] 'ear'

The concept of an affricate offered here is at the phonetic level of description. Whether the affrication of some oral stop in a particular language is solely a matter of phonetic realization, (either as an extralinguistic idiosyncrasy of the individual speaker, or as an accent-specific allophonic adjustment to the stop's contextual or structural environment), or plays a phonological role in serving to represent a unitary phoneme in that accent, is a question that can only be settled at the phonological level. Equally, there are often phonological reasons in particular languages, mostly to do with distributional facts and symmetry of patterning, to analyse phonetic affricates as representing a phonological sequence of a stop and a fricative, as two phonologically independent elements.

In a phonetic affricate, the audible friction is a property of the overlap phase of two adjacent segments where the first is a stop and the second a resonant. In a triple sequence of an oral stop followed by a full fricative followed by a resonant, the friction that is audible is a property of the medial phase of the full independent fricative segment (as well as necessarily of the overlap phase with the preceding stop). As such, the friction in a full fricative is normally of longer duration than that in the affricated case. The reason for the cautious use of the term 'normally' in the above statement, however, is that it is impossible, in a strict analysis, to avoid appeal to general phonological criteria in assessing how long the duration of audible friction needs to be to distinguish between a phonetic affricate and a sequence of oral stop plus full fricative. In English, a distinction which depends partly on the relative duration of audible friction in the two cases is made between *why choose* [waɪʧuz], with a palato-alveolar affricate [ʧ], and *white shoes* [waɪtʃuz], with a sequence of an alveolar stop [t] followed by a full palato-alveolar fricative [ʃ] (Jones 1931). The friction in *why choose* is relatively short, and the friction in *white shoes* is relatively long.

There are comparable cases in modern Standard Turkish (H. Kopkalli, personal communication), where [ɪʧɪmdɪ] 'it was my "inside"' is pronounced with an affricate, and is phonologically distinct from [ɪtʃɪmdɪ] 'push now', which is pronounced as a sequence of a stop followed by a full fricative. Another Turkish example is found in [saʧonun] 'it's his/her hair', with a

365

voiceless palato-alveolar affricate, versus [sɑtʃonun] 'sell that', with a sequence of a stop followed by a phonetically and phonologically independent palato-alveolar fricative.

In many accents of English, syllable-initial /tr/ and /dr/ are pronounced as post-alveolar affricates [ʈɹ̝] and [ɖɹ̝], where the onset of [ɹ] is fricative in both cases before reaching its resonant medial phase. The phrase *we dressed* [widɹ̝est] shows an affricated pronunciation of the [d], while *we'd rest* [widɹest], shows no audible friction on the release of [d] (Jones 1931). Similarly, *nitrate* [naɪʈɹ̝eɪt] shows affrication while *night rate* [naɪtɹeɪt] does not.

Affrication is sometimes confused by beginning students with aspiration. There are crucial differences between the co-ordinatory phenomena of affrication and aspiration. Affrication must involve a stop segment, while aspiration can apply to both stops and fricatives. Affrication is a co-ordinatory relationship solely of articulatory control, while aspiration is a co-ordinatory relationship involving both the articulatory and the phonatory systems. The confusion is nevertheless not entirely without basis. An affricated voiceless stop where the affrication in the overlap phase before a voiced vocoid is also voiceless, as in English *cheap* [ʧip], simultaneously also satisfies the technical conditions for aspiration, in that normal voicing for the vocoid is audibly delayed beyond the release of the stop. Equally, the English (RP) example of *nitrate* [naɪʈɹ̝eɪt] quoted in the paragraph above is an instance of the overlap phase between a stop and a resonant displaying both affrication and aspiration, in that it is characterized both by momentarily audible friction (homorganic with the stop) and by voice-onset delay beyond the release of the stop.

In the cases just described it is the stop that participates in the aspirated relationship, not the affricate, since normal voicing starts immediately at the termination of the affricate (or, more strictly, at the termination of the affricated overlap phase, and hence at the beginning of the medial phase of the resonant segment). Affricates can themselves be aspirated, however, in that the onset of voicing can be audibly delayed beyond the end of the fricative overlap phase into the medial phase of the following vocoid articulation. This is found contrastively in Igbo, the language of Eastern Nigeria (Williamson 1969a: 92):

> *Aspirated and unaspirated palato-alveolar affricates in Igbo*
> [eʧʰe] 'to rub/smear'   [eʧe] 'to laugh'

A similar example comes from Neo-Aramaic, the modern form of Old Aramaic spoken by Christian minorities in the Middle East, where aspiration is used contrastively to distinguish between two voiceless palato-alveolar affricates (Odisho 1977: 80):

> *Aspirated and unaspirated palato-alveolar affricates in Neo-Aramaic*
> [ʧʰamʧʰim] 'to hurl'   [ʧanʧin] 'to hum'

Another example is found in Thai, where voiceless alveolo-palatal affricates can be either unaspirated or aspirated (Henderson 1949). Sample words, though with different tonal pitch patterns, are:

> *Aspirated and unaspirated alveolo-palatal affricates in Thai*
> [t͡ɕʰon] 'water'   [t͡ɕoŋ] 'noise of Malay drum'

Sherpa, a Sino-Tibetan language spoken by some 50,000 people in Eastern Nepal, uses aspiration contrastively on two sets of affricates, alveolar and palatal. Examples of this, on tonally matching pairs of words, are (Maddieson, Hargus and Nartey 1980: 140–1):

> *Aspirated and unaspirated alveolar and palatal affricates in Sherpa*
> [t͡sʰa] 'salt'   [t͡sa] 'grass'
> [c͡ɕʰaːn] 'beer'   [c͡ɕaːn] 'north'

Affricates where the stop element is voiceless but the fricative offset phase is voiced are very much rarer in the languages of the world than the case where the two elements share the same phonatory state. Languages do exist, however, in which the fricative component of affrication has a different phonatory state from the stop component that precedes it. In Szechuanese, two alveolar affricates are used for lexical distinctions in which the stop component is voiceless in both cases. Examples are given by Scott (1947) (who does not provide word-glosses). The differences lie in two facts: in one case, voicelessness continues to run throughout the fricative component, and is prolonged beyond it into aspiration, giving [tsʰu]. In the other case, voicing may begin during the fricative component, so that voicelessness is not able to be prolonged beyond the end of frication into an audible period of aspiration, giving [t͡z̥u]. There is also a comparable pair of alveolo-palatal affricates, [t͡ɕʰe] and [t͡z̥e] (Scott 1947).

A language with an unusually large number of phonological contrasts between four voiceless affricates (alveolar, alveolar with trilled fricative release, palato-alveolar, retroflex palato-alveolar) is the San Vicente Coyotepec dialect of Popoloca, a Mesoamerican Otomanguean language. Suárez (1983: 44–5) cites Barrera and Dakin (1978) as stating that this language contrasts /t, t͡s, tʳ, t͡ʃ, t͡ʃ/. (The voiced/voiceless status of the trilled element of the affricate [tʳ] is not made clear in Suárez's account).

12.4.5.1 *Lateral affricates*

All the examples of affrication discussed so far have involved release of the stop element of the sequence as having occurred centrally. It is also possible, however, for the stop closure to be released into (homorganic) lateral frication. Instances can occur in English. In the RP pronunciations of *Atlantic*, one often hears not only lateral release of the first [t], but also lateral affrication fading into a resonant, as in [ətɬlantɪk]. A comparable example would be *cut lip*, pronounced as [kʰʌtɬlɪp]. Such pronunciations can be called **lateral affricates**.

Suárez (1983) mentions the occurrence of lateral affricates in some of the languages of Mesoamerica and Mexico. He draws information on central and lateral affricates in Nahuatl (a Uto-Aztecan language) from Andrews (1975) and Newman (1967), and gives examples from Texcoco Nahuatl (Suárez 1983: 32) and Classical Nahuatl (1983: 47):

Central and lateral affricates in Texcoco Nahuatl
[ʃi'tɬali] 'sit down!'   [ʃimoɬali't͡sino] 'sit down please!'

Central and lateral affricates in Classical Nahuatl
[nikt͡ʃiˑwa] 'I do it'   [mit͡stoˑkaˑjoˑti] 'he named you'
[ɬaˑkatekoloɬ] 'demon'

Maddieson (1984: 225), in his survey of 317 languages, lists a small number of languages (nearly all of them Amerindian) as exploiting pulmonic egressive lateral affricates of various sorts: voiceless dental or alveolar lateral affricate (Haida, Tlingit, Chipewyan, Nootka, Squamish); voiceless aspirated dental or alveolar lateral affricate (Chipewyan); palatalized voiceless dental lateral affricate (Kabardian); voiced dental or alveolar lateral affricate (Haida, Tlingit); voiceless alveolar lateral affricate (Navaho, Wintu, Quileute); voiceless aspirated alveolar lateral affricate (Kwakw'ala [Kwakiutl]); voiced alveolar lateral affricate (Navaho, Kwakw'ala).

12.4.5.2 *Ejective affricates*

Affricated stop segments made on an egressive glottalic airstream mechanism are uncommon, but not rare. An example comes from Tigre, the language of Eritrea mentioned earlier. In Tigre, both ejective alveolar and ejective palato-alveolar affricates occur (Palmer 1956):

Ejective alveolar and palato-alveolar affricated stops in Tigre
[falət͡s'] 'wood'   [hat͡s'hət͡s'] 'pebbles'
[ramat͡ʃ'] 'embers'   [t͡ʃ'abɐl] 'ashes'

Maddieson (1984) lists the following voiceless ejective affricates (given here with his labels, phonetic symbols in the style of this book and names of languages, or figures for larger language numbers, in his 317-language survey in brackets):

> voiceless dental ejective affricate [t͡θ'] (Chipewyan);
> voiceless dental sibilant ejective affricate [t͡s'] (Tzeltal, Squamish, Acoma, Gununa-Kena, Kabardian);
> voiceless dental/alveolar or alveolar sibilant ejective affricate [t͡s'] (29 languages);
> labialized voiceless dental/alveolar sibilant ejective affricate [t͡sʷ'] (Lak);
> voiceless palato-alveolar sibilant ejective affricate [t͡ʃ'] (35 languages);
> labialized voiceless palato-alveolar sibilant ejective affricate [t͡ʃʷ'] (Lak);
> voiceless retroflex sibilant ejective affricate [t͡ʂ] (Tolowa, Acoma, Jaqaru);
> voiceless palatal ejective affricate [c͡ç'] (Gununa-Kena);
> voiceless velar ejective affricate [k͡x'] (Tlingit);
> voiceless dental/alveolar or alveolar lateral ejective affricate [t͡ɬ'] (13 languages);
> voiceless laterally released velar ejective affricate [k͡ɬ'] (Zulu).

It would not be unreasonable to think that the label 'voiceless' is redundant in the above list. But it is used here to draw attention to the inclusion in the same list by Maddieson of a 'voiced palato-alveolar sibilant ejective affricate' ([d͡ʒ']) in !Xũ, the Khoisan language of Southern Africa, citing Snyman (1969). Earlier presentations of ejective segments in this book may have led the reader to conclude that these ejective sounds are always voiceless. Physiologically, however, there is no reason why the respiratory system should not supply the rising larynx of the glottalic egressive airstream mechanism with vigorous enough subglottal pressure from the pulmonic egressive mechanism to cause the vocal folds to vibrate for voicing. But this particular combination of airstream mechanisms, though physiologically possible, is certainly exploited extremely rarely in the languages of the world, if at all.

The reason for the caveat 'if at all' in the last sentence above is that it seems dubious whether a voiced ejective sound is really used in !Xũ itself. Snyman (1969: 37–45) describes those !Xũ sounds which are orthographically indicated as combining voicing and ejectiveness as in reality being made up of a rapid sequence of a voiced element and a voiceless ejective stop. Snyman (1969: 37fn) states that 'What actually happens is that the vocal cords are activated by pulmonary air and they produce a voiced unemitted sound ... Both the nasal and oral passages are closed ... The unemitted sound ... is swiftly followed by the articulation of the ejected sound ... In close sequence [they] are perceived as a vocalised sound.' Snyman applies this description to the pronunciation of six different phonemes, including the sound that Maddieson lists as a 'voiced palato-alveolar sibilant ejective affricate'. An appropriate phonetic symbolization for the complex !Xũ sound in question would therefore be [ᵈʧ']. The phonetic label for what Snyman calls 'a voiced unemitted sound' would in the terms of this book be **pre-voicing**, in that the brief period of pulmonically initiated voicing can be regarded as a property of the beginning of the medial, closure phase of the stop, before the initiation of the glottalic airstream starts. It can be thought of as analogous in its timing to the pre-nasal element of complex pre-nasal stops. The complex affricated stop [ᵈʧ'] would then be characterized as 'a pre-voiced voiceless palato-alveolar ejective affricated stop'.

Examples of voiceless alveolar lateral ejective affricates are found in several of the languages of the Pacific Northwest. One of them, mentioned earlier, is Wenatchee-Columbia (Hoard 1978: 64):

> *Alveolar lateral ejective affricates in Wenatchee-Columbia*
> [t̩ɬ'+ˈt̩ɬ'ikʰ+t̩ɬ'ikʰ] 'Brewer's blackbird'   [t̩ɬ'+ˈt̩ɬ'əkʷ+t̩ɬ'əkʷ] 'spotted fawn'

Another language exploiting voiceless alveolar lateral ejective affricates is Nitinaht (also called Ditidaht by its speakers), a Nootkan group member of the Wakashan family spoken on Vancouver Island. A phonemic opposition between the pulmonic egressive affricate and its ejective counterpart is shown in the following examples from Esling (1991: 2):

> *Alveolar lateral pulmonic egressive versus ejective affricates in Nitinaht*
> [t̂ɬʊɬ] 'good'   [t̂ɬ'uɬ] 'touch, lay hands on'
> [t̂ɬuːjaːs] 'pole on the ground'   [t̂ɬ'uːjaːs] 'dry ground'

An example of a language which exploits voiceless alveolar lateral ejective affricates in a way which provokes an interesting problem for descriptive phonetic theory is Akhwakh, a Caucasian language of the Andi group of

West Dagestan (Catford 1977a). In this language, a phonemic contrast is maintained not only between a glottalic egressive voiceless alveolar lateral ejective affricate [tɬ'] and a corresponding pulmonic egressive voiceless alveolar lateral affricate [tɬ], but each of these also counts as a 'plain' or 'weak' version in phonemic contrast with a 'strong' version. Each of the so-called 'strong' affricates is characterized by a 'relatively long and noisy fricative phase, lasting on average 160 ms [tɬɬ], 84 ms [tɬɬ'] in isolated words. The weak lateral affricate, however, has a fricative phase of on the average 70 ms [tɬ] 43 ms [tɬ'], that is, no longer than the aspiration of many an aspirated stop' (Catford 1977a: 214). Catford gives the following illustrations.

Weak and strong pulmonic egressive voiceless alveolar lateral
affricates and glottalic egressive voiceless alveolar lateral ejective
affricates in Akhwakh

[tɬutɬu] 'blow! (imper.)'	[tɬɬut'] 'wedge'
[tɬ'ini] 'malt'	[tɬɬ'ini] 'sleeps'

A similar durational pattern exists in the weak and strong central velar and uvular affricates of Avar, another Caucasian language (Catford 1977a: 202). To the extent that increased muscular effort is necessary to prolong the fricative phase of the 'strong' affricates (especially in the case of the strong ejective affricate), these 'strong' affricates are in principle not unlike the tense members of the tense/lax pairings of consonants in languages such as Etsako. But the provocative element of the Akhwakh and Avar strong affricates lies in the role that duration plays in the theoretical characterization of the fricative phase of affricates in general. This situation is quite different from the one where it is the stop closure phase that is prolonged to give long affricates, which is unproblematic from the point of view of classificatory phonetic theory.

The 'weak' affricates in the Akhwakh and Avar pairings clearly meet the durational prescription of 'momentary friction' for normal affricates in the framework of this book in a satisfactory way. The fricative release is short enough to be plausibly attributable to a normal intersegmental overlap phase between the stop and the following resonant. But the fricational elements of the 'strong' affricates equally clearly meet plausible durational criteria for phonetic status as independent fricative segments.

One solution might be to regard the strong Akhwakh and Avar affricates as a special type of affricate, made up of a stop with a prolonged fricative release. But this would then impair the capability of distinguishing at a phonetic level between affricates versus sequences of a stop followed by an independent homorganic fricative, for those languages (such as English) which exploit both possibilities.

In order to resolve the theoretical phonetic problem of how to classify these 'strong' lateral affricates with longer fricative elements, the position that will be taken in this book will be to preserve momentary frication in the overlap phase as the criterion for the classification of affricates at a phonetic level of analysis. From a phonetic point of view, the 'strong' affricates of Akhwakh and Avar would then be regarded as affricates followed by homorganic independent fricatives. The phonological analysis of these complexes as affricates functioning as unitary phonemes would (as elsewhere) have to be based on phonological criteria such as symmetry of patterning with other comparable phonological units, rather than on phonetic criteria.

12.4.5.3   *The status of affrication and aspiration as co-ordinatory phenomena*

Both affrication and aspiration are more complicated phenomena than their initial presentation suggested. These complexities put the simple structures of the proposed phonetic theory to a test which now calls for some justification.

The proposition that affrication is a co-ordinatory relationship contracted between a stop and a following resonant segment, with the friction realized as a property of the brief overlapping phase between the two segments, can reasonably be defended when the two segments share the same airstream mechanism and phonation. In such cases, affrication is plausibly suggested to be a mutual attribute of the two segments, without primary affiliation to either. When either the type of airstream initiation or the phonation type differs between the two segments, then the balance of affiliation of the frical element might be thought to alter somewhat towards the segment whose initiatory or phonatory characteristics it shares.

One case in point would be an ejective affricate, where the frictional phase shares a glottalic egressive airstream with the preceding stop segment, but where the following resonant is made on a pulmonic egressive airstream. In this case, and to this degree, the affrication might be thought to have a more primary affiliation to the stop than to the resonant. The opposite affiliation might be thought to obtain in the case of an affricate where the frictional element was voiced, like the following resonant, while the preceding stop was voiceless (as in the example from Szechuanese given in section 12.4.5 above).

This reservation is mentioned in order to draw attention to the fact that designing the shape of a phonetic theory necessarily involves choices being made between options on a cost–benefit basis. In the case of affrication, the preferred choice in this book is to opt for treating affrication as a co-ordinatory relationship between adjacent segments rather than as a property of one single segment of the two involved. The benefit lies in the treatment being more general, in that it covers the vast majority of cases of affrication in the languages of the world. Cases where the fricational element differs from the stop in its phonatory state, or differs from the resonant in its initiatory state, and hence supporting a single-segment-affiliation model, constitute a small minority of affricated sounds in the languages of the world. The benefit of the generality also lies in putting affrication as an intersegmental phenomenon on a par with comparable intersegmental processes such as aspiration and devoicing. That the generality of the proposed solution is not fully universal, however, is the cost that should not be overlooked.

It should be noted that the same type of arguments apply to the phenomena of aspiration. Voiceless aspiration shares its phonatory state with the preceding stop and not with the following resonant, but the phonetic quality of the aspiration is conditioned more by the articulatory characteristics of the resonant than by those of the stop. In voiceless stops which show voiced aspiration (such as in Changchow Chinese or Javanese, as mentioned in section 12.2.1 above) before voiced resonants, the whispery/breathy voicing phonation type of the aspiration is more akin to that of the resonant than to that of the stop. In cases of voiced aspiration, where both the stop and the resonant segments involved show normal voicing (such as in the examples from Sindhi in section 12.2.1), the phonation type of the aspirated phase is equally similar (or dissimilar) to that of the medial phases of the two segments. Voiceless aspiration between a voiceless stop and a voiced resonant is by far the most frequent type of aspiration in the languages of the world, and the theoretical status of aspiration in this book as a feature shared by two adjacent segments is therefore set by that generality.

12.4.5.4   *Symbols for pulmonic and non-pulmonic affricated stops*
Symbols for pulmonic affricated stops can be formed from the combinations of the individual stop and fricative symbols found in the IPA alphabet reproduced in appendix I.

12.4.6   *Pre-affrication of stop segments*
As with affrication, **pre-affrication** is a property of a co-ordinatory relationship between two segments, but in this case the relationship is between a vocoid and a following oral stop. In pre-affrication, the

onset phase of the stop is made briefly but audibly fricative in the transition to full closure. The friction is by definition homorganic with the place of articulation of the stop.

The transcription of pre-affricated stops can follow the pattern set by affricated stops. The pre-affrication can be identified by a superscript small fricative symbol of the same place of articulation as the relevant stop, as in [ˣk] in the Gaelic examples below, or it can be made linear and joined to the stop symbol by a linker, as in [x͡k].

The phonetic differentiation of a pre-affricated stop of this sort from a sequence of an independent fricative followed by an oral stop will normally be a matter of relative duration. But the final arbitration of this decision, as with the comparable situation with affrication, once again rests on general phonological criteria, such as typical distributional and durational facts. The decision about how to treat a phonetically pre-affricated stop in the phonology of the language concerned will always necessarily rest on phonological criteria particular to that language.

A brief comment was made earlier about this (apparently rare) possibility of stop segments being pre-affricated, in a mirror-image process to affrication of the offset phase of an oral stop preceding a segment with open approximation. The example given was that of Gaelic, where pre-affrication in the accents associated with some dialects was the (phonetically stronger) reflex of pre-aspiration in cognate languages such as Irish. It is worth pointing out that, in the examples given in chapter 17 of general phonetic transcriptions of utterances from native speakers of a number of languages made by the author of this book and a colleague, the Gaelic of both Harris and the more inshore Hebridean island of Islay shows pre-affrication in the (very few) words examined from single informants. Anticipating chapter 17 for the purposes of this section, those examples are:

Pre-affrication in Scottish Gaelic (Harris)
[ʃaˣkʰ] 'seven'   [əhʷɔˣkʰ] 'eight'

Pre-affrication in Scottish Gaelic (Islay)
[kʰʷuˣʷt̪ʷs̬ʷ] 'cat'   [kʰʷʉˣʷt͡ʃʷ] 'cats'

Since labialization runs throughout both the examples cited from the Scottish Gaelic of Islay, a more economical transcription could isolate the labialization component, and signal it by a prefacing utterance-general symbol, as in Vʷ[kʰuˣt̪s̬] 'cat' and Vʷ[kʰʉˣt͡ʃ] 'cats'. This convention of indicating utterance-general settings applicable to all susceptible segments within the utterance is discussed more fully in chapter 13.

12.4.7   *Co-ordinatory features in click releases*

Some of the most complex co-ordinatory actions occur at the release of velaric ingressive click articulations. Perhaps this is not so surprising, given that the initiation of a velaric ingressive airstream involves two closures, one posterior (which can be velar or uvular), and one anterior, both of which have to be released in the overlap phase with the next segment. The release of the anterior closure normally takes place while the posterior closure is still being maintained, so that co-ordinatory options such as affrication can be applied to either stage of release. If affrication is applied to an anterior lingual release, then this may take the form of central or lateral frication. If the affrication is a characteristic of the posterior release, then the local friction will normally be central, and will be velar or uvular.

The phonatory component of clicks, since the formation of the velaric ingressive airstream is physiologically independent of the pulmonic mechanisms, can potentially take any form from voicelessness to normal, whispery, breathy or creaky voicing. It is also straightforward to accompany a click with a glottal stop, to prolong the glottal stop beyond the supraglottal release stages of the click, or to make the posterior closure of the click into a velar (or uvular) ejective or implosive or voiced implosive stop. Clicks can therefore be voiced, voiceless, whispery voiced (murmured) or creaky voiced (laryngealized), and can involve a velar or uvular ejective or implosive element. The velic state of a click has been described in chapter 6 as free from the intra-oral constraints of click formation, and it was noted that clicks can therefore be oral or nasal. The posterior release of a click can also be made either orally, without or with local velar (or uvular) friction, or nasally. The articles by Traill (1991) and Ladefoged and Traill (1993) are recommended for very clear descriptions of the phonetic intricacies of click articulations in the Khoisan languages such as !Xóõ, !Xū and Nama, Bantu languages such as Zulu and Xhosa, and the Tanzanian languages Sandawe and Hadzapi. No other general category of speech sound seems to involve such extreme complexities of production.

All the phenomena described so far that can be related to the activities of the posterior element of click formation have been called **click accompaniments** (Ladefoged and Traill 1993). But we need to distinguish between those accompaniments that are an integral part of the medial phase of the click, such as the voicing state or velic state during the medial phase, and those which are a matter of co-ordinatory control. Affrication, aspiration and nasal release all qualify as options of co-ordination. Ladefoged and Traill (1993) give examples from Nama (all with high tone, explained in chapter 15) of contrasts between a voiced nasal click, a voiceless unaspirated click, a voiceless aspirated click (i.e. with voicing delay), and a click with delayed aspiration (i.e. with yet further delayed onset of voicing, also involving voiceless nasal escape of the air-pressure that would have built up behind a velar + velic closure), and a click with an accompanying glottal stop. Some of these are shown in table 12.2. A full account of the articulatory and phonatory basis of Nama clicks is given in Ladefoged and Traill (1984).

Table 12.2 *Co-ordinatory phenomena in contrasting clicks in Nama*

Anterior stricture	Voiced nasal	Voiceless unaspirated	Voiceless aspirated	Delayed aspiration	Glottal closure
Dental	[ŋǀo] 'measure'	[kǀoa] 'out into'	[kǀʰo] 'play music'	[ŋǀho] 'push into'	[ʔkǀoa] 'sound'
Alveolar	[ŋǃoras] 'pluck maize'	[kǃoas] 'hollow'	[kǃʰoas] 'belt'	[ŋǃhoas] 'narrating'	[ʔkǃoas] 'meeting'
Palatal	[ŋǂais] 'turtledove'	[kǂais] 'calling'	[kǂʰaris] 'small one'	[ŋǂhais] 'baboon's arse'	[ʔkǂais] 'gold'
Lateral	[ŋǁaes] 'pointing'	[kǁaros] 'writing'	[kǁʰaos] 'strike'	[ŋǁhaos] 'special cooking place'	[ʔkǁaos] 'reject a present'

Source: Ladefoged and Traill (1993)

12.5   Articulatory feature sharing

A close examination of the phonetic make-up of any utterance often reveals that neighbouring segments exercise a certain degree of mutual influence on each other's articulatory characteristics. This influence can be exerted at a number of different levels of analysis. Phonetically, adjacent segments can show an articulatory 'feature-copying' process at work as part of their accommodation to their occurrence in the particular context. Phonologically, segments can show an (optional) mutual influence being exercised across word-boundaries, in **assimilation**. Finally, **segment harmony** is a phonological phenomenon which constrains the choice of segments within a word to either of two mutually exclusive sets, each characterized by one or more shared phonological feature(s). This phenomenon is usually called **vowel harmony**, or **consonant harmony**. Each of these feature-sharing phenomena will be considered in turn.

12.5.1   *Co-articulatory feature spreading*

Accommodation of at least some of the articulatory characteristics of any segment to those of its contextual neighbours is so universal a phenomenon in the languages of the world that it is reasonable to suppose that it reflects inherent principles of strategic neuromuscular control. The purpose of this section is to consider some of the phonetic details of the ways in which adjacent segments exercise their mutual accommodatory influence on articulatory features.

Figure 12.3 Sagittal cross-sections of the vocal organs during the production of the medial closure phases of: (a) a voiceless pre-velar stop [k̟]; (b) a voiceless post-velar stop [k̠]; (c) a voiceless fully velar stop [k]

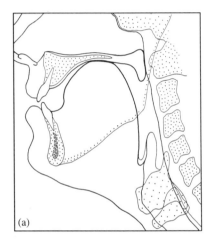

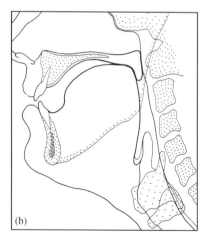
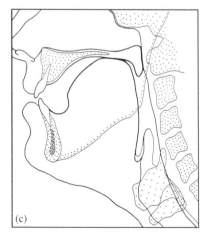

The pronunciations of the two English (RP) words *keys* /kiz/ and *cars* /kɑz/ can be transcribed phonetically as [k̟ʰiz] and [k̠ʰɑz], using the subscript diacritics [˰] and [˭] to mean **advanced** and **retracted** places of articulation within the relevant zone. The pronunciations reflect a tendency, present in virtually all languages, for accommodations of place and aspect of articulation to occur between adjacent segments, particularly, but not only, within the same syllable. This tendency is normally strongest in accommodations between syllable-initial consonant and syllable-nuclear vowel realizations, and less strong between vowel and syllable-final consonant realizations.

The accommodatory adjustments visible in the transcribed examples can be thought of as a 'spreading' of articulatory features from one segment to another. The detailed place of articulation of the [k] segments in both cases is an anticipatory copy to some degree of that for the following vocoid, with the advanced, pre-velar [k̟] anticipating the front tongue-body position for [i] and the post-velar [k̠] anticipating the back tongue-body position for [ɑ]. In the case of a third word *cool* [kʰʷulˠ], there is no adjustment of the velar stop away from a centrally velar position, because the articulatory position for the body of the tongue in the performance of the following vocoid is also centrally below the soft palate, in the middle of the velar zone. Figures 12.3a–c show the articulatory positions for these three types of [k]-segment, in sagittal cross-section.

Lip position is also anticipated in an accommodatory way, as could be seen from the English example of *cool* quoted above. In English *keel* [kʰilˠ] and *cool* [kʰʷulˠ], the (unmarked) lip-spreading of [k] in *keel* and the rounded labial position of [kʷ] in *cool* anticipate the lip positions of their respective vocoid neighbours.

Velic position participates in feature-copying in a similar way. In the English words *seen* [sĩn] and *soon* [sʷũn], the velic position for the syllable-final [n] is anticipated during the production of both vocoids, though the effect here is less strong, with the velum opening before alveolar closure for the [n] is reached, but late in the course of production of the vocoids. In all three cases, the features of tongue position, labial position and velic position have spread anticipatorily from their segmental 'origin'. Conversely, the tongue position for the vocoids has exercised a perseverative influence on the detailed place of articulation of the syllable-final [n] segments, with the back vocoid [u] causing the articulation of the following [n] to be made slightly further back on the alveolar ridge than is the case in *seen*. Perseverative effects tend usually to be weaker than anticipatory effects (Gay 1978), and the lip-rounding in 'cool' is normally fading by the onset to the final [lˠ].

The co-ordinatory phenomenon of accommodatory spreading of articulatory features of this sort has come to be known as **co-articulation**. This term was first introduced by Menzerath and Lacerda (1933), but its use became widespread in phonetics only after the publication of two influential papers by the Swedish phonetician Sven Öhman (1966, 1967). The phenomenon has also been called 'similitude' (Jones 1918, 9th edn 1960: 217) and 'articulatory smoothing' (Fujimura and Lovins 1978: 108). The term **anticipatory co-articulation** will be used here to mean the articulatory influence exercised by a segment on segments that precede it in an utterance. **Perseverative co-articulation** will be the term used for the articulatory influence exercised by a segment on segments that follow it in the utterance. The direction of co-articulatory influence in the chain of speech here labelled 'anticipatory' has also been called 'right-to-left' co-articulation (Lubker 1981: 129), and alternatives to 'perseverative' have been 'carry-over', 'retention' and 'left-to-right' co-articulation (Lubker 1981: 128).

Co-articulatory feature-copying makes the segments involved more similar to each other than they are in other contexts. Some of this increased similarity may conceivably be due to mechanical factors constraining the actions of the vocal apparatus. Ohala (1981b: 112) mentions such factors as 'inertial properties of the articulators, the anatomical connections between articulators, the elasticity of articulator tissues, aerodynamic factors etc.'. It deserves emphasis, however, that many characteristics of co-articulation reflect options of positive co-ordinatory control, and are not solely the consequence of mechanical necessity. This point of view is based on the fact that both speakers and languages differ in the degree of co-articulatory influence exercised on adjacent segments.

Such lingual adjustments of velar stops as there are in English, in anticipation of front and back vowels, are relatively small in comparison with some other languages. Robins (1956) describes anticipatory and perseveratory adjustments applied to velar consonants in Sundanese in the following terms:

> Consonants of the velar group enjoy the greatest phonetic latitude of any of the Sundanese consonants in their realization, being articulated as pre-velar, mid-velar, or post-velar according to the nature of the preceding or following vowel, with noticeably greater variation than occurs in the Standard English k- and g- sounds in their different phonetic contexts.

The timing and degree of labial co-articulation also differs from speaker to speaker, and from language to language. Perkell (1986) measured the degree of lower-lip protrusion in the repeated performance of the segment-sequences [katu] and [kantu] in individual speakers of English, Spanish and French (presumably pronounced as [katu] and [kan̪tu] by the Spanish and

Lower lip protrusion vs. time
Line-up point: onset of voicing for [u]

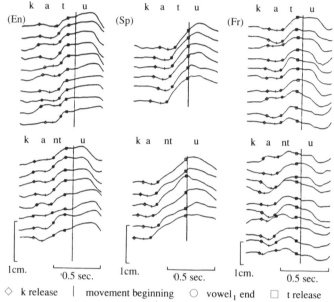

◇ k release ⁣ | movement beginning ⁣ ○ vowel₁ end ⁣ □ t release

Figure 12.4 Differences of timing of lip-protrusion during the performance
of [katu] and [kantu] in English, and [kaṯu] and [kanṯu] in French and
Spanish (from Perkell 1986: 261)

French speakers). The segment-sequences were embedded within carrier
phrases appropriate to each language. Figure 12.4 shows the results of his
experiment (Perkell 1986: 261), in which the jaw position of each speaker
was standardized by the insertion of a small bite-block. The traces are mutually aligned in time with respect to the onset of voicing for the vocoid [u].
Perkell describes the data in the figure in the following terms:

> Note that in all cases, protrusion beginning occurs just before the end
> of the [a]. However, other aspects of the movement patterns are quite
> different for the different speakers. Protrusion for the speaker of
> English, at the left, reaches the target for the [u] just before the [t]
> release, then a second, more gradual protrusive movement occurs after
> onset of voicing for the [u], presumably to produce an appropriate
> pattern of diphthongization. The protrusion movement for the Spanish
> speaker, in the middle, consists of one single gesture which reaches its
> extreme after the almost coincident [t] release and onset of voicing for
> the vowel. Protrusion for the French speaker, on the right, reaches a

maximum before release of the [t], and gradual retraction with some hesitation occurs throughout the vowel. (Perkell 1986: 260)

It was also pointed out earlier that in French the velum opens anticipatorily on vocoids before nasal consonant realizations, as it does in English, but with a characteristically later onset.

The timing of the phonetic features involved in co-articulatory action does not respect segmental boundaries. Lisker (1978: 133), describing co-articulation, states that

> When we examine closely the operation of the various structures
> making up the vocal tract we find that they do not in general shift
> position in close synchrony and at the rate at which the phonetic
> segments are emitted. Thus lip-rounding and nasalization are
> segmental features of English that refuse to be contained within their
> 'proper' segmental boundaries, as these are commonly placed.

In co-articulation, articulatory features by definition spread across more than one segment. This is also precisely the major attribute of a 'setting' where a setting is characterized as an articulatory property shared by two or more segments which are either adjacent or in close proximity.

Settings are more fully discussed in chapter 13, but we can note here that the segmental domain of co-articulatory settings tends to vary with the type of setting involved. The hierarchy of co-articulatory effects in terms of typical span of influence is as follows: the co-articulatory setting with the smallest span is the adjustment of tongue position, which seems typically to exercise its chief effect within the syllable. Secondly, the velic setting of nasality can cross both syllable and word boundaries – Moll and Daniloff (1971) showed that in English the velum can lower in anticipation of a nasal consonant several segments earlier, across such boundaries, provided that the segments influenced are all vocoids. Lastly, a co-articulatory labial setting seems to have the longest potential segmental span. Kozhevnikov and Chistovich (1965) showed that when a string of consonants (whose phonological requirements for labial position are neutral) precede a lip-rounded vowel in Russian, then the onset of rounding can begin on the first consonant in the string, for up to three such consonants. This was shown to extend to four such consonants in English by Daniloff and Moll (1968), and up to six for French (Benguerel and Cowan 1974). In Swedish, Lubker, McAllister and Carlson (1975) showed that the onset of lip-rounding in such a consonantal string can start up to 600 msec ahead of a rounded vowel, in terms of the onset of electrical activity in the lip muscles chiefly responsible for moving the lips to a rounded position.

Within the category of co-articulatory influences that seem to operate over a small span of segments, certain effects such as palatalization and retroflexion seem to have interesting directional constraints. Palatal and palatalized contoids chiefly affect following segments, while retroflexed contoids affect mostly preceding segments (Bhat 1974: 235). According to Bhat, the perseverative effect of palatalization, namely fronting and raising following vocoids, is found in Russian, Marshallese, Yagua, Korean, Irish, Higi and Kannada.

The fact that retroflexion should exercise its influence chiefly in an anticipatory direction is perhaps transparent. The articulatory aspect of retroflexion involves the tongue tip/blade being curled upwards, and this action must be completed before the medial phase of the segment chiefly concerned. Any susceptible segment immediately preceding the retroflexed segment will therefore tend to suffer the consequences of this preparatory action. Bhat suggests that this finding is typical of languages such as Mundari, Konda, Tamil, Tulu, Marathi, Armenian, Pitta-Pitta, Mantjiltjara and Chrau.

A co-articulatory phenomenon complementarily related to that of retroflexion is the effect in certain languages of segments with a tapped aspect of articulation. In most tapped segments, the tongue hits the passive articulator at a perpendicular angle. In a minority of types of tapped stops, however, there is a tendency for the tongue tip/blade to strike the alveolar ridge on an oblique rather than a perpendicular angle, and to follow a retracting trajectory after making momentary closure. The consequence of this action is to inject a certain degree of retroflexion on the following segment. Bhat (1974: 235) states that in languages such as Sanskrit, Yidgha, Sanglechi, Pasha, Tiwi, Ngarluma, Burera, Kunjen, Norwegian, Swedish and Faroese, apical tapped stops (and trilled stops) have 'induced retroflexion on a following consonant'.

Co-articulatory settings may have important perceptual benefits. Anticipatory co-articulation may provide auditory cues which a listener can exploit to predict segments before the speaker has produced them, and perseverative co-articulation can give 'carry-over' cues which usefully add to the general perceptual redundancy of the speech signal (Lubker 1981: 129).

12.5.2 *Feature copying in assimilation*

The concept of assimilation was briefly introduced in chapter 3. It can now be discussed in more detail, as an example of co-ordination at the phonological level. Assimilation is seen here as an optional process consisting of one segment exercising a modifying influence on the articulatory or phonatory characteristics of another segment across a word-boundary, or across the boundary between the components of a compound word. The influence can be exercised in a forward direction along the chain of speech, from a segment at the end of one word to a segment at the beginning of the next, as an instance of **perseverative assimilation**. When the influence is exercised in the other direction, from a segment at the beginning of one word to a segment at the end of the preceding word, this is said to be an instance of **anticipatory assimilation**. The fact of assimilation is established by comparison with the form of the word when pronounced in isolation. The segments can be made more similar in terms of phonation, place of articulation, nasal aspect of articulation, or degree of stricture.

Examples of perseverative assimilation of voicelessness from English (RP) can be seen in the following pronunciations of *is* and *has*, where a preceding phonological process of elision has deleted vowel phonemes intervening between the assimilating and assimilated consonants (Jones 1962: 225):

> *Perseverative assimilation of voicelessness in English*
> /wɒt ɪz ðə taɪm/ ⇒ [wɒt s ðə tʰaɪm] What is the time?
> /ðə ʃɒp ɪz oʊpn̩/ ⇒ [ðə ʃɒp s oʊpn̩] The shop is open
> /dʒak haz bɪn hɪə/ ⇒ [dʒak s bɪn hɪə] Jack has been here
> /wɒt haz hi dʌn/ ⇒ [wɒt s hi dʌn] What has he done

Examples of anticipatory assimilation of place of articulation, which is much more common, can be seen in the following English pronunciations of *that* and *this*:

> *Anticipatory assimilations of place of articulation in English*
> /ðat man/ ⇒ [ðap man] that man
> /ðat gɜl/ ⇒ [ðak gɜl] that girl
> /ðɪs ʃɒp/ ⇒ [ðɪʃ ʃɒp] this shop
> /ðɪs jɪə/ ⇒ [ðɪʃ jɪə] this year

The last example is revealing, in that, unlike all the other examples cited above of assimilation, the assimilatory process here has resulted not in a complete copy of the place of articulation of the assimilating segment by the assimilated segment, but only in a partial adjustment of the place of articulation. The original alveolar fricative [s] has become a palato-alveolar fricative [ʃ], in response to the influence of the palatal approximant [j].

An example of an anticipatory assimilation in English involving a change from an oral to a nasal aspect of articulation is the pronunciation of *good morning* (canonically /gʊd mɔnɪŋ /) as [gʊm mɔnɪŋ].

A third type of assimilation is the case where both segments change their characteristics, under their mutual influence across the word boundary, which Gimson (1962: 271) refers to as 'coalescence'. An example of this would be a more extreme assimilation of *this year*, being pronounced as [ðɪʃ ʃɪə]. This **coalescent assimilation** would involve adjustments of phonation type, place of articulation and degree of stricture, in that the normal voiced palatal approximant [j] in *year* would be replaced by a voiceless palato-alveolar fricative, as well as the normal voiceless alveolar fricative [s] in *this* being replaced by a voiceless palato-alveolar fricative [ʃ]. Another coalescent assimilation would be the instance of the sequence [-t j-] in *hit you* [hɪt ju] being jointly replaced by a voiceless palato-alveolar affricated stop in [hɪt͡ʃu].

All the examples quoted above are of assimilations which are the outcome of optional phonological processes. Assimilations which are internal to compound words tend over time to become fixed patterns, and lose their optionality. Many compound words in English show such traces of **historical assimilation** (Jones 1962: 221). An example in transition is *newspaper*, which is more commonly heard as [njuspeɪpə], rather than [njuzpeɪpə], though both are heard. An example that has become fully institutionalized in the language is *orchard*, which has lost the signs of its historical origin as *ort + yard*, with the earlier sequence /-t/ + /j-/ coalescing to the modern /-tʃ-/, in the RP pronunciation [ɔtʃəd].

Assimilation patterns are accent-specific and language-specific. Received Pronunciation of English shows no examples of anticipatory assimilation of voicing. In some accents of Scottish English, on the other hand, this is quite common, in assimilated forms such as [bɪrðde] for *birthday*, in place of [bɪrθde]. Equally, anticipatory assimilation of voicing is not uncommonly heard in French, in assimilated forms such as [yn̪tazd̪œte] for *une tasse de thé* ('a cup of tea'), in place of [yn̪tasd̪œte].

12.5.3   *Segmental harmony*

Segment harmony is a phonological phenomenon where there is a phonotactic restriction of choice of the type of segments that can co-occur in a word, or sometimes in a morphological component of a word, such that the segments have to be chosen from either one or another of two entirely or largely exclusive sets. The segments of each set usually share one or more characterizing phonetic features. This phenomenon is usually called **vowel harmony**, or **consonant harmony**, though in fact co-articulatory constraints necessarily operate on neighbouring segments, resulting in the harmony process applying allophonically throughout all or most of the syllable concerned.

The general concept of segment harmony would normally perhaps be more appropriately treated in a textbook on phonology, rather than in one on phonetics as such. But discussion of segment harmony is included here as an illustration of the fact that it is in matters of co-ordination, whether this is at a subsegmental or intersegmental phonetic level, or at an intersegmental phonological level of word-construction, that some of the most interesting problems in phonetics and phonology tend to be found.

Vowel harmony is a phenomenon found in many different language areas of the world. Examples are found in languages as diverse as Efik, Igbo and Twi (Akan) from West Africa; Turkana from East Africa; Yaka from the Bantu area of central Africa; Palestinian Arabic from the Eastern Mediterranean; Telugu and Bengali from the Indian sub-continent; Finnish, Hungarian and Turkish from Europe; Kirghiz from the southernmost part of the CIS, near the Afghanistan-China border; Khalkha Mongolian from the area north of central China; and Chukchi from the north-eastern tip of Siberia.

In Igbo, one of the major languages of Nigeria, Ward (1936) suggested that eight vowel phonemes could be distinguished, and arranged and numbered as follows:

Igbo vowel phonemes

1. i   5. u
2. e   6. ə
3. ɛ   7. o
4. a   8. ɔ

Ward suggested a vowel-harmony rule that applies to this organization to the effect that vowels within a polysyllabic word could be drawn from either the even-numbered set or the odd-numbered set, but, with few exceptions, not both. Carnochan (1960) illustrates this vowel-harmony principle in Igbo operating in trisyllabic verb forms (where the first segment represents a pronominal prefix). Tone is omitted in the following examples:

Vowel harmony in Igbo

/isiri/ 'you cooked'	/esere/ 'you said'
/osiɛ/ 'he cooks'	/ɔsea/ 'he says'
/isɛrɛ/ 'you quarrelled'	/esara/ 'you washed'
/otɛɛ/ 'he rubs'	/ɔsaa/ 'he washes'
/izuru/ 'you stole'	/ezərə/ 'you bought'
/ozuo/ 'he steals'	/ɔzeɔ/ 'he buys'
/izoro/ 'you hid'	/ezɔrɔ/ 'you got up'
/ogoo/ 'he buys'	/ɔbɔɔ/ 'he cuts up'

A second illustration of vowel harmony comes from Lyons (1962), writing here in a Firthian vein. He describes the phonological process of vowel harmony as it applies to Turkish in the following terms, which speak eloquently of the problems to which a phonemic monosystemic analysis gives rise in such areas (vowel symbols are as in Lyons' original):

> To illustrate the difference between the phonemic and the prosodic approach to analysis, we may briefly consider what is generally called 'vowel harmony' in Turkish. It seems that any phonemically-based analysis of Turkish must recognize eight vowels: *viz*, /i ï u ü e a o ö /. Any one of these vowels may occur in monosyllabic words: in words of more than one syllable, however, there are systematic restrictions on the co-occurrence of the several vowel phonemes. Thus, in words of native Turkish origin, front vowels / i ü e ö/, and back vowels /ï u a o/, do not occur together; nor do rounded vowels /ü ö u o/, and unrounded vowels /i e ï a/. Moreover, the phoneme /o/ occurs generally only in the first syllable of a word (with the exception of certain verbal forms). A phonemic representation of polysyllabic words is therefore very highly redundant, since it represents each vowel in the structure as a selection from eight contrasting units, whereas all but two of the eight vowel phonemes are excluded from occurrence by the occurrence of any other given vowel phoneme of the word. It is to be noticed, however, that the redundancy is of (the analyst's) own making, and the corrective distributional statement a consequence of the phonemic preconceptions of the analysis in the first place. (Lyons 1962: 129)

Lyons goes on to give a 'prosodic' analysis of modern Standard Turkish, in the Firthian tradition, which, although undoubtedly harder to read and interpret, more succinctly captures the mutual phonological constraints at work in this language – and which brings morphological facts more directly into play, in that in this analysis 'stems and suffixes have everywhere the same phonological form' (Lyons *ibid.*). An illustration from Lyons is given in table 12.3, with a phonemic transcription for comparison, to give a flavour of this Firthian approach. Space does not permit more extensive illustration, and the interested reader is referred to the collections of articles in the Firthian tradition cited in section 2.5.7.

The prosodic transcription in table 12.3 exploits 'two binary PROSODIC contrasts of front/back and rounding/non-rounding, and ... only two contrasting segmental PHONEMATIC units, high/low ... For the phonematic contrast between the high vowel and the low vowel, *i:a* (is used); for the prosodies of front/back and rounding/non-rounding *F:B* and *R:N* (is used) respectively' (Lyons *ibid.*). The interest of the illustration should not be diminished by Lyons' use of phonetically unorthodox symbols for his phonemic transcription. The meanings of the individual items are due to H. Kopkalli (personal communication).

Table 12.3 *Phonemic and prosodic (Firthian) analysis of modern Standard Turkish*

Word meaning	Phonemic transcription	Prosodic transcription
eyes (eye + pl. marker)	/gözler/	FRgazlar
houses	/evler/	FNavlar
arms	/kollar/	BRkallar
men	/adamlar/	BNadamlar
roses	/güller/	FRgillar
matches	/kibritler/	FNkibritlar
clouds	/bulutlar/	BRbilitlar
girls	/kïzlar/	BNkizlar
my eye (eye + poss. marker)	/gözüm/	FRgazim
my house	/evim/	FNavim
my arm	/kolum/	BRkalim
my man	/adamïm/	BNadamim
my rose	/gülüm/	FRgilim
my matches	/kibritim/	FNkibritim
my cloud	/bulutum/	BRbilitim
my girl (daughter)	/kïzïm/	BNkizim

Source: Based on Lyons (1962)

Another 'prosodic' analysis of vowel harmony in Turkish is available in Waterson (1956), and a more conventional account is given in Kornfilt (1987). It should be noted that there are many loanwords in Turkish which violate the harmony rules (and thereby reveal themselves as not part of the native stock of the language). Instances of loanwords from languages such as Arabic and English, cited by Ringen (1980: 38), are:

Violations of vowel harmony in loanwords in Turkish
/kitab/ 'book'   /zafer/ 'victory'
/aruz/ 'prosody'   /boksit/ 'bauxite'
/zijaret/ 'visit'   /goril/ 'gorilla'

The work of writers in the Firthian prosodic school is based on principles of analysis some of which are not dissimilar to those of the more modern school of autosegmental and metrical phonology. Indeed, Shibatani (1990: 179) goes as far as to suggest that, in separating specific phonological features from the segmental representation of a morpheme or word 'The Firthian tradition of prosodic analysis has ... been resurrected in the name of autosegmental phonology'. Vowel harmony, which specifically involves a phonological domain larger than the individual segment, has attracted a substantial contribution from researchers in these perspectives, and interested readers are referred to articles on the topic listed under Further Reading at the end of the chapter.

Treatments of phonological harmony processes often concentrate on the harmonization of vowel phonemes within words or parts of words of vowel phonemes. It was pointed out above that allophonic co-ordination will also entail phonetic adjustments to the segments representing the consonantal elements of such words. In these circumstances, an alternative phonological solution is feasible, where the harmony process is analysed as being carried by the consonants rather than the vowels, with consequential statements having to be made about the allophonic adjustments applicable to the realizations of the vowels concerned. That most languages showing harmony are analysed as displaying vowel harmony rather than consonant harmony is possibly a consequence of the fact that the relevant phonetic distinctions are in some way perceptually more blatant for the differences between the segments representing vowels than for those representing consonants. Another reason for opting for a solution which is based on harmonic relations between vowel rather than consonant phonemes is often economy of presentation, in that vowel systems are usually smaller than consonant systems.

Some languages invite a treatment of consonant harmony, however, in that the harmonic realizations are perceptually more salient for the realizations of the consonants than for those of the vowels. One instance is the Aywele accent of Etsako, the Niger-Congo Kwa language spoken by some 9,000 speakers around the confluence of the Niger and Benue rivers in the mid-western part of Nigeria. It will be recalled that this language has been cited earlier as exploiting differences of muscular tension during the articulation of syllables as the basis for a phonological opposition. Laver (1967) suggests that a possible phonological solution for this language is to focus the harmony process on the consonants, and to posit three sets of consonants:

> *Consonant harmony sets in Etsako*
> *Tense*   /w m v z r ñ k g/
> *Lax*   /wh mh vh zh rh ñh kh gh/
> *Neutral* /p b f t d s l n j ɥ kp gb/

The symbol 'h' is being used here solely as a phonological indicator that the consonant concerned is a member of the lax set of consonants, which are articulated with markedly less muscular tension than tense consonants, and with typically shorter duration. Consonant harmony operates in the sense

388

that, with a very small number of exceptions, 'in any morpheme consonants from either the tense set or the lax set can occur, but no co-occurrence ... is possible. Consonants from the neutral set can occur in any morpheme with the consonants from either the tense set or the lax set' (Laver 1967: 53).

There are seven monophthongal vowels in Etsako /i e ɛ a ɔ o u/, with phonetically long vowels and phonetic diphthongs all being treated as sequences of two (tone-bearing) single vowels. Examples of words from Etsako obeying the consonant-harmony rules are given in Table 12.4. Instances of words in Etsako with mixed tense and lax consonants, which by violating the consonant-harmony rules thereby show their morphologically compound construction, are: /ùkòkòrhê/ 'to gather' < /úkókô/ 'to collect' + /-rhê/ 'away from original position'; /ùrèkháà/ 'to accompany' < /ùrê/'to use' + /-kháà/ 'together, jointly'; and /ígwóghò/ 'dried stems of elephant grass' < /ígwà/ 'bones' + /òghò/ 'elephant grass'.

Table 12.4 *Consonant harmony in Etsako*

Tense	Lax
/ùmê/ 'camwood, ochre'	/úmhè/ 'salt'
/ ìvì/ 'kernels'	/ívhìlì/ 'boundaries'
/úzò/ 'antelope'	/ùzhò/ 'animal trap'
/ɔ́kà/ 'maize'	/ɔ́khà/ 'tooth'
/àgógô/ 'bell'	/àghòghò/ 'brains'

Source: Based on Laver (1967: 56)

The availability of the option of treating Etsako as showing vowel harmony instead of consonant harmony can be judged from the following description of allophonic interactions (Laver 1967: 55):

> The allophones of /i e o u/ tend to be slightly closer and more peripheral when they occur in tense morphemes, and slightly more open and more central when they occur in lax morphemes. Interconsonantal allophones of all vowels are of longer duration after tense consonants than after lax consonants. Utterance-final allophones tend to be glottalised after tense consonants, and pronounced with breathy voice after lax consonants; utterance-initial allophones before a tense consonant are shorter than before a lax consonant.

Further reading

Docherty (1992) gives an account of co-ordinatory features associated with the production of stops and fricatives. Kohler (1984) considers the concepts of **fortis** and **lenis sounds** from a phonetic and a phonological viewpoint, as does Braun (1988).

Co-articulation is explored by Farnetani (1990), Fowler (1980), Harris (1983), Keating (1990), Kent (1983), Kent and Minifie (1977), Lindblom (1983), Lubker and Gay (1982), Recasens (1984a, 1984b, 1987) and Sharf and Ohde (1981).

Readers interested in modern treatments of **vowel harmony**, especially in the autosegmental tradition, can consult publications by Abu-Salim (1987), Clements (1977, 1981), Goldsmith (1985), Halle and Vergnaud (1981), van der Hulst (1985, 1989), van der Hulst and Smith (1985b, 1987, 1989) and Steriade (1979).

13

Phonetic similarity and multisegmental settings

One of the most basic concepts in phonetics, and one of the least discussed, is that of **phonetic similarity**. An adequate general phonetic theory should permit any two phonetic events to be compared and rated on a scale of relative similarity, within a coherent account of the physiological, acoustic and perceptual ways in which the events are related to each other. Such a theory has not yet been completely developed. No explicit metric exists to date which would allow such a graded comparison to be carried out across the full range of phonetic entities with any great sensitivity of comparison, though the phonetic schemes for the descriptive featural classification of contoids and vocoids do enable a more limited comparison within each of those broad categories.

Part of the reason for the relative inadequacy of current phonetic theory in this area is possibly that, as noted earlier, the concept of phonetic quality itself is not concrete but abstract, and that the nature of this abstraction has not yet been fully explored. In addition, the detailed nature of the relationship between the phonetic and the organic contributions to speech events is still not well understood. Issues of phonetic similarity, though underlying many of the key concepts in phonetics, are hence often left tacit.

13.1   Phonetic similarity and segments

There are two different approaches to the notion of phonetic similarity in speech. The first is the relatively straightforward question of the degree to which any two segments under comparison are similar to each other, at the given level of comparison – articulatory, auditory or acoustic. This question can be addressed in scalar terms, such that one could for instance ask whether [p] is auditorily (say) more similar to [k] than it is to [t]. Equally, it would be hypothetically possible to locate all segment-types in multidimensional auditory space in such a way that a statement could be made of the nearest neighbours of any given segment-type, together with a description of their respective positions and mutual distances. The greater the phonetic similarity between any two segment-types, the greater their proximity in this multidimensional auditory space.

The number of different dimensions one might explore in such a model of auditory space is very large (Boves 1984), with many of them, such as 'bright/dark', 'rough/smooth', or 'clear/dull', being able to be identified only by means of metaphorical labels derived from other sensory modalities. The method to be followed here will use a phonetic model, though it should be noted that metaphorical elements are not completely absent from such a phonetic approach, when it is the auditory domain that is under discussion.

For convenience in the figures that follow, phonetic similarity is presented as its inverse – **phonetic distance**. Figure 13.1 is an initial attempt to give a global suggestion of auditory distance (and hence of acoustic dissimilarity) between segment-types representing the consonantal phonemes of English (RP). It is a simplistic statement, organizing the comparisons in a pair-wise matrix, with the convention that every comparison of distance is judged on a percentage scale, with 0 meaning 'identical' and 100 meaning 'with no

Figure 13.1 Auditory distances between segment-types representing the consonantal phonemes of English (Received Pronunciation)

percentage auditory distance from other segment ⟶

	p	t	k	f	θ	s	ʃ	v	ð	z	ʒ	b	d	g	m	n	ŋ	w	j	ɹ	l	h
p		25	15	65	70	90	95	80	85	95	95	20	55	30	60	70	65	60	70	75	85	85
t			20	85	65	80	85	80	75	90	90	45	20	35	75	65	75	75	70	65	85	85
k				80	85	95	90	85	95	95	85	35	45	20	65	70	55	60	80	90	85	85
f					25	65	70	20	65	70	65	75	85	80	80	85	85	80	95	95	95	65
θ						70	65	35	25	70	65	80	75	85	85	85	90	85	95	95	95	65
s							35	85	80	40	60	95	85	95	95	90	95	95	95	95	95	85
ʃ								80	75	55	45	95	90	95	95	85	95	90	95	95	95	85
v									25	65	30	55	60	65	55	65	65	55	60	60	60	80
ð										60	25	50	45	75	65	65	70	70	70	70	70	80
z											20	85	65	85	85	75	80	85	80	70	90	85
ʒ												80	70	85	85	65	75	80	75	75	90	85
b													30	25	25	65	60	55	85	85	80	95
d														30	60	30	65	80	80	80	75	95
g															55	65	30	50	70	85	70	95
m																20	20	55	75	85	75	90
n																	25	65	75	80	70	90
ŋ																		35	70	85	75	90
w																			30	30	30	85
j																				50	45	85
ɹ																					40	85
l																						85
h																						

hypothesized segments

auditory features in common'. The information in figure 13.1 was developed by the author from subjective auditory impressions (supported by some theoretical assumptions). But it nevertheless has some potential objective usefulness. It is possible, for example, to make use of figure 13.1 as a hypothesized confusion-matrix which predicts the perceptual confusions that human subjects are likely to make when asked to identify segment-types presented as stimuli in perceptual labelling experiments. The smaller the distance between two segments, the greater the proposed phonetic similarity, and the more likely the subjects are to confuse the two segments, particularly when the stimuli are presented under conditions of masking noise, or at low intensities. The claims made about degrees and rankings of intersegmental phonetic similarity in figure 13.1 are thus directly open to experimental test.

Figure 13.1 can also serve as a confusion-matrix for use in the design of automatic speech recognition systems. When these computer-based systems attain a performance which is at all comparable to human performance, then the greatest number of false identifications made should be those of the acoustically nearest neighbours of the true segments. In the design of automatic speech recognition systems which exploit phonetic segments as basic units of recognition, it is hence important that the mistakes made by such systems should not be random, but related in a principled way to the properties of the segments concerned. The relationships of phonetic similarity indicated in figure 13.1 therefore effectively constitute a type of distance measure which can be exploited in the design process of such automatic recognition systems.

An example may make the above point clearer. If a recognition machine hypothesizes the presence of a [p] segment at some point in the stream of speech, then the possibility that the segment concerned is not actually a [p] but is really a [k] is greater, to the degree hypothesized by the values given in figure 13.1, than that it is actually a [t]. This allows the system to say to itself, in effect, 'I think I recognize a [p] here. But I have limited perceptual experience, and I may be wrong. I therefore will also hypothesize, at a slightly lower level of probability, that I am dealing with a [k], and at a slightly lower level of probability yet, with a [t]. I will take these different graded possibilities into account when I come to the stage of looking up in my dictionary the possible words in which these segment-types participate in order to choose the most probable word.'

The distance measure implied by figure 13.1 could help to seed the initial values for the probability gradings of such segment hypotheses in the development of an automatic speech recognition system, though clearly other factors (such as the relative frequency of occurrence of the segment-types in the vocabulary of the application concerned) would also have to play their part. It will be recalled that relative frequency of occurrence was mentioned in section 9.6 as a factor contributing to the response bias of subjects in the experiments reported on perceptual confusions of fricative segments sharing low auditory prominence (i.e. confusions by listeners between the members of a class of confusable and therefore phonetically similar segments).

Figure 13.2 shows the actual values for a confusion-matrix developed from these initial 'seedings' by an automatic speech recognition system built at the Centre for Speech Technology Research at the University of Edinburgh (F. McInnes, personal communication). The system was trained by exposure to a set of 200 sentences of about twenty words each, designed to give representative coverage of the distribution of diphones (effectively two-phoneme sequences) in British English (RP), read by each of four male speakers. The values are expressed in mean negative log probabilities, with large values truncated to 99. The entries in the matrices reflect the probability of confusion of recognition by the system based on the training material described. The results are asymmetric, in that the system's performance is not identical in recognizing [p] as [b] versus [b] as [p], for instance. Compared with the values in figure 13.1, the results for the automatic recognition system are non-linear, in that they are concentrated towards the ends of the scale. But the ranking of the acoustic scores is not too dissimilar to those of the auditory hypotheses. With considerably more exposure to known acoustic training material, the results of the automatic system would probably converge with the performance of human judges to a greater degree.

13.2   Phonetic similarity and settings

The above approach to the topic of phonetic similarity considered a comparison between any two segment-types, arbitrarily chosen. The second approach to phonetic similarity concerns the ways in which the segments of a given stretch of connected speech from a given speaker are phonetically related to each other. The phonetic realizations of the phonemic sequence of that stretch of speech can show gradations of phonetic similarity to each other that make them audibly different from the phonetic realizations of the same string of phonemes said by that speaker on different occasions in different tones of voice, or by a different speaker with a different voice quality. Any tendency towards phonetic similarity in the segmental realizations that make up a given stretch of speech is the basis of what, earlier in this book, has been called a **phonetic setting**.

Segment identity	Scored phoneme																							
	p	t	k	f	θ	s	ʃ	ʧ	v	ð	z	ʒ	ʤ	b	d	g	m	n	ŋ	w	j	r	l	h
p	2	3	3	11	9	13	18	11	15	99	16	19	14	5	10	7	17	18	26	18	58	18	17	15
t	6	2	4	9	8	10	15	10	12	99	11	16	12	9	6	8	16	14	20	16	41	16	14	12
k	4	3	2	9	9	12	15	10	13	99	14	17	13	8	9	6	17	15	23	15	84	16	16	12
f	9	4	6	1	4	8	11	11	9	99	9	17	14	13	9	13	18	17	20	17	30	17	15	10
θ	9	8	9	4	1	6	13	12	25	99	7	17	13	14	19	14	19	25	38	31	99	23	16	14
s	18	7	15	12	6	1	13	10	99	99	4	14	13	20	76	26	65	81	99	66	99	51	29	36
ʃ	17	9	11	11	13	13	1	3	75	99	13	17	8	20	98	22	46	82	99	61	99	64	36	33
ʧ	14	7	9	16	12	10	5	1	99	99	11	18	5	20	5	69	99	24	99	79	99	64	41	55
v	8	6	8	8	10	14	15	15	2	16	11	18	15	8	5	14	10	9	16	12	17	14	10	11
ð	14	8	14	15	13	18	25	25	9	2	15	23	25	13	6	12	18	18	99	62	52	27	9	12
z	16	5	13	11	9	4	13	12	39	99	1	12	12	18	30	14	20	38	51	37	55	33	25	20
ʒ	16	8	8	12	14	10	6	7	18	99	9	2	5	19	13	16	19	19	21	20	49	19	17	17
ʤ	13	6	9	14	13	7	3	5	21	99	10	8	1	16	23	14	19	34	45	23	99	27	25	24
b	4	5	6	13	13	15	19	15	9	99	16	2	15	2	5	6	12	12	18	12	28	17	16	16
d	8	5	8	13	13	15	18	15	8	21	16	7	14	7	2	8	11	9	16	14	19	16	12	13
g	7	6	4	13	13	15	17	13	11	45	15	2	14	7	6	2	12	12	15	14	19	15	15	13
m	13	12	12	18	18	20	21	21	11	20	17	19	19	10	9	10	1	3	9	9	16	12	11	16
n	14	11	13	17	17	19	20	21	11	17	16	19	18	11	6	11	4	1	7	13	16	13	10	15
ŋ	16	13	11	19	19	20	21	22	15	20	20	20	18	14	11	7	5	4	1	13	15	17	14	17
w	14	12	13	17	17	18	20	20	14	62	18	19	20	9	16	15	12	13	18	2	25	12	8	16
j	18	14	14	18	18	19	19	20	17	52	18	19	20	18	15	13	16	13	14	17	2	15	12	15
r	17	15	16	18	18	20	21	19	16	27	19	19	20	17	15	18	18	18	13	13	17	1	14	17
l	16	14	16	18	17	19	19	19	12	9	16	18	18	15	16	16	15	13	17	13	16	13	1	16
h	10	6	7	9	11	14	16	16	12	24	16	17	17	13	10	11	15	13	17	13	16	13	12	1

Figure 13.2 Acoustic distances between segment-types representing the consonantal phonemes of English (Received Pronunciation), as assessed by an automatic speech-recognition system (F. McInnes, personal communication)

A close examination of the segmental make-up of most utterances in the speech of any speaker will reveal different densities of phonetic similarity between the segments concerned, both in the apparent degree of similarity and in the timespan of such relationships. The analysis of such fluctuating concentrations of phonetic similarity in utterances offers a fresh perspective on some particularly important areas in the description of speech. These include the description of linguistically relevant co-ordinatory phenomena such as co-articulation, assimilation and segment harmony, the phonetic specification of paralinguistic communication by tone of voice, and the characterization of individual speakers in terms of the phonetic component of their extralinguistic voice quality. The idea of a setting can be applied to the phonetic analysis of all these areas, from co-articulation to voice quality.

The function of the remainder of this chapter is to develop this notion of a phonetic setting, in the context of analysing phonetic similarity in the linguistic, paralinguistic and extralinguistic domains of speech. The discussion presented here is an extension of the analysis of settings published in Laver (1980, 1991), Laver and Hanson (1981) and Mackenzie Beck (1988). Laver (1980) is accompanied by a cassette recording which illustrates many of the settings discussed in this chapter.

13.2.1   *Definition of a phonetic setting*

A **phonetic setting** can be defined as any co-ordinatory tendency underlying the production of the chain of segments in speech towards maintaining a particular configuration or state of the vocal apparatus. More specifically, a setting consists of one or more featural properties held in common by two or more speech segments in close proximity in the stream of speech. The segments concerned can be regarded as carriers of the setting. Settings themselves are combinable, within physiological limitations. Any two segments displaying the effects of a given setting are by definition to that degree phonetically similar in terms of featural properties, and the greater the number of features shared between the two segments the greater the degree of their phonetic similarity.

13.2.2   *The segmental span of phonetic settings*

In assimilation, the minimum span of a setting extends over two segments, located on each side of a word-boundary. In the case of co-articulation, we have seen that the span of a setting in the chain of speech can range from a minimum of two adjacent segments up to six or seven segments. In segmental harmony, the span covers all the segments within a

396

word, or sometimes within a given morphological part of a word. In paralinguistic communication, the span can extend over a whole utterance pronounced in a particular tone of voice. The maximum possibility for the span of a setting lies in the extralinguistic area, where every single utterance produced by a particular speaker is phonetically coloured to some degree by his or her personal quality. It may be helpful, before going further, to review some brief examples of each of these possibilities.

In **co-articulation**, we can say that a setting finds its expression as an adjustment of the featural properties of one segment towards greater phonetic similarity to those of an adjacent segment within the word involved. It will be recalled that one instance of a co-articulatory (labial) setting is the tendency for [k] in *keep* [kip] in English to be pronounced with spread lips, as an adaptation to the lip-spread quality of the following vocoid. This can be contrasted with the instance of a different co-articulatory (labial) setting shown in the tendency of [kʷ] in *coop* [kʷup] to be pronounced with rounded lips, as an adaptation to the lip-rounded property of the following vocoid.

Comparable adaptive influences exercised across a word-boundary can be seen in **assimilation**. An example cited earlier was the adjustment of the /t/ in the English word *that*, normally realized as an alveolar [t] when pronounced in isolation as [ðat], to a labial [p] in the phrase *that man* pronounced as [ðap man], under the influence of the following labial [m] of *man*. A different example is the adjustment of the /t/ in *that* to a pronunciation as a velar [k] in *that girl* [ðak ɡɜl], under the influence of the following velar [ɡ] of *girl*. We can say that the [-pm-] sequence in *that man* shows a labial assimilatory setting, and the [-kɡ-] sequence in *that girl* shows a velar assimilatory setting.

The previous chapter discussed the role of settings in **segment harmony**, which tend to involve more complex strands of phonetic features being shared across corresponding segments in the successive syllables of a word or other linguistic unit. Similarly, in the phonetic analysis of paralinguistic communication through **tone of voice**, segments throughout a whole utterance are pronounced in such a way as to give the impression of a common featural tendency towards maintaining a particular configuration or state of the vocal apparatus – that is, towards displaying a common setting. An example of this is the case of a speaker maintaining a smiling lip position throughout a particular utterance. Another is the case where a speaker pronounces all the phonetically voiced segments in an utterance with whispery voice, marking the utterance as conspiratorially confidential.

It is in the case of the analysis of extralinguistic **voice quality** that the concept of a phonetic setting perhaps displays its greatest descriptive potential.

The sound of a person's voice was said in the Introduction to be an emblem of the speaker's personal identity. It is part of the general human experience of speech that listeners confidently identify their friends and acquaintances through the familiar consistency of their voices. One basis for such confidence is that the organic foundation of the speaker's vocal anatomy confers a distinctiveness on the voice which, while not approaching the uniqueness of fingerprints, is normally a fairly powerful index of identity. Another element of the identifiability of speakers' voices, however, lies in the fact that all speakers have acquired phonetic habits that confer a recognizably personal style on their production of speech. Part of this personal style lies in the way each speaker chooses to pronounce individual segments. But another part of the style lies in the settings that run through many of the individual segments, giving them a unifying quality that is to some degree particular to the speaker's accent-community, and to some degree idiosyncratic to the speaker.

One speaker might produce a habitually nasal quality of speech, so that vocoids representing vowels are all or mostly nasal rather than oral. Nasality of this sort is typical of very many regional accents, especially of Australian and New Zealand English, of many American accents, and to a smaller degree of British English spoken with an RP accent. Another speaker might adopt a habitually whispery voice as the preferred mode of phonation, so that all segments with phonetic voicing were perceptually coloured by the whispery effect. Whispery voice of this sort tends to act as an idiosyncratic marker of identity, rather than as a marker of membership of some regional or social accent-community. Another could tend to speak with a habitually spread lip position, so that the impression was given that the speaker had a permanent half-smile. This again would usually be a matter of personal style, rather than a marker of membership of some sociolinguistic community.

This last example of a labial setting being used to characterize trends in an individual's articulatory habits offers an opportunity to make an important comment on settings in general. The semiotic function of a setting, as between its potential linguistic, paralinguistic or extralinguistic role, is not dictated by the phonetic identity of the setting. We have seen that labial settings can be used for linguistic purposes, in co-articulation and assimilation, and for paralinguistic communication through tone of voice. We have also just seen an instance of their use for extralinguistic characterization of the speaker through voice quality. It is thus worth emphasis that, from a semiotic point of view, settings are able to fulfil both communicative and informative functions.

The structure of the main part of this chapter will be to consider first the phonetic description of settings of all types and the interactions of settings with segments, and then to explore some of the applications to which the notion of settings can be put.

13.3   The phonetic description of settings

The study of phonetic settings (mostly in their contribution to tone of voice and to voice quality) has had a very long history, from the time of Cicero and Quintilian onwards (Laver 1981). Honikman (1964) was the first to give them the name of 'settings', though Wallis (1653) and Wilkins (1668) described some of them in fair detail over three hundred years ago (Laver 1978). Laver (1980) includes detailed schematic presentations of the anatomy of the vocal apparatus and of the physiology of the muscle systems used for the adjustments which give rise to settings of the apparatus. The acoustic basis of settings has been initially explored by Laver (1980) and in more detail by Esling (1986), Esling and Dickson (1985) and Nolan (1983).

The idea of a setting as a constraining tendency imposing a discernible degree of phonetic similarity on the performance of individual segments is applicable at every level of phonetic analysis. Within the framework offered in this book, the following groups of settings will be considered: articulatory settings, phonatory settings, settings of overall muscular tension and prosodic settings. Their discussion will be prefaced by some comments on issues general to all four major groupings.

First, the notion of a **neutral reference setting**, as a baseline from which to measure deviation, is central to the ideas advanced in this chapter. Each group of settings can be related to its own neutral reference setting. The collected neutral reference settings will be described together in the next section.

Second, settings can be conceived in terms of one or more representative values of the trends underlying momentary segmental excursions. Relevant values are the **mean**, the **range** and the **variability** of the features concerned. The notion of a mean value is useful for all groups of settings, though the actual terms used to label any deviations from the mean will necessarily vary with the type of setting concerned. The idea of a range (from **narrow range** through neutral range to **wide range**) is most useful for application to prosodic settings of pitch and loudness, though it is also relevant to instances of different widths of excursion of articulatory movements. The concept of variability of a setting (from **low variability** through neutral variability to **high variability**) is probably most useful in the prosodic area, though it could also be applied to cases of articulatory and phonatory inconsistency.

Third, if a higher degree of resolution is needed for any descriptive purpose, then any deviation from neutral can be allocated some value in terms of three scalar degrees. 1 stands for a **slight** degree of deviation from neutral, 2 for a **moderate** degree, 3 for an **extreme** degree. The third scalar degree represents the limit of normal variation of settings in a sociolinguistic, accent-characterizing function. It would be necessary to create an extension of this scale when applications in speech pathology are considered, where more abnormal speech behaviour is sometimes encountered.

An illustration of these scalar degrees within the normal sociolinguistic range is that of a deviation from the neutral lip position in the case of a lip-rounded setting characterizing a speaker's habitual voice quality. If the articulatory position that the speaker favours during continuous speech is that of a just noticeable degree of lip-rounding, the setting can be described as showing lip-rounding of scalar degree 1. Scalar degree 2 describes open rounding of the same degree as an open back rounded vocoid [ɒ], and scalar degree 3 a habitual posture of open rounding of a degree appropriate for a half-open back rounded vocoid [ɔ]. A greater degree of habitual lip-rounding than scalar degree 3, which would correspond to the rounding of the half-close back rounded vocoid [o], or to that for [u], would have to be considered somewhat unusual.

Fourth, settings differ in the amount of perceptual evidence necessary for their identification. The representative value of some settings can be decided on very limited evidence. An example is the fact and degree of whisperiness in the phonation of a person who speaks with a habitually whispery voice. This can often be identified on the basis of hearing only a few syllables of phonation.

In order to detect a setting in a speaker's voice which exploits an articulatory bias on the shape of the vocoid area, habitually limiting the vocoid articulations to some restricted zone of the vocoid space, a listener would need more evidence, however, than simply a few syllables. An instance of this would be the voice of a speaker who biases all vocoid articulations forwards and upwards towards the hard palate, say, in what we shall later call **palatalized voice**. In order to conclude that this is the case, a listener would have to hear a sufficient number of vocoids to establish that a general trend exists, as a shift in the centre of gravity of the speaker's vocoid area away from the neutral location, which would be the position for the central vocoid [ə]. Figure 13.3 shows two hypothetical vocoid charts illustrating the locations of a set of vocoids for a neutral setting (figure 13.3a) versus a palatalized setting (figure 13.3b).

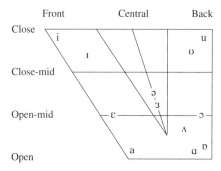

Figure 13.3a Vocoid chart of a set of selected vocoids in English (Received Pronunciation) pronounced with a neutral setting

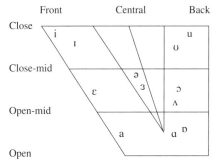

Figure 13.3b Vocoid chart of a set of selected vocoids in English (Received Pronunciation) pronounced with a palatalized setting

The fifth general concept is that of **segmental susceptibility** to the effects of a setting. Some segments are not susceptible to the influence of a setting because of the physiological independence of the muscle systems responsible for their production. The articulatory contribution of the body of the tongue to the production of a segment is relatively unaffected by a lip-rounded setting, for instance – although the overall acoustic effect is of course a composite of the two elements. In some cases, phonological requirements over-ride the potential susceptibility of given segments to the effect of settings which could otherwise change their production – nasality as a setting is not normally allowed to make oral stops into nasal stops, for example. The consequence of allowing the change would be a major loss of linguistic intelligibility.

Some settings have a very pervasive effect on a wide range of susceptible segment-types. Settings which involve the mode of voicing, for example, affect more than half of all segments in English. Settings of the body of the tongue where it might be biased towards taking up a long-term position towards the back wall of the pharynx, for instance, would have an impact on even more segments, affecting all segments made with the tongue as the active articulator.

Some segments are affected more than others by a given setting, in a gradient of susceptibility mostly dependent on the degree of shared muscular anatomy. Some segments will be maximally affected, and these can be considered to be **key segments** for an auditory analysis of settings, where the effect of the setting is most audible. The identification of these key segments will be used as a device for explaining the nature of individual settings in some of the groups discussed in detail below.

Whether the effect of a given setting is major or minor depends on the pervasiveness of its susceptibility relations with individual segments. It now becomes possible to be more precise about the definition of a setting. A setting can be abstracted from the chain of segmental performance in terms of featural properties shared by segments with a common susceptibility. Because segments vary in their susceptibility to the effect of given settings, any individual setting is only intermittently applicable in the stream of speech. This then means that such intermittency does not disqualify a phonetic feature from being the basis of a setting, and a setting does not need to be shared by segments which are necessarily adjacent in the stream of speech, so long as they are in reasonable proximity. Nasality is a good example of a setting which is typically intermittent, able to occur audibly only (in non-pathological speakers) on voiced segments in speech.

The sixth general concept is that settings co-occur, within limits of mutual physiological **compatibility**. The overall voice quality of every speaker is characterized by a constellation of co-occurrent settings (even though in many cases these may show neutral values). It is in this sense that Abercrombie may have intended his description of voice quality as 'those characteristics which are present more or less all the time that a person is talking: it is a quasi-permanent quality running through all the sound that issues from his mouth' (Abercrombie 1967: 91).

13.4 Neutral reference settings

The configuration that represents the neutral setting, by reference to which all other articulatory settings can be described, has already been introduced in chapter 5 as the neutral disposition of the vocal tract. This neutral disposition was described there in the following terms:

> the vocal tract is as nearly as anatomy allows in a posture giving
> equal cross-section to the vocal tract along its full length;

the tongue is in a regularly curved convex shape;
the velum is in a position of closure with the back wall of the
  pharynx, except for phonemically nasal segments;
the lower jaw is held slightly open;
the lips are held slightly open, without rounding or spreading.

Figure 5.12 illustrated this neutral configuration by means of a xeroradiographic picture of a vocal tract in sagittal cross-section, which represented
the vocoid position for [ə], the central unrounded vocoid. This figure is
repeated here as figure 13.4 for convenience.

The concept of a neutral setting can now be extended to that of a constellation of neutral reference settings which can act as the baseline for the
description of articulatory settings, phonatory settings, settings of overall
muscular tension and prosodic settings.

In order for the settings in the speech of a particular speaker to be
describable as neutral in every respect, his or her production of speech must
also show a number of other neutral characteristics:

voicing must show modal phonation;
the average muscular tension throughout the vocal apparatus
  must be moderate;
the prosodic features of pitch and loudness must be set at moderate values for mean, range and variability.

A question is perhaps begged as to what might count as 'moderate' in the

Figure 13.4 The neutral configuration of the vocal tract,
drawn from a xeroradiographic photograph

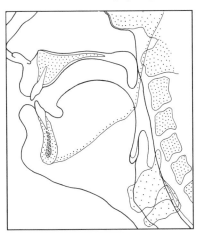

cases of muscular tension and prosodic settings, but it is possible to be a little more precise about some of the details of a neutral articulatory setting and a neutral phonatory setting. In order to satisfy the conditions for a neutral articulatory setting, the following factors should apply to the average articulatory configuration of the segments concerned:

> the length of the vocal tract must not be muscularly distorted, in that the lips must not be protruded, and the larynx must be neither muscularly raised nor lowered;
>
> the vocal tract must not be muscularly distorted at any point, by the action of the lips, the jaw, the tongue or the pharynx, and thereby prevented from approaching an optimally equal-cross-section configuration along its full length.

In order to satisfy the conditions for a neutral phonatory setting, the following factors should apply to the type of voicing characteristically displayed by the segments concerned, in order to produce modal phonation:

> only the true vocal folds must be in vibration;
>
> the vibration of the folds must be regularly periodic, without audible roughness arising from dysperiodicity;
>
> the vibration of the folds must be efficient in air use, without audible friction;
>
> the degree of muscle tension in all phonatory muscle systems must be moderate.

Virtually nobody speaks with a voice which is fully neutral in all categories of settings. Even if we disregard the fact that the presence of any nasal segments, other than ones which are phonemically nasal, will immediately disqualify the voice from fully neutral articulatory status, it seems to be the case that every speaker is characterized by some degree of deviation from one or another neutral setting. In any event, the concept of neutral settings should not be confused with any idea of 'normal' settings.

One reason for this is the way in which the phonology of the speaker's accent distributes the phonetic manifestations of vowels across the dimensions of vocoid space. In this respect, the speaker's articulatory setting is the joint outcome of the location in vocoid space of the different vocoids, and of their frequency of occurrence. These two factors combine to determine the centre of gravity of the speaker's vocoid distribution. Almost no language shows such symmetry of vocoid placements and their frequencies of occurrence such that the net result is a centre of gravity in

Category	Setting	Scalar degrees			
		neutral	1	2	3
Longitudinal	Laryngeal				
	raised larynx				
	lowered larynx				
	Labial				
	labiodentalization				
	labial protrusion				
Cross-sectional	Labial				
	lip-rounded				
	lip-spread				
	Mandibular				
	close jaw				
	open jaw				
	Lingual tip blade				
	advanced tip blade				
	retracted tip blade				
	Lingual body				
	advanced body				
	retracted body				
	raised body				
	lowered body				
	Lingual root				
	advanced root				
	retracted root				
Velopharyngeal	Velic coupling				
	nasal				
	denasal				

Figure 13.5 Protocol for recording scalar degrees of longitudinal, cross-sectional and velopharyngeal settings

vocoid space that falls exactly on the position for [ə], the central unrounded vocoid.

Deviations from the neutral specifications at the articulatory, phonatory, muscle tension or prosodic levels can be specifically labelled, and if necessary given a characterizing scalar degree of deviation from the neutral value. Comment here is confined to those settings that directly affect the quality of speech production. Descriptions of prosodic settings are discussed in chapter

15, where pitch and loudness settings are described in section 15.9. The different labels associated with the different articulatory, phonatory and muscle-tension categories of settings will be presented in the relevant sections below, together with comments about key segments, segmental susceptibility and inter-setting compatibilities. The settings will be described mostly in terms of their applicability to the segmental performance of English.

The presentation of the different types of settings directly influencing phonetic quality will be related to the categories of the overall protocol shown in figure 13.5. This protocol allows a written record to be made of the three groups of settings in any non-pathological voice, including an indication of the scalar degree of any non-neutral setting. Providing a written annotation of settings in this way gives the analyst a characterizing **vocal profile** of the voice of the speaker concerned. Conventions for transcribing settings will be described in section 13.9 after the presentation of the settings.

13.5   Articulatory settings

Deviations from the neutral reference setting at the articulatory level can be categorized in three groups, shown in figure 13.5. These are longitudinal settings, cross-sectional settings and velopharyngeal settings. They will partly be presented in the same general terminology as employed to describe secondary articulations, since the effect of a setting, from the point of view of segmental description, is usually that of a secondary, modifying influence.

13.5.1   *Longitudinal settings*

Longitudinal settings concern deviations from the requirement that the length of the vocal tract must remain undistorted by muscular bias on segmental articulations. The vocal tract can be shortened, either by the larynx being pulled upwards, or by the bottom lip being pulled inwards in the process of labiodentalization.The vocal tract can be lengthened by muscular adjustment, either by the larynx being pulled downwards, or by the lips being protruded. Comment can be made first on changes of larynx position, then on labial factors.

A **raised larynx setting** is achieved by muscular adjustments that also partly serve the function of raising the pitch of the voice. The higher level of mean pitch typically heard in raised larynx settings is also often associated with an increase in settings of overall muscular tension.

A **lowered larynx setting**, conversely, is achieved by muscular adjustments which can also partly serve the function of lowering the pitch of the voice. The impression of a somewhat sepulchral quality that is produced by the lengthened vocal tract in lowered larynx voice is reinforced by this lower average pitch.

The decrease in length of the vocal tract effected by a **labiodentalized setting** is minimal, though audible. It normally involves retraction of the lower lip to the point where it comes into contact with the outer surfaces of the lower teeth, and approximation towards the biting edge of the upper teeth. The element of retraction affects the longitudinal axis of the vocal tract, and the element of approximation towards the upper teeth affects the cross-sectional axis. Both elements will be described in this section.

There are two main consequences of a labiodentalized setting for key contoid segments. The first is that, with an increasing scalar degree of labiodentalization, the onsets and offsets of what would otherwise be simple labial stops tend to become double stops, with a joint labial–labiodental closure. At abnormal degrees of labiodentalized settings beyond scalar degree 3, these become single labiodental stops. The second consequence is that the apparent 'pitch' of the friction audible during the production of the alveolar fricatives [s] and [z] is lowered progressively with the scalar degree of the labiodentalized setting, as the intrusion of the lower lip into the escape of the egressive jet of air beyond the alveolar constriction becomes more extreme.

Labial protrusion is very often accompanied by a lip-rounded setting. Key segments and segmental susceptibility conditions for labial protrusion will be presented in the discussion of lip-rounding below. Occasionally, labial protrusion without rounding occurs, especially when the speaker concerned is also characterized by a protruded jaw setting.

13.5.2   *Cross-sectional settings*

Cross-sectional settings concern deviations from the requirement that the vocal tract must not be subjected to any habitual articulatory constriction (or expansion) which prevents it from maintaining a neutral long-term configuration. Deviations of this sort can be imposed by labial, mandibular, lingual or pharyngeal action, and the different articulatory settings in this cross-sectional group can be classified on this basis.

13.5.2.1   *Labial settings*

The neutral labial setting requires the lips to be held slightly open, without rounding or spreading. Deviations from this long-term configuration gives rise to two main settings – a **lip-rounded setting** and a **lip-spread setting**. Although lip-rounding can be physiologically achieved without labial protrusion, this seems to be seldom used as a setting, and the comments on the lip-rounded setting will assume that a component of protrusion is included.

Scalar degrees for lip-rounding have been described above: scalar degree 1 is defined as just noticeable rounding; scalar degree 2 corresponds to a setting configuration comparable to the open rounding for an open back rounded vocoid [ɒ]; scalar degree 3 to that for [ɔ]. Key segments for a lip-rounding setting at scalar degree 3 for English include /i/. Because the labial component of the pronunciation of vowels such as /i/ is not mandated by phonological requirements in English, in that lip-rounding on vocoids is not distinctive, the rounded effect of the setting tends to over-ride the lip-spreading more normally seen on this segment in other speakers. The result for this key segment therefore tends to be an under-rounded close front vocoid. Other key segments include [s] and [z], in which the apparent 'pitch' of the friction sounds lower when accompanied by lip-rounding than by lip-spreading.

It is physically possible to produce a lip-spread setting with labial protrusion. But this is very unusual, and it will be assumed here that a lip-spread setting does not typically involve labial protrusion. Scalar degrees for a lip-spread setting are as follows: scalar degree 1 is defined as just noticeable spreading; scalar degree 2 is comparable to the labial position for [e]; and scalar degree 3 to that for [i]. Key segments for a lip-spreading setting in English include those contoid segments where rounding is non-distinctive but otherwise often present, in the pronunciation of /r/, /ʃ/, /ʒ/, /tʃ/ and /dʒ/. Other key segments include [s] and [z], in which the 'pitch' of the friction sounds higher when accompanied by lip-spreading than by lip-rounding.

All segments are susceptible to the effects of labial settings. In the case of stop segments only, audible susceptibility is limited to the onset and offset phases of the stops. Labial settings are also compatible with normal degrees of all other types of settings, because of the physiological independence of the labial musculature from that underlying all other setting mechanisms. The one partial exception to this is the case of mandibular settings, where more extreme degrees of adjustment of the jaw begin to constrain the setting possibilities of labial adjustments.

13.5.2.2   *Mandibular settings*

The neutral setting for the jaw specifies that its long-term position should be one where it is held slightly open. This can be interpreted to mean that a small vertical gap should be just visible between the biting surfaces of the upper and lower teeth.

There is an asymmetry of adjustment in **close jaw settings** versus **open jaw settings**. In scalar degree 1 of a close jaw setting, the vertical gap between upper and lower teeth just disappears; in scalar degree 2 it closes a little more; and in scalar degree 3 a little more. A position with clenched teeth constitutes an abnormal degree of adjustment, though this is seen not too uncommonly, especially in individual speakers with unusual patterns of dentition. In settings with an open jaw, the intervals between the different scalar degrees have greater steps.

Given that the jaw is anatomically the carrier of the tongue and the lower lip, extreme adjustments of the jaw normally entail compensatory action by these other articulators if intelligibility is not to be endangered. A wide open jaw position thus typically entails rather large vertical articulatory movements of the tongue and lower lip. Key segments for an open jaw setting at scalar degree 3 show these compensatory actions. Instances are the diphthongs [aɪ] and [aʊ], which either show compensatory extensive vertical travel, or fail to reach the usual articulatory end-point targets. Equally, an expansion of the vertical dimension of the vocoid space tends to occur. Conversely, a close jaw position usually results in key segments such as these diphthongs showing minimized articulatory travel, together with a general reduction of the vertical axis of the vocoid space.

Other possibilities for mandibular adjustments exist, in other planes of movement than the vertical. Some individuals are characterized by lateral adjustments of the jaw to one side. In others, the jaw may be either protruded or retracted from its neutral position. Such adjustments are idiosyncratic only, and with the possible exception of slight adjustments of mandibular protrusion, do not seem to participate in settings which typify accent-communities. They do, however, figure to some extent in the range of conventional paralinguistic signals of attitude. Jaw protrusion, in the conventions of paralinguistic communication of many cultures, has a well-understood connotation of symbolic aggression, for instance.

13.5.2.3 *Lingual settings*

Lingual settings can be descriptively divided into three subgroups: settings of the tip/blade system; settings of the body of the tongue; and settings of the root of the tongue.

The neutral requirement for **tip/blade settings** is that relevant articulations should be performed by the active articulator that lies neutrally opposite the corresponding passive articulator. In this interpretation, dental segments should be performed by the tip of the tongue against or near the inner surfaces of the upper teeth, and alveolar segments by the blade articulating against or near the alveolar ridge. Deviations from this give rise to advanced versus retracted tip/blade settings.

In an **advanced tip/blade setting**, key susceptible segments such as [θ] and [ð] are made interdental rather than dental, in that the tip protrudes between the teeth, and the passive articulator is the biting edge rather than the inner surface of the upper teeth. Similarly, the blade of the tongue articulates /t, d, n, l/, and sometimes /s/ and /z/, at the denti-alveolar or dental place of articulation.

In a **retracted tip/blade setting**, [θ] and [ð] are made denti-alveolar rather than dental by the action of the tip of the tongue, and the pronunciations of /t, d, n, l/, and sometimes /s/ and /z/, are articulated at the post-alveolar place of articulation by the action of the blade of the tongue.

The neutral requirement for **tongue-body settings** is that its long-term position should correspond to that for the central vocoid [ə], in which the surface of the tongue body is convex and regularly curved, with the vocal tract as nearly as anatomy allows in equal cross-section along its full length. A great advantage of this specification of the neutral configuration is that, at an acoustic level of description, if the vocal tract is regarded as a tube of standard cross-section, then the ratio of the resonant frequencies (the formants) is such that the frequency of each successive formant is an odd multiple of that of the lowest formant (Fant 1960). For a vocal tract of 17.5 cm in length, this will give formant frequency values as follows: formant 1 = 500 Hz, formant 2 = 1500 Hz, formant 3 = 2500 Hz, and so on. This standard formant-ratio approach to the acoustic specification of the neutral setting means that an objective metric for comparing neutral settings in two speakers exists. This is true at least for adult male speakers. Female speakers and children tend to have vocal tracts in which the proportion of pharynx length to mouth length is different from that of typical males, such that direct comparability is made more complex (Fant 1973).

Taking the highest point of the tongue body as a point of location, settings of the body of the tongue can be described in terms of the movement of the long-term average position of this point away from its location in the neutral setting. This can be done in two dimensions, vertical and horizontal, so that the body of the tongue can show a fronted or a backed setting, or a raised or a lowered setting. All these will result in a manipulation of the vocoid space, as well as constraining the place of articulation of contoid segments for which the body of the tongue acts as an active articulator.

An **advanced tongue-body setting** compresses the vocoid space towards the front of the mouth, and results in fronting of the place of articulation of susceptible contoids such as [k], [g], [ŋ], [ɫ], [ɹ], [w], [j], [ʃ], [ʒ], [tʃ], [dʒ], [n], [s] and

[z]. Conversely, a **retracted tongue-body setting** compresses the vocoid space towards the pharynx, and results in retraction of the place of articulation of the same susceptible contoids. Raised and lowered tongue-body settings do not directly affect the place of articulation of the contoid segments mentioned above, but a **raised tongue-body setting** compresses the vocoid space towards the palate, and a **lowered tongue-body setting** expands the vocoid space downwards.

Tongue-body settings frequently co-occur with each other. A combination of advanced and raised tongue-body settings compresses the vocoid space towards the hard palate; a lowered and retracted tongue-body setting combination compresses the location of vocoids towards the back and open part of the vocoid space. The first can be called a **palatalized voice**, and the second a **pharyngealized voice**. These two combinations are the most common, but the other logical possibilities are also found. The combination of a raised with a retracted setting compresses the vocoid space towards the soft palate, and can be called a **velarized voice**. It is a major component of the Liverpool and Birmingham accents in Britain, of the Bronx accent in New York, and of some types of Houston accents in Texas (Esling and Dickson 1985).

One possibility of constricting the pharynx has just been mentioned, where the body of the tongue is retracted into the pharynx. This constricts the pharynx at a mid-pharynx level. The pharynx can also be constricted at a lower level, by adjustments of the root of the tongue. A **tongue-root retracted setting** is sometimes used in phonological contrast to a **tongue-root advanced setting** which expands the volume of the lower pharynx, in segmental harmony in languages such as Twi (Akan), spoken in Ghana (Lindau 1979: 176). Impressionistically, a setting which involves an advanced tongue root tends to sound rather 'hollow', whereas one with a retracted tongue root sounds rather 'muffled'.

Any setting of the body of the tongue will tend to affect the settings of the other sub-parts of the tongue, namely the tip/blade sub-system and the tongue-root sub-system. This interaction is not confined to simple, unidirectional mechanical constraints, however. It is not uncommon for the body of the tongue to be retracted and slightly raised towards the uvular location, with a simultaneous resistance to a retracted tip/blade setting. The mechanical consequence of this is, however, that the surface of the front of the tongue tends to be lowered by the antagonistic action of these two opposing constraints. In Algerian Arabic, the phonological process of 'emphasis' referred to earlier is manifested by either secondary pharyngealization or secondary uvularization. When this is applied to dental segments, they nevertheless seem to maintain their dental place of articulation, but with a lowering and retracting of associated vocoid segments. This is illustrated in the following pairs of words (Z. Chebchoub, personal communication):

Pharyngealization in Algerian Arabic

/siːn/ ⇒ [sɪːn̪] 'name of   /siːn/ ⇒ [seːn̪ˤ] 'China'
the letter "s" '

/brɪt̪/ ⇒ [brːt̪] 'a house'   /brːt̪/ ⇒ [beːt̪ˤ] 'eggs'

/taːt̪a/ ⇒ [tɛːt̪ˤæ] 'a spider'

13.5.2.4   *Pharyngeal settings*

A final possibility for settings involving pharyngeal constriction arises from sphincteric constriction of the pharynx by the muscles that surround the pharynx itself. These are U-shaped muscles, with their arms running forwards from the back of the pharynx to insert in the sides of the root and body of the tongue. When they contract, they constrict the aperture of the pharynx, and unless opposed tend to pull the body and root of the tongue backwards. Pharyngeal constriction of this sphincteric sort seems often accompanied by a setting of increased overall muscular tension. Impressionistically, constrictive and muscularly tense action of this sort gives the voice a tense, 'strangulated' quality.

Pharyngealized voice can thus be achieved by three partly different means: retraction of the body of the tongue to compress the mid-pharynx region; retraction of the root of the tongue, constricting the lower pharyngeal region; or sphincteric constriction of part of the pharynx involving both the body and the root of the tongue. In all three types, a major result is to compress the vocoid space towards the pharynx, because the mass of the tongue is drawn backwards in all cases. As a practical convention, therefore, all settings involving pharyngealization are attributed to retraction of either the body or the root of the tongue, or both; there is hence no separate category of 'pharyngeal' settings in figure 13.5 separate from the lingual category.

13.5.3   *Velopharyngeal settings*

The neutral requirement for velopharyngeal settings is that the velum should lie against the back wall of the nasopharynx, closing the entry to the nasal cavity, for all segments except those for which nasality is a phonologically contrastive requirement. This implies that a voice showing a neutral velopharyngeal setting will display the physiologically minimum possible anticipatory nasality on vocoids before nasal contoids. In this respect, French is closer to a neutral value than English, in that the typical onset of

412

anticipatory nasality in vocoids before nasal contoids is later than in all native accents of English. To the extent that English shows a greater amount of anticipatory nasality than the neutral requirement, all native accents of English would have to be classified as showing a nasal setting to some degree.

There are two non-neutral velopharyngeal settings. The first is a nasal setting, and the second is a denasal setting. A **nasal setting** shows more than the physiological minimum of nasality on some susceptible segments. Since all segment-types are susceptible to nasality, with the sole exception of stops whose primary place of articulation is below the level of the velum, such as a glottal stop, scalar degrees of nasality can be assessed in terms of the number of segment-types made with a nasal aspect of articulation by the speaker concerned.

A nasal setting at scalar degree 1 shows nasality only on those segments where there is a contextual justification for the nasality in co-articulatory terms. Such segments either anticipate the phonologically distinctive nasality of the immediately following segment, or perseverate that of the preceding segment. If, in addition to contextually determined nasality, the speaker shows nasality on open vocoids without contextual motivation, then this can be regarded as an instance of nasality at scalar degree 2. RP accents of British English often demonstrate nasality at scalar degree 2. Nasality without contrastive or contextual motivation occurring on close vocoids and/or on contoids, can be classified as an instance of a nasal setting at scalar degree 3. Accents of English spoken in Australia and New Zealand sometimes show a nasal setting at this scalar degree.

A **denasal setting** of the velopharyngeal system is one where the audible nasality which normally characterizes contrastively nasal segments in the language concerned is absent, such that these nasal segments are made oral, mimicking the organic conditions brought about by a cold in the head. By definition, a denasal setting can only exist in relation to listeners' expectations about due nasality. In this regard, it is conceivable that a given utterance might be heard in two quite different ways by a listener, depending on the expectations brought to its perception. An English utterance which could be transcribed phonetically as [bad] might be taken to represent either /bad/ or /man/, depending on the assumptions about nasality or denasality brought to bear by the listener. Denasality is, however, a more complex phenomenon than this brief description suggests, and a slightly more extended discussion can be found in Laver (1980: 88–92). It is probably not profitable to suggest criteria for different scalar degrees of denasality, and judgements can simply be made about presence versus absence of this setting.

413

13.6 Phonatory settings

The neutral phonatory setting in this framework is that of modal voicing, showing regular, efficient vibration of the true vocal folds, without audible friction. Any departure from these long-term conditions constitutes a non-neutral phonatory setting. Figure 13.6 shows the options for the annotation of the different phonatory settings involving modal voice, falsetto, creak or whisper. The phonetic description of how these modes of phonation are produced was given in chapter 7 above. Figure 13.7 repeats figure 7.7 from that chapter, to show the physiological compatibilities between the different phonation types involved. Susceptible segments for the phonatory settings included here are all segments which carry the phonetic feature of voicing.

Falsetto and modal voice show no scalar degree gradations on the protocol. This is because they should be regarded as simply present or absent, rather than graded. Since they are mutually incompatible modes of phonation, falsetto and voice cannot co-occur. But either can be modified by the presence of various degrees of whisperiness or creakiness. Whisper and creak can also occur by themselves, or can modify each other.

When whisper or creak combine in a compound phonatory setting, with either voice or falsetto, or with each other, conventions for judging the different scalar degrees of the components are based on the relative perceptual prominence of the ingredients involved. When any compound phonation includes whisperiness, then scalar degree 1 can be used to indicate a just noticeable presence of whisperiness. Scalar degree 2 is used when whisperiness is confidently audible, but where the vibratory component is still perceptually dominant. Scalar degree 3 can be used when it is judged that the whispery component and the vibratory component are of equal perceptual prominence. A voice in which the whispery component perceptually dominates the vibratory component can reasonably be judged to be somewhat

Figure 13.6 Protocol for recording scalar degrees of phonatory settings

Category	Setting	Scalar degrees				
		neutral	non neutral			
Phonatory	modal voice					
	falsetto					
				1	2	3
	creak(y)					
	whisper(y)					

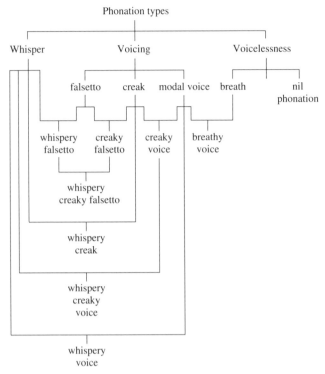

Figure 13.7 Some constraints on the combinability
of different modes of phonation

abnormal. The same conventions can be followed for marking the relative
contribution of creakiness in compound phonatory settings.

A phonatory setting of whispery voice is very common indeed as a personal characteristic, particularly among older speakers, and whispery creak
or whispery creaky voice is not uncommon among older males. In many
cases, the whispery component may not be strongly prominent, but in a
recent perceptual study of over 200 normal adult speakers of both sexes conducted by the author and colleagues at the University of Edinburgh, less
than 5 per cent of speakers were judged to be without at least some slight
degree of audible whisperiness in their habitual phonatory setting.

13.7   Settings of articulatory range

        The range of articulatory movements can be divided into three
types of settings, depending on the articulators involved – settings of labial
range, mandibular range and lingual range. A narrow range of labial arti-

culations minimizes the extent of the visible excursions of the lips from a neutral position. A wide range of labial articulations shows substantial excursions of movement from the neutral position, with the outer surfaces of the upper and lower teeth frequently visible. Most speakers of Received Pronunciation of British English show a slightly narrow range of labial articulation. By contrast, many French speakers use a slightly wide range of labial articulation.

A narrow range of mandibular articulation shows a restricted amount of movement of the lower jaw away from the neutral position, with the upper and lower jaw seldom separating enough to allow the tongue to be visible. A wide range of mandibular articulation is characterized by substantial vertical movements of the lower jaw, with the mouth often opening sufficiently on open vocoids to allow the surface of the tip, blade and front of the tongue to be seen. Received Pronunciation tends to be spoken with a slightly narrow range of mandibular movement, while French typically exploits a wider range.

The range-setting of lingual movements is most evident in the performance of the vocoid segments, in terms of the distribution within vocoid space of the actual vocoid articulations performed by the speaker. In a narrow range-setting, the location of vocoids clusters in a relatively restricted space around the centre of the vocoid chart. In a wide range-setting, the body of the tongue moves within a substantially larger area of the vocoid chart, with radial excursions reaching out towards the periphery. Received Pronunciation tends to use a slightly narrow range of lingual articulation, while many accents of Scots English use a wider range. Similarly, French is typically spoken with a wider range of lingual articulation than Received Pronunciation.

Range settings of labial, mandibular and lingual articulation are presented in figure 13.8. For practical purposes outside speech pathology, it is probably necessary only to distinguish gross differences of articulatory range, and divisions into scalar degrees beyond merely 'non-neutral' are therefore omitted.

13.8   Settings of overall muscular tension

Settings have so far been described largely as if it were possible for the speaker to manipulate them in isolation from each other. In fact this is seldom the case, with strong interdependence between settings being the norm rather than the exception. The discussion of the next group of settings takes a more global view of the interdependence of settings, and considers the constellation of co-occurring settings that result from overall adjust-

Category	Setting	Scalar degrees	
		neutral	non neutral
Articulatory range	Labial		
	narrow range		
	wide range		
	Mandibular		
	narrow range		
	wide range		
	Lingual		
	narrow range		
	wide range		

Figure 13.8 Protocol for recording scalar degrees of ranges of labial, mandibular and lingual articulatory settings

ments of the degree of muscular tension exercised throughout the vocal apparatus. Seen globally, such overall adjustments would have repercussions at every level of performance from the respiratory level through to the articulatory level. Comment here will focus on two major sub-sets of such adjustments, at the supralaryngeal and laryngeal levels.

13.8.1   *Overall tension modifications of supralaryngeal articulation*

The neutral requirement for overall muscular tension was said earlier to be that a moderate degree of tension should characterize the long-term articulatory adjustment of the vocal apparatus. The effects on segmental performance of increasing or decreasing the degree of muscular tension from this neutral specification are reflected in the comments of many authors on the topic of **lax** versus **tense** segments. **Lax vocoid** segments are said to involve a smaller degree of deformation of the vocal tract from the position for [ə], the central unrounded vocoid, than is the case for **tense vocoid** segments. In general, radial articulatory movements of the body of the tongue are said to be less extensive in lax voice than in tense voice. Correspondingly, lax segments are said to be shorter in duration, to be produced with less articulatory effort and less sub-glottal air pressure, than tense segments (Jakobson and Halle 1964: 97–100). They are also said to be characterized by greater acoustic attenuation, resulting from greater absorption of acoustic energy by the muscularly more lax walls of the vocal tract.

It is clear from these descriptions that one salient attribute of the performance of lax and tense segments is their susceptibility to narrow and wide settings of the range of lingual articulation. But range of lingual articulation

417

is not the only typical attribute of lax and tense segmental performance. Since laxness and tenseness in the definitions adopted here are a matter of overall muscular tension, range-settings throughout the supralaryngeal vocal tract are likely to be involved. Lax segments are therefore likely to participate not only in a narrow range of lingual articulation, but also in narrow ranges of labial and mandibular articulation. Conversely, tense segments are likely to be associated with wide ranges of labial, mandibular and lingual articulation. Echoing the comments mentioned in the previous section on instances of languages showing different range-settings of articulatory action, we can also say that Received Pronunciation typically shows a slight degree of lax voice and French a slight degree of tense voice.

The link between overall muscular-tension settings and range-settings is, however, typical rather than obligatory. It is also possible, for example, to produce speech under conditions of high but antagonistic muscular tension which is characterized by narrow labial, mandibular and lingual articulatory ranges.

Tense and lax settings of overall muscular tension in the supralaryngeal part of the vocal apparatus are able to be perceptually differentiated only in a fairly gross way. Comment can therefore be confined, in non-pathological cases, to a three-way choice between lax, neutral or tense settings, without further specification of scalar degrees. Supralaryngeal settings of muscular tension are included in figure 13.9.

13.8.2   *Overall tension modifications of phonation*

Taking the production of modal voicing as neutral on a scale of muscular tension, progressive relaxation or tensing of the laryngeal system results in audible changes in the quality of phonation. Two types of phonation need to be discussed at this point to account for such adjustments of laryngeal tension, over and above the presentation in chapter 7 on phonation, namely breathy voice and harsh voice.

When the whole laryngeal musculature is substantially more relaxed than in modal voicing, in a **lax setting**, then the result is for the vibrating vocal folds not to be brought very close together, and at maximum constriction the glottis is left somewhat open. If the gap left between the folds is small, as it is if the degree of relaxation is not excessive, then slightly **whispery voice** will be the result. If the gap is larger, as it is in conditions of more extreme relaxation, then provided the transglottal pulmonic airflow is copious enough, a mode of phonation which can be called **breathy voice** occurs. This type of phonation is a very inefficient use of air, with the folds 'flapping in the breeze', as it were. Catford (1977a: 99) gives the figures of 900–1000 cc/s for the range of airflow. Flow-rates at the top end of this range are

Category	Setting	Scalar degrees			
		neutral	1	2	3
Supralaryngeal tension	tense				
	lax				
Laryngeal tension	tense				
	slightly harsh				
	moderately harsh				
	lax				
	slightly breathy				
	moderately breathy				

Figure 13.9 Protocol for recording scalar degrees of supralaryngeal and laryngeal settings of overall muscular tension

produced in the breathy voice that results from speaking while sighing. Flow-rates towards the lower end of the range characterize the paralinguistic use of breathy voice in English, and in many other cultures, as a phonatory setting signalling intimacy.

Scalar degree 1 of a lax laryngeal tension setting is appropriate when whispery voice is the consequence of the muscular relaxation. Scalar degree 2 can be used when the phonation type becomes noticeably breathy, but where the voicing component is still perceptually dominant over the breathy component. Scalar degree 3 applies when the breathy component and the voicing component are of equal perceptual prominence. Perceptual dominance of the breathy component over the voicing component, where longer utterances cannot be sustained because the reservoir of pulmonic air is too rapidly exhausted, can be regarded as somewhat abnormal.

When the muscle tension of the laryngeal system is progressively boosted beyond the limits for normal voicing, as part of a **tense setting**, the result is first for the glottal aperture to be reduced in length, with the arytenoid cartilages pressed tightly together along their full horizontal extent, and for the upper larynx to begin to be constricted, giving what Catford (1977a: 103) calls 'anterior voice'. This he says impressionistically has a 'tight', 'hard' quality, and is characteristic of many North German speakers, and of some accents of Northeast Scotland, particularly Aberdeenshire and Banff (Catford, *ibid.*). It also seems to be used as a language-characterizing setting in Tamil, a Dravidian language of South India and Sri Lanka. Impressionistically, a tense setting of this sort lends a 'metallic' auditory quality to the voice.

When the whole larynx is subjected to extreme hypertension, the upper larynx becomes severely constricted, with the ventricular folds pressing down from above on the upper surfaces of the true vocal folds, making their vibration very inefficient. This hypertense inefficiency is reflected in the voice acquiring an audibly rough quality that is often called **harsh voice** (Laver 1980: 126–32). Harsh voice is used paralinguistically as a setting in English, and perhaps in all cultures, as a signal of anger and aggression, and is usually accompanied by heightened pitch and loudness.

Scalar degree 1 of a tense laryngeal tension setting is appropriate when a 'tight' phonatory quality of the sort described by Catford is the consequence of the increased muscular tension. Scalar degree 2 can be used when the phonation type becomes just noticeably harsh, but where the voicing component is still perceptually dominant over the harsh component. Scalar degree 3 applies when the harsh component and the voicing component are of equal perceptual prominence. Perceptual dominance of the harsh component over the voicing component can be regarded as abnormal. Such dominance can arise from extreme hypertension of the muscles responsible for adducting the vocal folds. This abuses the delicate tissues of the vocal-fold surfaces, and if habitual (shouting in a permanently noisy work environment, for instance) can lead to the development of vocal pathology such as nodules and polyps on the fold surfaces. The presence of these growths further perturbs the regularity of vocal-fold vibration, and exacerbates the auditory quality of harshness to a yet more extreme level.

Extremes of laryngeal tension are not used linguistically, so the concepts of breathy voice and harsh voice are not needed for linguistic description, though they are useful for both paralinguistic and extralinguistic purposes. It is true that many authors use the term 'breathy voice' in linguistic discussion, but the entity to which they are referring is more likely to be whispery voice, in the terms offered here, than breathy voice as defined above. Settings of laryngeal tension are included in figure 13.9.

13.9   Summary transcription conventions

There are two main methods of transcribing the effects of settings on segments. The first is simply to allow the phonetic similarities involved to be shown directly by the symbols and diacritics chosen for the segmental representation. It can be inferred from such a segmental transcription, for instance, that a nasal setting is running through susceptible vocoid segments of the following English phrase:

Orthographic version	An Englishman's home is his castle
Segmental transcription	[ə̃n ĩŋglĩʃmə̃nz h̃õm ĩz h ĩz kã̃sl̩]

The second method is more economical, but its interpretation puts a greater responsibility on the shoulders of the reader. This is the method where the identification of the setting is abstracted from the symbolization of the susceptible vocoid segments, and is written as a separate symbol, prefacing the segmental transcription (Laver 1980). Its applicability to susceptible segments is then tacit, and the writer relies on the reader's memory for the phonetic conventions specifying the relationship between settings and susceptible (and non-susceptible) segments. An example of this method of separate symbolization of the setting component, introduced as an extension to IPA conventions in 1989 and using the generic symbol V as the carrier for the setting within a pair of curly braces, is as follows:

> *Orthographic version*   An Englishman's home is his castle
> *Setting transcription*   [{Ṽ ən ɪŋglɪʃmənz həʊm ɪz hɪz kɑsl̩}]

A small degree of resolution is potentially lost by this method of using prefacing symbols. For example, had the nasality setting been applicable at scalar degree 3, then only [ɑ̃] would have been nasal amongst all the vocoids which were not followed by nasal segments, and [ɪ] as a non-open vocoid would not have been nasal, in that nasality at scalar degree 3 applies in non-nasal-neighbour contexts only to open vocoids. Such details would have been lost in the generalization indicated by the prefacing setting symbol that 'all susceptible segments are nasal'. This disadvantage can be overcome by including a scalar-degree value with the prefacing symbol, as in the following setting transcription (with the implied segmental transcription indicated below):

> *Orthographic version*   An Englishman's home is his castle
> *Setting transcription*   [{Ṽ3 ən ɪŋglɪʃmənz həʊm ɪz hɪz kɑsl̩}]
> *Segmental transcription*   [ə̃n ĩŋglɪʃmə̃nz hə̃ʊ̃m ɪz hɪz kɑ̃sl̩]

This second method (of prefacing the transcription with a setting symbol and a scalar-degree value) remains more legible than the segmental transcription method. Some extensions of the second method are given below.

Multiple settings can be indicated on a single utterance. For instance, if the above phrase showed not only nasality but also whispery voice, the transcription (without scalar degrees indicated) would be as follows:

> *Orthographic version*   An Englishman's home is his castle
> *Setting transcription*   [{Ṽ̬ ən ɪŋglɪʃmənz həʊm ɪz hɪz kɑsl̩]}

If scalar degrees of multiple different settings need to be indicated, then separate prefacing symbols could be used, as below:

421

Category	Setting	Scalar degrees			
		neutral	1	2	3
Longitudinal	Laryngeal				
	raised larynx				
	lowered larynx				
	Labial				
	labiodentalization				
	labial protrusion				
	Labial				
	lip-rounded				
	lip-spread				
	Mandibular				
	close jaw				
	open jaw				
Cross-sectional	Lingual tip blade				
	advanced tip blade				
	retracted tip blade				
	Lingual body				
	advanced body				
	retracted body				
	raised body				
	lowered body				
	Lingual root				
	advanced root				
	retracted root				
Velopharyngeal	Velic coupling				
	nasal				
	denasal				

Category	Setting	Scalar degrees			
		neutral	1	2	3
Supralaryngeal tension	tense				
	lax				
Laryngeal tension	tense				
	slightly harsh				
	moderately harsh				
	lax				
	slightly breathy				
	moderately breathy				

Category	Setting	Scalar degrees			
		neutral	non neutral	1	2	3
Phonatory	modal voice					
	falsetto					
	creak(y)					
	whisper(y)					

Figure 13.10 Summary protocol for recording the scalar degrees of settings of articulation, phonation and overall muscular tension in any non-pathological speaker as a vocal profile

Orthographic version	An Englishman's home is his castle
Setting transcription	[{Ṽ3 V̱2 ən ɪŋɡlɪʃmənz həʊm ɪz hɪz kɑsl̩}]

Figure 13.10 shows a composite protocol which allows the written annotation of all three groups of settings on the same form – articulatory, phonatory and tension settings, and figure 13.11 lists all the prefacing symbols for these settings.

13.10 Applications of setting-analysis

The protocols introduced above for annotating characteristic articulatory, phonatory, tension and prosodic settings in the speech of individuals can be used in a variety of applications in linguistic, paralinguistic and extralinguistic analysis.

Figure 13.11 Summary of the prefacing phonetic symbols for identifying settings of articulation, phonation and overall muscular tension

Articulatory settings

labial adjustments		labialization	V̫ or Vʷ
		labiodentalization	V̪ or Vᵛ
tongue-body adjustments	advanced and raised	palatalization	V̡ or Vʲ
	retracted and raised	velarization	̵V or Vˣ
	retracted and lowered	pharyngealization	̴V or Vˤ
tongue-root adjustments		advanced tongue root	V̘
		retracted tongue root	V̙
velopharyngeal adjustments	nasal		Ṽ
	denasal		V̾

Tension settings

supralaryngeal tension	tense vocal tract		T
	lax vocal tract		L
laryngeal tension	tense phonation	harsh voice	V!!
	lax phonation	breathy voice	V̤

Phonatory settings

simple phonation types	falsetto	F
	creak	C
	whisper	W
compound phonation types	creaky voice	V̰
	whispery voice	Ṿ
	whispery creaky voice	V̥

423

Linguistic applications already mentioned include the study of settings in co-articulation, assimilation and segment harmony. Other potential applications of linguistic relevance include the investigation of a number of sociolinguistic phenomena. One of these is the use of settings to characterize membership of a particular accent-community (Esling 1978; Trudgill 1974). Another is the involvement of settings in the phonetic and phonological characteristics of a given accent when they act as markers of prestige, status or power. Many of the sociolinguistic phenomena discussed in Labov (1972a), Milroy (1980) and Romaine (1982), for example, could potentially be analysed in this perspective.

A related application is the study of the way that settings participate in the evolution of the phonetic and phonological characteristics of one accent under the influence of another. This is of relevance not only in a study of the interaction of two accents within a single language, but also in analysing and resolving interference patterns in foreign-language learning. This is an area commented on at some length by Honikman (1964), where she found that teaching native-like English pronunciation to foreign speakers was very much facilitated by encouraging the students to learn appropriate 'postural' settings of the vocal organs as a foundation for the segmental pronunciations, rather than focusing on the articulatory patterns of the individual segments alone.

A further linguistic application lies in the area of speech therapy, where disordered speech patterns in acquisition or pathology can often be related to problems that are better approached at the co-ordinatory, integrative level of settings than at solely a segmental level. This interest focuses on the intelligibility of speech as a means of communication, rather than on the characterization of the speaker as an individual, which is an extralinguistic application.

Paralinguistic applications include the study of the contributions of settings to tone of voice in different cultures. This is an area still largely unresearched, where pervasive ethnocentric assumptions tend to prevail in support of beliefs that the phonetic substance of paralinguistic communication through tone of voice is universally and accurately understandable by all human beings. It may be that some types of informative emotional behaviour, such as anger and fear, tend to have a universal basis in biochemical endocrinal and hormonal conditions. But many other types of communicative paralinguistic behaviour, particularly more socially conditioned activities such as pleading, sarcasm, humour, annoyance, teasing, whining, soothing and so forth, are much less likely to be communicated by uniform means across all human societies. They will tend to be culturally specific, and as such will be governed by convention.

An objective analysis of the contribution of phonetic settings to the communication of such attitudes offers one thread towards unravelling the complexity of this paralinguistic topic. Success in such a study would have benefit not only in the understanding of mechanisms of social communication in general, but also in areas such as the nature of cues to deception and persuasion in both ordinary conversation and acting.

Extralinguistic applications of setting analysis include the study of social and psychological markers of personality and role in speech (Laver and Trudgill 1979). One such area is the investigation of gender-markers (not to be confused with the marking of speaker-sex, which concerns biological not social identity). Another is the marking of factors such as dominance and submissiveness as attributes of social and psychological identity.

A major area of extralinguistic application is in speech pathology, in the characterization of settings in the speech of individual speakers (where it is often necessary to extend the concept of scalar degrees of settings well beyond the normal range). One aspect of such an application is the use of vocal-profile analysis in a long-term monitoring function as a means of assessing improvement or deterioration of speech factors.

An example of this would be the measurement of progressive change in efficiency of vocal-fold vibration with radiotherapy for laryngeal cancer, with increasing or decreasing harshness as the condition deteriorated or improved with treatment. Another example would be assessment of the progressive reduction of perceived nasality in the speech of a child who had undergone late surgery for repair of a cleft palate, and who was benefiting from speech therapy. Another would be the progressive relaxation of overall muscle tension in the speech of a patient undergoing speech therapy to reduce the hypertensive phonatory habits that had given rise to vocal-fold nodules.

A different type of application in speech pathology, which is mentioned not least for the illumination it offers on the relationship between phonetic and organic facets of speech production, is that of characterizing the different consequences for speech that arise from normal and abnormal patterns of anatomy and physiology. One obvious example is the description of settings in the speech of hard-of-hearing and profoundly deaf speakers, where a prominent characteristic of speech is often abnormal nasality, and a reduced range of pitch and loudness, all of which can be the subject of remedial speech therapy in suitable cases.

A less obvious example is that of assessing the speech of individual speakers whose vocal-tract anatomy differs organically from that of the normal population for genetic reasons. A recent project was conducted by the author and colleagues into the typical voice quality associated with Down's Syndrome. In that study, a perceptual evaluation of settings in the voices of subjects with Down's Syndrome showed that a palatalized setting – that is, a pervasive tendency to constrict the vocal tract at the palatal location – was a very frequent component of their speech. One somewhat implausible explanation for this finding might be that speakers with Down's Syndrome all tend to adopt a raised and fronted setting of the body of the tongue. A preferable explanation is that the genetic consequences for anatomical growth patterns in Down's Syndrome equip such speakers with a specific tendency towards a particular type of vocal-tract geometry. There are frequent comments in the medical literature on Down's Syndrome to the effect that such speakers tend to have unusually large tongues. This would explain the articulatory tendency to constrict the vocal tract at the palatal location. Mackenzie Beck (1988: 209–27) summarizes the medical literature investigating organic variability in Down's Syndrome. In her account, biometric measurement of the tongues and jaws of speakers with Down's Syndrome in fact shows no consistent tendency to over-large tongue volume, although unusual variability between speakers is found. What has been established, however, is that there is a strong genetically-based trend in speakers with Down's Syndrome to show under-development of the mid-face, with relatively normal development of the mandible and tongue. This would have the same consequence of constricting the vocal tract at the palatal location.

The relevant conclusion for the purposes of this book is that a given perceptual effect can be produced by two different configurational influences, one phonetic and one organic. Such an equivalence might be called a **configurational equivalence**. A comparable equivalence could obtain at the phonatory level between two speakers producing whispery voice. In one speaker, this might be the result of a habitual adjustment of a normal laryngeal apparatus. In the other, it might be the consequence of one vocal fold being semi-paralysed in a half-open position, so that the glottis was unable to close completely. This equivalence might be called a **phonatory equivalence**.

It will be recalled from chapter 2 that the concept of phonetic equivalence was based on an idealizing assumption that organic differences between two speakers can be ignored in evaluating phonetic quality, 'as if both speakers could be held to be producing their performance on the same notional vocal apparatus'. The ground for such an assumption is clearly restricted to those speakers with an anatomy that can be regarded as falling within normal limits. But even with this limitation, the abstract nature of the concept of phonetic quality perhaps becomes a little clearer. The auditory quality of every speaker's voice arises from the balance in that speaker between on the one hand organic effects of the dimensions and geometry of the vocal apparatus, and on the other the phonetic adjustments of that apparatus which the speaker habitually makes. The exact balance in any individual case is difficult to quantify. But we conceptualize the phonetic quality that results by pretending that every speaker is organically the same, and attributing the differences of perceived quality to the phonetic adjustments that the speaker in question would make if he or she were indeed equipped with this standard vocal apparatus.

The assumption of configurational equivalence holds of course not just for the speakers in the discussion above of the effects of Down's Syndrome, or of a semi-paralysed vocal fold, but as a matter of principle for all speakers treated by descriptive phonetic theory, no matter how apparently 'normal' their anatomy might actually be. The concept of phonetic quality, and the related concept of phonetic similarity, both need to be coloured by an appreciation that organic factors play a role in their definition that is only beginning to be understood.

Further reading

Rush (1827) and Sweet (1877) were the two main phoneticians of the nineteenth century to deal with the phenomena of **articulatory settings** in voice quality. The articulatory analysis of settings has been discussed by Abercrombie (1967), Honikman (1964), Laver (1975, 1980), Laver and Trudgill (1979) and Mackenzie Beck (1988). Part II of Laver (1991) reproduces a number of articles on the articulatory and acoustic analysis of **normal and pathological voice quality**, several written with colleagues (Laver 1968, 1974, 1979; Laver and Hanson 1981; Laver *et al.* 1981, 1986; Laver, Hiller and Mackenzie Beck 1988; Mackenzie, Laver and Hiller 1983). Hiller (1985) describes an acoustic approach to measuring waveform perturbations in harsh and hoarse voices.

PART VI

Temporal, prosodic and metrical analysis

14

The temporal organization of speech: segmental duration

A statement was made in chapter 2 that there were only four perceptual domains available to the human auditory system for differentiating the elements of speech. These were the domains of perceptual quality, duration, pitch and loudness. The analysis offered in chapters 7–13 concentrated on those facets of the production of speech that modify the first of these domains – that of the perceived quality of speech at the subsegmental, segmental, intersegmental and suprasegmental levels. The present chapter will focus on the next of these domains, and will consider the temporal factor of segmental duration.

Chapter 15 will present an analysis of the third domain, discussing prosodic factors to do with the control of pitch and loudness, in speech melody and sonority respectively. Chapter 16 will then explore the question of how all four domains of quality, duration, pitch and loudness are integrated over a whole utterance, in which the interaction of syllabic, stress and rhythmic factors produce the metrical structure of speech. Chapter 17 will then consider the temporal organization of whole utterances, and will discuss matters of continuity and rate (or tempo) in speech.

14.1 The perception of duration

Duration itself is simply the amount of time taken up by a speech event, usually expressed in thousandths of a second (msec). Duration as such is thus a simple concept, though establishing adequate criteria for exactly where in time the start-point and end-point of an individual speech-segment might fall in an actual utterance, and therefore whether one segment is greater or less in duration than another, is often considerably more difficult. The discussion of the relative duration of sounds in speech should however be prefaced by some comment on the listener's perceptual ability to discriminate different durations. The human auditory system is psychophysically capable of registering very fine temporal differences of duration under favourable experimental conditions. In the perception of speech, and noting

431

that the duration of individual speech-segments ranges from about 30 msec to some 300 msec, the psychophysical threshold for just-noticeable differences in duration between two such sounds is of the order of 10–40 msec (Lehiste 1976: 226). This discriminability is affected by intensity and noise: making sounds softer and **masking** them by noise both diminish the listener's ability to discriminate small differences of duration (Lehiste 1970: 17). The acoustic frequency characteristics of the sounds concerned do not, however, seem to influence the listener's ability to discriminate their durations.

14.2   **Intrinsic versus conditioned factors of duration**
      The duration of individual units in speech, from the segment upwards, is responsive to a number of conditioning factors. Some of these will be described in more detail in the sections below, and in chapter 16 on metrical structure, but they include such global factors as the language and accent of the speaker, the overall tempo and continuity of the utterance and the current paralinguistic state of the speaker. They also include the more local influences of the structural linguistic context in which linguistic units find themselves. The influence of local linguistic structure can be exercised on the segment in terms of the articulatory characteristics of its neighbouring segments, the segmental structure of the syllable in which the segment finds itself, the stressed/unstressed nature of that syllable, the place of the syllable in the overall utterance (initial, medial or final in the utterance), and the number and type of syllables making up the local rhythmic unit concerned.

These global and local influences are mentioned here to set the scene for an assertion that, despite this wealth of conditioning factors, there exist some **intrinsic properties** of duration that constrain the relative manipulations of timing to which the units of speech can be subjected. These intrinsic properties apply at the segmental level and below, and reflect requirements of either or both speech production and perception. A given type of segment or feature will often have some **intrinsic duration** which it must exhibit before it can be perceived as a segment or feature of that type.

One example of an intrinsic constraint in this area is the duration of the very short-lived audible fricative energy that characterizes the release of a stop-closure. If the duration is longer than a certain minimum, the friction will be heard as constituting the fricative portion of an affricated stop. If the duration is slightly longer again, then a separate fricative segment may be perceived.

The performance of a tapped stop is another example of intrinsic constraints. A tapped stop requires a certain minimum duration to complete its rapid movement towards closure and away again, but must be completed within a certain maximum duration. Conversely, if the articulatory manoeuvre takes a tangibly longer duration to complete than the maximum, the stop will be heard as a simple stop rather than as a tapped stop. In this case, aerodynamic, articulatory and perceptual factors are all involved.

This discussion of intrinsic constraints should not be taken to imply that the speech patterns of any accent directly reflect mechanically unavoidable limitations on phonetic performance. It would be unsafe for speech communication to depend on performance at the very limits of the physical possibilities of a speaker's vocal apparatus. The relationship between absolute anthropophonic possibilities of speech performance on the one hand, and the phonetic selection by a language of some zone within those possibilities on the other, is not one which places phonetic performance at the very outer perimeter of anthropophonic space, as it were.

Languages seem characteristically to select zones of comfortable phonetic performance well within this anthropophonic space which allow both relative ease of articulation and security of perceptual distinctiveness, as discussed in chapter 4. To give one illustration of this principle, it might on first reflection appear that the typical duration of ejective fricatives is probably also their maximum duration, because of what one might conceive to be constraining physiological and aerodynamic reasons. It is however physiologically possible to maintain audible friction in an ejective fricative for a considerably longer maximum duration – about 2 seconds, with careful control of the size of the fricative stricture and the speed of the rising larynx (Catford 1977a: 196). It is therefore more appropriate to think of intrinsic constraints as setting boundary conditions within which an accent makes its communicative choice of comfortable phonetic performance.

The intrinsic constraints on the durations of segmental performance provide a background against which are set the contrastive and realizational patterns learned by speakers from their sociolinguistic accent-community during language acquisition. A further layer of constraint on realizational patterning is shown by the durational characteristics adopted by speakers as a matter of personal habit, which give their speech an idiosyncratic, individual flavour. Intrinsic limits and learned, volitional factors thus interact in a fine-grained way.

Realizational constraints set by a speaker's sociolinguistic accent-community can be seen in the different timing choices made by British English accents to distinguish a syllabic vocoid and a non-syllabic approximant of otherwise more or less the same articulatory characteristics. If the [j] in an

RP pronunciation of *year* [jɪə] were to be either abbreviated or prolonged to a significant degree, the listener would be thrown into doubt about whether the pronunciation was intended to represent *year* or *ear*. RP sets the phonetic boundary between the two percepts at a particular value. Some accents of Welsh English, however, while maintaining the same general distinction, set the phonetic boundary value at a longer duration for [j] (and, correspondingly, also for [w] versus [u]) than does RP. Part of a listener's ability to identify a speaker's accent as RP versus Welsh English is then based on this accent-distinguishing durational factor.

Finally, still at the most general level of discussion, the duration of any given segment in the speech of a given speaker, even when all conditioning circumstances are equal, will show quasi-random microvariability from one occasion to another. In the discussion that follows, such intra-speaker microvariability will be left aside, in order to concentrate on variabilities which can be attributed to a number of conditioning factors including the role of different accents and different languages. But it is included at this point to underline the fact that experimental observations of segmental timing are inevitably clouded by the mist of such intra-speaker **microvariability of duration**. Safe conclusions can be drawn only about general tendencies emerging from examination of adequate amounts of data gathered under sufficiently controlled experimental conditions.

The relative duration of segments has been the subject of much research. Good general summaries are available in Delattre (1965), Lehiste (1970, 1976), Ohala (1973) and Fletcher (1988). An influential theoretical and experimental account is given by Fowler (1980). Various authors will be cited in the text of the discussion, but relevant works on segmental duration in individual European languages which can be consulted are listed in Further Reading at the end of the chapter.

14.3   Intrinsic durations of contoids

Lehiste (1970: 27–30) offers some generalizations about the intrinsic factors in the durations of contoids, and the comments that follow are based in part on her summary. In the following discussion, however, it is important to be aware that disentangling the evidence for actual intrinsic constraints from language-specific influences is difficult, as indicated in section 14.1. The most sensible approach is perhaps to compare the typical durational values of different types of segments when pronounced at typical rates in connected speech, in comparable environments and structures.

With such a proviso, factors of place of articulation, voicing state and type of stricture all play a role. Other factors being held constant, within a language labial contoids are typically longer in duration than alveolars and velars, though the relationship between alveolars and velars is not stable across languages. In data from Danish, Fischer-Jørgensen (1964) showed that the duration of stop closures in monosyllabic words averaged 101 msecs for [b], whereas [d] and [g] averaged 92 and 94 msecs respectively. In other structures, labials maintained their value as the longest voiced stop, but the relationship between [d] and [g] was inconsistent. In Breton, Falc'hun (1951) showed that the closure for [b] in intervocalic position was longer than for [d] and [g], but that the stop closure of [p] was shorter than those of [t] and [k]. Falc'hun (1951) also showed that, after a stressed vowel in Breton, voiced stops were longer than voiced nasals and fricatives, while voiceless stops were shorter than voiceless fricatives. Fintoft (1961) was able to demonstrate that voiceless fricatives in Norwegian were longer than any other contoid. Using the symbols '>' to mean 'is of greater duration than' and '=' to mean 'is approximately the same duration as', the Norwegian series for the realizations of consonant phonemes in initial and medial position was as follows: /s, f/ > /r/ > /m, n/ > or = /l/ > /v/. For the realizations of consonants in final position, the series was: /s, f/ > /m, n/ = /v/ > or = /l/ > /r/.

14.4   Intrinsic durations of vocoids

Lehiste (1970: 18–27) summarizes findings on the intrinsic influences in the durations of vocoids with the generalization that, other factors being held constant, a close vocoid is shorter than an open vocoid. Amongst the authors cited in support of this generalization across a number of European languages are: Danish – Fischer-Jørgensen (1955); English – House and Fairbanks (1953), Peterson and Lehiste (1960); German – (Maack 1949); Lappish – Äimä (1918); Spanish – Navarro Tomás (1966); and Swedish – Elert (1964). The same phenomenon is evidenced in Thai (Abramson 1962).

The same caveat applies to considerations of intrinsic durations of vocoids as did in the section above on contoids. That intrinsic factors should contribute to variation in the typical durations of different types of vocoids is difficult to understand when thinking of the vocoid being performed in isolation. It perhaps becomes more readily understandable when one conceives of vocoid performance taking place in connected speech, as for example in a CVC syllable, where the vocoid is embedded in a contoidal context. Catford (1977a) explains the generalization that close vocoids are intrinsically shorter in duration than open vocoids by appeal to a contextual articulatory constraint of this sort. Implicitly taking a CVC structure as his illustration, he comments that 'the change of articulatory position from that of a consonant to that of an open vowel and back again involves a longer movement and hence requires more time than the movement to and from a less open vowel' (Catford 1977a:197). The consequences of this generalization for contextual allophonic constraints on vocoid duration are further explored in section 14.5.1 below.

14.5 Phonetic duration and phonological length

Over and above any contextual conditioning, segmental duration can itself be exploited as a contrastive phonological feature. The sections immediately below explore the phonological options of segmental length being available to languages for contrastive use. For clarity, a distinction will be maintained here between **duration** as a phonetic feature, and **length** as a phonological feature manifested by relative phonetic duration. Another term often used for phonological length is **quantity**. Daniel Jones (1944b) suggested that another terminology to express these concepts might include the terms **chrone** to denote any particular degree of phonetic duration, and the term **chroneme** to denote a distinctive degree of phonological length: 'In this way we should have chrones and chronemes parallel to phones (sound-qualities) and phonemes'.

After discussing contrastive segmental length, durational variation will then be described at the segmental allophonic level, in terms of differences of the co-ordinatory adjustments of the timing of segments conditioned by different contextual and structural positions.

14.5.1 *Contrastive segment length*

Contrastive length is utilized by many languages as a phonological property of either or both consonants and vowels. In order to function reliably as a contrastive phonological resource, durational differences between otherwise similar pairs of segments obviously have to be substantially greater than the minimum threshold of 10–40 msec described in the introductory section to this chapter. Allophonically conditioned durational differences need not be as great.

Contrastive vowel length is much more common in the languages of the world than consonant length, but there are some examples of languages that make use of contrastive length on both consonants and vowels. Examples of contrastive consonantal length are given here first, then of contrastive vowel length. Finally, examples are given of three languages (Finnish, Estonian and Maltese) that use both consonant- and vowel-length distinctions.

436

14.5.2   *Contrastive consonantal length*

Jones (1950: 114–34) offers instances from Italian and Hungarian:

Contrastive consonantal length in Italian

[faṭo] 'fate'   [faṭːo] 'made'

(It will be recalled that the diacritic [ː] in the above example is used as a marker of relatively greater length – in this case the medial, closure phase of the stop is prolonged perceptibly beyond that for the shorter stop.)

Contrastive consonantal length in Hungarian

[hal] 'fish'   [halː] 'hears'

[lap] 'sheet of paper'   [lapː] 'Laplander'

An unusual example of consonantal length is given by Abramson (1986:9) from Pattani Malay, a Malay dialect spoken in Southeastern Thailand. Pattani Malay, according to Abramson, who cites Chaiyanara (1983), 'has a length distinction for *all* consonants in word-initial position'. Abramson gives the following illustrations:

Contrastive length on initial consonants in Pattani Malay

[labɔ] 'to make a profit'   [lːabɔ] 'spider'

[makɛ] 'to eat'   [mːakɛ] 'to be eaten'

[siku] 'elbow'   [sːiku] 'hand-tool'

[bulɛ] 'moon'   [bːulɛ] 'many months'

[katoʔ] 'to strike'   [kːatoʔ] 'frog'

Abramson comments that:

> it is obvious that closure duration alone could be enough to differentiate the members of each pair in both production and perception. The first four pairs of examples are of that type, while the fifth pair, with voiceless unaspirated stops, is not. That is, in pairs of the last type, the difference in the closure durations appears only as shorter or longer medial silent gaps when the words are embedded in utterances. (Abramson 1986: 9)

Perceptual experiments confirmed the role of closure duration as a sufficient manifestation of the consonantal length distinction. Another language in which consonants in syllable-initial position participate in a quantity distinction is Pame, a language of central Mexico (Gibson 1956, cited by Abercrombie 1967: 82).

Nubian exploits a morphophonemic process which results in the realizations of certain consonants becoming **geminated** (being made long, across a syllable boundary), when an inflection meaning 'and' is added to the stem of a noun. Ohala (1983), citing Bell (1971), describes the process resulting in the examples given below in the following terms: 'In Nubian the noun inflection that means "and" involves the gemination of the stem-final consonant and the addition of the sequence /-ɔn/. When a final /b/ is geminated it remains voiced; /d, ʤ, g/, however, the stops (and affricate) with farther-back points of articulation, become devoiced to /t, ʧ, k/' (Ohala 1983:198).

Long geminate consonants in Nubian (Nobiin accent)

Noun stem	Stem + 'and'	Meaning
/fab/	/fabːɔn/	'father'
/sɛgɛd/	/sɛgɛtːɔn/	'scorpion'
/kaʤ/	/kaʧːɔn/	'donkey'
/mʊg/	/mʊkːɔn/	'dog'

When segments at the junction of two phonological syllables are judged to have an equal affiliation to both syllables, as in such geminate cases, they are said to be **ambisyllabic** segments.

Sounds made with phonetic differences of duration that could be analysed as representing either consonants of contrastively different length, or as single versus geminate consonants, occur in the Inuktitut (Pangnirtung) dialect of Inuit. This is an Eskimo-Aleut language spoken in the North Baffin area of the Canadian Arctic by some 15,000 people (Esling 1991):

Long consonants in Inuktitut (Inuit)

[ˈtʰunuɑni] 'behind'	[ˈunːuɑqʰ] 'night'
[ˈtɑkuvɑsi] 'you guys see him/her/it/them'	[siˈkukːutʰ] 'by ice'
[tiˈkiqɑtɑujutʰ] 'they arrive together'	[tiˈkiqɑtːɑqtutʰ] 'they arrive frequently'
[ˈqɪmːɪq ˈimiqtʊqʰ] 'the dog drinks'	[tiˈkimːɐt] 'because (s)he arrives'
[ˈnuliɑʁɑ] 'my wife'	[ˈaʁːɑːni] 'last year'

An unusual form of phonological lengthening creating geminate consonants occurs in Bengali and Marathi, where gemination of a word-medial consonant can act as a sign of pragmatic or semantic intensification. An example from Marathi is [ɑtɑ] 'now' versus [ɑtːɑ] 'now!' (Masica 1991: 122, citing Kavadi and Southworth 1965: 20). A particularly interesting instance of this process in Bengali lengthens a voiced retroflex alveolar flapped stop [ɽ] to a long voiced retroflex palato-alveolar stop [ɖ̣], as in [bɔɽɔ] 'large' versus [bɔɖːɔ] 'enormous' (Masica *ibid.*, citing a personal communication from C. Seely). This example is interesting not least for the light it throws on the perceptual and articulatory relationship between [ɽ] and [ɖ]. Even though the point of maximum stricture is different (alveolar versus palato-alveolar), the shared aspect of retroflexion plays a significant role in the phonetic basis of the phonological relationship between the two stops.

In some languages, affricated stops can participate in length distinctions. In such cases, it is usually the stop-closure component of the affricated stop that is phonetically lengthened. Prolongation of the stop component is indicated by placing the phonetic length diacritic after the affricate symbol, as in [ʧːʃ]. No change of relative duration in the fricative component is implied. This representation can also be used phonologically, giving /ʧː/, or alternatively the stop element of the symbol can be doubled, as in /tʧ/. Doubling of the composite affricate symbol is sometimes used, as for example by Arnott (1969a: 60) in the case of Fula, to indicate greater length of the affricates in words such as /ɗatɕce/ ⇒ [ɗatɕːe] 'gum (from tree)' and /baʤʣo/ ⇒ [baʣːo] 'only child'. However, length needs sometimes to be distinguished from repetition. Repeated affricates, for example, occur in Russian, in [ʧʧetniː] 'vain' (Jones 1950: 81). In the very rare cases involving a phonologically long affricate in which it is the fricative element that is prolonged rather than the stop-closure element (such as in Akhwakh, the Caucasian language discussed in section 12.4.5.2), the phonetic transcription can double the fricative symbol, as in [ʧʃ].

When stops or fricatives with an aspirated relationship with their following context participate in phonological length distinctions, it is normally the medial phase of the stop or the fricative that is phonetically prolonged. Once again, while the phonetic transcription places a length diacritic after the composite symbol for the aspirated segment, as in [tʰː], a phonological representation can either do the same, as /tʰː/, or can double the stop element of the symbol, as in /ttʰ/.

14.5.3   *Contrastive vowel length*

Contrastive vowel length is a phenomenon found in a very wide range of languages. One example is Qatari Arabic, as in the following examples from Bukshaisha (1985: 40):

Contrastive vowel length in Qatari Arabic
[tir] 'beg!'   [tiːr] 'fly!'
[ful] 'Arabian jasmine'   [fuːl] 'broad beans'

Sinhalese, Japanese, Somali, Kikuyu and Luganda also use vowel length contrastively (Jones 1950: 114–34), in word-pairs such as:

Contrastive vowel length in a number of languages

Sinhalese
[βelə] 'field'   [βeːlə] 'half-day'

Japanese
[ho] 'sail'   [hoː] 'law'

Somali
[kul] 'hot'   [kuːl] 'necklace'

Kikuyu
[igɔko] 'bark of tree'   [igoːko] 'thick thatching grass'

Luganda
[okusona] 'to sew'   [okusoːna] 'to take by surprise'

(Tonal patterns on some of the examples above have been omitted.)

A little known language in which a contrastive difference of length exists on vowel phonemes is Rarotongan Maori. This is an East Polynesian language of the Malayo-Polynesian family spoken on the island of Rarotonga in the South Cook islands in the Pacific, related to Tahitian and to New Zealand Maori. Buse (1966: 52–3) gives the following examples of length differences:

Contrastive vowel length in Rarotongan Maori
[pɑʔi] 'taro bed'   [pɑːʔi] 'ship'
[pɑku] 'dandruff'   [pɑːku] 'thump'
[tɑne] 'a skin disease'   [tɑːne] 'male'
[toto] 'blood'   [toːto] 'drag'
[kekeː] 'foreign'   [keːkeː] 'armpit'

An unusual use of vowel-length relationships is found in many southern dialects of Dutch, where the plural of nouns is signalled by the choice of a short vowel, and the singular by a lengthening of the vowel. The following illustrations come from the Weert dialect of Southern Dutch (J. Verhoeven, personal communication):

Contrastive vowel length in the Weert dialect of Southern Dutch
[kənin] 'rabbits'   [kəniːn] 'rabbit'
[bɛín] 'legs'   [bɛíːn] 'leg'
[ɛrm] 'arms'   [ɛːrm] 'arm'

A complex pattern of distributional relationships exists in Tigre, the Eritrean language studied by Palmer (1956), between short and long vowels and their mutual possibilities of occurrence. Palmer describes the relationships evidenced by the words below in the following terms:

> (i) A short open front vowel is always followed, within the same word, by a long open front vowel, with no long vowel of any other quality between them;

> (ii) a short half open central vowel is *either* followed, within the same word, by a long vowel other than open front, with no long open front vowel between them, *or* not followed, within the same word, by any long vowel;

> (iii) neither short open front vowels nor short half open central vowels are found word finally. (Palmer 1956)

Long and short vowels in Tigre

[sɛlsɛlɛt] 'bracelet'	[salsalaṭaː] 'her bracelet'
[n̪ɛbiːt̪] 'wine'	[maŋkaːhuː] 'his spoon'
[baːldɛŋgɛt̪] 'bean'	[sɛmbuːkaː] 'her boat'
[d̪ɛbeːlaː] 'he-goat'	[ṱɛkoːbaṭaː] 'her mat'

In Fula, the language spoken in many countries in West Africa, Chad, Cameroon and Southern Mauritania, all vowels can be contrastively either short or long, giving a ten-vowel system. Figure 14.1 shows the phonetic distribution of the qualities of these vowels on a vocoid chart, as exemplified by the following words cited by Arnott (1969a: 63) – the phonemic transcription given by Arnott is included as an instance of the use of romanized cover-symbols (discussed in chapter 16) that are often a consideration in the development of legible phonological transcriptions:

Figure 14.1 Vocoid chart of the phonetic qualities of the ten vowel phonemes of Fula (adapted from Arnott 1969: 63)

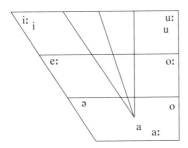

Long and short vowels in Fula

/kiːkiːɗe/ ⇒ [kiːkiːɗɛ]   /ɗiɗi/ ⇒ [ɗiɗi] 'two'
'evening'

/deːɗi / ⇒ [deːɗi]   /deɗe/ ⇒ [dɛɗɛ] 'leather
'stomachs'   loincloths'

/paɗe/ ⇒ [paɗɛ] 'shoes'   /baːɗe/ ⇒ [baːɗɛ] 'ant-heaps'

/koɗi/ ⇒ [kɔɗi] 'necklaces'   /ʃoːɗe/ ⇒ [ʃoːɗɛ] 'herons'

/kuɗi/ ⇒ [kuɗi] 'stalks   /ʃuːɗi/ ⇒ [ʃuːɗi] 'huts/rooms'
of grass'

A small number of languages make a triple length distinction in vowels, between **short**, **long** and **over-long** lengths. One example is Scottish Gaelic. The dialect of Applecross in Northwest Scotland distinguishes between three degrees of length on realization of vowels (Ternes 1973), as in the following examples, where the length diacritic [ː] is doubled to [ːː] to show an **over-long** (or **extra-long**) relative duration:

Three degrees of vowel length in Scottish Gaelic (Applecross)
[tuɬ] 'to go'   [uːɬ] 'apple'   [suːːɬ] 'eye'

Suárez (1983: 34) suggests that in Coatlan Mixe (Hoogshagen 1959) and San José El Paraíso Mixe (Van Haitsma and Van Haitsma 1976), two dialects of the Mesoamerican language Mixe, 'extra long vowels correspond to the long aspirated nuclei of Totontepec Mixe. That is, in these Mixe languages we find the typologically uncommon contrast between short, long and extra long vowels'. The example Suárez cites is a triplet from San José El Paraíso Mixe, taken from data by Van Haitsma and Van Haitsma (1976), where the first part of a diphthong carries the phonetic realization of length. The transcription has been adjusted to the conventions of this book:

Three degrees of vowel length in San José El Paraíso Mixe
[ʔoi] 'although'   [ʔoːi] 'he went'   [ʔoːːi] 'very'

Other languages where triple phonological length distinctions may be operating include Lappish (Ravila 1962) and Hopi (Whorf 1946). Catford (1977a: 199) also mentions the example of Nenets, a Samoyedic language, citing Tereščenko (1966), and the Amerindian languages Hopi and Mixe. A good general discussion of phonological considerations in length distinctions is available in Lehiste (1970).

The ratio of phonetic durations corresponding to short and long vowels (V/Vː) in a number of different languages is summarized by Lehiste (1970:34). The V/Vː ratio in Danish is about 50 per cent (Fischer-Jørgensen

1955); in Finnish around 44 per cent (Wiik and Lehiste 1968); in Serbo-Croatian roughly 67 per cent (Lehiste and Ivić 1963); in different accents of Thai between 28 per cent and 50 per cent (Abramson 1962); in German between about 90 per cent in the east to about 51 per cent in the west (Zwirner 1959).

14.5.4   *Length distinctions on both consonants and vowels*

Swedish is usually thought of as having contrastive long and short vowels. The allophones of consonants following short vowels are of greater duration than those following long vowels. However, at least two different phonemic solutions would be consistent with the Swedish data presented by Ladefoged (1975: 276). One would give allophonic status to 'long' consonantal pronunciations after contrastively short vowels, and the other allophonic status to the 'short' vowel pronunciations before contrastively long consonants:

Allophonic duration and contrastive length in Swedish

[ɹɪːta] 'draw'   [ɹeːta] 'tease'
[ɹɛːta] 'straighten'   [hæːɹ] 'here'
[ɹɑːta] 'refuse'   [ɹoːta] 'name of a valley'
[ɹuːta] 'root'   [ɹyːta] 'roar'
[ɹøːta] 'rot'   [ɹʉːta] 'window pane'
[ɹɪtː] 'ride (n.)'   [ɹɛtː] 'correct'
[hœɹ] 'hear!'   [hæːɹ] 'Mr'
[ɹatː] 'steering wheel'   [ɹɔtː] 'raw'
[ɹʊtː] 'rowed'   [nʏtːa] 'use (n.)'
[ɹœtː] 'red'   [ɹɵtː] 'route'

Finnish is an instance of a language that exploits contrastive length on both consonants and vowels (T. Lauttamus, personal communication). Examples of such contrasts can be seen in multiple sets as follows:

Contrastive length on consonants and vowels in Finnish

[rʋpːʏ] 'a crease'	[rʋpːʏ] 'a drink'	
[ʋaras] 'a thief'	[ʋarːas] 'a (roasting) spit'	
[ʋeli] 'a brother'	[ʋelːi] 'a gruel'	
[kisa] 'a game'	[kisːa] 'a cat'	
[katɔ] 'a crop failure'	[katːɔ] 'a roof/ceiling'	[kaːtɔ] 'a (bowling) strike'
[tuma] 'a cell nucleus'	[tumːa] 'dark'	[tuːma] 'an inch'

443

[ṭule] 'come!'   [ṭuleː] '(he) comes'
[ṭuːleː] 'it blows'   [ṭulːe] '(he) might come'

Another language that makes use of contrastive length on both consonants and vowels is Maltese. The following examples come from a speaker of Standard Maltese, from Gzira (M. Alexander, personal communication):

Contrastive length on consonants and vowels in Maltese
['kɪsɐɹ] 'he broke (some body part/accidentally)'
['kɪsːɐɹ] 'he broke (something/deliberately)'
['kɛsɑh] 'he became cold'   ['kɛsːɑh] 'he cooled
                                                                (something down)'
['ɹɑʔɑt] 'he fell asleep'
['ɹɑʔːɑt] 'he put (someone) to sleep'
[ɹɑˈʔːɑtː] 'I put (someone) to sleep'
['nɛzɑ] 'he undressed (himself)'   ['nɛz ːɑ] 'he undressed
                                                                (someone else)'
['nɪzɛl] 'he went downstairs/he got down'
['nɪzːɛl] 'he brought (something) down'
['nɪːzɛl] 'he is coming down'
['nɪʃɛf] 'he/it (became) dried'
['nɪːʃɛf] '(he/it is) dry'
['nɪʃːɛf] 'he dried (something)'
['wɛʤɑ] 'a hurt'   ['wɛʤːɑ] 'he hurt
                                                                himself/someone'
['dɛɹɑ] 'he got used to (something)'
['dɛɹːɑ] 'he got someone used to something'
['dɛːɹɑ] 'appearance'
[bɔtː] 'a tin'   [bɔːt] 'distance/far away'
[tɛmː] 'he ended (something)'   [tɛːm] 'he tasted
                                                                (something)'
[ɑːˈʤɪnɑ] 'he kneaded it'   [ɑːˈʤɪːnɑ] 'pastry'

An unusual case amongst the small minority of languages that exploit contrastive length on both consonants and vowels is Estonian. This language is highly atypical in being said to make contrastive use of three degrees of length on both consonants and vowels, as illustrated in the following examples from Jones (1944b), citing the work of Krass (1944):

Three degrees of consonant and vowel length in Estonian
[jama] 'nonsense' [jaːma] 'of the station' [jaːːma] 'to the station'
[lina] 'flax'   [linːa] 'of the town'   [linːːa] 'to the town'

In Jones' (1944b) terminology, 'in Estonian, there are three chronemes applicable to both vowels and consonants'. Lehiste (1970) cites Liiv (1962) as having shown that in the three degrees of vowel length in Estonian, in disyllabic words, the ratio of short vowels to long vowels is approximately 58 per cent, short to over-long vowels about 49 per cent, and long to over-long vowels around 85 per cent. The ratio of the absolute averages of the phonetic durations of short, long and over-long vowels in Estonian in the same study was 119:204:240 (msec).

14.6 Allophonic adaptations of duration

Part of the high degree of variability of speech lies in the principled ways that individual elements of speech are accommodated to their context and to their structural environment. Accommodations of duration contribute actively to this variability, and the next two sections will discuss adaptations of duration to factors first of segmental context, then of structural position.

14.6.1 *Allophonic adaptations of duration to segmental context*

A generalization about intrinsic constraints on articulation was quoted in section 14.4 above, to the effect that the longer the articulatory travel between a vocoid stricture and an adjacent contoid position, the longer the duration of the vocoid. Lehiste (1970) summarizes the results found for VC sequences by Fischer-Jørgensen (1964) in her study of segment duration and place of articulation in Danish, in the following terms:

> The duration of a vowel depends on the extent of the movement of the speech organs required in order to come from the vowel position to the position of the following consonant. The greater the extent of the movement, the longer the vowel. This explains the fact that all vowels were shorter before /b/ than before /d/ or /g/: since two different articulators are involved in the sequence vowel + labial, there is no time delay in moving ... the tongue from vowel target to consonant target. On the other hand /u/ was particularly long before /d/. Before /g/, /u/ had an intermediate value; the movement involved is relatively small, but the back of the tongue is not so mobile as the tip of the tongue and the closing process takes more time. (Lehiste 1970: 20)

The data for Danish presented above is broadly matched by comparable data for American English, though the variation in the detailed differences does not unequivocally support the articulatory principle offered. In detail, the scale of relative durations of vocoids representing short vowels before different consonants was shown by Peterson and Lehiste (1960) to be longest before /t/ > /k/ > /p/; longest before /g/ > /d/ > /b/; longest before /ʃ/ > /s/ > /f/; and longest before /z/ > /v/. A different order was shown for vocoids before nasal stop consonants, however, in that the realizations of short vowels were longest before /m/ > /ŋ/ > /n/, which perturbs the articulatory principle mentioned. In the case of long vowels, their realizations were longest before /t/ > /k/ > /p/; longest before /d/ > /g/ > /b/; longest before /ʃ/ > /s/ > /f/; longest before /ʒ/ > /z/ > /v/; and longest before /ŋ/ > /n/ > /m/.

Considering comparisons of relative duration of vocoids before different types of contoids, House and Fairbanks (1953) showed that in American English vocoids were longest before voiced fricatives > voiced stops > nasal stops > voiceless fricatives > voiceless stops. As a very broad generalization, Peterson and Lehiste (1960) suggest that in American English the ratio of the duration of vocoids before voiceless consonants to the duration of vocoids before voiced consonants is typically 2:3. On average, the duration associated with a vowel before /t/ was 147 msec, before /d/ 206 msec; before /s/ it was 199 msec, before /z/ 262 msec. The size of these contextually determined differences is language-specific, however, rather than language-universal. Elert (1964), cited by Lehiste (1970: 27), showed that in Swedish the difference in duration associated with short vowels before /t/ was only 13 msec less than that associated with vocoids before /d/. Lehiste suggests (*ibid.*) that the size of this difference is more likely to be typical of the general majority of languages than the rather extreme differences which typify English.

It is worthy of note that in English, the adaptation of duration of the segments representing a vowel and a following consonant is reciprocal, and depends on the voicing state associated with the consonant. In considering the relative durations of the individual segments in pairs of English words such as *sat* /sat/ versus *sad* /sad/, or *beat* /bit/ versus *bead* /bid/, the realization of the vowel is shorter before the voiceless consonant and longer before the voiced consonant, while the stop closure for the consonant is longer for the voiceless consonant and shorter for the voiced consonant. It is not clear how widespread this reciprocal durational adjustment conditioned by the voicing state of the consonant in a VC sequence within a syllable might be in the languages of the world.

As an example of contextual conditioning of duration at a subsegmental level, we can consider the duration of the delay in the onset of voicing in an aspirated relationship between a voiceless stop and a following vocoid. Lehiste (1970: 22–3) discusses experimental results found for American English by Peterson and Lehiste (1960) and Danish by Fischer-Jørgensen (1964). In the study on American English, the effect on the duration of the voice-onset delay of aspiration by place of articulation of the stop was studied. Peterson and Lehiste found that, for about eighty or so items each, the average duration of the delay for /p/ was 58 msec, for /t/ 69 msec and for /k/ 75 msec. Lehiste (1970: 22) comments that 'These data suggest that aspiration may become progressively longer as the point of articulation shifts farther back in the mouth', but goes on to say that this hypothesis was not sustained when a closer examination turned to consider the individual allophones of /k/. Peterson and Lehiste (1960) found here that the fronter allophones of /k/ showed longer voice onset delays for aspiration (78 msec on average over thirty-nine instances) than did the backer allophones (72 msec on average over forty-four tokens).

Fischer-Jørgensen's (1964) data for Danish showed that both place of articulation of the consonant and the quality of the vocoid influence the duration of the voice-onset delay between them. In the context /Ci/, the average duration of the aspiration phase was 57 msec for /pi/, 74 msec for /ti/ and 77 msec for /ki/. For /pu/ it was 66 msec and for /ku/ 74 msec.

14.6.2   *Allophonic adaptations of duration to structural position*

Over and above the intrinsic and contextually conditioned influences on the duration of speech segments, structural factors also make a contribution. These include the segmental structure of the syllable of which the segment is a part, the place of that syllable in the rhythmic structures of the utterance, the position of the syllable in the overall utterance and the role of the syllable in the particular tempo and continuity of the paralinguistic colouring of the utterance. We can briefly explore each of these in turn.

The phonological syllable was proposed in chapter 4 as a construct which was useful for organizing the mutual incidence of vowel and consonant phonemes. A number of different types of syllable structures were defined. Syllables with zero final consonants (such as *sea* /si/ in English), making a CVØ structure, were called open syllables, while syllables with a consonantal ending (such as *seat* /sit/), making a CVC structure, were called closed syllables. The duration associated with a vowel in an open syllable is typically longer than that associated with the same vowel in a closed syllable of otherwise the same segmental make-up. In closed syllables, other things being equal, the greater the number of segments making up the syllable the shorter the relative duration of each of the segments. Thus in the pronunciation of *sting* in English versus *string*, the duration associated with the vowel is slightly shorter in the latter word than the former.

The structural sequence in which the segment finds itself can also affect its duration. Tamil, the South Indian language which has a length distinction between short and long vowels, can be represented (allophonically) as having geminate plosive consonants of longer duration than their shorter-duration counterparts, in intervocalic contexts. Balasubramanian and Asher (1984), who comment that the duration of closure for a voiceless plosive is 'longer if it is preceded by a short vowel than if it is preceded by a long vowel … these are represented in these transcriptions by the length mark [ː] and the half-length mark [ˑ]', offer the following illustrations:

Allophonic variation of duration of geminate intervocalic consonants in Tamil

[paːli] 'milk'	[apːaː] 'father'	[kaːpˑɨ] 'bangle'
[ʈalɛ] 'head'	[aʈˑɛ] 'aunt'	[paːʈˑɨ] 'flower-bed'
[ʈiː] 'tea'	[paʈːɨ] 'silk'	[paːʈˑɨ] 'grandmother'
[kɑi] 'hand'	[akːɑ] 'elder sister'	[paːkˑɨ] 'areca nut'

The place of a syllable in the rhythmic structures of speech influences its duration in many languages, and hence that of its constituent segments. When a syllable in English is in a stressed position in the utterance, its duration is longer than when it is unstressed in an otherwise comparable utterance, as discussed in chapter 16. Comparing two versions of the sentence *Tom can't do it but Sue can*, when the sentence stresses are placed as indicated by underlining in the following utterances, then in each case the underlined syllables are pronounced with longer durations than their unstressed counterparts:

Tom can't do it but Sue can

Tom can't do it but Sue can

The number of syllables in a word is another factor which controls the relative duration of a given syllable and its individual segments. Comparing the syllables representing *west* /wɛst/ in the English words *west*, *western* and *westerly*, each instance becomes progressively shorter with the increasing number of syllables involved.

Finally, the overall rate of articulation of an utterance has an obvious effect on the relative duration of its parts, as has the temporal manipulation of an utterance for the regulative purposes of controlling speaker-turns in a conversation, as discussed in chapter 17.

Further reading

Details of experimental work on segmental duration in individual European languages can be found in the following publications: **Danish** – Fischer-Jørgensen (1964, 1979); **Dutch** – Nooteboom (1972), Nooteboom and Slis (1972); **English** – Allen (1973), Crystal and House (1982), House (1961), Kent (1983), Klatt (1976, 1979), Peterson and Lehiste (1960); Umeda (1975a, 1977); **French** – Crompton (1980), Fletcher (1988), O'Shaughnessy (1981, 1984), Wajskop (1979); **German** – Kohler (1986a); **Hungarian** – Olaszy (1991); and **Swedish** – Elert (1964) and Lindblom (1975).

15

The prosodic organization of speech: pitch and loudness

Syllables vary in their perceptual **prominence**. In the chain of continuous speech, the pronunciations of some syllables are made to stand out more strongly than others. As a very broad generalization, the more prominent the syllable to the listener, the greater the muscular effort that has been devoted by the speaker to the performance of its constituent segments. Other things being equal, one syllable is more prominent than another to the extent that its constituent segments display higher pitch, greater loudness, longer duration or greater articulatory excursion from the neutral disposition of the vocal tract.

The patterns of varying syllabic prominence that result from the interactions of these four elements – pitch, loudness, duration and articulatory quality – give each language a characteristic texture, over and above the segmental detail of the language. This texture is made up of the interweaving of three main patterns of suprasegmental organization. These three patterns are those of the prosodic, metrical and temporal organization of the speech material. Metrical organization will be described in chapter 16, and temporal organization in chapter 17. The function of the present chapter is to consider the contribution to the suprasegmental texture of speech of the patterns of **prosodic organization** of pitch and loudness, in the variations of melody and sonority in individual utterances. Matters of pitch will be discussed first, then matters of loudness.

15.1 The perception of pitch

The melody of an utterance is communicated chiefly by movements in time of the pitch of the voice. Pitch as such is a perceptual concept. The phonetic correlate of the pitch of the voice is the frequency (or rate) of vibration of the vocal folds during the voicing of segments. Its acoustic correlate is **fundamental frequency**, measured in cycles per second, for which the modern notation is **Hz** (Hertz), as was explained in chapter 7 on phonation. The phrase 'fundamental frequency' itself is sometimes abbreviated to 'FØ' (pronounced [ɛf zɪəɹoʊ]), for convenience.

450

Average values for fundamental frequency in conversational speech in European languages are approximately 120 Hz for men, 220 Hz for women and about 330 Hz for children about ten years old (Fant 1956). The maximum range of fundamental frequency in ordinary conversation is about 50–250 Hz for men, and about 120–480 Hz for women. Within these limits, the typical range exploited by a single speaker within one utterance is normally of the order of one octave – that is, where the Hz value of the top frequency is double that of the lowest frequency (Fant 1956).

There are a number of different metrics for describing differences of perceived pitch as auditory phenomena, and it is worth mentioning that the psychoacoustic scales applicable to the perception of pitch are linear only at relatively low frequencies. However, in the low ranges of absolute frequency that are relevant for the perception of the pitch of the male and female speaking voice, we can assume that a linear correlation between pitch and fundamental frequency is valid. 'Pitch' in this chapter, if mentioned without further qualification, will therefore be treated as synonymous with the fundamental frequency of vibration of the vocal folds.

The perception of fundamental-frequency differences by the human auditory system is remarkably accurate when listening to stimuli in ideal conditions. The just-noticeable difference (the psychophysical threshold or **limen**) in pitch-discrimination between two notes, in the span of fundamental frequencies from 80 to 160 Hz, is of the order of +/– 1 Hz (Flanagan 1957: 534). Differences of less than about 1 Hz are imperceptible, or **subliminal**. Above these frequencies the limen becomes progressively greater. However, this does not tell us very much about the performance of the auditory system when listening to continuous speech in noisy conversational surroundings, where pitch discrimination is rather less acute. An excellent summary of the experimental work that has been carried out on the psychophysical limits of speech perception is available in 't Hart, Collier and Cohen (1990: 26–37). They report several decades of international work that indicates that the judgement of pitch equivalence or difference between two speech stimuli depends on the fundamental frequency of the stimuli, their duration and intensity, whether their frequency is steady or changing, and on whether there is any accompanying noise masking the audibility of the stimuli. It is also strongly likely that the linguistic expectation of the listener will exercise a substantial influence on the resolution with which meaningful speech stimuli can be discriminated.

Readers interested in the elements of acoustic analysis of the pitch and loudness of the voice can find good explanations of fundamental frequency, intensity and related topics in Baken (1987). The characteristics of the auditory system are well described by Moore (1982), who gives a comprehensive account of the perception of pitch and loudness, and the general field of the biology, psychology and acoustics of hearing. The standard work on computer-based automatic extraction of fundamental-frequency information from the acoustic speech waveform is Hess (1983).

One brief word of caution is relevant at this point. It is conventional to describe the pitch of voicing as 'higher' when the frequency of vibration of the vocal folds increases, and 'lower' when the frequency decreases. It is easy to forget that this convention exploits a solely metaphorical connection between a temporal dimension of frequency of vibration and a spatial dimension of height. There is nothing natural about such a connection, and it is not surprising that students sometimes have difficulty adopting the metaphor with accuracy, often unwittingly inverting the conventional relationship.

15.2   Inherent and overlaid features

The full discussion of prosodic phenomena needs to be prefaced by saying, following Lehiste (1970: 2), that there is a difference in kind between segmental features as such and suprasegmental features of prosodic organization. A segment is defined by the mutual co-presence of particular features which can be regarded as 'inherent' to the identification of the segment concerned. Suprasegmental prosodic features are 'overlaid' on segments, and are not inherent to the definition of segments. One example is the relationship between voicing and pitch: the voicing of a phonetically voiced segment is an **inherent feature**, in that it must by definition figure in the production of the segment in order for the segment to qualify as phonetically voiced. The pitch of that voicing can be perceptually high or low without affecting the identity of the segment as phonetically voiced, and can therefore act as an **overlaid feature**. A similar example is offered by the relationship between phonetic voicing and loudness. The segment, as a complex of defining inherent features, thus acts (within the framework of the syllable) as a carrier for overlaid suprasegmental features.

15.3   Perturbations of pitch and loudness due to segmental performance

Another prefacing comment that needs to be made is that although the analysis of prosodic organization will be treated in this chapter mostly as being concerned with properties of syllables and larger units, there remain of course lower-level interactions between segments and suprasegmental features. The effects mostly concern fine-grained perturbations of suprasegmental features by the muscular and aerodynamic requirements of momentary segments (Ladefoged 1971: 14–15; Lehiste 1970: 68–74; Ohala 1978: 25–30). Reversing the image of the segment as a carrier for suprasegmental features, one could think of these segmental perturbations as being momentarily superimposed on the general trend-line of the pitch or loudness movements characterizing the utterance. The next two sections expand on this relationship between segmental and suprasegmental aspects of pitch behaviour.

15.3.1   *Microperturbation of pitch*

There is no recurrent biomechanical activity whose repetition is perfectly regular in its timing. The fundamental frequency of even a prolonged vocoid pronounced on a seemingly level monotone in fact shows very small deviations (or **excursions**) from the local moving average frequency (or **trend-line**) running through the train of cyclic pulses of the vocal folds in voiced vibration. If the duration of a single cycle of vibration of the vocal folds is taken to last from the instant that the folds close until the moment that they close again, which we shall refer to as the **period** of the cycle, then close inspection shows that successive periods are very seldom perfectly identical (Laver, Hiller and Mackenzie Beck 1992).

Such excursions tend to vary in size on a quite unpredictable basis, but the deviation from the general trend-line in the voice of a healthy young adult using modal phonation will seldom be larger than about +/– 2 per cent to +/–5 per cent of the local value of that trend. In durational terms, what this means is that the scale of these quasi-random excursions is of the order only of a small number of thousandths of a second. However, there are some locations in speech where the deviations tend typically to be larger. These are the onset and offset margins of episodes of voicing. The probability that an individual period will be markedly erratic from the trend is highest at a point up to about five cycles after the onset or before the offset of voicing. If one considers the actual physiological and aerodynamic detail of laryngeal vibration that obtains in voicing, this is not so surprising. The adjustments in the laryngeal and respiratory muscles needed to bring the vocal folds into just the right condition to vibrate at a given fundamental frequency for a given subglottal pressure are complex, delicate and interactive, and unlikely to be achieved with a rapid and high degree of efficiency. Similarly, in the transition from voicing to voicelessness, a perfectly smooth change of muscular and aerodynamic adjustments is seldom produced. We can call these very small-scale perturbations of laryngeal periodicity **microperturbations**.

The presence of these microperturbations in the train of individual pulses in a phonatory sequence is a reflection of the fact that virtually every act of voicing shows some minor **dysperiodicity**. Minor dysperiodicity of this sort is perceptible as a very slight 'roughness' in the audible quality of the phonation, rather than as a factor of perceived melody. (More extreme dysperiodicity is a characteristic of some types of laryngeal pathology, where growths on one of the vocal folds make the vibration yet more inefficient, and this is then audible as a 'harsh' or 'hoarse' perceptual quality (Mackenzie Beck 1988; Laver *et al.* 1986; Laver, Hiller and Mackenzie Beck 1992).

It is hence not quite accurate to say, as was suggested at the beginning of this chapter, that 'The phonetic correlate of the pitch of the voice is the frequency (or rate) of vibration of the vocal folds during the voicing of segments.' It would be more accurate to say that the phonetic correlate of perceived pitch is the general trend-line characterizing the frequency of vibration of the vocal folds during voicing.

This rather fine level of detail was introduced to dispel the impression that, even in ideal conditions of producing a sustained, monotone voiced vocoid, the larynx maintains a perfectly regular vibration in voicing. In the next two sections, discussion will concentrate on yet more substantial distortions imposed on the vibratory pattern of the larynx, with consequent effects on detailed pitch-movements, by the articulatory and aerodynamic transitions from one segment to the next. These more substantial segment-related distortions we shall call **microprosodic perturbations**, partly after Di Cristo and Chafcouloff (1976).

15.3.2   *Microprosodic perturbatory effects of segmental performance on pitch*

When sets of vocoids are pronounced by a given speaker in a standard context, measurements show that each vocoid is associated with a different average pitch. Ohala (1978: 29) states that 'It has been noted for over 50 years that, other things being equal, the average pitch of vowels shows a systematic correlation with vowel height, that is, the higher the vowel, the higher the pitch (Crandall 1925, House and Fairbanks 1953, Lea 1972). The difference in pitch may be as much as 25 Hz.' In an acoustic investigation of what they call **intrinsic pitch**, Lehiste and Peterson (1961) were able to show from data measured in over 1,200 different syllables from a single adult male speaker of American English that the following average pitches were found:

Intrinsic pitch on vocoids

Vocoid	Average Hz	Vocoid	Average Hz
[i]	183 Hz	[u]	182 Hz
[ɪ]	173 Hz	[ʊ]	171 Hz
[ɛ]	166 Hz	[o]	170 Hz
[ə]	164 Hz	[ɔ]	165 Hz
[æ]	162 Hz		

Lehiste (1976: 230) reports that similar results have been found for vocoids in languages as widely different as Serbo-Croatian and Itsekiri, a Nigerian language of West Africa. Hombert (1978) reports that the same correlation has been found in Danish (Petersen 1976), French (Di Cristo and Chafcouloff 1976) and Korean (Kim 1968). The reasons for intrinsic pitch differences on vocoids is therefore likely to be more a **language-universal** matter of the properties of the speech-production system than one which is **language-dependent**.

Ohala (1978: 29–30) advances two possible explanations for the correlation of vocoid height with pitch height. One is an acoustic explanation, to do with resonatory characteristics of the vocal tract in high vocoids favouring the fundamental frequency correlated with that particular articulatory configuration. This effect is calculated to be slight. The other is a physiological explanation, based on the muscular linkages between the tongue and the larynx. When the tongue is raised for the production of a high vocoid, it is hypothesized that the effect on the larynx is to pull it slightly upwards, and that this should tense the vocal folds, thus raising the frequency of their vibration and hence the pitch. This effect has had some support from experimental investigations by Lindblom and Sundberg (1971), and by Ohala and Eukel (1976). However, in the cases of some high vocoids, it has been noticed that the larynx actually tends to be lowered rather than raised (Ladefoged *et al.* 1972), so a full understanding of the intrinsic pitch effect on vocoids remains to be established.

Comparable microprosodic perturbations of pitch attributable to contoids also have their effect on neighbouring vocoids, most dominantly on following vocoids. Lehiste (1976: 230) states that 'The influence of an initial consonant may counterbalance the influence of intrinsic pitch.' In a study by Lehiste and Peterson (1961), the average pitch for [kæ] sequences was found to be 171 Hz, as against 170 Hz for [ɡi] sequences. Lehiste also points out that the distribution of the pitch-contour over the syllable concerned will differ according to the perturbing contoid (1976: 230–1):

> Higher fundamental frequencies are associated with voiceless
> consonants ... After a voiceless consonant, and especially after a
> voiceless fricative, the highest peak will occur immediately after the
> consonant. However, after a voiced consonant, especially a voiced
> resonant, the fundamental frequency will tend to rise slowly and the
> peak may be expected to occur approximately in the middle of the test
> word.

Clark and Yallop (1990: 283) note that prenasal stops and breathy voiced stops have a greater lowering effect on the pitch of following vocoids than plain voiced stops do. These effects are further discussed in section 15.6.2.4 below. Good discussions of the complex and still unresolved factors affecting the pitch-behaviour of contoids, and their influence on neighbouring vocoids, are available in Hombert (1978), Jeel (1975) and Ohala (1978).

Substantial though the microprosodic distortions may be that are physically imposed by segmental adjustments of vocoids and contoids on the vibratory pattern of the vocal folds, it seems that the listener, while engaged on the perceptual task of tracking the prosodic relevance of a given pitch-contour, has learned to discount such distortions. At a prosodic level of analysis, it is hence possible to say that two utterances of quite different segmental composition uttered by the same speaker nevertheless show what counts as the same prosodic pitch-contour. This is despite the fact that an instrumental analysis of the actual fundamental-frequency contour will show detailed and characteristic differences attributable to the microprosodic perturbing effect of the individual segments on one scale of inspection, and at a greater magnification will show differences attributable to the quasi-random microperturbations inherent in all biomechanical vibratory systems.

15.4 The prosodic analysis of pitch

The remainder of this account of pitch will take a prosodic viewpoint, and concentrate on the melodic pattern of pitch-movement over the syllables, words and phrases of an utterance, discounting both microperturbations and microprosodic distortions. An initial distinction will be drawn between the range within which pitch-movements take place, versus the shape, height and direction of these movements.

15.4.1 *Pitch-range and pitch-span*

The melody of a speaker's voice on any given occasion is not a matter of the absolute values of pitch displayed by the voice from syllable to syllable. Pitch is relative in two senses. Firstly, the estimation of the pitch-value of a single syllable as 'high' (or 'low', or 'mid' etc.), is a relative per-ceptual judgement made by the listener in terms of a hypothesized place-ment within the general range of pitch over which the speaker's voice is believed to move. The lowest pitches in the voice of a small child may be considerably higher, in terms of absolute frequency, than the highest pitches in the voice of a large man.

Secondly, the pitch-value of a given syllable in a train of syllables in con-nected speech is judged relative to the pitch-values of its immediate neigh-bours, as being the same, higher or lower. The **melody** of a speaker's voice on any given occasion is thus a matter of the train of relative pitch values that the listener perceives in the succession of syllables that make up the utterance, within the framework of the speaker's assumed **pitch-range** .

This definition of 'melody' leaves matters of rhythm largely out of account, to be considered in the next chapter. It also emphasizes the fact that the listener brings a number of assumptions to the assessment of the speaker's range of pitch. These assumptions bear on issues to do with differ-ent kinds of pitch-range typified by the particular speaker's voice. One is the **organic range** of the speaker's pitch, which is the maximum range of which the speaker's voice is physically capable, given the biologically determined factors of his or her laryngeal anatomy and physiology.

The second kind of pitch-range is the speaker's current **paralinguistic range**, which is the adjustment, within the organic range, of the range of pitch that is exploited for momentary paralinguistic purposes of signalling particular attitudinal information (such as, in any given utterance, surprise, anger, sorrow, impatience, concern etc.). Cultures vary in the way that they utilize pitch-settings as part of paralinguistic communication, and the rela-tion between a given linguistic pitch-contour and the paralinguistic pitch-range will therefore differ not only with respect to the particular tone of voice overlaying the linguistic message, but also possibly with the specific culture of the speaker. Which pitch-phenomena count as linguistically signif-icant cannot be dissociated from the complementary question of which pitch-phenomena count as paralinguistically communicative.

The third type is the **linguistic range**, which is the range within which the phonologically relevant pitch of the speaker's voice habitually varies in par-alinguistically unmarked, attitudinally neutral conversation. Languages differ to some degree in the placement of this linguistic range within the organic range. Spanish is said to be spoken on a typically lower average range of pitch than French, for example (Brosnahan and Malmberg 1970: 148). Languages also differ in the width of the linguistic range. The typical range in Mandarin is said by Sneppe and Wei (1984: 302) to be greater than in French.

Another term that has sometimes been used to try to represent this linguistic range is the **voice compass**, defined as the range of pitch stretching one standard deviation on either side of the mean pitch (Eady 1982; Sneppe and Wei 1984). An overall range of two standard deviations captures approximately 95 per cent of the different pitch values typically used by a speaker.

The fourth and for our purposes the most important type of pitch-range to be distinguished is the phonological **pitch-span**, which is the local range within which the speaker organizes relative values of pitch for prosodic purposes within the whole or part of a particular utterance (Brown, Currie and Kenworthy 1980: 23). This chapter will concentrate on the concept of the phonological pitch-span exploited by a speaker for organizing the limits of pitch-movement in particular utterances, and the placement of pitch-values for individual syllables within it.

Our perception as listeners of the linguistically relevant pitch-value of a given syllable on a single occasion from a particular speaker, in the terms introduced above, is thus highly relative, and very far from absolute. If we consider the linguistically relevant pitch-value as the figure in our perceptual attention, then the ground against which it is perceived is a perspective of several layers. Listeners have to have at least a (tacit) working hypothesis of the organic range of pitch that characterizes the speaker. They should also have an understanding of the current paralinguistic status of the speaker's attitudinal state, as expressed in his or her paralinguistic range of pitch. Furthermore, an estimate of the normal width of the speaker's linguistic range, and an assessment of the value of the speaker's current pitch-span, are both required. Once all these factors are known (or at least hypothesized), then it becomes possible for the listener to form a well-founded estimate of the relative pitch-value of the individual syllable. By extension, two melodic sequences uttered by two different speakers will be judged to be phonetically the same (or similar, or dissimilar) on the basis of perceptual operations that will have taken into account the relationships between the melodic patterns concerned and the organic and paralinguistic ranges of pitch within which they occur, as well as relevant factors of linguistic range and pitch-span.

The question of how many different relative pitch-patterns might meaningfully be distinguished in a given accent, and of what type, is identical in form to the question of how many consonantal or vocalic distinctions are exploited at the segmental level. It is a phonological question, but at the suprasegmental level rather than the segmental. The standard phonological concepts of opposition, distinctiveness, system, structure, distribution and phonetic similarity can equally be brought to bear.

The phonetic transcription of pitch-phenomena is conventionally limited to

I would like some oranges, lemons, and bananas

Figure 15.1 Annotating the pitch-pattern of a typical English (Received Pronunciation) utterance within a stave representing the upper and lower limits of an individual speaker's linguistic range of pitch

comment on relative pitch-movements within the linguistic range. Two parallel horizontal lines are usually drawn to act as a stave representing the upper and lower limits of the linguistic range. By annotating pitch as relative to the individual's own linguistic range, phonetic analysis thus chooses to ignore as linguistically irrelevant the absolute nature of organically influenced pitch differences between one speaker and the next. This procedure effectively **normalizes** the organically based differences between speakers. Figure 15.1 illustrates a typical English (RP) utterance within such a stave. In this case, the utterance ends with a falling pitch-pattern. The figure does not show typical temporal effects in English, such as the tendency to prolong the duration of syllables next to pauses at the beginning and end of utterances as indicated in figure 15.2 below.

Within the notion of a pitch-span, one can isolate two framing components, both exemplified in Figure 15.2. The first is the component contributed by the choice of the **baseline**, which is the series of pitch-values that is perceived as forming the floor of the current pitch-span. The second is the component contributed by the choice of **plateau** (Vaissière 1983: 55), or **topline** (Bruce and Gårding 1978), which is the series of pitch-values that is perceived as forming the ceiling of the current pitch-span. The interval between the baseline and the topline defines the width of the pitch-span.

An essential ingredient of the concepts of pitch-span, baseline and topline is that they are defined as trends over several syllables. One of the characteristic pitch-phenomena in many (but not all) languages is the downward slope of both the baseline and the topline, with a progressive narrowing of the pitch-span within the linguistic range, as illustrated in figure 15.2. This effect is usually called **declination**. The degree of any declination will condition and be conditioned by assumptions about the speaker's place in the present speaking-turn. In English, being willing to yield the floor is conventionally signalled partly by allowing final declination, and the placement of terminal falling intonation patterns within that declination, to reach an extra low pitch-value. However, not all speakers of English obey this rule in their idiolects, and not all languages behave exactly like English.

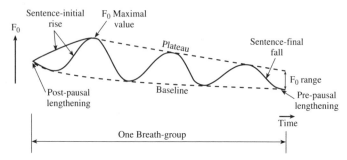

Figure 15.2 The pitch-span as the range of pitch-values used by a speaker for organizing pitch for prosodic purposes within a given utterance (after Vaissière 1983: 55). The baseline and plateau (or topline) form the floor and the ceiling of the pitch-span

Both the width of the pitch-span and the pitch-value of the baseline can be manipulated for phonological effect. The start of a new topic, for example, is often signalled in English by a sudden widening of the pitch-span, and/or by a step-like raising of the baseline. Equally, the parenthetic status of some remark embedded within the flow of the utterance can be identified in English by such devices as depressing the baseline and narrowing the width of the pitch-span for the duration of the parenthetic remark, then returning to the span and baseline values of the framing material. Figure 15.3 shows a sample transcription of the pitch-patterns used in the English utterance *David (who is Welsh) broke into song* to signal the parenthetic status of the phrase *who is Welsh*.

15.4.2   *Pitch-height and pitch-contour*

Within the constraints of the pitch-span and any declination, a distinction can be drawn between the relative height of the pitch of an individual syllable and the contour of any dynamic pitch-movement involved. We can deal first with the notion of **pitch-height**. This refers to the relative placement of the syllable within the values of the pitch-span. Different levels can be categorized as 'high', 'mid', 'low', 'mid-high' (meaning an intermedi-

Figure 15.3 Parenthetic intonation in an English (Received Pronunciation) utterance *David, who is Welsh, broke into song*

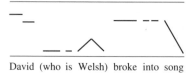

David (who is Welsh) broke into song

Table 15.1 *Some pitch-patterns and their associated labels*

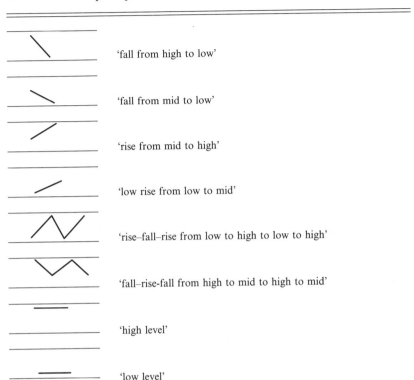

	'fall from high to low'
	'fall from mid to low'
	'rise from mid to high'
	'low rise from low to mid'
	'rise–fall–rise from low to high to low to high'
	'fall–rise-fall from high to mid to high to mid'
	'high level'
	'low level'

ate value between mid and high), 'mid-low' (meaning an intermediate value between mid and low) etc., as appropriate.

The concept of a **pitch-contour** refers to the shape and direction of the trajectory shown by any perceptible change in pitch-value through the duration of the syllable. Different contours can be referred to as 'level', 'rise', 'fall', 'rise–fall', 'fall–rise', 'rise–fall–rise' etc., as required. The question of placement of the pitch-values within the pitch-span is then a matter of combining relevant labels from the choices of pitch-height and pitch-contour, to give composite labels such as 'high level', 'high-to-low fall', 'low-to-high rise', 'low-to-mid rise', and so forth. Table 15.1 illustrates some pitch-values and their associated labels.

Within the general notion of a pitch-contour, one can informally distinguish a number of other physical features of such movements. These include the steepness of the changing contour ('gentle rise', 'steep fall' etc.), and the duration over which the pitch-change is distributed ('abrupt fall', 'extended rise' etc.). Languages do not seem to distinguish pitch-contours on the systematic basis of positive or negative accelerations of pitch-contours. There seems therefore to be no need to posit characteristics of contours such as a 'steepening fall'.

Another relevant characteristic of pitch-contours is their alignment with respect to the segmental strand of speech production. A given pitch-movement may begin its salient movement in the early, middle or late part of the syllable concerned ('t Hart, Collier and Cohen 1990: 153). A different facet of alignment is the question of whether a given pitch-contour is distributed over only a syllable or more than a single syllable. When it is desirable to analyse the sequence of melodic movement as distributed patterns over stretches of speech greater than an individual syllable, the same names for pitch-contours as are used for single-syllable patterns ('level', 'rise', 'fall', 'rise–fall' etc.) can also be used for the pattern distributed over the longer domain. This brings out the point that a distributed contour labelled a 'fall', for example, may take the form of a relationship between two syllables of level but different pitch, where it is the difference of level that constitutes the linguistically relevant fact, rather than the existence of a continuously changing pitch-pattern as such. An illustration of this double possibility is shown in figure 15.21 later in this chapter.

15.5   The analysis of melody in language

Armed with these descriptive concepts, we can now come to a discussion of the phonological use of pitch-patterns to identify different units in the chain of language. A distinction will be drawn between two different phonological uses of pitch, on the basis of the linguistic domain over which pitch-patterns can be held to be serving contrastive functions. The first category is the use of pitch in **tone systems**, where it serves to differentiate units at the level of individual words and individual syllables. The second is the use of pitch in **intonation systems**, where it serves to identify linguistic entities at levels higher than the word, at the phrase and sentence level.

15.6   The analysis of pitch-patterns in tone systems

In **tone systems**, where patterns of pitch contribute to the lexical identification of the individual words, one can draw a distinction between uses of lexical tone in two main types of tone system – those where the domain of linguistically significant pitch-behaviour is the whole word, versus those where the significant domain is the syllable.

15.6.1   *Word-based tone systems*

In the first type of tone system, a contour-pattern of pitch is associated with the entire word, over a variable number of syllables. This can be referred to as a word-based use of lexical tone. The use of **word-based tones** of this sort can be found in Slovenian, and possibly in the Lewis dialect of Scots Gaelic (Abercrombie 1967: 109). Swedish and Norwegian are the most-cited examples of the use of word-tones in this type of tonal system, where all dialects (except the Finnish dialects of Swedish and some of the northern dialects of Norwegian) are said to exploit two contrasting tonal patterns on many words of two or more syllables, of which the first syllable is stressed (Brosnahan and Malmberg 1970: 149–50). Monosyllabic words show no tonal contrast.

Typical Swedish (Stockholm accent) realizations of these word-tone patterns, which are usually called 'accent I' and 'accent II', are described by Fant and Kruckenberg (1989) in the following terms:

> The Swedish word accent is primarily encoded in a local F0 contour which includes the domain of the stressed syllable and to some extent a previous or a following unstressed syllable. In standard Swedish (Stockholm area), accent I, also referred to as acute, is realized by an essentially level or rising F0 in the syllable carrying primary stress, whereas accent II, the grave accent, is realized by a falling F0 in the primary syllable. Accent II is also associated with a domain of secondary or weak stress in the next or in a later syllable within the word, where a second F0 maximum may appear. It is apparent in compound words and is usually weak or absent in single words except under the influence of a sentence or focal stress, when it may equal or even override the primary accent II F0 maximum. Under such conditions of a higher level of stress, the main syllable of accent I words attain a clear rising contour. (Fant and Kruckenberg 1989: 5)

Figure 15.4 is adapted from the figure Fant and Kruckenberg give, originally published by Fant (1959), to illustrate the acoustic parameters of pitch and amplitude which serve to distinguish the representative Swedish word-pair *anden* 'the duck' (accent I) versus *anden* 'the spirit' (accent II). Also shown in figure 15.4 is the analysis of the acoustic parameter of amplitude when the word-pair is whispered (and hence when fundamental frequency, because of the absence of voicing, is absent). It can be seen that the contrast is maintained, though the distinctiveness now lies chiefly in the second syllable.

There are some 500 such pairs of words in Swedish which are distinguished by the use of accent I versus accent II (Cruttenden 1986: 11). Phonologically sophisticated analyses of Scandinavian word-tones can be found in Bruce and Gårding (1978) and Ladd (1983).

A detailed phonetic transcription of pairs of Swedish words differentiated by accent I versus accent II is given by J. Verhoeven (personal communication) of a female speaker from the north of Sweden. The over-low termina-

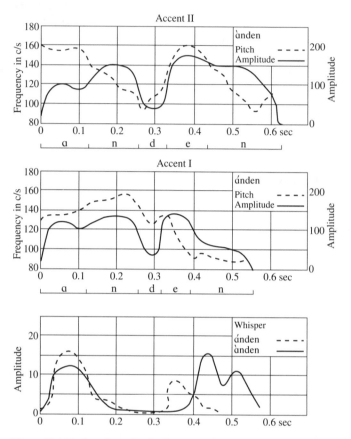

Figure 15.4 Pitch and amplitude characteristics distinguishing accent 1 (*anden*, 'duck') from accent 2 (*anden*, 'spirit') in Swedish (from Fant and Kruckenberg 1989, following Fant 1959)

tion to the final part of the falling tone in accent I in these examples is shown as having a creaky phonation:

Word-tones in Northern Swedish

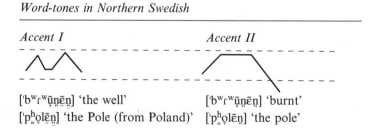

Accent I	*Accent II*
[ˈbʷɾʷũnɛ̃n] 'the well'	[ˈbʷɾʷũnɛ̃n] 'burnt'
[ˈpʰolɛ̃n] 'the Pole (from Poland)'	[ˈpʰolɛ̃n] 'the pole'

A sub-variety of the use of word-tone for lexical identification can be found in **partial tone** languages, which have significant pitch on some syllables only. Examples are Lithuanian and Serbo-Croatian (Fischer-Jørgensen 1975: 98). A discussion of Serbo-Croatian tonal phenomena can be found in Lehiste (1970: 85–105).

15.6.2   *Syllable-based tone systems*

In the second major type of tone system, every syllable is associated with a characteristic relative pitch-value. Pike (1948), in his seminal work on languages exploiting tone systems, defines these as having lexically significant, contrastive but relative pitch on each syllable. It is the pattern made up by the series of such tones on the syllables of the word that serve to identify the word. This can therefore be referred to as a syllable-based use of lexical tone.

The use of **syllable-based tones** of this sort is widespread in the languages of Central America, Africa and Southeast Asia, and languages using syllable-tone systems make up not only by far the larger part of the languages of the world known to make use of tone systems, but in fact the majority of all of the known languages of the world.

The claim that the domain of tone in languages in fact is using syllable-based tones the syllable is reinforced by the case of those languages where individual tone-bearing syllables are represented by single syllabic contoid segments, as in Efik [ɲ́sànà] 'I am walking' and [ŋ̀kà] 'I am going' (Cook 1969: 39). Using the acute-accent diacritic above a segmental symbol to refer to a high level tone, as in [á], and the grave-accent diacritic to mark a low level tone, as in [à], a word-pair in Bafang (the Bamileke language of Cameroon) such as [lɔ́x] 'sleep' and [lɔ̀x] 'stone' are distinguished only by their tonal properties (Westermann and Bryan 1952: 130).

Pike (1948) suggested a typological division of languages using syllable-based tone systems into two categories, depending on what feature of the pitch behaviour was significant. He described the first type as 'register tone languages', and the second as 'contour tone languages', though it may be more appropriate to refer to 'languages using register tone systems' and 'languages using contour tone systems', to facilitate the analysis of other facets of pitch-use in both types of languages as exhibiting an 'intonational' function. The phrase **register tone system** can be taken to mean a system where the relevant feature of word-identifying pitch behaviour is the relative height of the syllabic pitches concerned within the speaker's pitch-span. In such register tone systems, syllables may show only level pitches, only changing pitches (rises or falls), or a mixture of both level and changing pitches. In the case of changing

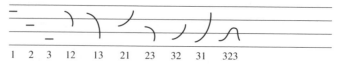

Figure 15.5 Ten tonal patterns in Tlapanec (from Suárez 1983: 48)

pitches, each of the end-points of the falls and rises are identified with one of the level pitches. This is exemplified in figure 15.5, which is adapted from Suárez (1983: 48), representing the ten tonal patterns of Tlapanec, an Otomanguean Mesoamerican Indian language of Central America.

The phrase **contour tone system** applies to the system of tones of a language where the relevant feature of word-identifying pitch behaviour is less the relative height of the syllabic pitch concerned, but more its shape as a trajectory, together with its general placement in the speaker's pitch-span. An example of this type of contour tone system can be seen in figure 15.6, adapted from Speck (1978, cited by Suárez 1983: 49), for the Texmelucan dialect of Zapotec, another Otomanguean language.

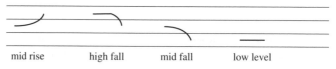

mid rise   high fall   mid fall   low level

Figure 15.6 Contour tone system in Texmelucan Zapotec (from Suárez 1983: 49, following Speck 1978)

Finally, **mixed register/contour tone systems** are also found. Hollenbach (1977, cited by Suárez 1983: 49) gives the example of the Copala dialect of Trique, a Mixtecan Otomanguean language, whose pitch-patterns are shown in figure 15.7. In the case of the last two tone-patterns shown here, the end-points cannot be identified directly with any of the level tones, and their contrastive function is thus manifested more by their identity as rises, at two different general heights in the pitch-span.

Yoruba, a Kwa language spoken in Nigeria, is an example of a language making use of a register tone system (Bamgbose 1969: 168), in which there

Figure 15.7 Mixed register/contour tone system in Copala Trique (from Suárez 1983: 49, following Hollenbach 1977)

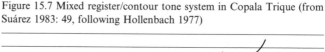

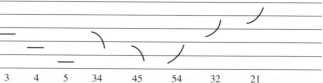

3   4   5   34   45   54   32   21

are three level tones – 'high', marked as [´], 'mid' (unmarked) and 'low' marked as [`], (and a contextually conditioned 'rise' to high):

Register tones in Yoruba

High–high	[ó bé]	‒ ‒	'he jumped'
High–mid	[ó bɛ]	‒	'he is forward'
High–low	[ó bɛ̀]	⎯	'he asks for pardon'

Acoustic analysis reveals, not surprisingly, that in real speech the pitches of the so-called 'level' tones are seldom strictly level. Gandour (1978: 47–8), following Hombert (1976), showed that in the Yoruba triplet [wá] 'to come', [wɑ] 'to look' and [wà] 'to exist', speakers produce the pitch-patterns shown in figure 15.8.

Etsako is another Nigerian example of a language which exploits a register tone system. In the example below, the illustrations show two level tones (high and low), together with a fall from high to low – marked as [ˆ] – (Laver 1969: 52–3):

Register tones in Etsako

[íg͡bà]	⎯	'fences/thorns'
[ìg͡bà]	‒ ‒	'chins'
[ìg͡bâ]	⎯ ↘	'locust beans/gathering(s)'

The languages of Southeast Asia characteristically make use of **contour tone systems**. Examples of languages using such contour tone systems are Mandarin Chinese, Thai and Vietnamese. In Central Thai, for instance, five tones are used to distinguish monosyllabic words of CV structure with long vowels, when produced in isolation. They are often called 'mid', 'low', 'falling', 'rising' and 'high' (Abramson 1975; Davies 1979; Gandour 1975a), and are conventionally divided into three relatively level tones ('mid', 'low' and 'high'), and two more dynamically changing contour tones ('falling' and

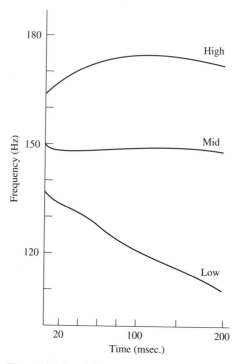

Figure 15.8 Tonal differences in Yoruba (from Gandour 1978: 47–8, following Hombert 1976)

'rising'). Illustrative words carrying these tonal contrasts are as follows (Abramson 1975: 3):

Level and contour tones in Central Thai

mid	[khaː]	———	'a grass (*Imperata cylindrica*)'
low	[khaː]	___	'galangal, a rhizome'
falling	[khaː]	⟍	'slave, servant'
high	[khaː]	—	'to engage in trade'
rising	[khaː]	⟋	'leg'

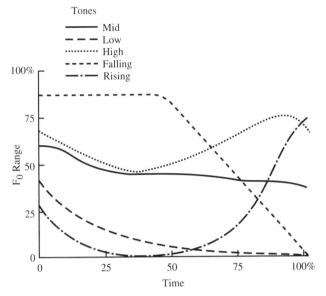

Figure 15.9 Acoustic analysis of tonal patterns in Thai, showing some pitch movement on 'level' tones (after Abramson 1979: 3)

Acoustic analysis of the fundamental frequency actually used confirms once again that the so-called level tones display a certain amount of movement, though substantially less than the so-called rises and falls. Figure 15.9, from Abramson (1979: 3), demonstrates this clearly. Gandour's (1979: 96) descriptive terms ('*mid* falling', '*low* falling', 'high *falling*', '*high* rising' and 'low *rising*') match the acoustic patterns more closely. Gandour (1979: 96) gives the following examples from Central Thai. (It should be noted that Gandour's notation uses '5' to represent the highest pitch-value and '1' to indicate the lowest. This reverses the practice of the Mesoamerican language researchers described above, where '1' indicates the highest pitch and '5' the lowest.)

Tonal contrasts in Central Thai

mid falling	32	[naː]	'field'
low falling	21	[nàː]	'(a nickname)'
high *falling*	51	[nâː]	'face'
high rising	45	[náː]	'aunt'
low *rising*	24	[nǎː]	'thick'

Gandour (1978: 45–6), following Chuang *et al.* (1972), gives a summary acoustic analysis (shown in figure 15.10) of the four contrastive tonal patterns of monosyllables in the Beijing dialect of Mandarin, on the following set of words:

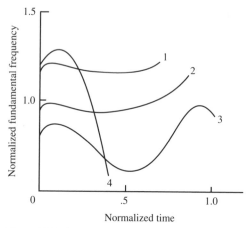

Figure 15.10 Acoustic analysis of four contrastive tonal patterns in Beijing Mandarin (from Gandour 1978: 45–6, following Chuang, Hiki, Sone and Nimura 1972)

Contour tones in Mandarin

high level (1)	[mā]	'mother'
high rising (2)	[má]	'hemp'
low dipping (3)	[mǎ]	'horse'
high falling (4)	[mà]	'to scold'

15.6.2.1   *Discrete-level and terraced-level tone systems*

Welmers (1959), working in the Africanist tradition of tone-system analysis, described **discrete-level tone systems** as ones where the pitch-values of the different tones are maintained in approximately a standard relationship to each other. Connell and Ladd (1990: 3–4) characterize discrete-level tone systems as ones in which 'the realisations of the tone phonemes are not supposed to trespass on each other's phonetic space, but are realised in discrete frequency bands that remain more or less fixed throughout the utterance'. An example of a language maintaining this continuing separation of syllabic pitch-heights is Navajo, according to Anderson (1978: 139), which has two level tones.

Welmers (1959) also introduced the notion of **downstep**, which is a lowering process in tonal phonology which can be applied to the second of two high-tone syllables. This means that the choice of tone after a low tone syllable is different from the choice after a high-tone syllable. After a low tone, the tone of the next syllable can only be low or high. After a high tone, however, the next tone can be low, high or downstepped high (i.e. a pitch

di^{l}o^l-ko^l↓ tu $^{?l}$tu^l↓ vi^{l}ı^l↓ lu $^{?l}$ku^l 'I want crazy cold paper'

Figure 15.11 Downstepped high tones in Coatzospan Mixtec
(after Suárez 1983: 50, following Pike and Small 1974)

slightly lower than the preceding high but not so low as it would need to be
to count as a low tone). A high tone after a downstepped high is on the
same level as that downstepped high. An illustration of a sequence of high
tones, with some of them downstepped, is given in figure 15.11. It is adapted
from Suárez (1983: 50, citing Pike and Small 1974), and cites a phrase
(invented for the purpose) from the Coatzospan dialect of the Otomanguean
language Mixtec meaning 'I want crazy cold paper'. The use of the diacritic
'↓' is intended to indicate the application of the downstep process to the
high tone concerned.

Urhobo is a Nigerian example of a language making use of a register tone
system with two basic tones, one high and one low, with downstep able to
be applied to high tones (Kelly 1969: 158). Pairs of words such as [èβé]
'goat' versus [èβè] 'kola nut' are contrastively identified by their syllabic
tonal patterns alone (low–high versus low–low). The following examples
(phonetically transcribed) illustrate the application of downstep in phrasal
examples, with the '↓' diacritic after the vocoid symbol again identifying the
downstepped tone (Kelly 1969: 159):

Downstep tone in Urhobo

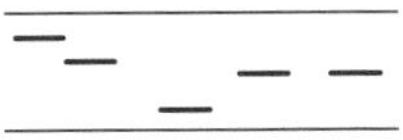

[ì ɣo↓kùɡ͡bír̨wó] 'money and work'

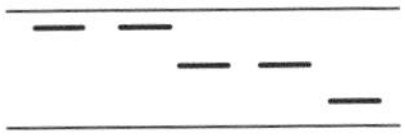

[ɡ͡béxákā↓β̄ár̨è̄] 'dance for us!'

(In the above examples from Urhobo, [r̨] is a voiced nasal retroflex alveolar
flap, but with a lateral onset.) Downstep of the type described, where downstepping is a process applicable only to high tones (or rather to non-low
tones, strictly), is a phonological characteristic of many tone languages. But
in a very small number of languages, such as Zulu, a phonological feature

called **upstep** has also been discovered (Schuh 1978), where successive high tones can spread upwards. In a similar vein, Anderson (1978: 140) cites an unpublished manuscript by Eunice Pike on tone systems in the Mesoamerican Indian languages of Central America, where she describes the tones of Acatlán Mixtec, in which:

> the step-up tone contrasts with the three classical tones, high, mid, and low, but it differs structurally from these tones in that it is always higher than any preceding tone. It is not only higher than a preceding high, but is also higher than a preceding step-up tone. Therefore a sequence of step-up tones is a sequence of progressively higher tones. (E. Pike, n.d.)

Suárez (1983: 50) cites a publication by Eunice Pike and Wistrand (1974) on the same language, with an illustration of the upstep process being applied to high tones in the phrase 'he will not skin the deer the day after tomorrow', shown in adapted form in figure 15.12. Upstep is indicated by the diacritic '↑'.

A yet more elaborated system situation has been reported by Tadadjeu (1974) and Hyman (1985) for Bamileke-Dschang, a Bantu language of Cameroon, where the tonal choice after a low tone can include what one might call a high tone, a downstepped tone and an upstepped tone.

Downstep as a phonological feature is to be distinguished from a feature of many tone languages called **downdrift**. This is the process which results in high tones after low tones being phonetically less high than any preceding high tone in the utterance, which can be regarded as a type of tonal assimilation with the low tone influencing the height of the succeeding high tone (Hyman 1973: 154). To the extent that downdrift is a characteristic of potentially a whole utterance, it can be regarded as an intonational use of pitch. Schachter (1965) also showed that downdrift,

Figure 15.12 Upstepped high tones in Coatzospan Mixtec
(after Suárez 1983: 50, following E. Pike and Wistrand 1974)

$$\text{—}$$
$$\text{—}$$
$$\text{— —}$$
$$\text{—}$$
$$\text{— —}$$
$$\text{—}$$

ma³ⁿne^l e^l te^l ↑ sa^l ↑ ᵏw a^l a^l· ʔi^l ↑ da^l ↑
'he will not skin the deer the day after tomorrow'

in a language such as Hausa, can be suspended to indicate emphasis. Downdrift and downstep give a language with a tone system a **terraced-level** effect (Welmers 1973). The repeated application of upstep adjustments similarly results in a terraced-level effect (Connell and Ladd 1990: 4).

Downdrift can result in several different types of intonational patterns. In Urhobo of Southeastern Nigeria, Kelly (1969:159) shows that successive high tones remain at the same pitch-height, and successive low tones maintain a common level. High tones interspersed with low tones drift downwards, but the low tones interspersed with the high tones are represented by Kelly as maintaining their standard baseline:

Tonal downdrift in Urhobo

[ódibó] 'banana'

[ûw̃ékùɡ͡bé̞ɹɔ́] 'a nose and an ear'

[ɔ́kàáβáɾ̃ēↆ] 'our guinea corn'

(In the above example from Urhobo, the pronunciation of [ɹ] is in free variation with [r], or can be replaced in careful speech by [ɽ] (Kelly 1969: 156).)

Etsako, the Edo language of Nigeria spoken around the confluence of the Niger and Benue rivers, also exploits downstep on high tones, but here the baseline constituted by the phonetic realizations of the low tones in such interspersed sequences also drifts downwards, as in the following example (Laver 1969: 53):

Tonal downdrift in Etsako

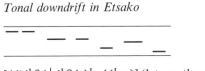

[ɔ́ɔ́jɔ́ᴸβéↆéᴸβé̞ɾ̞è̞ᴸxááᴸmè̞] 'let another person follow me'

(In this Etsako example, the segments marked with a preceding superscript [ᴸ] are articulated with lax articulation.)

The downdrift effect, as an intonational device, can be manipulated for syntactic purposes. Schuh (1978: 239) reports that in Hausa, 'a downdrift pattern is used in statements, but downdrift is suspended when question intonation is used'. Schachter (1969: 80) confirms that 'Yes/No questions in Hausa lack downdrift' (though 'questions that include an interrogative word normally have a downdrift type of intonation').

Hombert (1974) and Schuh (1978) suggest that in most languages with downdrift, low tones drift down more slowly than do the intervening high tones. Hombert (1974) also states that in downdrift languages, while successive high tones typically maintain a standard pitch-level, successive low tones tend to drift downwards even if no high tones intervene. This may be a reflection of the declination process described earlier. But the detailed nature of possible phonetic, phonological and higher-level contributions to the interaction of declination and downdrift remains to be fully established (Connell and Ladd 1990: 3–5).

Tone itself can often be used for grammatical purposes. An example comes from Bini, an Edo language of Eastern Nigeria, where tone is exploited for signalling differences of tense (Ladefoged 1975: 227):

Tonal distinctions of tense in Bini
[i mà] 'I show' (timeless)
[í mà] 'I am showing' (continuous)
[ì mà] 'I showed' (past)

15.6.2.2 *Tonal sandhi*

The patterns of tone on isolated citation forms of words often differ from their manifestations in different contextual positions in connected speech, under the influence of adjacent tones and other factors. There are close parallels between the analysis of the phonetic variants of tones due to such contextual influences of other tones, of intonation, and of structural position, and the analysis of the allophones of segmental phonemes. Indeed the closeness of the analogy between these is reflected in the invention of a parallel terminology: phoneme and **toneme**, phonemic and **tonemic**, allophone and **allotone**, phonetic and **tonetic**, phonology and **tonology**.

A revealing study of tonal phenomena in connected speech in the accent associated with the Chengtu Szechuanese dialect of Chinese was carried out by Nien-Chuang Chang (1958). Chang uses another useful method of annotating tone. This is the method called 'tone letters', designed by her father, Y.R. Chao (1930). It indicates the phonetic realization of pitch in individual syllables, by showing the pitch-movement relative to a vertical line representing the width of the pitch-span, instead of using a stave of

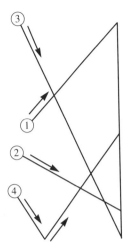

Figure 15.13 Y.R. Chao's 'tone letters' method of annotating relative pitch, applied to the 'naming tones' of Szechuanese (from Chang 1958, following Chao 1930)

parallel horizontal lines. This is illustrated in figure 15.13, showing the tonal pattern for monosyllabic one-word utterances, called the 'naming tone' by Chang.

There are four such naming tones in the Chengtu Szechuanese dialect, and they can be taken here as reference patterns, representing the contextually unmodified realizations of the four tonemes. In Chang's terms, toneme 1 is characterized as 'high–rising', starting between mid-high and mid, and rising to high. Toneme 2 is 'low–falling', starting lower than mid and falling to between mid-low and low. Toneme 3 is 'high–falling', starting at mid-high and falling to a position just above low. Toneme 4 is 'low–falling–rising', starting at mid-low, falling to low, then rising to mid or a little higher. (Chang also points out that the pitch-value of toneme 4, at its lowest, 'often ... reaches so low a point that the voice is almost creaky' (Chang 1958).)

The four tonemes can distinguish a minimal quadruplet of words in Szechuanese (Chang 1958). Adopting a convention of placing the identifying number of the toneme before the tonemic bracket of the word's transcription, the minimal quadruplet is as follows:

Table 15.2 *Allotonic sandhi in Szechuanese*

Toneme	Naming tone	Initial	Medial	Final
I	1	1	┥	┥
II	↓	↓	↓	↓
III	\	˥	˥	\
IV	⟋	⟋	⌐	⌐

Source: Adapted from Chang 1958

> *Tonal contrasts in Chengtu Szechuanese*
> 1/tʃin/ 'clear'
> 2/tʃin/ 'fine (weather)'
> 3/tʃin/ 'to invite'
> 4/tʃin/ 'to celebrate'

One particularly relevant facet of Chang's study was the analysis of the allotonic variation in the phonetic realization of the tonemes in Szechuanese due to contextual effects exercised by neighbouring tonemes in the stream of speech. These variations are sometimes called **tonal sandhi**, after the term used by the Sanskrit grammarians. Table 15.2 shows the allotonic realizations of the four tonemes of Szechuanese when four syllable groups are produced.

15.6.2.3 *Tone and intonation*

Some of the simpler effects of intonational influence on tonal behaviour have been mentioned in the sections above. In some languages with both tonal and intonational systems, however, the interaction of these two systems can be quite complex. Luksaneeyanawin (1993: 289–91) describes this interaction in Thai, for which she posits three intonational patterns (generally falling, generally rising, and a mixed pattern which she calls the 'Convolution' pattern) superimposed on the five contrastive syllable tones (three of which, it will be recalled, are relatively static, or level, and two dynamic, or changing in pitch). She states that 'the system of tone and the system of intonation interplay and are systematically concerted to form the speech melody in spoken Thai. It is clear from the studies of intonation in Thai that each tone has its own behaviour when superimposed by different intonations' (Luksaneeyanawin 1993: 289). She suggests that the Falling intonation pattern 'conveys semantic finality, closedness, and definiteness'. The Rising pattern signals 'semantic non-finality, openness, and non-definiteness', and the Convolution pattern indicates 'semantic contrariety, conflicts and emphasis' (*ibid.*). The interaction of tone and intonation whose analysis she discusses is illustrated in table 15.3 on the next page.

15.6.2.4 *Tones and phonation*

The aerodynamic and physiological requirements of different phonation types have discernible repercussions on the manifestation of pitch-patterns, with the mode of phonation exercising a constraining influence on pitch height. The two examples to be considered in this section both concern a lowering influence on pitch. The first instance to be discussed is the effect of breathy voice on tonal realizations, and the second is the association between creaky voice and low tones in certain languages.

Breathy voice, whether used extralinguistically to characterize the speaker, paralinguistically to signal attitudinal or emotional information, or as the basis for linguistic contrasts, is almost invariably associated with lower values of both intensity and pitch than would be the case for a comparable utterance pronounced with normal (modal) voice (Fairbanks 1960: 179; Laver 1980: 133).

The breathy voiced nasal stops in Tsonga, the Bantu language of Mozambique and South Africa mentioned in section 8.7, are examples of what are sometimes called **depressor consonants** in the phonological analysis of languages with tonal systems. Traill and Jackson (1988: 387) give the following account:

> The consonants of Tsonga may be divided into two classes according to their effect on a following high tone. Those that cause a high tone to become a rising tone are termed depressors (Louw 1968). The distinction between depressor and non-depressor nasals has always been described as involving a clear phonation type contrast. The [former] are breathy (the literature on Tsonga uses the term 'murmured') (Baumbach 1974; Louw 1968) and the [latter] have normal voice.

In the breathy voiced (murmured) nasal stops of Tsonga, the effect of

Table 15.3 *The interaction of tone and intonation in Thai*

Static Tones		Dynamic Tones	
the high		the fall	
the mid			
the low		the rise	

The five tones with the Fall intonation

Static Tones		Dynamic Tones	
the high		the fall	
the mid			
the low		the rise	

The five tones with the Rise intonation

Static Tones		Dynamic Tones	
the high		the fall	
the mid			
the low		the rise	

The five tones with the Convolution intonation

Source: Adapted from Luksaneeyanawin 1993: 290–1

breathy voicing on high tones can be a lowering of fundamental frequency by as much as 35 Hz, and on low tones by as much as 22 Hz (Traill and Jackson 1988: 396). The acoustic effect of such depression of pitch-height in Tsonga can be regarded to some extent as a language-specific exaggeration of the inherent pitch-lowering tendency of breathy voice, in that it is more extreme than is found in some other languages. Maddieson and Hess (1986) report a pitch-lowering effect of lax breathy voice on high tones in Jingpho (a minority language of China) of some 12 Hz.

An association between low falling tones and syllable-final creaky phonation, often associated with a tendency to laryngealization, is common in the languages of Southeast Asia. Ramsey (1987: 45–6) describes the four tones of Standard Chinese (Mandarin) in the following terms:

> The first tone is high and level. It is pitched near the top of the speaking range and is held on a steady, sustained note. The second tone is high and rising. It begins near the middle of the normal conversational range of the voice but quickly rises to the top. The third tone is low. When a word with this tone is pronounced in isolation, the voice starts off low, drops to the bottom, then rises to or above the middle of its range. When the word is not in isolation and is followed by another word, the voice stays down low. Either way, this tone goes down so low the voice often gets creaky. The fourth tone is high and falling. It begins on a pitch at the very top of the vocal range and falls immediately to the bottom. It is very short in duration.

The illustrations quoted by Ramsey (1987: 46) include the following minimal quadruplet, further to the examples cited in section 15.6.2:

Lexical tones in Mandarin

Tone 1	Tone 2	Tone 3	Tone 4
[dā] 'to put up'	[dá] 'to answer'	[dǎ] 'to beat'	[dà] 'to be big'

In Khamti Shan, spoken in Assam and Northwest Burma, the Maan Chong Kham dialect shows a tendency to glottal constriction not only on the low falling tone, but also on a tone that begins at mid and rises. Khamti Shan has five lexical tones on open monosyllables (Harris 1976: 114):

Contour tones and glottal constriction in Khamti Shan

Mid falling	[kau]	⌐⌐⌐	'I (pers. pron.)'
Low falling, with glottal constriction	[kauˀ]	⌐⌐⌐	'a type of night bird'

High falling	[kau]	╲	'to have bad luck'
High level	[kau]	──	'old (of things)'
Mid rising, with glottal constriction	[kauˀ]	╱	'nine'

15.6.2.5 *Tonogenesis*

Since the form of any given language evolves with time, languages which were once **atonal** can develop tonal systems, in a process called **tonogenesis**. (Languages may also lose the use of tonal distinctions and become atonal.) One of the ways that a tonal system may arise springs from microprosodic influences on perception. The statement made in section 15.3.2 that the listener has learned to discount microprosodic distortions of pitch superimposed on the melody of the utterance by segmental constraints when tracking the prosodic melody of utterances should not be interpreted to mean that such distortions are not perceived at all. There is good evidence that, in the historical evolution of a language, the perception of distortions of this contextual sort can give rise to the development of tonal differentiations of words and other grammatical units. Ohala (1978: 25) discusses 'the commonly observed phenomenon that voiceless oral obstruents produce high tone (or a higher variant of a tone) on the following vowel, whereas voiced oral obstruents produce low tone (or a lower variant) on the following vowel (Haudricourt 1961, Cheng 1973)'. (The term 'obstruent' here means stops and fricatives.)

Hombert gives a helpful summary of this area, where he looks at the particular case of the possible tonal consequences of a loss of the voiced/voiceless distinction in consonants represented by stops:

> The historical development of tones ... can result from the reinterpretation by listeners of a previously intrinsic cue after the recession and disappearance of the main cue ... The development of contrastive tones on vowels due to the loss of a voicing distinction on obstruents in prevocalic position is probably the most well documented type of tonogenesis. When such a development occurs, a relatively lower pitch register develops on vowels following the previously voiced series, and a relatively higher pitch is found after the previously voiceless or voiceless aspirated series. The process can lead to a multiplication by two of the number of tones. If the language is atonal, it will have two tones after this development; an already existing two-

tone system can be transformed into a four-tone system, and so on. (Hombert 1978: 78)

Research by a number of authors cited by Hombert (1978: 78–9) attesting to historical developments of this type of tonogenesis is listed in the section on Further Reading at the end of the chapter.

Microprosodic factors constitute one type of contribution to the tonogenesis process. Another (often related) factor is phonation type. The allotonic lowering effect of breathy voice on high tones leading in time to tonal change is one plausible example of such an influence.

15.6.2.6 *Communication of tonal patterns by whistling*

Tonal patterns in languages with tone systems can make a sufficiently important contribution to lexical identification that in some cultures they can be abstracted for linguistic communication as a **speech surrogate** by whistling the tonal melody alone. Effective communication of quite extended linguistic messages has been observed to take place in this way in a number of Mesoamerican languages (Hymes 1964: 310; Suárez 1983: 54–5). Cowan (1948: 280) describes a conversation held solely by whistling in the Huautla dialect of the Mazatec language. This is a Popolocan-Mazatec Otomanguean language of Mexico spoken by some 60,000 speakers in the Oaxaca, Puebla and Vera Cruz regions of Mexico:

> The Mazatecos frequently converse by whistling to one another. The whistles are not merely signals with limited semantic value arrived at by common agreement, but are parallel to spoken conversations as a means of communication. Eusebio Martinez was observed one day standing in front of his hut, whistling to a man a considerable distance away. The man was passing on the trail below, going to market to sell a load of corn leaves which he was carrying. The man answered Eusebio's whistle with a whistle. The interchange was repeated several times with different whistles. Finally the man turned round, re-traced his steps a short way and came up the footpath to Eusebio's hut. Without saying a word he dumped his load on the ground. Eusebio looked the load over, went into his hut, returned with some money, and paid the man his price. The man turned and left. Not a word had been spoken. They had talked, bargained over the price, and come to an agreement satisfactory to both parties – using only whistles as a medium of conversation.

Cowan (1948) makes the sociolinguistic comment that in the Huautla Mazatec culture only males whistle, though females understand the whistling equally well. He also reports that conversations begun by whistling at a distance may be carried on in normal speech when the whistlers come close enough to each other to speak, and that in large meetings conversations lateral to the main spoken conversation may be carried on by group members in subdued whistles. Ambiguities of lexical identification sometimes arise, especially with proper names as a limited lexical set, but in general the linguistic and situational context apparently sufficiently resolves such problems. From a phonetic point of view, Cowan (*ibid.*) describes the whistling, made with a lip-rounded labial whistle-stricture, as preserving the rhythmic and syllabic structure of the spoken equivalents of the whistled phrases. The key of the whistle is set by the first whistler and copied by the second, and the height of the whistle-pitch is higher for longer distances.

Cowan (1948) refers to reports that speakers of other Otomanguean languages such as Chinantec and Zapotec use surrogate communication by whistling tonal patterns, but that the speakers of the Soyaltepec Mazatec language, although it too uses a lexical tonal system, do not. He quotes Gudschinsky (1958) to the effect that Soyaltepec Mazatec speakers 'do not focus on abstracted tone without teaching' (Cowan 1948: 286).

Hymes (1964: 310) describes a number of other languages which use whistling for surrogate communication. He cites Holmberg (1950) as stating that the Sirionó of Eastern Bolivia use whistling for communication while hunting, and Ritzenthaler and Peterson (1954) as describing the whistling of the Mexican Kickapoo Indians during courtship. He also cites Hasler (1960), as stating that whistling as a speech surrogate characterizes communication in cultures which live in mountainous terrain. This would be true of the whistled speech found in La Gomera, one of the Canary Islands (Classe 1957), in the Turkish of Kusköy (Busnel and Classe 1976), and in the French–Spanish dialect of Aas (now dying out) in the French Pyrenees (Busnel, Moles and Vallancien 1962). These latter three examples, however, are not languages which use tonal systems. In these cases, the pitch of the whistle is largely controlled by 'modulating a labial whistle by the articulatory tongue movements of the segments of normal speech, thus producing patterns of pitch variation which are distinctive and recognizable, though they have no connection with the speech melody of the language' (Abercrombie 1967: 107). This is also the basis for the whistled communication used by the speakers of Tepehua, a non-tonal Totonac-Tepehua Mesoamerican language, which Suárez (1983: 55) describes as producing whistles in which 'changes in tongue position, as well as changes in lip tension and contour, are used to reproduce, in modified form, vowels and consonants'.

15.6.2.7   *Communication of tonal patterns by drumming*

An analogue of imitating tonal patterns for surrogate speech communication by whistling is reproducing these pitch-patterns by the so-called 'talking drums' of Africa, which are usually instruments whose pitch can be changed at will by the drummer by tightening or slackening the tension of cords bracing the skin of the drum-head. Abercrombie (1967: 106) describes the 'secret of the talking drums in Africa' in the following way: 'Drum signalling is not by means of a code: the signals are a direct transfer of linguistic pitch patterns and rhythm patterns to the drums. The advantages of this for long distance communication are obvious. Various other instruments are used in some tone-language communities for conveying the pitch patterns of words – flutes or horns, for instance.'

The relationship between linguistic features and drum-signalling can become quite elaborate. Herzog (1945) gives an account of drum-signalling in the Jabo culture of Eastern Liberia, where hollowed-out tree-trunks are used as slit-drums, rather than the variable-tension skin-drums of most of the rest of West Africa. Pitch is controlled by hitting on different places on the variable-thickness lips of the slit with sticks, or by holding the sticks differently. The relationship between pitch and rhythm in Jabo is quite complex, and the drums are mostly used in ceremonial functions. Partly because of the specialized aesthetic tradition that has arisen in such functions, and partly because of the complex interaction with features relevant to speech patterns, Herzog (1945) comments that 'the bulk of signalling is apt to be practised and fully understood only by specialists'. The interested reader is referred to Herzog's detailed article.

15.7   The analysis of pitch-patterns in intonation systems

Pitch is used phonologically in an intonational function when significant melodic patterns of pitch-movement are distributed over units larger than the single word. One such language is English. The pitch patterns of English intonation have received more detailed study than those of any other language, particularly by phonologists, and the section of Further Reading at the end of the chapter contains a list of recommended publications on this topic, as well as on the study of intonation in other languages.

15.7.1   *Basic concepts in intonational analysis*

The preliminary comments made in section 15.3, about the need in the prosodic analysis of pitch to discount both the inherent microperturbations of fundamental frequency in voiced laryngeal vibration, and the microprosodic effects due to the influence of segmental articulation, apply as much to the analysis of the phonetic basis of intonation as they do to that of lexical tone. The initial data for intonational analysis therefore consists of the fundamental-frequency contour of the speaker's utterance, from which the microperturbatory and microprosodic disturbances have been smoothed. This contour is quasi-continuous, in the sense that the intermittent gaps caused by any stretches of voicelessness are left out of analytic account except for purposes of alignment. Also left out of account are any pitch-factors that are to be ascribed to organic influences from such sources as the size of the speaker's larynx. In other words, the fundamental-frequency contour has to be **speaker-normalized** before further analysis, to allow comparability between the intonational patterns of different speakers. A further abstraction then has to be made, to allow for the exploitation of pitch for other linguistic uses than intonation. These include lexical stress and lexical tone. (The phonetic correlates of lexical stress are discussed in chapter 16 on the metrical organization of speech, as are those of rhythm.)

The object of attention in intonation analysis is hence a somewhat idealized contour of pitch movement over the full duration of the given utterance. There are several different ways in which the intonational pattern represented by such an idealized contour could be analysed. One (holistic) way would be to identify the whole 'tune' of the pitch sequence as one of a small set of intonational tunes recognized as associated with that language. The second (atomistic) way would be to apply the standard linguistic notions of structure and system to the intonation of the overall contour, in a perspective where the speaker exercised communicative options of choice at relevant points in the intonation of the utterance. The first of these can be called the **tune-based approach to intonation**, the second the **tone-based approach to intonation**. The next two sections will explore each of these approaches in turn.

15.7.1.1   *Tune-based analysis of intonation*

A long-established tradition of intonational analysis, particularly identified originally with Jones (1962) and Armstrong and Ward (1931) for English, and with Coustenoble and Armstrong (1934) for French, reduces the inventory of significant pitch-patterns in each of these languages to a very small number of options. The work by Jones and his colleagues on English specified the intonation of English in terms of two holistic tunes, 'tune I' and 'tune II', which differ chiefly in the pitch tendencies on the final syllable of the utterance. Couper-Kuhlen (1986: 69) characterizes these tunes as follows:

> Whereas in Tune I the pitch of the voice *falls* to a low level at the end,
> in Tune II the voice *rises* on any unstressed syllables that follow the
> last stressed syllable. If there are none, then the rise occurs within the

last stressed syllable ... Although admittedly 'there are other varieties
and greater wealth of detail than are here recorded' (1931: 1)
Armstrong and Ward claim that for all practical purposes, English
intonation can be reduced to these two tunes, one with final falling,
one with final rising pitch movement. Variations for emphatic
sentences include increased stress as well as widened, or narrowed and
lowered pitch range.

Couper-Kuhlen (1986: 69) gives the following illustrations of the two tunes
(with dashes and dots representing the pitch of stressed syllables and
unstressed syllables respectively):

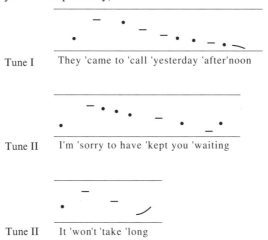

Tune I   They 'came to 'call 'yesterday 'after'noon

Tune II   I'm 'sorry to have 'kept you 'waiting

Tune II   It 'won't 'take 'long

The purpose of this tune-based approach was largely pedagogic, teaching
English to foreign learners, and distinguishing between unemphatic declarative sentences and other types. Its controversial linguistic claim was to limit
the location of relevant pitch-behaviour to the final part of each tune, effectively setting up a contrast between two terminal tendencies, falling versus
rising. Within a constrained pedagogic objective, this use of holistic pitch-
contours to characterize intonation retains a certain influence.

Leach (1988) characterizes the intonation of French in a way that consciously returns to the tune-based tradition of Coustenoble and Armstrong
(1934). Leach suggests that:

> the total configuration of simple one-group utterances in French can
> best be accounted for by an analysis in terms of tune. Although two or
> three major points are identified within the rhythmic group as being
> intonationally relevant (onset, (pre-final) and final syllable), the
> semantic contrasts discerned lie not in the differences of pitch at those
> points but rather in the overall contour of the tune section. Seven

major tunes are identified on the basis of the relationship between onset, (pre-final) and final syllable, and of whether the final is pronounced on a glide, as in Tunes 1, 2, 3, and 4, or on a level pitch, in Tunes 1-, 2- and 4-; in the latter three, the pitch of the penultimate syllable is also relevant. (...) Pre-tune syllables within the group typically hover around a mid pitch but are attracted towards the onset pitch of the tune. (Leach 1988: 138)

Figure 15.14 shows six of Leach's tunes of French, given in stylized form from a recorded corpus of material. The six utterances are all of a standard phrase *c'est Marie-Jeanne* ('it's Marie-Jeanne'). In this figure, adapted from Leach (1988: 134–5), non-initial syllables are represented as dots indicating the pitch-height of the syllable concerned, and the final syllable (which is typically lengthened) is represented as a dash, indicating the terminal tendency of the pitch-movement.

Tranel (1987: 202–4) uses the concept of 'phonological groups' as a basis for analysing the finer detail within the overall intonational tune of French phrases. He shows that the overall contours of intonational patterns of French phrases (globally falling or rising–falling for declarative phrases, or rising for questions) are actually segmented into component stretches, whose boundaries conform more or less to those of grammatical phrase-structure. Figure 15.15a shows the components of a globally rising-falling tune on a complex declarative phrase, figure 15.15b the segmented pattern for a question whose intonation rises overall, and figure 15.16 the structure of a generally rising–falling tune on a yet more complex declarative phrase (analysed

Figure 15.14 Six tunes of French intonation (after Leach 1988: 134–5)

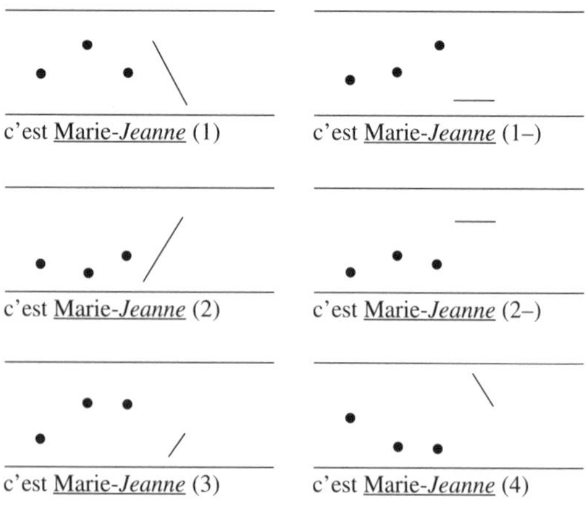

c'est Marie-*Jeanne* (1)

c'est Marie-*Jeanne* (1–)

c'est Marie-*Jeanne* (2)

c'est Marie-*Jeanne* (2–)

c'est Marie-*Jeanne* (3)

c'est Marie-*Jeanne* (4)

Il s'enfuit | en courant   'He runs away'

Figure 15.15a Components of a globally rising-falling tune on a complex declarative phrase in French (after Tranel 1987: 204)

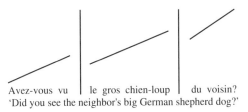

Avez-vous vu | le gros chien-loup | du voisin?
'Did you see the neighbor's big German shepherd dog?'

Figure 15.15b Components of a globally rising tune on a question in French (after Tranel 1987: 204)

first at a global level, then into a finer level of detail, and finally into the lowest level of Tranel's analysis, which he calls 'phonological phrases').

The tune-based approach to intonation also characterizes much of the work that has been conducted on the intonation of Spanish. Cid Uribe and Roach (1990: 1) suggest that Spanish intonation

> has always been described in a global rather than in an atomistic way, in terms of intonation contours where the end of the contour is the

Figure 15.16 Successively detailed analyses of the intonation of a French declarative utterance (after Tranel 1987: 202)

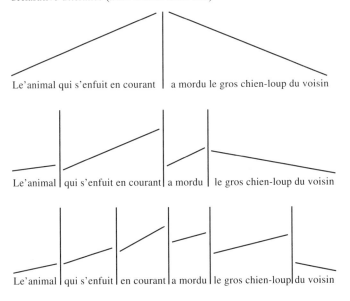

Le'animal qui s'enfuit en courant | a mordu le gros chien-loup du voisin

Le'animal | qui s'enfuit en courant | a mordu | le gros chien-loup du voisin

Le'animal | qui s'enfuit | en courant | a mordu | le gros chien-loup | du voisin

factor that bears the linguistic significance ... Navarro Tomás (1974) and others after him (e.g. Canellada and Madsen 1987) claim that Spanish intonation is to be described in terms of three different levels at the end of an intonation contour which are manifested in five inflexions: *cadencia*, a low fall (*terminacion grave*), which expresses absolute finality; *anticadencia*, which constitutes the end of a subordinate clause and is a high rise; *semicadencia*, which is a fall but less complete than the *cadencia* and expresses non-finality, series of elements or uncertainty; *semianticadencia*, which is a rise but less high than that of the *anticadencia* reflecting oppositions and contrasts of a secondary kind; and 'level' which ends at the same level as the body of the group, reflecting the interruption of an idea.

Cid Uribe and Roach (1990: 1) go on to say that the five different pitch-patterns, each with its final pitch-value, and intended to account for all intonational patterns in Spanish, were claimed by Navarro Tomás to be reducible to just two basic patterns, A and B. Figure 15.17 shows these two basic patterns claimed to represent typical intonational patterns in Spanish.

The tune-based approach to intonation is also finding an application in new developments in speech technology, where it is being used as a simplified teaching strategy in a computer-assisted system for teaching pronunciation to learners of foreign languages (Hiller *et al.* 1991). Figure 15.18 shows some of the overall contours used in this system for neutral, unemphatic utterances in English, French and Italian.

Finally, the tune-based approach to intonation has re-surfaced in the work of a number of modern phonologists working on intonation. Couper-Kuhlen (1986: 70) draws attention to the work of Liberman (1975) as the source of a '[view of] English intonation as a lexicon whose words are holistic contours, or tunes, which are associated with units of meaning. Among the tunes which have been investigated so far are the "contradiction" contour (Liberman and Sag 1974), the "surprise/redundancy" contour (Sag and Liberman 1975) and the "warning/calling" contour (Liberman 1975).' Figure 15.19 shows a representation of the overall contour that Liberman and Sag (1974) associate with the function of 'contradiction'. However, as Cutler (1977) has pointed out, a one-to-one connection between contradiction and

Figure 15.17 Two tunes of Spanish intonation (after Cid Uribe and Roach 1990: 1, following Navarro Tomás 1974)

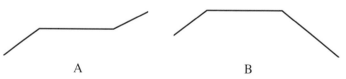

A   B

French

'Vous avez du fromage'

English

'I live in Manchester now'

Italian

'Vorrei una informazione'

Figure 15.18 Intonational contours for neutral, unemphatic utterances in English, French and Italian (after Hiller *et al.* 1991)

such a contour is not tenable in a strong form. Cutler suggests that it is possible to utter phrases such as *Go and see what the fellow wants!* (in a situation in which a father chides his son, who had persisted in ignoring a friend's attempt to attract attention from outside the window), without any contradictory function being conveyed, with exactly the same intonational contour as shown in figure 15.19 (cited in Couper-Kuhlen 1986: 164).

15.7.1.2 *Tone-based analysis of intonation*

The remainder of this presentation of intonation will be couched in terms of a tone-based perspective. In order to introduce some basic concepts for the description of intonational phenomena in such a perspective, it will be helpful to begin with a brief discussion of some aspects of intonational phenomena in English (RP), and use this as the background for making comparative comments about tone-based intonational data in other accents of English and other languages. Cruttenden (1986: 59–60) illustrates five different patterns of pitch on an English 'Yes/No' question. In Cruttenden's diagrams of these patterns, reproduced here in adapted form as figure 15.20, the upper and lower limits of the speaker's pitch-span are depicted by parallel upper and lower horizontal lines. The pitch-pattern

Figure 15.19 A contour of American English intonation said to be associated with contradiction (Liberman and Sag 1974) and chiding remonstrance (Cutler 1977) (after Couper-Kuhlen 1986: 164)

Elephantiasis isn't incurable!

Figure 15.20 Five possible intonation patterns on a 'Yes/No' question in English (Received Pronunciation) (after Cruttenden 1986: 59–60)

associated with each syllable is separately analysed, level pitch is shown by dots, the heavier dots represent syllables which are stressed, and moving pitch is indicated by a line of changing height. Declination effects are disregarded.

A number of properties of the pitch-patterns in figure 15.20 can be isolated which are relevant to possible linguistic functions, with the assumption that the analysis implicit in the diagrams reflects the broad consensus that exists at this level of observation between researchers investigating intonational phenomena from a tone-based perspective. First, the patterns of pitch are temporally aligned with the segmental, syllabic and lexical units of the utterance, but are nevertheless also free to make their own distinctive contribution to the overall utterance. They are constrained in time by being coterminous (by definition) with voiced segments, but they are free to vary in pitch-value. This partial independence of the phonetic phenomena of intonation from the segmental strand of performance raises issues of integration shared with other suprasegmental strands of phonology.

Second, the pitch-pattern for the first five syllables *Are you going a-* in each of the utterances is identical, and the intonational discrimination of the five utterances from each other rests on the pitch behaviour associated with the last syllable *-way*, with respect to the rest of the pattern. This suggests that intonational behaviour is analysable in structural terms, like many other phonological entities.

490

Third, the diagram represents differences between the component syllables which are thought to correspond to their different grades of perceptual prominence for the listener, with unstressed syllables being the least prominent, stressed syllables being slightly greater in prominence, and the syllable marked as showing moving pitch being the most prominent. This suggests that one function of intonation may be to signal that particular parts of an intonational structure are in some way more pivotal for the interpretation of the meaning of the intended message than other less prominent parts. Another facet of the organization of graded prominence in speech is that the prominence signals relevant to intonation have to be co-ordinated with those relevant to the metrical organization of stress and rhythm. Since pitch is exploited by very many languages as a realization of word-stress, the local contribution of word-stress to a given pitch-contour has to be distinguished from the global role of the contour as a realization of a given intonational unit.

Fourth, although the five phrases are syntactically identical, their intonation is heard as conveying intended differences of interpretation. This suggests that syntax and intonation can be to some extent decoupled, and that each can make its own contribution to the overall interpretation of the composite message.

Finally, the actual patterns of pitch on the final most-prominent syllable vary. This is reminiscent of the way that a paradigm of minimally contrasting word-structures can vary by commutation of one element, and suggests that a categorial system of intonational choices can be made at this point in the intonational structure concerned. It also suggests that differences of interpretation can be attached to the different choices of pitch-pattern made at this most-prominent syllable.

Taken together, these five properties of pitch-patterning support the idea that intonation can be treated as a linguistic form of behaviour, capable of phonological analysis in structural and systemic terms, with a communicative role to play in association with (but partially independent of) lexical and syntactic levels of language. Couper-Kuhlen (1986: 118–19) suggests a partly different set of criteria for recognizing intonation as potentially linguistic in nature. With some reservations, she would regard intonation as linguistic to the extent that it is:

> systematic (displaying paradigmatic systems and syntagmatic structures);
> conventional ('determined by cultural tradition rather than by human physiology alone');

purposive (used for conscious communication);

arbitrary (with a linkage between sign and meaning that is free of necessity);

discrete (with units that are categorial rather than gradient);

language-specific (differing in pattern and realization from one language to another).

Accepting intonation as linguistic in nature, the phonological unit of intonational structure will for convenience of reference be called an **intonational phrase**, and the most prominent syllable within the intonational phrase will be called the **intonational nucleus**. The phonological system of pitch-patterns operating at the nuclear place in the structure of the intonational phrase will be called the system of **nuclear tones**. Any legitimate utterance of English is made up of one or more intonational phrases, and each intonational phrase contains one intonational nucleus at which one of the possible nuclear tones is chosen. In English, the intonational phrase is often but not always co-terminous with the syntactic clause (Cruttenden 1986: 75). Any material in the intonational phrase before the nucleus can be called the **pre-nucleus**, and any after the nucleus can be described as the **post-nucleus**. Every utterance in English which can be regarded as intonationally complete must contain an intonational nucleus, but pre-nuclear and post-nuclear material are optional elements.

A question remains to be answered which is as much phonetic as phonological in nature: what properties of prominence achieved through modification of pitch qualify for nuclear intonational status? The answer will vary from language to language, but in English there are two properties of pitch that have to be taken into account in deciding on the intonationally relevant pitch-prominence of a stressed syllable. The first, which is visible in the examples in figure 15.20, is an intonationally significant dynamic change in pitch, giving either a **fall** or a **rise** in pitch, or a change which reverses direction either once, giving a **fall–rise**, or a **rise–fall**, or twice, giving a **rise–fall–rise**, or a **fall–rise–fall**. The use of the term 'intonationally significant' here means that the change in pitch must be more prominent than that produced by word-stress alone, since stressed syllables in English tend to be not only longer in duration and louder in intensity, but also generally more prominent in pitch than their unstressed counterparts, as indicated in the earlier comments in this section.

The second means of achieving intonationally significant prominence does not necessarily involve a dynamic change in pitch, but is based on a step in the relative pitch-difference between adjacent syllables. Figure 15.21 illus-

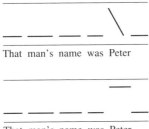

That man's name was Peter

That man's name was Peter

Figure 15.21 Two different types of pitch prominence in English (Received Pronunciation), showing a fall from high to low pitch versus a step down from a high-level pitch to a low-level pitch

trates these two ways of making a syllable prominent. In the first utterance, the first syllable of *Peter* has a falling pitch from high to low in the pitch span. In the second utterance, the first syllable of *Peter* is said with a high level pitch, having stepped up from the low level pitch on the preceding material. The pitch then steps down to a low level on the second syllable of *Peter*.

This is a reflection of the more general principle that Bolinger (1958: 112) enunciated when he suggested that what is responsible for provoking the perception of intonational prominence is **pitch obtrusion** – 'a rapid and relatively wide departure from a smooth or undulating contour' (obtruding in either direction from the local trend-line of pitch). Bolinger (1958) proposed the term 'pitch-accent' for the configurations of pitch that give rise to the impression of prominence. He also insisted that pitch and lexical stress collaborated in defining such prominence, neither alone being sufficient to make a syllable sound accented. Commenting on Bolinger's seminal work, Couper-Kuhlen (1986: 30) states that

> [When] we learn the lexicon of our language, we learn that some syllables shun pitch accents. Consequently, when these 'unaccentables' do appear with pitch prominence, our foreknowledge prevents us from hearing them as accented. Thus it is the interaction of our knowledge of lexical stress patterns, *stress* being understood as potential for pitch accent, together with (primarily) pitch obtrusion, which accounts for perception of accent.

We can adopt the term **pitch-accent** for any pitch configuration that makes a syllable prominent, whether the pitch obtrusion involved is phonetically **dynamic** (rising, falling, rising–falling, falling–rising) or phonetically **stepping** (from or to a given pitch value) in nature.

15.7.2   *Linguistic functions of intonation*

In any utterance in English, the prosodic structure of the utterance will reflect choices made by the speaker about how many intonational phrases the utterance should be divided into, where in each phrase the nuclear tone should be placed, and which nuclear tone should be selected at the nucleus of each intonational phrase. It is then legitimate in a general linguistic perspective to ask what the communicative function of such choices might be. This goes well beyond the limits of phonetic description, into phonological matters of discourse structure and pragmatics. But a very short discussion of the linguistic functions of intonation may be helpful, in order to give an indication in principle of how the phonological options of intonation allow speakers to communicate the intent of their messages to listeners. For a more extended discussion on the communicative function of intonation in English, the reader might consult Bolinger (1986, 1989), Couper-Kuhlen (1986) and Cruttenden (1986). Bolinger (1989) also discusses intonational functions in many other languages.

Two central concepts in considerations of these linguistic functions of intonation are those of 'focus' and 'pre-supposition'. Couper-Kuhlen (1986: 42) cites Jackendoff (1972: 230) to the effect that focus 'denotes "the information in the sentence that is assumed by the speaker not to be shared by him and the hearer"', while pre-supposition 'denotes "the information in the sentence that is assumed by the speaker to be shared by him and the hearer"'. The prime function of intonational **focus** will be taken below to signal the location of **new information**, and the chief **pre-supposition** assumed in intonational performance will be taken to concern the identification of **given information**.

The discussion that follows is founded on a simplified and abbreviated version of the tone-based phonological analysis of British English (RP) intonation proposed by Halliday (e.g. 1963, 1967, 1970). Halliday's detailed approach (which is not uncontroversial in terms of more modern developments) is an integrative one, combining the phonological statement of intonational patterns with an account of rhythmic structure, but the involvement of rhythm in his model will be left out of account here.

We can say, following Halliday, that there are three different phonological systems at work in the intonation of English, namely 'tonality', 'tonicity' and 'tone', whose use enables the speaker to signal focus and pre-suppositions to the listener. **Tonality** is the system of options for dividing the utterance into units of intonational phrases. Halliday called the intonational phrase a 'tone-group'. **Tonicity** is the system of options for the location within the intonational phrase of the intonational nucleus. Halliday called the syllable carrying the intonational nucleus the 'tonic syllable'. **Nuclear tone** is the system of choices of the type of pitch-pattern made on the intonational nucleus. Halliday's term for the nuclear tone system was simply the 'tone' system.

It was said in section 15.7.1.2 above that every utterance in English must consist of at least one intonational phrase, which means that every intonationally complete utterance must make a selection from the system of nuclear tone on at least one syllable in the utterance. Halliday suggests that the nuclear tone system is made up of five principal tones. At an initial level of analysis (several of the nuclear tones having a number of sub-types), the pitch-patterns that make up the manifestations of these five tones are shown in table 15.4.

Table 15.4 *Pitch-patterns on tonic syllables in English*

Name of tone	Pitch pattern	Contour name	Terminal tendency
Tone 1	\	fall	low
Tone 2	/\/	rise or fall–rise	high
Tone 3	__/	rise	mid
Tone 4	/\/	rise–fall–rise	mid
Tone 5	\/\	fall–rise–fall	low

Source: After Halliday (1963, 1967, 1970)

Using the symbol '//' to signal the boundary of each intonational phrase, and underlining to identify the syllable carrying the intonational nucleus, then a typical contour for the pitch patterning over one intonational phrase might be:

Orthographic //1 Why don't you come to the <u>cin</u>ema with me?//

Pitch contour

495

In this illustration, *Why don't you come to the* – is the intonational pre-nucleus. The nuclear tone has been selected on the <u>*ci*</u>- of *cinema*, and is identified as an instance of tone 1 by the prefacing '1' symbol after the initial intonational phrase-boundary symbol. The remaining part of the utterance, -*nema with me*, is the intonational post-nucleus.

The choice of pitch-contour shown by the pre-nuclear stretch is contextually somewhat limited by the nature of the choice of nuclear tone. Tone 1 has the widest choice of different pre-nuclear patterns that can precede the nuclear tone. The post-nuclear choice of pitch-pattern however is completely mechanical in this accent of English, in that a choice of nuclear tone with a low terminal tendency can only be followed by a low level post-nuclear element, as in the above example. Any nuclear tone with a rising, non-low terminal tendency can only be followed within the same intonational phrase by a post-nuclear pattern that continues the rising tendency of the nuclear tone. An example of this is:

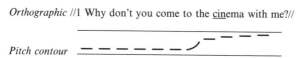

Orthographic //1 Why don't you come to the <u>ci</u>nema with me?//

Pitch contour

The fully predictable nature of post-nuclear patterns in this accent means that no extra information is carried by this element in the structure of the intonational phrase, over and above the information conveyed by the nuclear tone.

The system of tonality, where a choice is made about the number and location of intonational phrase boundaries, is illustrated in table 15.5 (with the syllables bearing the nuclear tone being underlined in all three cases).

Table 15.5 *Choices of tonality on an English utterance*

Orthographic	//1 Every diplomat is a skilled <u>linguist</u>//
Pitch contour	
Orthographic	//1 Every <u>dip</u>lomat is a //1 skilled <u>linguist</u>//
Pitch contour	
Orthographic	//1 Every <u>dip</u>lomat is a //1 <u>skilled</u> //1 <u>linguist</u>//
Pitch contour	

Source: After Halliday (1963, 1967, 1970)

One of the functions of tonality is to signal the number of 'information points' carried by the utterance, with one such **information point** per intonational phrase. It has been said that pitch prominence is a generalized 'pay attention' signal to the listener (Ladd and Cutler 1983: 7), and the choice of tonality is a demarcative indication of the informational 'chunking' of the utterance. In the above examples, each intonational phrase carries one major information point. But Halliday also allows the concept of an intonational phrase with a double intonational nucleus in certain cases of combined nuclear tones, with the second nucleus identifying information of importance which is seen by the speaker as subordinated to the information signalled by the first. In this case, both information points are new, but the first is of more major and the second of more minor importance. The two instances in RP English where this is possible are sequences of tone 1 followed by tone 3, and tone 5 followed by tone 3. An example is the major information point (*there's another one*) and the minor information point (*in the kitchen*) carried by the following utterance:

Orthographic //13 There's a<u>no</u>ther one in the <u>ki</u>tchen//

Pitch-contour

The system of tonicity, which chooses the placement of the nuclear tone within the intonational phrase, can signal either that information is thought to be new to the listener, or is pre-supposed to be knowledge already held by the listener, or is meant to be contrastive with such knowledge. This is analysed in the following way. Tonicity in English is held to be neutral, and to signal that the information in the intonational phrase is considered to be new information for the listener, if the nuclear tone is placed on the stressed syllable of the last lexical item in the intonational phrase. If the nuclear tone is 'non-neutral', by being placed elsewhere, then the information conveyed is held to be given – that is, already known by the listener, or is meant to be conveyed contrastively. These different possibilities can be seen in the following examples:

Orthographic   //1 There's another one in the <u>ki</u>tchen//

Pitch-contour

Orthographic   //1 There's a<u>no</u>ther one in the kitchen//

Pitch-contour

The first example above is a case of neutral tonicity, and the information is assumed to be all new to the listener. In the second case, the intonational phrase carries non-neutral tonicity, and *kitchen* is thereby marked as given information that the listener is thought already to possess.

Halliday also cites a range of more narrowly linguistic functions fulfilled by intonation. They include the identification of the 'mood' of clauses – affirmative, interrogative, imperative and moodless – and the support of contextual sentence functions such as 'statement', 'question', 'command', 'answer' and 'exclamation'. More subtle functions are also supported, such as 'echo statements', as in:

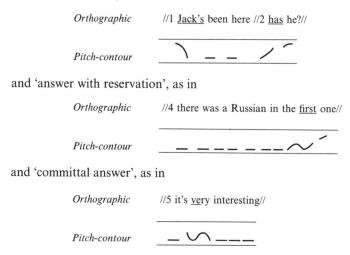

| *Orthographic* | //1 <u>Jack's</u> been here //2 <u>has</u> he?// |

and 'answer with reservation', as in

| *Orthographic* | //4 there was a Russian in the <u>first</u> one// |

and 'committal answer', as in

| *Orthographic* | //5 it's <u>very</u> interesting// |

15.7.3 Contour interaction theories versus tone sequence theories of intonational description

Finally, it is necessary to say that the presentation offered above of intonational (and tonal) phenomena in language has stayed relatively close to matters of phonetic realization, whose description is after all the prime purpose of this book. The discussion so far has also been coloured by an attitude that it is reasonable to try to allocate functional uses of intonation (such as 'declarative statement') to the patterns discriminated, and that it is feasible to relate the description of the contours used to a concept of a 'neutral' pattern which is distinctively opposed to some 'contrastive' pattern. The reader should be aware that a considerably more abstract phonological perspective on tone and intonation has gathered pace in the last fifteen or so years, partly as a companion to advances in autosegmental and metrical phonology.

Ladd (1984), one of the significant scholars working in this more abstract perspective, suggests that in the approach taken by the authors mostly cited in the account of intonation in this book, they

> assume a fairly traditional view of intonation, which we may call the CONTOUR INTERACTION (CI) theory. In this view, the basic units of intonation (at least in the European languages) are taken to be phrase- or utterance-level contours: approximate over-all shapes that are correlated with grammatical meanings like 'declarative' and 'continuation'. Other factors affecting F_0 (such as emotional colouring, syntactic boundaries, accent, emphasis, and segment-related effects) are thought of as independent components overlaid on the phrase contour, generating their own local F_0 configurations which interact with the phrase contour's basic abstract shape. (Ladd 1984: 722)

Ladd criticizes the **contour interaction** (CI) approach as assuming too strict a division between grammatical and expressive uses of intonation, over-simplifying the possibility of a distinction between 'neutral' and 'contrastive' patterns of intonation (*ibid.*), and above all as being concerned with the communicative function of intonation, at the expense of specifying its phonological form.

Ladd (1984: 721–3) discusses the more phonological, more abstract approach as growing partly from the intonational work of the Dutch researcher 't Hart and his colleagues (e.g. Collier and 't Hart 1975; 't Hart and Cohen 1973; 't Hart and Collier 1975, 1979), of the Swedish researchers Bruce and Gårding (e.g. Bruce 1977, 1982; Bruce and Gårding 1978) and of the American researcher Pierrehumbert (e.g. 1980, 1981). He characterizes this approach as a **tone sequence** (TS) view, in the following terms:

> Unlike the CI model, which treats 'sentence intonation' as a phonological primitive in itself, the TS theory treats intonational tunes as sequences of simpler tonal elements or pitch accents. The difference between the two views thus revolves around their conceptions of the relationship between accent and intonation. The CI model assumes that the individual accent-related pitch movements are specified by a separate component, and then *interact with* an overall tune; the TS view assumes that those pitch movements are simply concatenated to *make up* the tune, so that 'sentence intonation' is merely the sum of its accent-related parts. (Ladd 1984: 723)

Ladd refers to 't Hart and Collier (1975) and Pierrehumbert (1980) for 'well-developed arguments for the TS model, emphasizing in particular its formal simplicity and theoretical restrictiveness'. This foundational book on phonetics is not the place to say more about this phonologically very interesting and advanced perspective on intonation, which the reader is urged to explore. But one particular advantage that might be borne in mind by the reader in this exploration is that the TS model of intonation allows a better unification of treatment, at least at the phonological level, of both tonal and intonational prosodic phenomena. Further reading on the CI and TS models is specified at the end of this chapter.

15.7.4   *Paralinguistic functions of pitch behaviour*

The properties of intonation discussed above can perhaps all be defended as formal properties of language, but it is also the case that the phonetic substance of pitch behaviour, especially because of its gradient, scalar nature, lends itself to the service of paralinguistic communication as well. The details of how these features are actually taken up by the paralinguistic conventions of different cultures have so far received only a little research, except by pioneers such as Bolinger (1986, 1989) and Crystal (1969). Features such as the exact placement and interval of pitch-movement, and the width and mean of the pitch range involved, are all available for communicating attitudinal and emotional information paralinguistically through manipulation of tone of voice. Some of these features are, however, also used linguistically (e.g. the use of a change in pitch range to signal the parenthetic status of comment inserted in the main linguistic message). The absence of well-codified information about the contribution of paralinguistic functions to the control of pitch behaviour then makes the construction of adequate accounts of linguistic intonation particularly problematic. The boundary between linguistic and paralinguistic uses of pitch thus remains a somewhat undefined frontier (Couper-Kuhlen 1986: 184). The nebulous status of this borderland territory was well captured by Bolinger (1972: 19) in his comment that intonation is a phenomenon 'around the edge of language'.

15.8   **The analysis of loudness**

The loudness of the speech of any individual speaker will vary with a number of factors. First, the sociolinguistic accent-community of which he or she is a member will be characterized by a typical average loudness of speech. The speech of Gaelic communities in Scotland seems markedly less loud than the speech of urban Egyptian Arabic communities, for instance. Sometimes, the sociolinguistic community will tacitly prescribe different ranges of loudness for males and females, as a matter of social convention. Within such sociolinguistic constraints, a speaker's loudness will vary with factors with relatively direct linguistic relevance such as the place of the utterance in the speaking-turn, with paralinguistic factors such as the tone of voice used, and extralinguistic factors such as the physical and social location in which the conversation is taking place, and the distance apart of the participants. Linguistic factors to do with the loudness of speaking-turns, of utterances, and of their constituent syllables, are explored in section 15.8.3 below. Paralinguistic details of loudness in speech are discussed in section 15.8.4.

The extreme possibilities of loudness obviously have a biological basis in the organic nature of the speech apparatus in every speaker, notably in the capacity of the respiratory system. But beyond saying that in general the speech of men is louder than that of women, possibly for organic reasons, it is not possible to associate habitual loudness of speech with physique, for instance, in any confident way. The organic possibilities of loudness in speech are overlaid by the way that the individual speaker has learned to control loudness phonetically. The phonetic capacity to produce loud speech is not merely a matter of the available power of the speaker's respiratory apparatus. Phonation types vary substantially in the loudness they can project. A tense modal phonation without the persistent air leakage of whisperiness will typically result in a louder voice than one which uses a breathy-voice phonation. Additionally, for any given input of voiced sound energy at the larynx, the intensity of the acoustic transmission that reaches the listener will be conditioned by other articulatory contributions such as the muscular tension of the vocal-tract walls and the amount of damping imposed by nasality.

The same considerations of the relationship between quasi-random variability, short-term segmental perturbations and the longer-term trend-line apply to loudness behaviour as did to pitch behaviour. The inherent effects which typify the performance of individual segments is discussed in section 15.8.2 below. Before embarking on that discussion, however, it will be helpful to explore some basic concepts in the perception of loudness.

15.8.1   *The perception of loudness*

Good descriptions of the perception of loudness can be found in the book by Moore (1982), which is particularly recommended. Other references are given in the suggestions for Further Reading at the end of the chapter.

We need first to distinguish between physical measures and their perceptual correlates in this area. Just as in the earlier discussion pitch was taken as the perceptual correlate of frequency as a physical measure, so we shall take **loudness** as the perceptual feature relating to the physical concept of **intensity**. Intensity is proportional to (the square of) the amplitude of oscillations of air molecules in sound-waves passing through the atmosphere. Intensity (or power) of a sound is usually measured in terms of a scale whose units are called **decibels**. The abbreviation for a decibel is **dB**. The decibel scale is a relative scale, with 0 dB corresponding to the sound-pressure level (SPL) of a reference sound, namely one close to the absolute limit of detectability by the average listener of a sound whose frequency is 1 kHz. A doubling of intensity corresponds to a difference of 3 dB. Moore (1982: 48) describes the early work of a pioneer in the field of hearing, S.S. Stevens (1957), where he suggested that the relationship between perceived loudness and physical intensity, is one where the 'loudness of a given sound will be proportional to its intensity raised to the power 0.3'. A doubling of loudness therefore corresponds to a rise in sound-level of approximately 10 dB (Moore *ibid.*).

The human auditory system is remarkably sensitive to the intensity of sounds, and can cope with an astonishing range of intensities. The minimum movement of the ear-drum that can be heard as an audible sound, in the ear's most sensitive frequency zone (about 3 kHz), is about 4×10^{-10} cm, or about 0.04 of a nanometre (Moore 1982: 43), which is about the diameter of a hydrogen molecule. Compared with such a minimum, the most intense sound we can hear without physical damage to the auditory apparatus has a power which is about 1,000 billion times greater (i.e. a ratio of 1,000,000,000,000 to 1), at 120 dB SPL. Exposure to 120 dB SPL can be tolerated only for a very short time before grave risk of permanent damage.

Moore (1982: 8) gives some illustrations of different sources of sound which put the sound-levels of human speech into context. A Saturn rocket being launched 45 metres away would have a sound level of 180 dB SPL, far beyond the threshold of physical damage to the auditory apparatus. Amplified music at a rock concert is often played at about 140 dB SPL, still very substantially above the range of loudness which will cause long-lasting and often permanent damage to hearing. A speaker shouting with maximum strength at a listener at very close range will produce noise at about 100 dB SPL. Normal conversation is conducted at about 70 dB SPL, quiet conversation at about 50 dB, and a soft whisper at about 30 dB. The apparent silence of an area deep in the country late at night, which is probably the quietest environment most of us have experienced, produces a sound level of about 20 dB SPL.

Sensitivity to loudness varies with frequency. The most sensitive zone lies between about 1 kHz and 5 kHz (where much of the crucial acoustic information for speech is found). Below 1 kHz, loudness-sensitivity drops off steeply with descending frequency. Above 5 kHz, sensitivity also decreases, but slightly more slowly. Overall loudness sensitivity diminishes with age, just as sensitivity to pitch does. Young children can hear faint sounds of low intensity at frequencies up to about 20 kHz, but the intensity thresholds for the perception of such sounds by adults tend to be considerably higher, if they can hear them at all, and typically increase with age.

A variety of scales of loudness have been suggested. One scale which has been suggested is the sone scale (S.S. Stevens 1957). In Stevens' scale, one **sone** is defined as the perceived loudness of a pure tone note at 40 dB SPL. The scale was constructed by asking listeners to adjust the level of the tone until it sounded half as loud as this reference. This level was then given the value of 0.5 sones, another heard as twice as loud a value of 2 sones, and so on. Intermediate values were assessed by interpolation between the experimental values. Other experimenters have found slightly different relations between such perceptual values and their physical correlates (Moore 1982: 48–50), and the exact nature of the psychoacoustic relationship between loudness and intensity remains a research area. Taking the viability of some such 'sonic' scale of comparison of perceptual loudness, we can now move on to consider the concept of 'sonority'. This concept has a pedigree of over a century in the phonetic and phonological literature, but the length of its lineage does not necessarily reflect the reliability of its character.

15.8.2   *The sonority principle*

Ladefoged (1975: 219) defines the **sonority** of a segment as 'its loudness relative to that of other sounds with the same length, stress, and pitch'. Goldsmith (1990: 110–11) describes sonority as 'roughly speaking, ... a ranking on a scale that reflects the degree of openness of the vocal apparatus during speech production, or the relative amount of energy produced during the sound – or perhaps it is a ranking that is motivated by, but distinct from, these notions'.

We shall see in a moment one of the reasons for Goldsmith's caveat in his last phrase of the above quotation. First, it can be noted that the organization of segment-types on a scale of **intrinsic sonority**, if perceptually valid, could open the door to a phonetically realistic definition of the syllable, which would be attractive to phoneticians and phonologists alike. The necessary conditions would be that the segment-types typically representing the syllabic nucleus should be intrinsically more sonorous than those representing the syllable margins, and that relative proximity to the nucleus should be reflected in relatively greater sonority. This would allow a **sonority principle** to operate, such that (in Goldsmith's own explicit formulation):

> (i) the segmental material in the onset of the syllable must be arranged in a linear order of increasing sonority from the beginning of the syllable to the nucleus of the syllable; and (ii) conversely, the segmental

material in the rhyme of the syllable must be arranged in a linear order of descending sonority from the nuclear vowel of the syllable to the final segment of the syllable. (Goldsmith 1990: 110)

The onset of the syllable is made up of all segments up to, but not including, the segment representing the syllabic nucleus, while the rhyme consists of all the segments from and including the nucleus to the end of the syllable. In the English word *treats* /triːts/, the onset is made up of the cluster /tr-/, and the rhyme by the sequence /-iːts/. These structural elements of the syllable are discussed further in chapter 16.

The **sonority hierarchy** that is generally accepted, in the phonologically oriented terminology used by Goldsmith (1990: 110), is the following:

most sonorous
    vowels
        low vowels
        mid vowels
        high vowels
    glides
    liquids
    nasals
    obstruents
        fricatives
        affricates
        stops
least sonorous

There are some problems with such a sonority hierarchy. Equally, there are some promising avenues offered for future development. Restricting our discussion to English, the problems include the fact that while some syllables fit the pattern predicted by the sonority principle, others violate the principle. In yet other syllable types, the way that individual speakers produce the sound-types concerned may differ sufficiently to effect a re-ordering of the hierarchy. Thus the segments making up the syllables corresponding to the words *elephant, compensation, liquidity* obey the suggested sonority hierarchy. Those containing syllable onset-clusters beginning with [s], such *spy, string, scrape* do not obey it, in that [s] is normally thought by most people to be more perceptually salient than the [p], [t] or [k] that follows it, while nevertheless being more distant from the syllabic nucleus. In some speakers, especially with nuclear syllabic constituents such as [m̩] in words like *prism* /prɪzm̩/, the syllabic nasal stop may be less salient (sonorous) than the preceding syllable-initial /z/ (Ladefoged 1975: 220).

One reason for Goldsmith's caveat in the quotation above, therefore, to the effect that perhaps the sonority hierarchy 'is a ranking that is motivated by, but distinct from', notions of precise perceptual salience, is that the motivation is essentially phonological in nature. As such, like so many other phonologically-motivated characterizations of speech, the truth it reflects is general rather than comprehensive, and sufficiently rich as a concept that a deeper exploration may reveal useful further phonological principles of organization at work. One such principle may be, as Goldsmith suggests (1990: 111), citing the work of Selkirk (1982), that the sonority hierarchy may be able to be used not only as a scale for organizing the segmental membership of syllable structures, but as a distance metric for asserting phonological constraints on the nature of segmental adjacency within those structures in a quantified way. Although the distance metric ultimately found to be useful may be quite complex, it would be of significant benefit to our attempt to understand the organizational principles of phonology to be able to 'characterize languages with respect to how much sonority distance they demand of successive segments' (Goldsmith 1990: 112).

Assuming that a relative sonority principle could be established for language-general rules governing privileges of segmental sequence within syllables, then two consequences follow. First, each syllable would be internally characterized by a **sonority profile** across its constituent segments, as explored above. Second, whole syllables would be able to be related to their neighbouring syllables in an utterance in a hierarchy of relative syllabic prominence. This second consideration will be seen in chapter 16 to contribute to a 'syllable-weight' approach to explaining the perceived rhythm of utterances.

15.8.3 *Linguistic functions of loudness*

Loudness seems to be exploited by linguistic communication to a much smaller degree than pitch. We shall see in the next chapter that differences of loudness can contribute to the perceived stress of a given syllable in particular languages. Beyond the syllable, the linguistic use of loudness as a prosodic feature is comparable to that of pitch in some limited respects. As with pitch, it is reasonable to think of an utterance as having a **loudness contour**. In most types of utterances in most languages, the loudness contour of the utterance shows a **loudness declination** not unlike that of pitch-declination, with a corresponding **loudness baseline** and **topline**. The concepts of **loudness range** and **loudness span** are also analogous to the corresponding concepts applied to pitch.

Unlike pitch in either lexical tone systems or intonation systems, the trajectories of the loudness contour do not seem to be subjected in any versatile way to structured short-term manipulation within the utterance for communicative purposes. One limited exception in English (and in many languages with intonational systems) is a linguistic function of loudness correlated directly with that of intonational uses of pitch, in the re-setting of the loudness range to signal the start of a new topic within an utterance, or to indicate the parenthetic status of some intercalated material in an utterance. As with pitch, as indicated in section 15.4.1, the start of a new topic can be signalled by a widening of the loudness-span, and/or by a step-like raising of the baseline. Similarly, the parenthetic status of a remark inset within an utterance can be identified by depressing the baseline and narrowing the width of the loudness span for the duration of the parenthetic remark, then returning to the span and baseline values of the framing material.

15.8.4 *Paralinguistic functions of loudness*

The momentary **loudness value** of a speaker's utterance, as reflected in the loudness declination, disregarding the local influence of segmental material and the stressed or unstressed nature of the syllables concerned, has a regulative paralinguistic role to play in a participant's claiming the floor at the beginning of the speaking-turn. During continuing competition for the floor, with the other participant speaking simultaneously, loudness (and often pitch as well) is usually either boosted, or the loudness declination suspended, until the conflict is resolved. With the floor successfully claimed, normal loudness declination can proceed.

Manipulation of the **loudness mean** is a frequent ingredient of paralinguistic control of tone of voice. Many of the agonist emotions, such as anger, exasperation, irritation, grief and horror, tend to be expressed in very many cultures in a loud tone of voice. Exceptions exist in individual habits, and extreme anger, for instance, is signalled by some speakers (at least in English) by speaking more quietly, not more loudly. Tenderness is expressed in most cultures in a quiet voice.

15.9 Prosodic settings of pitch and loudness

Neutral references in prosodic settings of pitch and loudness are considerably less satisfactorily defined than in articulatory settings. In the articulatory case, the neutral reference settings were able to be defined in ways which were largely common to speakers in general. In the case of prosodic settings, this is more difficult. Trying to answer a question such as 'What is meant by "high" in the phrase "a high mean pitch-setting"?', for example, one is obliged to choose between two possible answers. One is 'A high mean pitch-setting should be interpreted as "high with respect to pitch-values encountered in the population at large"'. The other is 'A high mean pitch-setting should be interpreted as "high with respect to the pitch-values that might be expected from a speaker of that age, sex, height and physique"'.

The first answer gives rise to difficulties of comparison between males and females, children and adults. The second, which will be the preferred answer here, gives rise to difficulties about the relationship between organic and phonetic facts. Listeners usually have confident views about the existence of a strong positive correlation between a speaker's age, sex, height and physique on the one hand, and the size of the speaker's larynx on the other. In the light of this confidence, they are often ready to draw conclusions about the mean pitch-setting in a particular speaker's voice in such terms as 'the mean pitch of this speaker's voice is high compared with what one would have expected from the visible physical characteristics of the speaker'.

The implication of such a conclusion is that, if a correlation of the sort described actually exists, then the speaker must be imposing a constraining setting on the activities of the larynx. No positive (or negative) correlation has yet been shown to exist by experimental investigation, and the basis for the confidence shown by listeners must remain somewhat tentative at best. Nevertheless, it will be taken here for practical purposes to be a valid assumption. Neutral prosodic reference settings will thus be taken to refer to organically based values specific to the individual speaker, rather than to values defined as standard for the whole population of speakers.

Figure 15.22 shows a protocol for written annotation of prosodic settings. Pitch-settings include high and low mean pitch, wide and narrow ranges of pitch, and high and low variability of pitch. Loudness settings are duplicates of this arrangement. Because of the tentative nature of the assumptions built into the definition of the neutral reference settings concerned, no scalar degrees of strength of the settings are included.

The settings for **pitch mean** and **loudness mean** should be understood to refer to the average pitch-value or loudness-value shown by the speaker relative to an assumption about what one would normally expect from a speaker of that particular age, sex, height and physique. **Pitch-range** or **loudness-range settings** are defined as the linguistic range within which the speaker's voice habitually varies in paralinguistically unmarked, attitudinally neutral conversation. When setting-analysis is used for paralinguistic investigation, then paralinguistic range can be substituted for linguistic range. **Variability of pitch** and **variability of loudness** concern the degree

Category	Setting		Scalar degrees			
			neutral	1	2	3
Prosodic	Pitch					
	mean	high				
		low				
	range	wide				
		narrow				
	variability	high				
		low				
	Loudness					
	mean	high				
		low				
	range	wide				
		narrow				
	variability	high				
		low				

Figure 15.22 Protocol for recording scalar degrees of prosodic settings.

to which pitch or loudness varies from moment to moment within the relevant range. Voices which tend to be monotonous with respect to pitch, or which tend to show nearly uniform loudness, can be scored as low in variability. Conversely, voices with a substantial amount of dynamic movement of pitch or loudness within the relevant range can be scored as high in variability.

Further reading

Recommended publications on the **acoustics of speech** and **auditory perception** are Borden and Harris (1980), Fry (1979), Ladefoged (1962, 1967), Lieberman and Blumstein (1988) and Pickett (1980). The anatomy, physiology, neurology and physics of hearing are well covered in Yost and Nielsen (1985), and Kuehn, Lemme and Baumgartner (1989) is an excellent edited summary of many topics in the **neuroanatomy and neurophysiology of hearing**. The biological bases of the sensory systems relevant to speech production are presented in Hardcastle (1976) and Kaplan (1960). The psychophysical and biological characteristics of the full range of human perceptual systems are well described in Ludel (1978) and Uttal (1973).

A good general reference on **tone** is the book edited by Fromkin (1978), in which Hombert (1978: 78–9) cites the following research on historical developments of **tonogenesis** in languages in South Africa (Beach 1938), and the following languages and language groups in Southeast Asia: **Chinese** (Karlgren 1926, Maspero 1912); **Karen** (Burling 1969, Haudricourt 1946, 1961, Henderson 1973, Jones 1961); **Miao-Yao** (Chang 1973); **Thai** (Brown 1965, Gandour 1975b, Gedney 1973, Li 1954, Sarawit 1973); **Tibeto-Burman** (Matisoff 1971, 1972, 1973a, 1973b, Mazaudon 1977); and **Vietnamese** (Haudricourt 1954). A good general reference on the topic of the interaction of consonants and tone is the book edited by Hyman (1973). A general article on the use of drumming and whistling as **speech surrogates** is Stern (1957).

Accounts of the systematic patterns of **English intonation**, and discussions of theoretical methodology and issues in the prosodic analysis of intonation, are available in Beckman and Pierrehumbert (1986), Bolinger (1972, 1986, 1989), Brown, Currie and Kenworthy (1980), Chafe (1970), Cooper and Sorensen (1981), Couper-Kuhlen (1986), Cruttenden (1986), Crystal (1969), Cutler and Ladd (1983), Gibbon (1976), Halliday (1963a, 1963b, 1966, 1967, 1970), Hirst (1977), Kingdon (1958a), Ladd (1980, 1983, 1984, 1986), Leben (1976), Liberman (1975), Liberman and Pierrehumbert (1984), Maeda (1976), O'Connor and Arnold (1961), O'Shaughnessy (1976, 1979), Pierrehumbert (1980), de Pijper (1984), Pike (1945), Schubiger (1958) and Willems (1982).

Descriptions of the **intonation** of a number of other languages are available as follows: **Danish** is described by Thorsen (1978, 1979, 1980, 1983, 1985); **Dutch** by Collier and 't Hart (1981), Collier (1989), 't Hart, Collier and Cohen (1990) and Keijsper (1983); **French** by Coustenoble and Armstrong (1934), Faure (1973), Grundstrom (1973), Kenning (1979, 1983), Leach (1980, 1988), Martin (1975, 1982), Touati (1987), Tranel (1987), Vaissière (1971), Wunderli (1987) and Zwanenburg (1965); **German** by Adriaens (1984), Bannert (1985), Fox (1984) and Isačenko and Schädlich (1970); **Greek** by Botinis (1989); **Hungarian** by Varga (1975, 1983); **Italian** by Avesani (1987), Chapallaz (1979), D'Eugenio (1976) and Martin (1978); **Japanese** by Beckman and Pierrehumbert (1986), Fujisaki (1981), Fujisaki and Hirose (1984), Fujisaki *et al.* (1990), Fujisaki, Hirose and Takahashi (1990), Fujisaki and Nagashima (1969), Fujisaki and Sudo (1971), Haraguchi (1977), Kubozono (1988, 1989), Pierrehumbert and Beckman (1988) and Poser (1984); **Russian** by Keijsper (1983), Leed (1965), Odé

(1986, 1989) and van Schooneveld (1961); **Spanish** by Canellada and Madsen (1987), Cid Uribe (1989), Cid Uribe and Roach (1990), Kvavik (1974, 1976), Quilis (1981) and Quilis and Fernandez (1985); **Swahili** by Maw and Kelly (1975); **Swedish** by Bruce and Gårding (1978), Gårding (1979), Hadding-Koch (1961), and Touati (1987); and **Thai** by Luksaneeyanawin (1983).

The volume edited by Cutler and Ladd (1983) is a balanced starting-point for comparing the two **contour interaction** (CI) and **tone sequence** (TS) perspectives on prosodic analysis, which Ladd and Cutler (1983: 1–10) characterize in their introduction to that volume as 'concrete' versus 'abstract'. The publications by Beckman and Pierrehumbert (1986), 't Hart and Collier (1975), Ladd (1980, 1983, 1984, 1986), Liberman (1975), Liberman and Pierrehumbert (1984), Pierrehumbert (1980) and Pierrehumbert and Beckman (1988) are particularly recommended to the reader wishing to pursue the more abstract TS perspective.

16

The metrical organization of speech: stress, syllable weight, prominence and rhythm

The previous chapter described the prosodic structure of speech in terms of melody and loudness. Any musical phrase is characterized not only by these factors, however, but also by its metrical structure - the grouping, accentuation and rhythm of the delivery of its component parts. Continuing this musical metaphor, this chapter considers the metrical structure of speech in terms of the relationships between its syllables, stress and rhythm.

The **metrical organization** of speech is the most complex of all the different levels to analyse, in that its temporal structure integrates facets of all four basic dimensions of speech - quality, duration, loudness and pitch. In the previous chapter, it was said that 'Other things being equal, one syllable is more prominent than another to the extent that its constituent segments display higher pitch, greater loudness, longer duration or greater articulatory excursion from the neutral disposition of the vocal tract.' This description tacitly compares two syllables of the same phonological structure. Where one of two otherwise identical syllables is made more prominent than the other by an exaggeration of the value of one or more of the phonetic parameters of pitch, loudness, duration or quality in this way, the more prominent syllable can be said to receive more **stress**. In this definition, **phonetic stress** is a gradient phenomenon, and the phonetic realization of any syllable can be said to show a greater or less degree of stress relative to the manifestation of some other syllable.

Stress can also be regarded as a phonological property of the syllable, and a distinction can initially be drawn between stressed and unstressed syllables, using two degrees of **phonological stress**. The placement of phonological stress on a particular syllable within a word is a defining property of that word, and this can be referred to as **word-stress** or **lexical stress**. The term **accent** or **word-accent** is also used for the concept of lexical stress, which can be useful when one wants to distinguish between 'word-accent' as the potential for the normal syllabic location of stress in a word, and 'stress' as the actual placement on a given occasion.

Using the diacritic '' before the first segment of the syllable concerned to indicate its stressed status, the two Pashto words ['guʈa] 'knot' and [guʹʈa] 'pochard' (Shafeev 1964: 5) and the two Asmat words ['eco] 'kind of frog' and [eʹco] 'revenge' (Voorhoeve 1965: 26), both cited by Hyman (1977a: 39), are phonologically distinguished only by the different location of word-stress. (Asmat is one of the New Guinean languages, spoken in Irian Jaya).

The phonetic manifestation of stress varies from language to language, with some (such as English) exploiting all four parameters of pitch, loudness, duration and quality. The majority of languages with phonological stress seem to make use of only three parameters, however. Pitch, loudness and duration alone, without manipulation of phonetic quality, are the triplet of phonetic parameters used by most languages that exploit stress as a phonological device.

Manipulating the degree of stress is one way of differentiating the prominence of syllables. A second way in which syllables may differ in prominence is through **syllable weight**, which is partly a phonological concept based on the segmental constituency of the structure of syllables. Depending on their structural make-up, we shall see in section 16.2 that syllables can be regarded as metrically 'heavy' or 'light' in prominence. The third way that syllables can differ in prominence, within the general constraints of syllable weight, is in the sonority characteristics of the individual segmental members of the syllable, as discussed in section 15.8.2.

Utterances are generally perceived as being spoken with a certain rhythm. The perception of rhythm in speech is predicated on the listener's recognition of a quasi-periodic recurrence in time of a given type of speech unit, such as syllables carrying peaks of prominence (achieved through either or both syllable stress or syllable weight), or syllables themselves. The study of rhythm in speech is a highly controversial area of research, however, as we shall see in section 16.4.

The structure of this chapter will be to look first at prominence achieved through syllable stress. Then the nature of prominence achieved through syllable weight will be considered. Next, the typology of the different patterns of lexical stress found in the languages of the world will be explored. Finally, the relationship between syllabic prominence and the perceived rhythm of utterances will be discussed.

16.1   Prominence achieved through syllable stress

We can begin this section on prominence achieved through syllable stress by considering the nature of the mechanisms used to produce phonetic stress. A view of respiratory activity in speech was presented in chapter

6, where a pulmonic egressive airflow was provided by a smoothly controlled dynamic balance of expiratory and inspiratory effort. It was suggested that no good evidence had been found by modern experimental research to support Stetson's (1928, 1951) early contention that each syllable is produced on an individual pulse of egressive airflow created by a specific contraction of the muscles of the respiratory system. By investigating the electrical activity correlated with the contractions of the muscles involved in the activities of the respiratory system during speech, Ladefoged, Draper and Whitteridge (1958) showed that on some occasions an English utterance made up of two phonological syllables (such as *pity*) may be pronounced with only one major contraction of the expiratory muscles. Conversely, some single-syllable utterances such as *sport* showed a double burst of electrical activity in the respiratory muscles. In general, however, the realizations of at least the phonologically stressed syllables of an utterance of connected speech seem to correlate fairly closely with these bursts of electrical activity in the contracting respiratory muscles (Lehiste 1970: 109).

This broad correlation does not prove the necessity of pulsatile behaviour in the respiratory system for supporting stressed syllables. Lehiste (*ibid.*) cites work by Peterson (1956) with paralysed patients who could only breathe with the help of a respirator. Despite having to time their utterances to coincide with the perfectly regular outflow phase of the machine, their speech was apparently perceived as notably normal in its syllable and stress patterns (Lehiste *ibid.*). The implication of such findings is that a significant part of the phonetic control of syllabification and stress can lie downstream of the respiratory process, in the laryngeal and articulatory processes - for instance by control of the pitch correlates of stress by vocal fold tension rather than by subglottal pressure (Ohala 1977: 146).

Fry (1955, 1958, 1965) investigated the acoustic and perceptual correlates of lexical stress in English noun/verb word-pairs such as 'object/ob'ject, 'permit/per'mit, 'contract/con'tract etc. He was able to show very clearly the existence of a hierarchy of acoustic cues to the stressed status of a syllable in English. The perceptually most influential cue was (higher) pitch, especially when this was dynamically changing rather than level. The second most important cue in the hierarchy was (longer) duration, the third was (greater) intensity and the last was segmental quality (with stress being correlated with a more peripheral location in the vocoid space).

Lass comments that the phonetic realization of lexical stress in different languages can differ widely. In the English spoken in Southern England, the stressed syllables 'tend to be louder, longer and higher than [unstressed syllables]; in Northern Irish English and Danish they are louder, longer and lower. The only "universal" requirement is that [stressed syllables] be different from [weak syllables], and that this difference be perceived as a difference in prominence' (Lass 1987: 108).

The dominant role of pitch in conveying stress patterns gives stress the most intimately interactive relationship with other linguistic and pragmatic uses of pitch, notably in intonation. We can conclude from the previous chapter, for example, that the placement of the nuclear intonational tone in all languages using an intonational system is always, except in very special circumstances, coincident with a lexically stressed syllable. When the intonational nuclear tone does fall on the lexically stressed syllable of a word, the pitch-pattern used for the manifestation of the tone will reinforce and exaggerate that used for the realization of lexical stress, if both involve a falling pitch-pattern. If the nuclear tone is rising, it will over-ride the falling pitch-pattern normally associated with the phonetic realization of lexical stress.

The term 'stress' occurs in many usages in the conventional vocabulary of phonetics and phonology in ways which involve intonation, and which can cause confusion if not well understood. These usages include 'sentence stress', 'nuclear stress' and 'emphatic stress'. **Sentence stress** is simply another term for the placement of the nuclear intonational tone. Given the role of the nuclear tone in boosting the stressed syllable of a given word by ensuring that it is the most prominent of all the words in the intonational phrase, the use of a term like 'sentence stress' has an obvious interpretability. The interaction of lexical stress and sentence stress can be seen in the four different patterns of sentence stress (shown by underlined syllables), superimposed on an utterance with an unvarying pattern of lexical stress, illustrated below:

> The 'pictures that are dis'<u>played</u> in the '<u>li</u>brary are '<u>cer</u>tainly '<u>com</u>petent
>
> The '<u>pic</u>tures that are dis'played in the '<u>li</u>brary are 'certainly '<u>com</u>petent
>
> The '<u>pic</u>tures that are dis'played in the 'library are 'certainly '<u>com</u>petent
>
> The 'pictures that are dis'played in the 'library are 'certainly '<u>com</u>petent

Nuclear stress is a term used by generative phonology (e.g. in Chomsky and Halle 1968) for the location of greatest syllabic prominence on phrases. As such it has implications for intonational structure. The 'Nuclear Stress Rule' in generative phonology, for example, is formulated to express the requirement in English that 'in a noun phrase primary stress is assigned to the last primary-stressed syllable (e.g *a black boárd, a big Univérsity*)' (Fischer-Jørgensen 1975: 246).

The function of **emphatic stress** is to call the listener's attention to a given syllable or word with greater insistence than is afforded merely by neutral patterns of intonation or lexical stress. In the case where intonation and lexical stress are neutral, with a falling nuclear tone being placed on the lexically stressed syllable of the last content word in the utterance, as in the English utterance *The dog ate the biscuit*, emphatic stress can be used to give special emphasis to this syllable, as in *The dog ate the BIScuit*, with a wider pitch excursion, greater loudness and possibly a longer duration for the realization of the vowel. The effect on the listener is then to convey that there is a particular reason for insisting on the identification of the word receiving emphatic stress (for instance, implying that it was 'not the bone'). A paralinguistic effect of emphatic stress can also be to signal the degree of intensity felt by the speaker about the topic under discussion, as in the French utterance *C'est aTROCE* 'it is atrocious' (Tranel 1987: 201). This element of insistence on the part of the speaker in the function of emphatic stress is reflected in the French translation of the phrase 'emphatic stress' as 'l'accent d'insistance' (Tranel 1987: 194).

Emphatic stress can also be used to highlight a syllable not normally receiving lexical stress (i.e. on a syllable other than the normally word-accented syllable), in order to draw the listener's attention to a choice made by the speaker between potentially competing forms. An example of emphatic stress in this function would be the pronunciations *ENable* and *DISable* instead of the normal *en'able* and *dis'able*, in the English utterance *I said ENable, not DISable*. Another example of placing stress on a syllable other than the normally word-accented syllable (in a compound word) would be the utterance *He lives in SOUTH Dakota*, insisting on an implied contrast with *North Dakota* (normally accented as 'North Da'kota'). In such cases the placement of the nuclear tone is also non-neutral.

A French example of emphatic stress in this type of displacement of stress-location from the normal word-accented syllable for paralinguistic effect of increased intensity of feeling is the utterance *C'est éPOUvantable* 'It's terrible' (Tranel 1987: 202). The French example achieves part of its emphasis by virtue of the fact that stress in French is normally placed on the last syllable of the word (unless the vowel is /ə/). Normal word-stress patterns would have given *C'est épouvan'table*.

An initial distinction was drawn above between two degrees of phonological stress, 'stressed' and 'unstressed'. But many phonologists set up not just two categories of stress in the syllables of a single word, but three - **primary stress, secondary stress** and **unstressed**. They point to the graded differences of prominence that characterize individual syllables in words in English such as ',resig'nation', ',syste'matic', ',intro'ductory', "ve̡to' and "anec̡dote' (using "' and ',' to indicate primary and secondary stress respectively). Differences in the distribution of primary and secondary stress can also typify different accents. Fromkin and Rodman (1974: 90) compare the word-stress patterns of American English *láboratòry*, (['labəɹˌtɔɹɪ]) which shows both primary and secondary stress on the stressed syllables, with Received Pronunciation's *labóratory* ([lə'bɒɹətɹɪ]), which uses only primary stress.

The contribution of segmental quality to lexical stress in English can be seen in a diminution of the relative degree of stress on a syllable by a process called **vowel reduction** (Lindblom 1963). This phonological process replaces a peripheral vowel with a more central vowel in unstressed syllables. The most frequent type of vowel reduction in English and other languages making use of this phonological process such as Russian and Swedish is the replacement of a more peripheral vowel by /ə/. Possible pronunciations in English (RP) of the noun/verb pairs mentioned earlier, showing vowel reduction on the (unstressed) first syllable of the verb, would be:

Differentiation of noun/verb pairs in English by lexical stress and vowel reduction

Noun	Verb
/'ɒbʤɛkt/ 'object	/əb'ʤɛkt/ ob'ject
/'pɜmɪt/ 'permit	/pə'mɪt/ per'mit
/'kɒntrakt/ 'contract	/kən'trakt/ con'tract

Householder (1971: 268–9) investigated a very large corpus of everyday English, and found only 135 pairs of words of identical orthography which like these could occur either as nouns (with stress on the penultimate syllable) or as verbs (with stress on the final syllable). In a very small number of cases the location of lexical stress alone was the differentiating factor, as in 'import (noun) versus im'port (verb), and 'insult (noun) versus in'sult (verb). In these cases, pitch, loudness and duration alone were the phonetic parameters used to make the distinction. The very large majority of word-pairs, however, used vowel reduction as a manipulation of quality together with differences of pitch, loudness and duration to signal the difference of word-stress location. A selection of the words in Householder's list is given in table 16.1.

Table 16.1 *Some orthographically identical word-pairs in English differentiated by word-stress as nouns (penultimate stress) or verbs (final stress)*

abstract	colleague	defect	exploit	insert	rebel
accent	collect	detail	export	intern	recess
addict	combat	digest	extract	outrage	recoil
address	combine	discard	ferment	perfume	record
affect	commerce	discharge	fragment	pervert	recount
affix	commune	discount	impact	present	refuse
ally	compound	discourse	impress	proceed	reject
alloy	compress	entrance	imprint	project	segment
annex	concert	escort	incense	protest	survey
assay	conscript	essay	incline	purport	torment

Most words in most languages that use stress linguistically do not enjoy partnership in minimal pairs based on stress, and in this sense stress cannot properly be said to be used in a contrastive function. It is said rather to show a **culminative** function, being a characteristic property of the word without normally contributing to contrastive paradigms (Martinet 1954). As such, this culminative property is thought to help the listener to judge how many individual words the speaker has produced in a given utterance.

16.2   Prominence achieved through syllable weight

The notion of syllable weight is a phonological one, underpinning metrically-relevant rules of stress-placement. It will be helpful first to expand on the structure of the syllable, following the introduction in the previous chapter of the concepts of the onset and the rhyme of the syllable. It will be recalled that the overall syllable consists of an optional onset, followed by an obligatory rhyme. The rhyme is divided into the nucleus and the coda. The **onset** is defined as any consonant(s) preceding the **nucleus**, which is the structural place filled by the vowel of the syllable. The nucleus is the perceptually most prominent part of the syllable. The **coda** is made up of any consonant(s) following the nuclear vowel. The **rhyme** therefore comprises the (obligatory) nuclear vowel and any consonant(s) following it (Hogg and McCully 1987: 36). The rhyme is sometimes called the **core**, and the nuclear vowel the **peak** of the syllable. These relationships are summarized in figure 16.1.

Syllable weight encompasses two kinds of syllable: 'light' syllables and 'heavy' syllables. A **light syllable** is one whose rhyme is made up of a nucleus consisting of a short vowel, followed by a maximum of one short consonant. Light syllables are sometimes called **weak syllables**, and heavy syllables

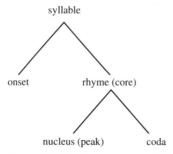

Figure 16.1 Metrical structure of syllables

strong syllables (Sloat, Taylor and Hoard 1978: 64). As a measure of **syllable quantity**, the phonological length of a light syllable has been called a **mora** (Trubetzkoy 1939). A **heavy syllable** is any other type of syllable, and its phonological length is greater than one mora. The structure of the rhyme in heavy syllables can hence take any of the following shapes:

> a long vowel, with or without a coda of any sort;
> a short vowel, with a coda made up of two or more consonants;
> a short vowel, followed by at least one long consonant.

The concepts set out above (onsets, nuclei, codas, light and heavy syllables, and moraic considerations) will be seen to be relevant in specifying the constraints for locating lexical stress in different languages. They also provide a suitable descriptive terminology for discussing the fluctuations of prominence in a train of syllables in connected speech. The phonetic realizations of heavy syllables, with their longer nuclear vowels and/or their more substantial codas, stand out more prominently in the perceived flow of speech than do light syllables. The mora has also been suggested as providing the basis for rhythmic organization in languages such as Japanese. Prominence achieved by syllable weight will be germane to the discussion below of the perceived rhythm of speech.

16.3   The typology of lexical stress

The typology of lexical stress in the languages of the world is a matter primarily of phonological interest. The limited discussion offered below is intended to provide sufficient background for the discussion to follow of the perception of rhythm, in which the location and recurrence of stressed syllables play a relevant part.

The most extensive survey to date of the incidence and distribution of stress as a linguistic phenomenon is given by Hyman (1977b), who considered data reported from 444 languages (taken partly from Ruhlen 1975). If a language makes linguistic use of stress, then it will fall into one of two broad types: locating the word-stress predominantly on a given syllabic location in the word, or allowing much more freedom for placement of the stress. We can call the first type a language which uses (predominantly) **fixed lexical stress**, and the second type one which permits **variable lexical stress**. Out of the set of 444 languages (which were drawn from every inhabited continent, but were not completely balanced genetically as a sample), Hyman (1977a: 56) found 306 with fixed lexical stress versus 138 others. These others were made up of sixteen languages which did not exploit stress (or tone either); nine languages with stress-placement dominantly based on syllable weight, which did not result in fixed stress-placement; and 113 languages for which 'no statement can be made as to any dominant tendency in stress-placement'. The following three sections illustrate the patterns that characterize fixed and variable lexical stress in these and comparable languages.

16.3.1 *Fixed lexical stress*

The languages in Hyman's survey which showed predominantly fixed lexical stress location fall into strongly different proportions, depending on the syllable-placement chosen. The data show the following totals (Hyman 1977a: 41, 56):

> *306 languages with predominantly fixed lexical stress-placement*
> | | | |
> |---|---|---|
> | Dominant initial syllable stress | 114 languages | 37.3% |
> | Dominant second syllable stress | 12 languages | 3.9% |
> | Dominant antepenultimate syllable stress | 6 languages | 2.0% |
> | Dominant penultimate syllable stress | 77 languages | 25.2% |
> | Dominant final syllable stress | 97 languages | 31.7% |

The relatively strong tendency (about 57 per cent) for languages to prefer the trailing edge of words (final or penultimate syllable) for the location of fixed lexical stress is to some extent explainable by suggesting that such placement gives stress a **demarcative** function, indicating where the word-boundaries are without making the listener expend too much cognitive effort in calculating them. The same argument holds for initial syllable stress-placement at the leading edge of the word. The final, penultimate and initial syllable word-marginal positions together account for 94 per cent of the 306 languages with fixed-stress systems.

A number of examples of words from languages with predominantly fixed lexical stress are given below. A case where the lexical stress obligatorily falls on the final syllable is Tatar, the Altaic language spoken in the central area of the Commonwealth of Independent States (Comrie 1981: 67), where it is the fifth largest language of the CIS. It is also spoken by some 4,000 speakers just across the border in the Xinjiang region of China. Ramsey (1987: 182–3), gives the following examples:

> *Fixed lexical stress (final syllable) in Tatar*
> [ba'la] 'child' [bala'lar] 'children'
> [balala'rə] 'child's' [balalarə'nəŋ] 'of his children'
> [ur'man] 'forest' [urman'li?] 'forest hut'
> [urman'ʧi] 'forested area' [urmanʧi'li?] 'forestry'

French, as indicated earlier, is another language where word-stress is normally fixed on the last syllable (though normally this is chiefly audible only on the last syllable of the final word of the utterance, and therefore is a restricted instance of the use of lexical stress). Adding a suffix elongates the structure of the word and therefore requires word-stress to be shifted rightwards (Tranel 1987: 195):

> *Fixed lexical stress (final syllable) in French*
> [kyl̩'tyʁ] 'culture' [kyl̩ty'ʁɛl̩] 'cultural' [kyl̩tyʁɛl̩'mɑ̃]
> 'culturally'

An instance of lexical stress being fixed on the penultimate syllable of words can be seen in the Texcoco dialect of Nahuatl, the Uto-Aztecan Mesoamerican Indian language mentioned in chapter 12, where suffix-addition similarly requires a stress-shift (Suárez 1983: 32):

> *Fixed lexical stress (penultimate syllable) in Texcoco Nahuatl*
> [ʃi'tɬali] 'sit down!' [ʃimotɬali'tsino] 'sit down please!'

Fixed lexical stress seems to be a fairly firm areal characteristic of Mesoamerican languages. Suárez (1983: 33) suggests that, although there are occasional languages in which lexical stress placement is variable within narrow limits, in that stress falls 'unpredictably on either of the last two syllables in the word' (such as in Cuitlatec, a language-isolate), 'there are few languages in Mesoamerica in which the placement of stress is completely unpredictable'.

Hyman (1977a: 52) states that fixed final syllable stress is an areal characteristic of Turkic languages, Iranian languages and Armenian. Other examples of individual languages with fixed lexical stress are Finnish and Czech, both with initial syllable stress, some Macedonian dialects with antepenultimate syllable stress (Lehiste 1970: 148), and Polish and Swahili, both with penultimate syllable stress. For a much more extensive list of fixed lexical stress languages, the reader might like to consult Hyman (1977a).

16.3.1.1   *Lexical stress location governed by syllable weight*
The placement of lexical stress can sometimes be prescribed by rules based on considerations of syllable weight. Lehiste describes the stress-pattern of (modern) Classical Arabic as being one where stress normally falls on the 'long syllable that is closest to the beginning of the word, and on the first syllable if the word consists only of short syllables' (Lehiste 1970: 148).

The mora, as a concept related to that of syllable weight, is a useful concept in expressing the rules for stress location in a number of languages, for instance Northern and Southern Paiute, which are members of the Western and Southern branches of the Numic sub-group of the Uto-Aztecan language family spoken in western North America and central Mexico (Munro 1977: 305–6). Munro describes the participation of vowel length (and hence moraic considerations) in placing stress in these two languages as follows:

> Vowel length is contrastive in most modern Uto-Aztecan languages ...
> In some cases, vowel length is important in determining the placement
> of stress. The term 'second mora' ... is used to describe a situation in
> which the first syllable of a word is stressed if it contains a long vowel
> or a diphthong, but the second syllable is stressed if the first vowel is
> short. If long vowels count as two moras, or vowel-units, and short
> vowels count as one mora, it is clear that in such languages stress
> always falls on the second mora of the word. (Munro 1977: 304)

A further regularity in various Uto-Aztecan languages discussed by Munro (1977: 308) is the use of an 'alternating stress rule', by which 'after primary stress is placed, every second mora or syllable away from the primary stressed vowel receives a secondary stress'. She cites Sapir's (1930) investigation of Southern Paiute, in which he analyses the word-complex meaning 'even if he says it to me' as [áijuʃàmpaːáŋanı]. The second syllable, as an unstressed syllable, is devoiced, and the final syllable may not receive stress. Munro (*ibid.*) describes the application here of the stress-placement rule in Southern Paiute in the following terms: 'Stress falls on the first syllable, a diphthong, since it contains the second mora of the word, and every second mora thereafter gets a secondary stress.'

16.3.2   *Variable lexical stress*
A relatively small proportion of the languages of the world allow a range of different locations of lexical stress. Examples of such languages using relatively free placement of stress include Assamese (Goswami 1966, cited in Masica 1991: 121, in a use of free lexical stress atypical of the other Indo-Aryan languages of the Indian subcontinent); Dutch (V. van

Heuven, personal communication); English (as discussed earlier) and Greek (Jones 1944); Italian (Vincent 1988: 284); Rumanian (Mallinson 1988: 392); Russian (Brosnahan and Malmberg 1970: 157); Spanish (Green 1988: 87); Swedish (Brosnahan and Malmberg 1970: 157), where its use on the final syllable excludes the use of the tonal accent mentioned in the preceding chapter; and Uzbek (in a few word-pairs, mentioned by Comrie 1981: 66 as exceptions to its general fixed-stress pattern):

Variable lexical stress in a number of languages

Assamese
['bɑːndfiʊ] 'friend'   [bɑːnˈdfiʊ] 'you fasten'
['pise] 'he is drinking'   [piˈse] 'then'

Dutch
['kaːnɔn] 'canon'   [kaːˈnɔn] 'cannon'

English (Received Pronunciation)
['fɔbɛə] 'forbear (n.)'   [fɔˈbɛə] 'forbear (vb)'

Greek
['poli] 'city'   [poˈli] 'much'

Italian
['prinʧipi] 'princes'   [prinˈʧipi] 'principles'
['kapiṭo] 'I turn up'   [kaˈpiṭo] 'understood'   [kapiˈṭo] 'he turned up'

Spanish
['ampljo] 'ample'   [amˈpljo] '(s)he broadened'
[kɔnˈṭiṇwo] 'I continue'   [kɔnṭiˈṇwo] '(s)he continued'

Swedish
['jɑːpan] 'Japan'   [jɑːˈpan] 'Japanese'

Rumanian
['ʧinta] 'he sings'   [ʧinˈta] 'he sang'
['aʧele] 'the needles'   [aˈʧele] 'those'

Russian
['pravda] 'truth'   ['zolətə] 'gold'
[daˈrogə] 'road'   [səmaˈvar] 'samovar'

Uzbek
['olma] 'don't take'   [olˈma] 'apple'

16.3.3   *Syntactic stress*

A small number of languages use word-stress in a syntactic function, to distinguish between different grammatical roles taken up by words in sentences. Brosnahan and Malmberg (1970: 158) cite Bendor-Samuel's (1962) investigations of the Southwest Brazilian language Terena, where stress-placement is used:

> to distinguish the subject from the object in a verb in an independent clause as *kúti otopíko* 'who chopped?' but *kúti otópiko* 'what did he chop?'; to mark certain sequences of independent clauses in coordinative relationship as *tokopónu namukónu* 'he found me, took me' in comparison with *tokóponu namúkonu* 'he found and took me'; to mark the verb introduced by a sequence particle as *ína aunkópovo* 'then I returned home' in comparison with *aúnkopovo* 'I returned home'; and so on.

16.4   **Rhythm in speech**

Phonetic theories of rhythmic phenomena in speech have persisted for centuries in suggesting that **isochrony**, as the regular recurrence in time of some given unit of speech rhythm, is a pervasive attribute of all spoken languages. Abercrombie (1967), who adopted the categories of speech rhythm introduced by Pike (1946), was a leading proponent of such a model. He distinguished between two types of isochronous recurrence of movement in rhythmic speech production:

> As far as is known, every language in the world is spoken with one kind of rhythm or with the other. In the one kind, known as *syllable-timed* rhythm, the periodic recurrence of movement is supplied by the syllable-producing process: ... the syllables recur at equal intervals of time - they are *isochronous*. French, Telugu, Yoruba illustrate this mode ...: they are syllable-timed languages. In the other kind, known as a *stress-timed* rhythm, the periodic recurrence of movement is supplied by the stress-producing process: ... the stressed syllables are isochronous. English, Russian, Arabic illustrate this other mode: they are stress-timed languages. (Abercrombie 1967: 97)

Empirical investigations have unfortunately failed to show any such regularity, on any absolute basis. At best, the available empirical evidence could be said sometimes to have shown the existence of timing characteristics that fluctuate around a very approximately regular rhythm, with explanations usually being offered for the deviations by appeal to the varying structural identity of the constituent parts of the utterance.

Physical evidence from measurements of the actual timing of speech has therefore obliged these theories to retreat from 'objective isochrony', as it were, to 'subjective isochrony', where the physical regularity of isochrony is described as a 'tendency' (Beckman 1992: 458). The implication offered by such subjectively oriented theories is that true isochrony is an underlying constraint, the regularity of whose surface realization is perturbed by factors to do with the phonetic, phonological and grammatical structure of the utterance, in a patterning whose rule-based complexity remains to be fully explained.

Much more research is clearly needed, and the general area of metrical structure is one of the most active fields in modern phonology. Some key publications are listed in Further Reading at the end of the chapter. However, the concept of an approximately isochronous rhythm in speech has been so tenacious in the history of phonology and phonetics that it seems unlikely that it is completely without foundation. It will therefore be explored in somewhat more detail in the sections below.

16.5   The constructive perception of rhythm

A perception of rhythm appears to be a nearly ubiquitous element of our experience of sequences of events in the time domain (Nord 1991; Pöppel 1989). We can note first that the auditory system is extremely sensitive to phenomena that are genuinely rhythmic. Listeners seem particularly good at registering the regularity of the rhythmic beat in music, for example, and are just as good at noticing deviations from an established musical rhythm, as in syncopated phrasing. We notice such a deviation immediately, and can decide that a single syncopated beat was clearly out of step, as it were, with the rhythm of the rest of the phrase, before the resumption of the previous rhythm. It seems plausible that a prerequisite for noticing the rhythmic deviation of the single syncopated beat is that the listener has developed an expectation of rhythmic performance against which to judge such deviation.

The perception of rhythm is not only analytic and predictive, however. It can be constructive as well. The human cognitive system seems unable to resist the temptation to impose a constructed rhythm on suitable sensory material in the time domain. For instance, the regular ticking of a clock is often perceptually grouped into sequences of two (or more) ticks, with one tick heard as dominant over the other(s) in an arbitrary and reversible rhythmic grouping. A similar example is in the rhythm perceptually imposed on cyclic events like walking. In both of these examples, the stimuli available to the perceptual system are already regular in their successive timing, and the rhythmic grouping is superimposed by the cognitive system.

Speech offers a fairly clear illustration of the brain's predilection for constructively seeking out rhythmic interpretations of auditory material. A simple view of the perception of underlying rhythmicity in speech is that it depends on constructing a hypothesis about what the rhythm of an utterance might have been had it been free of the distorting accidents of the variety of individual lexical and other linguistic structures used. When asked to tap a pencil on a desk in time with rhythmic beats perceived in continuous speech, for instance, listeners tap at a more regular rhythm than is typically justified by the speech material (Allen 1975; Beckman 1992, Scott, Isard and de Boysson-Bardies 1985). One explanation for this is that the listeners discount momentary variations from a truly regular rhythm in the speech, through their knowledge of the perturbations of timing necessitated by the different phonological structures of the utterances involved. If such an explanation is acceptable, it would suggest that listeners have a cognitive readiness to impose a regularized temporal grouping on utterances they hear, as a construct organizing the perception of the component parts of those utterances.

An important consideration in developing an understanding of the perception of rhythm is to establish what the listener might be attending to as a relevant percept. In watching a conductor, the percept used by members of an orchestra to control their rhythmic performance is thought to be the moment of maximum acceleration of the conductor's baton. The movements of a conductor's baton, though complicated, are much more simple than the complex structures that are available for the perception of rhythmic timing in speech. The instant that is perceptually equivalent in speech to the perceived beat of the baton in music could be the leading edge of the first segment of a syllable, the beginning of the nuclear segment of the syllable, the moment of reaching the most steady state in the performance of the syllable-nuclear vowel, and so on.

One way of approaching this question experimentally is to establish how listeners perceptually synchronize two speech events. Morton, Marcus and Frankish (1976) and Marcus (1981) gave the term **perceptual centre** or **P-centre** to the perceptually relevant instant in speech material that listeners use for such alignment. Two problems arise which complicate the attempt to decide the identity of relevant percepts of this sort: one is that different individuals can employ different perceptual strategies; the other is that the same individual, on different occasions, can vary in the choice of perceptual strategy. In a task where Swedish subjects were asked to adjust the duration of a silent interval 'so as to make a string of synthetic syllables sound rhythmically steady' (Nord 1991: 109), subjects varied in their results. Nord explains this, in the cases where syllables such as /spa/ were involved, by suggesting that subjects listened in different ways, 'either to let the rhythmic pulse agree with the early consonantal percept or with the vowel percept' (*ibid.*).

The view of speech as typically rhythmic might be able to be defended if the sole problem were the variable nature of perceptual strategies. Unfortunately, there are indeed other problems. The view presented above that speech production would be rhythmic were it not for the distorting but predictable influences of the varying segmental make-up of the syllables of speech is over-simplified. If the phonological structure of the constituents of an utterance were the sole influence responsible for distorting the properly rhythmic nature of the utterance, it is not unreasonable to think that phonologists would by now have developed a fully successful rule-based account of rhythm in speech, and that consequently the rhythm heard in the best rule-based speech synthesis, for example, would be indistinguishable from that of real speech. Neither situation obtains. It is the nature of speech production itself that makes it difficult to maintain the position that real speech is performed rhythmically. Over and above the variabilities in timing introduced by the phonological structure of the linguistic units of the utterance, the additional variabilities due to differences of speaker, accent, style, rate and tone of voice, together with the inevitable and random microvariabilities of timing from one occasion to another, will always ensure that the actual material pronounced by a human speaker will bear a less than perfect correspondence to prototypical norms.

The material of speech is hence never completely predictable. The listener's perceptual task is therefore to recover the linguistic intent of the speaker from such temporally distributed evidence as can be discerned in the speech signal. Language is made more efficient as a communicative system by listeners being able to make a rapid transition from initial auditory percepts to the symbolic linguistic levels of cognitive decoding. A readiness to accept perceptual evidence that is suggestive rather than conclusive helps such a process, and it is easy to understand that conversion processes of a stereotyping nature might be involved in such categorial decoding. It seems equally persuasive that an empathetic hypothesizing of the speaker's future intent might play a useful anticipatory role in accelerating the progress of the decoding of clues to structure. If analysis consists partly of grouping such clues in our cognitive attention in order to examine their inter-relationships, it may then be that setting up rhythmic hypotheses functions as an effective organizing principle for doing this. In this perspective, the formation of rhythmic hypotheses about speech is seen as part of the brain's cognitive strategies for constructively imposing pattern on sensory material, in order to make it available for further processing.

16.6   The typology of speech rhythm

Leaving on one side these detailed reservations springing from the variability inherent in speech, this section explores the phonetic basis of differences of rhythm perceived in different languages. Comparing two syllables for relative prominence, it was said at the beginning of this chapter that there are three chief ways they may differ. If they are made up of different segments, one syllable may be of heavier metrical weight than the other. Within the same category of metrical weight, one syllable may contain segments of greater sonority than the other. If the two syllables are made up of the same segments, one syllable may receive more overlaid stress than the other. These factors may combine, so that two syllables of different segmental make-up may differ in metrical weight, segmental sonority and the degree of lexical stress applied.

It was suggested in the preceding section that rhythm in speech is partly imposed, as an organizing construct of the cognitive system for speech perception. The following working assumption will therefore be adopted:

> *Perceived rhythm is a property of speech emerging from the coincidence of segmental sonority, syllabic weight and lexical stress in the lexicon of a language, and of the pragmatic use of the lexicon in the utterances of that language.*

The latter part of this characterization needs to be offered in order to explain the fact that some utterances are (by the combined accident of their lexical and pragmatic construction) more regularly rhythmic than some other utterances of the same language, with intonational requirements of timing adding their influence.

It follows directly from this working assumption of rhythm as an emergent property that the perception of rhythm in steady-tempo utterances of a given language will be directly dependent on the way that the prominence of successive syllables is able to fluctuate. Given that relative prominence is seen as basically the combined product of segmental sonority, syllabic weight and lexical stress, we can explore the continuum of rhythmic possibilities that results from the permutations of their combination. To make the discussion sharper, we can invent two fictitious languages of maximally different metrical properties, as polar extremes of the continuuum of possible types of linguistic rhythm.

At one extreme of the logical set of possibilities of speech rhythm would be a language with the following properties:

> only one syllable structure (say CV) is allowed;
>
> only a small set of consonants of broadly similar sonority is available;

only a small set of vowels of the same phonological length, comparable phonetic durations and similar sonority are available;
words are typically composed of a standard number of syllables
(say two);
lexical stress is not exploited.

The result would be utterances made up of trains of syllables of nearly equal duration, without notable fluctuations of prominence. It would be reasonable to describe the patterns of prominence characterizing the rhythm of such a language as 'syllable-timed', with its implication of a fairly strict obedience to isochronous regularity.

As soon as any of the above conditions vary, the rhythm of the language would necessarily depart from a fully syllable-timed classification. French was said by Abercrombie (1967) in the quotation above to have a syllable-timed rhythm. But it is immediately obvious that French departs in some important ways from the strict syllable-timing template just described. French syllable structure is much more varied, with at least the following structures being used: V, CV, CCV, VC, VCC, CVC, CCVC, CCVCC. Equally, the French consonant and vowel systems have numerous members, and their sonority is highly variable. Unless speakers of French managed to exercise a fully successful strategy of timing compensation to keep the syllable duration relatively constant despite such structural variation, then the frequency in the lexicon and usage of the language of these syllable types of varying structure and weight will conspire to distort the rhythm of French away from a fully syllable-timed model of the sort described above. It is therefore preferable, in the perspective offered by this book, to use the more general term **syllable-based**, rather than 'syllable-timed', to describe the perceived rhythm of French and comparable languages. Other languages with perceived rhythms said to be syllable-based in ways similar to French are Italian, Greek, Hindi, Indonesian, Spanish and Tamil (Dauer 1983: 56).

At the other extreme of the logical set of possibilities of speech rhythm would be a language with the following different set of properties:

many syllable structures are used;
a large set of consonants of widely differing sonority is available;
a large set of vowels of more than one phonological length,
widely varying phonetic durations and differing sonority is
available;
words are composed of a widely varying number of syllables;
lexical stress is relatively free in its location;
unstressed syllables exploit a vowel-reduction process.

The result would be utterances made up of trains of syllables of widely varying duration, with significant fluctuations of prominence dominated by syllables of heavy metrical weight, syllables receiving lexical stress, or both, with unstressed syllables being made particularly non-prominent through vowel reduction. It would be reasonable to describe the rhythm of such a language as **prominence-based rhythm**. To the extent that metrically heavy syllables tend to receive phonologically secondary stress, when not receiving primary stress, one could describe the patterns of prominence characterizing the rhythm of such a language as **stress-based rhythm**. Once again, the more general term 'stress-based' is recommended for use to describe the perceived rhythm of languages such as English, rather than the more limiting term 'stress-timed'. Other languages with perceived rhythms which can be said to be stress-based are Brazilian Portuguese, German, Swedish and conversational Thai (Dauer 1983: 56).

As well as rhythms that might be said to be perceived as syllable-based and stress-based, a unit that has been suggested as influencing the perceived rhythmic organization of speech is the mora. The perceived rhythm of Japanese, as mentioned earlier, is said to be a **mora-based rhythm** (Beckman 1992: 458; Ladefoged 1975: 224; Port, Dalby and O'Dell 1987), though very few other languages have been claimed to show such a rhythm.

Intermediate between the two logical extremes of syllable-based and stress-based accounts of the fluctuations of prominence in languages is another hypothetical type, identical to the first syllable-based type except in that fixed lexical stress is exploited on every word (say on the first syllable of the two-syllable words characterizing this language). The only way that prominence could then fluctuate significantly (disregarding the effects of intonation) would be as a realization of this lexical stress. Because the placement of lexical stress in this hypothetical language is fixed, and the words of standard length, the realizations of word-stress would tend to recur at nearly equal intervals of time. If we assume that the unstressed syllables each lasted for approximately the same duration as other unstressed syllables, these too would tend to recur at approximately equal intervals of time, intermitting with the stressed syllables of greater duration.

There would thus be two trains of recurrent perceptual events, unstressed syllables and stressed syllables. Rather than hearing such trains as separate, listeners tend to hear the members of a stressed and an unstressed series as linked into groups which we can call **feet**, following Abercrombie (1967: 131). The internal organization of the foot can be categorized in terms of the relative prominence of the constituent syllables. If the individual foot (made up in this language of one stressed and one unstressed syllable) is heard as a pattern in which the stressed syllable is perceived as initial, the foot can be said to show **leader-timing**; if the unstressed syllable is heard as the initial syllable, the foot can be said to show **trailer-timing** (Wenk and Wioland 1982).

Discussion of a rhythm perceived as stress-based is mostly conducted in the phonetic and phonological literature in terms of the tendency towards isochrony of feet showing leader-timing, with the initial stressed syllables of the feet being said to recur at approximately equal intervals of time. We shall make no further appeal in the descriptive apparatus of this book to the notion of isochrony, but will rather follow Dauer (1983) in concentrating on the relationships of the constituent syllables within a foot. In her meticulous experimental investigations of English, Spanish, Italian and Greek, she was able to show that the mean duration between stressed syllables in all these languages is proportional to the number of syllables in that interval, and that 'there is no more of a tendency for interstress intervals to clump together in English than in the other languages' (Dauer 1983: 54). Dauer also concludes that the perceived rhythmic differences between languages such as English and Spanish, both using lexical stress, and traditionally considered as two languages representing stress-based and syllable-based rhythm respectively, have 'nothing to do with the durations of interstress intervals. Furthermore, stresses recur no more regularly in English than they do in any other language with clearly definable stress' (Dauer, *ibid.*).

Dauer looked elsewhere for the explanation of the perceived rhythmic differences between such languages, and turned to an examination of differences of syllable-structure and its consequences for speech rhythm. Restricting comment here to her comparison of English and Spanish, we can note that she established substantial differences between the most frequently occurring syllable structures in the two languages (Dauer 1983: 56):

Incidence of most frequent syllable structures in English and Spanish

Syllable type	English (%)	Spanish (%)
CV	34	58
V	8	6
CVC	30	22
VC	15	6
CVCC	6	—

Open syllables thus make up a minority of the total in English, compared with a majority in Spanish. Closed syllables make up a majority of the total in English, against a small minority in Spanish. Dauer notes that in addition to the greater variety of syllable structures typically found in a stress-timed language, there is also a strong tendency for 'heavy' syllables (those containing many segments) to be stressed and 'light' syllables (those containing few segments) to be unstressed. That is, syllable structure and stress are more likely to reinforce each other in a stress-timed language than in a syllable-timed language. (Dauer 1983: 55–6)

(Dauer is here using the traditional terms 'stress-timed' and 'syllable-timed' in the same general senses as proposed in this book for 'stress-based' and 'syllable-based' rhythms.)

Gimson (1989: 149) cites the work of Fry (1947), who analysed the relative frequency of occurrence of English vowels in Received Pronunciation. Vowels accounted for some 40 per cent of the occurrence of phonemes of all types. Fry established that [ə] and [ɪ] contributed considerably more frequently than any other vowels to this total. The values he found were as follows:

Relative frequency of occurrence (%) of vowel phonemes in English (Received Pronunciation)

/ə/	10.74	/ɔː/	1.24
/ɪ/	8.33	/uː/	1.13
/e/	2.97	/ʊ/	0.86
/aɪ/	1.83	/ɑː/	0.79
/ʌ/	1.75	/aʊ/	0.61
/eɪ/	1.71	/ɜː/	0.52
/iː/	1.65	/ɛə/	0.34
/əʊ/	1.51	/ɪə/	0.21
/a/	1.45	/ɔɪ/	0.14
/ɒ/	1.37	/ʊə/	0.06

Short central vocoids are thus the most frequent of all English vowels in running speech, and can be thought of as a continually present background against which the less-frequently occurring longer stressed vowels can be perceived as standing out more prominently. Dauer also observed that vowels in 92 per cent of the unstressed CV English syllables she analysed were realized phonetically as relatively short central vocoids, while the nuclei of 90 per cent of the unstressed CV syllables in Spanish were manifested by longer peripheral vocoids. Taken together, these observations suggest that the perceived durational contrast between stressed and unstressed vowels is likely to be less striking in Spanish than in English (Dauer 1983: 57).

Dauer also considers the contribution of the realizations of lexical stress to perceived rhythm. She cites a finding by Delattre (1966) to the effect that stressed syllables in Spanish are typically about 1.3 times longer than unstressed syllables, while English stressed syllables are characteristically about 1.5 times longer. The differential effects in Spanish and English are especially noticeable in utterance-medial open syllables, where Spanish stressed syllables are only 1.1 times longer than unstressed syllables, while English stressed syllables are 1.6 times as long as unstressed syllables (Dauer 1983: 58). It is plausible that these relationships will combine with the effects described in the previous paragraph to support a perceptual impression of greater equality of the duration of individual syllables in Spanish versus English.

Conversely, we can note that one of the phenomena that characterize the rhythmic organization of a language such as English is **foot-level shortening** (Rakerd, Sennett and Fowler 1987). This is the phenomenon where adding an unstressed syllable to a foot shortens the duration of the stressed syllable, with the overall duration of the foot growing by less than the duration of the unstressed syllable.The fact that the syllables within a foot seem to contract interactive durational relations of this sort then supports the notion that the foot can be perceived as an integral unit of rhythmic performance in English.

Dauer's overall conclusion is that 'the rhythmic differences we feel to exist between languages such as English and Spanish are more a result of phonological, phonetic, lexical and syntactic facts about the language than any attempt on the part of the speaker to equalize interstress or intersyllable intervals' (Dauer 1983: 55). She ends her study with the following comment:

> the differences summed up by the terms 'stress-timed' and 'syllable-timed' refer to what goes on within rhythmic groups, the characteristics of successive syllables and their interrelationships, which are ultimately a product of the entire linguistic system. As Classe (1939, p. 132), who carried out the first experimental study on isochrony in English, concluded, 'in ordinary speech and everyday prose ... the rhythmic effect is a purely automatic consequence of linguistic circumstances'. (Dauer 1983: 60)

16.7 Utterance-marginal lengthening

One of the assumptions in the discussion of speech rhythm above was that the speaking rate (to be discussed further in the next chapter) was held constant. In fact it is a characteristic of many languages including English that the onset and offset of utterances show an adjustment of tempo, especially on the utterance-initial and utterance-final syllables, compared with the utterance-medial rate of speech. Beckman (1992),

Delattre (1966) and Fletcher (1991) can be consulted for discussions of phrase-final lengthening of final syllables in French, and Campbell (1992) and Kaiki and Sagisaka (1992) for descriptions of the lengthening of the last mora in an utterance in Japanese.

Further reading

Significant phonological publications on **metrical structure** are Durand (1990), Giegerich (1985), Halle and Vergnaud (1987), Hogg and McCully (1987), Kaye (1989), Liberman and Prince (1977) and Selkirk (1984).

Good accounts of **stress** in English are given by Fudge (1984), Kingdon (1958b) and Poldauf (1984). Thompson (1980), on the interaction of stress and salience in (American) English, is also recommended.

Two interesting general works on the psychology of our experience of rhythm and time are Fraisse (1956) and Fraisse (1963) respectively. Good reviews of studies on **rhythm** in speech can be found in Allen (1973, 1975), Lehiste (1977) and Dauer (1983).

17

The temporal organization of speech: continuity and rate

The phonological length of individual segments, and the allophonic variation of duration of segments in response to their contextual and structural environment, were described in chapter 14 as part of the temporal structure of speech. At the other end of the scale of temporal organization lie the timing characteristics of whole utterances. This chapter discusses the continuity of utterances, in terms of fluency and hesitation, and the rate of speech, as a matter of overall tempo.

The continuity of speech and the rate of articulation of individual utterances are best thought of as non-linguistic in nature. To the degree that continuity and rate of speech are subject to conventional interpretation, reflecting the communication of such attitudinal or emotional states as impatience, deliberation, excitement, happiness, disappointment or sadness, for instance, then they are paralinguistic in nature. To the extent that continuity and rate are simply characteristic of the speaker as an individual, without culturally specific conventional paralinguistic interpretability, then they should be considered extralinguistic in nature.

A linkage exists between paralinguistic and extralinguistic attributions, however, in that the same speech phenomena may be involved in both cases. The momentary affective mood of the speaker may be perceived as exploiting a given phenomenon for short-term communicative purposes of paralinguistic communication, while habitual use of the same phenomenon may result in informative conclusions being drawn about the long-term marking of personality and identity. On first hearing a speaker produce a very hesitant utterance, for example, one might initially conclude that the speaker was uncertain about the message being expressed by the utterance. If further exposure to the speaker revealed that such hesitance was a characteristic trait, one might develop a view of the speaker's personality as tentative and unconfident. Similarly, on first hearing a speaker with a markedly slow rate of articulation, for instance, one might conclude that the speaker was depressed or sad. If it turned out that the speaker habitually spoke slowly, compared with other speakers from the same sociolinguistic community, then one might build a picture of the speaker's personality as depressive or lugubrious. On longer acquaintance, one might eventually, of course, conclude that the speaker's slow speech was merely idiosyncratic, and had no reliable relevance in this case for judgements about personality.

Only familiarity with a given speaker's habitual performance allows a listener to make an accurate assessment on any given occasion of the paralinguistic versus extralinguistic status of that speaker's patterns of continuity and rate of speech. Given that paralinguistic patterns of continuity and rate are culturally specific, the most erratic conclusions by listeners in this area are likely to be found in unwitting misjudgements in cross-cultural conversations where the paralinguistic norms of the speaker's sociolinguistic community are not known.

The concept of a setting could conceivably be extended to the analysis of temporal organization, with settings of continuity being classified as neutral, continuous or non-continuous, and settings of rate divided into neutral, fast and slow. But the definition of 'neutral' in this context is yet more problematic than in the case of modifications of phonetic quality, pitch or loudness, and the phenomena of temporal organization will not be analysed here in setting terms.

17.1   Continuity of speech

A speaking-turn of spontaneous speech is very different from the idealized version usually reproduced in a written version of that utterance, say in a secretary's typed document corresponding to notes taken in shorthand. Unlike the continuous, heavily edited text of the written account, a speaking-turn in real spontaneous speech is normally replete with false starts, repetitions, silent pauses, gaps in the verbal content filled by articulations such as [ɜː], [ɑː] or [mː], prolongations of parts of the utterance, and the occasional slip of the tongue and (sometimes) its subsequent correction. Also, in between the utterances which make up one speaker's speaking-turn, there are often silences of considerable duration. Whether the speaker feels safe from potential attempts by the other participant to take over the speaker-role during such silences will partly depend on how successfully the desire to maintain the role of speaker has been signalled. Such floor-protection signals depend partly on speech behaviour, particularly on intonational patterns, and partly on non-vocal behaviour such as avoidance of eye-contact.

The analysis of continuity in speech draws on two related distinctions, the first between continuous versus non-continuous speech, and the second between fluent versus interrupted speech. The first distinction requires the prior definition of the concept of a pause. Pauses can be either 'silent' or 'filled'. A **silent pause** within a speaking-turn can be operationally defined as any silence which is of 200 msec or more in duration. The reason for setting a minimum threshold to the duration of a silent pause is that the silence associated with the closure phase of a voiceless stop segment can sometimes last for up to about 180 msec or so, depending on the overall rate of speech. A **filled pause** is any gap in the verbal structure of a speaking-turn filled by non-linguistic material, for example in English by articulations such as [ɜː], [ɑː] or [mː]. **Continuous speech** can then be defined as a speaking-turn containing no silent or filled pauses, nor any non-linguistic prolongation of linguistic elements of its constituent utterances. **Non-continuous speech** is any speech showing one or more of these signals.

Continuous speech can be regarded as **fluent** speech. But whether a given instance of non-continuous speech can be regarded on a particular occasion of speaking as fluent rather than **interrupted** (or **hesitant**) **speech**, however, will depend in turn on the concept of hesitation. **Hesitation** can be signalled in many ways, including silent or filled pauses, or prolongations of parts of an utterance. Hesitation is the outcome of a speaker's indecision about what to say next. In order to come closer to an understanding of whether some particular example of non-continuous speech is interrupted by hesitation we need to consider briefly the cognitive process of planning and performing utterances.

The cognitive process of planning speech is typically episodic. That is, an episode of speech is cognitively planned as a unitary entity, and uttered and perceived as an integrated act. Boomer (1965, 1978) argued that this entity was what he called a **phonemic clause** (after Trager and Smith 1951), which was sometimes but by no means always coincident with the syntactic clause. He suggested that

> In spontaneous speech there are discernible 'chunks', sequences of a few syllables, usually from one to seven or eight, that seem to be spoken as a unit, ... speech is formulated in phonemic clauses, each of which is planned and executed as an organized speech act. ... We believe that the perception of speech is also based on a chunking strategy in which incoming phonemic clauses are processed as successive coherent packages of sound, syntax and sense. (Boomer 1978: 246–9)

Boomer used an illustration of an utterance consisting of two phonemic clauses (using '|' as an indication of phonemic clause boundaries) as follows:

| the man who called me yesterday | just telephoned again |

The phonemic clause is marked off by 'patterns of voice pitch, rhythm and loudness' (Boomer 1978: 246). Pitch is the most obvious of these parameters, and the pitch-patterns which correspond to the phonemic clause were discussed in chapter 15 under the heading of the 'intonational phrase'. Briefly, the pitch-pattern of the phonemic clause is hence intonationally marked by one and only one perceptually very prominent word, preceded and optionally succeeded by less prominent stretches of speech (Boomer and Laver 1968). In the structure of the phonemic clause, the stressed syllable of one informationally important word (the 'intonational nucleus', here the *yes* of *yesterday* in the first clause and the *gain* of *again* in the second clause of the example above) is made more intonationally prominent than the other syllables of the phonemic clause, usually by displaying a large movement in its pitch contour. Within the phonemic clause, the preceding and the succeeding material is subordinated in prominence to the intonational nucleus by having less dynamic pitch-movements associated with them.

If we can accept the argument that speech is produced in short episodes whose coherence is marked in part by intonational behaviour, then the way is open to characterizing fluent versus hesitant speech. When a speaking-turn composed of several phonemic clauses is produced without pauses, it was said above that this counted as continuous, fluent speech. When the speaking-turn is broken into individual utterances by the insertion of silent or filled pauses at the junctures between the phonemic clauses, it can be regarded as non-continuous but fluent, in that the linguistic material of the phonemic clauses is uninterrupted. When a silent or filled pause falls internally within a phonemic clause, breaking its coherent intonational structure, then the speaking-turn can be regarded as non-continuous and interrupted, or hesitant. If the clause-internal pause is silent, the effect of inserting the pause into the speaking-turn will be to multiply the number of separate utterances making up the speaking-turn.

A similar characterization can be applied to phonemic clauses whose tempo is altered by non-linguistic prolongations of the duration of one or more of their constituent syllables. The presence of such prolongations counts as a signal of hesitation, and interrupts the continuity and fluency of the speech concerned.

If we call pauses internal to phonemic clauses **hesitation pauses**, and those at the juncture between two phonemic clauses **juncture pauses**, then we can say that the conversational function of a pause seems to differ according to whether the pause is a hesitation pause or a juncture pause. While a speaker is talking, a listener will often make audible interjections such as *uh huh*, *yes*, *I see*, *mm*, *really* and visible gestures such as head-nods. These are not attempts to capture the speaker-role, but are rather signals that the listener is paying attention, and successfully decoding the utterances of the speaker. Boomer (1978: 256) describes how two of his colleagues, Dittmann and Llewellyn (1967), annotated 124 such listener-responses made in simulated telephone conversations. One hundred and ten of these listener-responses were synchronized with the speaker's juncture pauses. By contrast, listener-responses coincided with only four of 123 hesitation pauses made by the speaker. Dittmann and Llewellyn (1968) then looked at head-nods as listener-responses. The ratio of head-nods made during juncture pauses to those made within phonemic clauses was in excess of 50:1. Both these sets of findings support the notion that the phonemic clause (i.e. the intonational phrase) is a plausible candidate for a psycholinguistic unit of speech decoding, as well as for speech encoding.

Finally, we can consider the question of where in speech speakers tend to pause. In Butterworth's (1980: 166) history of this research area, Lounsbury is described as having put forward the earliest cognitively oriented hypothesis about the illumination that pausing behaviour might shed on psycholinguistic operations of speech production, when he wrote that 'hesitation pauses correspond to points of highest statistical uncertainty in the sequencing of units' (Lounsbury 1954: 99). In other words, the larger the set of linguistic candidates for inclusion in the plan for an utterance, the more likely a speaker is to pause while considering the choice. This was supported to some extent by Maclay and Osgood (1959), who found that in a corpus of 50,000 words taken from tapes of conference discussions, hesitation pauses 'were more likely to occur before content words than function words' (Butterworth 1980: 167). Boomer (1965), however, showed that in a corpus of 1,593 phonemic clauses in spontaneous American English speech, containing a total of 1,127 hesitations, 749 pauses and 378 filled pauses, a strongly significant percentage of hesitations occurred after the first word in the clause (though it should be noted that Butterworth (1980: 169), in replicating the Boomer study, found a considerably lower incidence of hesitations after the first word).

There are several possible explanations for the tendency, if one truly exists, for speakers to pause after the first word of a phonemic clause. One is that speakers launch into the utterance of a phonemic clause while the planning for it is still incomplete. The articulation of the clause outruns the plan, and the speaker has to pause to clarify the plan. An alternative explanation lies in the conversational competition between the participants to occupy and maintain the role of speaker. One strategy for pre-empting any bid by the other participant is to launch an utterance while it is still only sketchily planned, and thereby seize the floor. Having succeeded in gaining the floor, one can then resist attempts by the other participant to take over the speaker-role (by eye-contact avoidance etc.), while planning the fuller detail of the rest of the utterance. This is a very tentative explanation, however, and the issue of how speakers construct their psycholinguistic and neuro-muscular plans for utterances, and how they execute and monitor the performance of such plans, remains very much a research topic. For interested readers, a number of relevant publications are listed in Further Reading at the end of the chapter.

Some of the hesitation phenomena discussed above, together with repetition, can be seen in the following transcript of part of an interview with an applicant for a job (Cheepen 1988: 37). The symbols used in the illustration to indicate hesitation behaviour are as follows: '.' = short pause; '–' = longer pause (of one second or more); [ə, m, a] = phonetic quality of segments used for filled pause (adapted from Cheepen 1988: 8).

> *Pausing behaviour in interview speech in English*
> 'the the panel here have got various things to [ə] ask you
> obviously about this job . and [əm] – Mrs [ə] . Scott here will .
> [əm] take . you know . descr [əm] . y talk to you about the . [a]
> the job . itself'

17.2   Articulation rate and speaking rate

Definitions of the tempo of speech need to distinguish between the speed with which an individual utterance is produced, versus the rate at which an overall multi-utterance speaking-turn is performed. The tempo with which an individual utterance is spoken can be called the 'articulation rate', and the overall tempo of a speaking-turn can be called the 'speaking rate'.

Articulation rate describes the tempo of articulating an utterance, excluding any silent pauses, but including non-linguistic speech material such as filled pauses and prolongations of syllables. Articulation rate thus refers to the tempo of performance of all audible, 'vocalized' speech within an individual utterance, whether that speech consists of the manifestation of linguistic units or of paralinguistic signals of hesitation. **Speaking rate** refers to the overall tempo of performance not only of all the utterances in the particular speaking turn, including any filled pauses and prolongations of syllables within the utterances, but also the durations of any silent pauses between the utterances making up the speaking-turn.

The units in which articulation rate and speaking rate are expressed can be syllables per second. (Equally, it could be segments per second or words per second, depending on the motivation of the analysis.) The consequence of choosing the syllable as a unit of measurement requires some explanation, however. The syllable has so far been defined in this book as a phonological concept, though in practice it has been convenient to allow a certain ambivalence, speaking of the phonetic realization of phonological syllables as 'syllables' also, without necessarily making their manifestatory role explicit in every instance. Hesitation behaviour has been analysed above as paralinguistic in nature, signalling in part the progress of the speaker in the mental planning of utterances. The question then emerges as to whether the concept of the syllable can be extended, by analogy with the concept of linguistic phonology, to what one might call the **paraphonology** of speech, including the production of **paraphonological syllables** of hesitant filled pauses. If so, then the calculation of articulation rate (and, by extension, speaking rate) is relatively straightforward. If not, then a situation arises where two utterances containing the same phonological syllables, where their syllabic duration was the same, might nevertheless not be regarded as having the same articulation rate, because of the duration of one of the two utterances being augmented by one or more filled pauses which would contribute to the overall duration but not to the number of qualifying syllables.

We have seen that the phonetic manifestations of filled pauses differ across sociolinguistic communities, though the communities are perhaps more tolerant of individual paraphonological eccentricity than in the case of the realizations of their phonological code. Their phonetic make-up does seem to be relatable to that of (rather simple) syllables of the speaker's phonology in most cases, and the practical step will be taken here of positing paraphonological syllables of the same potential structure and constituency as simple phonological syllables. When calculating the number of syllables per second in the articulation rate of a given utterance, therefore, the analyst would include not only the realizations of the phonological syllables produced, but also the manifestations of any paraphonological syllables of filled pauses. Prolongation of the duration of a phonological syllable, as a paraphonological signal of hesitation, would be factored into the calculation of the duration of the phonological syllable concerned.

One final point needs to be made about the methods of calculating the rate of speech production in terms of syllables or words per second. Such a definition cannot hope to be applicable in a fully language-general way, since the structural make-up of syllables or words in different languages is likely to be (often quite widely) different.

Speech can obviously be performed at a large number of different rates, and these rates can be either steady or changing. But until circumstances oblige one to increase the number of categories, it is probably sufficient to distinguish only three steady tempos, **medium, fast** and **slow rates**, and two types of changes of tempo, **accelerating** and **decelerating rates**.

Several different relationships between articulation rate and speaking rate are possible, depending on the continuity of the speech. A fast articulation rate could be combined with a fast overall speaking rate if the speech is fluent, without frequent or long inter-utterance silent pauses. A fast articulation rate could be combined with a slower overall speaking rate if the speech is interrupted, with frequent or long inter-utterance silences. A relatively slow articulation rate could be part of an overall fast speaking rate, if combined with unusual fluency. There seems, at least in the English-speaking world, to be no necessary tendency for articulation rate and speaking rate to share the same tempo category. Goldman-Eisler (1968: 24), a pioneer in investigations of both continuity and rate, showed experimentally that while speaking rate is positively correlated with the proportional duration of silent pauses in the speech material, speaking rate and articulation rate have no significant correlation.

Goldman-Eisler (*ibid.*) represents the typical range of a medium rate of articulation (in English speakers) as being between 4.4 and 5.9 syllables per second, with a physiologically conditioned maximum somewhere between 6.7 and 8.2 syllables per second depending on the articulators involved (Miller 1951). For English, a medium speaking rate can be thought of as one where 'An average syllable's duration is 0.18 seconds, yielding about 5 to 5.5 syllables/second. Most adults read orally from 150 to 180 words/minute and produce 200 or more words/minute in conversational speech' (Calvert 1986: 178). Lindblom (1983: 238) reports the average duration of syllables as ranging between 160 and 200 msec. Grosjean (1980: 309) mentions a figure of 224 words per minute for reading a standard text (the Goldilocks passage) at a medium rate. Ramsaran (1978), cited in Gimson (1989: 308, as revised by Ramsaran), found in a detailed study of twenty hours of tape-recorded spontaneous speech from six RP speakers that the range of speaking rates varied from 189 syllables per minute (3.1 syllables/sec, 7.6 segments/sec) at the slowest to 324 syllables per minute (5.4 syllables/sec, 13.4 segments/sec) at the fastest.

Data for the average range of syllables per second in the speaking rate characteristic of some other languages has been summarized by Gósy (1991b: 66)

Average speaking rate in a number of languages

Language	Syllables/sec
Dutch	5.5–9.3
French	4.7–6.8
Spanish	4.6–7.0
Arabic	4.6–7.0
Italian	5.3–8.9

This gives an approximate account of the differences of average speaking rate in these languages, but for an interpretation of what the figures mean for articulation rate, that is, the number of segments articulated per second, one would need to know details of the range of syllable structures used by each language, and their typical frequency of occurrence in utterances of the language.

In order to establish norms for speaking rate, one might conclude as a somewhat arbitrary rule of thumb that a speaking rate of more than 240 words per minute would count paralinguistically as a notably fast speaking rate, and fewer than 160 as a notably slow rate. A more considered approach would be to establish what counted as medium, fast or slow speaking rates for individual sociolinguistic communities, in terms of the paralinguistic conventions of their culture, without seeking to define universal values for the different speaking rates.

The analysis of phenomena such as rate is dangerously open to subjective bias. Most listeners seem willing to attach judgements of rate to utterances in their own language, and these tend to correlate reasonably well with experimental counts of the number of syllables uttered per unit time. But the perception of rate is strongly tied to expectations of segmental and suprasegmental temporal patterning typical of the listener's own phonological experience. This has the consequence that listeners' judgements rapidly begin to lose objectivity when the utterance concerned comes either from an unfamiliar accent, or (even worse) from an unfamiliar language.

As in many other domains of phonetic performance, the capacities of perception exceed those of production. Maximum rates of perception are faster than maximum rates of production. Calvert (1986: 178) describes this situation in the following terms:

> [the] maximum rate of producing speech appears to be limited by articulatory control. With simple repetitive articulatory movements, speakers reach maximum rates of about 8 syllables/second but cannot exceed this even with practice. Although the time it takes to produce different speech sounds varies greatly, it is interesting to note that speakers average a rate of 10 sounds/second in conversation. At faster rates it is difficult to co-ordinate articulation and errors begin to occur.

At the rate of 15 sounds/second, errors are frequent and speech is distorted. Comprehending speech, on the other hand, occurs much faster, as does silent reading and thinking in general. While we typically produce speech at 10 sounds/second, we can understand it at as much as 30 sounds/second when paying careful attention.

Comments about overall rate of articulation mask the underlying 'quasi-random microvariability from one occasion to another' that was mentioned in section 14.2 of segmental and syllabic durations in the production of speech, even at a notionally standard tempo. Figure 17.1 shows the results of an acoustic analysis by Kent (1983: 58) of the temporal patterns found in the speech of ten young adult speakers of American English, each repeating the sentence *I took a spoon and a knife* four times. Kent takes a number of anchor points amongst the seven utterance-internal segments [tʊkəspu], and measures the time distances between them on the four occasions of repeti-

Figure 17.1 Temporal patterns in four repetitions each of the American English phrase *I took a spoon and a knife* by ten young adult speakers, showing a number of acoustic anchor points amongst the seven utterance-internal segments [tʊkəspu] (after Kent 1983: 58)

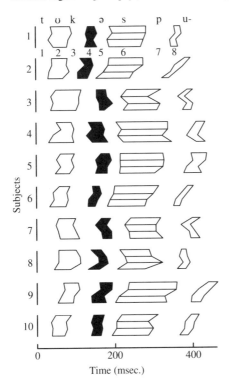

543

tion. It is clear from an inspection of the results that the segmental durations, within narrow limits, were quite variable for each speaker across the
four repetitions of the phrase.

Leaving aside this reservation about inter-occasion variability of segments
even when subjects try to maintain a standard tempo, languages differ in
how they distribute the relative compressions and expansions of syllable
durations to achieve variations of rate of articulation. Changing the rate of
articulation of an utterance from medium to fast (for instance) can be
achieved in either a linear or a non-linear way. In some languages, the
decrease in duration of the overall utterance is proportionally distributed
over the whole utterance, with the duration of individual segments and syllables being reduced in a linear fashion. In others, like English, non-linear
changes are preferred, with the overall rate of articulation of the utterance
being increased by preferentially shortening unstressed syllables or by re-
organizing syllable structures, or by combining both (Lehiste 1970: 38).

The place of a syllable in the utterance can also influence its relative duration, as noted in section 16.7. A characteristic of English and many other
languages is that utterance-finality is often signalled for regulative purposes
of yielding the floor to the other participant by a deceleration of the rate of
articulation on the last part of the utterance. Comparing the two pronunciations of the monosyllabic word *car* in the phrase *the only reliable car is a*
new car shows that the duration of the last *car* is noticeably longer than the
first. In some circumstances in English, the first syllable or two of an
utterance can also be pronounced at a slower tempo than any syllables of
otherwise comparable make-up which are medial in the utterance. These
utterance-marginal effects apply to stretches of speech which are either
isolated utterances or part of a speaking-turn broken up by pauses.

Speaking rate and formality of speech style seem to have no direct correlation, at least in English. In Ramsaran's (1978) study of spontaneous
speech in RP, the style of speech was controlled by arranging conversations
in social situations likely to provoke either formal or casual styles. A
markedly formal style, for example, was achieved by recording 'an undergraduate in conversation with a professor who was a stranger to her', and a
markedly casual style by recording 'a man in conversation with his wife'
(Gimson 1989: 308, edited by Ramsaran). In all such formal and casual situations, Ramsaran found that the degree of formality and the rate of speaking were quite independent, with no necessary association between formality
and slow tempo, or between a casual style and fast tempo. Ramsaran, in her
edition of Gimson (1989: 286), does make the point, however, that the rate
of speaking may be correlated with the mood of a speaker, in that 'a rapid

rate of delivery, for instance, may express irritation or urgency, whereas a slower rate may show hesitancy, doubt, or boredom in statements, or sympathy or encouragement in questions and commands'.

Siptár (1991: 29), analysing speech style and tempo in Hungarian, reflects the same point of view as that of Ramsaran – that rate and style have no necessary correlation. He sets up three categories of speech style ('formal', 'neutral' and 'intimate'), and shows that any of these can be spoken at either a 'normal' or a 'fast' tempo. Siptár calls the intersections of the three categories of speech style with normal tempo 'guarded speech' (formal style), 'colloquial speech' (neutral style) and 'casual speech' (intimate style). The intersections of speech style with fast tempo he calls 'accelerated speech' (formal style), 'swift speech' (neutral style) and 'fast-casual speech' (intimate style).

Illustrations of these types of speech offered by Siptár (1991), showing different strategies of segment deletion and syllable re-organization, and a number of phonetic effects such as replacement of nasal contoids by nasalization of vocoids, are shown in table 17.1. (The symbol '++' in the 'guarded speech' example in the table represents a short silent pause, ','

Table 17.1 *Combinations of different speech styles and tempos in Hungarian*

Meaning	'I think we should go to the theatre at last'
Orthography	Azt hiszem, el kellene már egyszer menni színházba
Guarded speech	[ˈɔst hisɛm ++ ˈɛl kɛlːɛnɛ maːr ˈɛcsɛr ˈmɛnːi ˈsiːnhaːzbɔ]
Colloquial speech	[ˈɔsi sɛm ˈɛl kɛlːɛnɛ maː ɛtsɛr ˈmɛnːi s̃iːfiaːzbɔ]
Casual speech	[ɔsːɛmˈeːkɛːnɛmaː ɛtsːɛ mɛnːi s̃iːazbɔ]
Swift speech	[ˈɔsisɛm ˈɛkɛɛnɛ maɛtsɛ mɛːnɪ ˈs̃iãzbɔ]
Fast-casual speech	[ɔsmˈɛːknɛmatsɛmɛnɪˌsjãzbɔ]

Source: Based on Siptár (1991: 27–9)

stands for secondary stress and '·' for primary stress.) Siptár points out that this 'guarded speech' version can be uttered at a fast tempo (for example by a well-trained professional broadcaster) without necessarily undergoing the structural and phonetic changes that would classify it as 'colloquial' or 'casual' speech. A fast version of such 'guarded' speech would be classified as 'accelerated' speech in Siptár's terms. He also comments that, although to utter the 'fast-casual' example above would typically take less time than it would to pronounce any of the other versions given, 'all three varieties may occur in a protracted, extremely slow tempo as well' (Siptár 1991: 28).

Further reading

Further reading on **psycholinguistic** and **neuromuscular planning** of speech programs can be found in Butterworth (1980), Cooper and Walker (1979), Fromkin (1973, 1980), Laver (1991) and Levelt (1989). The theoretical models discussed in these publications are usually thought to be examples of what has been called 'Translation Theory', in that their architecture consists of a series of stages, translating the representation of speech successively from one stage to the next. An alternative approach to modelling neuromuscular planning in speech is that of **Action Theory**, which is a model borrowed from the general physiological study of the muscular control of repetitive actions such as walking. Foundational articles on Action Theory applied to speech are Fowler (1980) and Fowler *et al.* (1980). Laver (1989) and Nolan (1982) discuss the differences of approach between Translation Theories and Action Theory.

The topic of **pausing** in speech is explored in Beattie and Butterworth (1979), Boomer and Dittman (1962), Butterworth (1975), Dechert and Raupach (1980), Deese (1980), Duez (1982, 1991), Goldman-Eisler (1968) and Grosjean, Grosjean and Lane (1979).

Investigations of **rate** in speech have been reported by Gay (1981), Kohler (1986b), Levelt (1989), Miller (1981), den Os (1985), Osser and Peng (1964), Rietveld and Gussenhoven (1987) and Vaane (1982).

PART VII

Principles of transcription

18

Types of transcription

Frequent comment has been made in passing in the chapters above on matters of transcription, and a variety of types of transcription have been used for different purposes. These different types of transcription can be classified on a principled basis. It would clearly be possible to classify different ways of notating units at all linguistic levels of analysis from phonetics and phonology to semantics and pragmatics, and to classify phonetic notation covering both segmental and suprasegmental effects. This chapter will address the question of the classification of transcription only at the levels of phonetics and phonology, and within those levels will consider issues of transcription related only to the segment. Furthermore, consideration will be confined to phonemic models of phonology. The classificatory criteria employed will be partly linguistic, reflecting a view of the relationship between phonetics and phonology, and partly typographical, reflecting a view of the relationship between the spoken medium and the written medium of language.

18.1   Phonological and phonetic transcriptions

The first classificatory division of types of transcription depends on whether the motivation for constructing the transcription is primarily phonological or directly phonetic. Phonologically motivated transcriptions include phonemic and allophonic transcription. In the case of both phonemic and allophonic transcriptions, the intention is to bring into the foreground of analytic attention comments on phonological abstractions about the utterances concerned. In the case of a **phonemic transcription**, the object of attention is the system of phonemic contrasts exploited by the accent of the language concerned, and the ways in which these are distributed over phonological and higher-level units of the language. In the case of an **allophonic transcription**, the focus is on the ways in which the spoken material of the accent reveals differences associated with structural and environmental context. In both cases, the transcriptions reflect generalizations about the typical habits of speakers of the accent in question, and are normally relevant to the speaker as an individual only in his or her capacity as a representative of the accent-community to which the accent marks the speaker's affiliation. Both phonemic and allophonic transcriptions are used to make explicit observations on rule-based generalizations about regular, patterned activities in the accent concerned. They can therefore both be regarded as types of **systematic transcription**.

Phonetically motivated transcriptions are usually called **general phonetic transcriptions**, or **impressionistic transcriptions**. They pay no attention to the phonological value of the material transcribed. The account of speech offered by a phonetic transcription is normally specific to the occasion of utterance and, within the framework of a general phonetic theory, specific to the performance of the individual speaker concerned.

18.2 Systematic phonemic and allophonic transcriptions

The choice of symbols in a **phonemic transcription** is limited to one symbol per phoneme. The symbol can be made up of one written character such as /a/, or two, in the case of a digraph symbol such as /tʃ/, (or more), so long as the given phoneme, in whatever context it occurs, is always and only transcribed by means of that particular symbol. Any transcription that represents the occurrences of even a single phoneme by different symbols when the phoneme appears in different structural or environmental contexts becomes by definition an **allophonic transcription**. From this point of view, transcriptions can be less or more allophonic (depending on how many phonemes in the accent's phonemic system are treated allophonically), but they can only be phonemic or not phonemic. An alternative to this practice would be to say that a given transcription was phonemic with respect to some sub-set (a sub-system) of the phonemic system of the accent, and allophonic with respect to the remainder of the phonemic system (the other sub-systems).

The following set of transcriptions of a single utterance from British English (RP) illustrates the possibility of changing a phonemic transcription of an utterance to an allophonic one by giving allophonic specifications of selected parts of the utterance. The orthographic version of the utterance is given first. The second version is a phonemic transcription. The third is an allophonic transcription where only the /p/ phoneme has been transcribed allophonically, with the remainder being transcribed phonemically. The allophonic specifications are of structurally governed details of aspiration (in *pink* and *port*) versus non-aspiration (in *spot*); with glottal-stopped reinforcement of utterance-final non-release (in *top*); and of contextually determined anticipatory co-articulation of labialization of the instances of /p/ before lip-rounded vowels (in *spot* and *port*):

Orthographic   A pink spot of port stained the clean
                      table-top
Phonemic   /ə pɪŋk spɒt əv pɔt steɪnd ðə klin teɪbl tɒp /
Allophonic (for /p/) [ə pʰɪŋk spʷɒt əv pʰʷɔt steɪnd ðə klin teɪbl
                      tɒʔp˺]

The salient objective of a phonemic transcription is to provide a unique identification for each separate linguistic unit of the language that is phonemically differentiated by the accent in question. It is assumed that supporting each phonemic symbol there is, notionally available from the analyst, a detailed statement of conventions about the specific pronunciation of the phoneme as appropriate to its contrastive and contextual characteristics. Using one symbol per phoneme is therefore adequate to the purpose. Furthermore, the function of the symbol chosen to represent the phoneme is to communicate the fact of distinctiveness, and to be broadly mnemonic in reminding the reader about the phonetic manifestation typically associated with the phoneme. It is therefore not normally necessary, in developing a phonemic transcription as such, to choose symbols whose purpose is to make highly specific comments on detailed subtleties of pronunciation. For these reasons, a phonemic transcription is sometimes called a **broad transcription**.

Phonological transcriptions (both phonemic and allophonic) constitute generalized, abstract statements about the pronunciatory behaviour which typifies a given accent. The most general level of comment is perhaps represented by a form of transcription which indicates the pronunciations of the individual words of the utterance as if they had been spoken one word at a time, in isolation from the context of neighbouring words, and in a formal style. Such pronunciations can be thought of as **canonical forms**, and this type of transcription (phonemic or allophonic) can therefore be referred to as a **canonical transcription**. The transcriptions of the individual words in almost all pronouncing dictionaries are canonical phonemic transcriptions. An instance of a canonical phonemic transcription of an utterance in British English (RP) would be:

Orthographic   These sheep will actually bite the hands
                      that feed them
Canonical phonemic /ðiz ʃip wɪl akʧuəlɪ baɪt ðə handz ðat fid
                      ðɛm/

Phonological transcriptions (both phonemic and allophonic) can also be used, however, to comment on facts of pronunciation which are relevant to particular occasions or styles of utterance, provided that the comment is framed in terms of choices made from options which are part of the phonological repertoire of the accent concerned. It is thus possible to use phonemic or allophonic transcriptions to note occasion-specific choices of assimilation at word-boundaries, together with instances of syllable-reorganization specific to a particular style of informality, for example. Instances would be the following phonemic and allophonic transcriptions (with selected allophonic detail) of an informal utterance in British English (RP) of the sentence cited immediately above:

Orthographic	These sheep will actually bite the hands that feed them
Phonemic	/ðiʒ ʃip l akʃlɪ baɪt ðə hanz ðət fid ðm/
Allophonic	[ðiʒ ʃip l̩ akʃlɪ baɪt̪ ðə hã̠n̠z ðət fid̪ ðm̩]

Phonemic transcriptions are often required either to provide a writing system for a previously unwritten language, or to furnish an analysis of the segmental phonology of a given language on which to base further linguistic work in suprasegmental phonology, morphology, syntax and semantics. Fine phonetic detail is not often at a premium in such circumstances. In designing a phonemic transcription for these purposes, therefore, typographic criteria of legibility and printability are often relevant. A practical reflection of this is that the typographic shapes of the symbol inventory in phonemic transcriptions are most often drawn from the stock of letter-shapes familiar to us from the lower-case roman alphabet.

Abercrombie (1964) offers a distinction between transcriptions which relies on a criterion based on the shape of the symbols chosen to represent the sounds concerned. He introduces the notion of **romanic** attributes of a symbol, where a symbol is less or more romanic in terms of its degree of similarity to the shapes of orthographic symbols used in the roman alphabet. Abercrombie distinguishes between transcriptions utilizing the most 'romanic' possible choice of symbol in all cases, to which he gives the name **simple transcriptions**, and those which (in the interest, for instance, of drawing attention to phonetic facts of detailed pronunciation specific to the particular language or accent) choose more exotic symbols. To this latter type he gives the name **comparative transcriptions**. In order to qualify as a **simple** notation, a phonemic transcription has to prefer the most romanic symbol available wherever general phonetic theory allows a choice. This becomes a particular issue whenever cover-symbols exist for a group of phonetically related sounds. If a transcription for any reason uses a less romanic symbol than is theoretically available, then that transcription becomes by definition a comparative transcription.

The symbols available from the roman alphabet are of course not selectable on some arbitrary basis: the phonetic conventions governing their selectability are formalized by the International Phonetic Association (IPA 1949 and appendix I in this book; Albright 1958; Pullum and Ladusaw 1986; Roach 1987), stating the range of possible associations between particular typographic symbols and specific phonetic values. These conventions tie individual symbols in many cases to phonetic interpretations of high specificity. But in the case of **cover-symbols**, one general symbol can stand for a whole class of different types of segments. An example is the symbol 'r', which can conventionally be used as a cover-symbol for all types of 'r-sounds' (which, it will be recalled, are normally referred to as a group as **rhotic sounds**) in different languages. These different members of the rhotic class of segments include [r, ɾ, ɹ, ʀ, ʁ, ɽ, ɺ, ɻ], their voiceless counterparts, and a number of other sounds.

There is a problem that arises from the existence of such cover-symbols, which often gives rise to misunderstanding in the minds of students. It is that, typographically, a single letter can act both as the superordinate cover-symbol for a phonetically defined class of sounds, and as a subordinate symbol specific to an individual member of that class. We have seen, for example, that the class of phonetic events called rhotic sounds is quite wide, and the symbol 'r' stands not only as the cover-symbol for rhotic sounds in general, but also for a voiced alveolar trilled stop (or 'trill'), as a specific phonetic pronunciation within this general class.

This example can be used to sharpen the distinction drawn between **simple** and **comparative transcriptions**. When one is dealing with an accent where the pronunciation of the 'r' sounds is typically not a trill, then a phonemic transcription of that accent which aspires to be considered a simple transcription would be obliged to select 'r' as the symbol for the /r/-phoneme in all its occurrences. The phrase *three rabid rabbits* spoken in an RP accent would therefore be transcribed as /θri reɪbɪd rabɪts/, for instance.

Attention might alternatively need to be drawn to the fact in a particular English accent that the 'r'-sounds are typically pronounced without trilling, technically as a voiced post-alveolar approximant [ɹ]. If /ɹ/ were then preferred to /r/ in the transcriptional stock of symbols for the phonemes of this accent, this would become a **comparative transcription**, and it would be necessary to transcribe the phrase *three rabid rabbits* as /θɹi ɹeɪbɪd ɹabɪts/. It would be 'comparative' because (for motivations of making comments which compared the phonetic habits of different accents of English, or of different languages) the analyst had chosen to prefer the symbol /ɹ/, as a less romanic but phonetically more specific symbol, to the romanically more familiar but phonetically more general /r/ symbol. The two transcriptions of the phrase *three rabid rabbits* are equally phonemic, however, because they both respect the criterion of consistently using only one symbol per phoneme.

The use of a simple transcription, as opposed to a comparative transcription, does not diminish the phonetic specificity of the whole transcription, if a transcription is considered to be made up of a visible part (the **text**), and an invisible part, which consists of the **interpretive conventions** detailing the phonetic values of the symbols concerned (Abercrombie 1964). To change from a simple phonemic transcription to a comparative phonemic transcription merely changes the location of information from the interpretive conventions to the visible text.

A **simple phonemic transcription**, therefore, would be one which in all contexts consistently used one (single or digraph) symbol per phoneme, of the most romanic typographic shape available under IPA conventions. It is worth emphasizing that two different types of criterion are used in making this classification. The criterion for classifying the transcription as phonemic or allophonic, namely the number of symbols for representing a given phoneme, is a **linguistic criterion**. The criterion for classifying the transcription as simple or comparative, namely the shape of the letters used, is a **typographic criterion**. The linguistic phonemic/allophonic dimension for classifying transcriptions is thus independent of the typographic simple/comparative dimension of classification.

The above comments about the simple/comparative dimension of classification of transcriptions apply to allophonic transcriptions as well as to phonemic transcriptions. In practice, however, the usefulness of the typographic dimension for classifying allophonic transcriptions is somewhat diluted by the progressive arbitrariness of the scale of 'romanicness' when applied to the large numbers of highly specific phonetic symbols for subtly different allophones. This is especially true in the area of detailed pronunciations of different allophones of vowel phonemes. How might one organize the scale of romanicness of symbols in the general area of [a] and [ɑ], such as [a, ɑ, ɒ, ɐ, æ]? The potential and somewhat unproductive intricacies of the simple/comparative dimension of classification when applied to allophonic transcription will therefore here be left aside.

A final (minor) classification of phonemic transcriptions arises from the way that combined length and quality differences are handled. In many languages, including English, some pairs of vowel phonemes are phonetically characterized by differences both of relative duration and of phonetic quality. Examples of this in British English (RP) are:

> *Relative duration and articulatory quality as the phonetic basis*
> *for stressed monophthongal vowel distinctions in British English*
> *(RP)*
>
> [biːt] beat   [bɪt] bit
> [kʰɑːt] cart   [kʰat] cat
> [tʰɔːt] taut   [tʰɒt] tot
> [pʰuːl] pool   [pʰʊl] pull

Transcriptional issues arise in decisions about the phonemic representation of relative duration and articulatory quality relations of this sort. This is because the phonetic basis for the phonological contrast is not one single distinguishing feature, but two. Since both duration and articulatory quality are involved, either or both of the phonetic differences can be utilized as the basis for choosing an appropriate phonemic transcription. If phonetic duration alone is preferred, giving priority to the visible expression of the phonological feature of **quantity**, then the same vowel symbol differentiated by the presence versus the absence of a length mark, as in /biːt/ versus /bit/, can be used. (Another way of representing exactly the same solution would be to double the vowel symbol and dispense with the length mark, as in /biit/ versus /bit/.) If articulatory quality alone is preferred, giving priority of visible expression to the phonological feature of **quality**, then different vowel symbols can be used without any appeal to a length mark, as in /bit/ versus /bɪt/.

The statement of the fully detailed nature of the phonetic manifestations of both quantity and quality would reside in each case in the conventions explaining the phonetic values of the transcriptional symbols. A less economical solution, which is nevertheless sometimes helpful for particular pedagogical applications in the teaching of English as a foreign language, is to combine both quantity and quality in the phonological representation, transcribing the above pair as /biːt/ versus /bɪt/. All these solutions have been used at different times in the design of English pronouncing dictionaries for foreign learners.

All the transcriptions indicated immediately above would count as phonemic, provided that each phoneme were transcribed in all contexts with an unvarying choice of symbol. Taking the distinction between the vowels in *beat* and *bit* as representative, a transcription of Received Pronunciation which preferred a solution which used the symbols /iː/ versus /i/ (or /ii/ versus /i/) could be classified as a **quantitative transcription**. One which preferred to use the symbols /i/ versus /ɪ/ could be called a **qualitative transcription**

(Abercrombie 1964). One which preferred a solution with the symbols /iː/ and /ɪ/, could be termed a **quantitative/qualitative transcription**.

18.3   Allophonic and phonetic transcriptions

The transcription of both allophones and phones is conventionally enclosed in square brackets. The appearance of a transcription surrounded by square brackets is hence ambiguous between a transcription at the level of discriminable phones (a general phonetic transcription) and one at the level of somewhat more abstract allophones (an allophonic transcription). This is not normally a harmful ambiguity. General phonetic and allophonic transcriptions share the property of making more or less narrowly specific comment on phonetic details of pronunciation. For this reason, both of these types of transcription are sometimes called a **narrow transcription**.

There are two characteristics of general phonetic transcription, as distinct from phonological allophonic transcription, which are specially worth mentioning. The first is that observation of phonetic performance, as communicated in general phonetic transcription, is supposedly free of phonological motivation. This amounts to saying that the commentary on speech afforded by a transcription couched in terms of the descriptors of general phonetic theory is as language-neutral as possible. The second characteristic is that general phonetic transcription is especially suitable for occasion-specific observations of the speech of a particular speaker, where a commentary on phonetic performance at high resolution may be important. Allophonic transcription is more suited to commentaries on regularities about the typical phonetic performance of a given accent by the speech-community concerned, and this type of transcription is by definition dense with phonological assumptions of an accent-specific kind.

A phonetic transcription is often used, as mentioned above, in the very early stages of a phonological investigation of a language new to the analyst, when the phonemic and allophonic details are yet to be established. It is in this use of phonetic transcription that one of the most insidious problems faced by phoneticians can arise. Listeners are magnificently skilled at decoding utterances in their native language: they have, after all, invested a lifetime's effort in learning, using and maintaining this skill. The over-learned nature of the skill seems to result, however, in a petrification of their perceptual ability when it comes to listening to novel material from another language. Listeners tend to force the new material through the perceptual grid of the phonological categories of their own language. In the ideal case, a phonetician working on a new language should be able to exercise a language-independent perceptual skill, free of such categorical contamination.

In reality, however, despite long training, phoneticians are rather unlikely fully to escape their status as listeners whose normal language-centred perceptual habits are as deeply ingrained as those of any other speakers of their own language. Learning to become as independent as possible of this prejudicial bias is a central part of the perceptual training of phoneticians. Conscious attention is often needed to avoid the risk of suffering native-language-centred perceptual bias when beginning to work on the analysis of an unfamiliar language.

Early in the exploratory phase of the investigation of a new language, with the possibility of language-centred personal bias borne in mind, the phonetician is likely to use a very detailed phonetic transcription, and to try to use a relatively high degree of resolution in order to differentiate the phonetic events presented. In addition, the type of symbols chosen is likely to vary, as one refines one's phonetic opinion about what one hears on different occasions of repetition by the consultant, and as one progressively settles to an understanding of the relationship between the voice quality of the consultant and the phonetic events being heard.

The following illustrative transcriptions reproduce the text of actual written notes of general phonetic analysis of utterances in a number of languages from consultants who were native speakers, made by the author (JL) and a colleague (SH) while teaching postgraduate courses in the use of general phonetic transcription for linguistic investigation. The pattern in a given session with an adult native consultant of the language in question was one where the consultant would first pronounce a selected word or phrase some ten to twelve times, at a normal rate and in a conversational style. Both transcribers would write down their initial analysis of the word or phrase, using the full potential repertoire of general phonetic symbols and diacritics. Then the consultant would repeat the item in the same way about six times. The transcribers would then amend their transcriptions if necessary. This process would be reiterated a number of times, until the transcribers reached the point of diminishing returns. The transcriptions would then be compared, but not changed. In a later session, the process would be repeated with a group of postgraduate students taking the role of transcribers, to allow them to experiment with their own transcriptional ability, and the staff transcriptions would finally be used as the basis for discussion and comparison.

It is worth emphasis that, as implied earlier, the most difficult language to transcribe in general phonetic terms, for native English-speaking analysts, is without question English itself. For a phonetician, the insidious prejudice of one's own phonologically-biased perceptual habits is at its most forceful, and least suspected, when one's own language is concerned.

Single transcriptions in the illustrations represent these final transcriptions from one or other of the two staff transcribers. Multiple transcriptions in the Czech examples represent successive notations by a single transcriber of the same item repeated by the consultant, to show the progression of phonetic hypotheses. Parentheses ( ) denote uncertainty. Some symbols have been adjusted to match the conventions of this book, but no other changes have been introduced. In some cases, examples from more than one consultant have been included, and more than one accent may therefore be illustrated for a given language. Readers might like to try to perform the transcribed words, and this might also serve as a useful practical rehearsal of the phonetic meanings of some of the symbols introduced in this book.

A number of items in the list might have been transcribed slightly differently with the benefit of either greater familiarity with the phonetic characteristics of the languages in question, or of knowledge about the phonological value of some of the components. It should be noted that, apart from knowing that the utterances represented single words or sometimes phrases in the language concerned, no linguistic knowledge about such phonologically relevant details as word-boundaries, phonemic system, syllabic structure, assimilation, liaison or syllabic affiliation was taken into account. It should be clear, nevertheless, after reading this book, that a wealth of more or less inevitable assumptions at a general phonological level pervades the transcriptions.

Illustrations of detailed general phonetic transcriptions of words and phrases in a number of languages from native-speaker consultants

---

Australian English (Brisbane)
[ˈp̥ɹʷēnsəˈpɑɫ̩əti̩] principality
[kɑɫ̩ɜ̩s̩θēnə̩ʔk̩s̩] callisthenics

Czech

[ˈʋiɛɾɛtskiː] 'scientific'	2. [ˈʋi̯e̯d̥e̯tskiː]
[pɾɒstʃi] 'simpler'	2. [ˌb̥ɾʷɒsːtʃʷiˑ]
	3. [pɾʷɒstʃʷiˑ]
	4. [pʷɾʷɒ̥stʃʷiː]
[sɛɹɲaːhᵃtm̩i] 'it is thundering loudly'	2. [ˈsɛ̯ɹɛɲaːhɾ̩tmiː],
	3. [ˈsɛ̯ɹɛɲɛːhɾ̩tmiː]
[ˈɟɾɛcɛ̩] 'children'	
[ˈkɾɑːsnaˑᵉɟɛcɛ̩ʰ] 'beautiful children'	

[ˌɾiːt̪k̠ɑːml̩fia̪ː] 'mist'

[ˈk̠ʲn̪ɛfiɒvˈnɑ̩ˑ] 'library'

[kʷr̥ŝʷiːdɑ̩] 'chalk'

[ˈdʷr̪ᶻʷɛʋǫ̪] 'wood'

[ˌfiʷeɾᶻʷb̪it̪ɒvʷɲʷĩː] 'cemetery-like'

[ˈbɲ̊ɛ̃ᵑɲŋkɑ̩] 'female citizen of Brno'

[ˈraɾɑːʃʷɛk̪] 'little devil'

Danish

[kʷʰø̥ᴸpm̥hã̰ʊ̃ʔʷn̪̥] 'Copenhagen'

[ø̥sʷtʷø̥hʷǫʊ̰ʔʷl̩ʲʷ] 'cheese-slicer'

Dutch (Amsterdam)

[kʰɜʔt̪ˢ] 'calf'

[kˣɑ̪ʊtʷ] 'cold'

Finnish (Kouvola)

[pa̪ːlʲø̥s̪ʋɑ̪ːt̪ɛ̥] 'cloak'

[mʲʷøn̪̊t̪æ] 'to admit'

Scottish Gaelic (Skye)

[kʲa̪ʎiç̪ː] 'of an old woman'

[kʰɑ̪ːl̥ᶾɾiʃ] 'accompanying him/along with him'

[ɲiᵊd̪̥θɾʌx̪ːk̪] '(family) washing'

Scottish Gaelic (Islay)

[kʰʷʘ̪ʲˣʷt̪ʷʃʲ] 'cat'

[n̪̥d̪ᶻɑ̪ʔ̪ʒ̪] 'the day'

Scottish Gaelic (Harris)

[ʃʲa̪xkʰ] 'seven'

[əfiʷɔx̪ʷkʷʰ] 'eight'

[kʲehe̪ð] 'four'

Hindi

[n̪e̪ɾɜ̃n̪t̪ʰɜɾ̥] 'continuously'

[paɾe̪ʃ̥ːɹ̩ãmˑ] 'labour, hard work'

[kʰɑ̪ɾɜ̃t̪ᶾᵊ] 'reason (for doing something)'

[ˈhʷo̪li] 'a (particular) festival'

[saɦasi̯ʋʲɛɹt̪i] 'courageous person'

Icelandic

[hɑ̃ũŋʷʝʲe̞] 'clothes peg'

['kʰahple̞ⁿkʰʷu̠ᵂ] 'match (game)'

[ɡe̞ɾʷœn̠ʷtʷœ̞] 'shallow'

[ʝʲʷjo̠ᵘsmĩn̪ta̠ʋʲe̞ɹ] 'camera'

Norwegian (Southeastern, Larvik)

[va̠ʃtɛ̞zkɾa̠n̪ɑ̠] 'overalls'

[hʷɔ̠ːrfa̠ɾʋɛ̞ɾ] 'hair colours'

[sʷyːʝʲʷt̪ʷe̞n̪ʲ] 'as thin as an awl'

[sʷu̠ʃʷe̞ʔt̪ə̠ʔ] 'sweet and sour'

Panjabi (Central-Southern)

[lə'kɾi̯ð̞ɑːʳre̞ʈa̠] 'a wooden cart'

[kˣʌ'te̞ð̞ikʰʌ'tɑe̞ʔ] 'the sourness of the sour-fruit'

['ɡʷɦʷɔ̞mbə̠ʳ'ɡɦɛ̞ːɾ] 'whirlpool'

Polish

[prɒʃʷã̠ɣ̃] 'please'

[prɒʃʲã̠ɣ̃] 'pig'

[ɣʲʒ̃ãõ̃] 'he took it'

[tʃʷt͡ʃʲiːna] 'swamp plant'

[ʃʷt͡ʃã̠ʊ̃ʃʲt͡ʃʲɛ] 'luck'

As soon as early phonological decisions are taken about systemic, structural or contextual regularities that are hypothesized, a tentative stabilization of the transcription tends to take place. The degree of resolution of the transcription then often lowers drastically as the transcription changes function and character from a phonetic to a phonological mode. The phonic analysis that characterizes the earliest stages gives way to allophonic interpretations, and information often begins to be transferred from the visible text to the tacit interpretive conventions. Once the allophonic basis of hypothesized phonemes is understood by the analyst, the complexity of using contextually and structurally specific symbols yields place to the convenience and legibility of a small stock of phonemic symbols. Where feasible, these phonemic symbols will tend to be romanic cover symbols, for reasons of legibility and printability.

A strong reduction thus occurs in the data explicitly represented by the symbols used. One of the chief differences between phonetic and phonological transcriptions is that the former maximizes the amount of information explicit in the symbols that make up the text, while the latter maximizes the weight of information in the interpretive conventions that explain the symbols of the text. In this sense, an allophonic transcription is intermediate between a phonetic transcription and a phonemic one.

18.4   General phonetic transcription and the IPA

General phonetic transcription, as indicated earlier, typically uses the stock of symbols available in the alphabet of the IPA. The acronym 'IPA' strictly refers, as in this usage, to the 'International Phonetic Association'. But it is now such a common practice to use the acronym also to refer to the alphabet itself (from the phrase 'International Phonetic Alphabet') that resistance seems pedantic. Context usually serves to disambiguate the two usages.

The international community of phoneticians who constitute the membership of the International Phonetic Association expend considerable effort to ensure that the symbols of the IPA alphabet and their possible interpretations are well understood by the community, through articles in the *Journal of the International Phonetic Association* and elsewhere. Such revisions as are from time to time agreed are the subject of a good deal of preliminary discussion. The rescrutiny of the stock of IPA symbols that was conducted by the Association in 1989 at the Kiel Convention, coinciding with the centenary of the Association, has been mentioned a number of times earlier in the book. This book has followed the Kiel conventions of the IPA in matters of phonetic transcription wherever possible, unless some particular transcriptional point was being made, or unless innovations were being suggested because relevant symbols have not been satisfactorily established.

The virtues of a standardized approach to a topic as intricate as phonetic transcription cannot be overemphasized. Without standard interpretability, the plethora of symbols necessary for precise identification of the sounds exploited by the many thousands of different languages of the world threatens to become a written version of Babel. With international agreement on standard usage, relatively accurate communication becomes feasible, and the subject of phonetics itself is able to be coherent. The difficulty of maintaining such international standards, however, should not be underestimated. The only safe way to minimize confusion is to use a standard symbol for a standard description of a given phonetic event, in practice and theory. But this is a counsel of perfection, and some degree of confusion over symbols

561

and interpretations will undoubtedly reign for as long as an adequate and widely accepted general phonetic theory eludes pursuit.

Further reading

The major book on the **typology of phonetic transcription** is still Abercrombie (1964), which contains a good bibliography of previous work. An early article on defining the properties of a 'letter' in transcription and orthography, which retains its importance, is Abercrombie (1949). The book by Pullum and Ladusaw (1986) has become a standard guide to the names and shapes of letters used as individual phonetic symbols. Articles, pamphlets and books discussing **IPA conventions** and possible revisions are: Albright (1958), Fox (1974), Henton (1987), IPA (1949), Ladefoged (1987a, 1987b), Ladefoged and Roach (1986), MacMahon (1986), Maddieson (1987a), Pullum and Ladusaw (1986), Roach (1987) and Wells (1975, 1976). The outcome of the 1989 Kiel Convention of the IPA, revising the symbols of the International Phonetic Alphabet to its current form, is described in a set of articles in the *Journal of the International Phonetic Association* (1989: vol 19, no. 2). **Computer coding of phonetic characters** is discussed by Esling (1990), IPA Workgroup 9 (1989) and Wells (1987, 1989). A book discussing many practical issues in phonetic and phonological transcription is Kelly and Local (1989).

Phonetic and phonological transcription, as well as having the status of types of observational notation, are also instances of writing systems. The history and analysis of the writing systems of the world have a mutual relevance, in most instances, for the study of the spoken language of the culture concerned. Recommended publications on **writing systems** are Chadwick (1958), Coulmas (1989), Diringer (1962, 1968), Gelb (1952), Healey (1990), Kemp (1981), Nakanishi (1980), Ong (1982), Sampson (1985) and Senner (1989).

PART VIII

Conclusion

19

Evaluating general
phonetic theory

The study of speech was described in the Introduction as covering 'a remarkably wide domain, embracing aspects of the social sciences, the life sciences, the physical sciences, the engineering sciences and the information sciences'. As one might imagine in a field which attracts the interest of so diverse a range of disciplines, each of these specialisms has developed its own perspective on speech, coloured by the conceptual filter through which it views its own subject (Beckman 1988). One might then ask whether there is some common framework of understanding about how speech works and how it is used, which all these subjects share. To the extent that an answer exists, it is probably fair to say that the only well-developed model of speech description which commands really widespread international acceptance is the one represented by the International Phonetic Association's phonetic alphabet, with its attendant segmentally oriented assumptions.

It was suggested in section 5.2 that the classificatory architecture shaping the IPA alphabet has remained largely unchanged for over a hundred years, even after the adjustments made by the 1989 Kiel Convention. The IPA alphabet thus has the great strength of having withstood the test of time. Its prime virtue lies in offering a readily understandable, reasonably objective and above all internationally accepted and standard means of describing the substance of speech, usable by phonetic research of all varieties as a point of departure into more specialized and diversified territory. This is not at all to say that a segmentally oriented approach of the IPA variety is without problems, nor that theories built on other less segmental perspectives may not in principle provide equally usable foundations for future research into speech. The purpose of this chapter is to consider such issues in the evaluation of a general phonetic theory, and to take the opportunity to reflect on some of the strengths and weaknesses of the approach to phonetic description presented in this book.

The stated objective of this book was to equip beginning phoneticians, and those embarking on speech-related interests in other disciplines such as speech pathology, speech science, speech technology, foreign-language learning, psycholinguistics and sociolinguistics, with a systematic, comprehensive and workable foundation for independent research into the substance of speech. Readers will have developed their own views about whether this objective has been successfully reached, but some comments on the nature of the foundation presented here may be timely.

An emphasis throughout the book has been on the architectural structure of the general phonetic theory being offered. The design of any theory is systematic to the degree that the relations between its components show a structural coherence; it is comprehensive to the extent that it adequately covers all currently known phenomena in the field of interest; and it is workable to the point that researchers find it a useful tool for the operations to which they apply it. It is these three dimensions that shape the architecture of a descriptive model into a habitable mental environment for the researcher.

In such terms, many versions of general phonetic theory would find acceptability. One of the basic attitudes that this book has tried to communicate is that every serious approach to the study of speech has something in it of value. Each such approach will invariably also have limitations and disadvantages. The most valuable scientific attitude that the beginning phonetician can acquire is that an eclectic openness to the merits of different theories, provided it is coupled with a critical eye for the strengths and weaknesses of the theoretical architecture concerned, has more to commend it than the adoption of any doctrinaire approach. The theoretical model offered in this book is no less deserving of critical evaluation, not least for the exposure that might result of avenues of further necessary research.

19.1   General phonetic theory and the segment

In conventional scientific usage, a theory is supposed to be able to describe data, explain the relationships between them and enable the formulation of testable hypotheses predicting the nature of hitherto-uninvestigated phenomena within the general domain of the theory. We shall return to the testability of general phonetic theory in a later section. The descriptive responsibility of the theory is partly characterized in terms of comprehensiveness of coverage. We have seen that the theory offered here is largely but not entirely comprehensive. Some limitations have perhaps been visible – for example the relative inability of the theory to cope gracefully with subsegmental complexities such as those found in the complex oral/nasal stops discussed in chapter 8. Another example was the theory's difficulty in maintaining both its phonetic definition of affrication and a plausible support for phonology when faced with the prolongation of the fricative element in the 'strong' lateral affricates of Akhwakh described in chapter 12. Such limitations spring in part from the nature of the fundamental descriptive constructs adopted, especially that of the segment.

Problematic issues that derive from exploiting the essentially linear concept of the segment are discussed more fully below, but one might simply note here that these difficulties are the acknowledged price to be paid for the convenience of the segmental concept as a means of introducing data from a wealth of languages to the intended audience of this book, for whom no prior technical knowledge of speech was assumed. The segment has been, and continues to be, the descriptive vehicle for the overwhelming majority of the phonetic analysis of the languages of the world. We have seen that it is one of the longest-lived of all descriptive concepts applied to speech, and it has been a remarkably helpful enabling device for the discussion of speech over the centuries. While segment-based descriptions of the world's languages abound, non-segmental descriptions of more than the most limited number of languages simply do not yet exist.

This book was written during a period in which the concept of the segment has been somewhat under attack as an unduly constraining unit in the descriptive theory of phonetics. Criticism has come particularly from phonologists concerned to develop effective means of relating the phonology of articulatory events to suprasegmental temporal, prosodic and metrical phenomena of word-stress, tone, intonation and rhythm. Recent publications produced under the banner of autosegmental and metrical phonology display some of the most perceptive and inventive work in modern phonology. Much has been achieved by these non-linear approaches to phonology, and more is anticipated. Their chief focus, however, has been mostly on the phonological level of analysis, rather than the phonetic level. An exception to this has been the parametrically oriented work in **laboratory phonology** by Browman and Goldstein, which has attempted to provide what they call **articulatory phonology** in an autosegmental vein (e.g. 1986, 1990). The reader is encouraged to consult the publications by Browman and Goldstein on this significant initiative, for which Steriade (1990) and Ladefoged (1990) provide an opposing critique, the first from the perspective of autosegmental phonology, the second from the viewpoint of phonetics.

Non-linear theories that try to dispense with a pivotal role for the phonetic segment are almost all theories whose prime motivation is the foregrounding of the distinctiveness of phonological relations, rather than the highlighting of details of phonetic realizations. In this phonological emphasis, non-linear models of phonology have much to recommend them. But few non-linear phonologies, from the prosodic approach of J.R. Firth to the most recent developments in autosegmental and metrical phonology, could yet claim to offer comprehensively developed schemes of phonetic description, since this has not been their priority.

It might be noted that even those non-linear theories that seek to dispense with the idea of the segment tend to use it as a procedural entity in their initial approach to data-handling. Provided it is kept firmly in mind that the concept of the segment is an imposed analytic construct, then the theoretical architecture supporting the segment is perhaps not as intellectually constraining as is sometimes claimed. This book has tried to make it clear that the concept of the segment is neither natural nor (in some ultimate analysis) necessary. It is merely one rather convenient way of organizing our initial analytic thinking about speech. It does not stand in the way of extending that thinking to other correlatable approaches, linear or non-linear.

Since the principal focus of this book has been an attempt to give a comprehensive and principled picture of the phonetic substance underlying the spoken languages of the world, it was felt preferable to present a theoretical architecture which included a considered version of the concept of the segment. Whether the convenience of the segment as a descriptive unit of phonetic theory will continue to be acknowledged by the phoneticians of the twenty-first century and beyond, only time will tell. But our alphabetic inheritance predisposes us to a segmental view of speech, and with the benefit of time-travel it would not be surprising to learn that the segment figured as a basic descriptive concept in phonetic discussion well into the future.

19.2 The role of convenient fictions in theory-building

As a preliminary to the following discussion, it is perhaps important to note the role that convenient fiction plays in the status of any units proposed for the description of speech. If one accepts the metaphorical function of convenient fictions in theory-building, then for every fiction postulated, a compensating counter-fiction needs to be invented. We can take the segment as the most obvious example of this. Proposing the notion of the segment encourages us also to posit the compensating fiction of co-articulation, to explain the properties which a given segment seems to acquire, and which we construe as belonging to it, in different contexts. If we describe a segment 'as if' it had an abiding identity in different contexts, then we have to invent another concept (co-articulation) to compensate for the error we have thereby introduced, as a deliberate step in the construction of theory.

A limited version of this approach has been adopted here, in that not all units proposed for the description of speech are claimed to be convenient fictions. Some, such as the speaking-turn and the utterance itself, have been regarded as more natural units of analysis, given that both are objectively definable with respect to silence at their borders. The feature, the syllable and the setting, as well as the segment, must be said to be analytically imposed.

19.3   Linear and non-linear characteristics of speech units

The phonetic theory set out in this book was initially characterized in chapter 4 as a 'linear' approach. This is not completely accurate, and merits some discussion. It is worth pointing out that two different cross-cutting series of units are involved, in terms of the alignability in time of their respective boundaries. The speaking turn, the utterance, and the segment constitute one series, with all their boundaries being mutually aligned in time. They are **chain-exhausting** in the sense that at the relevant level, the chain of speech can be parsed without residue into a chained sequence of the units concerned. The feature and the setting (which is itself featurally defined) are in a different series, with mutually aligned boundaries within that series. This alignment does not necessarily extend to that of the other series (except trivially in that the marginal boundaries of the speaking-turn and the utterance as natural units coincide with the beginning and end of speaking). Phonetic features are chain-exhausting, but settings (being a secondary analysis of the mutual properties of features) are not necessarily so.

Because at least some phonetic features are independent of the alignment constraints of the segment/utterance series, the feature/setting series has to be regarded as being in a non-linear relationship with the segment/utterance series. A clear example of this is the feature of nasality, in anticipatory co-articulation in the medial phase of resonant segments. In its contextual occurrence in different languages this has different onset locations, as in English which shows an earlier onset of anticipatory nasality on vocoids than is the case in French. The freedom of this feature from phasal segmental constraints arises partly from the relative anatomical and physiological independence of the velopharyngeal system from the other organic structures of the vocal tract.

A similar organic explanation applies to the relative independence of labial action from that of other articulatory actions except those of the jaw. Equally, a general organic explanation applies to the relative independence, except in very fine detail, of all the laryngeal features (phonation, as well as pitch and loudness) from the articulatory features of performance. It also applies to the general non-linear relationship between the segment/utterance series and the feature/setting series.

We can now return again to the notion of the segment. In chapter 4, it was acknowledged that the origins of the idea of dividing speech into a train of segments (as theoretical constructs) lay in a linear rather than a parametric approach to the description of speech. The central task of theory-building is of course to engineer the best conceivable match between the constructs of the theory and the external 'reality' they are designed to describe. The responsibility of theorists, correspondingly, is to be critical about this goodness of fit, and to strive constantly to improve it. It has to be said that the fit between the segment as a theoretical construct and the 'reality' it addresses is not completely satisfactory, even within the linear approach in which it is set. A number of related concepts therefore needed to be recruited to mitigate, if not remedy, some of the deficiencies of a thorough-going segmental concept. One of these related concepts was the notion of the segment having internal structure, being made up of three articulatorily defined phases – the onset, medial and offset phases. Given that the two marginal phases are seen as overlapping with the marginal phases of neighbouring segments, or as being utterance-marginal transitions from or to utterance-external silence, the concept of a segment having a multiphasal internal structure enabled some problematic phenomena to be brought more comfortably within the descriptive ability of the model.

One such problem was the issue of the segmental affiliation of segmentally ambivalent events. Traditional phonetic theory tends to describe such events as primarily associated with one rather than the other of two adjacent segments. Examples are aspiration and affrication, which in chapter 12 were both identified explicitly as a matter of segmental co-ordination, and as a property of a relationship between two segments rather than a characteristic of a single segment. In this respect, aspiration and affrication are treated in this book in a non-linear rather than a linear fashion. A further example can be found in the treatment of different types of stop release as co-ordinatory choices for the relationship between the stop and its segmental context.

An antidote of a different type to over-reliance on the concept of the segment was introduced in the idea of a setting as a phonetic property common to two or more segments, sometimes common to the majority of segments in a whole utterance. The availability of the notion of a setting also means that the theoretical mechanisms for describing linguistic phenomena in speech are able to be unified to some extent with the mechanisms for describing certain paralinguistic and extralinguistic phenomena.

19.4   Default assumptions and language statistics

This section will consider the empirical justification for the shape of the descriptive theory offered in this book by appeal to a major principle of theory-building, that of **architectural parsimony**. The economy principle enshrined in Occam's Razor enjoins us not to complicate explanations before we must. Applying this principle to the construction of descriptive phonetic theory, a well-designed and efficient model would be one where the most basic theoretical structures offered the most comprehensive coverage of the data to be described. Another way of putting this is to say that maximal simplicity of theoretical structure in phonetic description should reflect the greatest frequency of occurrence in the languages of the world of the sounds described. The more elaborated the descriptive structure used, the more limited should be the incidence of the sound-types described.

In the philosophical view of scientific method as the construction of provisional truth promoted by Karl Popper, the testability of hypotheses means their potential for falsifiability. The claim that the structure of the descriptive theory offered here successfully reflects patterns of incidence of sound-types in the known languages of the world is clearly open to empirical test, provided that an acceptably representative sample of the world's languages is available. The section immediately below offers some preliminary comments about the typical size and content of the consonant systems exploited by the languages of the world. The claim about simplicity of theoretical description being directly correlated with frequency of occurrence of the sound-types concerned will then be assessed against the statistics of segmental take-up by the languages represented in the largest database for which systematic data is readily available – the UPSID database assembled by Maddieson and colleagues at UCLA (Maddieson 1984). The hypothesis to be tested about the architectural parsimony shown by the descriptive phonetic model will be the following:

> *The more elaborated the phonetic description of a consonantal segment-type, the greater will be its articulatory complexity, and the less widespread will be its take-up by the languages of the world.*

This hypothesis takes its point of departure from the discussion of phonetic universals in consonant systems in Lindblom and Maddieson (1988), who divide consonant realizations into three sets along a scale of **articulatory complexity**, 'basic', 'elaborated' and 'complex' articulations. The last of these is constituted by combinations of elaborated articulations. Elaborated articulations for Lindblom and Maddieson (1988: 67) involve departures from a **default mode of production** in initiation, phonation or articulation, and include such segment-types as ejectives, implosives and clicks, breathy or creaky voiced segments, pre-nasalized stops, aspirated and pre-aspirated stops, and segments made with a secondary or displaced articulation. Examples of 'complex' articulations in their terms would include 'breathiness combined with [a] click airstream', as in !Xũ, or 'retroflexion combined with breathy voice', as in Hindi (*ibid.*). 'Basic' articulations are then all types of segments other than such elaborated types.

We shall follow the interesting precedent set by Lindblom and Maddieson in describing **elaborated segments** as those which depart from a specified default mode of initiation, phonation, articulation or co-ordination characterizing **basic segments**. We shall not adopt their concept of 'complex' segment-types, however, but treat these as lying at the more extreme end of a scale of elaboration (and hence of a hypothesized scale of articulatory complexity). The term 'complex' will be reserved in this book for segments such as the complex oral/nasal stops discussed in chapter 8.

Section 19.4.2 specifies the conventions for characterizing the default cases of basic segments, and section 19.4.3 details the relevant statistics of the take-up by the languages of the UPSID database of segments of both basic and elaborated types. The discussion below will concentrate on segments representing consonants, but the reader interested in universal properties of vowel systems might like to consult the publications listed in the section on Further Reading at the end of the chapter.

19.4.1 The size of typical phonemic inventories in the languages of the world

Maddieson (1984: 7–9) discusses the overall size of the phonemic inventories in the 317 languages of the UPSID database. The inventories ranged in size from only 11 (6 consonants and 5 vowels) for Rotokas and 13 for Hawaiian (8 consonants and 5 vowels) to 141 (95 consonants and 46 vowels) for !Xũ. Obviously, these figures revolve crucially on how one defines an individual segment, and Maddieson does not economize by abstracting common distinctive features such as nasality or length from multiple vowels as single phonemic entities. Nasality and length thus have the effect in these calculations of multiplying the numbers of vowels which they distinguish. Within his conventions, the typical size of a combined consonant and vowel inventory for a language is between 20 and 37 segments, with 70 per cent of the 317 languages falling in this range. The average number of segments used contrastively by the languages of the UPSID database is just over 31.

In general, a large inventory size is achieved by increased sizes of consonantal systems (Maddieson 1984: 9). Some consonants are more frequent in the languages of the UPSID database than others. Maddieson therefore explores the hypothesis that 'a smaller inventory has a greater probability of including a common segment than a larger one, and a larger inventory has a greater probability of including an unusual segment type than a smaller one' (p. 10). He defines a 'small' inventory as one with 20–24 consonants, and a 'large' one as having more than 40 consonants; he investigated the consonants in the languages of the database, and found the relationships shown in table 19.1.

Table 19.1 *Percentage incidence of frequent and infrequent consonant-types in languages with small versus large consonant systems, compared with their incidence in 317 languages*

		% in small C-systems	% in 317 languages	% in large C-systems
Group I: more likely	/p/	89.5	82.6	77.8
to occur in small systems	/k/	93.0	89.3	79.3
	/ŋ/	59.6	52.7	51.9
Group II: equally likely	/m/	94.7	94.3	92.6
in small or large systems	/w/	75.4	75.1	77.8
Group III: more likely	/b/	45.6	62.8	77.8
to occur in large systems	/g/	42.1	55.2	75.9
	/ʔ/	33.3	30.3	55.6
	/ʧ/	22.8	44.5	64.8
	/f/	15.8	42.6	51.8
	/ʃ/	17.5	46.1	70.4
	/j/	78.9	85.5	94.4
	/ɲ/	22.8	33.8	37.0

Source: After Maddieson (1984: 11)

Maddieson investigated the statistical basis of these differences. The consonants in groups I and III show a very significant difference ($p < 0.005$) from the overall frequency of occurrence, while those in group II show no significant difference. There are already indicative clues in the phonetic nature of the differences between the segments in groups I and III for answering the hypothesis framed in section 19.4: the segments in group I are place-neutral contoids without elaborated co-ordinatory complexities, whereas the segments in group III include at least two elaborated segments – a segment with a displaced place of articulation (/f/), and one involving affricated co-ordination (/ʧ/).

573

Maddieson (1984: 11) concludes from his examination of the data that 'the relationship between the size and the content of an inventory is a matter that concerns individual types of segments, rather than being amenable to broad generalizations'. Section 19.4.3 processes the consonantal data in Maddieson's (1984: 263–422) tables of characteristic segments occurring in the 317 languages of the database, to match directly against the hypothesis in section 19.4 above, after an account of default assumptions.

19.4.2   *Default assumptions and label-structure conventions for segmental description*

Segments were said in chapter 5 to be able to be classified by reference to their initiation, phonation, articulation and co-ordination. In the interests not only of characterizing the default cases of basic segments, but also of standardization of everyday usage in using phonetic terminology, it would be convenient to constrain the possible structure of the composite descriptive labels for segments by obeying a number of practical conventions.

It is already customary in phonetics to standardize the sequence of the individual elements of a composite label in four groups. The groups refer to different elements of speech production, and are ordered in the following way:

> airstream mechanism and airflow direction;
> phonation type;
> place of articulation;
> stricture type.

If we take the composite label for [θ] at the beginning of the English word *thin* [θɪn] as an instance, [θ] would customarily be called 'a pulmonic egressive voiceless dental fricative'. This is often shortened in practice to 'a voiceless dental fricative'. The choice of phonation type is made explicit in such labels, as are place-neutral or displaced choices of place of articulation. But it is clear from the discussion above that even the slightly longer label fails to make explicit a number of choices of speech-production possibilities that are involved in the pronunciation of [θ]. One is that [θ] is an oral not a nasal fricative. Another is that it is a central not a lateral fricative. Another is that it is assumed in this case that [θ] constitutes a segment made by a single stricture rather than by multiple strictures. Another is that the surface of the tongue as the active articulator does not depart from its neutral convex shape to show grooving, retroflexion or cupping. Another, finally, is that the production of the fricative is relatively steady-state, and during its medial phase shows no significant transitional tendencies to flapping, tapping or trilling.

A more complete list of label-groups within which choices of individual labels are chosen to make up a full composite label would therefore be:

> airstream mechanism and airflow direction;
> phonation type;
> aspect of articulation;
> place of articulation;
> options of co-ordination;
> stricture type.

A more complete label for [θ] would then be 'a pulmonic egressive voiceless oral central single-stricture plain steady-state unaspirated dental fricative'. An alternative location for the label(s) referring to co-ordination could be before the label for the airstream mechanism, giving 'an unaspirated pulmonic egressive voiceless ...'.

Composite labels of this degree of comprehensiveness are useful only on the most limited number of occasions, even though the ability to be as explicit as this if needed is important from the point of view of theory. In order to marry convenient practice to sound theory, it is therefore helpful to set up the notion of **default assumptions** about segmental labelling, where certain segmental properties can be taken to be true if no specific mention is made to the contrary in the label concerned. These default assumptions will directly reflect the concept of neutral values of the descriptive architecture.

Firstly, a **general default assumption** can be adopted to the effect that, if no mention is made of different choices, the following properties will be held to be true of a segment of any stricture type:

> the airstream mechanism is pulmonic;
> the direction of airflow is egressive;
> the active articulator is the one which lies opposite the passive articulator in the neutral configuration;
> there is only a single stricture;
> the conformational routing for the airflow is oral and central;
> no relevant comment needs to be made about any co-ordinatory details of the segment's relationship to any contextual neighbours.

In addition, some more **specific default assumptions** can be made in the case of individual segment types:

> in a segment made with the tongue as the active articulator, the topographical aspect of articulation can be assumed to reflect a convex choice of shape of the tongue surface;

in contoidal segments, the choice of transitional aspect of articulation can be taken to be one which reflects a relatively steady-state articulation during the medial phase, so that no flapping, tapping or trilling is involved;

in vocoidal segments, the choice of transitional aspect of articulation can be taken to reflect a monophthongal production, with no divergence during the medial phase from a relatively steady state;

in vocoidal segments, the phonation type can be assumed to be that of normal voicing.

These labelling conventions, in conformity with the default assumptions, allow the use of abbreviated labels such as the following:

'a voiceless labial stop';
'a whispered dental fricative';
'a voiced velar approximant';
'a close front vocoid'.

When one or more departures from either the general or the specific default assumptions are made, these should be labelled explicitly, as in the following:

'a voiceless alveolar grooved fricative';
'a whispered lamino-dental fricative';
'a voiced retroflex palato-alveolar stop';
'a voiced labialized alveolar nasal stop';
'a voiced alveolar lateral resonant';
'a voiced close front rounded vocoid';
'a voiceless close front vocoid'.

The structure of labels that obey the general or specific default conditions is intended to constitute the description of basic segments, and under the hypothesis to be tested should ideally offer a direct reflection of the relative frequency of the segment-types found in the languages of the world. But a moment's thought is sufficient to show that the fit between the two is not completely perfect. For example, the voiceless alveolar grooved fricative [s], which is elaborated in that its topographical aspect is not neutral, seems much more common in the languages of the world (though possibly merely more familiar to phoneticians who speak European languages) than the non-grooved (i.e. basic) alveolar fricative.

A possible explanation for the apparent preponderance of the voiceless grooved alveolar fricative over its non-grooved counterpart may be that the greater auditory salience which results from the aerodynamic and acoustic consequences of the narrow groove adds to the distinctiveness of this fricative, and to its perceptual robustness against background noise. Be that as it may, a practical by-product of the preponderance of the voiceless alveolar grooved fricative is the habitual abbreviation of the label 'grooved alveolar fricative' simply to 'alveolar fricative'. By extension, the same treatment is given to the voiced alveolar grooved fricative [z]. For experienced users, this may be convenient. For the beginning phonetician, however, it is probably desirable initially to retain the more elaborate labels.

In general, except for the anomaly of the more elaborated grooved alveolar fricatives being more frequent than their more basic non-grooved counterparts, the basic segment-types which fit the default assumptions seem more frequent than their more elaborated counterparts. This is only an intuitive impression, however, and we can move now to the firmer ground of a quantified examination of the statistics of the UPSID database.

19.4.3 The statistical incidence of basic and elaborated segment-types in the languages of the world

Maddieson (1984) and his colleagues at UCLA gathered data for the UPSID database on 317 languages for which trustable phonetic description was available. A quota rule was applied, to the effect that only one language from any small family grouping could be included, and an effort was made to cover the principal language families of the world. The entries in the UPSID database are phonetic segments, constituting the 'most representative' allophones of the phonemes concerned. In making his selection of this most representative allophone, Maddieson (1984: 162–3) asked himself the following three questions:

> Which allophone has the widest distribution (i.e. appears in the widest range of and/or most frequently occurring environments)?
>
> Which allophone most appropriately represents the phonetic range of variation of all allophones?
>
> Which allophone is the one from which other allophones can be most simply and naturally derived?

In cases of conflicting answers being yielded by these three considerations, Maddieson preferred the answer that 'did least violence to all three considerations taken together' (p. 163). These questions (especially the third, and to some extent the second) inevitably have a phonological colouring to their motivation. In addition, underlying the difficulty of any comparable enterprise is the practical problem of deciding on the number of allophones per phoneme to be admitted into the arena of interest (which concerns the answers to both the first and the second question). The occurrence of a phoneme in different contextual environments generates a phonetically differentiable allophone of that phoneme in virtually every such environment, through the process of co-articulation. Different structural environments also often generate differentiable allophones of a phoneme, usually characterized by aspectual and co-ordinatory differences. The union of contextual and structural influences thus gives birth to a multitude of allophonic offspring, which make up the family of sounds representing a given phoneme in any language. Reaching a practical selection of such 'most representative' allophones, if the full power of descriptive phonetic theory were to be applied, would therefore have to appeal to very wide-ranging and often perhaps somewhat intuitive criteria.

In practice, Maddieson limited the resolution of the descriptive apparatus he used to specify the phonetic detail of the allophones to 'that attained by the traditional 3-term label of phonetics, specifying *voicing*, *place* and *manner* for consonants, ... plus additional labels required for features [of] secondary articulations' (p. 163). He uses some forty-five classificatory phonetic parameters for the description of segments representing consonants (Maddieson 1984: 164–7), which are in all cases either directly equivalent to or readily translatable into the phonetic dimensions described in this book. The UPSID database, and Maddieson's (1984) analysis, is an immensely valuable source of raw data on which to test hypotheses about the statistical distribution of sound types, though one could hope for future expansion of the number of languages contained.

The following analysis of the UPSID data is suggestive rather than exhaustive. It gathers evidence to begin to help in answering two questions about the incidence of different types of segments in the languages of the world. The first question addresses the raw frequency of occurrence of individual types of segments in the set of 317 languages of the database:

> *What is the frequency of occurrence in the 317 languages of the*
> *UPSID database of different categories of segments within a*
> *given manner of articulation?*

The second question addresses the depth of take-up by the consonantal phonemic systems of the different languages of the world of different manners of articulation:

> *How many distinctions of place of articulation do the 317*
> *languages of the UPSID database make within a given manner of*
> *articulation?*

The answers to the first question will give some indication of the degree of parsimony in the fit between the classificatory theory presented in this book and the data it seeks to describe. The answers to the second will speak to issues of phonetic and phonological 'universals', in giving some quantified probabilistic impression of what range of places of articulation might be expected to be found in the segment-types representing consonants in some hypothetical stereotypic language.

19.4.3.1   *The frequency of occurrence in the languages of the world of different categories of segments*

In addressing the first question, voiced and voiceless categories were calculated separately (except for lateral segments), and the total number of languages making use of each different place of articulation, aspect of articulation, mode of co-ordination and type of initiation within a given manner of articulation was established. This was done independently of the statistics offered by Maddieson (1984: 25–122), who gives a much more comprehensive treatment, often using different bases for calculation from those used in this book. For a more detailed account of the statistics to be found by examination of the UPSID database, Maddieson's version is recommended to the reader.

The following manners of articulation were selected for examination: oral stops, aspirated stops, affricated stops, ejective stops, implosive stops, nasal stops, pre-nasal and post-nasal complex stops, central oral fricatives, lateral and rhotic segments. Tables 19.2a–p show the totals and percentages for each of these categories of manner of articulation in turn, answering the first question in terms predominantly of data on place of articulation. For example, table 19.2a indicates that 255 of the 317 languages of the UPSID database (i.e. 80 per cent) make phonologically distinctive use in their consonant systems of a voiceless labial oral stop [p], and that 281 languages (89 per cent) use a voiceless velar oral stop [k]. Overall, 1,087 single voiceless oral stops figure in the consonant systems of the 317 languages.

To allow direct comparisons of categories within the focus of this chapter, the manners of articulation were interpreted strictly. Thus in Maddieson's general category of 'ejective stop', to take one example, he includes 'plain', 'labialized', 'palatalized' and 'pre-voiced' sub-categories in the overall calculation, making a total of 188 ejective stops by his own criteria, against only 157 in the investigation carried out for this book, which only considered 'plain' ejective stops. That this strictness of interpretation biased the overall results to a serious degree in favour of the hypothesis being tested is possible, and needs further research. It seems unlikely, though, that the rank-ordering of results was significantly affected.

It should be noted that in tables 19.2a–p information about the segments in the dental and alveolar regions are difficult to disentangle. This is because the otherwise reliable sources of phonetic and phonological information used by Maddieson often failed to offer specific comment about the exact place of articulation concerned in this zone. It was not always clear whether the term 'dental', for example, was being used strictly to indicate that the passive articulator was the upper front teeth, or rather as a cover term of a phonological colouring for articulations that might have been phonetically either dental (strictly) or alveolar (strictly). A section has therefore been added to each table combining the results for 'dental', 'dental or alveolar' and 'alveolar'.

Table 19.2a *Numbers of languages exploiting differences of place of articulation and aspectual categories on single voiceless oral stops in 317 languages*

Labial [p	Dental t̪	Dent/Al t̪ ~ t	Alveol t	Post-al t̠	R'flex ʈ	Palatal c	Velar k	Uvular q	Glottal ʔ]	**Total**
255	74	130	103	7	28	38	281	35	136	**1087**
80%	23%	41%	32%	2%	9%	12%	89%	12%	43%	
		Dental + Dnt/Al + Alveolar 307 97%								

Source: Calculated from information in the UPSID database given in Maddieson (1984: 263–422)

Table 19.2b *Numbers of languages exploiting differences of place of articulation and aspectual categories on single voiced oral stops in 317 languages*

Labial [b	Dental d̪	Dent/Al d̪ ~ d	Alveol d	Post-al d̠	R'flex ɖ	Palatal ɟ	Velar g	Uvular ɢ]	**Total**
195	52	74	64	2	23	26	166	8	**610**
62%	16%	23%	20%	1%	7%	8%	52%	3%	
		Dental + Dnt/Al + Alveolar 190 60%							

Source: Calculated from information in the UPSID database given in Maddieson (1984: 263–422)

Table 19.2c *Numbers of languages exploiting differences of place of articulation, aspectual and co-ordination categories on single post-aspirated voiceless oral stops in 317 languages*

Labial [pʰ	Dental t̪ʰ	Dnt/Al t̪ʰ ~ tʰ	Alveol tʰ	Post-al t̠ʰ	R'flex ʈʰ	Palatal cʰ	Velar kʰ	Uvul qʰ	Glottal ʔʰ]	Total
81	23	48	22	0	10	13	81	11	0	**289**
26%	7%	15%	7%	0%	3%	4%	26%	3%	0%	
		Dental + Dnt/Al + Alveolar 93 29%								

Source: Calculated from information in the UPSID database given in Maddieson (1984: 263–422)

Table 19.2d *Numbers of languages exploiting differences of place of articulation, aspectual and co-ordination categories on single post-affricated voiceless oral stops in 317 languages*

Labial [pᶲ	Lab-dnt pᶠ	Dental t̪ᶿ	Dent/Al t̪ᶿ ~ tˢ	Alveol tˢ	Post-al t̠ʃ	R'flex ʈʂ	Palatal cᶜ	Velar kˣ	Uvular qˣ]	Total
0	3	2	63	46	153	11	10	3	3	**294**
0%	1%	1%	20%	15%	48%	3%	3%	1%	1%	
		Dental + Dnt/Al + Alveolar 111 35%								

Source: Calculated from information in the UPSID database given in Maddieson (1984: 263–422)

Table 19.2e *Numbers of languages exploiting differences of place of articulation, aspectual and co-ordination categories on single post-affricated voiced oral stops in 317 languages*

Labial [bᵝ	Lab-dnt bᵛ	Dental d̪ᶞ	Dent/Al d̪ᶞ ~ dᶻ	Alveol dᶻ	Post-al d̠ʒ	R'flex ɖʐ	Palatal ɟʲ	Velar gᵞ	Uvular ɢʁ]	Total
0	1	1	20	15	84	4	6	0	0	**131**
0%	1%	1%	6%	5%	26%	1%	2%	0%	0%	
		Dental + Dnt/Al + Alveolar 36 11%								

Source: Calculated from information in Maddieson (1984: 263–422)

Table 19.2f *Numbers of languages exploiting differences of place of articulation, aspectual and initiatory categories on single voiceless ejective stops in 317 languages*

Labial [p'	Dental ţ'	Dent/Al ţ' ~ t'	Alveol t'	Post-al ţ'	R'flex ţ'	Palatal c'	Velar k'	Uvular q']	Total
33	13	18	18	0	0	7	49	19	**157**
10%	4%	6%	6%	0%	0%	2%	16%	5%	
		Dental + Dnt/Al + Alveolar							
		49 15%							

Source: Calculated from information in the UPSID database given in Maddieson (1984: 263–422)

Table 19.2g *Numbers of languages exploiting differences of place of articulation, aspectual and initiatory categories on single voiced implosive stops in 317 languages*

Labial [ɓ	Dental ḍ	Dent/Al ḍ ~ d	Alveol d	Post-al ḍ	R'flex ḍ	Palatal ʄ	Velar ɠ	Uvular ɠ]	Total
29	3	14	11	0	0	7	4	1	**69**
9%	1%	4%	3%	0%	0%	2%	1%	1%	
		Dental + Dnt/Al + Alveolar							
		28 9%							

Source: Calculated from information in the UPSID database given in Maddieson (1984: 263–422)

Table 19.2h *Numbers of languages exploiting differences of place of articulation, aspectual and initiatory categories on single voiceless implosive stops in 317 languages*

Labial [ɓ̥	Dental ţ̣	Dent/Al ţ̣ ~ ţ	Alveol ţ	Post-al ţ̣	R'flex ţ	Palatal c̓	Velar ƙ	Uvular ɗ]	Total
2	0	0	2	0	0	0	1	0	**5**
1%	0%	0%	1%	0%	0%	0%	1%	0%	
		Dental + Dnt/Al + Alveolar							
		2 1%							

Source: Calculated from information in the UPSID database given in Maddieson (1984: 263–422)

Table 19.2i *Numbers of languages exploiting differences of place of articulation and aspectual categories on single voiced nasal stops in 317 languages*

Labial [m	Lab-dnt ɱ	Dental n̪	Dent/Al n̪ ~ n	Alveol n	Post-al ṇ	R'flex ɳ	Palatal ɲ	Velar ŋ	Uvular N]	Total
298	1	58	151	105	16	20	107	160	0	**916**
94%	1%	18%	48%	33%	5%	6%	34%	50%	0%	
		Dental + Dnt/Al + Alveolar 314 99%								

Source: Calculated from information in the UPSID database given in Maddieson (1984: 263–422)

Table 19.2j *Numbers of languages exploiting differences of place of articulation and aspectual categories on single voiceless nasal stops in 317 languages*

Labial [m̥	Lab-dnt ɱ̥	Dental n̪̥	Dent/Al n̪̥ ~ n̥	Alveol n̥	Post-al n̥̠	R'flex ɳ̥	Palatal ɲ̥	Velar ŋ̥	Uvular N̥]	Total
10	0	1	6	2	0	1	6	8	0	**34**
3%	0%	1%	2%	1%	0%	1%	2%	3%	0%	
		Dental + Dnt/Al + Alveolar 9 3%								

Source: Calculated from information in the UPSID database given in Maddieson (1984: 263–422)

Table 19.2k *Numbers of languages exploiting differences of place of articulation, aspectual and phasal categories on complex voiced pre-nasal oral stops in 317 languages*

Labial [ᵐb	Dental ⁿd̪	Dent/Al ⁿd̪ ~ ⁿd	Alveol ⁿd	Post-al ⁿd̠	R'flex ⁿɖ	Palatal ᶮɟ	Velar ᵑg	Uvular ᴺɢ]	Total
17	2	8	7	1	1	4	17	0	**57**
5%	1%	3%	2%	1%	1%	1%	5%	0%	
	Dental + Dnt/Al + Alveolar 17 5%								

Source: Calculated from information in the UPSID database given in Maddieson (1984: 263–422)

Table 19.2l *Numbers of languages exploiting differences of place of articulation, aspectual and phasal categories on complex voiced post-nasal oral stops in 317 languages*

Labial $[b^m$	Dental $\d{d}^n$	Dent/Al $\d{d}^n \sim d^n$	Alveol d^n	Post-al $\d{d}^n$	R'flex $ɖ^n$	Palatal $ɟ^n$	Velar g^n	Uvular $ɢ^N]$	**Total**
1	0	1	1	1	1	0	1	0	**6**
1%	0%	1%	1%	1%	1%	0%	1%	0%	

Dental + Dnt/Al + Alveolar
2 1%

Source: Calculated from information in the UPSID database given in Maddieson (1984: 263–422)

Table 19.2m *Numbers of languages exploiting differences of place of articulation and aspectual categories on single voiceless central fricatives in 317 languages*

Lab $[\phi$	Lab-dnt f	Dent θ	Dent/Al $\theta \sim s$	Alv s	Pal-al $\int$	R'flex $ʂ$	Al-pal $ɕ$	Pal $ç$	Velar x	Uv χ	Phar h	Epigl $ʜ$	Gl $h]$	**Total**
18	117	17	129	111	139	17	0	11	76	25	11	0	2	**673**
6%	37%	5%	41%	35%	44%	5%	0%	3%	24%	8%	3%	0%	1%	

Dent + Dent/Al + Alveolar
257 81%

Source: Calculated from information in Maddieson (1984: 263–422)

Table 19.2n *Numbers of languages exploiting differences of place of articulation and aspectual categories on single voiced central fricatives in 317 languages*

Lab $[\beta$	Lab-dnt v	Dent $ð$	Dent/Al $ð \sim z$	Alv z	Pal-al $ʒ$	R'flex $ʐ$	Al-pal $ʑ$	Pal j	Velar $ɣ$	Uv $ʁ$	Phar $ʕ$	Epigl $ʕ$	Gl $ɦ]$	**Total**
32	62	18	45	37	44	4	0	7	36	15	7	0	4	**311**
10%	20%	6%	14%	12%	14%	1%	0%	2%	11%	5%	2%	0%	1%	

Dent + Dent/Al + Alveolar
100 32%

Source: Calculated from information in the UPSID database given in Maddieson (1984: 263–422)

Table 19.2o *Numbers of languages exploiting differences of place of articulation and aspectual categories on single voiced lateral resonant segments in 317 languages*

Labial [–	Dental ḷ	Dent/Al ḷ ~ l	Alveolar l	R'flex ɭ	Palatal ʎ	Velar ʟ]	**Total**
0 0%	27 9%	125 43%	91 31%	27 9%	19 7%	1 0%	**290**
		Dent + Dent/Alv + Alveolar 243 84%					

Source: Calculated from information in the UPSID database given in Maddieson (1984: 263–422)

Table 19.2p *Numbers of languages exploiting differences of place of articulation and aspectual categories on single rhotic segments in 317 languages*

Lab- Trill [B	Dent- Tap ɾ̪	Alv- Tap ɾ	Alv- Trill r	Fric- Trill r̝	Post- Al ɹ	Retr- App ɻ	Retr- Flap ɽ	Uv- Trill ʀ	Uv- App ʁ]	**Total**
2 1%	2 1%	17 5%	137 43%	1 1%	11 3%	23 7%	78 25%	2 1%	0 0%	**273**

Source: Calculated from information in the UPSID database given in Maddieson (1984: 263–422)

For convenience of presentation, table 19.3 abstracts from tables 19.2a–p the combined total of segments contrastively exploited by the 317 languages of the UPSID database within each **manner of articulation** (i.e. segments sharing the same features of initiation, phonation, degree of stricture, aspect of articulation and co-ordination but differing by place of articulation), and presents them in rank order of implied frequency of occurrence in the languages of the world. (The difference between voicelessness and voicing will not be explicitly considered in the discussion below).

The information in table 19.3 can be related to the architectural-parsimony hypothesis that the segment-types described in the phonetic theory presented here as most neutral and most basic are more numerous in the languages of the world than the more elaborated types. The overall result is that the hypothesis is broadly upheld by these results, in that with one exception (voiced nasal stops in second position), basic segments are more frequent (ranks 1–5) than the more elaborated segments (ranks 6–16). Nasal stops are categorized in this book as elaborated articulations in that they involve a non-neutral choice of

Table 19.3 *Total numbers of segments contrastively exploited by 317 languages within a given manner category*

Rank order	Manner category	Combined total of segments in 317 languages
1	Voiceless oral stops	1087
2	Voiced nasal stops	916
3	Voiceless central fricatives	673
4	Voiced oral stops	610
5	Voiced central fricatives	311
6	Voiceless affricated oral stops	294
7	Voiced lateral resonant segments	290
8	Voiceless aspirated oral stops	289
9	Voiced rhotic segments	273
10	Voiceless ejective stops	157
11	Voiced affricated oral stops	131
12	Voiced implosive stops	69
13	Voiced pre-nasal oral stops	57
14	Voiceless nasal stops	34
15	Voiced post-nasal oral stops	6
16	Voiceless implosive stops	5

Source: Calculated from information in the UPSID database given in Maddieson (1984: 263–422)

the conformational aspect of articulation. In this they are by definition more elaborate than the basic categories in third and fourth rank (voiceless central fricatives and voiced oral stops), which are both defined as making neutral choices as far as the conformational aspect of articulation is concerned.

The conventional descriptive phonetic theory adopted by the IPA phonetic alphabet gives 'nasals' the status of an independent category, and does not treat them in the way suggested in this book as a modified sub-category of 'stop'. The IPA treatment is also consistent with studies of infant speech acquisition which suggest that nasal stops such as [m] are amongst the very earliest anthropophonic sounds recruited for use in speech, which is perhaps not surprising from a biological point of view (S. Hutcheson, personal communication). To that extent, the data in table 19.3 suggest that the IPA assumptions better reflect both this biological priority and the principle of architectural simplicity than do the proposals in this book. However, the disadvantage of the IPA classification of nasal stops as an independent segment-type on a par with oral stops is that the commonality of nasality being applicable as a modifying feature to all three basic stricture types (stop, fricative and resonant), with oral versions of these counting as neutral, is then lost.

19.4.3.2   *The phonological take-up by the languages of the world of*
            different manners of articulation
Table 19.4 gives the results for the second question, approaching
the matter of **phonetic** and **phonological universals**. It calculates the percentage of the languages of the database exploiting a particular number of
places of articulation within a given manner category for contrastive purposes. This percentage can be thought of as the take-up by languages of the
contrastive opportunities within a given manner category.

Table 19.4 *Numbers of languages in the UPSID database using zero, one or*
more phonetic segment-types within a manner category for contrastive
purposes

SEGMENT TYPE	Number of segments used within a manner category per language for contrastive purposes								Percentage of languages using one or more segments
	0	1	2	3	4	5	6	7	
Voiced nasal stops	12	8	102	97	81	12	5	0	96.2
Voiceless oral stops	15	13	18	103	119	41	8	0	95.3
Voiceless fricatives	25	28	70	94	56	33	9	2	92.1
Voiced and voiceless lateral segments	69	190	44	10	3	1	0	0	78.2
Voiced rhotic segments	88	197	30	2	0	0	0	0	72.2
Voiceless affricated oral stops	116	132	58	10	1	0	0	0	63.4
Voiced oral stops	117	16	25	104	48	7	0	0	63.1
Voiced fricatives	158	62	43	36	12	6	0	0	50.2
Voiced affricated oral stops	210	88	16	3	0	0	0	0	33.8
Voiceless aspirated oral stops	225	6	7	53	20	6	0	0	29.0
Voiceless ejective stops	265	5	12	17	13	5	0	0	16.4
Voiced implosive stops	286	5	18	4	4	0	0	0	9.8
Voiced pre-nasal oral stops	298	1	1	11	4	1	0	0	6.0
Voiceless nasal stops	307	0	1	4	5	0	0	0	3.2
Voiceless implosive stops	315	0	1	1	0	0	0	0	0.6
Voiced post-nasal stops	316	0	0	0	0	0	1	0	0.3

Source: Calculated from data in Maddieson (1984: 263–422)

Some very clear patterns of segmental exploitation are visible from table 19.4, in terms of the take-up by languages of one or more instances of a given manner category. The results fall into five groups: nearly universal take-up, high, moderate, low and minority take-up. Virtually all 317 languages in the UPSID database exploit one or more voiceless oral stops (95.3 per cent), voiced nasal stops (96.2 per cent) and voiceless fricatives (92.1 per cent). Falling in the high range of take-up of one or more types of segment within the manner category concerned are the two categories of lateral segments (78.2 per cent) and rhotic segments (72.2 per cent). Moderate exploitation of one or more voiceless affricated stops (63.4 per cent), voiced oral stops (63.1 per cent) and voiced fricatives (50.2 per cent) is also a characteristic of the languages represented in the database. Falling in the low range, with less take-up than the moderate group but more than the minority group that follows, is the use of one or more voiced affricated stops (33.8 per cent) and voiceless aspirated stops (29.0 per cent). Minority usage of categories of manner of articulation is seen in the take-up of one or more voiceless ejective stops (16.4 per cent), voiced implosive stops (9.8 per cent), voiced pre-nasal stops (6.0 per cent), voiceless nasal stops (3.2 per cent), voiceless implosive stops (0.6 per cent) and voiced post-nasal stops (0.3 per cent).

The percentages given in table 19.4 can be thought of as an indication of the probability that any given manner of articulation will be represented by at least one phoneme in the consonant system of a given language. They give only a partial view of the segmental take-up by languages, however, since they summarize only the proportion of languages making contrastive use of one or more segments in a given manner category. Another way of analysing the information in table 19.4 is to look at the different depths of take-up by a language of a given manner category (i.e. the range of differentiations of place of articulation by the language within that manner of articulation). For example, the maximal depth of take-up is by the manner category of voiceless fricatives, which ranges from 28 languages using only one segment-type contrastively to 2 languages making use of seven, with a fairly flat distribution peaking at 94 languages exploiting three such segments. The depths of take-up of voiceless oral stops and voiced nasal stops are similar to each other in range, at six contrastive segments, but the distribution of voiced nasal stops has a broad though salient peak at two or three segments being contrasted by place of articulation, while the distribution of voiceless stops has a broad though salient peak of three or four. Voiceless affricates, on the other hand, range only up to four segments being used contrastively, with the very large majority of languages that exploit voiceless affricates using only one. This is similar to the pattern for rhotic segments, which range up to three segments being used contrastively, with the large majority that use rhotic segments using only one.

19.4.3.3   *The phonological take-up by the languages of the world of different places of articulation*

Table 19.4 analyses segmental take-up at a rather coarse grain. For detail on place of articulation, tables 19.2a–p allow one to examine the relative frequencies within a manner category of single consonants in the phonemic systems of the 317 languages. We can consider the most frequently occurring segments, noting whether they are characterized by a neutral place of articulation (supporting the architectural-parsimony hypothesis) or by a non-neutral, displaced articulation (contradicting the hypothesis).

We have seen that voiceless oral stops dominate the consonant systems of the UPSID languages, in terms of raw frequency of occurrence (table 19.3). Within voiceless oral stops, table 19.2a shows that labial (80 per cent of languages), 'dental + dental/alveolar + alveolar' (97 per cent) and velar stops (89 per cent) are by far the most numerous. Voiced nasal stops (table 19.2i), as the next most frequent category, do not show quite the same pattern, with labial (94 per cent) and 'dental + dental/alveolar + alveolar' nasal stops (99 per cent) predominating, but with only 50 per cent of languages exploiting the velar place of articulation. Voiceless fricatives (table 19.2m), show yet a different pattern, with the dental/alveolar category most numerous. This category is hard to quantify, given the uncertainty of interpreting the original observations of the dental (flat) [θ] versus alveolar (grooved) [s] contribution to the 'dental + dental/alveolar + alveolar' collapsed category. But if we reasonably assume that the label 'dental' was used in the original sources for a (strictly) alveolar [s] only when [θ] was absent from the investigation of the language concerned, then a (phonetically strict) alveolar [s] probably accounts for about 241 languages out of the 257 listed for the 'dental + dental/alveolar + alveolar' category. If so, it would suggest that about 76 per cent of languages exploit an alveolar [s]. Palato-alveolar [ʃ] is next in frequency, being used by 44 per cent of languages. The frequency of usage of the non-neutral, displaced labiodental [f] is lower, though still highish, at 37 per cent of languages.

In lateral resonant segments (table 19.2.o, which excludes lateral fricative segments), 'dental + dental/alveolar + alveolar' segments predominate at 84%, with no other place of articulation being taken up by even 10 per cent of languages. The membership of the rhotic class of segments is determined by considerations of phonological function to a greater extent than by phonetic criteria, and is in any case a mixed category from a phonetic point of view, in that it includes stops made with various different aspects of articulation (taps, flaps and trills) as well as approximants. In rhotic segments (table 19.2p), the voiced alveolar trilled stop predominates (43 per cent of languages), but with retroflex alveolar flapped stops [ɽ] being taken up by 25 per cent of languages. The retroflex alveolar flapped stop [ɽ] does not count as displaced from the point of view of the place of articulation of its moment of greatest stricture (complete alveolar closure), though it does count as non-neutral in terms of its retroflex topographical aspect of articulation.

From the point of view of place of articulation, the most frequent sounds in the most frequently used manner-categories found in the UPSID database are therefore all place-neutral, far outweighing those with displaced articulations. The hypothesis of architectural parsimony therefore seems tenable as far as place of articulation is concerned.

19.4.3.4   *The phonological take-up by the languages of the world of*
             different aspects of articulation, co-ordination and initiation

      Inspecting tables 19.2a–p for other potential violations of the hypothesis by elaborated segmental performance, we find that retroflexion (as a non-neutral topographic aspect of articulation), aspiration and affrication (as non-neutral choices of co-ordination), and ejective/implosive initiation (as a non-neutral option of type of airstream mechanism) all occur with substantially less frequency than the types of segments which can be regarded as basic. They thus support the hypothesis. Grooving of alveolar [s], as a non-neutral topographic aspect of articulation, in the voiceless central fricative probably used by about 76 per cent of languages, remains problematic for the architectural parsimony hypothesis, as noted above.

19.4.3.5   *Conclusion*

      The issue that has been addressed in the sections immediately above is whether the structural principles underlying the design of the architecture of the descriptive phonetic model offered in this book bear a parsimonious relation to the major trends of segmental choice by the languages of the world. Much more research is needed to explore this hypothesis in detail, and to consider methods of subjecting the geometry of the descriptive model to a more graded, quantified and searching test against hierarchies of occurrence of segments and features. Whether the choice of languages in the UPSID database is fully representative of segmental usage by languages in general will also become clearer only when more languages are incorporated in the database. But with the exception of nasality on stops, and the anomalously high incidence of the non-neutrally grooved alveolar fricative [s], inspection of the statistics of segmental characterization offered in tables 19.2a–p, 19.3 and 19.4 seems to give preliminary support to the hypothesis suggested in section 19.4. As a broad conclusion, it thus seems a sustainable view that the architecture of the phonetic theory set up in this book bears a fairly parsimonious relationship to the sounds of the world's languages that it seeks to describe.

Further reading

The typology of **consonant systems** in the languages of the world is discussed by Lass (1984a: 147-59) and Maddieson (1984). The typology of **vowel systems** is explored by Crothers (1978), Disner (in a chapter she wrote on insights into vowel spacing, in Maddieson 1984: 136-55), Lass (1984a: 134-47, 1984b) and Lindblom (1986).

Greenberg (1978) edited a volume on **phonological universals** in the languages of the world (which contains the chapter by Crothers listed above). John Ohala was the chairman of an interesting symposium on **phonetic universals** in phonological systems held during the Ninth International Congress of Phonetic Sciences in Copenhagen (Fischer-Jørgensen 1979) and in his chairman's remarks discusses the nature of these phonetic universals, the role they play in phonological systems, and how they might be explained (Ohala 1979). In a later publication, he goes on to explore the source of some types of sound patterning in constraints set by the way the vocal organs work (Ohala 1983).

Envoi

The objective of this book has been to offer the reader an analytic perspective on phonetics, as a foundation for research in speech. The Introduction began by saying that speech is our most human characteristic. To speak is to display the most open declaration of our social identity. Speaking is also our prime means of communicating cognitive, emotional and attitudinal information to other people. More personal and symbolic communication is conducted through spoken conversation than is ever achieved through writing. Speech thus has a most central place in our social, cognitive and affective lives.

It remains true, nevertheless, that although as speakers and listeners we all have a very well-developed operational understanding of the many-stranded messages transmitted every day through speech, not many people know very much about either the semiotic or the physical basis of how speech actually works. Nor do many people have more than the most fragmentary experience of the range and variety of patterns found in the speech of different language-communities around the world. It is the privilege and the pleasure of phoneticians, with their colleagues from related disciplines professionally concerned with speech, to engage themselves in the analysis of this most intricate of our communicative skills, in all its richness and variety.

I have tried to give an account of the full phonetic range of spoken language. Above all, as I said in the Introduction, I have tried to give the reader the opportunity to appreciate the paradox that underlying the apparently extraordinary diversity shown by the thousands of mutually incomprehensible languages of the world, there is a remarkable, elegant and principled unity in the way that these languages exploit the phonetic resources of speech. It is these principles of phonetics that I have tried to describe.

APPENDIX I

The phonetic alphabet of the International Phonetic Association

CONSONANTS

	Bilabial	Labiodental	Dental	Alveolar	Postalveolar	Retroflex	Palatal	Velar	Uvular	Pharyngeal	Glottal
Plosive	p b			t d		ʈ ɖ	c ɟ	k ɡ	q ɢ		ʔ
Nasal	m	ɱ		n		ɳ	ɲ	ŋ	ɴ		
Trill	ʙ			r					ʀ		
Tap or Flap				ɾ		ɽ					
Fricative	ɸ β	f v	θ ð	s z	ʃ ʒ	ʂ ʐ	ç ʝ	x ɣ	χ ʁ	ħ ʕ	h ɦ
Lateral fricative				ɬ ɮ							
Approximant		ʋ		ɹ		ɻ	j	ɰ			
Lateral approximant				l		ɭ	ʎ	ʟ			
Ejective stop	p'			t'		ʈ'	c'	k'	q'		
Implosive	ɓ ɓ			t' ɗ			c' ʄ	k' ɠ	q' ʛ		

Where symbols appear in pairs, the one to the right represents a voiced consonant. Shaded areas denote articulations judged impossible.

DIACRITICS

̥	Voiceless	n̥ d̥	̹	More rounded	ɔ̹	
̬	Voiced	s̬ t̬	̜	Less rounded	ɔ̜	
ʰ	Aspirated	tʰ dʰ	̟	Advanced	u̟	
̤	Breathy voiced	b̤ a̤	̠	Retracted	i̠	
̰	Creaky voiced	b̰ a̰	̈	Centralized	ë	
̼	Linguolabial	t̼ d̼	̽	Mid-centralized	ë̽	
̪	Dental	t̪ d̪	̩	Syllabic	ṇ	
̺	Apical	t̺ d̺	̯	Non-syllabic	e̯	
̻	Laminal	t̻ d̻	˞	Rhoticity	ɚ a˞	

ʷ	Labialized	tʷ dʷ	̃	Nasalized	ẽ
ʲ	Palatalized	tʲ dʲ	ⁿ	Nasal release	dⁿ
ˠ	Velarized	tˠ dˠ	ˡ	Lateral release	dˡ
ˁ	Pharyngealized	tˁ dˁ	̚	No audible release	d̚
̃	Velarized or pharyngealized	ɫ			
̝	Raised	e̝ (ɹ̝ = voiced alveolar fricative)			
̞	Lowered	e̞ (β̞ = voiced bilabial approximant)			
̘	Advanced Tongue Root	e̘			
̙	Retracted Tongue Root	e̙			

VOWELS

Where symbols appear in pairs, the one to the right represents a rounded vowel.

OTHER SYMBOLS

ʍ	Voiceless labial-velar fricative
w	Voiced labial-velar approximant
ɥ	Voiced labial-palatal approximant
ʜ	Voiceless epiglottal fricative
ʢ	Voiced epiglottal fricative
ʡ	Epiglottal plosive

ʘ	Bilabial click
ǀ	Dental click
ǃ	(Post)alveolar click
ǂ	Palatoalveolar click
ǁ	Alveolar lateral click

ɕ ʑ Alveolo-palatal fricatives
ɺ Alveolar lateral flap
ɧ Simultaneous ʃ and x

Affricates and double articulations can be represented by two symbols joined by a tie bar if necessary. k͡p t͡s

SUPRASEGMENTALS

ˈ	Primary stress	ˌfoʊnəˈtɪʃən
ˌ	Secondary stress	
ː	Long	eː
ˑ	Half-long	eˑ
̆	Extra-short	ĕ
.	Syllable break	ɹi.ækt
ǀ	Minor (foot) group	
‖	Major (intonation) group	
‿	Linking (absence of a break)	

TONES & WORD ACCENTS

LEVEL		CONTOUR	
e̋ or ˥	Extra high	ě or ˩˥	Rising
é ˦	High	ê ˥˩	Falling
ē ˧	Mid	e᷄ ˦˥	High rising
è ˨	Low	e᷅ ˩˨	Low rising
ȅ ˩	Extra low	e᷈ ˧˦˧	Rising falling etc.
↓	Downstep	↗	Global rise
↑	Upstep	↘	Global fall

593

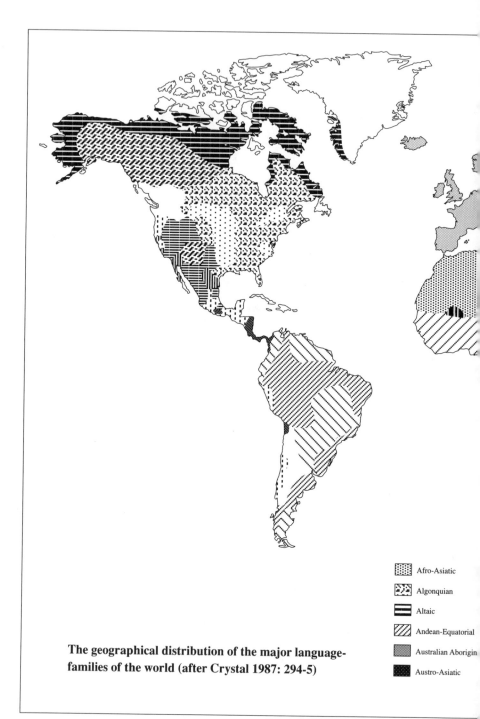

The geographical distribution of the major language-
families of the world (after Crystal 1987: 294-5)

▦	Afro-Asiatic
▨	Algonquian
▤	Altaic
▨	Andean-Equatorial
▦	Australian Aborigin
▨	Austro-Asiatic

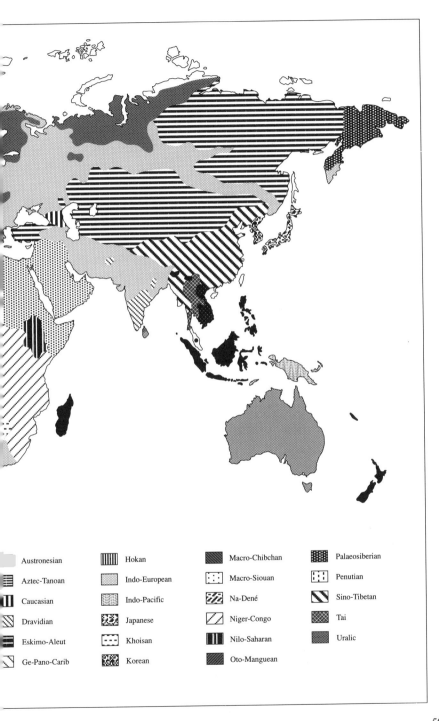

Austronesian	Hokan	Macro-Chibchan	Palaeosiberian
Aztec-Tanoan	Indo-European	Macro-Siouan	Penutian
Caucasian	Indo-Pacific	Na-Dené	Sino-Tibetan
Dravidian	Japanese	Niger-Congo	Tai
Eskimo-Aleut	Khoisan	Nilo-Saharan	Uralic
Ge-Pano-Carib	Korean	Oto-Manguean	

APPENDIX II

Index of languages

This appendix was compiled partly by reference to publications by Bright (1992), Campbell (1991), Comrie (1987), Crystal (1987), Grimes (1988), Harris and Vincent (1988), Ruhlen (1987) and Voegelin and Voegelin (1977), which are recommended as authoritative sources on the genetic affiliation and geography of the world's languages. Further reading on this topic is also listed at the end of chapter 3.

Language	Alternative name	Language family	Geographical location	Page
Abaza	Abazin	Northwest Caucasian	Karachay-Cherkes Oblast, Dagestan (CIS), Turkey	322, 324
Abazin	*see* Abaza			324
Abdzakh	dialect of Adyghe			
Aberdeen English	dialect of Scottish English			419
Abkhaz	Abkhazian	Northwest Caucasian	Abkhaz (CIS), Georgia, Black Sea coast, Turkey	194, 316, 318, 322–3, 324, 328
Abkhazian	*see* Abkhaz			
Acatlán Mixtec	dialect of Mixtec			472
Acoma	Western Keresan	Keresan	New Mexico (USA)	369
Adyghe	Circassian	Northwest Caucasian	Adyget Oblast, Cherkes (CIS), Turkey, Jordan, Iraq, Syria, Israel	172, 248, 303, 322
Adynya-mathanha	*see* Wailpi			
African English	a number of dialects of English			61
Afrikaans		Indo-European	South Africa, Malawi, Namibia, Zimbabwe and in Southern Africa as a *lingua franca*	61, 81
Ainu		*language isolate*	Hokkaido Island (Northern Japan)	86

596

Language	Alternative name	Language family	Geographical location	Page
Akan	*see* Twi			
Akhvakh	*see* Akhwakh			
Akhwakh	Akhvakh	Northeast Caucasian	Southern Dagestan (CIS)	370–2, 439, 567
Alabama	*see* Alabama-Koasati			
Alabama-Koasati	Alabama	Eastern Muskogean	Louisiana, Texas (USA)	257
Alawa		Australian	Roper River, Arnhem Land, Northern Territory (Australia)	231
Alexandrian Arabic	dialect of Egyptian Arabic			328, 329
Algerian Arabic	dialect of Arabic			411
Amahuaca		Panoan	Peru, Brazil	231–2, 256
American English	a number of dialects of English			60, 72–3, 89, 90–1, 218, 227, 243, 285, 299, 300, 307, 315, 333, 398, 445, 446–7, 454–5, 489, 516, 533, 538, 543–4
Amharic	Amharik	Semitic	Ethiopia	266
Amuzgo		Otomanguean-Amuzgoan	Mexico	220, 231
Andalucian Spanish	dialect of Continental Spanish			358
Apinayé		Macro-Gê	Goiás State (Brazil)	231, 232
Applecross Gaelic	dialect of Scottish Gaelic			295, 334, 442
Arabana	*see* Arapana			
Arabic		Semitic	from West Africa to Afghanistan, and as a *lingua franca* throughout this area	81, 83, 285–7, 327–8, 329, 333–4, 387, 411, 521, 523, 542
Aranda		Pama-Nyungan	Alice Springs, Northern Territory (Australia)	362
Arapaho	Arapahoe	Algonquian	Wyoming USA	89
Arapahoe	*see* Arapaho			
Arapana	Arapani, Arabana	Pama-Nyungan	South Australia	362
Arapani	*see* Arapana			
Arbili Kurdish	dialect of Kurdish			253, 254
Armenian		Indo-European (independent branch)	Armenia, Iran, Turkey, the countries of the Eastern Mediterranean, and many countries of emigration	382

Appendix II

Language	Alternative name	Language family	Geographical location	Page
Asian English	a number of dialects of English			59
Asmat		Papuan	Irian Jaya	512
Assamese		Indo-European	Assam (India), Bangladesh, Bhutan	200, 522
Ateso	*see* Teso			
Australian English	a number of dialects of English			59, 61, 90, 398, 413, 558
Avar		North East Caucasian	Southern Dagestan, Azerbaijan, Terek and Sulk Rivers area (CIS)	371–2
Aywele Etsako	dialect of Etsako			388
Azerbaijani		Turkic	Azerbaijan, Nagorno-Karabakh Oblast (CIS), Iran, Iraq, Turkey, Syria, Afghanistan	294
Aztec	*see* Nahuatl			
Bafang	*see* Fe'Fe			281
Bamileke		Niger-Congo	Cameroon	465, 472
Bamun		Niger-Congo	Cameroon	359
Banff English	dialect of Scottish English			419
Bangkok Thai	dialect of Thai			326
Banjalang		Pama-Nyungan	New South Wales (Australia)	325
Basque		*language isolate* of disputed affiliation	Southeastern France and Northeastern Spain, and a language of emigration to the New World	86
Beijing Chinese	*see* Mandarin Chinese			
Belfast English	dialect of Ulster English			90
Bella Coola		Salishan *language isolate*	British Columbia (Canada)	239, 240, 265
Bengali		Indo-European	Bangladesh, India, Singapore and many other countries of emigration	172, 200, 295, 354, 385, 438
Berber		Afro-Asiatic	Morocco, Algeria	327–8
Berta		Nilo-Saharan	Ethiopia, Sudan	231
Bhele	*see* Bili			
Bhojpuri	Bihari	Indo-European	Bihar, Assam, Madhya Pradesh, Uttar Pradesh (India), Nepal, and many countries of emigration	

598

Language	Alternative name	Language family	Geographical location	Page
Bihari	*see* Bhojpuri			
Bili	Bhele	Niger-Congo	Kivu region (Zaïre)	312
Bini		Niger-Congo	Nigeria	474
Birmingham English	dialect of English English			411
Bisara Japanese	dialect of Japanese			348
Bishnupriya		Indo-European	Assam, Tripura (India), Bangladesh	172
Brazilian Portuguese	a number of dialects of Portuguese			212, 287–9, 292, 291–3, 329, 529
Breton		Indo-European	Brittany (France)	296, 435
Brisbane English	dialect of Australian English			558
British English	a number of dialects of English			73, 74–6, 89, 90, 243, 265, 267, 270, 284, 394, 398, 413, 416, 433–4, 552–7
Bronx English	dialect of New York English			411
Bura		Afro-Asiatic	Nigeria	195, 316
Burarra	Burera, Bawera, Bureda	Australian	Maningrida, Arnhem Land, Northern Territory (Australia)	382
Burera	*see* Burarra			
Burmese		Sino-Tibetan	Burma, Bangladesh	211, 311, 351, 509
Burushaski		*language isolate*	Hunza-Nagir and Yasin areas of the Gilgit Agency (Pakistan), Northwest India	216, 217, 320
Bushman		Khoisan	Southern Africa	174
Bwe Karen	dialect of Karen			332
Bzhedug Adyghe	dialect of Adyghe			322
Bzyb Abkhaz	dialect of Abkhaz			318, 328
Cakchiquel		Mayan	Guatemala	173, 181–2
Californian English	a number of dialects of American English			250
Canadian English	a number of dialects of English			59, 61, 72–3, 85–7, 225, 270

Appendix II

Language	Alternative name	Language family	Geographical location	Page
Cantonese	Yue, dialect of Chinese		Kwantung, and southern part of Kwangsi, China	194
Carcha K'ekchi	dialect of K'ekchi			181–2
Cardiff English	dialect of Welsh English			90
Caribbean English	a number of dialects of English			59
Catalan		Indo-European	Catalonia, Spain	86
Cayapa	*see* Chachi			
Central-Southern Punjabi	dialect of Punjabi			560
Central Thai	dialect of Thai			467–9
Chachi	Cayapa	Macro-Chibchan	Northwestern Ecuador	295
Chagga	Chaga	Niger-Congo	Tanzania	215, 311
Chamelco K'ekchi	dialect of K'ekchi			181–2
Changchow Chinese	dialect of Chinese (also called Wu)			355
Chechen		North Caucasian	Chechen Ingush, Kazakh, Georgia, Northern Caucasus (CIS)	358
Chengdu		*see* Chengtu Szechuanese		
Chengtu Szechuanese	Chengtu sub-dialect of the Szechuanese dialect of Chinese			298, 349, 353, 474–6
Chewelah Kalispel	dialect of Kalispel			238
Cheyenne		Algonquian	Montana, Oklahoma (USA)	189, 296–7
Chinantec		Otomanguean	Mexico	241, 295, 482
Chinese	large family of dialects	Sino-Tibetan	China, Taiwan, Singapore, Hongkong, Malaysia, Vietnam and many countries of emigration	252, 260, 285–6, 319, 509
Chinook Jargon		a *pidgin*	Pacific Northwest Coast of North America	84
Chipewyan		Athabaskan	Northwest Territories, Saskatechewan, Alberta, Manitoba (Canada)	294, 368, 369
Chontal		Tequistlatecan Hokan	Mexico	226, 310

Language	Alternative name	Language family	Geographical location	Page
Chrau		Austro-Asiatic	Vietnam	382
Chuana	*see* Tswana			
Chukchi		Chokotko-Kamchatkan	Chukotka Peninsula, Siberia (CIS)	385
Circassian	*see* Adyghe			
Classical Arabic	dialect of Arabic			521
Classical Nahuatl	dialect of Nahuatl			368
Coastal Chontal	dialect of Chontal			226, 310
Coatlan Mixe	dialect of Mixe			442
Coatzospan Mixtec	dialect of Mixtec			471
Coban K'ekchi	dialect of K'ekchi			181–2
Cockney English	dialect of English English			70
Coeur d'Alène		Salishan	Idaho (USA)	34
Columbian	Wenatchee-Columbia	Salishan	Washington State (USA)	241
Comanche		Uto-Aztecan	Oklahoma (USA)	189, 296
Continental Portuguese	a number of dialects of Portuguese		Portugal	259, 347
Continental Spanish	a number of dialects of Spanish		Spain	225, 358
Copala Trique	dialect of Trique		Mexico	466–7
Cree		Algonquian	Canada, Montana (USA)	88
Cuitlatec (now extinct)		Meso-American *language isolate*	Mexico	520
Czech		Indo-European	Czechoslovakia and many countries of emigration	264, 520, 560–1
Dafla	*see* Nisi			
Damin		(Pama-Nyungan)	secret ritual language of the Lardil tribe, Northern Queensland (Australia)	170
Danish		Indo-European	Denmark, Greenland, Faroe Islands	77, 169, 195, 196, 281, 282, 303, 330–2, 333, 435, 442, 445, 447, 448, 455, 509, 513, 559
Delaware		Algonquian	Ontario (Canada), Oklahoma (USA)	294
Dido	Tsez	North Caucasian	Southern Dagestan (CIS)	328

Appendix II

Language	Alternative name	Language family	Geographical location	Page
Diegueño	Digueño	Hokan	Baja California (Mexico), California (USA)	257
Ditidaht	*see* Nitinaht			
Dogri-Kangri		Indo-European	Jammu and Kashmir (India)	222
Dutch		Indo-European	Netherlands, Belgium, Suriname Netherlands Antilles	83, 220, 281, 286, 440, 448, 509, 522, 542, 559
Dyirbal		Pama-Nyungan	Northern Queensland (Australia)	213
Eastern English	a number of dialects of American English			59
Edinburgh English	dialect of Scottish English			60, 61
Efik		Niger-Congo	Nigeria, Cameroon	315, 360, 385
Egyptian Arabic	dialect of Arabic			328, 329, 500
Enga		Papuan	Enga Province (Papua New Guinea)	296
English		Indo-European	United Kingdom, United States of America, Canada, Australia, New Zealand, South Africa, Ireland, India, Pakistan, Singapore, the Caribbean, in many countries of emigration and worldwide as a *lingua franca*	15, 18, 22, 31–3, 35, 36–7, 38, 40, 60, 61, 64, 71, 79, 85–6, 90, 111, 149–50, 152, 155, 157, 169, 175, 189, 194, 207, 215, 241, 250, 258–9, 261–2, 293–4, 297, 298, 299, 305, 307, 308, 315, 322, 324, 333, 345, 348, 352–3, 359, 360, 361, 362, 365, 366, 378–81, 387, 397, 408, 413, 420, 435, 446, 447, 448, 449, 484, 485, 492–6, 506, 507, 513, 515, 516–17, 523, 530, 531–3, 541, 544, 569
English English	a number of dialects of British English			9, 42–3, 46, 250, 251, 273,

602

Language	Alternative name	Language family	Geographical location	Page
Erse	*see* Irish			
Estonian		Uralic	Estonia, Latvia	436, 444–5
Etsako	Esako	Niger-Congo	Nigeria	35, 263, 371, 388–9, 467, 473
Ewe		Niger-Congo	Ghana, Togo	218, 253, 254
Faroese		Indo-European	Faroe Islands, Denmark	356, 357, 382
Fe'Fe	Bafang	Niger-Congo	Cameroon	281, 465
Fijian		Oceanic	Fiji, Vanuatu, New Zealand	230
Finnish		Uralic	Finland, Estonia	35, 151, 170, 356, 385, 436, 443–4, 520, 559
Finnish Swedish	dialect of Swedish			463
Fox		Algonquian	Iowa, Oklahoma, Kansas (USA)	88
French		Indo-European	France, Canada, Belgium, Luxembourg, Switzerland, Haiti, French Guiana, Monaco, parts of Polynesia, in many countries of emigration and worldwide as a *lingua franca*	40, 78, 85, 86, 87, 170, 189, 194, 212, 264, 284, 293–4, 295, 297, 298, 307–9, 311, 345, 352, 360, 379–81, 384, 412, 416, 418, 449, 455, 457, 484, 485–7, 488, 489, 509, 515, 520, 523, 528, 533, 542, 569
Fula	Fulfulde, Pulaar, Pulle	Niger-Congo	Northern West Africa, and from Northern Sudan west to the Atlantic as a *lingua franca*	230, 238, 360, 439, 441–2
Fulfulde	*see* Fula			
Gaelic		Indo-European	Scotland, Nova Scotia, Prince Edward Island (Canada)	73, 150, 151 *see also* Scottish Gaelic
Gaididj		*see* Kaititj		
Ganda	*see* Luganda			
Gbaya	Gbeya	Adamawa (Eastern)	Sudan, Central African Republic, Cameroon, Northwestern Congo	224, 231
Gbeya	*see* Gbaya			
General American	a number of dialects of American English			58–9, 62, 63, 65, 90, 263–4, 298
Georgian		South Caucasian	Georgia (CIS), Turkey	34, 172

Appendix II

Language	Alternative name	Language family	Geographical location	Page
German		Indo-European	Germany, Austria, Switzerland, Poland, CIS, Czechoslovakia, Hungary, Rumania, Liechtenstein, and many countries of emigration	77, 253, 254–5, 308–9, 362, 435, 443, 449, 509, 529
Gikuyu	*see* Kikuyu			
Gilbertese	*see* Ikiribati			
Glasgow English	dialect of Scottish English			90
Greek		Indo-European	Greece, Cyprus, Turkey, Rumania, Bulgaria, Albania, Egypt and many countries of emigration	86, 170, 189, 209, 253, 255, 297, 346–7, 509, 522, 528, 530
Greenlandic	*see* Inuit		Greenland	
Guajiro		Arawakan	Colombia, Venezuela	358
Guéré		Niger-Congo	Ivory Coast	238
Gujarati	Gujerati	Indo-European	Gujarat, Maharashtra (India), Bangladesh, Pakistan, and many countries of emigration	172, 200, 222, 312, 353, 354
Gujerati	*see* Gujarati			
Gujuri	Rajasthani	Indo-European	Himachal Pradesh, Madhya Pradesh, Uttar Pradesh, Rajasthan, Jammu and Kashmir (India), Pakistan, Afghanistan	222, 312
Gununa-Kena	Tehuelche	Patagon	Patagonia (Argentina)	369
Hadzapi	*see* Hatsa			
Haida		Na-Dené *language isolate*	British Columbia (Canada), Alaska (USA)	257, 368
Hakka	*see* Kèjià			
Hanunóo		Austronesian	Mindoro (Philippines)	170
Harris Gaelic	dialect of Scottish Gaelic			356, 357, 374, 559
Hatsa	Hadzapi	Khoisan *language isolate*	Tanzania	174, 375
Hausa		Afro-Asiatic	Nigeria, Niger, Chad, Togo, Burkina Faso, Ghana, Cameroon and elsewhere in West Africa as a *lingua franca*	35, 80, 180, 181, 195, 219, 222, 226, 237, 266, 286–7, 473, 474
Hawaiian		Austronesian	Hawaii (USA)	35, 248, 572
Haya		Benue-Congo	Uganda, Kenya, Tanzania, Zaïre	311
Hebridean Gaelic	a number of dialects of Scottish Gaelic			226–7, 304, 356–7, 358, 374, 463, 559
Herero		Niger-Congo	Namibia	218
Highland Totonac	dialect of Totonac			296

Language	Alternative name	Language family	Geographical location	Page
Higi		Afro-Asiatic	Nigeria	382
Hindi		Indo-European	India, Fiji, Guyana, Mauritius, East Africa, South Africa, Suriname, Trinidad	86, 200, 222, 291, 292, 528, 559–60, 572
Hmong	*see* Miao-Yao			
Hmong-Mien	*see* Miao-Yao			
Hopi		Uto-Aztecan	Arizona (USA)	442
Hottentot	*see* Nama (NOTE: 'Hottentot' is now considered a derogatory term for this language)			
Houston English	dialect of Texan English			411
Huautla Mazatec	dialect of Mazatec			481–2
Huichol		Uto-Aztecan	Mexico	198, 223
Hungarian		Uralic	Hungary, Rumania and parts of the Balkans	385, 437, 449, 509, 545
Hupa		Athabaskan	Northwestern California (USA)	257, 295
Icelandic		Indo-European	Iceland	260, 356, 357, 358, 560
Içúa Tupí	*see* Tupí			
Idoma		Niger-Congo	Nigeria	314
Igbo	Ibo	Niger-Congo	Nigeria	86, 221, 255–6, 291, 306, 355, 366, 385
Ijọ	Ijaw	Niger-Congo	Nigeria	225, 238–9
Ik		Nilo-Saharan	Uganda	296
Ikiribati	Gilbertese	Austronesian	Gilbert Islands, Solomon Islands, Nauru, Fiji, Vanuatu	326
Indonesiam	Malay	Austronesian	Indonesia	528
Ingush		North Caucasian	Chechen Ingush (CIS)	358
Inuit	Eskimo, Greenlandic	Eskimo-Aleut	Greenland west through Canada and Alaska and the Aleutians to Siberia	294, 438
Inuktitut	dialect of Inuit		West of Hudson's Bay, east through Baffin Island, Quebec and Labrador (Canada)	438
Iranian	Persian	Indo-European	Iran, Afghanistan, India, Oman, United Arab Emirates, CIS, Turkey	86
Irish	Erse	Indo-European	Eire, Northern Ireland	73, 356, 357, 358, 374, 382
Irish English	a number of dialects of English			260, 513
Isekiri	*see* Itsekiri			

605

Language	Alternative name	Language family	Geographical location	Page
Islay Gaelic	dialect of Scottish Gaelic			374, 559
Isoko		Niger-Congo	Nigeria	207, 253, 254, 304, 314
Isthmus Zapotec	dialect of Zapotec			220
Italian		Indo-European	Italy, Switzerland, France, San Marino, Yugoslavia and many countries of emigration	44, 46, 78, 86, 87, 219, 307, 360, 437, 489, 509, 522, 528, 530, 542
Itsekiri	Isekiri	Niger-Congo	Nigeria	455
Jamaican Creole		a *creole* based on English	Caribbean	83
Japanese		unclear, possibly Altaic	Japan	157, 189, 347–8, 353, 439, 440, 509, 518, 529, 533
Jaqaru		Jaqí	Peru	369
Javanese		Austronesian	Java (Republic of Indonesia)	212–13, 216, 355
Jibbali		Semitic South Arabian	Dhofar	317
Jingpho		Sino-Tibetan	Burma, China, India	479
Jordanian Arabic	dialect of Arabic			327–8
Kabardian		North Caucasian	Kabard-Balkar, Karachay Cherkes (CIS), Turkey, and a number of countries of emigration	44, 266, 368, 369
Kagoshima Japanese	dialect of Japanese			348
Kaingang		Macro-Gẽ	Brazil	232, 233
Kaititj	Gaididj	Pama-Nyungan	Northern Territory (Australia)	310
Kalabari Ịjọ	dialect of Ịjọ			
Kalam		Papuan	Madang Province and Western Highlands Province, East New Guinea Highlands (Papua New Guinea)	230–1
Kalispel		Salishan	Washington State, Montana (USA)	238
Kalispel-Flathead	dialect of Kalispel			237
Kamassian		Uralic	Siberia (recently became extinct)	51
Kanite		Papuan	Eastern Highlands Province (Papua New Guinea)	310
Kannada		Dravidian	India	382
Karen		Sino-Tibetan	Burma, Thailand	509
Karok	*see* Karuk			
Karuk	Karok	Hokan	California (USA)	259
Kashmiri		Indo-European	India, Pakistan	222, 294

Language	Alternative name	Language family	Geographical location	Page
Kèjià	Hakka	Sino-Tibetan	Guangdong and south of Yellow River (China), Hongkong, Taiwan, and as a language of emigration in Hawaii, Brunei, Malaysia, Suriname, Panama	231
K'ekchi		Mayan	Guatemala, Belize	172
Kele		Austronesian	Manus Province (Papua New Guinea)	220, 235
Kentucky English	dialect of American English			57
Kewa		Papuan	Southern Highlands Province (Papua New Guinea)	231
Khalkha Mongolian	dialect of Mongolian			385
Khamti Shan		Tai	Burma, India, China (possibly)	479
Khvarshi	Khwarshi	North Caucasian	Dagestan (CIS)	328
Khwarshi	*see* Khvarshi			
Kikuyu	Gikuyu	Niger-Congo	Kenya	229, 253, 439, 440
Kirghiz	Kirgiz	Turkic	CIS, China, Afghanistan, Turkey	385
Kirgiz	*see* Kirghiz			
Kiteke	*see* Teke			
Konda	Konda-Dora	Dravidian	Koraput district of Orissa (India)	382
Korean		Altaic	Korea, China, CIS, Japan and a number of countries of emigration	353, 382, 455
Kouvola Finnish	dialect of Finnish			559
Krio		a *creole* based on English	Sierra Leone	83
Kumamoto Japanese	dialect of Japanese			348
Kumauni		Indo-European	India, Nepal	222, 312
Kunjen		Pama-Nyungan	Queensland (Australia)	294, 382
Kurdish		Indo-European	Iraq, Turkey, Iran, Syria, Armenia	209, 225, 253, 254, 282, 365
Kurux		Dravidian	India, Bangladesh	294
Kwakiutl	Kwakw'ala	Wakashan	Vancouver Island and mainland British Columbia (Canada)	84, 257, 368
Kwakw'ala	*see* Kwakiutl			
Kwarshi		North Caucasian	Dagestan (CIS)	328
Kwoma	*see* Washkuk			
Kyoto Japanese	dialect of Japanese			347

Language	Alternative name	Language family	Geographical location	Page
Lak		North Caucasian	Southern Dagestan (CIS)	369
Lama-Lama	*see* Lamu-Lamu			
Lamu-Lamu	Lama-Lama, Lamalama	Pama-Nyungan	Queensland (Australia)	234
Land Dayak		Malayo-Polynesian	Borneo, Sarawak (Malaysia), Kalimantan (Indonesia)	294
Lango		Nilo-Saharan	Sudan	195
Lappish	*see* Lule Sami			
Latin		Indo-European	Extinct language of central Italy, and the imperial language of the Roman Empire; language of administration, science, culture and international diplomacy until the seventeenth century, and of Catholic Christianity	86, 87
Léonais Breton	dialect of Breton			295
Lewis Gaelic	dialect of Scottish Gaelic			226, 304, 356, 357, 358, 463
Lhasa Tibetan	dialect of Tibetan			207, 281
Lingua Franca (the pidgin that gave its name to the general concept of 'lingua francas')	Sabir	a *pidgin* based on Italian, Provençal, French, Spanish, Portuguese	spoken from the time of the Crusades for some seven centuries in the countries of the Mediterranean and the Barbary Coast of North Africa	80
Lisbon Portuguese	dialect of Continental Portuguese			259, 347
Lithuanian		Indo-European	Lithuania, CIS, many countries of emigration	464
Liverpool English	dialect of English English			411
Loma		Niger-Congo	Liberia, Guinea	294
Luganda	Ganda	Niger-Congo	Uganda	322, 439, 440
Luiseño		Uto-Aztecan	California (USA)	259
Lule Sami	Lappish	Uralic	Lapland, Sweden, Norway	356, 357, 435, 442
Lushootsheed	*see* Puget Salish			
Luvale		Niger-Congo	Angola, Zambia	231
Maan Chong Kham	Khamti Shan dialect of Khamti Shan			479–80
Machiguenga		Arawakan	Urubamba River (Peru)	296
Maidu	*see* Maiduan			
Maiduan	Maidu	Penutian	California (USA)	180

Language	Alternative name	Language family	Geographical location	Page
Maithili		Indo-European	Bihar, Madhya Pradesh, Maharashtra, West Bengal (India), Nepal	222
Malaysian	Malaysian, Indonesian			
Malagasy	Malay	Austronesian	Madagascar, Comoro Islands	297
Malay		Malayo-Polynesian	Malaysia, Singapore, Indonesia, Brunei, Thailand and some countries of emigration	80, 294, 437
Malayalam		Dravidian	Kerala, Laccadive Islands (India), Fiji and a number of other countries of emigration	216, 220, 334
Maltese		Semitic	Malta, and as a language of emigration in Australia, Canada, United States of America and United Kingdom	436, 444
Mandarin Chinese	Beijing Chinese, dialect of Chinese			80, 252, 260, 285–6, 319, 457, 467, 469–70, 479
Mantjiltjara		Pama-Nyungan	Jigalong area (Western Australia)	382
Maori		Polynesian	New Zealand and some Pacific islands	440
Marathi		Indo-European	Maharashtra and adjacent states (India)	200, 222, 314, 354, 382, 438
Margany		Pama-Nyungan	Queensland (Australia)	218
Margi		Afro-Asiatic	Nigeria	180, 196, 224, 236, 257, 304–5
Marshallese		Austronesian	Marshall Islands, Nauru	327, 382
Marwari	Rajasthani	Indo-Aryan	Rajastan, Pakistan and India	222, 314
Maung		Australian	Goulburn Island (Australia)	222
Maxakali		Macro-Gê	Minas Gerais State (Brazil)	233
Mayan	group of languages	affiliation unclear	Mexico, Belize, Guatemala, Honduras	181–2
Mazatec	Mazateco	Otomanguean	Mexico	294, 481–2
Mazateco	*see* Mazatec			
Medlpa	*see* Melpa			
Melpa	Medlpa	Papuan	Western Highlands Province (Papua New Guinea)	309–10
Menomini		Algonquian	Wisconsin (USA)	88
Miao-Yao	Hmong, Hmong-Mien, Miao	Sino-Tibetan	Southern China, Northern Vietnam, Laos, Thailand	509
Mid-West English	a number of dialects of American English			59, 64
Miskito Coast Creole	English	a *creole* based on English	Northeast coast of Honduras to the east coast of Nicaragua	83
Mixe		Penutian	Mexico	196, 200, 442
Mixtec		Otomanguean	Mexico	471, 472

Language	Alternative name	Language family	Geographical location	Page
Mongolian		Altaic	Outer and Inner Mongolia, and adjacent provinces in China	385
Mooré	Mossi	Niger-Congo	Burkina Faso, Togo	253
Morelos Aztec	dialect of Nahuatl			257–8
Moscow Russian	dialect of Russian			334, 345–6
Mossi	*see* Mooré			
Mundari		Austro-Asiatic	Assam, Northeastern India, Andaman and Nicobar Islands, Nepal, Bangladesh	382
Mura	*see* Pirahã			
Náhual	*see* Nahuatl			
Nahuat	*see* Nahuatl			
Nahuatl	Náhual, Nahuat, Aztec	Uto-Aztecan	Mexico	294, 368, 522
Nama	Hottentot, Khoikhoi	Khoisan	Namibia, South Africa	174, 177, 294, 375, 376
Nambakaengo	*see* Santa Cruz			
Navaho	*see* Navajo			
Navajo	Navaho	Athabaskan	Arizona, Utah, New Mexico (USA)	257, 258, 368, 470
Ndau		Benue-Congo	Zimbabwe, Mozambique	350
Ndebele	Nde'bele	Benue-Congo	Zimbabwe, Botswana, South Africa, Swaziland, Lesotho	200, 236, 354
Nenets		Uralic	from the mouth of the northern Dvina River in Northeastern Europe to the delta of the Yenesei in Asia, Kola Peninsula (CIS)	442
Neo-Aramaic		Semitic	Lebanon	366–7
Nepali		Indo-European	Eastern Nepal, India, Bhutan	222
New England English	dialect of American English			90
Newfound-land English	dialect of Canadian English English			59
New York English	a number of dialects of American English			71, 325–6, 411
New Zealand English	a number of dialects of English			398, 413
New Zealand Maori	dialect of Maori			440
Nez Perce		Penutian	Idaho (USA)	240, 257, 265, 294

Language	Alternative name	Language family	Geographical location	Page
Ngarluma		Pama-Nyungan	Northwest coast of Western Australia	382
Ngembi Tikar	dialect of Tikar			298
Ngizim		Afro-Asiatic	Borno State, Nigeria	231
Ngoni	*see* Sutu			
Ngwe		Bantoid	Cameroon	220, 281
Nisi	Dafla	Sino-Tibetan	Assam, Arunachal Pradesh (India)	296
Nitinaht	Nitinat, Ditidaht	Wakashan	British Columbia (Canada)	189, 370
Nobiin	dialect of Nubian			438
Nootka		Wakashan	Western British Columbia (Canada)	189, 257, 368
Northern English	dialect of English English			74, 196
Northern Norwegian	dialect of Norwegian			463
Northern Paiute		Uto-Aztecan	California, Idaho, Nevada (USA)	521
Northern Puget Sound Salish	*see* Puget Salish			
Northern Sotho	Pedi	Niger-Congo	Transvaal (South Africa)	253, 254
Northern Swedish	dialect of Swedish			463
North German	a number of dialects of German			419
North Uist Gaelic	dialect of Hebridean Gaelic			356
North Welsh	dialect of Welsh			258, 286
Northwest Gaelic	dialect of Scottish Gaelic			357, 442
Norwegian		Indo-European	Norway	77, 169, 382, 435, 463, 560
Nubian		Nilo-Saharan	along the Nile, Southern Egypt, Northern Sudan	437–8
Nupe		Niger-Congo	Nigeria	364
Nyangumarda	*see* Nyangumarta			
Nyangumarta	Nyangumarda	Pama-Nyungan	Western Australia	217, 296
Nyanja		Niger-Congo	Malawi, Zambia, Mozambique, Zimbabwe, Tanzania	230
Oaxaca Chontal	dialect of Chontal			211
Occitan	*see* Provençal			

Language	Alternative name	Language family	Geographical location	Page
Ojibwa		Algonquian	Ontario, Saskatchewan, Manitoba, Ontario, Quebec (Canada), Montana, North Dakota, Minnesota, Wisconsin, Michigan (USA)	88
Olgolo		Pama-Nyungan	Cape York (Australia)	234
Okinawa Japanese	dialect of Japanese			348
Oriya		Indo-European	Orissa, Bihar, West Bengal, Assam, Andhra Pradesh (India), Bangladesh	312
Orkney English	dialect of Scottish English			74
Ottawa English	dialect of Canadian English			90
Pacific English	a number of dialects of English			59
Paez	*see* Páez			
Páez	Paez	Paezan	Central Andes Mountains (Colombia)	231, 294
Palantla Chinantec	dialect of Chinantec			295
Palestinian Arabic	dialect of Arabic			385
Pame		Otomanguean	Mexico	437
Panamanian Spanish	dialect of South American Spanish			294
Panjabi	*see* Punjabi			
Pasha	*see* Pashayi			
Pashayi	Pasha	Indo-European	Afghanistan	382
Pashto		Indo-European	Afghanistan border with Pakistan, Northwest Frontier Province (Pakistan), and a number of countries of emigration	216
Pattani	dialect of Malay	Austronesian	East coast of South Thailand below Songkhla	437
Pedi	*see* Northern Sotho			
Peking Chinese	*see* Beijing Chinese			
Persian	*see* Iranian			
Pidgin English	many versions, depending on the substrate	a *pidgin* language lexically based on English	Pacific basin, Africa	81–2

Language	Alternative name	Language family	Geographical location	Page
Pirahã	Múra-Pirahã	*language isolate*	Maici River, Amazonas (Brazil)	215
Pitta-Pitta		Pama-Nyungan	Queensland (Australia)	382
Pocomchí	Pokomchí	Mayan	Guatemala	181–2
Pokomchí	*see* Pocomchí			
Polish		Indo-European	Poland, CIS, Germany, and many countries of emigration	253, 291, 292, 520, 560
Popoloca	Popoloc	Otomanguean	Mexico	367, 481
Portuguese		Indo-European	Portugal, Brazil, Angola, Mozambique, Guinea Bissau, Timor (Indonesia) and a number of countries of emigration	83, 189, 212, 225, 250, 253, 255 259, 297, 309, 347
Provençal	Occitan	Indo-European	Southeastern France	86, 220, 316
Puget Salish	Lushootsheed, Northern Puget Sound Salish	Salishan	Puget Sound, Washington State (USA)	34, 211, 237, 257, 265
Puget Sound	*see* Puget Salish			
Pulaar	*see* Fula			
Pulle	*see* Fula			
Punjabi	Panjabi	Indo-European	Punjab State (Pakistan) and many countries of emigration	222, 312, 560
Qatari Arabic	dialect of Arabic			33, 189, 297, 327, 346, 361, 362, 439
Quechua		Quechua	Peru, Ecuador, Bolivia, Colombia, Argentina, Chile	207
Quiche	*see* Quiché			
Quiché	Quiche	Mayan	Guatemala	181–2
Quileute		unaffiliated	Olympic peninsula, Washington State (USA)	34, 211, 257, 265, 368
Quiotepec Chinantec	dialect of Chinantec			241
Rajasthani	*see* Marwari, Gujuri			
Rarotongan Maori	dialect of Maori; also called Cook Islands Maori		Cook Islands (New Zealand and French Polynesia)	440
Reading English	dialect of English English			71, 90

Language	Alternative name	Language family	Geographical location	Page
Received Pronunciation	accent of English English			9, 34, 57–8, 62, 63, 64, 65, 80, 89–90, 146, 147–8, 151, 189, 196, 265, 280, 284–5, 286–7, 298, 306, 332–3, 340–1, 351, 364, 368, 377–8, 383–4, 392, 394, 398, 401, 413, 416, 418, 434, 459–60, 489–90, 494–8, 516, 531–2, 550–6
Rotokas		Papuan	central mountains of Kieta sub-province, North Solomons Province (Papua New Guinea)	211, 572
Rumanian		Indo-European	Rumania, Moldavia, Yugoslavia, Bulgaria, Greece, Albania and many countries of emigration	522
Russian		Indo-European	Russia, CIS and many countries of influence	86, 194, 297, 324, 325, 333–4, 345–6, 353, 381, 382, 439, 509, 516, 522, 523
Sabir	*see* Lingua Franca			
San Cristobal Pocomchí	dialect of Pocomchí			181–2
Sandawe		Khoisan *language isolate*	Tanzania	174, 375
Sanglechi		Indo-European	Afghanistan, Tajikistan (CIS)	382
San José El Paraíso Mixe	dialect of Mixe			442
Sanskrit		Indo-European	(ancient language of North India)	86, 382
Santa Cruz	Nambakaengo	Papuan	Santa Cruz Islands, Eastern Solomon Islands	231
San Vicente Coyotepec Popoloca	dialect of Popoloca			367–8
São Paolo Portuguese	dialect of Brazilian Portuguese			212, 287–9, 309
Sara		Nilo-Saharan	Central African Republic	231

Language	Alternative name	Language family	Geographical location	Page
Scottish English	a number of dialects of English			60, 61, 62, 63, 64, 65, 73, 225, 299, 384, 416, 419
Scottish Gaelic	a number of dialects of Gaelic			73, 150, 151, 226, 295, 304, 334, 356, 357, 358, 374, 442, 463, 500, 561
Sedang		Austro-Asiatic	Vietnam	231
Selepet		Papuan	Morobe Province (Papua New Guinea)	231
Serbo-Croatian		Indo-European	Yugoslavia, Hungary, Austria, Turkey, Rumania, Greece, Czechoslovakia and many countries of emigration	33–4, 443, 455, 464
Shapsugh Adyghe	dialect of Adyghe			248, 303
Sherpa		Sino-Tibetan	Nepal, Sikkim, India, China	150, 367
Shetland English	dialect of Scottish English			74
Shina		Indo-European	Gilgit Agency, Kashmir (Pakistan)	222
Shona		Niger-Congo	Zimbabwe, Mozambique, Zambia	22, 198, 200, 224, 252, 317, 318, 354
Sindhi		Indo-European	Sindh (Pakistan), India	150, 180, 181, 200, 222, 282, 354–5
Sinhalese		Indo-European	Sri Lanka	229
Sioux	language group	Amerindian	Central North America from the plains of Canada south to the southern Mississippi valley	291, 292
Sirionó		Tupian	Bolivia	231, 482
Skagit	dialect of Puget Salish			238
Skåne	dialect of Swedish			316–17
Skye Gaelic	dialect of Scottish Gaelic			559
Swedish Slovenian	Swedish	Indo-European	Slovene Republic of Yugoslavia, Italy, Austria, Hungary and a number of countries of emigration	463
Solomon Islands Pidgin	Pijin	a *pidgin/ creole* based on English	Solomon Islands	82
Somali		Afro-Asiatic	Somalia, Ethiopia, Djibouti, South Yemen, United Arab Emirates, Kenya	253, 254, 439, 440

Language	Alternative name	Language family	Geographical location	Page
S. African English	a number of dialects of English			61
S. American Spanish	a number of dialects of Spanish			81, 358
Southeastern Norwegian	dialect of Norwegian			560
Southern English	a number of dialects of English English			42–3, 75–6, 513
Southern English	a number of dialects of American English			58, 250
Southern Paiute		Uto-Aztecan	California, Arizona (USA)	521
Southwestern English	a number of dialects of English English			299
Soyaltepec Mazatec	dialect of Mazatec			482
Spanish		Indo-European	Spain, Equatorial Guinea, 19 countries in North, Central and South America from the United States of America to Cape Horn, and many countries of emigration	46, 78, 81, 83, 86, 87, 156, 219, 225, 302, 307–9, 358, 360, 379–80, 435, 457, 487–8, 510, 522, 530, 531–2, 542
Spokane Kalispel	dialect of Kalispel			237
Squamish		Salishan	Southwestern British Columbia (Canada)	368, 369
Standard Chinese	dialect of Chinese			252, 260, 319, 479
Standard English	dialect of English			56–9, 60, 61, 89
St John's English	dialect of Newfoundland English			90
Stockholm Swedish	dialect of Swedish			320, 463–4
Suleimaniya Kurdish	dialect of Kurdish			209, 226, 365
Sundanese	Sunda	Malayo-Polynesian	Western third of Java	213, 220, 282, 294, 364, 379
Suto	*see* Sutu			
Sutu	Suto, Ngoni	Niger-Congo	Tanzania, Mozambique, Malawi	350, 351

Language	Alternative name	Language family	Geographical location	Page
Swahili		Niger-Congo	Zanzibar, Tanzania, Kenya, Oman, United Arab Emirates, Uganda, Rwanda, Burundi, Somalia and throughout East Africa as a *lingua franca*	80, 83, 350, 510, 520
Swedish		Indo-European	Sweden, Finland	170, 219, 282, 316–17, 319, 320, 333, 381, 435, 446, 449, 463–4, 510, 516, 522, 525, 529
Swiss German	a number of dialects of German			170
Sydney English	dialect of Australian English			90
Szechuanese	dialect of Chinese		Szechuan	319, 367, 474–6
Tabasaran	*see* Tabassaran			
Tabassaran	Tabasaran	North Caucasian	Southern Dagestan (CIS)	322, 323
Tactic Pocomchí	dialect of Pocomchí			181–2
Tagalog		Malayo-Polynesian (*language isolate* within the Central Philippine group)	Philippines and many countries of emigration	294
Tahitian		Polynesian	Society Islands, North Tuamotus, French Polynesia, New Zealand, New Caledonia	440
Tamazight Berber	dialect of Berber			327
Tamil		Dravidian	Tamil Nadu (India), Sri Lanka, Vietnam, South Africa, Malaysia, Fiji, Singapore Mauritius, United Arab Emirates and many other countries of emigration	216–17, 282, 283, 299, 309, 382, 419, 447–8, 528
Tarascan		Mesoamerican *language isolate*	Mexico	224
Tarawa Gilbertese	dialect of Ikiribati			326
Tatar		Altaic	Tatar (CIS), Turkey, Afghanistan, China and a number of countries of emigration	520
Tehuelche	*see* Gununa-Kena			
Teke	Kiteke	Niger-Congo	Congo, Zaïre	215
Telegu	*see* Telugu			

Appendix II

Language	Alternative name	Language family	Geographical location	Page
Telugu	Telegu	Dravidian	Andhra Pradesh (India), Fiji, United Arab Emirates, Singapore and other countries of emigration	385, 525
Tepehuán		Uto-Aztecan	Mexico	220, 482
Terena	Tereno	Arawakan	Brazil	212, 256, 305, 525
Tereno	*see* Terena			
Teso	Ateso	East Sudanic	Kenya, Uganda	195
Tewa		Timor-Alor-Pantar	Pantar Island (Indonesia)	294
Texan English	a number of dialects of American English			90, 411
Texcoco Nahuatl	dialect of Nahuatl			368, 520
Texmelucan Zapotec	dialect of Zapotec			466
Tfuea Punguu Tsou	dialect of Tsou			168
Thai	Siamese	Tai	Central Thailand, Singapore, and many countries of emigration	53, 326, 349–50, 352, 367, 435, 467–9, 478–9, 510, 529
Thompson		Salishan	South Central British Columbia (Canada)	322
Tibetan		Sino-Tibetan	Tibet, Ladakh, Lahul, Baltistan, India, Nepal, Sikkim, Bhutan, China	207, 281, 509
Ticuna		South American *language isolate*	Northeastern Amazon River area, Brazil, Peru, Colombia	294
Tigre		Semitic	Eritrea, Ethiopia, Northern Sudan	54, 209, 213, 219, 237, 250, 253, 254, 368–9, 441
Tikali	*see* Tikar			
Tikar	Tikali	Niger-Congo	Western Cameroon	298
Titan		Oceanic	Manus Province (Papua New Guinea)	219, 230
Tiv		Niger-Congo	Nigeria and Cameroon	230
Tiwa		Kiowa-Tanoan	New Mexico (USA)	257
Tiwi		Australian *language isolate*	Northern Territory (Australia)	382
Tlapanec	*see* Tlapaneco			
Tlapaneco	Tlapanec	Hokan	Mexico	466
Tlingit		Na-Dené Tlingit	Southeastern Alaska (USA), British Columbia (Canada)	257, 296, 368, 369
Tojolabal		Mayan	Mexico	173

Language	Alternative name	Language family	Geographical location	Page
Tok Pisin		a *pidgin* based on English	Papua New Guinea	81–2
Tokyo Japanese	dialect of Japanese			347
Tolowa		Athabaskan	Northwestern California (USA)	257, 294, 369
Totonac		Penutian	Mexico	296, 482
Totontepec Mixe	dialect of Mixe			196, 200, 442
Trique		Otomanguean	Mexico	466
Tsakhur		North Caucasian	Southern Dagestan, Azerbaijan (CIS)	328
Tsez	*see* Dido			
Tsonga		Niger-Congo	Transvaal (South Africa), Mozambique, Swaziland	200, 237, 354, 477–9
Tsou		Austronesian	Taiwan	168–9
Tsutujil	*see* Tzutujil			
Tswana	Chuana	Niger-Congo	Botswana, Namibia, South Africa, Zimbabwe	253, 254
Tulu		Dravidian	Karnataka (India) and adjacent areas	382
Tunica		North American *language isolate*	lower Mississippi valley (USA)	294
Tupí		Andean-Equatorial	Eastern Brazil	232
Turkana		Nilo-Saharan	Kenya, Sudan, Ethiopia	189, 297, 385
Turkish		Altaic	Turkey, Bulgaria, Yugoslavia, Greece, Cyprus, Rumania, CIS and many countries of emigration	36, 209, 364, 365–6, 385, 386–7, 483
Twi	Akan	Niger-Congo	Southeast Ghana	289, 291, 322, 385, 411
Tzeltal		Mayan	Mexico	22, 196, 198, 369
Tzutujil		Mayan	Guatemala	181
Ubykh		North Caucasian	Turkey	316, 322, 328
Uduk		Nilo-Saharan	Sudan	180
Uist Gaelic	dialect of Hebridean Gaelic			356, 357
Ulster English	a number of dialects of English			90, 513
Urhobo		Niger-Congo	Nigeria	35, 207, 226, 253, 317, 471, 473
Uzbek		Altaic	Northern Uzbekestan, Russia, China, North Afghanistan, Pakistan and a number of countries of emigration	522
Vancouver English	dialect of Canadian English			90

Language	Alternative name	Language family	Geographical location	Page
V'enen Taut		Austronesian	Vanuatu (Pacific)	215, 250
Vietnamese		Austro-Asiatic	Vietnam, Cambodia, Laos, Thailand, and many countries of emigration	216, 467, 509
Waalubal	dialect of Banjalang			325
Waffa		Papuan	Morobe Province (Papua New Guinea)	256
Wailbi	*see* Wailpi			
Wailpi	Wailpi, Adynya-mathanha	Pama-Nyungan	South Australia	362
Walmatjari		Pama-Nyungan	Fitzroy Crossing area (Western Australia)	214
Wantoat		Papuan	Morobe Province (Papua New Guinea)	231
Warja	*see* Warji			
Warji	Warja	Afro-Asiatic	Nigeria	257
Warlpiri		Pama-Nyungan	Northern Territory (Australia)	222
Washkuk	Kwoma	Papuan	Sepik River area in East Sepik Province (Papua New Guinea)	231
Watjari	*see* Watjarri			
Watjarri	Watjari	Pama-Nyungan	Western Australia	310
Welsh		Indo-European	Wales, Patagonia (Argentina) and a number of other countries of emigration	258, 286
Welsh English	a number of dialects of English			73, 434
Wenatchee-Columbia	dialect of Columbian			241, 265, 370
Western Aranda	dialect of Aranda			362
Western Keresan	*see* Acoma			
Western English	a number of dialects of American English			58, 64, 300–1
West Norwegian	dialect of Norwegian			356
Wintu		Penutian	California (USA)	368
Wiyot (extinct)		Algic	Northeastern California (USA)	257
Wolof		Niger-Congo	Mauritania, the Gambia, Senegal	294, 362
Wu	*see* Changchow Chinese			

Language	Alternative name	Language family	Geographical location	Page
Xhosa		Niger-Congo	Cape Province (South Africa), the Transkei	61, 174, 237, 238–9, 257, 266, 375
!Xóõ		Khoisan	Botswana, Angola	174, 177–9, 375
!Xū		Khoisan	Angola, Namibia	174, 369–70, 375, 572
Yagua		Macro-Carib	Peru	382
Yaka		Niger-Congo	Zaïre, Angola	385
Yanuwa	*see* Yanyuwa			
Yanyuwa	Yanuwa	Australian	Northern Territory, Queensland (Australia)	214
Yidgha		Indo-European	Pakistan	382
Yoruba		Niger-Congo	Nigeria, Benin, Togo, Benin, Sierra Leone	86, 225–6, 227, 291, 292, 314, 466, 467, 468, 523
Yuchi		Yuchi	East Central Oklahoma, Tennessee (USA)	257, 291, 292, 294
Yulu	dialect of Yulu-Binga			231
Yulu-Binga		Nilo-Saharan	Sudan	231
Zande		Niger-Congo	Zaïre, Southern Sudan, Central African Republic	221, 256
Zapotec		Otomanguean	Mexico	220, 466, 482
Zibiao Guéré	dialect of Guéré			238
Zulu		Niger-Congo	South Africa, Lesotho, Swaziland, Malawi	61, 117, 172, 174, 180, 200, 257, 354, 369, 375, 471
Zuni		Aztec-Tanoan *language isolate*	New Mexico (USA)	257

621

REFERENCES

Abberton, E. (1972) 'Some laryngographic data for Korean stops', *Journal of the International Phonetic Association* 2: 67–78.

Abercrombie, D. (1949) 'What is a "letter"?', *Lingua* 2: 54–62.

(1964) *English Phonetic Texts*, London: Faber and Faber.

(1965) *Studies in Phonetics and Linguistics*, London: Oxford University Press.

(1967) *Elements of General Phonetics*, Edinburgh University Press.

(1968) 'Paralanguage', *British Journal of Disorders of Communication* 3: 55–9; reprinted in J. Laver and S. Hutcheson (eds.) (1972) *Communication in Face to Face Interaction*, Harmondsworth: Penguin.

(1977) 'The accents of Standard English in Scotland', *Edinburgh University Department of Linguistics Work in Progress* 10: 21–32; reprinted in A.J. Aitken and T. McArthur (eds.) (1979) *The Languages of Scotland*, Edinburgh: Chambers, pp. 68–84.

(1985) 'Daniel Jones's teaching', in V.A. Fromkin (ed.), *Phonetic Linguistics: Essays in Honor of Peter Ladefoged*, Orlando FL: Academic Press, pp. 15–24.

Abercrombie, D., D.B. Fry, P.A.D. MacCarthy, N.C. Scott and J.L.M. Trim (eds.) (1964) *In Honour of Daniel Jones*, London: Longmans Green.

Abramson, A.S. (1962) *The Vowels and Tones of Standard Thai: Acoustical Measurements and Experiments*, Publication 20 of Indiana University Research Center in Anthropology, Folklore, and Linguistics, Bloomington IN.

(1968) 'Contrastive distribution of phoneme classes in Içũa Tupi', *Anthropological Linguistics* 10: 11–21.

(1975) 'The tones of Central Thai: some perceptual experiments', in J.G. Harris and J.R. Chamberlain (eds.) *Studies in Tai Linguistics in Honor of William J. Gedney*, Bangkok: Central Institute of English Language, Office of State Universities, pp. 1–16.

(1979) 'The co-articulation of tones: an acoustic study of Thai', in T.L. Thongkum, V. Panupong, P. Kullavanijaya and M.R.K. Tingsabadh (eds.), *Studies in Tai and Mon-Khmer Phonetics and Phonology: in Honour of Eugénie Henderson*, Bangkok: Chulalongkorn University Press, pp. 1–9.

(1986) 'The perception of word-initial consonant length: Pattani Malay', *Journal of the International Phonetic Association* 16: 8–16.

Abu-Salim, I.M. (1987) 'Vowel harmony in Palestinian Arabic: a metrical perspective', *Journal of Linguistics* 23: 1–24.

Adriaens, L.M.H. (1984) 'A preliminary description of German intonation', *Annual Progress Report* 19: 36–41, Institute for Perception Research, Eindhoven.

Ager, D. (1990) *Sociolinguistics and Contemporary French*, Cambridge University Press.

Agostoni, E. and J. Mead (1964) 'Statics of the respiratory system', in W. Fenn and H. Rahn (eds.) *Handbook of Physiology: Respiration 1*, Section 3, American Physiological Society, Washington DC, pp. 387–409.

Äimä, F. (1918) 'Phonetik und lautlehre des Inarilappischen', *Mémoires de la Société Finno-Ougrienne* (Helsinki, Finland) 42: 1–118, 43: 1–249.

Ainsworth, W.A. (1988) *Speech Recognition by Machine*, London: Peter Peregrinus.

Aitchison, J. (1987) *Words in the Mind: an Introduction to the Mental Lexicon*, Oxford: Basil Blackwell.

(1991) *Language Change: Progress or Decay?*, Cambridge University Press.

Aitken, A.J. and T. McArthur (eds.) (1979) *The Languages of Scotland*, Edinburgh: Chambers.

Al-Ani, S.H. (1970) *Arabic Phonology: an Acoustical and Physiological Investigation*, Janua Linguarum 61, Series Practica, The Hague: Mouton.

Al-Ani, S.H. and M.S. El-Dalee (1984) 'Tafkhim in Arabic: the acoustic and [physiological] parameters', in M.P.R. van den Broecke and A. Cohen (eds.), *Proceedings of the Tenth International Congress of Phonetic Sciences* (Utrecht), Dordrecht, and Cinnaminson NJ: Foris, pp. 385–9.

Albright, R.W. (1958) 'The International Phonetic Alphabet: its backgrounds and development', *International Journal of American Linguistics*, Publication 7 as Part III, vol. XXIV.1.

Albrow, K.H. (1966) 'Mutation in "Spoken North Welsh"', in C.E. Bazell, J.C. Catford, M.A.K. Halliday and R.H. Robins (eds.), *In Memory of J.R. Firth*, London: Longmans Green, pp.1–7.

Ali, L., Gallager, T., Goldstein, J. and Daniloff, R. (1971) 'Perception of coarticulated nasality', *Journal of the Acoustical Society of America* 49:538–40.

Allen, G. D. (1973) 'Segmental timing control in speech production', *Journal of Phonetics* 1: 219–37.

(1975) 'Speech rhythm: its relation to performance universals and articulatory timing', *Journal of Phonetics* 3: 75–86.

Allen, H.B. (1973–1976) *The Linguistic Atlas of the Upper Midwest*, 3 vols., Minneapolis MN: University of Minnesota Press.

(1977) 'Regional dialects', *American Speech* 52: 163–261.

Allen, H.B. and M.D. Linn (eds.) (1986) *Dialect and Accent Variation*, Orlando FL: Academic Press.

Allen, H.B. and G.N. Underwood (eds.) (1971) *Readings in American Dialectology*, New York: Meredith Corporation, Appleton-Century-Crofts.

Allen, J., M.S. Hunnicutt and D. Klatt, with R.C. Armstrong and D.B. Pisoni

References

(1987) *From Text to Speech: the MITalk System*, Cambridge University Press.

Allerhand, M. (1987) *Knowledge-Based Speech Pattern Recognition*, London: Kogan Page.

Allwood, J., L-G. Andersson and Ö. Dahl (1977) *Logic in Linguistics*, Cambridge University Press.

Anderson, J.M. (1969) 'Syllabic or non-syllabic phonology', *Journal of Linguistics* 5: 136–43.

Anderson, J.M. and C. Jones (1977) *Phonological Structure and the History of English*, Amsterdam: North-Holland.

Anderson, J.M., C. Ewen and J. Staun (1985) 'Phonological structure: segmental, suprasegmental and extrasegmental', *Phonology Yearbook* 2: 203–24.

Anderson, S. (1974) *The Organization of Phonology*, New York: Academic Press.
　(1976) 'Nasal consonants and the internal structure of segments', *Language* 52: 326–44.

　(1978) 'Tone features', in V.A. Fromkin (ed.) *Tone: a Linguistic Survey*, New York: Academic Press, pp. 133–176.

　(1985) *Phonology in the Twentieth Century: Theories of Rules and Theories of Representations*, University of Chicago Press.

Andrésen, B.S. (1968) *Pre-glottalization in English Standard Pronunciation*, Oslo: Norwegian Universities Press, and New York: Humanities Press.

Andrews, J.R. (1975) *Introduction to Classical Nahuatl*, Austin TX: University of Texas Press.

Appley, M.H. and R. Trumbull (eds.) (1986) *Dynamics of Stress*, New York: Plenum.

Armstrong, L.E. (1940) *The Phonetic and Tonal Structure of Kikuyu*, London: Oxford University Press.

Armstrong, L.E. and I.C. Ward (1931) *A Handbook of English Intonation*, Cambridge: W. Heffer and Sons.

Arnason, K. (1980) *Quantity in Historical Phonology*, Cambridge University Press.

Arnott, D.W. (1969a) 'Fula', in E. Dunstan (ed.), *Twelve Nigerian Languages*, London: Longmans, Green, pp. 57–72.

　(1969b) 'Tiv', in E. Dunstan (ed.), *Twelve Nigerian Languages*, London: Longmans, Green, pp. 143–52.

Aronoff, M. and R.T. Oehrle (eds., with F. Kelley and B.W. Stephens) (1984) *Language Sound Structure: Studies in Phonology Presented to Morris Halle by his Teacher and Students*, Cambridge MA: Massachusetts Institute of Technology Press.

Ashby, M.G. (1990) 'Articulatory possibilities for implosives', *Journal of the International Phonetic Association* 20: 15–18.

Asher, R.E. (1982) *Tamil*, Lingua Descriptive Studies vol. VII, Amsterdam: North-Holland, (republished in 1985 by Croom Helm, London, and in 1989 by Routledge, London, under the same title on both occasions).

624

Asher, R.E. and E.J.A. Henderson (eds.) (1981) *Towards a History of Phonetics*, Edinburgh University Press.

Asher, R.E. and J.M.Y. Simpson (eds.) (1993) *Encyclopedia of Language and Linguistics*, 10 vols., Oxford: Pergamon Press.

Atkinson, J.M. and J. Heritage (eds.) (1984) *Structures of Social Action: Studies in Conversation Analysis*, Cambridge University Press and Paris: Editions de la Maison des Sciences de l'Homme.

Atwood, E.B. (1962) *The Regional Vocabulary of Texas*, Austin TX: University of Texas Press.

(1963) 'The methods of American dialectology', *Zeitschrift für Mundartforschung* 30: 1–39; reprinted in H.B. Allen and M.D. Linn (eds.) (1986) *Dialect and Accent Variation*, Orlando FL: Academic Press, pp. 63–97.

Austin, J.L. (1962) *How to do Things with Words*, Oxford: Clarendon Press.

Avesani, C. (1987) 'Declination and sentence intonation in Italian', *Proceedings of the Eleventh International Congress of Phonetic Sciences*, Tallinn, pp. 153–6.

Avis, W.S. (1986) 'The contemporary context of Canadian English', in H.B. Allen and M.D. Linn (eds.) *Dialect and Language Variation*, Orlando FL: Academic Press, pp. 212–16.

Bailey, R.W. and M. Görlach (eds.) (1982) *English as a World Language*, Ann Arbor MI: University of Michigan Press.

Baken, R.J. (1987) *Clinical Measurement of Speech and Voice*, Boston MA: Little, Brown, London: Taylor and Francis.

Balasubramanian, T. (1972) 'The phonetics of Colloquial Tamil', PhD dissertation, University of Edinburgh.

(1979) 'Timing in Tamil', *Edinburgh University Department of Linguistics Work in Progress* 12: 58–75.

Balasubramanian, T. and R.E. Asher (1984) 'Intervocalic plosives in Tamil', in J.A. Higgs and R. Thelwall (eds.), *Topics in Linguistic Phonetics: in Honour of E.T. Uldall*, Occasional Papers in Linguistics and Language Learning no. 9, March, Department of Linguistics, The New University of Ulster, pp. 49–63.

Bamgbose, A. (1969) 'Yoruba', in E. Dunstan (ed.), *Twelve Nigerian Languages*, London: Longmans Green, pp.163–72.

Bannert, R. (1985) 'Towards a model for German prosody', *Folia Linguistica* 19: 312–41.

Barbour, S. and P. Stevenson (1990) *Variation in German: a Critical Approach to German Sociolinguistics*, Cambridge University Press.

Barentsen, A.A., B.N. Groen and R. Sprenger (eds.) (1986) *Dutch Studies in Russian Linguistics*, Amsterdam: Rodopi.

Barrera, B. and K. Dakin (1978) *Vocabulario Popoloca de San Vicente Coyotepec*, Cuadernos de la Casa Chata 11, Centro de Investigaciones Superiores del Instituto Nacional de Antropologia e Historia, Mexico.

Barry, S.M.E. (1989) 'Aspects of sonorant devoicing in Russian', *Speech, Hearing and Language: Work in Progress* 3: 45–60, Department of Phonetics and Linguistics, University College, London.

Basbøll, H. (1972) 'Some remarks concerning the stød in a generative grammar of Danish', in F. Kiefer (ed.) *Proceedings of the KVAL Seminar: Derivational Processes*, Stockholm: KVAL, pp. 5–30.

—— (1985) 'Stød in modern Danish', *Folia Linguistica* 19: 1–50.

—— (1988) 'Phonological theory', in F.J. Newmeyer (1988) *Linguistics: the Cambridge Survey*, vol. I, *Linguistic Theory: Foundations*, Cambridge University Press, pp. 192–215.

Bauer, L. (1983) *English Word Formation*, Cambridge University Press.

Bauernschmidt, A. (1965) 'Amuzgo syllable dynamics', *Language* 41: 471–83.

Baumbach, E.J.M. (1974) *Introduction to the Speech Sounds and Speech Sound Changes of Tsonga*, Pretoria, South Africa: van Schaik.

Bazell, C.E., J.C. Catford, M.A.K. Halliday and R.H. Robins (eds.) (1966) *In Memory of J.R. Firth*, London: Longmans Green.

Beach, D.M. (1938) *The Phonetics of the Hottentot Language*, Cambridge: Heffer.

Beattie, G. and B. Butterworth (1979) 'Contextual probability and word frequency as determinants of pauses and errors in spontaneous speech', *Language and Speech* 22: 201–11.

Beckman, M. (1982) 'Segment duration and the "mora" in Japanese', *Phonetica* 39: 113–35.

—— (1986) *Stress and Non-stress Accent*, Dordrecht: Foris.

—— (1988) 'Phonetic theory', in F.J. Newmeyer (ed.) *Linguistics: the Cambridge Survey*, vol. I, *Linguistic Theory: Foundations*, Cambridge University Press, pp. 216–38.

—— (1992) 'Evidence for speech rhythms across languages', in Y. Tohkura, E. Vatikiotis-Bateson and Y. Sagisaka (eds.) *Speech Perception, Production and Linguistic Structure*, Tokyo: Ohmsha and Amsterdam: IOS Press, pp. 457–63.

Beckman, M.E. and J.B. Pierrehumbert (1986) 'Intonational structure in English and Japanese', *Phonology Yearbook* 3: 255–309.

Bell, A. and J.B. Hooper (eds.) (1978) *Syllables and Segments*, Amsterdam: North-Holland.

Bell, A.M. (1867) *Visible Speech: the Science of Universal Alphabetics*, London: Simpkin Marshall.

Bell, H. (1971) 'The phonology of Nobiin Nubian', *African Language Review* 9: 115–59.

Bendor-Samuel, J.T. (1960) 'Some problems of segmentation in the phonological analysis of Terena', *Word* 16.3: 348–55; reprinted in F.R. Palmer (ed.) (1970) *Prosodic Analysis*, London: Oxford University Press, pp. 214–21.

—— (1962) 'Stress in Terena', *Transactions of the Philological Society*, pp. 105–23.

Benguerel, A.-P. and H.A. Cowan (1974) 'Coarticulation of upper lip protrusion in French' *Phonetica* 30: 41–55.

Berg, J. van den (1958) 'Myoelastic-aerodynamic theory of voice-production', *Journal of Speech and Hearing Research* 1: 227–44.

(1962) 'Modern research in experimental phoniatrics', *Folia Phoniatrica* 14: 81–149.

(1968) 'Mechanism of the larynx and the laryngeal vibrations', in B. Malmberg (ed.) *Manual of Phonetics*, Amsterdam: North-Holland, pp. 278–308.

Berg, J. van den, J.F. Zantema and J.P. Doornenbal (1959) 'On the air resistance and Bernoulli effect of the human larynx', *Journal of the Acoustical Society of America* 29: 626–31.

Bernard, J.R.L. (1969) 'On the uniformity of spoken Australian English', *Orbis* 18: 62–73.

Bezooyen, R. van (1984) *Characteristics and Recognizability of Vocal Expressions of Emotion*, Dordrecht, and Cinnaminson NJ: Foris.

Bhat, D.N.S. (1974) 'Retroflexion and retraction', *Journal of Phonetics* 2: 233–7.

Biber, D. (1988) *Variation across Speech and Writing*, Cambridge University Press.

Bickerton, D. (1981) *Roots of Language*, Ann Arbor MI: Karoma.

(1990) *Language and Species*, University of Chicago Press.

Birdwhistell, R.L. (1961) 'Paralanguage twenty-five years after Sapir', in H.G. Brosin (ed.) *Lectures in Experimental Psychiatry*, Pittsburgh University Press, pp. 43–63; reprinted in J. Laver and S. Hutcheson (eds.) (1972), *Communication in Face to Face Interaction*, Harmondsworth: Penguin.

Björk, L. (1961) 'Velopharyngeal function in connected speech. Studies using tomography and cineradiography synchronized with speech spectrography', *Acta Radiologica* (Stockholm), Supplement no. 202.

Bladon, R.A.W. and F.J. Nolan (1977) 'A video-fluorographic investigation of tip and blade alveolars in English', *Journal of Phonetics* 5: 185–93.

Bladon, R.A.W., C. Clark and K. Mickey (1987) 'Production and perception of sibilant fricatives: Shona data', *Journal of the International Phonetic Association* 17: 39–65.

Blakemore, D. (1992) *Understanding Utterances*, Oxford: Blackwell.

Bless, D. and Abbs, J. (eds.) (1983) *Vocal Fold Physiology*, San Diego CA: College Hill Press.

Bogers, K., H. van der Hulst and M. Mous (eds.) (1986) *The Phonological Representation of Suprasegmentals: Studies on African Languages Offered to John M. Stewart on his 60th Birthday*, Dordrecht, and Cinnaminson NJ: Foris.

Bolinger, D.L. (1958) 'A theory of pitch accent in English', *Word* 14: 109–49.

(1964) 'Around the edge of language', *Harvard Educational Review* 34: 282–93; reprinted in D. Bolinger (ed.) (1972) *Intonation*, Harmondsworth: Penguin, pp. 19–29.

(ed.) (1972) *Intonation*, Harmondsworth: Penguin.

(1986) *Intonation and its Parts: Melody in Spoken English*, Stanford University Press, and London: Edward Arnold.

(1989) *Intonation and its Uses: Melody in Grammar and Discourse*, Stanford University Press, and London: Edward Arnold.

References

Bolozky, S. (1982) 'Remarks on rhythmic stress in Modern Hebrew', *Journal of Linguistics* 18: 275–90.

Boomer, D.S. (1965) 'Hesitation and grammatical encoding', *Language and Speech* 8: 148–58.

(1978) 'The phonemic clause: speech unit in human communication', in A.W. Siegman and S. Feldstein (eds.) (1978), *Nonverbal Behavior and Communication*, Hillsdale NJ: Lawrence Erlbaum Associates, pp. 245–62.

Boomer, D.S. and A.T. Dittman (1962) 'Hesitation pauses and juncture pauses in speech', *Language and Speech* 5: 215–20.

Boomer, D.S. and J. Laver (1968) 'Slips of the tongue', *British Disorders of Communication* 3: 2–11; reprinted in V.A. Fromkin (ed.) (1973) *Speech Errors as Linguistic Evidence*, The Hague: Mouton; also reprinted in J. Laver (1991) *The Gift of Speech: Papers in the Analysis of Speech and Voice*, Edinburgh University Press.

Borden, G.J. and K.S. Harris (1980) *Speech Science Primer: Physiology, Acoustics and Perception of Speech*, Baltimore MD: Williams and Wilkins.

Borgstrøm, C.H. (1940) *A Linguistic Survey of the Gaelic Dialects of Scotland*: vol. I, *The Dialects of the Outer Hebrides*, Norsk Tidsskrift for Sprofvidenskap Suppl.1.

(1941) *A Linguistic Survey of the Gaelic Dialects of Scotland*: vol. I, *The Dialects of Skye and Ross-shire*, Norsk Tidsskrift for Sprofvidenskap Suppl. 2.

Bortoni-Ricardo, S.M. (1985) *The Urbanization of Rural Dialect Speakers: a Sociolinguistic Study in Brazil*, Cambridge University Press.

Botinis, A. (1989) *Stress and Prosodic Structure in Greek*, Lund University Press.

Boves, L. (1984) *The Phonetic Basis of Perceptual Ratings of Running Speech*, Dordrecht, and Cinnaminson NJ: Foris.

Bowen, J.D. (1975) *Patterns of English Pronunciation*, Cambridge MA: Newbury House.

Braun, A. (1988) *Zum Merkmal 'Fortis/Lenis': phonologische Betrachtungen und instrumentalphonetische Untersuchungen an einem mittelhessischen Dialekt*, Stuttgart: Franz Steiner.

Breen, J.G. (1981) 'Margany and Gunya', in R.M.W. Dixon and B.J. Blake (eds.) (1981) *Handbook of Australian Languages*, vol. II, *Wargamay, the Mpakwithi Dialect of Anguthimri, Watjarri, Margany and Gunya, Tasmanian*, Canberra: Australian National University Press, pp. 274–393.

Brend R. M. (ed.) (1974) *Advances in Tagmemics*, Amsterdam: North-Holland.

(1975) *Studies in Tone and Intonation by Members of the Summer Institute of Linguistics*, Basel: Karger.

Bright, W. (1978) 'Sibilants and naturalness in aboriginal California', *Journal of California Anthropology, Papers in Linguistics* 1: 39–63.

(ed.) (1992) *International Encyclopedia of Linguistics*, 4 vols., New York and Oxford: Oxford University Press.

Bristow, G. (ed.) (1984) *Electronic Speech Synthesis: Techniques, Technology and Applications*, London: Granada.

Brito, G. (1975) 'The perception of nasal vowels in Brazilian Portuguese: a pilot study', in C.A. Ferguson, L.M. Hyman and J.J. Ohala (eds.), *Nasálfest. Papers from a Symposium on Nasals and Nasalization*, Language Universals Project, Stanford University, pp. 49–66.

Broad, D. (1973) 'Phonation', in F. Minifie, T. Hixon and F. Williams (eds.) *Normal Aspects of Speech, Hearing and Language*, Englewood Cliffs NJ: Prentice-Hall, pp. 127–67.

Brosin, H.G. (ed.) (1961) *Lectures in Experimental Psychiatry*, Pittsburgh University Press.

Brosnahan, L.F. and B. Malmberg (1970) *Introduction to Phonetics*, Cambridge University Press.

Browman, C.P. and L.M. Goldstein (1986) 'Towards an articulatory phonology', *Phonology Yearbook* 3: 219–52.

—— (1990) 'Tiers in articulatory phonology, with some implications for casual speech', in J. Kingston and M. Beckman (eds.) *Papers in Laboratory Phonology: Between the Grammar and the Physics of Speech*, Cambridge University Press, pp. 341–76.

Brown, E.K. and M. Millar (1978) 'Auxiliary verbs in Edinburgh speech', *Edinburgh University Department of Linguistics Work in Progress* 11: 146–84.

Brown, G. (1983) 'Prosodic structure and the given/new distinction', in A. Cutler and D.R. Ladd (eds.) *Prosody: Models and Measurements*, Berlin: Springer-Verlag, pp. 67–78.

Brown, G. and Yule, G. (1983) *Discourse Analysis*, Cambridge University Press.

Brown, G., K. Currie and J. Kenworthy (1980) *Questions of Intonation*, London: Croom Helm.

Brown, J.M. (1965) *From Ancient Thai to Modern Dialects*, Bangkok: Social Science Association Press of Thailand.

Brown, P. and S.C Levinson (1978) 'Politeness: some universals in language usage', in E.N. Goody (ed.) *Questions and Politeness: Strategies in Social Interaction*, Cambridge University Press, pp. 56–310; revised and published as an independent volume by P. Brown and S.C. Levinson (1987) *Politeness: Some Universals in Language Usage*, Cambridge University Press.

Bruce, G. (1977) *Swedish Word-accents in Sentence Perspective*, Lund: Gleerup.

—— (1982) 'Developing the Swedish intonation model', *Department of Linguistics Working Papers* 22: 51–116, University of Lund.

Bruce, G. and E. Gårding (1978) 'A prosodic typology for Swedish dialects', in E. Gårding, G. Bruce and R. Bannert (eds.) *Nordic Prosody*, Lund: Gleerup, pp. 219–28.

Buchler, J. (ed.) (1940) *The Philosophy of Peirce: Selected Writings*, London: Kegan Paul, Trench and Trubner.

Buck, R. (1984) *The Communication of Emotion*, New York: The Guilford Press.

Bukshaisha, F.A.M. (1985) 'An experimental phonetic study of some aspects of Qatari Arabic', PhD dissertation, University of Edinburgh.

References

Burks, A.W. (1949) 'Icon, index, symbol', *Philosophy and Phenomenological Research* 9: 673–89.

Burling, R. (1969) 'Proto-Karen: a re-analysis', *Occasional Papers of the Wolfenden Society on Tibeto-Burman Linguistics* 1: 1–116.

Buse, J.E. (1966) 'Number in Rarotongan Maori', in C.E. Bazell, J.C. Catford, M.A.K. Halliday and R.H. Robins (eds.) *In Memory of J.R. Firth*, London: Longmans Green, pp. 52–65.

Busnel, R.G. and A. Classe (1976) *Whistled Languages*, Berlin: Springer-Verlag.

Busnel, R.G., A. Moles and B. Vallancien (1962) 'Sur l'aspect phonétique d'une langage sifflée des Pyrénées françaises', *Proceedings of the Fourth International Congress of Phonetic Sciences*, Helsinki, pp. 533–46.

Butlin, R.T. (1936) 'On the alphabetic notation of certain phonetic features of Malayalam', *Bulletin of the School of Oriental and African Studies* 8: 437–47; reprinted in W.E. Jones and J. Laver (eds.) (1973) *Phonetics in Linguistics: a Book of Readings*, London: Longman.

Butterworth, B. (1975) 'Hesitation and semantic planning in speech', *Journal of Psycholinguistic Research* 4: 75–87.

—— (1980) 'Evidence from pauses in speech', in B. Butterworth (ed.) *Language Production*, vol. I, *Speech and Talk*, London: Academic Press, pp. 155–76.

Buxton, H. (1983) 'Temporal predictability in the perception of English speech', in A. Cutler and D.R. Ladd (eds.) *Prosody: Models and Measurements*, Berlin: Springer-Verlag, pp. 111–22.

Bynon, T. (1977) *Historical Linguistics*, Cambridge University Press.

Cagliari, L.C. (1977) 'An experimental study of nasality with particular reference to Brazilian Portuguese', PhD dissertation, University of Edinburgh.

Callow, J.C. (1962) 'The Apinayé language', PhD dissertation, University of London.

Calvert, D.R. (1986) *Descriptive Phonetics*, 2nd edn, New York: Thieme, and Stuttgart: Georg Thieme.

Campbell, G.L. (1991) *Compendium of the World's Languages*, 2 vols., London and New York: Routledge.

Campbell, L. (1973) 'On glottalic consonants', *International Journal of American Linguistics* 39: 44–6.

Campbell, N. (1992) 'Segmental elasticity and timing in Japanese speech', in Y. Tohkura, E. Vatikiotis-Bateson and Y. Sagisaka (eds.) *Speech Perception, Production and Linguistic Structure*, Tokyo: Ohmsha, and Amsterdam: IOS Press, pp. 403–18.

Canellada, M.J. and J. Madsen (1987) *Pronunciacion del Español*, Madrid: Editorial Castalia.

Canonge, E. D. (1957) 'Voiceless vowels in Comanche', *International Journal of American Linguistics* 23: 63–7.

Caplan, D. (1987) *Neurolinguistics and Linguistic Aphasiology*, Cambridge University Press.

(1988) 'The biological basis for language', in F.J. Newmeyer (ed.) *Linguistics: the Cambridge Survey*, vol. III, *Language: Psychological and Biological Aspects*, Cambridge University Press, pp. 237–55.

Carnochan, J. (1960) 'Vowel harmony in Igbo', *African Language Studies* 1: 155–63; reprinted in F.R. Palmer (ed.) (1970) *Prosodic Analysis*, London: Oxford University Press.

Carré, R. and M. Mrayati (1990) 'Articulatory–acoustic–phonetic relations and modeling, regions and modes', in W.J. Hardcastle and A. Marchal (eds.) *Speech Production and Speech Modelling*, Dordrecht: Kluwer Academic, pp. 211–40.

Carter, H. and G.P. Kahari (1979) *Kuverenga chiShona, an Introductory Shona Reader with Grammatical Sketch*, School of Oriental and African Studies, University of London.

Carver, C.M. (1987) *American Regional Dialects*, Ann Arbor MI: University of Michigan Press.

Casagrande, J.B. (1954) 'Comanche linguistic acculturation', *International Journal of American Linguistics* 20: 140–51.

Cassidy, F.G (ed.) (1985) *Dictionary of American Regional English*, Cambridge MA: Harvard University Press.

Catford, J.C. (1957) 'Vowel-systems of Scots dialects', *Transactions of the Philological Society*, pp. 107–17.

(1964) 'Phonation types', in D. Abercrombie, D.B. Fry, P.A.D. MacCarthy, N.C. Scott and J.L.M. Trim (eds.), *In Honour of Daniel Jones*, London: Longmans, Green, pp. 26–37.

(1977a) *Fundamental Problems in Phonetics*, Edinburgh University Press.

(1977b) 'Mountain of tongues: the languages of the Caucasus', *Annual Review of Anthropology* 6: 283–314.

(1984) 'Instrumental data and linguistic phonetics', in J.A. Higgs and R. Thelwall (eds.), *Topics in Linguistic Phonetics: in Honour of E.T. Uldall*, Occasional Papers in Linguistics and Language Learning no. 9, Department of Linguistics, The New University of Ulster, pp. 23–48.

(1988) *A Practical Introduction to Phonetics*, Oxford: Clarendon Press.

Chadwick, J. (1958) *The Decipherment of Linear B*, Cambridge University Press.

Chafe, W. (1970) *Meaning and the Structure of Language*, Chicago University Press.

Chaika, E. (1989) *Language: the Social Mirror*, 2nd edn, New York: Newbury House, Harper and Row.

Chaiyanara, P.M. (1983) 'Dialek Melayu Patani dan Bahasa Malaysia: Satu Kaijian Perbandingan dari segi Fonologi, Morfologi dan Syntaksis', Master's thesis, University of Malaya.

Chambers, J.K. and P. Trudgill (1980) *Dialectology*, Cambridge University Press.

Chang, K. (1973) 'The reconstruction of proto-Miao-Yao tones', *Bulletin of the Institute of History and Philology – Academica Sinica* 44: 541–628.

Chang, N.-C. T. (1958) 'Tones and intonation in the Chengtu dialect (Szechuan,

China)', *Phonetica* 2: 59–84; reprinted in D. Bolinger (ed.) (1972) *Intonation*, Harmondsworth: Penguin.

Chao, Y.R. (1930) 'A system of tone letters', *le maître phonétique* 30: 24–7.

—— (1970) 'The Changchow dialect', *Journal of the American Oriental Society* 90: 45–59.

Chapallaz, M. (1979) *The Pronunciation of Italian: a Practical Introduction*, London: Bell and Hyman.

Chasaide, A. Ní (1985) 'Preaspiration in phonological stop contrasts', PhD dissertation, University College of North Wales, Bangor.

Chasaide, A. Ní and C. O Dochartaigh (1984) 'Some durational aspects of preaspiration', in J.A. Higgs and R. Thelwall (eds.) *Topics in Linguistic Phonetics: in Honour of E.T. Uldall*, Occasional Papers in Linguistics and Language Learning no. 9, March, Department of Linguistics, The New University of Ulster, pp. 141–57.

Cheepen, C. (1988) *The Predictability of Informal Conversation*, London: Pinter.

Cheng, C.C. (1973) 'A quantitative study of tone in Chinese', *Journal of Chinese Linguistics* 1: 93–110.

Cheshire, J. (ed.) (1991) *English Around the World*, Cambridge University Press.

Chomsky, N. (1965) *Aspects of the Theory of Syntax*, Cambridge MA: Massachusetts Institute of Technology Press.

Chomsky, N. and M. Halle (1968) *The Sound Pattern of English*, New York: Harper and Row.

Christopherson, P. (1952) 'The glottal stop in English', *English Studies* 33: 156–63.

Chuang, C.K., S. Hiki, T. Sone and T. Nimura (1972) 'The acoustical features and perceptual cues of the four tones of standard colloquial Chinese', *Proceedings of the 7th International Congress of Acoustics*, vol. III, Budapest: Akadémai Kiadó, pp. 297–300.

Cicero: *Brutus*, and *De Oratore*, trans. J.S. Watson (1899), London: George Bell and Sons.

Cid Uribe, M.E. (1989) 'Contrastive analysis of English and Spanish intonation using computer corpora – a preliminary study', PhD dissertation, University of Leeds.

Cid Uribe, M.E. and P. Roach (1990) 'Spanish intonation: design and implementation of a machine-readable corpus', *Journal of the International Phonetic Association* 20: 1–8.

Clark, H.H. and E.V. Clark (1977) *Psychology and Language: an Introduction to Psycholinguistics*, New York: Harcourt Brace Jovanovich.

Clark, J.E. and C. Yallop (1990) *An Introduction to Phonetics and Phonology*, Oxford: Basil Blackwell.

Clarke, S. (1985) 'Sociolinguistic variation in a small urban context: the St John's survey', in H.J. Warkentyne (ed.) *Papers from the Fifth International Conference on Methods in Dialectology 1984*, Department of Linguistics, University of Victoria, British Columbia, pp. 143–53.

Classe, A. (1939) *The Rhythm of English Prose*, Oxford: Basil Blackwell.

(1957) 'Phonetics of the Silbo Gomero', *Archivum Linguisticum* 9: 44–61.

Clements, G.N. (1977) 'The autosegmental treatment of vowel harmony', in W.U. Dressler and O.E. Pfeiffer (eds.) *Phonologica 1976*, Innsbrucker Beiträger zür Sprachwissenschaft, pp. 111–19.

(1981) 'Akan vowel harmony: a nonlinear analysis', *Harvard Studies in Phonology* 2: 108–77.

Clements, G.N. and S.J. Keyser (1983) *CV Phonology: a Generative Theory of the Syllable*, Cambridge MA: Massachusetts Institute of Technology Press.

Clumeck, H. (1971) 'Degrees of nasal coarticulation', Monthly internal memorandum (July), Phonology Laboratory, University of California at Berkeley.

(1975) 'A cross-linguistic investigation of vowel nasalization: an instrumental study', in C.A. Ferguson, L.M. Hyman and J.J. Ohala (eds.) *Nasálfest: Papers from a Symposium on Nasals and Nasalization*, Language Universals Project, Stanford University CA.

(1976) 'Patterns of soft palate movements in six languages', *Journal of Phonetics* 4: 337–52.

Cohen, J.M. and M.J. Cohen (1971) *The Penguin Dictionary of Modern Quotations*, Harmondsworth: Penguin.

Cohen, A. and Nooteboom, S.G. (eds.) (1975) *Structure and Process in Speech Perception*, Berlin, Heidelberg and New York: Springer-Verlag.

Collier, R. (1975) 'Physiological correlates of intonation patterns', *Journal of the Acoustical Society of America* 58: 249–55.

(1983) 'Some physiological and perceptual constraints on tonal systems', *Linguistics* 21: 237–47.

(1989) 'On the phonology of Dutch intonation', in F.J. Heyvaert and F. Steurs (eds.) *Worlds behind Words: Essays in Honour of Professor Dr F.G. Droste*, Leuven University Press, pp. 245–59.

Collier, R. and J. 't Hart (1975) 'The role of intonation in speech perception', in A. Cohen and S.G. Nooteboom (eds.), *Structure and Process in Speech Perception*, Berlin, Heidelberg and New York: Springer-Verlag, pp. 107–23.

(1981) *Cursus Nederlandse Intonatie*, Limburg: Wetenschappelijk Onderwijs.

The Collins Dictionary of the English Language (1986), (P. Hanks, W.T. McLeod and L. Urdang, Chief Editors), 2nd edn, London and Glasgow: Collins.

Comrie, B. (1976) *Aspect: an Introduction to the Study of Verbal Aspect and Related Problems*, Cambridge University Press.

(1981) *The Languages of the Soviet Union*, Cambridge University Press.

(1985) *Tense*, Cambridge University Press.

(ed.) (1987) *The World's Major Languages*, London: Croom Helm.

Conklin, H. C. (1959) 'Linguistic play in its cultural context', *Language* 35: 631–6.

Connell, B. and D.R. Ladd (1990) 'Aspects of pitch realization in Yoruba', *Phonology* 7: 1–29.

References

Cook, T.L. (1969) 'Efik', in E. Dunstan (ed.), *Twelve Nigerian Languages*, London: Longmans Green, pp. 35–46.

Cooper, W.E. and J. Paccia-Cooper (1980) *Syntax and Speech*, Cambridge MA: Harvard University Press.

Cooper, W.E. and J.M. Sorensen (1981) *Fundamental Frequency in Sentence Production*, New York: Springer-Verlag.

Cooper, W.E and E.C.T. Walker (1979) *Sentence Processing: Psycholinguistic Studies Presented to Merrill Garrett*, Hillsdale NJ: Lawrence Erlbaum Associates.

Corbett, G.G. (1991) *Gender*, Cambridge University Press.

Coulmas, F. (ed.) (1981) *Conversational Routine*, The Hague: Mouton.

(1989) *The Writing Systems of the World*, Oxford: Basil Blackwell.

Couper-Kuhlen, E. (1986) *An Introduction to English Prosody*, London: Edward Arnold.

Coupland, N. (1988) *Dialect in Use: Sociolinguistic Variation in Cardiff English*, Cardiff: University of Wales Press.

Coustenoble, H.N. (1929) 'Quelques observations sur la prononciation de la langue Wolof', *le maître phonétique*, 3rd Series, Jan.-Mar., pp. 1–3.

(1945) *La Phonétique du Provençal Moderne en Terre d'Arles*, Hertford: Stephen Austin.

Coustenoble, H.N. and L.E. Armstrong (1934) *Studies in French Intonation*, Cambridge University Press.

Cowan, G.M. (1948) 'Mazateco whistled speech', *Language* 24: 280–6; reprinted in D. Hymes (ed.) (1964) *Language in Culture and Society: a Reader in Linguistics and Anthropology*, New York: Harper and Row.

Crandall, I.B. (1925) 'The sounds of speech', *Bell System Technical Journal* 4: 586–622.

Crawford, J.C. (1963) *Totontepec Mixe phonotagmemics*, Summer Institute of Linguistics Publications no. 8, Summer Institute of Linguistics and University of Oklahoma, Norman OK.

Di Cristo, A. and M. Chafcouloff (1976) 'An acoustic investigation of microprosodic effects in French vowels', paper presented at the 14th Conference on Acoustics, High Tatra, Czechoslovakia.

Croft, W. (1990) *Typology and Universals*, Cambridge University Press.

Crompton, A. (1980) 'Timing patterns in French', *Phonetica* 37: 205–34.

Crothers, J. (1978a) 'Typology and universals of vowel systems', in J.H. Greenberg (ed.) (1978b) *Universals of Human Language*, vol. I, *Theory and Methodology*, Stanford University Press, pp. 93–152.

Crowley, T. (1978) *The Middle Clarence Dialects of Bandjalang*, Canberra: Australian Institute of Aboriginal Studies.

Cruse, D.A. (1986) *Lexical Semantics*, Cambridge University Press.

Cruttenden, A. (1986) *Intonation*, Cambridge University Press.

(1992) 'Clicks and syllables in the phonology of Dama', *Lingua* 86: 101–17.

Crystal, D. (1969) *Prosodic Systems and Intonation in English*, Cambridge University Press.

(1975) *The English Tone of Voice*, London: Edward Arnold.

(1985) *A Dictionary of Linguistics and Phonetics*, 2nd edn, Oxford: Basil Blackwell, in association with André Deutsch, London (*see also* Crystal 1991).

(1987) *The Cambridge Encyclopedia of Language*, Cambridge University Press.

(1988) *The English Language*, London: Penguin.

(1991) *A Dictionary of Linguistics and Phonetics*, 3rd edn, Oxford: Basil Blackwell

Crystal, D. and R. Quirk (1964) *Systems of Prosodic and Paralinguistic Features in English*, The Hague: Mouton.

Crystal, T. and A. House (1982) 'Segmental durations in connected speech signals: preliminary results', *Journal of the Acoustical Society of America* 72: 705–16.

Cutler, A. (1977) 'The context-dependence of "intonational meaning" ', *Papers from the 13th Regional Meeting*, Chicago Linguistic Society, pp. 104–15.

Cutler, A. and D.R. Ladd (eds.) (1983) *Prosody: Models and Measurements*, Berlin: Springer-Verlag.

Daniloff, R.G. (ed.) (1983) *Articulation Assessment and Treatment Issues*, San Diego CA: College-Hill Press.

Daniloff, R.G. and R.E. Hammarberg (1973) 'On defining co-articulation', *Journal of Phonetics* 1: 239–48.

Daniloff, R.G. and K. Moll (1968) 'Coarticulation of lip rounding', *Journal of Speech and Hearing Research* 11: 707–21.

Darby, J. (ed.) (1981) *Speech Evaluation in Psychiatry*, New York : Grune and Stratton.

Darwin, C. (1872) *The Expression of Emotion in Man and Animals*, London: John Murray.

Dauer, R.M. (1978) 'Tonal patterns in the Kyooto-Osaka accent of Standard Japanese', *Edinburgh University Department of Linguistics Work in Progress* 11: 87–106.

(1980a) 'Stress and rhythm in modern Greek', PhD dissertation, University of Edinburgh.

(1980b) 'The reduction of unstressed high vowels in modern Greek', *Journal of the International Phonetic Association* 10: 17–27.

(1983) 'Stress-timing and syllable-timing re-analyzed', *Journal of Phonetics* 11: 51–62.

Davies, S. (1979) 'A comparative study of Yong and Standard Thai', in T.L. Thongkum, V. Panupong, P. Kullavanijaya and M.R.K. Tingsabadh (eds.), *Studies in Tai and Mon-Khmer Phonetics and Phonology: in Honour of Eugénie Henderson*, Bangkok: Chulalongkorn University Press, pp. 26–48.

Davis, S. (1988) 'Syllable onsets as a factor in stress rules', *Phonology* 5: 1–19.

Dechert, H.W. and M. Raupach (eds.) (1980) *Temporal Variables in Speech: Studies in Honour of Frieda Goldman-Eisler*, The Hague: Mouton.

Deese, J. (1980) 'Pauses, prosody and the demands of production in language', in

References

H.W. Dechert and M. Raupach (eds.) (1980) *Temporal Variables in Speech: Studies in Honour of Frieda Goldman-Eisler*, The Hague: Mouton, pp. 69–84.

(1984) *Thought into Speech: the Psychology of a Language*, Englewood Cliffs: Prentice-Hall.

Delattre, P. (1965) *Comparing the Phonetic Features of English, French, German and Spanish: an Interim Report*, Heidelberg: Julius Groos.

(1966) 'A comparison of syllable length conditioning among languages', *International Review of Applied Linguistics* 7: 295–325.

Delbridge, A. (ed.) (1981) *The Macquarie Dictionary*, McMahon's Point, NSW, Australia: Macquarie Library.

Dickson, D.R. and W. Maue-Dickson (1982) *Anatomical and Physiological Bases of Speech*, Boston MA: Little, Brown.

Dieth, E. (1950) *Vademecum der Phonetik*, Bern: Francke.

Dimmendaal, G. (1983) *The Turkana Language*, Dordrecht: Foris.

Diringer, D. (1962) *Writing*, London: Thames and Hudson.

(1968) *The Alphabet: a Key to the History of Mankind*, 2 vols., 3rd rev. edn, New York: Funk and Wagnalls.

Dittmann, A.T. and L.G. Llewellyn (1967) 'The phonemic clause as a unit of speech decoding', *Journal of Personality and Social Psychology* 6: 341–9.

(1968) 'Relationship between vocalization and head nods as listener responses', *Journal of Personality and Social Psychology* 9: 79–84.

Dixon, N.R. and T.B. Martin (eds.) (1979) *Automatic Speech and Speaker Recognition*, New York: Institution of Electrical and Electronic Engineers and John Wiley and Sons.

Dixon, R.M.W. (1972) *The Dyirbal Language of North Queensland*, Cambridge University Press.

(1977) *A Grammar of Yidiɲ*, Cambridge University Press.

(1980) *The Languages of Australia*, Cambridge University Press.

Dixon, R.M.W. and B.J. Blake (eds.) (1981) *Handbook of Australian Languages*, vol. II, *Wargamay, the Mpakwithi Dialect of Anguthimri, Watjarri, Margany and Gunya, Tasmanian*, Canberra: Australian National University Press.

Docherty, G.J. (1992) *The Timing of Voicing in British English Obstruents*, Berlin: Foris.

Doke, C.M. (1926) *The Phonetics of the Zulu Language*, special issue of *Bantu Studies*.

(1931a) *Report on the Unification of the Shona Dialects, Containing an Outline of Shona Phonetics*, Report carried out under the auspices of the Government of Southern Rhodesia and the Carnegie Corporation.

(1931b) *A Comparative Study in Shona Phonetics*, Johannesburg: University of Witwatersrand Press.

Douglas, W.H. (1981) 'Watjarri', in R.M.W. Dixon and B.J. Blake (eds.) *Handbook of Australian Languages*, vol. II, Canberra: Australian National University Press, pp. 197–274.

Dressler, W.U. and O.E. Pfeiffer (eds.) (1977) *Phonologica 1976*, Innsbrucker Beiträger zur Sprachwissenschaft.

Duez, D. (1982) 'Silent and non-silent pauses in three speech styles', *Language and Speech* 25: 11–28.

(1991) *La Pause dans la Parole de l'Homme Politique*, Paris: Editions du Centre National de la Recherche Scientifique.

Dunstan, E. (ed.) (1969) *Twelve Nigerian Languages: a Handbook on their Sound Systems for Teachers of English*, London and Harlow: Longmans, Green.

Durand, J. (1990) *Generative and Non-Linear Phonology*, London and New York: Longman.

Eady, S.J. (1982) 'Differences in the F0 patterns of speech: tone language versus stress language', *Language and Speech* 25: 29–42.

Einstein, A. (1933) 'On the method of theoretical physics', Spencer Lecture, University of Oxford.

Ekman, P. (1984) 'Methods for measuring facial action', in K.R. Scherer and P. Ekman (eds.) *Handbook of Methods in Nonverbal Behavior Research*, Cambridge University Press and Paris: Editions de la Maison des Sciences de l'Homme, pp. 45–90.

Ekman, P. and W.V. Friesen, (1978) *Facial Action Coding System*, Palo Alto CA: Consulting Psychologists Press.

Ekman, P., W.V. Friesen and P. Ellsworth (1972) *Emotion in the Human Face: Guidelines for Research and an Integration of Findings*, New York: Pergamon.

Elert, C. (1964) *Phonologic Studies of Quantity in Swedish*, Stockholm: Almqvist and Wiksell.

Elliot, A.J. (1981) *Child Language*, Cambridge University Press.

Engstrand, O. (1987) 'Preaspiration and the voicing contrast in Lule Sami', *Phonetica* 44: 103–16.

Engstrand, O. and C. Kylander (eds.) (1991) *Proceedings of the Symposium on Current Phonetic Research Paradigms: Implications for Speech Motor Control*, Stockholm, 13–16 August, 1991, published as vol. XIV of *Phonetic Experimental Research at the Institute of Linguistics, University of Stockholm (PERILUS)*.

Esling, J.H. (1978) 'The identification of features of voice quality in social groups', *Journal of the International Phonetic Association* 8: 18–23.

(1986) 'The setting component of accent in Vancouver: spectral analyses of vowels by social group in the Survey of Vancouver English', Final Report on Research Grant no. 410–85–1481, Social Sciences and Humanities Research Council of Canada.

(1991) *Phonetic Database* (Instruction Manual), joint project of Kay Elemetrics Corp., Pine Brook NJ, and Speech Technology Research Ltd, University of Victoria, British Columbia.

Esling, J.H. and B.C. Dickson (1985) 'Acoustical procedures for articulatory setting

References

analysis in accent', in H.J. Warkentyne (ed.), *Papers from the Fifth International Conference on Methods in Dialectology*, University of Victoria, British Columbia, pp.155–70.

Essien, O.E. (1979) 'Length and nasalization in Ibibio', *Edinburgh University Department of Linguistics Work in Progress* 12: 109–21.

D'Eugenio, A. (1976) 'The intonation systems of Italian and English', *Rassegna Italiana di Linguistica Applicata* 8: 57–85.

Everett, D.L. (1982) 'Phonetic rarities in Pirahã', *Journal of the International Phonetic Association* 12: 94–6.

Everett, D.L. and K. Everett (1984) 'Syllable onsets and stress placement in Pirahã', *Proceedings of the West Coast Conference on Formal Linguistics* 3: 105–16.

Ewan, W.G. (1979) *Laryngeal Behavior in Speech*, Report of the Phonology Laboratory, University of California at Berkeley, no. 3.

Ewen, C.J. (1982) 'The internal structure of complex segments', in H. van der Hulst and N. Smith (eds.) *The Structure of Phonological Representations*, vol. II, Dordrecht: Foris, pp.26–67.

Fairbanks, G. (1960) *Voice and Articulation Drill-book*, 2nd edn, New York, NY: Harper and Row.

Falc'hun, F. (1951) *Le système consonantique du breton avec une étude comparative de phonétique expérimentale*, Rennes: Imprimeries Réunies.

Fallside, F. and W. Woods (eds.) (1985) *Computer Speech Processing*, London: Prentice-Hall International.

Fant, G. (1956) 'On the predictability of formant levels and spectrum envelopes from formant frequencies', in M. Halle, H. Lunt and H. MacLean (eds.), *For Roman Jakobson*, The Hague: Mouton, pp.109–20.

—— (1959) 'Acoustic analysis and synthesis of speech with applications to Swedish', *Ericsson Technics Report*, no. 1, Stockholm.

—— (1960) *Acoustic Theory of Speech Production*, The Hague: Mouton.

—— (1973) *Speech Sounds and Features*, Cambridge MA: Massachusetts Institute of Technology Press.

Fant, G. and A. Kruckenberg (1989) 'Preliminaries to the study of Swedish prose reading and reading style', *Quarterly Progress and Status Report* 2: 1–80, Speech Transmission Laboratory, Royal Institute of Technology (KTH), Stockholm.

Farnetani, E. (1990) 'V–C–V lingual coarticulation and its spatiotemporal domain', in W.J. Hardcastle and A. Marchal (eds.) *Speech Production and Speech Modelling*, Dordrecht: Kluwer Academic, pp. 93–130.

Fasold, R. (1984) *The Sociolinguistics of Society*, Oxford: Blackwell.

—— (1989) *The Sociolinguistics of Language*, Oxford: Blackwell.

Faure, G. (1973) 'La description phonologique des systèmes prosodiques', in A.W. Grundström and P.R. Léon (eds.) *Interrogation et intonation en français standard et en français canadien*, Montréal: Didier, pp. 1–16.

Feibleman, J.K. (1970) *An Introduction to the Philosophy of Charles S. Peirce*,

Interpreted as a System, Cambridge MA: Massachusetts Institute of Technology Press.

Fengtong, Z. (1989) 'The initials of Chengdu speech', *Journal of the International Phonetic Association* 15: 59–68.

Ferguson, C.A. and M. Chowdhury (1960) 'The phonemes of Bengali', *Language* 36: 22–59.

Ferguson, C.A., L.M. Hyman and J.J. Ohala (eds.) (1975) *Nasálfest. Papers from a Symposium on Nasals and Nasalization*, Language Universals Project, Stanford University.

Fintoft, K. (1961) 'The duration of some Norwegian speech sounds', *Phonetica* 7: 19–39.

Firchow, I. and Firchow, J. (1969) 'An abbreviated phoneme inventory', *Anthropological Linguistics* 11: 271–6.

Firth, J.R. (1948) 'Sounds and prosodies', *Transactions of the Philological Society*, pp. 127–52; reprinted in W.E. Jones and J. Laver (eds.) (1973) *Phonetics in Linguistics: a Book of Readings*, London: Longman.

—— (1957) *Papers in Linguistics 1934–1951*, London: Oxford University Press.

Fischer-Jørgensen, E. (1955) 'Om vokallaengde i dansk rigsmål', *Nordisk Tidsskrift for Tale og Stemme* 15: 33–56.

—— (1964) 'Sound duration and place of articulation', *Zeitschrift für Phonetik* 17: 175–207.

—— (1967) 'Phonetic analysis of breathy (murmured) vowels in Gujarati', *Indian Linguistics* 28: 71–139.

—— (1975) *Trends in Phonological Theory: a Historical Introduction*, Copenhagen: Akademisk Forlag.

—— (1979) 'Temporal relations in consonant-vowel syllables with stop consonants based on Danish material', in B. Lindblom and S. Öhman (eds.) *Frontiers of Speech Communication Research*, New York: Academic Press, pp. 51–68.

—— (1985) 'Some basic vowel features, their articulatory correlates, and their explanatory power in phonology', in V.A. Fromkin (ed.) (1985) *Phonetic Linguistics: Essays in Honor of Peter Ladefoged*, Orlando FL: Academic Press, pp. 79–100.

—— (1987) 'A phonetic study of the stød in Standard Danish', *Annual Report of the Institute of Phonetics of the University of Copenhagen* 21: 55–265.

—— (1990) 'Intrinsic F_0 in tense and lax vowels with special reference to German', *Phonetica* 47: 99–140.

Fischer-Jørgensen, E., J. Rischel and N. Thorsen (eds.) (1979) *Proceedings of the Ninth International Congress of Phonetic Sciences*, 2 vols., Institute of Phonetics, University of Copenhagen.

Fishman, J.A. (ed.) (1968) *Readings in the Sociology of Language*, The Hague: Mouton.

Flanagan, J.L. (1957) 'Estimates of the maximum precision necessary in quantizing certain "dimensions" of vowel sounds', *Journal of the Acoustical Society of America* 24: 533–4.

(1965) *Speech Analysis, Synthesis and Perception*, Berlin: Springer-Verlag.

Flanagan, J.L. and L.R. Rabiner (eds.) (1973) *Speech Synthesis*, Stroudsburg PA: Dowden, Hutchinson and Ross.

Fletcher, J.M. (1988) 'An acoustic study of timing in French', PhD Dissertation, University of Reading, England.

(1991) 'Rhythm and final lengthening in French', *Journal of Phonetics* 19: 193–212.

Flores d'Arcais, G.B. (1988) 'Language perception', in F.J. Newmeyer (ed.) (1988) *Linguistics: the Cambridge Survey*, vol. III *Language: Psychological and Biological Aspects*, Cambridge University Press, pp. 97–123.

Fodor, J.A., T.G. Bever and M.F. Garrett (1974) *The Psychology of Language: an Introduction to Psycholinguistics and Generative Grammar*, New York: McGraw-Hill.

Foldvik, A.K. (1981) 'Voice quality in Norwegian dialects', in T. Fretheim (ed.), *Nordic Prosody* 2: 228–32, Trondheim.

Foley, W.F. (1986) *The Papuan Languages of New Guinea*, Cambridge University Press.

Fortune, G. (1955) *An Analytical Grammar of Shona*, London: Longmans, Green.

Foss, D.J. and D.T. Hakes (1978) *Psycholinguistics: an Introduction to the Psychology of Language*, Englewood Cliffs NJ: Prentice-Hall.

Fowler, C.A. (1980) 'Coarticulation and theories of extrinsic timing control', *Journal of Phonetics* 8: 113–33.

Fowler, C.A., P. Rubin, R.E. Remez and M.T. Turvey (1980) 'Implications for speech production of a general theory of action', in B. Butterworth (ed.) *Language Production*, vol. I, *Speech and Talk*, London: Academic Press, pp. 373–420.

Fox, A. (1974) 'The IPA alphabet: remarks on some proposals for reform', *Journal of the International Phonetic Association* 4: 76–9.

(1984) *German Intonation: an Outline*, Oxford: Clarendon Press.

Fox, G.J. (1979) *Big Nambas Grammar*, Pacific Linguistics, Series B, no. 60.

Fraisse, P. (1956) *Les structures rhythmiques*, Louvain: Publications Universitaires de Louvain.

Fraisse, P. (1963) *The Psychology of Time*, New York: Harper and Row.

Francis, W.N. (ed.) (1958) *The Structure of American English*, New York: The Ronald Press.

Frauenfelder, U. H. and L. K. Tyler (eds.) (1987) *Spoken Word Recognition*, Cambridge, MA: Massachusetts Institute of Technology Press (originally published as a special issue of *COGNITION: an International Journal of Cognitive Science*, vol. 25, (1987) ed. J. Mehler, Amsterdam: Elsevier Science).

Fromkin, V.A. (ed.) (1973) *Speech Errors as Linguistic Evidence*, The Hague: Mouton.

(ed.) (1978) *Tone: a Linguistic Survey*, New York: Academic Press.

(ed.) (1980) *Errors in Linguistic Performance: Slips of the Tongue, Ear, Pen, and Hand*, New York: Academic Press.

(ed.) (1985) *Phonetic Linguistics: Essays in Honor of Peter Ladefoged*, Orlando FL: Academic Press.

Fromkin, V.A. and R. Rodman (1974) *An Introduction to Language*, New York: Holt, Rinehart and Winston.

Fry, D.B. (1947) 'The frequency of occurrence of speech sounds in Southern English', *Archives Néerlandaises de Phonétique Expérimentale* 20: 103–6.

—— (1955) 'Duration and intensity as physical correlates of linguistic stress', *Journal of the Acoustical Society of America* 27: 765–8.

—— (1958) 'Experiments in the perception of stress', *Language and Speech* 1: 126–52; reprinted in D.B. Fry (ed.) (1976) *Acoustic Phonetics: a Course of Basic Readings*, Cambridge University Press.

—— (1965) 'The dependence of stress judgments on vowel formant structure', in E. Zwirner and W. Bethge (eds.), *Proceedings of the Sixth International Congress of Phonetic Sciences*, Basel: Karger, pp. 306–11; reprinted in D.B. Fry (ed.) (1976) *Acoustic Phonetics: a Course of Basic Readings*, Cambridge University Press.

—— (ed.) (1976) *Acoustic Phonetics: a Course of Basic Readings*, Cambridge University Press.

—— (1979) *The Physics of Speech*, Cambridge University Press.

Fudge, E.C. (1969) 'Syllables', *Journal of Linguistics* 5: 253–86.

—— (1984) *English Word-Stress*, London: Allen and Unwin.

Fujimura, O. and J. Lovins (1978) 'Syllables as concatenative phonetic units', in A. Bell and J.B. Hooper (eds.) *Syllables and Segments*, Amsterdam: North-Holland.

Fujimura, O. and M. Sawashima (1971) 'Consonant sequences and laryngeal control', *Annual Bulletin of the Research Institute of Logopedics and Phoniatrics* 5: 1–6, Tokyo.

Fujisaki, H. (1981) 'Dynamic characteristics of voice fundamental frequency in speech and singing', paper presented at the *Federation of Acoustical Societies of Europe Fourth Symposium*, Venice.

Fujisaki, H. and K. Hirose (1984) 'Analysis of voice fundamental frequency contours for declarative sentences of Japanese', *Journal of the Acoustical Society of Japan* 5: 233–42.

Fujisaki, H. and S. Nagashima (1969) 'A model for synthesis of pitch contours of connected speech', *Annual Report of the Engineering Research Institute* 28: 53–60, University of Tokyo.

Fujisaki, H. and H. Sudo (1971) 'Synthesis by rule of prosodic features of connected Japanese', *Proceedings of the Seventh International Congress on Acoustics* 3: 133–6, Budapest: Akadémai Kiadó.

Fujisaki, H., K. Hirose and N. Takahashi (1990) 'Manifestation of linguistic and para-linguistic information in the voice fundamental frequency contours of spoken Japanese', *Proceedings of the First International Conference on Spoken Language Processing* (Kobe, Japan) 12.1–12.4.

Fujisaki, H., K. Hirose, H. Kawai and Y. Asano (1990) 'A system for synthesis of high quality speech from Japanese text', in H. Fujisaki (ed.) *Recent Research toward Advanced Man-Machine Interface through Spoken Language*, published by the Steering Group of the Priority Research Area 'Advanced Man-Machine Interface through Spoken Language', Ministry of Education, Science and Culture, Japan, pp. 302–20.

Fuller, M. (1990) 'Pulmonic ingressive fricatives in Tsou', *Journal of the International Phonetic Association* 20: 9–14.

Gandour, J.T. (1975a) 'On the representation of tone in Siamese', in J.G. Harris and J.R. Chamberlain, (eds.) *Studies in Tai Linguistics in Honor of William J. Gedney*, Bangkok: Central Institute of English Language, Office of State Universities, pp.170–95.

(1975b) 'The features of the larynx: N-ary or Binary?', *Phonetica* 32: 241–53.

(1978) 'The perception of tone', in V.A. Fromkin (ed.), *Tone: a Linguistic Survey*, New York: Academic Press, pp. 41–76.

(1979) 'Tonal rules for English loanwords in Thai', in T.L. Thongkum, V. Panupong, P. Kullavanijaya and M.R.K. Tingsabadh (eds.) *Studies in Tai and Mon-Khmer Phonetics and Phonology: in Honour of Eugénie Henderson*, Bangkok: Chulalongkorn University Press, pp. 94–105.

Gårding, E. (1977) *The Scandinavian Word Accents*, Travaux de l'Institut de Linguistique de Lund 11, Lund: Gleerup.

(1979) 'Sentence intonation in Swedish', *Phonetica* 36: 207–15.

(1983) 'A generative model of intonation', in A. Cutler and D.R. Ladd (eds.) *Prosody: Models and Measurements*, Berlin: Springer-Verlag, pp. 11–26.

Gårding, E., G. Bruce and R. Bannert (eds.) (1978) *Nordic Prosody*, Travaux de l'Institut de Linguistique de Lund 13, Lund: Gleerup.

Garman, M. (1990) *Psycholinguistics*, Cambridge University Press.

Garnes, S. (1973) 'Phonetic evidence supporting a phonological analysis', *Journal of Phonetics* 1: 272–83.

Garrett, M.F. (1988) 'Processes in language production', in F.J. Newmeyer (ed.) *Linguistics: the Cambridge Survey*, vol. III *Language: Psychological and Biological Aspects*, Cambridge University Press, pp. 69–96.

Gauffin, J. (1977) 'Mechanisms of larynx tube constriction', *Phonetica* 34: 307–9.

Gay, T. (1968) 'Effect of speaking rate on diphthong formant movements', *Journal of the Acoustical Society of America* 44: 1570–5.

(1978) 'Articulatory units: segments or syllables?' in A. Bell and J.B. Hooper (eds.) *Syllables and Segments*, Amsterdam: North-Holland, pp. 121–31.

(1981) 'Mechanisms in the control of speech rate', *Phonetica* 38: 148–58.

Gedney, W. (1973) 'A checklist for determining tones in Tai dialects', in M.E. Smith (ed.) *Studies in Linguistics in Honor of G.L. Trager*, The Hague: Mouton, pp. 423–37.

Gelb, I.J. (1952) *A Study of Writing*, University of Chicago Press, (2nd edn 1963).

Gibbon, D. (1976) *Perspectives of Intonation Analysis*, Forum Linguisticum 9, Frankfurt: Peter Lang.

Gibson, L.F. (1956) 'Pame (Otomi) phonemics and morphophonemics', *International Journal of American Linguistics* 22: 242–65.

Giegerich, H.J. (1985) *Metrical Phonology and Phonological Structure*, Cambridge University Press.

⸺ (1992) *English Phonology: an Introduction*, Cambridge University Press.

Giles, H., K.R. Scherer and D.M. Taylor (1979) 'Speech markers in social interaction', in K.R. Scherer and H. Giles (eds.) *Social Markers in Speech*, Cambridge University Press and Maison des Sciences de l'Homme, Paris, pp. 343–82.

Gillies, W. (1988) 'The Atlas of Gaelic dialects: an interim report', *Scottish Gaelic Studies* 15: 1–5.

Gimson, A.C. (1962) *An Introduction to the Pronunciation of English*, London: Edward Arnold.

⸺ (1967) *English Pronouncing Dictionary* (13th edn, originally compiled by Daniel Jones), London: Dent.

⸺ (1977) *English Pronouncing Dictionary* (14th edn, originally compiled by Daniel Jones), London: Dent.

⸺ (1989) *An Introduction to the Pronunciation of English* (4th edn, edited by S. Ramsaran), London: Edward Arnold.

Gleason, H.A., Jr (1961) *An Introduction to Descriptive Linguistics*, rev. edn, New York: Holt, Rinehart and Winston.

Goldman-Eisler, F. (1968) *Psycholinguistics: Experiments in Spontaneous Speech*, London: Academic Press.

Goldsmith, J. (1985) 'Vowel harmony in Khalkha Mongolian, Yaka, Finnish and Hungarian', *Phonology Yearbook* 2: 251–74.

⸺ (1990) *Autosegmental and Metrical Phonology: an Introduction*, Oxford: Blackwell.

Goldstein, L. (1977) *Three Studies in Speech Perception: Features, Relative Salience and Bias, UCLA Working Papers in Phonetics 39*, Phonetics Laboratory, Department of Linguistics, University of California at Los Angeles.

Goody, E.N. (ed.) (1978) *Questions and Politeness: Strategies in Social Interaction*, Cambridge University Press.

Goswami, G.C. (1966) *An Introduction to Assamese Phonology*, Poona: Deccan College.

Gósy, M. (ed.) (1991a) *Temporal Factors in Speech: a Collection of Papers*, Budapest: A Magyar Tudományos Akadémia Nyelvtudományi Intézete (Research Institute for Linguistics, Hungarian Academy of Sciences).

⸺ (1991b) 'The perception of tempo', in M. Gósy (ed.) *Temporal Factors in Speech: a Collection of Papers*, Budapest: A Magyar Tudományos Akadémia Nyelvtudományi Intézete (Research Institute for Linguistics, Hungarian Academy of Sciences), pp. 63–106.

Green, J. (1988) 'Spanish', in M. Harris and N. Vincent (eds.) *The Romance Languages*, London: Croom Helm, pp. 79–130.

References

Greenberg, J.H. (1955) 'The click languages', *Southwestern Journal of Anthropology* 6: 223–7.

(1970) 'Some generalizations concerning glottalic consonants, especially implosives', *International Journal of American Linguistics* 36: 123–46.

(ed.) (1978) *Universals of Human Language*, vol. II, *Phonology*, Stanford University Press.

Gregg, R.J. (1984) 'An urban dialect survey of the English spoken in Vancouver', Final Report to the Social Sciences and Humanities Research Council of Canada, Department of Linguistics, University of British Columbia, Vancouver.

Grimes, B. (1988) *Ethnologue*, parts I and II, Fort Worth, TX: Summer Institute of Linguistics.

Grimes J.E. (1955) 'Style in Huichol structure', *Language* 31: 31–5.

(1959) 'Huichol tone and intonation', *International Journal of American Linguistics* 25: 221–32.

Grosjean, F. (1980) 'Comparative studies of temporal variables in spoken and sign languages: a short review', in H.W. Dechert and M. Raupach (eds.) *Temporal Variables in Speech: Studies in Honour of Frieda Goldman-Eisler*, The Hague: Mouton, pp. 307–12.

(1982) *Life with Two Languages: an Introduction to Bilingualism*, Cambridge MA: Harvard University Press.

Grosjean, F., L. Grosjean and H. Lane (1979) 'The patterns of silence: performance structures in sentence production', *Cognitive Psychology* 11: 58–81.

Grundström, A.W. (1973) 'L'intonation des questions en français standard', in A.W. Grundstrom and P.R. Léon (eds.) *Interrogation et intonation en français standard et français canadien*, Montreal: Didier, pp. 19–50.

Grundström, A.W. and P.R. Léon (eds.) (1973) *Interrogation et intonation en français standard et français canadien*, Montreal: Didier.

Gudschinsky, S.C. (1956) 'The ABC's of lexicostatistics (glottochronology)', *Word* 12: 175–210.

(1958) 'Native reactions to tones and words in Mazatec', *Word* 14: 338–45.

Gudschinsky, S., H. Popovitch and F. Popovitch (1970) 'Native reaction and phonetic similarity in Maxakalí phonology', *Language* 46: 77–88.

Gumperz, J.J. (ed.) (1983) *Language and Social Identity*, Cambridge University Press.

Gumperz, J.J. and D. Hymes (eds.) (1986) *Directions in Sociolinguistics: the Ethnography of Communication*, Oxford: Blackwell.

Gussenhoven, C. (1984) *On the Grammar and Semantics of Sentence Accents*, Dordrecht: Foris.

Hadding-Koch, K. (1961) *Acoustico-phonetic Studies in the Intonation of Southern Swedish*, Lund: Gleerup.

Halá, B., M. Romportl and P. Janota (eds.), (1970) *Proceedings of the 6th International Congress of Phonetic Sciences*, Prague: Academia.

Hall, R.A. Jr (1966) *Pidgin and Creole Languages*, Ithaca: Cornell University Press.

Hall, T.A. (1989) 'Lexical phonology and the distribution of German [ç] and [x]', *Phonology* 6: 1–18.

Halle, M. and K.N. Stevens (1979) 'Some reflections on the theoretical bases of phonetics', in B. Lindblom and S. Öhman (eds.) *Frontiers of Speech Communication Research*, London: Academic Press, pp. 335–50.

Halle, M. and J.-R. Vergnaud (1981) 'Harmony processes', in W. Klein and W. Levelt (eds.) *Crossing the Boundaries in Linguistics*, Dordrecht: Reidel, pp. 1–22.

— (1987) *An Essay on Stress*, Cambridge MA: Massachusetts Institute of Technology Press.

Halliday, M.A.K. (1963a) 'The tones of English', *Archivum Linguisticum* 15: 1–28.

— (1963b) 'Intonation in English grammar', *Transactions of the Philological Society*, pp. 143–69.

— (1966) 'Intonation systems in English', in A. McIntosh and M.A.K. Halliday (eds.) *Patterns of Language: Papers in General, Descriptive and Applied Linguistics*, London: Longmans Green, pp. 111–33.

— (1967) *Intonation and Grammar in British English*, The Hague: Mouton.

— (1970) *A Course in Spoken English: Intonation*, London: Oxford University Press.

Hammond, M. (1989) 'Lexical stresses in Macedonian and Polish', *Phonology* 6: 19–38.

Hancock, I.F. (1971) 'A survey of the pidgins and creoles of the world', in D. Hymes (ed.) *Pidginization and Creolization of Languages*, Cambridge University Press, pp. 509–25.

Haraguchi, S. (1977) *The Tone Pattern of Japanese*, Tokyo: Kaitakusha.

Hardcastle, W.J. (1973) 'Some observations on the *tense–lax* distinction in initial stops in Korean', *Journal of Phonetics* 1: 263–72.

— (1976) *Physiology of Speech Production: an Introduction for Speech Scientists*, London: Academic Press.

Harrington, J. (1988) 'Automatic recognition of English consonants', in M.A. Jack and J. Laver (eds.) (1988) *Aspects of Speech Technology: a Survey*, Edinburgh University Press, pp. 69–143.

Harris, J. (1985) *Phonological Variation and Change: Studies in Hiberno-English*, Cambridge University Press.

Harris, J.G. (1976) 'Notes on Khamti Shan', in T.W. Gething, J.G. Harris and P. Kullavanijaya (eds.) *Tai Linguistics in Honor of Fang-Kuei Li*, Bangkok: Chulalongkorn University Press, pp.113–41.

Harris, K.S. (1958) 'Cues for the discrimination of American English fricatives in spoken syllables', *Language and Speech* 1: 1–7.

— (1983) 'Coarticulation as a component in articulatory description', in Daniloff, R.G. (ed.) *Articulation Assessment and Treatment Issues*, San Diego CA: College-Hill Press, pp. 147–67.

Harris, M. and N. Vincent (eds.) (1988) *The Romance Languages*, London: Croom Helm.

References

Harris, Z.S. (1951) *Structural Linguistics*, University of Chicago Press.
't Hart, J. and A. Cohen (1973) 'Intonation by rule: a perceptual quest', *Journal of Phonetics* 1: 309–21.
't Hart, J. and R. Collier (1975) 'Integrating different levels of intonation analysis', *Journal of Phonetics* 3: 235–55.
 (1979) 'On the interaction of accentuation and intonation in Dutch', in E. Fischer-Jørgensen, J. Rischel and N. Thorsen (eds.) *Proceedings of the Ninth International Congress of Phonetic Sciences* , vol. 2, Institute of Phonetics, University of Copenhagen, pp. 395–402.
't Hart, J., R. Collier and A. Cohen (1990) *A Perceptual Study of Intonation: an Experimental-Phonetic Approach to Speech Melody*, Cambridge University Press.
Hartshorne, C. and P. Weiss (eds.) (1931–5) *The Collected Papers of Charles Sanders Peirce*, Cambridge MA: Harvard University Press.
Hasler, J.A. (1960) 'El linguaje silbado', *La Palabra y el Hombre* (Revista de la Universidad Veracruzana)15: 25–36, Xalapa, Mexico.
Haudricourt, A.G. (1946) 'Restitution du Karen commun', *Bulletin de la Société Linguistique de Paris* 42: 103–11.
 (1954) 'De l'origine des tons en vietnamien', *Journal Asiatique* 242: 69–82.
 (1961) 'Bipartition et tripartition des systèmes de tons dans quelques langages d'Extrême Orient', *Bulletin de la Société Linguistique de Paris* 56: 163–80.
Haugen, E. (1956) *Bilingualism in the Americas: a Bibliography and Research Guide*, Publications of the American Dialect Society, University of Alabama.
 (1958) 'The phonemics of Modern Icelandic', *Language* 34: 55–88.
Haugen, E. and M. Joos (1952) 'Tone and intonation in East Norwegian', *Acta Philologica Scandinavica* 22: 41–64; reprinted in Bolinger, D. (ed.) (1972) *Intonation*, Harmondsworth: Penguin, pp. 414–36.
Healey, J.F. (1990) *The Early Alphabet*, London: British Museum Publications.
Heine, B. (1975) 'Ik – eine östafrikanische Restsprache', *Afrika und Übersee* 59: 31–56.
Heinz, J.M. and K.N. Stevens (1961) 'On the properties of voiceless fricative consonants', *Journal of the Acoustical Society of America* 33: 589–96.
Henderson, E.J.A. (1949) 'Prosodies in Siamese: a study in synthesis', *Asia Major* (New Series) 1: 189–215; reprinted in F.R. Palmer (ed.) (1970) *Prosodic Analysis*, London: Oxford University Press, pp. 27–53; and in W.E. Jones and J. Laver (eds.) (1973) *Phonetics in Linguistics: a Book of Readings*, London: Longman.
 (1952) 'The main features of Cambodian pronunciation', *Bulletin of the School of Oriental and African Studies* 14: 1.
 (1971) *The Indispensable Foundation: a Selection from the Writings of Henry Sweet*, London: Oxford University Press.
 (1973) 'Bwe Karen as a two-tone language? An enquiry into the interrelations of

pitch tone and initial consonants', Paper presented at the 6th Sino-Tibetan Conference, San Diego.

(1975) 'Phonetic description and phonological function: some reflection upon back unrounded vowels in Thai, Khmer and Vietnamese', in J. Harris and J.R. Chamberlain (eds.) *Studies in Tai Linguistics in Honor of William J. Gedney*, Bangkok: Central Institute of English Language, Office of State Universities, pp. 259–70.

(1982) 'Tonogenesis: some recent speculations on the development of tone', *Transactions of the Philological Society*, 1–24.

Henry, J. (1936) 'The linguistic expression of emotion', *American Anthropologist* 38: 250–56.

Henton, C.G. (1987) 'The IPA consonant chart: mugwumps, holes and therapeutic suggestions', *Journal of the International Phonetic Association* 17: 15–25.

Henton, C.G. and A. Bladon (1988) 'Creak as a sociophonetic marker', in L.M. Hyman and C.N. Li (eds) *Language, Speech and Mind: Studies in Honour of Victoria A. Fromkin*, London: Routledge, pp. 3–29.

Herbert, R.K. (1977) 'Language universals, markedness theory, and natural phonetic processes: the interaction of nasal and oral consonants', PhD dissertation, Ohio State University.

(1986) *Language Universals, Markedness Theory, and Natural Phonetic Processes*, New York and Amsterdam: Mouton de Gruyter.

Herzog, G. (1945) 'Drum-signalling in a West African tribe', *Word* 1: 217–38; reprinted in D. Hymes (ed.) (1964) *Language in Culture and Society: a Reader in Linguistics and Anthropology*, New York: Harper and Row, pp. 312–23.

Hess, W. (1983) *Pitch Determination of Speech Signals: Algorithms and Devices*, Berlin: Springer-Verlag.

Higginbottom, E. (1964) 'Glottal reinforcement in English', *Transactions of the Philological Society*, pp. 129–42.

Higgs, J.-A.W. and R. Thelwall (eds.) *Topics in Linguistic Phonetics: in Honour of E.T. Uldall*, The New University of Ulster, Coleraine.

Hiller, S.M. (1985) 'Automatic acoustic estimation of waveform perturbations', PhD dissertation, University of Edinburgh.

Hiller, S.M., E. Rooney, J. Laver, M.-G. Di Benedetto and J.-P. Lefèvre (1991) 'Macro and micro features for automated pronunciation improvement in the SPELL system', in *Proceedings of ESPRIT 91*, Brussels: Commission of the European Communities, pp. 378–92.

Hinde, R.A. (ed.) (1972) *Non-Verbal Communication*, Cambridge University Press.

(1974) *Biological Bases of Human Social Behavior*, New York: McGraw-Hill.

Hirano, M. (1981) *Clinical Examination of Voice*, Berlin: Springer-Verlag.

Hirose, H. (1976) 'Posterior cricoarytenoid as a speech muscle', *Annals of Otology, Rhinology and Laryngology* 85: 334–43.

(1992) 'The behavior of the larynx in spoken language production', *Proceedings of the International Conference of Spoken Language Processing* 1: 457–8.

References

Hirsh, I.J. (1959) 'Auditory perception of temporal order', *Journal of the Acoustical Society of America* 31: 759–67.

Hirst, D. J. (1977) *Intonative Features: a Syntactic Approach to English Intonation*, The Hague: Mouton.

Hixon, T.J. (1973) 'Respiratory function in speech', in F.D. Minifie, T.J. Hixon and F. Williams (eds.) *Normal Aspects of Speech, Hearing and Language*, Englewood Cliffs, NJ: Prentice-Hall, pp. 73–125.

(1987) *Respiratory Function in Speech and Song*, London: Taylor and Francis.

Hoard, J.E. (1978) 'Syllabication in Northwest Indian languages, with remarks on the nature of syllabic stops and affricates', in A. Bell and J.B. Hooper (eds.) *Syllables and Segments*, Amsterdam: North-Holland, pp. 59–72.

Hoard, J.E. and G.N. O'Grady (1976) 'Nyangumarda phonology: a preliminary report', in R.M.W. Dixon (ed.) *Grammatical Categories in Australian Languages*, Canberra: Australian Institute of Aboriginal Studies, pp. 51–77.

Hockett, C.F. (1955) 'A manual of phonology', *International Journal of American Linguistics* 21.4, part 1; republished as Indiana University Publications in Anthropology and Linguistics no. 11.

(1958) *A Course in Modern Linguistics*, New York: Macmillan.

Hoffmann, C. (1963) *A Grammar of the Margi Language*, Oxford University Press.

Hoffmann, C. and P. Schachter (1969) 'Hausa', in E. Dunstan (ed.) *Twelve Nigerian Languages: a Handbook on their Sound Systems for Teachers of English*, London and Harlow: Longmans, Green, pp. 73–84.

Hogg, R. and C.B. McCully (1987) *Metrical Phonology: a Coursebook*, Cambridge University Press.

Hollenbach, B.E. (1977) 'Phonetic vs. phonemic correspondence in two Trique dialects', in W.R. Merrifield (ed.) (1977) *Studies in Otomanguean Phonology*, Arlington: Summer Institute of Linguistics, and University of Texas at Arlington, pp. 35–68.

Hollien, H. (1972) 'Three major vocal registers: a proposal', in *Proceedings of the Seventh International Congress of Phonetic Sciences* (Montreal), pp. 320–31.

Hollien, H. and R.H. Colton (1969) 'Four laminagraphic studies of vocal fold thickness', *Folia Phoniatrica* 21: 179–98.

Hollien, H. and J. Michel (1968) 'Vocal fry as a phonational register', *Journal of Speech and Hearing Research* 11: 600–4.

Hollien, H., P. Moore, R.W. Wendahl and J.F. Michel (1966) 'On the nature of vocal fry', *Journal of Speech and Hearing Research* 9: 245–7.

Holm, J. (1988) *Pidgins and Creoles*, vol. I, *Theory and Structure*, Cambridge University Press.

(1989) *Pidgins and Creoles*, vol. II, *Reference Survey*, Cambridge University Press.

Holmberg, A.R. (1950) *Nomads of the Long Bow: the Siriono of Eastern Bolivia*, Washington DC: Institute of Social Anthropology, Publication no. 10, Smithsonian Institution.

Holmer, N.M. (1949) 'Goajiro (Arawak) I: Phonology', *International Journal of American Linguistics* 14: 45–56.

Holmes, J.N. (1972) *Speech Synthesis*, London: Mills and Boon.

(1988) *Speech Synthesis and Recognition*, Wokingham: Van Nostrand Reinhold.

Hombert, J.-M. (1974) 'Universals of downdrift: their phonetic basis and significance for a theory of tones', in W.R. Leben (ed.) *Papers from the Fifth Annual Conference on African Linguistics. Studies in African Linguistics* Supplement 5: 164–83.

(1976) 'Development of tones from vowel height', in J.M. Hombert (ed.) *Studies on Production and Perception of Tones*, University of California at Los Angeles *Working Papers in Phonetics* 33: 55–66.

(1978) 'Consonant types, vowel quality and tone', in V.A. Fromkin (ed.) *Tone: a Linguistic Survey*, New York: Academic Press, pp.77–111.

(1986) 'The development of nasalized vowels in the Teke language group (Bantu)', in K. Bogers, H. van der Hulst and M. Mous (eds.) *The Phonological Representation of Suprasegmentals: Studies on African Languages Offered to John M. Stewart on his 60th Birthday*, Dordrecht, and Cinnaminson, NJ: Foris, pp. 359–79.

Honikman, B. (1964) 'Articulatory settings', in D. Abercrombie, D.B. Fry, P.A.D. MacCarthy, N.C. Scott and J.L.M. Trim (eds.) *In Honour of Daniel Jones*, London: Longmans Green, pp. 73–84.

Hoogshagen, S. (1959) 'Three contrastive vowel lengths in Mixe', *Zeitschrift für Phonetik, Sprachwissenschaft und Kommunikationsforschung* 12: 111–15.

Horne, E.C. (1961) *Beginning Javanese*, New Haven CT: Yale University Press.

Horvath, B.M. (1985) *Variation in Australian English: the Sociolects of Sydney*, Cambridge University Press.

House, A.S. (1961) 'On vowel duration in English', *Journal of the Acoustical Society of America* 33: 1174–8.

House, A.S. and G. Fairbanks (1953) 'The influence of consonant environment upon the secondary acoustical characteristics of vowels', *Journal of the Acoustical Society of America* 25: 105–13.

Householder, F.W. (1971) *Linguistic Speculations*, Cambridge University Press.

Huddleston, R. (1984) *Introduction to the Grammar of English*, Cambridge University Press.

(1988) *English Grammar*, Cambridge University Press.

Hudson, J. (1978) *The Core of Walmatjari Grammar*, Canberra: Australian Institute of Aboriginal Studies.

Hudson, R. (1980) *Sociolinguistics*, Cambridge University Press.

Huggins, A.W.F. (1964) 'Distortion of the temporal pattern of speech: interruption and alternation', *Journal of the Acoustical Society of America* 36: 1055–64.

Hughes, A. and P. Trudgill (1979) *English Accents and Dialects*, London: Edward Arnold.

Hulst, H. G. van der (1985) 'Vowel harmony in Hungarian: a comparison of segmental and autosegmental analyses', in H. van der Hulst and N. Smith (eds.) *Advances in Non-linear Phonology*, Dordrecht: Foris, pp. 267–303.

(1989) 'Atoms of segmental structure: components, gestures and dependency', *Phonology* 6: 253–84.

Hulst, H. G. van der and N. Smith (eds.) (1982) *The Structure of Phonological Representations*, vol. II, Dordrecht: Foris.

(eds.) (1985a) *Advances in Non-linear Phonology*, Dordrecht: Foris.

(1985b) 'Vowel harmony in Djingili, Nyangumarda and Warlpiri', *Phonology Yearbook* 2: 277–303.

(1987) 'Vowel harmony in Khalkha and Buriat (east Mongolian)', in F. Beukema and P. Coopmans (eds.) *Linguistics in the Netherlands*, Dordrecht: Foris, pp. 81–90.

(1989) *Features, Segmental Structure and Harmony Processes*, 2 parts, Dordrecht: Foris.

Hurford, J.R. and B. Heasley (1983) *Semantics: a Coursebook*, Cambridge University Press.

Hyman, L. (1973) *Consonant Types and Tone* (Southern California Occasional Papers in Linguistics 1), Department of Linguistics, University of Southern California, Los Angeles, CA.

(1975) *Phonology: Theory and Analysis*, New York: Holt, Rinehart and Winston.

(ed.) (1977a) *Studies in Stress and Accent*, Southern California Occasional Papers in Linguistics 4, Department of Linguistics, University of Southern California, Los Angeles, CA.

(1977b) 'On the nature of linguistic stress', in L. Hyman (ed.) (1977a) *Studies in Stress and Accent*, Southern California Occasional Papers in Linguistics 4, Department of Linguistics, University of Southern California, Los Angeles, CA, pp. 37–82.

(1985) 'Historical tonology', in V.A. Fromkin (ed.) *Phonetic Linguistics: Essays in Honor of Peter Ladefoged*, Orlando FL: Academic Press, pp. 257–70.

Hymes, D.H. (1960) 'Lexicostatistics so far', *Current Anthropology* 1: 344.

(ed.) (1964) *Language in Culture and Society: a Reader in Linguistics and Anthropology*, New York: Harper and Row.

(1971a) *On Communicative Competence*, Philadelphia PA: University of Pennsylvania Press.

(ed.) (1971b) *Pidginization and Creolization of Languages*, Cambridge University Press.

(1974) *Foundations in Sociolinguistics: an Ethnographic Approach*, University of Philadelphia Press (2nd edn, 1977).

International Phonetic Association (1949) *Principles of the International Phonetic Association*, University College, London.

Isačenko, A. and H.J. Schädlich (1970) *A Model of Standard German Intonation*, The Hague: Mouton.

Isshiki, N. (1964) 'Regulatory mechanisms of voice intensity variation', *Journal of Speech and Hearing Research* 7: 17–29.

Izard, C. (1971) *The Face of Emotion*, New York: Appleton.

Jack, M.A. and J. Laver (eds.) (1988) *Aspects of Speech Technology*, Edinburgh University Press.

Jackendoff, R.S. (1972) *Semantic Interpretation in Generative Grammar*, Cambridge MA: Massachusetts Institute of Technology Press.

Jackson, K.H. (1958) 'The situation of the Scottish Gaelic language and the work of the Linguistic Survey of Scotland' *Lochlann* 1: 229–34.

(1967) *A Historical Phonology of Breton*, Dublin: Dublin Institute for Advanced Studies.

Jackson, M., P. Ladefoged and N. Antoñanzas-Barroso (1985) 'Automated measures of spectral tilt', *UCLA Department of Linguistics Working Papers in Phonetics* 62: 77–88.

Jakobson, R. (1949) 'On the identification of phonemic identities', *Recherches Structurales, Travaux du Cercle Linguistique de Prague* 5: 205–13.

Jakobson, R. and M. Halle (1956) *Fundamentals of Language*, The Hague: Mouton.

(1957) 'Phonology in relation to phonetics', in L. Kaiser (ed.) *Manual of Phonetics*, Amsterdam: North-Holland, pp. 215–51.

(1964) 'Tenseness and laxness', in D. Abercrombie, D.B. Fry, P.A.D. MacCarthy, N.C. Scott and J.L.M. Trim (eds.), *In Honour of Daniel Jones*, London: Longmans Green, pp. 96–101.

(1968) 'Phonology in relation to phonetics', in B. Malmberg (ed.) *Manual of Phonetics*, 2nd edn, Amsterdam: North-Holland, pp. 411–49.

Jakobson, R. and J. Lotz (1949) 'Notes on the French phonemic pattern', *Word* 5: 151–8.

Jakobson, R., C.G.M. Fant and M. Halle (1952) *Preliminaries to Speech Analysis*, Technical Report no. 13, Acoustics Laboratory, Cambridge MA: Massachusetts Institute of Technology; also published under the same title in 1963 by Massachusetts Institute of Technology Press, Cambridge MA.

Jassem, W. (1965) 'The formants of fricative consonants', *Language and Speech* 8: 1–16.

Jeel, V. (1975) 'An investigation of the fundamental frequency of vowels after various Danish consonants, in particular stop consonants', *Annual Report of the Institute of Phonetics* 9: 191–211, University of Copenhagen.

Jeffress, L.A. (ed.) (1951) *Cerebral Mechanisms in Behavior*, New York: John Wiley.

Jensen, P.J. and K.M.N. Menon (1972) 'Physical analysis of linguistic vowel duration', *Journal of the Acoustical Society of America* 52: 708–10.

Johns, C.M. (1972) 'Slips of the tongue in Portuguese', MLitt dissertation, University of Edinburgh.

Johnson, S.V. (1975) 'Chinook Jargon variation: towards the compleat Chinooker', *International Conference on Pidgins and Creoles*, Honolulu HI.

Jones, C. (1989) *A History of English Phonology*, Harlow: Longman Group.

Jones, D. (1917) *An English Pronouncing Dictionary,* 1st edn, London: Dent.

(1918) *An Outline of English Phonetics*, (1960, 8th edn) Cambridge: Heffer.

References

(1931) 'The word as a phonetic entity', *le maître phonétique* (3rd Series) 36: 60–5; reprinted in W.E. Jones and J. Laver (eds.) *Phonetics in Linguistics: a Book of Readings*, London: Longman.

(1937) 'The aims of phonetics', *Archiv für die gesamte Phonetik* 1: 4–10.

(1944a) 'Some thoughts on the phoneme', *Transactions of the Philological Society* pp.119–35; reprinted in W.E. Jones and J. Laver (eds.) (1973) *Phonetics in Linguistics: a Book of Readings*, London: Longman.

(1944b) 'Chronemes and tonemes: a contribution to the theory of phonemes', *Acta Linguistica* vol. IV, fasc. I:1–10; reprinted in W.E. Jones and J. Laver (eds.) *Phonetics in Linguistics: a Book of Readings*, London: Longman.

(1950) *The Phoneme: its Nature and Use*, Cambridge: Heffer.

(1957) 'The history and meaning of the term "phoneme" ', (pamphlet), *International Phonetic Association*, London; also printed as an appendix to D. Jones (1967) *The Phoneme: its Nature and Use*, (3rd edn), Cambridge: Heffer; and reprinted in W.E. Jones and J. Laver (eds.) *Phonetics in Linguistics: a Book of Readings*, London: Longman.

(1962) *An Outline of English Phonetics*, 9th edn., Cambridge: Heffer.

Jones, R.B. (1961) *Karen Linguistic Studies*, University of California Publications in Linguistics 25.1.

Jones, W.E. and J. Laver (eds.) (1973) *Phonetics in Linguistics: a Book of Readings*, London: Longman.

Jungraithmayr, H. (1967) 'A brief note on certain characteristics of "West Chadic" languages', *Journal of West African Languages* 4: 57–8.

Kaiki, N. and Y. Sagisaka (1992) 'The control of segmental duration in speech synthesis using statistical methods', in Y. Tohkura, E. Vatikiotis-Bateson and Y. Sagisaka (eds.) *Speech Perception, Production and Linguistic Structure*, Tokyo: Ohmsha, and Amsterdam: IOS Press, pp. 391–402.

Kaplan, H.M. (1960) *Anatomy and Physiology of Speech*, New York: McGraw-Hill.

Karlgren, B. (1926) *Etudes sur la Phonologie Chinoise*, Archives d'Etudes Orientales 15.

Kavadi, N.B. and F.C. Southworth (1965) *Spoken Marathi*, Book 1, *First-year Intensive Course*, Philadelphia: University of Pennsylvania Press.

Kawasaki, H. (1986) 'Phonetic explanations for phonological universals: the case of distinctive vowel nasalization', in J.J. Ohala and J.J. Jaeger (eds.) *Experimental Phonology*, Orlando FL: Academic Press, pp. 81–103.

Kaye, J. (1989) *Phonology: a Cognitive View*, Hillsdale NJ, Hove and London: Lawrence Erlbaum Associates.

Keating, P. (1984) 'Phonetic and phonological representation of stop consonant voicing', *Language* 60: 286–319.

(1990) 'The window model of coarticulation: articulatory evidence', in J. Kingston and M. Beckman (eds.) *Papers in Laboratory Phonology I: Between the Grammar and Physics of Speech*, Cambridge University Press, pp. 451–70.

Keijsper, C.E. (1983) 'Comparing Dutch and Russian pitch contours', *Russian Linguistics* 7: 101–54.

Kelly, J. (1969) 'Urhobo', in E. Dunstan (ed.) *Twelve Nigerian Languages*, London: Longmans Green, pp. 153–62.

Kelly, J. and J. Local (1989) *Doing Phonology: Observing, Recording, Interpreting*, Manchester University Press.

Kemp. J.A. (ed.) (1981) *Richard Lepsius' Standard Alphabet for Reducing Unwritten Languages and Foreign Graphic Systems to a Uniform Orthography in European Letters*, (2nd edn 1863, London: Williams and Norgate), Amsterdam: John Benjamins.

Kempson, R.M. (1977) *Semantic Theory*, Cambridge University Press.

Kendon, A. (ed.) (1981) *Nonverbal Communication, Interaction and Gesture*, The Hague: Mouton.

Kenning, M.M. (1979) 'Intonation systems in French', *Journal of the International Phonetics Association* 9: 15–30.

(1983) 'The tones of English and French', *Journal of the International Phonetics Association* 13: 32–48.

Kent, R.D. (1983) 'The segmental organization of speech', in P.F. MacNeilage (ed.) *The Production of Speech*, New York: Springer-Verlag pp. 57–89.

Kent, R.D. and F.D. Minifie (1977) 'Coarticulation in recent speech production models', *Journal of Phonetics* 5: 115–33.

Kent, R.D. and Read, C. (1992) *The Acoustic Analysis of Speech*, San Diego CA: Singular Publishing Group.

Kenworthy, J. (1987) *Teaching Pronunciation*, London: Longman.

Kenyon, J.S. (1930) *American Pronunciation: an Introduction for Students*, 4th edn, Ann Arbor MI: George Wahr.

Kenyon, J.S. and T.A. Knott (1944) *A Pronouncing Dictionary of American English*, Springfield MA: Merriam.

Key, M.R. (1975) *Paralanguage and Kinesics (Nonverbal Communication)*, Metuchen NJ: The Scarecrow Press.

(ed.) (1980) *The Relationship of Verbal and Nonverbal Communication*, The Hague: Mouton.

Kim, C.W. (1967) 'The linguistic specification of speech', *UCLA Working Papers in Phonetics* 5: 1–126.

(1968) Review of P. Lieberman (1967) *Intonation, perception and language*, Cambridge MA: Massachusetts Institute of Technology Press, in *Language* 44: 830–42.

(1970) 'A theory of aspiration', *Phonetica* 21: 107–16.

Kingdon, R. (1958a) *The Groundwork of English Intonation*, London: Longman.

(1958b) *The Groundwork of English Stress*, London: Longman.

Kiparsky, P. (1982) 'From cyclic phonology to lexical phonology', in H. van der Hulst, and N. Smith (eds.) *The Structure of Phonological Representations*, vol. II, Dordrecht: Foris, pp. 131–76.

References

(1988) 'Phonological change', in F.J. Newmeyer (ed.) (1988) *Linguistics: the Cambridge Survey*, vol. I, *Linguistic Theory: Foundations*, Cambridge University Press, pp. 363–415.

Kirk, J.M., S. Sanderson and J. Widdowson (eds.) (1985) *Studies in Linguistic Geography: the Dialects of English in Britain and Ireland*, London: Croom Helm.

Klatt, D.H. (1974) 'The duration of [s] in English words', *Journal of Speech and Hearing Research* 17: 51–63.

(1975) 'Vowel lengthening is syntactically determined in a connected discourse', *Journal of Phonetics* 3: 129–40.

(1976) 'Linguistic uses of segmental durations in English: acoustic and perceptual evidence', *Journal of the Acoustical Society of America* 59: 1208–21.

(1979) 'Synthesis by rule of segmental durations in English sentences', in B. Lindblom and S. Öhman (eds.) *Frontiers of Speech Communication Research*, London: Academic Press, pp. 287–300.

Klein, W. and W. Levelt (eds.) (1981) *Crossing the Boundaries in Linguistics*, Dordrecht: Reidel.

Kloster Jensen, M. (1963) 'Die Silbe in der Phonetik und Phonemik', *Phonetica* 9: 17–38.

Kohler, K.J. (1966a) 'Is the syllable a phonological universal?', *Journal of Linguistics* 2: 207–8.

(1966b) 'Towards a phonological theory', *Lingua* 16: 337–51.

(1984) 'Phonetic explanation in phonology: the feature Fortis/Lenis', *Phonetica* 41: 150–74.

(1986a) 'Invariance and variability in speech timing: from utterance to segment in German', in J. Perkell and D.H. Klatt (eds.) *Invariance and Variability in Speech Processes*, Hillsdale, NJ: Lawrence Erlbaum Associates, pp. 268–89.

(1986b) 'Parameters of speech rate perception in German words and sentences: duration, F0 movement, and F0 level', *Language and Speech* 29: 115–41.

Köhler, O., P. Ladefoged, J. Snyman, A. Traill and R. Vossen (1988) 'The symbols for clicks', *Journal of the International Phonetic Association* 2: 140–2.

Kornfilt, J. (1987) 'Turkish and the Turkic languages', in B. Comrie (ed.) *The World's Major Languages*, London: Routledge, pp. 619–44.

Kozhevnikov, V.A. and L. A. Chistovich (1965) *Speech: Articulation and Perception*, Washington DC: Joint Publications Research Service no. 30, (originally published in Russian, 1965).

Krapp, G.P. (1925) *The English Language in America*, 2 vols., New York: Century (for the Modern Language Association of America).

Krass, L. (1944) 'The phonetics of Estonian', MA thesis, University of London.

Kreidler, C.W. (1989) *The Pronunciation of English: a Course Book in Phonology*, Oxford: Blackwell.

Kubozono, H. (1988) 'The organization of Japanese prosody', PhD dissertation, University of Edinburgh.

654

(1989) 'Syntactic and rhythmic effects on downstep in Japanese', *Phonology* 6: 39–67.

(1990) 'The role of the mora in speech production in Japanese', *Proceedings of the First International Conference on Spoken Language Processing*, vol. 1, Kobe, Japan, pp. 501–4.

Kuehn, D.P., M.L. Lemme and J.M. Baumgartner (eds.) (1989) *Neural Bases of Speech, Hearing and Language*, Boston MA: Little, Brown.

Kuipers, A.N. (1960) *Phoneme and Morpheme in Kabardian*, The Hague: Mouton.

Kunze, L.H. (1964) 'Evaluation of methods of estimating sub-glottal air pressure', *Journal of Speech and Hearing Research* 7: 151–64.

Kurath, H. (1949) *A Word Geography of the Eastern United States*, Ann Arbor: University of Michigan Press.

(1964) *A Phonology and Prosody of Modern English*, Heidelberg: Carl Winter, Universitätsverlag.

(1972) 'The sociocultural background of dialect areas in American English', *Studies in Areal Linguistics*, pp. 39–53; reprinted in H.B. Allen and M.D. Linn (eds.) (1986) *Dialect and Accent Variation*, Orlando FL: Academic Press.

Kurath, H. *et al.* (1939–43) *The Linguistic Atlas of New England*, 3 vols. in 6 parts, Providence RI: Brown University Press.

Kurath, H., M.L. Hanson, J. Block and B. Bloch (1939) *Handbook of the Linguistic Geography of New England*, Providence RI: American Council of Learned Societies.

Kurath, H. and R.I. McDavid, Jr. (1961) *The Pronunciation of English in the Atlantic States*, Ann Arbor MI: University of Michigan Press.

Kuriyagawa, F., M. Sawashima, S. Niimi and H. Hirose (1988) 'Electromyographic study of emphatic consonants in Standard Jordanian Arabic', *Folia Phoniatrica* 40: 117–22.

Kvavik, K. (1974) 'An analysis of sentence-initial and final intonational data in two Spanish dialects', *Journal of Phonetics* 2: 351–61.

(1976) 'Research and pedagogical materials on Spanish intonation: a re-examination', *Hispania* 59: 406–17.

(1984) 'On Spanish fall-rise intonations', in D.F. Solá (ed.) *Language in the Americas, Proceedings of the Ninth PILEI Symposium*, Ithaca : Language Policy Research Program, Latin American Studies Program, Cornell University, pp. 167–87.

Kylstra, A.D. (1972) 'Die Präaspiration im Westskandinavischen und Lappischen', *Orbis* 21: 367–82.

Labov, W. (1966) *The Social Stratification of English in New York City*, Washington DC: Center for Applied Linguistics.

(1972a) *Sociolinguistic Patterns*, Philadelphia: University of Pennsylvania Press.

(1972b) *Language in the Inner City: Studies in the Black English Vernacular*, Philadelphia: University of Pennsylvania Press.

References

Ladd, D.R. (1980) *The Structure of Intonational Meaning: Evidence from English*, Bloomington: Indiana University Press.

(1983) 'Peak features and overall slope', in A. Cutler and D.R. Ladd (eds.) *Prosody: Models and Measurements*, Berlin: Springer-Verlag, pp. 39–52 .

(1984) 'Declination: a review and some hypotheses', *Phonology Yearbook* 1: 53–74.

(1986) 'Intonational phrasing: the case for recursive prosodic structure', *Phonology Yearbook* 3: 311–40.

Ladd, D.R. and A. Cutler (1983) 'Introduction: models and measurements in the study of prosody', in A. Cutler and D.R. Ladd (eds.) *Prosody: Models and Measurements*, Berlin: Springer-Verlag, pp. 1–10.

Ladefoged, P. (1962) *Elements of Acoustic Phonetics*, University of Chicago Press.

(1964) *A Phonetic Study of West African Languages*, Cambridge University Press.

(1967) *Three Areas of Experimental Phonetics*, London: Oxford University Press.

(1971) *Preliminaries to Linguistic Phonetics*, University of Chicago Press.

(1972) 'Phonological features and their phonetic correlates', *Journal of the International Phonetic Association* 2: 2–12.

(1975) *A Course in Phonetics*, New York: Harcourt Brace Jovanovich.

(1980)) 'What are linguistic sounds made of?', *Language* 56: 485–502.

(1983a) 'Cross-linguistic studies of speech production', in P.F. MacNeilage (ed.) *The Production of Speech*, New York: Springer-Verlag, pp. 177–88.

(1983b) 'The linguistic use of different phonation types', in D. Bless and J. Abbs (eds.) *Vocal Fold Physiology*, San Diego CA: College Hill Press, pp. 351–60.

(1987a) 'Revising the International Phonetic Alphabet', paper presented to the *Eleventh International Congress of Phonetic Sciences*, Tallinn.

(1987b) 'Updating the theory', *Journal of the International Phonetic Association* 17: 8–9.

(1990) 'On dividing phonetics and phonology: comments on the papers by Clements and by Browman and Goldstein', in J. Kingston and M. Beckman (eds.) *Papers in Laboratory Phonology: Between the Grammar and the Physics of Speech*, Cambridge University Press, pp. 398–405.

Ladefoged, P. and Maddieson, I. (1986) 'Some of the sounds of the world's languages: preliminary version', *UCLA Department of Linguistics Working Papers in Phonetics* 64.

(1988) 'Phonological features for places of articulation', in L.M. Hyman and C.N. Li (eds.) *Language, Speech and Mind: Studies in Honor of Victoria A. Fromkin*, London and New York: Routledge, pp. 49–61.

Ladefoged, P. and P. Roach (1986) 'Revising the International Phonetic Alphabet: a plan', *Journal of the International Phonetic Association*, 16: 22–9 (IPA Centenary Volume).

Ladefoged, P. and A. Traill (1980) 'The phonetic inadequacy of phonological specifications of clicks', UCLA Department of Linguistics Working Papers in Phonetics 49: 1–27.

(1984) 'Linguistic phonetic description of clicks', *Language* 60: 1–20.

(1993, forthcoming) 'Clicks and their accompaniments', *Journal of Phonetics* (in press).

Ladefoged, P., Williamson, K., Elugbe, B. and Uwalaka, A.A. (1976) 'The stops of Owerri Igbo', *Studies in African Linguistics*, Suppl. 6:147–63.

Ladefoged, P. and Z. Wu (1984) 'Places of articulation: an investigation of Pekingese fricatives and affricates', *Journal of Phonetics* 12: 267–78.

Ladefoged, P., A. Cochran and S. Disner (1977) 'Laterals and trills', *Journal of the International Phonetic Association* 7: 46–54.

Ladefoged, P., M. Draper and D. Whitteridge (1958) 'Syllables and stress', *Miscellanea Phonetica* 3: 1–15.

Ladefoged, P., P. de Clerk, M. Lindau and G. Papçun (1972) 'An auditory-motor theory of speech production', *UCLA Working Papers in Phonetics* 22: 48–75.

Langdon, M. (1977) 'Stress, length, and pitch in Yuman languages', in L. Hyman (ed.) *Studies in Stress and Accent,* Southern California Occasional Papers in Linguistics 4, Department of Linguistics, University of Southern California, Los Angeles CA, pp. 239–60.

Langendoen, D.T. (1968) *The London School of Linguistics: a Study of the Linguistic Theories of B. Malinowski and J.R. Firth*, Cambridge MA: Massachusetts Institute of Technology Press.

Lashley, K.S. (1951) 'The problem of serial order in behavior', in L.A. Jeffress (ed.) (1951) *Cerebral Mechanisms in Behavior*, New York: John Wiley, pp. 112–36.

Lass, N.J. (ed.) (1976) *Contemporary Issues in Experimental Phonetics*, New York: Academic Press.

Lass, R. (1976) *English Phonology and Phonological Theory: Synchronic and Diachronic Studies*, Cambridge University Press.

(1980) *On Explaining Language Change*, Cambridge University Press.

(1984a) *Phonology: an Introduction to Basic Concepts*, Cambridge University Press.

(1984b) 'Vowel system universals and typology: prologue to theory', *Phonology Yearbook* 1: 75–111.

(1987) *The Shape of English: Structure and History*, London: Dent.

Lass, R. and J.M. Anderson (1975) *Old English Phonology*, Cambridge University Press.

Lass, R. and J. Higgs (1984) 'Phonetics and language history: American /r/ as a candidate', in J.-A.W. Higgs and R. Thelwall (eds.) *Topics in Linguistic Phonetics in Honour of E.T. Uldall*, Coleraine: The New University of Ulster, pp. 65–90.

Laver, J. (1967) 'A preliminary phonology of the Aywele dialect of Etsako', *Journal of West African Languages* IV, 2: 53–6.

(1968) 'Voice quality and indexical information', *British Journal of Disorders of Communication* 3: 43–54; reprinted in J. Laver (1991) *The Gift of Speech: Papers in the Analysis of Speech and Voice*, Edinburgh University Press.

References

(1969) 'Etsako', in E. Dunstan (ed.) *Twelve Nigerian Languages*, London: Longmans, Green, pp. 47–56.

(1970) 'The production of speech', in J. Lyons (ed.) (1970), *New Horizons in Linguistics*, Harmondsworth: Penguin, pp. 53–75; reprinted in J. Laver (1991) *The Gift of Speech: Papers in the Analysis of Speech and Voice*, Edinburgh University Press.

(1974) 'Labels for voices', *Journal of the International Phonetic Association* 4: 62–75; reprinted in J. Laver (1991) *The Gift of Speech: Papers in the Analysis of Speech and Voice*, Edinburgh University Press.

(1975) 'Individual features in voice quality', PhD dissertation, University of Edinburgh.

(1976) 'Language and nonverbal communication', in E.C. Carterette and M.P. Friedman (eds.) (1976), *Handbook of Perception* , vol. VII, *Language and Speech*, New York: Academic Press, pp. 345–62; reprinted in J. Laver (1991) *The Gift of Speech: Papers in the Analysis of Speech and Voice*, Edinburgh University Press.

(1978) 'The concept of articulatory settings: an historical survey', *Historiographia Linguistica* 5: 1–14; reprinted in J. Laver (1991) *The Gift of Speech: Papers in the Analysis of Speech and Voice*, Edinburgh University Press.

(1979) 'The description of voice quality in general phonetic theory', *Edinburgh University Department of Linguistics Work in Progress* 12: 30–52; reprinted in J. Laver (1991) *The Gift of Speech: Papers in the Analysis of Speech and Voice*, Edinburgh University Press.

(1980) *The Phonetic Description of Voice Quality*, Cambridge University Press.

(1981) 'The analysis of vocal quality: from the classical period to the twentieth century', in R.E. Asher and E.J.A. Henderson (eds.) *Towards a History of Phonetics*, Edinburgh University Press, pp.79–99; reprinted in J. Laver (1991) *The Gift of Speech: Papers in the Analysis of Speech and Voice*, Edinburgh University Press.

(1989) 'Cognitive science and speech: a framework for research', in Schnelle, H. and N.-O. Bernsen (eds.), *Logic and Linguistics*, Hillsdale NJ, Hove and London: Lawrence Erlbaum Associates, pp. 37–69; reprinted in J. Laver (1991) *The Gift of Speech: Papers in the Analysis of Speech and Voice*, Edinburgh University Press.

(1991) *The Gift of Speech: Papers in the Analysis of Speech and Voice*, Edinburgh University Press.

(1993) 'Speech technology: an overview', in R.E. Asher and J.Y.M. Simpson (eds.) *Encyclopedia of Language and Linguistics*, (10 vols.), Oxford: Pergamon Press.

Laver, J. and R. Hanson (1981) 'Describing the normal voice', in J. Darby (ed.) *Speech Evaluation in Psychiatry*, New York : Grune and Stratton, pp. 51–78; reprinted in J. Laver (1991) *The Gift of Speech: Papers in the Analysis of Speech and Voice*, Edinburgh University Press.

Laver, J. and S. Hutcheson (1972) *Communication in Face to Face Interaction*, Harmondsworth: Penguin.

Laver, J. and P. Trudgill (1979) 'Phonetic and linguistic markers in speech', in K.R. Scherer and H. Giles (eds.) *Social Markers in Speech*, Cambridge University Press, and Paris: Editions de la Maison des Sciences de l'Homme, pp. 1–32; reprinted in J. Laver (1991)*The Gift of Speech: Papers in the Analysis of Speech and Voice*, Edinburgh University Press.

Laver, J., S.M. Hiller and J. Mackenzie Beck (1988) 'Acoustic waveform perturbations and voice disorders', *Report to the Voice Committee of the International Association of Logopedics and Phoniatrics*, pp. 1–26; published (1992) in *Journal of Voice* 6: 115–26; reprinted in J. Laver (1991) *The Gift of Speech: Papers in the Analysis of Speech and Voice*, Edinburgh University Press.

Laver, J., S.M. Hiller, J. Mackenzie and E. Rooney (1986) 'An acoustic system for the detection of laryngeal pathology', *Journal of Phonetics* 14: 517–24; reprinted in J. Laver (1991) *The Gift of Speech: Papers in the Analysis of Speech and Voice*, Edinburgh University Press.

Laver, J., S. Wirz, J. Mackenzie and S.M. Hiller (1981) 'A perceptual protocol for the analysis of vocal profiles', *Edinburgh University Department of Linguistics Work in Progress* 14: 139–55; reprinted in J. Laver (1991) *The Gift of Speech: Papers in the Analysis of Speech and Voice*, Edinburgh University Press.

Lea, W.A. (1972) 'Intonational cues to the constituent structure and phonemics of spoken English', PhD dissertation, Purdue University.

Leach, P. (1980) 'Linguistic aspects of French intonation', PhD dissertation, University of Leeds.

—— (1988) 'French intonation: tone or tune?', *Journal of the International Phonetics Association* 18: 125–39.

Leben, W.R. (1976) 'The tones of English intonation', *Linguistic Analysis* 2: 67–107.

Leden, H. von (1961) 'The mechanism of phonation', *Archives of Otolaryngology* 74: 660–76.

Leed, R. (1965) 'A contrastive analysis of Russian and English intonation contours', *Slavic and East European Journal* 9: 62–75.

Lehiste, I. (1967) *Readings in Acoustic Phonetics*, Cambridge MA: Massachusetts Institute of Technology Press.

—— (1970) *Suprasegmentals*, Cambridge MA: Massachusetts Institute of Technology Press.

—— (1976) 'Suprasegmental features of speech', in N.J. Lass (ed.) *Contemporary Issues in Experimental Phonetics*, New York: Academic Press, pp. 225–42.

—— (1977) 'Isochrony reconsidered', *Journal of Phonetics* 5: 253–63.

Lehiste, I. and P. Ivić (1963) 'Accent in Serbo-Croatian: an experimental study', *Michigan State Slavic Materials* 4, Ann Arbor MI: University of Michigan.

Lehiste, I. and G.E. Peterson (1961) 'Some basic considerations in the analysis of intonation', *Journal of the Acoustical Society of America* 33: 419–25.

References

Lehmann, W.P. (1962) *Historical Linguistics: an Introduction*, New York: Holt, Rinehart and Winston.

Lenneberg, E. H. (1967) *Biological Foundations of Language*, New York: John Wiley.

Lepsius, C.R. (1855) *Standard Alphabet for Reducing Unwritten Languages and Foreign Graphic Systems to a Uniform Orthography in European Letters*, London: Williams and Norgate; 2nd edn 1863, reprinted with an Introduction by J.A. Kemp, Amsterdam: John Benjamins.

Levelt, W.J.M. (1989) *Speaking: from Intention to Articulation*, Cambridge MA: Massachusetts Institute of Technology Press.

Levinson, S.C. (1983) *Pragmatics*, Cambridge University Press.

Li, F.K. (1954) 'Consonant clusters in Tai', *Language* 30: 368–79.

Liberman, A.M. (1976) 'The origin of Scandinavian accentuation', *Arkiv för Nordisk Filologi* 91: 37–58.

—— (1984) 'On finding that speech is special', in M.S. Gazzaniga (ed.) *Handbook of Cognitive Neuroscience*, New York: Plenum Press, pp. 169–98.

Liberman, M. (1975) 'The intonational system of English', PhD Dissertation, Massachusetts Institute of Technology (distributed by Indiana Linguistics Club).

Liberman, M. and J. Pierrehumbert (1984) 'Intonational invariance under changes in pitch range and length', in M. Aronoff and R.T. Oehrle (eds.) *Language Sound Structure: Studies in Phonology Presented to Morris Halle by his Teacher and Students*, Cambridge MA: Massachusetts Institute of Technology Press, pp. 157–233.

Liberman, M. and A. Prince (1977) 'On stress and linguistic rhythm', *Linguistic Inquiry* 8: 249–336.

Liberman, M. and I. Sag (1974)) 'Prosodic form and discourse function', in *Papers from the Tenth Regional Meeting*, Chicago Linguistic Society, pp. 416–26.

Lieberman, P. and S. Blumstein (1988) *Speech Physiology, Speech Perception, and Acoustic Phonetics*, Cambridge University Press.

Liiv, G. (1962) 'On the acoustic composition of Estonian vowels of three degrees of length', *Eesti NSV Teaduste Akadeemia Toimetised*, XI Köide, Ühiskonnateaduste seeria 3, pp. 271–90.

Lindau, M. (1979) 'The feature "expanded" ', *Journal of Phonetics* 7: 163–76.

—— (1980) 'The story of /r/', *University of California at Los Angeles Working Papers in Phonetics* 51: 114–19.

Lindau, M., K. Norlin and J. Svantesson (1990) 'Some cross-linguistic differences in diphthongs', *Journal of the International Phonetic Association* 20: 10–14.

Lindblad, P. (1980) 'Svenskans sje- och tje-ljud i ett allmänfonetisk perspektiv', *Travaux de l'Institut de Linguistique de Lund* 16, Lund: Gleerup.

Lindblom, B. (1963) 'Spectrographic study of vowel reduction', *Journal of the Acoustical Society of America* 35: 1173–81.

—— (1975) 'Some temporal regularities of spoken Swedish', in G. Fant and M. Tatham (eds.) *Auditory Analysis and Perception of Speech*, London: Academic Press and New York, pp. 387–96.

(1983) 'Economy of speech gestures', in P.F. MacNeilage (ed.) (1983) *The Production of Speech*, New York: Springer-Verlag, pp. 217–46.

(1986) 'Phonetic universals in vowel systems', in J.J. Ohala and J.J. Jaeger (eds.), *Experimental Phonology*, Orlando FL: Academic Press, pp. 13–44.

Lindblom, B. and I. Maddieson (1988) 'Phonetic universals in consonant systems', in L.M. Hyman and C.N. Li (eds.) *Language, Speech and Mind: Studies in Honor of Victoria A. Fromkin*, New York: Routledge, pp. 62–80.

Lindblom, B. and S. Öhman (eds.) (1979) *Frontiers of Speech Communication Research*, London: Academic Press.

Lindblom, B. and J. Sundberg (1971) 'Acoustical consequences of lip, tongue, jaw, and larynx movement', *Journal of the Acoustical Society of America* 50: 1166–79.

Lindqvist-Gauffin, J. (1969) 'Laryngeal mechanisms in speech', *Quarterly Progress and Status Report* 2–3: 26–32, Speech Transmission Laboratory, Royal Institute of Technology (KTH), Stockholm.

(1972) 'A descriptive model of laryngeal articulation in speech', *Quarterly Progress and Status Report* 2–3: 1–9, Speech Transmission Laboratory, Royal Institute of Technology (KTH), Stockholm.

Linell, P. (1979) *Psychological Reality in Phonology*, Cambridge University Press.

Lisker, L. (1978) 'Segment duration, voicing, and the syllable', in A. Bell and J.B. Hooper (eds.) *Syllables and Segments*, Amsterdam: North-Holland, pp. 133–42.

Lisker, L. and A.S. Abramson (1964) 'A cross-language study of voicing in initial stops: acoustical measurements', *Word* 20: 384–422.

(1967) 'Some effects of context on voice onset time in English stops', *Language and Speech* 10: 1–28.

(1970) 'The voicing dimension: some experiments in comparative phonetics', in B. Halá, M. Romportl and P. Janota (eds.) *Proceedings of the 6th International Congress of Phonetic Sciences*, Prague: Academia, pp. 563–7.

Lorimer, D.L.R. (1935) *The Burushaski Language*, Oslo: Institut for Sammenlignende Kulturforskning.

Lounsbury, F.G. (1954) 'Transitional probability, linguistic structure, and systems of habit-family hierarchies', in C.E. Osgood and T.A. Sebeok (eds.) *Psycholinguistics: a Survey of Theory and Research Problems*, Baltimore: Waverley Press, pp. 93–101.

Louw, J.A. (1968) *The Intonation of the Sentence and its Constituent Parts in Xhosa and Tsonga*, Pretoria: Human Sciences Research Council.

Lubker, J.F. (1981) 'Representation and context sensitivity', in T. Myers, J. Laver and J. Anderson (eds.) *The Cognitive Representation of Speech*, Amsterdam: North-Holland, pp. 127–32.

Lubker, J. and T. Gay (1982) 'Anticipatory labial coarticulation: experimental, biological and linguistic variables', *Journal of the Acoustical Society of America* 71: 437–48.

Lubker, J., R. McAllister and P. Carlson (1975) 'Labial co-articulation in Swedish:

a preliminary report', in C.G.M. Fant (ed.) *Proceedings of the Speech Communication Seminar*, Stockholm: Almqvist and Wiksell, pp. 55–64.

Ludel, J. (1978) *Introduction to Sensory Processes*, San Francisco CA: W.H. Freeman.

Luksaneeyanawin, S. (1983) 'Intonation in Thai', PhD Dissertation, University of Edinburgh.

(1993) 'Speech computing and speech technology in Thailand', in S. Luksaneeyanawin, P. Vongvipanond, K. Thepkanjana, V. Vuwongse, T. Koanantakool and W.S. Wharton (eds.), *Proceedings of the Symposium of Natural Language Processing in Thailand*, Bangkok: Chulalongkorn University, pp. 276–321.

Luksaneeyanawin, S., P. Vongvipanond, K. Thepkanjana, V. Vuwongse, T. Koanantakool and W.S. Wharton (eds.) (1993), *Proceedings of the Symposium of Natural Language Processing in Thailand*, Bangkok: Chulalongkorn University.

Lyons, J. (1962) 'Phonemic and non-phonemic phonology: some typological reflections', *International Journal of American Linguistics* 28: 127–33; reprinted in W.E. Jones and J. Laver (eds.) *Phonetics in Linguistics: a Book of Readings*, London: Longman.

(1968) *Introduction to Theoretical Linguistics*, Cambridge University Press.

(1972) 'Human language', in R. Hinde (ed.) *Non-verbal Communication*, Cambridge University Press, pp. 49–85.

(1977) *Semantics*, 2 vols., Cambridge University Press.

(1981) *Language and Linguistics: an Introduction*, Cambridge University Press.

(1991) *Natural Language and Universal Grammar: Essays in Linguistic Theory*, Cambridge University Press.

Maack, A. (1949) 'Die spezifische Lautdauer deutscher Sonanten', *Zeitschrift für Phonetik* 3: 190–232.

Macaulay, R.K.S. (1977) *Language, Social Class and Education: a Glasgow Study*, Edinburgh University Press.

Mackenzie, J., J. Laver and S.M. Hiller (1983) 'Structural pathologies of the vocal folds and phonation', *Edinburgh University Department of Linguistics Work in Progress* 16: 80–116; reprinted in J. Laver (1991) *The Gift of Speech: Papers in the Analysis of Speech and Voice*, Edinburgh University Press.

Mackenzie Beck, J.M. (1988) 'Organic variation and voice quality', PhD dissertation, University of Edinburgh.

Mackridge, P. (1985) *The Modern Greek Language*, Oxford: Clarendon Press.

Maclay, H. and C.E. Osgood (1959) 'Hesitation phenomena in spontaneous English speech', *Word* 15:19–44.

MacMahon, M.K.C. (1986) 'The International Phonetic Association: the first 100 years', *Journal of the International Phonetic Association*, 16: 30–8 (IPA Centenary Volume).

MacNeilage, P.F. (ed.) (1983) *The Production of Speech*, New York: Springer-Verlag.

Maddieson, I. (1978) 'Tone effects on consonants', *Journal of Phonetics* 6: 327–44.

(1980) *The UCLA Phonological Segment Inventory Database (UPSID)*, UCLA Department of Linguistics Working Paper in Phonetics no. 50.

(1981) *The UCLA Phonological Segment Inventory Database (UPSID): Data and Index*, UCLA Department of Linguistics Working Paper in Phonetics no. 53.

(1983) 'The analysis of complex phonetic elements in Bura and the syllable', *Studies in African Linguistics* 14: 286–310.

(1984) *Patterns of Sounds*, Cambridge University Press.

(1987a) 'Revision of the IPA: linguo-labials as a test case', *Journal of the International Phonetic Association* 17: 26–30.

(1987b) 'Linguo-labials', paper presented at the 113th Meeting of the Acoustical Society of America, Indianapolis, May 1987. Abstract in *Journal of the Acoustical Society of America* 81/S1, S65.

(1989) 'Prenasalized stops and speech timing', *Journal of the International Phonetic Association* 19: 57–66.

Maddieson, I. and S. Hess (1986) '"Tense" and "lax" revisited: more on phonation types in minority languages of China', *University of California Department of Linguistics Working Papers in Phonetics* 63: 103–9.

Maddieson, I., S. Hargus and J.N.A. Nartey (1980) 'Pitch in Sherpa', *UCLA Department of Linguistics Working Papers in Phonetics* 51: 132–43.

Maeda, S. (1976) 'A characterization of American English intonation', PhD dissertation, Massachusetts Institute of Technology, Cambridge MA.

Mafeni, B. (1969) 'Isoko', in E. Dunstan (ed.) *Twelve Nigerian Languages: a Handbook on their Sound Systems for Teachers of English*, London and Harlow: Longmans, Green, pp. 115–24.

Mallinson, G. (1988) 'Rumanian', in M. Harris and N. Vincent (eds.) *The Romance Languages*, London: Croom Helm, pp. 391–419.

Malone, K. (1923) *The Phonology of Modern Icelandic*, Menasha WI.

Marcus, S.M. (1981) 'Acoustic determinants of perceptual centre (P-centre) location', *Perception and Psychophysics* 30: 247–56.

Markel, J.D. and A.H. Gray (1976) *Linear Prediction of Speech*, New York: Springer-Verlag.

Martin, P. (1975) 'Analyse phonologique de la phrase française', *Linguistics* 146: 35–68.

(1978) 'L'intonation de la phrase en italien', *Studi di Grammatica Italiana* 8: 395–417.

(1982) 'Phonetic realizations of prosodic contours in French', *Speech Communication* 1: 283–94.

Martinet, A. (1954) 'Accents et tons', *Miscellanea Phonetica* 2: 13–24.

Masek, C.S., R.A. Hendrick and M.F. Miller (eds.) (1981), *Papers from the Parasession on Language and Behavior*, Chicago Linguistic Society, University of Chicago.

Masica, C.P. (1991) *The Indo-Aryan Languages*, Cambridge University Press.

Maspero, H. (1912) 'Etudes sur la phonétique historique de la langue annamite: les initiales', *Bulletin des Ecoles Françaises d'Extrême Orient* 12.

References

Mather, J.Y. and H.H. Speitel (eds.) (1975) *The Linguistic Atlas of Scotland* (Scots Section, vol. I), London: Croom Helm.

Matisoff, J.A. (1970) 'Glottal dissimilation and the Lahu high-rising tone: a tonogenetic case study', *Journal of the American Oriental Society* 90.1.

—— (1971) 'The tonal split in Loloish checked syllables', *Occasional Papers of the Wolfenden Society on Tibeto-Burman Linguistics* 2.

—— (1972) *The Loloish Tonal Split Re-Visited*, Center for South and Southeast Asia Studies 7, University of California at Berkeley.

—— (1973a) 'Tonogenesis in Southeast Asia', in L.M. Hyman (ed.) *Consonant Types and Tone*, Southern California Occasional Papers in Linguistics 1, Department of Linguistics, University of Southern California, Los Angeles, pp. 71–6.

—— (1973b) *The Grammar of Lahu*, Berkeley: University of California Press.

Matteson, E. (1965) *The Piro (Arawak) Language*, Berkeley: University of California Press.

Matthews, P. (1974) *Morphology: an Introduction to the Theory of Word Structure*, Cambridge University Press.

—— (1981) *Syntax*, Cambridge University Press.

—— (1991) *Morphology*, 2nd edn, Cambridge University Press.

Maw, J. and J. Kelly (1975) *Intonation in Swahili*, School of Oriental and African Studies, University of London.

Mazaudon, M. (1977) 'Tibeto-Burman tonogenetics', *Linguistics of the Tibeto-Burman Area* 3(2).

McCarthy, J.J. (1988) 'Feature geometry and dependency: a review', *Phonetica* 45: 84–108 (special issue on 'Articulatory organization: from phonology to speech signals', guest editor O. Fujimura).

McClelland, J.L. and D.E. Rumelhart (1986) *Parallel Distributed Processing: Explorations in the Microstructure of Cognition*, vol. II, *Psychological and Biological Models*, Cambridge MA: Massachusetts Institute of Technology Press (*see also* Rumelhart and McClelland 1986).

McDavid, R.I. Jr (1958) 'The dialects of American English', in W.N. Francis (ed.) *The Structure of American English*, New York: The Ronald Press, pp. 480–543.

McDavid, R.I. Jr and V. McDavid (1956) 'Regional Linguistic Atlases in the United States', *Orbis* 5: 349–86.

McDavid, R.I. Jr, R.K. O'Cain, G.T. Dorrill and G.S. Lowman, Jr (1980) *Linguistic Atlas of the Middle and South Atlantic States*, vol. 1, fascicles 1–2, University of Chicago Press.

McIntosh, A. (1952) *An Introduction to a Survey of Scottish Dialects*, Edinburgh: Nelson.

McIntosh, A. and M.A.K. Halliday (1966) *Patterns of Language: Papers in General, Descriptive and Applied Linguistics*, London: Longmans Green.

McKaughan, H. (ed.) (1973) *The Languages of the Eastern Family of the East New Guinea Highland Stock*, Seattle: University of Washington Press.

McNeill, D. (1987) *Psycholinguistics: a New Approach*, Cambridge MA: Harper and Row.

Meillet, A. and M. Cohen (1952) *Les Langues du Monde*, Paris: Champion.

Menzerath, P. and A. de Lacerda (1933) *Koartikulation, Steuerung und Lautabgrenzung*, Bonn: Dümmler.

Merrifield, W.R. (1963) 'Palantla Chinantec syllable types', *Anthropological Linguistics* 5.5: 1–16.

—— (ed.) (1977) *Studies in Otomanguean Phonology*, Arlington: Summer Institute of Linguistics, and University of Texas at Arlington.

Meyer-Eppler, W. (1957) 'Realization of prosodic features in whispered speech', *Journal of the Acoustical Society of America* 29: 104–6; reprinted in D. Bolinger (ed.) (1972) *Intonation*, Harmondsworth: Penguin.

Michailovsky, B. (1975) 'On some Tibeto-Burman sound changes', *Proceedings of the Annual Meeting of the Berkeley Linguistics Society* 1: 322–32.

Miller, G.A. (1951) *Language and Communication*, New York: McGraw-Hill.

Miller, G.A. and P.E. Nicely (1955) 'An analysis of perceptual confusions among some English consonants', *Journal of the Acoustical Society of America* 27: 338–52.

Miller, G.A., E. Galanter and K. Pribram (1960) *Plans and the Structure of Behavior*, New York: Holt Rinehart and Winston.

Miller, J. (1981) 'Some effects of speaking rate in phonetic perception', *Phonetica* 38: 159–81.

Milroy, L. (1980) *Language and Social Networks*, Oxford: Blackwell.

—— (1987) *Observing and Analysing Natural Language: a Critical Account of Sociolinguistic Method*, Oxford: Basil Blackwell.

Milroy, J. and L. Milroy (1978) 'Belfast: change and variation in an urban vernacular', in P. Trudgill (ed.) (1978) *Sociolinguistic Patterns in British English*, London: Edward Arnold, pp. 19–36.

—— (1985) *Authority in Language: Investigating Language Prescription and Standardisation*, London: Routledge and Kegan Paul.

Mish, F.C. (ed.) (1983) *Webster's Ninth New Collegiate Dictionary*, Springfield MA: Merriam-Webster.

Mitchell, A.G. and A. Delbridge (1965) *The Speech of Australian Adolescents*, Sydney: Angus and Robertson.

Mitchell, T.F. (1975) *Principles of Firthian Linguistics*, London: Longman.

Moll, K. and R. Daniloff (1971) 'Investigation of the timing of velar movements in speech', *Journal of the Acoustical Society of America* 50: 678–84.

Moore, B.C.J. (1982) *An Introduction to the Psychology of Hearing*, 2nd edn, Orlando FL: Academic Press.

Moore, P. and H. von Leden (1958) 'Dynamic variations of the vibratory pattern in the normal larynx', *Folia Phoniatrica* 10:205–38.

Morris, C.W. (1946) *Signs, Language and Behavior*, Englewood Cliffs NJ: Prentice-Hall.

Morris, W. (ed.) (1969) *The American Heritage Dictionary*, Boston MA: Houghton Mifflin.

References

Morton, J., S. Marcus and C. Frankish (1976) 'Perceptual centres (P-centres)', *Psychological Review* 83: 405–8.

Mühlhäusler, P. (1986) *Pidgins and Creole Linguistics*, Oxford: Basil Blackwell.

Munro, P. (1977) 'Towards a reconstruction of Uto-Aztecan', in L.M. Hyman (ed.) *Studies in Stress and Accent*, Southern California Occasional Papers in Linguistics no. 4, pp.303–26.

Myers, T., J. Laver and J. Anderson (eds.) (1981) *The Cognitive Representation of Speech*, Amsterdam: North-Holland.

Nakanishi, A. (1980) *Writing Systems of the World: Alphabets, Syllabaries, Pictograms*, Rutland VT: Charles E. Tuttle.

Nakatani, L.H., K.D. O'Connor and C.H. Aston (1981) 'Prosodic aspects of American English speech rhythm', *Phonetica* 38: 84–106.

Nartey, J.N.A. (1982) 'On fricative phones and phonemes: measuring the phonetic differences within and between languages', *UCLA Department of Linguistics Working Papers in Phonetics* no. 55.

Navarro Tomás, T. (1966) 'Cantidad de las vocales accentuadas', *Revista de Filologia Española* 3:387–408.

Navarro Tomás, T. (1974) *Manual de Entonacion Española*, Madrid: Ediciones Guadarrama.

Newman, S. (1947) 'Bella Coola I: phonology', *International Journal of American Linguistics* 13: 129–34.

(1967) 'Classical Nahuatl', in R. Wauchope and N.A. McQuown (eds.) *Handbook of Middle American Indians*, vol. V, *Linguistics*, Austin: University of Texas Press pp. 179–99.

Newmeyer, F.J. (ed.) (1988) *Linguistics: the Cambridge Survey*, 4 vols.: vol. I, *Linguistic Theory: Foundation*; vol. II, *Linguistic Theory: Extensions and Implications*; vol. III, *Language: Psychological and Biological Aspects*; vol. IV, *Language: the Sociocultural Context*, Cambridge University Press.

Newnham, R. (1971) *About Chinese*, Harmondsworth: Penguin.

Nihalani, P. (1973) 'Lip and jaw movements in the production of stops in Sindhi', *Journal of the International Phonetic Association* 3: 75–80.

(1975) 'Velopharyngeal opening in the formation of voiced stops in Sindhi', *Phonetica* 32: 89–102.

Nofsinger, R.E. (1991) *Everyday Conversation*, Newbury Park CA: Sage.

Nolan, F. J. (1982) 'The role of Action Theory in the description of speech production', *Linguistics* 20: 287–308.

(1983) *The Phonetic Bases of Speaker Recognition*, Cambridge University Press.

Nooteboom, S.G. (1972) 'Production and perception of vowel duration', PhD dissertation, University of Utrecht, Netherlands.

Nooteboom, S.G. and I.H. Slis (1972) 'The phonetic feature of vowel length in Dutch', *Language and Speech* 15: 301–16.

Nord, L. (1991) 'Rhythmical – in what sense? Some preliminary considerations', in

O. Engstrand and C. Kylander (eds.) *Proceedings of the Symposium on Current Phonetic Research Paradigms: Implications for Speech Motor Control*, Stockholm, 13–16 August, 1991, published as vol. XIV of *Phonetic Experimental Research at the Institute of Linguistics, University of Stockholm (PERILUS)*, pp. 107–11.

Norlin, K. (1985) 'Pharyngealization in Cairo Arabic', *Working Papers* 28: 139–50, Phonetics Laboratory, University of Lund.

Norman, J. (1988) *Chinese*, Cambridge University Press.

O'Connor, J.D. (1952) 'RP and the reinforcing glottal stop', *English Studies* 33: 214–18.

O'Connor, J.D. and G.F. Arnold (1961) *Intonation of Colloquial English*, London: Longmans.

O'Connor, J.D. and J.L.M. Trim (1953) 'Vowel, consonant and syllable – a phonological definition', *Word* 9: 103–22; reprinted in W.E. Jones and J. Laver (eds.) (1973) *Phonetics in Linguistics: a Book of Readings*, London: Longman.

Odé, C. (1986) 'Towards a perceptual analysis of Russian intonation', in A.A. Barentsen, B.N. Groen and R. Sprenger (eds.) *Dutch Studies in Russian Linguistics*, Amsterdam: Rodopi, pp. 395–442.

(1989) *Russian Intonation: a Perceptual Description*, Amsterdam: Rodopi.

Odisho, E.Y. (1977) 'The opposition /tʃ/ vs. /tʃh/ in Neo-Aramaic', *Journal of the International Phonetic Association* 7: 79–83.

O'Donnell, W.R. and L. Todd (1991) *Variety in Contemporary English*, (2nd edition), London and New York: HarperCollins Academic.

Oftedal, M. (1956) *The Gaelic of Leurbost Isle of Lewis*, Oslo: Norwegian University Press.

(1975) Review of E. Ternes (1973) *The Phonemic Analysis of Scottish Gaelic. Based on the Dialect of Applecross, Ross-shire*, Forum Phoneticum 1, Hamburg: Helmut Buske Verlag, *Phonetica* 32: 130–40.

O'Grady, G.N., C.F. Voegelin and F.M. Voegelin (1966) *Languages of the World: Indo-Pacific* (fascicule VI), *Anthropological Linguistics* 8, 2: 1–197.

Ohala, J.J. (1973) 'The temporal regulation of speech', *Project on Linguistic Analysis*, Second Series, 1: 1–23, University of California at Berkeley.

(1975) 'Conditions for vowel devoicing and frication', *Journal of the Acoustical Society of America* 58: S39.

(1976) 'A model of speech aerodynamics', *Report of the Phonology Laboratory* 1: 93–107, University of California at Berkeley.

(1977) 'The physiology of stress', in L. Hyman (ed.) *Studies in Stress and Accent*, Southern California Occasional Papers in Linguistics 4, Department of Linguistics, University of Southern California, Los Angeles, pp. 145–68.

(1978) 'The production of tone', in V.A. Fromkin (ed.) *Tone: a Linguistic Survey*, New York: Academic Press, pp. 5–39.

(1979) 'Moderator's introduction (summary) to Symposium on phonetic universals in phonological systems', in E. Fischer-Jørgensen, J. Rischel and N.

Thorsen (eds.) *Proceedings of the Ninth International Congress of Phonetic Sciences*, 2 vols., Institute of Phonetics, University of Copenhagen, pp. 5–8.

(1981a) 'The listener as a source of sound change', in C.S. Masek, R.A. Hendrick and M.F. Miller (eds.), *Papers from the Parasession on Language and Behavior*, Chicago Linguistic Society, University of Chicago, pp. 178–203.

(1981b) 'Articulatory constraints on the cognitive representation of speech', in T. Myers, J. Laver and J. Anderson (eds.) *The Cognitive Representation of Speech*, Amsterdam: North-Holland, pp. 111–22.

(1983) 'The origin of sound patterns in vocal tract constraints', in P.F. MacNeilage (ed.) *The Production of Speech*, New York, Heidelberg and Berlin: Springer-Verlag, pp. 189–216.

(ed.) (1989) *On the Quantal Nature of Speech*, theme issue of *Journal of Phonetics* 17.

(1990) 'Respiratory activity in speech', in W.J. Hardcastle and A. Marchal (eds.) *Speech Production and Speech Modelling*, Dordrecht: Kluwer Academic, pp. 23–53.

Ohala, J.J. and B.W. Eukel (1976) 'Explaining the intrinsic pitch of vowels' *Journal of the Acoustical Society of America* 60:S44.

Ohala, J.J. and J.J. Jaeger (eds.) (1986) *Experimental Phonology*, Orlando FL: Academic Press.

Ohala, M. (1975) 'Studies in nasals and nasalization in Hindi', *Report of the Phonology Laboratory, University of California at Berkeley* 1: 108–16.

(1983) *Aspects of Hindi Phonology*, Delhi: Motilal Banarsidass.

Öhman, S. (1966) 'Coarticulation in VCV utterances: spectrographic measurements', *Journal of the Acoustical Society of America* 39: 151–68.

(1967) 'Numerical model of coarticulation', *Journal of the Acoustical Society of America* 41: 310–20.

Olaszy, G. (1991) 'The inherent time structure of speech sounds', in M. Gósy (ed.) *Temporal Factors in Speech: a Collection of Papers*, Budapest: A Magyar Tudományos Akadémia Nyelvtudományi Intézete (Research Institute for Linguistics, Hungarian Academy of Sciences), pp.107–38.

Ong, W. (1982) *Orality and Literacy: the Technologizing of the Word*, London: Methuen.

Orton, H. (1962) *The Survey of English Dialects: Introduction*, Leeds: Arnold.

Orton, H. and M.V. Barry (1969–71) *The Survey of English Dialects:* vol. II, *The West Midland Counties*, 6 parts, Leeds: Arnold.

Orton, H. and W.H. Halliday (1962–3) *The Survey of English Dialects:* vol. I, *The Six Northern Counties and the Isle of Man*, Leeds: Arnold.

Orton, H. and P.M. Tilling (1969–71) *The Survey of English Dialects:* vol. III, *The East Midland Counties and East Anglia*, 3 parts, Leeds: Arnold.

Orton, H. and M.F. Wakelin (1967–8) *The Survey of English Dialects:* vol. IV, *The Southern Counties*, 3 parts, Leeds: Arnold.

Orton, H., S. Sanderson and J. Widdowson (1978) *The Linguistic Atlas of England*, London: Croom Helm.

Os, E. den (1985) 'Perception of speech rate of Dutch and Italian utterances', *Phonetica* 42: 124–34.

Osborn, H. and W.A. Smalley (1949) 'Formulae for Comanche stem and word formation', *International Journal of American Linguistics* 15: 93–9.

Osgood, C.E. and T.A. Sebeok (eds.) (1954) *Psycholinguistics: a Survey of Theory and Research Problems*, Baltimore: Waverley Press.

O'Shaughnessy, D. (1976) 'Modelling fundamental frequency and its relation to syntax, semantics and phonetics', PhD dissertation, Massachusetts Institute of Technology, Cambridge MA.

—— (1979) 'Linguistic features in fundamental frequency patterns', *Journal of Phonetics* 7: 119–45.

—— (1981) 'A study of French vowel and consonant durations', *Journal of Phonetics* 9: 385–406.

—— (1984) 'A multispeaker analysis of durations in read French paragraphs', *Journal of the Acoustical Society of America* 76: 1664–72.

Osser, H. and F. Peng (1964) 'A cross-linguistic study of speech rate', *Language and Speech* 7: 120–5.

Painter, C. (1973) 'Cineradiographic data on the feature "covered" in Twi vowel harmony', *Phonetica* 28: 97–120.

—— (1978) 'Implosives, inherent pitch, tonogenesis and laryngeal mechanisms', *Journal of Phonetics* 6: 249–74.

Palmer, F.R. (1956) ' "Openness" in Tigre: a problem of prosodic statement', *Bulletin of the School of Oriental and African Studies* 18: 561–77; reprinted in F.R. Palmer (ed.) (1970) *Prosodic Analysis*, London: Oxford University Press.

—— (ed.) (1970) *Prosodic Analysis*, London: Oxford University Press.

—— (1986) *Mood and Modality*, Cambridge University Press.

Pamp, B. (1978) *Svenska Dialekter*, Stockholm: Natur Och Kultur.

Pappenheimer, J., J.H. Comroe, Jr, A. Cournand, J. Ferguson, G. Filley, W. Fowler, J. Gray, H. Helmholz, Jr, A. Otis, H. Rahn and R. Riley (1950) 'Standardization of definitions and symbols in respiratory physiology', *Federal Proceedings* 9: 602–15.

Paradis, C. and J.-F. Prunet (1989) 'On coronal transparency', *Phonology* 6: 317–48.

Parkinson, S. (1988) 'Portuguese', in M. Harris and N. Vincent (eds.) *The Romance Languages*, London: Croom Helm, pp. 131–69.

Parsons, T. (1987) *Voice and Speech Processing*, New York: McGraw Hill.

Passy, P. (1899) *Les Sons du Français*, 5th edn, Paris: Association Fonétique Internationale.

Paulian, C. (1975) *Le Kukuya, Langue Teke du Congo*, Paris: Bibliothèque de la SELAF.

Pawley, A. (1966) 'The structure of Kalam: a grammar of a New Guinea Highlands language', PhD dissertation, University of Auckland.

Pedersen, P. (1973) 'An instrumental investigation of the Danish stød', *Annual Report of the Institute of Phonetics, University of Copenhagen* 7: 195–234.

References

Pederson, L. (1969) 'The linguistic atlas of the Gulf States: an interim report', *American Speech* 44: 279–86.

(1971) 'Southern speech and the *Linguistic Atlas of the Gulf States* project', *Orbis* 20:79–89.

(1974) 'The linguistic atlas of the Gulf States: interim report two', *American Speech* 49: 216–23.

(1976) 'The linguistic atlas of the Gulf States: interim report three', *American Speech* 51: 201–7.

(1977) 'Studies of American pronunciation since 1945', *American Speech* 52: 262–327.

Pederson, L., S. McDaniel and M. Bassett (1984) 'The LAGS concordance', *American Speech* 59: 332–59.

Peirce, C.S. (1931–5) *Collected Papers*, (ed. C. Hartshorne and P. Weiss), Cambridge MA: Harvard University Press.

(1985) 'Logic as semiotic: the theory of signs'; reprinted in R.E. Innis (ed.) *Semiotics: an Introductory Reader*, Bloomington: Indiana University Press, pp. 1–23.

Perkell, J.S. (1986) 'On sources of invariance and variability in speech production', in J.S. Perkell and D.H. Klatt (eds.) *Invariance and Variability in Speech Processes*, Hillsdale NJ: Lawrence Erlbaum Associates, pp. 260–3.

Perkell, J.S. and D.H. Klatt (eds.) (1986) *Invariance and Variability in Speech Processes*, Hillsdale NJ: Lawrence Erlbaum Associates.

Petersen, N.R. (1976) 'Intrinsic fundamental frequency of Danish vowels', *Annual Report of the Institute of Phonetics* 10: 1–27, University of Copenhagen.

Peterson, G.E. (1956) 'Some curiosities of speech', paper presented at the University of Michigan Summer Speech Conference, Ann Arbor MI.

Peterson, G.E. and I. Lehiste (1960) 'Duration of syllabic nuclei in English', *Journal of the Acoustical Society of America* 32: 693–703.

Pétursson, M. (1971) 'Étude de la réalisation des consonnes θ, ð, s, dans la prononciation d'un sujet islandais à partir de la radiocinématographie', *Phonetica* 23: 203–16.

(1972) 'La préaspiration en islandais moderne. Examen de sa réalisation phonétique chez deux sujets', *Studia Linguistica* 26: 61–80.

Petyt, K.M. (1980) *The Study of Dialect: an Introduction to Dialectology*, London: André Deutsch.

Pheby, J. (1975) *Intonation und Grammatik im Deutschen*, Berlin: Akademie-Verlag.

Pickett, J.M. (1980) *The Sounds of Speech Communication: a Primer of Acoustic Phonetics and Speech Perception*, Baltimore MD: University Park Press.

Pierrehumbert, J.B. (1979) 'The perception of fundamental frequency declination', *Journal of the Acoustical Society of America* 66: 362–9.

(1980) 'The phonology and phonetics of English intonation', PhD dissertation, Massachusetts Institute of Technology, Cambridge MA.

(1981) 'Synthesizing intonation', *Journal of the Acoustical Society of America* 70: 985–95.

Pierrehumbert, J.B. and M.E. Beckman (1988) *Japanese Tone Structure*, Cambridge MA: Massachusetts Institute of Technology Press.

Pijper, J.R. de (1984) *Modelling British English Intonation*, Dordrecht: Foris.

Pike, E.V. (1963) *Dictation Exercises in Phonetics*, Santa Ana CA: Summer Institute of Linguistics.

Pike, E.V. and P. Small (1974) 'Downstepping terrace tone in Coatzospan Mixtec', in R. M. Brend (ed.) *Advances in Tagmemics*, Amsterdam: North-Holland pp. 105–34.

Pike, E.V. and K. Wistrand (1974) 'Step-up terrace tone in Acatlán Mixtec', in R. M. Brend (ed.) (1974), *Advances in Tagmemics*, Amsterdam: North-Holland, pp. 81–104.

Pike, K.L. (1943) *Phonetics*, Ann Arbor: University of Michigan Press.

(1945) *The Intonation of American English*, 1st edn, Ann Arbor: University of Michigan Press.

(1946) *The Intonation of American English*, 2nd edn, Ann Arbor: University of Michigan Press.

(1947) *Phonemics: a Technique for Reducing Languages to Writing*, Ann Arbor: University of Michigan Press.

(1948) *Tone Languages*, Ann Arbor: University of Michigan Press.

Pinkerton, S. (1986) 'Quichean (Mayan) glottalized and nonglottalized stops: a phonetic study with implications for phonological universals', in J.J. Ohala and J.J. Jaeger (eds.), *Experimental Phonology*, Orlando FL: Academic Press, pp. 125–39.

Pisoni, D. (1977) 'Identification and discrimination of the relative onset time of two component tones: implications for voicing perception in stops', *Journal of the Acoustical Society of America* 61: 1352–61.

Pittenger, R.E., C.F. Hockett and J.J. Danehy (1960) *The First Five Minutes*, Ithaca NY: Paul Martineau.

Poldauf, I. (1984) *English Word Stress: a Theory of Word-Stress Patterns in English*, Oxford: Pergamon Press.

Pongweni, A. (1977) 'The phonetics and phonology of the Karanga dialect of Shona as spoken in the Midlands Region of Rhodesia', PhD dissertation, University of London.

(1984) 'An acoustic study of Karanga fricatives', *Zeitschrift für Phonetik, Sprachwissenschaft und Kommunikationsforschung* 37: 328–47.

Pöppel, E. (1989) 'The measurement of music and the cerebral clock: a new theory', *LEONARDO* 22: 883–9.

Port, R.F., J. Dalby and M. O'Dell (1987) 'Evidence for mora timing in Japanese', *Journal of the Acoustical Society of America* 81: 1574–85.

Poser, W.J. (1984) 'The phonetics and phonology of tone and intonation in Japanese', PhD dissertation, Massachusetts Institute of Technology, Cambridge MA.

Poyatos, F. (1983) *New Perspectives in Nonverbal Communication: Studies in*

References

Cultural Anthropology, Social Psychology, Linguistics, Literature and Semiotics, Oxford: Pergamon Press.

Procter, P. (ed.) (1978) *Longman Dictionary of Contemporary English*, Harlow: Longman Group.

Pullum, G.K. and W.A. Ladusaw (1986) *Phonetic Symbol Guide*, University of Chicago Press.

Quilis, A. (1981) 'Funciones de la entonación', *Homenaje al Ambrosio Rabanales, Boletín de Filología* (Santiago de Chile) 31: 443–60.

Quilis, A. and J.A. Fernandez (1985) *Curso de Fonetica y Fonologia Españolas*, 11th edn, Madrid: Consejo Superior de Investigaciones Cientificas.

Quintilian *Institutiones Oratoriae*, trans. J.S. Watson (1899) *Quintilian's Institutes of Oratory, or, Education of an Orator*, London: George Bell and Sons.

Rabiner, L.R. and R.W. Shafer (1978) *Digital Processing of Speech Signals*, Englewood Cliffs NJ: Prentice-Hall.

Radford, A. (1981) *Transformational Syntax*, Cambridge University Press.

(1988) *Transformational Grammar*, Cambridge University Press.

Rakerd, B., W. Sennett and C.A. Fowler (1987) 'Domain-final lengthening and foot-level shortening in spoken English', *Phonetica* 44: 147–55.

Ramsaran, S.M. (1978) 'Phonetic and phonological correlates of style in English: a preliminary investigation', PhD dissertation, University of London.

(1988) *English Pronouncing Dictionary*, (14th edn, revised, with a supplement; originally compiled by Daniel Jones), London: Dent.

(ed.) (1990) *Studies in the Pronunciation of English: a Commemorative Volume in Honour of A.C. Gimson*, London: Routledge.

Ramsey, S.R. (1987) *The Languages of China*, Princeton University Press.

Ravila, P. (1962) 'Quantity and phonemic analysis', *Proceedings of the Fourth International Congress of Phonetic Sciences*, Helsinki, Finland, 1961, The Hague: Mouton, pp. 490–3.

Ray, P.S. (1967) 'Dafla phonology and morphology', *Anthropological Linguistics* 9: 9–14.

Recasens, D. (1984a) 'V-to-C coarticulation in Catalan VCV sequences: an articulatory and acoustic study', *Journal of Phonetics* 12: 61–73.

(1984b) 'Vowel-to-Vowel coarticulation in Catalan VCV sequences', *Journal of the Acoustical Society of America* 76: 1624–35.

(1987) 'An acoustic analysis of V-to-C and V-to-V coarticulatory effects in Catalan and Spanish VCV sequences', *Journal of Phonetics* 15: 299–312.

Rietveld, A.C.M. and C. Gussenhoven (1987) 'Perceived speech rate and intonation', *Journal of Phonetics* 15: 273–85.

Riggs, V. (1949) 'Alternate phonemic analyses of Comanche', *International Journal of American Linguistics* 15: 229–31.

Ringaard, K. (1960) *Vestjysk Stød*, Åarhus: Universitetsforlaget i Åarhus.

(1962) 'The pronunciation of a glottal stop', *Phonetica* 8: 203–8.

(1978) 'Distribution af stød og tonal accent i danske dialektområder', in E.

Gårding, G. Bruce and R. Bannert (eds.) *Nordic Prosody*, Travaux de l'Institut de Linguistique de Lund 13, Lund: Gleerup, pp. 145–52.

Ringen, C. (1980) 'Uralic and Altaic vowel harmony: a problem for natural generative phonology', *Journal of Linguistics* 16: 37–44.

Ritzenthaler, R.E. and F.A. Peterson (1954) 'Courtship whistling of the Mexican Kickapoo Indians', *American Anthropologist* 56: 1088–9.

Roach, P.J. (1973) 'Glottalization of English /p/, /t/, /k/ and /tʃ/ - a re-examination', *Journal of the International Phonetic Association* 3: 10–21.

(1979) 'Laryngeal/oral coarticulation in glottalized English plosives' *Journal of the International Phonetic Association* 9: 1–6.

(1983a) *English Phonetics and Phonology: a Practical Course*, Cambridge University Press.

(1983b) *English Phonetics and Phonology: a Practical Course (Tutor's Book)*, Cambridge University Press.

(1987) 'Rethinking phonetic taxonomy', *Transactions of the Philological Society*, pp. 24–37.

(1991) *English Phonetics and Phonology: a Practical Course*, 2nd edn, Cambridge University Press.

Robbins, F.E. (1975) 'Nasal words without phonetic vowels in Quiotepec Chinantec', in R. M. Brend, (ed.), *Studies in Tone and Intonation by Members of the Summer Institute of Linguistics*, Basel: Karger, pp. 126–30.

Robins, R.H. (1953) 'The phonology of the nasalized verbal forms in Sundanese', *Bulletin of the School of Oriental and African Studies* 15: 138–45; reprinted in R.H. Robins (1970) *Diversions of Bloomsbury: Selected Writings on Linguistics*, Amsterdam: North-Holland.

(1957) 'Aspects of prosodic analysis', *Proceedings of the University of Durham Philosophical Society* vol. I, series B (Arts), 1: 1–11; reprinted in R.H. Robins (1970) *Diversions of Bloomsbury: Selected Writings on Linguistics*, Amsterdam: North-Holland.

(1964) *General Linguistics: an Introductory Survey*, London: Longmans, Green.

(1966) 'Word classes in Yurok', *Lingua* 17: 210–29; reprinted in R.H. Robins (1970) *Diversions of Bloomsbury: Selected Writings on Linguistics*, Amsterdam: North-Holland.

(1970) *Diversions of Bloomsbury: Selected Writings on Linguistics*, Amsterdam: North-Holland.

Robinson, M. (1985) *The Concise Scots Dictionary*, Aberdeen University Press.

Romaine, S. (ed.) (1982) *Sociolinguistic Variation in Speech Communities*, London: Edward Arnold.

(1988) *Pidgin and Creole Languages*, Harlow: Longman Group.

(1989) *Bilingualism*, Oxford: Basil Blackwell.

Rubach, J. (1977) 'Nasalization in Polish', *Journal of Phonetics* 5: 17–25.

Ruhlen, M. (1975) *A Guide to the Languages of the World*, (self-published) Stanford CA.

References

(1978) 'Nasal vowels', in J.H. Greenberg (ed.) *Universals of Human Language,* vol. II, *Phonology,* Stanford University Press, pp. 203–41.

(1987) *A Guide to the World's Languages,* vol. I: *Classification,* Stanford University Press, and London: Edward Arnold.

Rumelhart, D.E. and J.L. McClelland (1986) *Parallel Distributed Processing: Explorations in the Microstructure of Cognition,* vol. I, *Foundations,* Cambridge MA: Massachusetts Institute of Technology Press (*see also* McClelland and Rumelhart 1986).

Rush, J. (1827) *The Philosophy of the Human Voice,* Philadelphia PA: Griggs and Elliot.

Sacks, H., E.A. Schegloff and G. Jefferson (1974) 'A simplest systematics for the organization of turn-taking in conversation', *Language* 50: 696–735.

Sag, I. and M.Y. Liberman (1975) 'The intonational disambiguation of indirect speech acts', *Papers from the 11th Regional Meeting,* Chicago Linguistic Society, pp. 487–97.

Saib, J. (1978) 'Segment organization and the syllable in Tamazight Berber', in A. Bell and J.B. Hooper (eds.), *Syllables and Segments,* Amsterdam: North-Holland, pp. 93–106.

Saito, S. and K. Nakata (1985) *Fundamentals of Speech Signal Processing,* Tokyo, Orlando FL and London: Academic Press.

Sampson, G. (1980) *Schools of Linguistics: Competition and Evolution,* London: Hutchinson.

(1985) *Writing Systems: a Linguistic Introduction,* London: Hutchinson.

Sapir, E. (1921) *Language: an Introduction to the Study of Speech,* New York: Harcourt, Brace and World.

(1927) 'Speech as a personality trait', *American Journal of Sociology* 32: 892–905.

(1930) 'Southern Paiute, a Shoshonean language', *Proceedings of the American Academy of Arts and Sciences* 65: 1–3.

Sarawit, M. (1973) 'The Proto-Tai vowel system', PhD dissertation, University of Michigan.

Saussure, F. de (1916 (1966)) *Cours de linguistique générale,* ed. C. Bally, A. Sechehaye and A. Riedlinger, Paris: Payot. (*Course in General Linguistics,* ed. C. Bally, A. Sechehaye and A. Riedlinger, trans. W. Baskin, New York: McGraw-Hill.)

Saville-Troike, M. (1989) *The Ethnography of Communication: an Introduction,* Oxford: Blackwell.

Schachter, P. (1965) 'Some comments on J.M. Stewart's "The typology of the Twi tone system" ', *Bulletin of the Institute of African Studies* 1: 28–42, Ghana: Legon University.

(1969) 'Hausa', in E. Dunstan (ed.) *Twelve Nigerian Languages: a Handbook on their Sound Systems for Teachers of English,* London: Longmans Green, pp. 73–84.

Scherer, K. R. (1982) 'Methods of research on vocal communication: paradigms and parameters', in K.R. Scherer and P. Ekman (eds.) *Handbook of Methods in Nonverbal Behavior Research*, Cambridge University Press, and Paris: Editions de la Maison des Sciences de l'Homme, pp. 136–98.

(1984) 'On the nature and function of emotion: a component process approach', in K.R. Scherer and P. Ekman (eds.) (1984) *Approaches to Emotion*, Hillsdale NJ: Lawrence Erlbaum Associates, pp. 293–317.

(1986a) 'Voice, stress and emotion', in M.H. Appley and R. Trumbull (eds.) *Dynamics of Stress*, New York: Plenum, pp. 159–81.

(1986b) 'Vocal affect expression: a review and a model for future research', *Psychological Bulletin* 99: 143–65.

(1989) 'Vocal correlates of emotion', in E. Wagner and A. Manstead (eds.) *Handbook of Psychophysiology: Emotion and Social Behavior*, London: John Wiley, pp. 165–97.

Scherer, K.R. and P. Ekman (eds.) (1982) *Handbook of Methods in Nonverbal Behavior Research*, Cambridge University Press, and Paris: Editions de la Maison des Sciences de l'Homme.

Scherer, K.R. and H. Giles (1979) *Social Markers in Speech*, Cambridge University Press, and Paris: Editions de la Maison des Sciences de l'Homme.

Scherer, K.R., H. Wallbott and A.B. Summerfield (eds.) (1986) *Experiencing Emotion: a Cross-Cultural Study*, Cambridge University Press.

Schooneveld, C.H. van (1961) *The Sentence Intonation of Contemporary Standard Russian*, The Hague: Mouton.

Schubiger, M. (1958) *English Intonation, its Form and Function*, Tübingen: Max Niemeyer.

Schuh, R. (1978) 'Tone rules', in V.A. Fromkin (ed.) *Tone: a Linguistic Survey*, New York: Academic Press, pp. 221–56.

Scott, D.R., S.D. Isard and B. Boysson-Bardies (1985) 'Perceptual isochrony in English and French', *Journal of Phonetics* 13: 155–62.

Scott, N.C. (1947) 'The monosyllable in Szechuanese', *Bulletin of the School of Oriental and African Studies* 12: 197–213; reprinted in W.E. Jones and J. Laver (eds.) (1973) *Phonetics in Linguistics: a Book of Readings*, London: Longman.

(1964) 'Nasal consonants in Land Dayak (Bukar-Sadong)', in D. Abercrombie, D.B. Fry, P.A.D. MacCarthy, N.C. Scott and J.L.M. Trim (eds.) *In Honour of Daniel Jones*, London: Longmans Green, pp. 432–6.

Searle, J. (1969) *Speech Acts*, Cambridge University Press.

Sebeok, T.A. (ed.) (1963–76) *Current Trends in Linguistics*, Vols. I–XIV, The Hague: Mouton.

(1991) *A Sign is Just a Sign*, Bloomington: Indiana University Press.

Selinker, L. (1972) 'Interlanguage', *International Journal of Applied Linguistics* 10: 209–31.

Selkirk, E. O. (1980) 'The role of prosodic categories in English word stress', *Linguistic Inquiry* 11: 563–605.

(1982) 'The syllable', in H. van der Hulst and N. Smith (eds.) (1982) *The Structure of Phonological Representation*, part II, Dordrecht, and Cinnaminson NJ: Foris, pp. 337–83.

(1984) *Phonology and Syntax: the Relation between Sound and Structure*, Cambridge MA: Massachusetts Institute of Technology Press.

Senner, W. (ed.) (1989) *The Origins of Writing*, Lincoln NA: University of Nebraska Press.

Shadle, C. H. (1985) 'The acoustics of fricative consonants', PhD dissertation, Massachusetts Institute of Technology, Cambridge MA.

(1990) 'Articulatory–acoustic relationships in fricative consonants', in W.J. Hardcastle and A. Marchal (eds.) *Speech Production and Speech Modelling*, Dordrecht: Kluwer Academic, pp. 187–209.

Shafeev, D.A. (1964) *A Short Grammatical Outline of Pashto*, (trans. Paper, H.H.), *International Journal of American Linguistics* Publication 33.

Sharf, D.J. and R.N. Ohde (1981) 'Physiologic, acoustic and perceptual aspects of coarticulation', in N.J. Lass (ed.) *Speech and Language, Advances in Basic Research and Practice*, New York: Academic Press, pp. 153–247.

Shibatani, M. (1990) *The Languages of Japan*, Cambridge University Press.

Shopen, T. (ed.) (1985) *Language Typology and Syntactic Description*, 3 vols.: vol. I, *Clause Structure*; vol. II, *Complex Constructions*; vol. III, *Grammatical Categories and the Lexicon*, Cambridge University Press.

Shuken, C. (1979) 'Aspiration in Scottish Gaelic stop consonants', in H. Hollien and P. Hollien (eds.) *Current Issues in the Phonetic Sciences*, vol. I, Amsterdam: John Benjamins, pp. 451–8.

(1980) 'An instrumental investigation of some Scottish Gaelic consonants', PhD dissertation, University of Edinburgh.

(1984) '[ʔ], [h] and parametric phonetics', in J.A. Higgs and R. Thelwall (eds.), *Topics in Linguistic Phonetics: in Honour of E.T. Uldall*, Occasional Papers in Linguistics and Language Learning no. 9, March, Department of Linguistics, The New University of Ulster, pp. 111–39.

Siegman, A.W. and S. Feldstein (eds.) (1978), *Nonverbal Behavior and Communication*, Hillsdale NJ: Lawrence Erlbaum Associates.

Siptár, P. (1991) 'Fast-speech processes in Hungarian', in M. Gósy (ed.) *Temporal Factors in Speech: a Collection of Papers*, Budapest: A Magyar Tudományos Akadémia Nyelvtudományi Intézete (Research Institute for Linguistics, Hungarian Academy of Sciences), pp.27–62.

Sivers, F. de (1965) 'L'unité intonationelle d'interrogation en Hongrois', *La Linguistique* 1: 75–112.

Sloat, C., S.H. Taylor and J.E. Hoard (1978) *Introduction to Phonology*, Englewood Cliffs NJ: Prentice-Hall.

Smalley, W.A. (1953) 'Phonemic rhythm in Comanche', *International Journal of American Linguistics* 19: 297–301.

Smith, M.E. (ed.) (1973) *Studies in Linguistics in Honor of G.L. Trager*, The Hague: Mouton.

Smith, N.V. (1969) 'Nupe', in E. Dunstan (ed.) *Twelve Nigerian Languages: a Handbook on their Sound Systems for Teachers of English*, London: Longmans, Green, pp. 133–42.

Sneppe, R. and V. Wei (1984) 'F0 behaviour in Mandarin and French: an instrumental comparison', in M.P.R. van den Broecke and A. Cohen (eds.) *Proceedings of the Tenth International Congress of Phonetic Sciences* (Utrecht), pp. 299–303.

Snyman, J.W. (1969) *An Introduction to the !Xũ Language*, Cape Town: Balkema.

Solá, D.F. (ed.) (1984) *Language in the Americas, Proceedings of the Ninth PILEI Symposium*, Ithaca NY: Language Policy Research Program, Latin American Studies Program, Cornell University.

Sommerstein, A.H. (1977) *Modern Phonology*, London: Edward Arnold.

Soundararaj, F. (1986) 'Acoustic phonetic correlates of prominence in Tamil words', *Edinburgh University Department of Linguistics Work in Progress* 19: 16–35.

Speck, C.H. (1978) 'The phonology of Texmelucan Zapotec verb irregularity', M.A. thesis, University of North Dakota.

Sperber, D. and D. Wilson (1986) *Relevance: Communication and Cognition*, Oxford: Blackwell.

Spolsky, B. (1988) 'Bilingualism', in F.J. Newmeyer (ed.) *Linguistics: the Cambridge Survey*, vol. IV, *Language: the Socio-cultural Context*, Cambridge University Press, pp. 100–18.

Sprigg, R.K. (1961) 'Vowel harmony in Lhasa Tibetan: prosodic features applied to interrelated vocalic features of successive syllables', *Bulletin of the School of Oriental and African Studies* 24: 116–38; reprinted in F.R. Palmer (ed.) (1970) *Prosodic Analysis*, London: Oxford University Press.

— (1978) 'Phonation types: a re-appraisal', *Journal of the International Phonetic Association* 8: 2–17.

Stein, J. (ed.) (1983) *The Random House Dictionary of the English Language*, New York NY: Random House.

Steriade, D. (1979) 'Vowel harmony in Khalkha Mongolian', *Massachusetts Institute of Technology Working Papers in Linguistics* 1: 25–50.

— (1990) 'Gestures and autosegments: comments on Browman and Goldstein's paper', in J. Kingston and M. Beckman (eds.) *Papers in Laboratory Phonology: Between the Grammar and the Physics of Speech*, Cambridge University Press, pp. 382–97.

Stern, H.H. (1983) *Fundamental Concepts in Language Teaching*, Oxford University Press.

Stern, T. (1957) 'Drum and whistle languages: an analysis of speech surrogates', *American Anthropologist* 59: 487–506.

Stetson, R.H. (1928) 'Motor phonetics', *Archives Néerlandaises de Phonétique Expérimentale*, vol. III (2nd edn published as *Motor Phonetics*, Amsterdam: North-Holland, 1951).

Stevens, K.N. (1972) 'The quantal nature of speech: evidence from articulatory-acoustic data', in E.E. David and P.B. Denes (eds.) *Human Communication: a Unified View*, New York: McGraw Hill, pp. 51–6.

Stevens, K.N. and D. Klatt (1974) 'Role of formant transitions in the voiced-voiceless distinction for stops', *Journal of the Acoustical Society of America* 55: 653–9.

Stevens, S.S. (1957) 'On the psychophysical law', *Psychological Review* 64: 153–81.

Stewart, J.M. (1967) 'Tongue root position in Akan vowel harmony', *Phonetica* 16: 185–204.

Stringer, M. and J. Hotz (1973) 'Waffa phonemes', in H. McKaughan (ed.) *The Languages of the Eastern Family of the East New Guinea Highland Stock*, Seattle: University of Washington Press, pp. 523–9.

Studdert-Kennedy, M. (ed.) (1983) *Psychobiology of Language*, Cambridge MA: Massachusetts Institute of Technology.

Suárez, J.A. (1983) *The Mesoamerican Indian Languages*, Cambridge University Press.

Subtelny, J.D., D. Oya and J.D. Subtelny (1972) 'Cineradiographic study of sibilants', *Folia Phoniatrica* 24: 30–50.

Swadesh, M. (1951) 'Diffusional cumulation and archaic residue as historical explanation', *Southwestern Journal of Anthropology* 7: 1–21.

Sweet, H. (1877) *A Handbook of Phonetics*, Oxford: Clarendon Press.

Tadadjeu, M. (1974) 'Floating tones, shifting rules, and downstep in Dschang-Bamileke', in W.R. Leben (ed.) *Proceedings of the Fifth Annual Conference on African Linguistics, Studies in African Linguistics* Supplement 5: 283–90.

Tench, P. (1978) 'On introducing parametric phonetics', *Journal of the International Phonetic Association* 8: 34–46.

Tereščenko, N.M. (1966) 'Nenetskij jazyk', in *Jazyki Narodov SSSR*, vol. III, Moscow: Nauka.

Ternes, E. (1973) *The Phonemic Analysis of Scottish Gaelic. Based on the Dialect of Applecross, Ross-shire*, Forum Phoneticum 1, Hamburg: Helmut Buske Verlag.

Terry, M., S. Hiller, J. Laver and G. Duncan (1986) 'The AUDLAB interactive speech analysis system', *Proceedings of IEE Conference on Speech Input/Output*, London, *IEE Publication* 258: 263–5.

Thomas, A.R. (1973) *The Linguistic Geography of Wales*, Cardiff: University of Wales Press.

Thompson, H.S. (1980) *Stress and Salience in English*, Pala Alto CA: Xerox Corporation.

Thorsen, N. (1978) 'An acoustical analysis of Danish intonation', *Journal of Phonetics* 6: 151–75.

(1979) 'Interpreting raw fundamental frequency tracings of Danish', *Phonetica* 36: 57–8.

(1980) 'A study of the perception of sentence intonation – evidence from Danish', *Journal of the Acoustical Society of America* 67: 1014–30.

(1983) 'Two issues in the prosody of standard Danish', in A.Cutler and D.R. Ladd (eds.) *Prosody: Models and Measurements*, Berlin: Springer-Verlag, pp. 27–38.

(1985) 'Intonation and text in standard Danish', *Journal of the Acoustical Society of America* 77: 1205–16.

Thráinsson, H. (1978) 'On the phonology of Icelandic preaspiration', *Nordic Journal of Linguistics* 1: 3–54.

Tohkura, Y., E. Vatikiotis-Bateson and Y. Sagisaka (eds.) (1992) *Speech Perception, Production and Linguistic Structure*, Tokyo: Ohmsha, and Amsterdam: IOS Press.

Touati, P. (1987) *Structures Prosodiques du Suédois et du Français*, Lund University Press.

Trager, G.L. (1942) 'The phoneme "t": a study in theory and method', *American Speech* 17: 144–8.

(1958) 'Paralanguage: a first approximation', *Studies in Linguistics* 13: 1–12; reprinted in D. Hymes (ed.) (1964) *Language in Culture and Society: a Reader in Linguistics and Anthropology*, New York: Harper and Row.

(1960) 'Taos III: Paralanguage', *Anthropological Linguistics* 2: 24–30.

(1961) 'The typology of paralanguage', *Anthropological Linguistics* 3: 17–21.

Trager, G.L. and H.L. Smith, Jr (1951) *An Outline of English Structure*, Norman OK: Battenburg.

Traill, A. (1973) 'A preliminary sketch of !Xū phonetics', *Edinburgh University Department of Linguistics Work in Progress* 6: 1–23.

(1985) *Phonetic and Phonological Studies of the !Xóõ Bushman*, Hamburg: Hemut Buske Verlag.

(1991) 'Pulmonic control, nasal venting, and aspiration in Khoisan languages', *Journal of the International Phonetic Association* 21:13–18.

Traill, A. and M. Jackson (1988) 'Speaker variation and phonation type in Tsonga', *Journal of Phonetics* 16: 385–400.

Tranel, B. (1987) *The Sounds of French: an Introduction*, Cambridge University Press.

Trubetzkoy, N.S. (1931) 'Die Konsonantsysteme der ostkaukasischen Sprachen', *Caucasica* 8: 1–52.

(1939) *Gründzuge der Phonologie, Travaux du Cercle Linguistique de Prague* no. 7, Prague: Cercle Linguistique de Prague; reprinted 1958, Göttingen: Vandenhoeck and Ruprecht; translated in 1949 by J. Cantineau as *Principes de Phonologie*, Paris: Librairie Klinksieck; translated in 1966 by C.A.M Baltaxe as *Principles of Phonology*, Berkeley: University of California Press.

Trudgill, P. (1974) *The Social Differentiation of English in Norwich*, Cambridge University Press.

(1975) 'Sex, covert prestige, and linguistic change in the urban British English of Norwich', in B. Thorne and N. Henley (eds.) *Language and Sex: Difference and Dominance*, Rowley MA: Newbury House.

(ed.) (1978) *Sociolinguistic Patterns in British English*, London: Edward Arnold.

References

(1983) *On Dialect: Social and Geographical Perspectives*, Oxford: Basil Blackwell.

(ed.) (1985) *Language in the British Isles*, Cambridge University Press.

(1989) 'The sociophonetics of /l/ in the Greek of Sphakiá', *Journal of the International Phonetics Association* 15: 18–22.

(1990) *The Dialects of England*, Oxford: Basil Blackwell.

Trudgill, P. and J.K. Chambers (eds.) (1991) *Dialects of English: Studies in Grammatical Variation*, London: Longman.

Trudgill, P. and J. Hannah (1985) *International English: a Guide to Varieties of Standard English*, 2nd edn, London: Edward Arnold.

Tucker, A.N. (1969) Review of A. Burssens (1969) *Problemen en inventarisatie van der verbale strukturen in het Dho Alur (Noordskkongo)*, Koninklijke Academie, *Journal of African Languages* 8: 125–6.

Tucker, A.N. and P.E. Hackett (1959) *Le Groupe Linguistique Zande*, Tervuren: Annales du Musée Royal du Congo Belge.

Uhlenbeck, E.M. (1950) 'The Krama-Ngoko opposition: its place in the Javanese language system', in E.M. Uhlenbeck (ed.) (1978) *Studies in Javanese Morphology*, The Hague: Martinus Nijhoff, pp. 278–99.

Uldall, E.T. (1958) 'American "molar" r and "flapped" t', *Revista do Laboratorio de Fonetica Experimental da Faculdade de Letres da Universidade de Coimbra* 4: 3–6.

(1960) 'Attitudinal meanings conveyed by intonation contours', *Language and Speech* 3: 223–34.

(1964) 'Dimensions of meaning in intonation', in D. Abercrombie, D.B. Fry, P.A.D. MacCarthy, N.C. Scott and J.L.M. Trim (eds.), *In Honour of Daniel Jones*, London: Longmans Green, pp. 271–9; reprinted in D. Bolinger (ed.) (1972) *Intonation*, Harmondsworth: Penguin.

Umeda, N. (1975a) 'Vowel duration in American English', *Journal of the Acoustical Society of America* 58: 434–55.

(1975b) 'Linguistic rules for text-to-speech synthesis', *Proceedings of the IEEE* 64: 443–51.

(1977) 'Consonant duration in American English', *Journal of the Acoustical Society of America* 61: 846–58.

Umeda, N. and C.H. Coker (1974) 'Allophonic variation in American English', *Journal of Phonetics* 2: 1–5.

Uttal, W.R. (1973) *The Psychobiology of Sensory Coding*, New York: Harper and Row.

Vaane, E. (1982) 'Subjective estimation of speech rate', *Phonetica* 39: 136–49.

Vaissière, J. (1971) 'Contribution à la synthèse par règles du français', doctoral dissertation, Université des Langues et Lettres de Grenoble.

(1983) 'Language independent prosodic features', in A. Cutler and D.R. Ladd (eds.) *Prosody: Models and Measurements*, Berlin: Springer-Verlag, pp. 53–66.

Van Haitsma, J.D. and W. Van Haitsma (1976) 'A hierarchical sketch of Mixe as spoken in San José El Paraíso', *Summer Institute of Linguistics Publications* 44,

Norman OK: Summer Institute of Linguistics and University of Oklahoma.

Van Riper, W.R. (1973) 'General American: an ambiguity', in H. Schaller and J. Reidy (eds.) *Lexicography and Dialect Geography: Festgabe für Hans Kurath*, Wiesbaden: Franz Steiner Verlag, pp. 232–42; reprinted in H.B. Allen and M.D. Linn (eds.) *Dialect and Accent Variation*, Orlando FL: Academic Press.

Varga, L. (1975) *A Contrastive Analysis of English and Hungarian Sentence Prosody*, Budapest: Linguistics Institute of the Hungarian Academy of Sciences and Centre for Applied Linguistics.

—— (1983) 'Hungarian sentence prosody: an outline', *Folia Linguistica* 17: 117–51.

Verhoeven, J.W.M. (1990) 'Perceptual aspects of Dutch intonation', PhD dissertation, University of Edinburgh.

Vinay, J.P. (1986) 'L'enseignement de la prononciation: l'un des buts de l'Association Phonétique Internationale', *Journal of the International Phonetic Association*, 16: 48–53 (IPA Centenary Volume).

Vincent, N. (1988) 'Italian', in M. Harris and N. Vincent (eds.) *The Romance Languages*, London: Croom Helm, pp. 279–313.

Voegelin, C.F. (1935) 'Tübatulabal grammar', *University of California Publications in Archeology, Anthropology and Ethnology* 34: 55–159.

Voegelin, C.F. and F.M. Voegelin (1977) *Classification and Index of the World's Languages*, New York: Elsevier.

Voorhoeve, C.L. (1965) *The Flamingo Bay Dialect of the Asmat Language*, The Hague: Martinus Nijhoff.

Wagner, E. and A. Manstead (eds.) (1989) *Handbook of Psychophysiology: Emotion and Social Behavior*, London: John Wiley.

Wagner, W. (1964–9) *Linguistic Atlas and Survey of Irish Dialects*, 4 vols., Dublin: Dublin Institute for Advanced Studies.

Wajskop, M. (1979) 'Segmental durations of French intervocalic plosives', in B. Lindblom and S. Öhman (eds.) *Frontiers of Speech Communication Research*, New York NY: Academic Press, pp. 109–23.

Wakelin, M.F. (1972) *English Dialects: an Introduction*, (revised edition 1977), London: The Athlone Press.

—— (1988) *The Archaeology of English*, London: B.T. Batsford.

Wallis, J. (1653) *Grammatica Linguae Anglicanae*, Oxford: Leon Lichfield; edited by J.A. Kemp (1972), London: Longman.

Walters, K. (1988) 'Dialectology', in F. J. Newmeyer (ed.) *Linguistics: the Cambridge Survey*, vol. IV *Language: the Sociocultural Context*, Cambridge University Press, pp. 119–39.

Ward, D. (1964) 'A critique of Russian orthography', in D. Abercrombie, D.B. Fry, P.A.D. MacCarthy, N.C. Scott and J.L.M. Trim (eds.) *In Honour of Daniel Jones*, London: Longmans Green, pp. 384–94.

Ward, I.C. (1929) *The Phonetics of English*, Cambridge: Heffer.

—— (1936) *An Introduction to the Ibo Language*, Cambridge: Heffer.

Wardhaugh, R. (1986) *An Introduction to Sociolinguistics*, Oxford: Blackwell.

681

References

Warren, D.W. (1976) 'Aerodynamics of speech production', in N.J. Lass (ed.) *Contemporary Issues in Experimental Phonetics*, New York: Academic Press, pp. 107–37.

Waterhouse, V. (1962) *The Grammatical Structure of Oaxaca Chontal*, *International Journal of American Linguistics* 28(2), part II, Bloomington: Indiana Research Center in Anthropology, Folklore and Linguistics, Publication 19.

Waterhouse, V. and M. Morrison (1950) 'Chontal phonemes', *International Journal of American Linguistics* 16: 35–9.

Waterson, N. (1956) 'Some aspects of the phonology of the nominal forms of the Turkish word', *Bulletin of the School of Oriental and African Studies* 18: 578–91; reprinted in F.R. Palmer (ed.) (1970) *Prosodic Analysis*, London: Oxford University Press.

Watson, I. (1983) 'Cues to the voicing contrast: a survey', *Cambridge Papers in Phonetics and Experimental Linguistics* 2: 1–34.

Wauchope, R. and N.A. McQuown (eds.) (1967) *Handbook of Middle American Indians*, vol. V, *Linguistics*, Austin: University of Texas Press.

Weitz, S. (ed.) (1974) *Nonverbal Communication: Readings with Commentary*, Oxford University Press.

Wells, J.C. (1970) 'Local accents in England and Wales', *Journal of Linguistics* 6: 231–52.

(1975) 'The Association's alphabet', *Journal of the International Phonetic Association* 5: 52–8.

(1976) 'The Association's alphabet', *Journal of the International Phonetic Association* 6: 2–3.

(1982) *Accents of English*, 3 vols., Cambridge University Press.

(1990) *Longman Pronunciation Dictionary*, Harlow: Longman Group.

Welmers, W. (1959) 'Tonemics, morphotonemics, and tonal morphemes', *General Linguistics* 4: 1–9.

(1973) *African Language Structures*, Berkeley: University of California Press.

Wenk, B.J. and F. Wioland (1982) 'Is French really syllable-timed?', *Journal of Phonetics* 10: 193–216.

Westermann, D. and M.A. Bryan (1952) *Handbook of African Languages*, part II, *Languages of West Africa*, London: Oxford University Press.

Westermann, D. and I.C. Ward (1933) *Practical Phonetics for Students of African Languages*, London: Oxford University Press; 2nd edn, Kelly, J. (ed.) (1990), London: Kegan Paul International.

Whorf, B.L. (1946) 'The Hopi language', in C. Osgood (ed.) *Linguistic Structures of Native America*, Viking Fund Publication in Anthropology no. 6, New York: Viking Fund, pp. 159–83.

Wiesemann, U. (1972) *Die phonologische und grammatische Struktur der Kaingang-Sprache*, The Hague: Mouton.

Wiik, K. and I. Lehiste (1968) 'Vowel quantity in Finnish di-syllabic words',

Congressus Secundus Internationalis Fennougristarum, Helsinki (1965), Helsinki: Societas Fenno-Ugrica.

Wilkins, J. (1668) *An Essay towards a Real Character and a Philosophical Language*, London: John Martyn.

Willems, N. (1982) *English Intonation from a Dutch Point of View*, Dordrecht: Foris.

Williams, C. (ed.) (1988) *Language in Geographic Context*, Clevedon PA: Multilingual Matters.

Williamson, J.V. and V.M. Burke (eds.) (1971) *A Various Language: Perspectives on American Dialects*, New York: Holt Rinehart and Winston.

Williamson, K. (1969a) 'Igbo', in E. Dunstan (ed.) *Twelve Nigerian Languages: a Handbook on their Sound Systems for Teachers of English*, London: Longmans Green pp. 85–96.

—— (1969b) 'Ịjọ', in E. Dunstan (ed.) *Twelve Nigerian Languages: a Handbook on their Sound Systems for Teachers of English*, London: Longmans Green pp. 97–114.

Windsor-Lewis, J. (1976) 'The official IPA vowel diagram', *Journal of the International Phonetic Association* 6: 29–31.

Wolf, G.D. de (1988) 'A study of selected social and regional factors in Canadian English: a comparison of phonological variables and grammatical items in Ottawa and Vancouver', PhD dissertation, University of Victoria, British Columbia.

Wolfram, W. and R.W. Fasold (1974) *The Study of Social Dialects in American English*, Englewood Cliffs NJ: Prentice-Hall.

Wood, S. (1977) 'A radiographic analysis of constriction locations for vowels', *Working Papers* 15: 101–31, Phonetics Laboratory, University of Lund; later published under the same title in *Journal of Phonetics* 7: 25–44 (1979).

Woods, H.B. (1979) 'A socio-dialectology of the English spoken in Ottawa: a study of sociological and stylistic variation in Canadian English', PhD dissertation, University of British Columbia.

Wright, J. (1986) 'The behavior of nasalized vowels in the perceptual vowel space', in J.J. Ohala and J.J. Jaeger (eds.) *Experimental Phonology*, Orlando FL: Academic Press, pp. 45–67.

Wunderli, P. (1987) *Manuel de Phonétique Française*, Copenhagen: Ejnar Munksgaard.

Wurm, S.A. (1972) *Languages of Australia and Tasmania*, The Hague: Mouton.

Yallop, C. (1982) *Australian Aboriginal Languages*, London: André Deutsch.

Yip, M. (1989) 'Feature geometry and cooccurrence restrictions', *Phonology* 6: 349–74.

Yost, W.A. and D.W. Nielsen (1985) *Fundamentals of Hearing: an Introduction*, 2nd edn, Fort Worth TX: Holt Rinehart and Winston.

Zawadski, P. and D. Kuehn (1980) 'A cineradiographic study of static and dynamic aspects of American English /r/', *Phonetica* 37: 253–66.

References

Zee, E. (1980a) 'The effect of aspiration on the F0 of the following vowel in Cantonese', *UCLA Department of Linguistics Working Papers in Phonetics* 49: 90–7.

—— (1980b) 'A spectrographic investigation of Mandarin tone sandhi', *UCLA Department of Linguistics Working Papers in Phonetics* 49: 98–116.

Zlatin, M. (1974) 'Voicing contrast: perceptual and productive voice onset time characteristics of adults', *Journal of the Acoustical Society of America* 56: 981–94.

Zue, V. (1976) *Acoustic Analysis of Stop Consonants*, Bloomington: Indiana University Linguistics Club.

Zwanenburg, W. (1965) *Recherches sur la prosodie de la phrase française*, Leiden: University Press.

Zwirner, E. (1959) 'Phonometrische Isophonen der Quantität der deutschen Mundarten', *Phonetica* Supplement 4: 93–125.

Zwirner, E. and W. Bethge (eds.) (1965), *Proceedings of the Sixth International Congress of Phonetic Sciences*, Basel: Karger.

INDEX OF NAMES

685

SUBJECT INDEX

Technical terms, on introduction or definition, and as topic identifiers in the recommendations for Further Reading at the ends of chapters, are printed in the book in **bold-face**. In this Subject Index, the page numbers of these boldened items are also printed in bold, for convenience of review.

695